lonely planet

Iceland

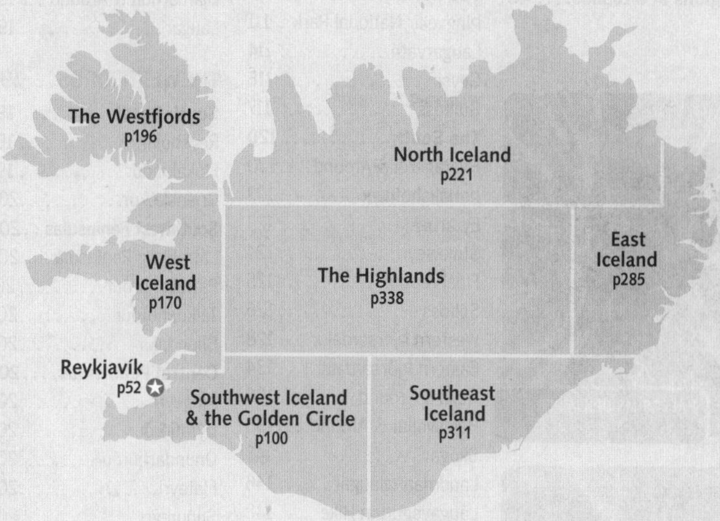

THIS EDITION WRITTEN AND RESEARCHED BY

Carolyn Bain, Alexis Averbuck

PLAN YOUR TRIP

HALLGRÍMSKIRKJA P59

MARION FARIA PHOTOGRAPHY/GETTY IMAGES ©

JÖKULSÁRLÓN P327

JAKKREETHAMPITAKKULL/GETTY IMAGES ©

ON THE ROAD

Contents

Welcome to Iceland

Hitting headlines, topping bucket lists, wooing nature lovers and dazzling increasing numbers of visitors – there seems no end to the talents of this breathtaking northern destination.

A Symphony of Elements

Iceland is, literally, a country in the making. It's a vast volcanic laboratory where mighty forces shape the earth: geysers gush, mudpots gloop, ice-covered volcanoes rumble and glaciers cut great pathways through the mountains. Its supercharged splendour seems designed to remind visitors of their utter insignificance in the greater scheme of things. And it works a treat: some crisp clean air, an eyeful of the cinematic landscapes, and everyone is transfixed.

The Power of Nature

It's the power of Icelandic nature to turn the prosaic into the extraordinary. A dip in a pool becomes a soak in a geothermal lagoon; a casual stroll can transform into a trek across a glittering glacier; and a quiet night of camping may mean front-row seats to the aurora borealis' curtains of fire, or the soft, pinkish hue of the midnight sun. Iceland has a transformative effect on people, too – its sagas turned brutes into poets, and its stories of *huldufólk* (hidden people) may make believers out of sceptics. Here you'll find some of the world's highest concentrations of dreamers, authors, artists and musicians, all fuelled by their surroundings.

A Personal Experience

The warmth of Icelanders is disarming, as is their industriousness – they've worked hard to recover from financial upheaval, and to transform Iceland into a destination that, thanks to its popularity with visitors, can host five times its population each year. Pause and consider a medium-sized city in your country – then give it far-flung universities, airports and hospitals to administer, 30-odd active volcanoes to monitor, and hundreds of hotels to run. How might they cope? Could they manage as well as the Icelanders – and still have time left over to create spine-tingling music and natty knitwear?

Nordic Nirvana

Don't for a minute think it's all about the great outdoors. The counterpoint to so much natural beauty is found in Iceland's cultural life, which celebrates a literary legacy that stretches from medieval sagas to contemporary thrillers by way of Nobel Prize winners. Live music is everywhere, as is visual art, handicrafts and locavore cuisine. The world's most northerly capital is home to the kind of egalitarianism, green thinking and effortless style that its Nordic brethren are famous for – all of which is wrapped in Iceland's assured individuality.

Why I Love Iceland

By Carolyn Bain, Writer

As I flew north to begin my third circuit of Iceland in four years, I was slightly anxious. The number of visitors to Iceland has doubled in that period, and I feared this might mean a little less magic to go around. At the end of this trip, 6000km later, I'm thrilled to report that the magic levels remain high. It's found in glorious football victories and Viking chants, kayaking among icebergs, sitting with puffins under the midnight sun and crunching across brand-new lava fields. The locals' resourcefulness, quirkiness, interconnectedness and warmth is undiminished. My smitten state continues.

For more about our writers, see p424

Above: Northern Lights over Jökulsárlón (p327)

Iceland

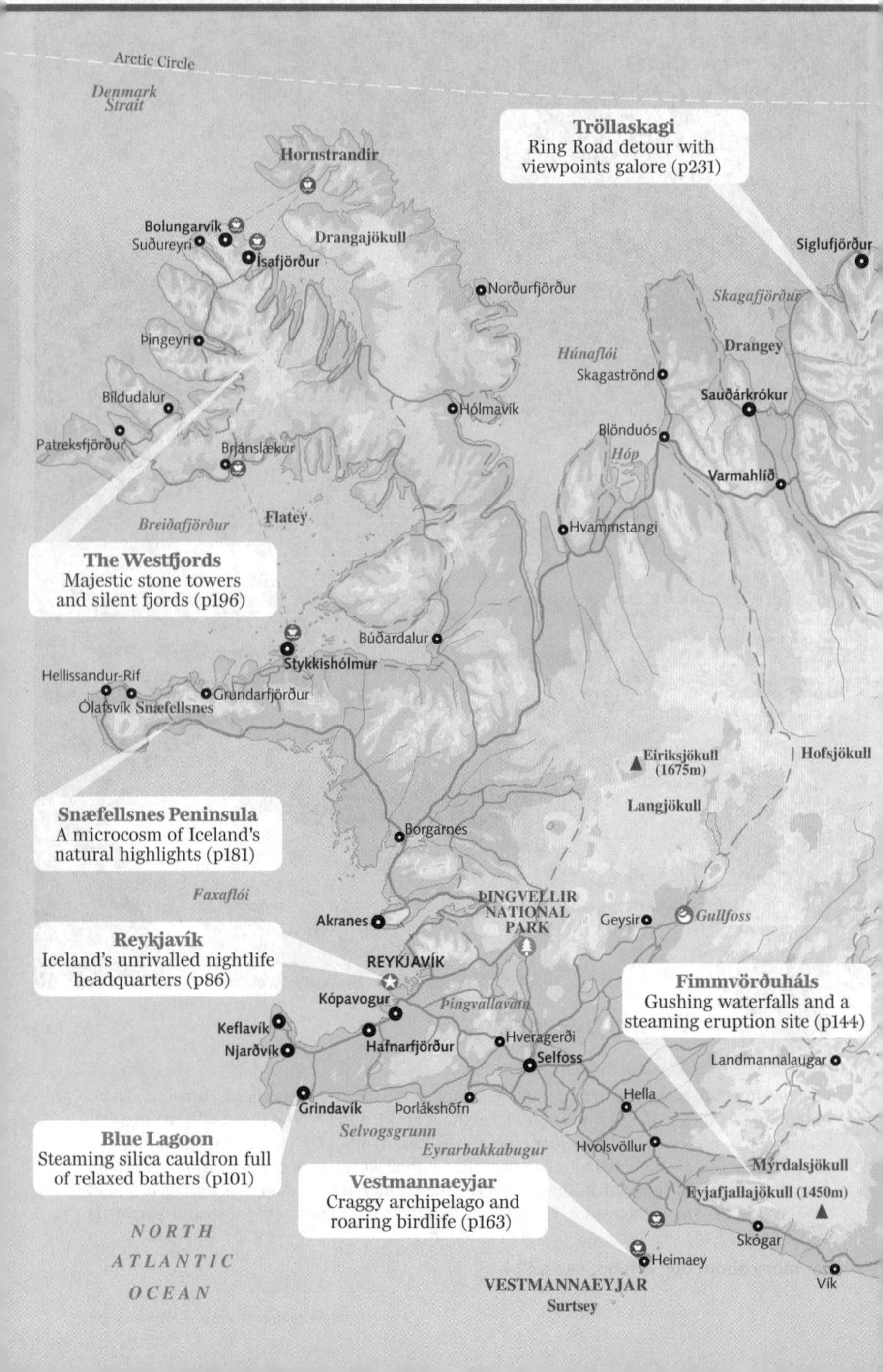

Arctic Circle
Denmark Strait
Tröllaskagi
Ring Road detour with viewpoints galore (p231)
Hornstrandir
Bolungarvík
Suðureyri
Drangajökull
Ísafjörður
Norðurfjörður
Siglufjörður
Skagafjörður
Þingeyri
Húnaflói
Drangey
Skagaströnd
Bíldudalur
Sauðárkrókur
Hólmavík
Patreksfjörður
Brjánslækur
Blönduós
Hóp
Varmahlíð
Breiðafjörður
Flatey
Hvammstangi
The Westfjords
Majestic stone towers and silent fjords (p196)
Búðardalur
Stykkishólmur
Hellissandur-Rif
Ólafsvík
Snæfellsnes
Grundarfjörður
Eiriksjökull (1675m)
Hofsjökull
Langjökull
Snæfellsnes Peninsula
A microcosm of Iceland's natural highlights (p181)
Borgarnes
Faxaflói
Þingvellir National Park
Akranes
Geysir
Gullfoss
Reykjavík
Iceland's unrivalled nightlife headquarters (p86)
REYKJAVÍK
Fimmvörðuháls
Gushing waterfalls and a steaming eruption site (p144)
Kópavogur
Þingvallavatn
Keflavík
Njarðvík
Hafnarfjörður
Hveragerði
Selfoss
Landmannalaugar
Grindavík
Þorlákshöfn
Hella
Blue Lagoon
Steaming silica cauldron full of relaxed bathers (p101)
Selvogsgrunn
Eyrarbakkabugur
Hvolsvöllur
Mýrdalsjökull
Vestmannaeyjar
Craggy archipelago and roaring birdlife (p163)
Eyjafjallajökull (1450m)
NORTH ATLANTIC OCEAN
Skógar
Heimaey
Vík
VESTMANNAEYJAR
Surtsey

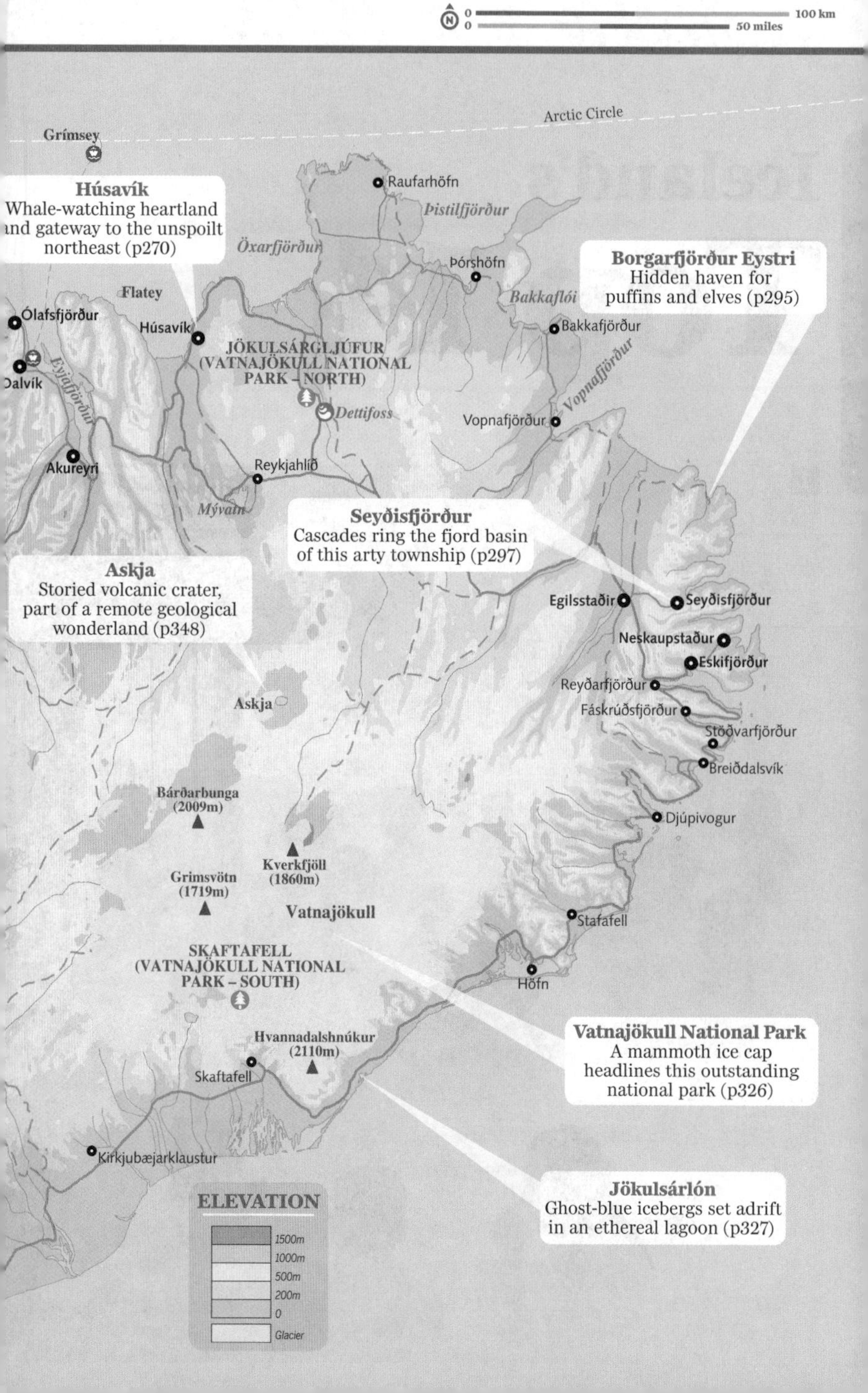
0
0
100 km
50 miles
Arctic Circle
Grímsey
Húsavík
Whale-watching heartland
and gateway to the unspoilt
northeast (p270)
Raufarhöfn
Þistilfjörður
Öxarfjörður
Þórshöfn
Borgarfjörður Eystri
Hidden haven for
puffins and elves (p295)
Bakkaflói
Flatey
Ólafsfjörður
Húsavík
Bakkafjörður
JÖKULSÁRGLJÚFUR
(VATNAJÖKULL NATIONAL
PARK – NORTH)
Vopnafjörður
Eyjafjörður
Dettifoss
Vopnafjörður
Akureyri
Reykjahlíð
Mývatn
Seyðisfjörður
Cascades ring the fjord basin
of this arty township (p297)
Askja
Storied volcanic crater,
part of a remote geological
wonderland (p348)
Egilsstaðir
Seyðisfjörður
Neskaupstaður
Eskifjörður
Reyðarfjörður
Fáskrúðsfjörður
Askja
Stöðvarfjörður
Breiðdalsvík
Bárðarbunga
(2009m)
Djúpivogur
Kverkfjöll
(1860m)
Grimsvötn
(1719m)
Vatnajökull
Stafafell
SKAFTAFELL
(VATNAJÖKULL NATIONAL
PARK – SOUTH)
Höfn
Vatnajökull National Park
A mammoth ice cap
headlines this outstanding
national park (p326)
Hvannadalshnúkur
(2110m)
Skaftafell
Kirkjubæjarklaustur
Jökulsárlón
Ghost-blue icebergs set adrift
in an ethereal lagoon (p327)
ELEVATION
1500m
1000m
500m
200m
0
Glacier

Iceland's Top 14

1

Getting into Hot Water

1 Iceland's unofficial pastime is splashing around in its surplus of geothermal water. You'll find 'hot-pots' everywhere, from downtown Reykjavík to the isolated peninsular tips of the Westfjords. Not only are they incredibly relaxing, they're the perfect antidote to a hangover and a great way to meet the locals (this is their social hub, the equivalent of the local pub or town square). The Blue Lagoon (p101) is the big cheese: its steaming lagoon full of silica deposits sits conveniently close to Keflavík airport, making it the perfect send-off before flying home. Below left: Blue Lagoon

Northern Lights

2 Everyone longs to glimpse the Northern Lights (p156), the celestial kaleidoscope known for transforming long winter nights into natural lava lamps. The lights, also known as aurora borealis, form when solar flares are drawn by the earth's magnetic field towards the North Pole. What results are ethereal veils of green, white, violet or red light, shimmering and dancing in a display not unlike silent fireworks. A good deal of luck is involved in seeing them, but look for the lights in clear, dark skies anytime between mid-September and mid-April.

SERGEY DIDENKO/SHUTTERSTOCK ©

2

NATTHAWAT/GETTY IMAGES ©

3

4

Westfjords

3 Iceland's sweeping spectrum of superlative nature comes to a dramatic climax in the Westfjords (p196) – the island's off-the-beaten-path adventure par excellence. Broad, multi-hued beaches flank the southern coast, roaring bird colonies abound, fjordheads tower above and then plunge into the deep, and a network of ruddy roads twists throughout, adding an extra edge of adventure. The region's uppermost peninsula, Hornstrandir, is the final frontier; its sea cliffs are perilous, the Arctic foxes are foxier, and hiking trails amble through pristine patches of wilderness that practically kiss the Arctic Circle. Top left: Hornbjarg sea cliffs (p216)

Jökulsárlón

4 A ghostly procession of luminous-blue icebergs drifts serenely through the 25-sq-km Jökulsárlón (p327) lagoon before floating out to sea. This surreal scene (handily, right next to the Ring Road) is a natural film set: in fact, you might have seen it in *Batman Begins* and the James Bond film *Die Another Day*. The ice calves come from Breiðamerkurjökull glacier, an offshoot of the mighty Vatnajökull ice cap. Boat trips among the bergs are popular, or you can simply wander the lakeshore, scout for seals and exhaust your camera's memory card.

Driving the Ring Road

5 There's no better way to explore Iceland than to hire a set of wheels and road-trip Rte 1, affectionately known as the Ring Road (p36). This 1330km tarmac trail loops around the island, passing through verdant dales decked with waterfalls, glacier tongues dripping from ice caps like frosting from a cake, desert-like plains of grey outwash sands, and velvety, moss-covered lava fields. It's supremely spectacular – but don't forget to detour. Use the Ring Road as your main artery and follow the veins as they splinter off into the wilderness. Above: Ring Road passing through Skaftafell (p319)

Tröllaskagi Peninsula

6 Touring Tröllaskagi (p231) is a joy, especially now that road tunnels link the spectacularly sited townships of Siglufjörður and Ólafsfjörður, once end-of-the-road settlements. Pit stops with pulling power include Hofsós' perfect fjordside swimming pool, Lónkot's fine local produce and Siglufjörður's outstanding herring museum. You'll find glorious panoramas, quality hiking, ski fields (including a growing trade in heliskiing), microbreweries, whale-watching tours, and ferries to offshore islands Grímsey and Hrísey. Below left: Swimming pool at Hofsós (p232)

Snæfellsnes Peninsula

7 With its cache of wild beaches, bird sanctuaries, horse farms and lava fields, the Snæfellsnes Peninsula (p181) is one of Iceland's best escapes – either as a day trip from the capital or as a relaxing long weekend. It's little wonder it's called 'Iceland in miniature' – it even hosts a national park and glacier-topped strato-volcano. Jules Verne was definitely onto something when he used Snæfellsjökull's icy crown as his magical doorway to the centre of the earth. Below right: Icelandic horse

6

HORSTGERLACH/GETTY IMAGES ©

7

SANTIAGO URQUIJO/GETTY IMAGES ©

Reykjavík's Cafe Culture & Beer Bars

8 Petite Reykjavík boasts all the treats you'd expect of a European capital – excellent museums and shopping – but the city's ratio of coffeehouses to citizens is staggering. In fact, the local social culture is built around such low-key hang-outs that crank up the intensity after hours, when tea is swapped for tipples and the dance moves are broken out. Handcrafted caffeine hits and designer microbrews are prepared with the utmost seriousness for accidental hipsters sporting well-worn *lopapeysur* (Icelandic woollen sweaters).

Vatnajökull National Park

9 Europe's largest national park covers nearly 14% of Iceland and safeguards mighty Vatnajökull (p326), the largest ice cap outside the poles (it's three times the size of Luxembourg). Scores of outlet glaciers flow down from its frosty bulk, while underneath it are active volcanoes and mountain peaks. Yes, this is ground zero for those 'fire and ice' clichés. You'll be spellbound by the diversity of landscapes, walking trails and activities inside this super sized park. Given its dimensions, access points are numerous – start at Skaftafell in the south or Ásbyrgi in the north. Above: Fjallsárlón (p327)

Borgarfjörður Eystri & Seyðisfjörður

10 A tale of two east-side fjords. Stunning Seyðisfjörður garners most of the attention – it's only 27 (sealed) kilometres from the Ring Road, and it welcomes the weekly ferry from Europe into its mountain- and waterfall-lined embrace. Beautiful Borgarfjörður Eystri (p295), on the other hand, is 70km from the Ring Road, and much of that stretch is bumpy and unsealed. Its selling points are understated: puffins and rugged rhyolite peaks. Both fjords have natural splendour and bumper hiking trails. Below: Seyðisfjörður (p297)

Fimmvörðuháls

11 If you haven't time to complete one of Iceland's multiday treks, the 23km, day-long Fimmvörðuháls trek (p144) will quench your wanderer's thirst. Start at the shimmering cascades of Skógafoss; hike up into the hinterland to discover a veritable parade of waterfalls; gingerly tiptoe over the steaming remnants of the Eyjafjallajökull eruption; and hike along the stone terraces of a flower-filled kingdom that ends in silent Þórsmörk, a haven for campers, hemmed by a crown of glacial ridges. Right: Fimmvörðuháls Pass (p144)

10

11

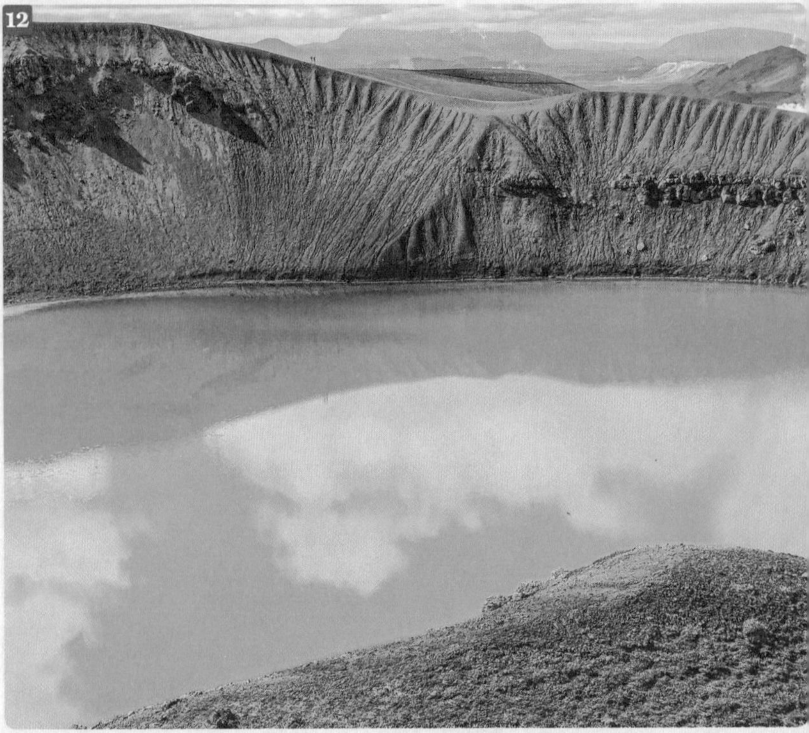

Askja & Surrounds

12 Accessible for only a few months each year, storied Askja (p348) is a mammoth caldera ringed by mountains and enclosing a sapphire-blue lake. To access this glorious, otherworldly place, you'll need a robust 4WD, a few days for hiking, or passage on a super-Jeep tour. Highlands excursions generally incorporate river crossings, impossibly vast lava fields, regal mountain vistas and outlaw hideouts – and possibly a naked soak in geothermal waters. Added bonus: head south from Askja to visit Iceland's freshest lava field at Holuhraun. Above: Víti crater, near Askja (p348)

Vestmannaeyjar

13 An offshore archipelago of craggy peaks, Vestmannaeyjar (p163) is a mere 30-minute ferry ride from the mainland, but feels miles and miles away in sentiment. A boat tour of the scattered islets unveils squawking seabirds, towering cliffs and postcard-worthy vistas of lonely hunting cabins perched atop rocky outcrops. The islands' 4000-plus population is focused on Heimaey, a small town of windswept bungalows with a scarring curl of lava that flows straight through its centre – a poignant reminder of Iceland's volatile landscape. Top right: Heimaey (p163)

Puffins & Whales

14 Iceland's two biggest wildlife drawcards are its most charismatic creatures: the twee puffin, which flits around like an anxious bumblebee, and the mighty whale, a number of species of which, including the immense blue whale, visit Iceland's coast. Opportunities to see both abound on land and sea. Whale-watching heartland is Húsavík (p270), and other northern towns and Reykjavík also offer cruises. Colonies of puffins are poised and ready for their close-up at numerous coastal cliffs and offshore isles, including Heimaey, Grímsey, Drangey, Látrabjarg and Borgarfjörður Eystri. Bottom right: Puffins

13

14

Need to Know

For more information, see Survival Guide (p387)

Currency
Icelandic króna (kr or ISK)

Language
Icelandic; English widely spoken

Visas
Generally not required for stays of up to 90 days.

Money
Iceland is an almost cashless society where credit cards reign supreme, even in the most rural reaches. PIN required for purchases. ATMs available in all towns.

Mobile Phones
Mobile (cell) coverage is widespread. Visitors with GSM phones can make roaming calls; purchase a local SIM card if you're staying a while.

Time
Western European Time Zone (equal to GMT)

When to Go

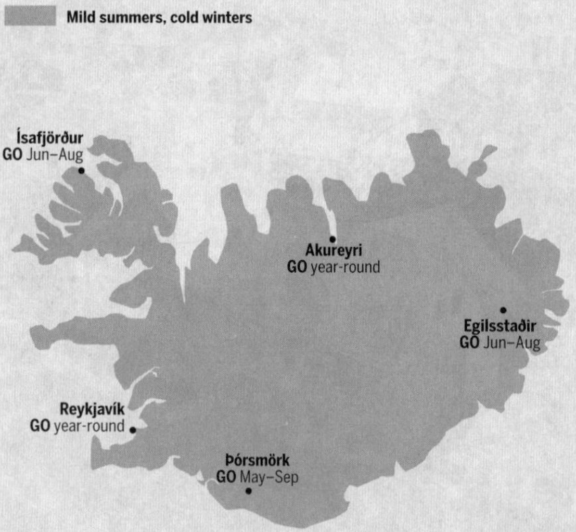

High Season
(Jun–Aug)

- Visitors descend en masse, especially to Reykjavík and the south. Prices peak; prebookings are essential.
- Endless daylight, plentiful festivals, busy activities.
- Interior mountain roads open to 4WDs, mid-June or later; hikers welcome.

Shoulder
(May & Sep)

- Breezier weather; occasional snows in the interior (access via mountain roads weather dependent).
- Optimal visiting conditions if you prefer fewer crowds and lower prices over cloudless days.

Low Season
(Oct–Apr)

- Mountain roads closed; some minor roads shut due to weather conditions.
- Winter activities on offer, including skiing, snowshoeing, visiting ice caves.
- Brief spurts of daylight; long nights with possible Northern Lights viewings.

Useful Websites

Visit Iceland (www.visiticeland.com) Official tourism portal.

Visit Reykjavík (www.visitreykjavik.is) Official site for the capital.

Icelandic Met Office (http://en.vedur.is) Best resource for weather forecasts.

Icelandic Road Administration (www.road.is) Details road openings and current conditions.

Lonely Planet (www.lonelyplanet.com/iceland) Destination information, traveller forum and more.

Important Numbers

To call from outside Iceland, dial your international access code, Iceland's country code (354) then the seven-digit number. There are no area codes in Iceland.

Emergency services (police, ambulance, fire, Search & Rescue)	☎112
Directory enquiries	☎118
Iceland country code (dialling in)	☎354
International access code (dialling out)	☎00
Weather	☎902 0600
Road condition information	☎1777

Exchange Rates

Australia	A$1	kr89
Canada	C$1	kr91
Europe	€1	kr132
Japan	¥100	kr116
NZ	NZ$1	kr85
UK	UK£1	kr152
US	US$1	kr116

For current exchange rates, see www.xe.com.

Daily Costs

Budget: less than kr18,000

- Camping: kr1200–1800
- Dorm bed: kr4500–7000
- Hostel breakfast: kr1800–2000
- Grill-bar grub or soup lunch: kr1500–2200
- One-way bus ticket Reykjavík–Akureyri: kr8800–9300

Midrange: kr18,000–35,000

- Guesthouse double room: kr18,000–28,000
- Cafe meal: kr2500–3500
- Museum entry: kr1000
- Small vehicle rental (per day): from kr10,000

Top end: more than kr35,000

- Boutique double room: kr30,000–40,000
- Main dish in top-end restaurant: kr4000–7000
- 4WD rental (per day): from kr20,000

Opening Hours

Opening hours vary throughout the year (some places are closed outside the high season). In general hours tend to be longer from June to August, and shorter from September to May.

Banks 9am–4pm Monday to Friday

Cafe-bars 10am–1am Sunday to Thursday, 10am to between 3am and 6am Friday and Saturday

Cafes 10am–6pm

Petrol stations 8am–10pm or 11pm

Restaurants 11.30am–2.30pm and 6pm–9pm or 10pm

Shops 10am–6pm Monday to Friday, 10am–4pm Saturday; some Sunday opening in Reykjavík malls and major shopping strips.

Supermarkets 9am–8pm (11pm in Reykjavík)

Vínbúðin (government-run alcohol stores) Variable; many outside Reykjavík only open for a couple of hours per day.

Arriving in Iceland

Keflavík International Airport Iceland's primary international airport, is 48km southwest of Reykjavík. Flybus (www.re.is), Airport Express (www.airportexpress.is) and public busline Strætó (www.bus.is) have buses connecting the airport with Reykjavík. Flybus and Airport Express offer pick-up/drop-off at many city accommodations (to bus station/hotel from kr2100/2700); Strætó is slightly cheaper (kr1680, to bus station only). Airport Express has a new connection between the airport and Akureyri. Note: if you are transferring to a domestic flight, you need to travel into Reykjavík to reach the domestic airport. Flybus offers transfers from Keflavík from kr2800.

Cars can be rented from the airport.

Taxis link KEF with Reykjavík but are expensive(about kr15,000),

Getting Around

Car Vehicles can be expensive to hire but provide great freedom. A 2WD vehicle will get you almost everywhere in summer. Driving into the highlands and on F roads requires 4WDs.

Bus A decent bus network operates from around mid-May to mid-September, shuttling you between major destinations and into the highlands. Outside these months, services are less frequent (even nonexistent). Check map at www.publictransport.is.

Air Domestic flights are good if you're short on time.

For much more on **getting around**, see p401

What's New

Everything Is Changing

Almost *everything* in Iceland is undergoing change. The country is one of the world's hottest travel destinations (it's seen a 20% growth in visitor numbers each year since 2010). The result: new sights and activities, increased tour options and operators, new and/or expanding accommodation, improved roads and tunnels, more airlines servicing Iceland. And increased demand has seen increased prices (websites are the best source of up-to-date rates).

Winter Appeal

Although most visitors come in summer, winter arrivals are surging – and this means more accommodation is staying open year-round, and more winter tours and activities are springing up, from ice cave visits to heliskiing. (p235)

Blue Lagoon Prebooking

The boom is having widespread consequences. It's getting tougher to be spontaneous, for example – visits to the Blue Lagoon must now be prebooked. (p101)

New lava at Holuhraun

Nature itself is changing the landscape: for instance, the 2014–15 eruption of Bárðarbunga has left Holuhraun, Iceland's newest lava field, deep in the highlands. (p348)

New Camping Laws

With so many visitors, Iceland's unspoilt nature is facing increased traffic, and authorities are looking at ways to protect it. New legislation prohibits wild camping for campervans and the like – make sure you know the ins and outs of this. (p391)

Hotels Booming

Every small town seems to have a handful of new guesthouses, while many farms are adding cottages and/or rooms. The hotel chains have big plans: Fosshótel has a shiny new option in Reykjavík, another just east of Skaftafell, a big renovation completed in Húsavík, and construction under way in Mývatn. Icelandair is partnering with Hilton to open several high-end properties in the capital. And yet, it's still tough to find a room in July!

New Sights, New Activities

In Reykjavík, new attractions range from the absorbing Culture House (p64) to a chocolate factory (p59). The Wilderness Center (p293) is a creative, multifaceted farm in east Iceland; there's fresh, frosty appeal at the Langjökull Ice Cave (p180); new hot springs at Krauma (p178) in the west; and a high-tech new LAVA Center (p138) planned near Hvolsvöllur. You can now kayak among icebergs on a glacier lagoon (p330), dive with puffins off Grímsey (p260), or go dog sledding near Mývatn (p262).

For more recommendations and reviews, see lonelyplanet.com/Iceland

If You Like...

Wildlife

Vestmannaeyjar's puffins The largest puffin colony in the world lives in this eye-catching archipelago. (p163)

Húsavík's whales View underwater marvels and bird life on a boat expedition from Iceland's whale-watching heartland. (p275)

Hornstrandir's Arctic foxes Iceland's only native mammal thrives in the faraway kingdom of towering cliffs and mossy stones. (p212)

Lake Mývatn's birds Twitchers adore the marshy surrounds of the lake, a magnet for migrating geese and all kinds of waterfowl. (p259)

Vatnsnes Peninsula's seals Take a seal-spotting cruise from Hvammstangi or drive the peninsula to scout for sunbaking pinnipeds. (p225)

Stunning Scenery

You realise that choosing between incomparable vistas is like trying to pick a favourite child? This list could be endless...

Þingeyri to Bíldudalur Zipper-like fjordheads resemble fleets of earthen ships engaged in battle. (p203)

Breiðafjörður Thousands of islets dot the sweeping bay as rainbows soar overhead in summertime sun showers. (p181)

Skaftafell to Höfn Glittering glaciers, brooding mountains and an iceberg-filled lagoon line this stretch along the Ring Road's southeast coast. (p319)

Eastfjords Supermodel Seyðisfjörður steals the limelight, but its fine fjord neighbours are just as photogenic. (p295)

Þórsmörk A magnificent forested kingdom nestled under volcanic peaks, wild stretches of desert and looming glaciers. (p152)

Askja A remote, sapphire-blue lake at the heart of an immense caldera accessed across vast, barren lava fields. (p348)

Tröllaskagi Peninsula The road hugs steep mountainsides, then emerges from tunnels to capture magical vistas of glistening waters. (p231)

Hiking

Landmannalaugar and Þórsmörk Striking realms offering endless foot fodder; the hike between these centres is the original flavour of wilderness walking. (p148)

Hornstrandir Pristine nature as far as the eye can see in this hiking paradise orbiting the Arctic Circle. (p214)

Skaftafell Follow trails through twisting birch woods or don crampons to tackle offshoots of mammoth Vatnajökull ice cap. (p319)

Jökulsárgljúfur A veritable smorgasbord of geological wonders, including thundering waterfalls and Iceland's 'Grand Canyon'. (p276)

Kerlingarfjöll A remote highland massif with geothermal activity, and a growing reputation among the hiking community. (p343)

Borgarfjörður Eystri The base for a superb series of trails – don't miss the giant boulders and green ponds of Stórurð. (p295)

Lagoons & Swimming Pools

Blue Lagoon It's hard not to adore a soak in this steaming silica soup surrounded by dramatic flourishes of frozen lava. (p101)

Mývatn Nature Baths Ease your aching hiking muscles at the north's scenic answer to the Blue Lagoon. (p268)

Krossneslaug A Valhalla at the edge of the world where lapping Arctic waters mingle with a toasty geothermal source. (p220)

Lýsuhólslaug Swimming in this pool's mineral-rich waters is like soaking in a warm gin fizz with a twist of algae. (p193)

Sundlaugin á Hofsósi This perfectly sited fjordside swimming pool puts the sleepy northern town of Hofsós on the map. (p232)

Gamla Laugin Mist rises from the 'Secret Lagoon' in Flúðir, surrounded by wildflower-filled meadows. (p119)

Víti The milky-blue waters are tepid, but the location – a crater beside the Askja caldera in the remote interior highland – is sizzling. (p348)

History

Settlement Exhibition Brilliantly curated exhibit constructed around the excavation site of an ancient Viking hall. (p54)

Settlement Centre Insight into Iceland's settlement and famous *Egil's Saga* through beautiful wooden sculptures. (p171)

Herring Era Museum Re-creates the heydey of herring fishing, which once brought frenzied activity and riches to Siglufjörður. (p233)

Víkingaheimar A fresh-faced museum whose centrepiece is a perfect reconstruction of the oldest known Viking-age ship. (p105)

Lakagígar Attempt to comprehend one of the most catastrophic volcanic events in human history. (p317)

Eldheimar The 'Pompeii of the North' museum gives insight into the devastating 1973 eruption on Heimaey. (p164)

Fáskrúðsfjörður The French flavour of this fjord is celebrated

Top: Dynjandi (p204)
Bottom: Fish soup

with a new hotel and museum development. (p306)

National Museum Great historical context and content, spanning Settlement to the modern age. (p65)

Icelandic Emigration Center How and why so many Icelanders headed to the New World for a new life in the late 19th century. (p231)

Local Food

Fish soup Any restaurant worth its salt has fish soup on the menu – try it at Narfeyrarstofa (p184) or Gamla Rif (p189).

Lamb Iceland's headliner meat is a locavore's dream; it falls off the bone at myriad restaurants, including Fjallakaffi. (p270)

Hákarl A pungent tribute to Iceland's unpalatable past – try a piece of this spongy-soggy oddity at Bjarnarhöfn. (p185)

Langoustine The Höfn fishing fleet pulls countless crustaceans from the icy local waters; Höfn's restaurants simply grill and add butter. (p333)

Skyr A delicious yoghurt-y snack available at any supermarket in Iceland. (p383)

Hverabrauð Sample this cake-like rye bread, baked underground using geothermal heat, around Mývatn. (p259)

Waterfalls

Dettifoss With the greatest volume of any waterfall in Europe, thundering Dettifoss is nature at its most awesome. (p280)

Goðafoss The 'Waterfall of the Gods', loaded with spiritual symbolism; looks like it's been ripped straight from a shampoo commercial. (p259)

Skógafoss Camp near this gorgeous gusher then hike up into the highlands for 20 more waterfalls just beyond. (p143)

Dynjandi Veins of Arctic water cascade 100m over terraces of stone and afford some of the most gorgeous fjord views. (p204)

Seljalandsfoss A (slippery) path in the rockface gives behind-the-scenes access to this postcard-perfect chute. (p141)

Hengifoss Iceland's second-highest falls plummet into a photogenic, brown-and-red-striped gorge. (p293)

Unique Sleeps

Hótel Egilsen A run-down merchant's house transformed into a gorgeous harbour inn with boutique-chic fixtures. (p183)

Hótel Djúpavík This legendary bolt-hole fulfils fjord fantasies; Sigur Rós shot part of their documentary here. (p220)

Dalvík HI Hostel Charming, vintage-inspired hostel like no other we've encountered. Budget prices belie boutique decor. (p241)

Silfurberg Soak in a glass-dome-enclosed hot-pot at this luxurious boutique guesthouse in view-blessed Breiðdalur valley. (p308)

Ion Luxury Adventure Hotel Swim in geothermal waters and dine on organic, local fare at this award-winning design hotel. (p114)

Wilderness Center Bunk down in a re-created *baðstofa* (historic living/sleeping room) on a farm in a glorious, remote eastern valley. (p293)

Skálanes Remote fjordside farm and nature reserve that gladdens the heart of retreat-seeking ecologists and birdwatchers. (p301)

Buubble Hotel Scouting for Northern Lights might prevent you catching any shut-eye in these unique clear domes. (p118)

Tungulending A secluded waterfront outpost designed to make you slow down and enjoy the knockout views. (p276)

Þakgil Camp in an emerald-green valley among stark mountains and dramatic rock formations. (p163)

Architecture & Design

Churches Some of Iceland's most intriguing architectural flourishes can be seen in churches in Stykkishólmur (p183), Akureyri (p243) and Reykjavík (p59).

Iceland Design Centre Promoting Iceland's designers and architects, and the brains behind the annual DesignMarch event. (p59)

Harpa Reykjavík's dazzling concert hall and cultural centre glows like the switchboard of an alien ship after dark. (p59)

Turf houses A paradigm of pre-modern Iceland, these hobbit houses offer a wonderfully whimsical insight into Iceland's past. (p227)

Reykjavík design boutiques From sleek, fish-skin purses to knitted *lopapeysur* (Icelandic woollen sweaters) and nature-inspired jewellery. (p90)

Þórbergssetur Honouring a local writer, this museum has an inspired exterior (resembling a giant bookshelf) that's a traffic-stopper. (p329)

Month by Month

TOP EVENTS

Iceland Airwaves, November

Reykjavík Culture Night, August

Þjóðhátíð, August

Bræðslan, July

Northern Lights, mid-September to mid-April

January

After December's cheer, the festive hangover hits. The first few weeks of the year can feel like an anticlimax – not helped by long dark nights and inclement weather.

Þorrablót

This Viking midwinter feast from late January to mid- or late February is marked nationwide with stomach-churning treats such as *hákarl* (fermented Greenland shark), *svið* (singed sheep's head) and *hrútspungar* (rams' testicles). All accompanied by shots of *brennivín* (a potent schnapps nicknamed 'black death'). Hungry?

February

The coldest month in many parts of Iceland, though life in the capital seems untouched. The countryside is scenic under snow, but it's mostly dark – there are only seven to eight hours of daylight per day.

Winter Lights Festival

Reykjavík sparkles mid-month with this winter-warmer encompassing Museum Night and Pool Night (late-opening museums and swimming pools), illuminated landmarks, light installations, concerts, and celebrations to mark International Children's Day. See www.vetrarhatid.is.

Food & Fun

International chefs team up with local restaurants and vie for awards at this capital feast held in February or March. Teams are given the finest Icelandic ingredients (lamb and seafood, natch) to create their masterpieces. See www.foodandfun.is.

Sónar Reykjavík

Music, creativity and technology: this festival brings all three together for three days in February at Harpa concert hall, with more than 70 bands and DJs from Iceland and abroad (www.sonarreykjavik.com).

March

Winter is officially over, but it's not quite time to start celebrating. The country wakes from its slumber; winter activities such as skiing are popular as daylight hours increase.

Beer Day

Hard to imagine, but beer was illegal in Iceland for 75 years. On 1 March, Icelanders celebrate the day in 1989 when the prohibition was overturned. Pubs, restaurants and clubs around Reykjavík are especially beer-lovin' on this night.

Iceland Winter Games

Snowy activities take centre stage in Akureyri, Iceland's winter-sports capital, including international free ski and snowboard competitions. Tour operators offer ways to get out into snowy scenes (dog sledding, snowmobiling, super-Jeep and helicopter tours). Get more details at www.icelandwintergames.com.

DesignMarch

The local design scene is celebrated in Reykjavík at this four-day fest of all things aesthetically pleasing: from fashion to furniture, architecture to food design. It's organised by the Iceland Design Centre (see www.designmarch.is).

April

Easter is celebrated in a traditional fashion (Easter-egg hunts and roast lamb), and spring is in the air. Days lengthen and the mercury climbs, meaning lots of greenery after the snow melts, plus thousands of migrating birds.

Sumardagurinn Fyrsti

Rather ambitiously, Icelanders celebrate the first day of summer (the first Thursday after 18 April) with celebrations and street parades. A case of winter-induced madness? No, it's a nod to the Old Norse calendar, which divided the year into just two seasons: winter and summer.

Puffins on Parade

To the delight of twitchers and photographers, the divinely comedic puffin arrives in huge numbers (an estimated 10 million birds) for the breeding season, departing for warmer climes by mid-August. There are puffin colonies all around the country.

May

May is shoulder season, and isn't a bad month to visit, just before the tourist season cranks up in earnest. Enjoy prices before they escalate, plus lengthening days, spring wildflowers and first-rate birdwatching.

Reykjavík Arts Festival

Culture-vultures flock to Iceland's premier cultural festival, which showcases two weeks of local and international theatre performances, film, dance, music and visual art. See www.listahatid.is.

June

Hello summer! The short three-month-long tourist season begins. Pros: the best weather, near-endless daylight, the pick of tours and excursions, the best choice of accommodation. Cons: big crowds, peak prices, the need to book all lodging.

Seafarers' Day

Fishing is integral to Icelandic life, and Seafarers' Day (Sjómannadagurinn) is party time in fishing villages. On the first weekend in June, every ship in Iceland is in harbour and all sailors have a day off. Salty-dog events include drinking, rowing and swimming contests, tugs-of-war and mock sea rescues.

Hafnarfjörður Viking Festival

The peace is shattered as Viking hordes invade this seaside town near Reykjavík for a four-day festival mid-June. Expect family-friendly storytelling, staged battles, archery and music. See www.vikingvillage.is.

Whale Watching

Some 11 species of whale are regularly spotted in waters around Iceland. Sightings happen year-round but the best time is from June to August. Whale-watching boats leave from the Reykjavík area, from Akureyri and surrounds, and from Húsavík, the country's whale-watching HQ.

National Day

The country's biggest holiday commemorates the founding of the Republic of Iceland, on 17 June 1944, with parades and general patriotic merriness. Tradition has it that the sun isn't supposed to shine. And it usually doesn't.

Opening of Mountain Roads

The highland regions of Iceland are generally blanketed in snow well into the warmer months. The opening of 4WD-only mountain roads is weather dependent, but generally occurs around mid-June; roads are closed again by late September/October. The website www.road.is keeps you updated.

Midnight Sun

Except for the island of Grímsey, Iceland lies just south of the Arctic Circle. Still, around the summer solstice (21 June) it's possible to view the midnight sun (when the setting sun doesn't fully dip below the horizon), especially in the country's north. The endless daylight is perfect for visiting natural attractions in the wee hours, avoiding peak daytime crowds.

Secret Solstice

This excellent music festival (www.secretsolstice.is) with local and international acts coincides with the summer solstice, so there's 24-hour daylight for partying. It's held at Laugardalur in Reykjavík.

Midsummer

Although midsummer isn't as major an event as in the rest of the Nordic countries, the longest day of the year is celebrated in Iceland with solstice parties and bonfires (staged anytime between 21 and 24 June).

Humar Festival

The tasty *humar* (often called lobster, but technically it's langoustine) is pulled fresh from Icelandic waters and served a delectable number of ways in the fishing town of Höfn during the Humarhátíð festival in late June/early July.

July

Iceland's festival pace quickens alongside a (hopefully) rising temperature gauge and a distinct swelling of tourist numbers. Expect busy roads, crowded trails, packed camping grounds, no-vacancy guesthouses etc and book ahead.

Landsmót Hestamanna

Horse lovers: the week-long national Icelandic horse competition is held in even-numbered years at rotating host towns. It's a beloved spectator event and excuse for a country festival. See www.landsmot.is.

Folk Music Festival

The tiny but perfect five-day folk music festival in Siglufjörður welcomes Icelandic and foreign musicians. Enjoy traditional tunes, courses on Icelandic music, dance and handicrafts. See www.folkmusik.is.

Skálholt Summer Concerts

The cathedral at the historic religious centre of Skálholt hosts around 40 public concerts, lectures and workshops over a six-week period from July to August. The focus is on contemporary religious music and early music. See www.sumartonleikar.is.

Eistnaflug

The remote Eastfjords town of Neskaupstaður goes *off* in the second week of July, when the population doubles to celebrate the heavy-metal festival Eistnaflug. Metal, hardcore, punk, rock and indie bands share the stage. See www.eistnaflug.is.

Bræðslan

The beloved Bræðslan pop/rock festival has earned a reputation for great music and an intimate atmosphere. Some big local names (and a few international ones) come to play in tiny, out-of-the-way Borgarfjörður Eystri on the third weekend in July. Check out www.braedslan.com.

August

The busy tourist season continues apace, with Southern Europeans flying north for vacation. By mid-month the puffins have departed (and some whales, too); by late August the local kids are back at school, and the nights are lengthening.

Verslunarmannahelgi

A public-holiday long weekend (the first weekend in August) when Icelanders flock to rural festivals, rock concerts and wild camping-ground parties.

Þjóðhátíð

This earth-shaking event occurs in Heimaey, Vestmannaeyjar, on the August long weekend, commemorating the day in 1874 when foul weather prevented the islanders from partying when Iceland's constitution was established. Up to 16,000 people descend to watch bands and fireworks, and drink gallons of alcohol. See www.dalurinn.is.

Herring Festival

On the August long weekend, Siglufjörður celebrates its heady herring-induced heyday with dancing, feasting, drinking and fishy-flavoured activities.

Reykjavík Culture Night

On Culture Night (Menningarnótt), held mid-month, Reykjavikers turn out in force for a day and night of art, music, dance and fireworks. Many galleries, ateliers, shops, cafes and churches stay open until late. See www.menningarnott.is for a full program.

Reykjavík Marathon

Your chance to get sporty, mid-month in Reykjavík sees more than 15,000 people get sweaty at full- and half-marathons, as well as fun runs. See www.marathon.is.

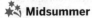

Reykjavík Jazz Festival

Mid-August, Reykjavík toe-taps its way through five days dedicated to jazz, man. Local and international musicians blow their own trumpets at events staged at Harpa. Check out www.reykjavikjazz.is.

Reykjavík Pride

Out and proud since 1999, this festival brings carnival colour to the capital on the second weekend of August. Up to 90,000 people (more than a quarter of the country's population) attend the Pride march and celebrations. See www.hinsegindagar.is/en.

Jökulsárlón Fireworks

Could there be a more beautiful location for a fireworks display than Jökulsárlón glacier lagoon? For one night in mid- to late August, an annual event is staged, with buses shuttling spectators from Höfn, Kirkjubæjarklaustur and Skaftafell. See www.visitvatnajokull.is.

September

Tourist arrivals decrease significantly and prices drop, making this a good time to visit. The weather can still be agreeable, but summer-only hotels, attractions and services are closed. Highland roads are closed by month's end.

Réttir

An autumn highlight, the *réttir* is the farmers' round-up of sheep that have grazed wild over summer. The round-up is often done on horseback and the animals are herded into a corral where the sorting takes place (participants and spectators welcome). Naturally, it's all accompanied by much merrymaking.

Reykjavík International Film Festival

This intimate 11-day event from late September features quirky programming that highlights independent film-making, both home-grown and international. There are also panels and masterclasses. Check the program at www.riff.is.

Reykjavík International Literary Festival

Feeling bookish? This venerable festival gathers international writers for four days of readings and panels in the capital. Check www.bokmenntahatid.is.

October

October marks the official onset of winter, with cooler temperatures, longer nights and the appearance of the Northern Lights.

Northern Lights

Also called aurora borealis, these colourful, dancing lights are caused by charged particles from solar flares colliding with the earth's atmosphere. They can only be viewed on a dark night with no cloud cover. The best months for viewing are from October to April (from mid-September, if you're lucky).

November

Summer is a distant memory. November sees nights lengthening (sunsets around 4pm) and weather cooling, but Reykjavík parties hard, with big crowds gathering for its music festival.

Iceland Airwaves

You'd be forgiven for thinking Iceland is just one giant music-producing machine. Since the first edition of Iceland Airwaves was held in 1999, this fab festival has become one of the world's premier annual showcases for new music (Icelandic and otherwise). Check out www.icelandairwaves.is.

Days of Darkness

East Iceland (Egilsstaðir and the fjords) perversely celebrates the onset of winter over 10 days in early to mid-November, with dark dances, ghost stories, magic shows and torch-lit processions during its unusual Days of Darkness (Dagar Myrkurs) festival.

Ice Caves

The frozen blue wonder of natural ice caves becomes accessible close to glacier edges from around November through to March. For safety reasons you *must* visit with a guide – arrange tours with local operators in the southeast, between Skaftafell and Höfn. (p321)

December

A festive atmosphere brings cheer to the darkest time of the year. Christmas markets, concerts and parties keep things bright and cosy, followed by New Year's Eve celebrations. Note that some hotels are closed between Christmas and New Year.

STOCKWITHME/SHUTTERSTOCK ©

Plan Your Trip
Itineraries

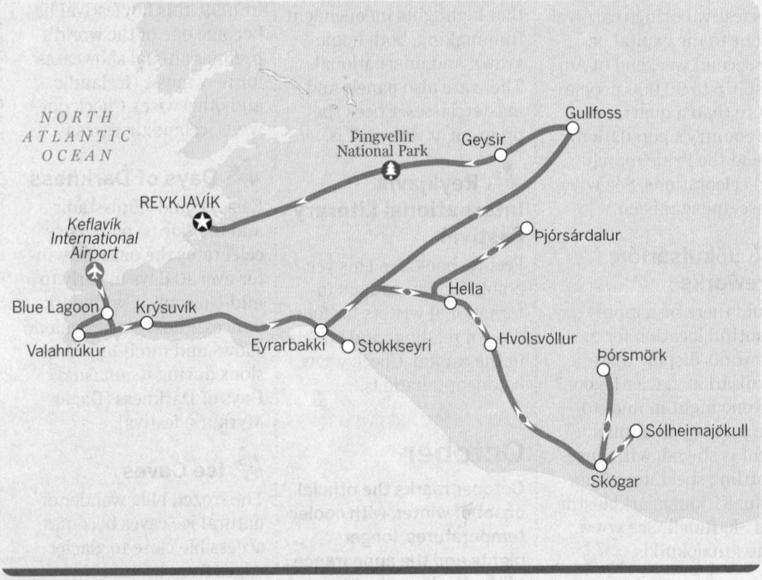

4 DAYS Reykjavík Minibreak

Whether you're on a lengthy layover or enjoying a long weekend away, don't miss the chance to get out into the countryside and take in some of the natural wonders located within a stone's throw of the capital. It's simple to string together the top sights, including the Golden Circle, with more off-the-beaten-path diversions, and still have a bit of time left to lap up Reykjavík's unique charm.

After landing in **Keflavík International Airport** make a beeline for the **Blue Lagoon** to soak away the jet lag in surreal waters and silica mud. Wander the Reykjanes Peninsula's steaming earth near **Valahnúkur** or **Krýsuvík** before barrelling down the coastal highway for fresh seafood in **Eyrarbakki** or **Stokkseyri**. Choose a base near **Hella** or **Hvolsvöllur** to get out in the open air on horseback: the lush waterfall-rimmed Fljótshlíð valley is a key candidate. Or try to spot the Northern Lights (in the colder months). Active bodies will enjoy the stunning Fimmvörðuháls hike from **Skógar** up through the ridge

Geysir (p116)

between two brooding ice caps (and the site of the Eyjafjallajökull eruption in 2010) then down into **Þórsmörk**, a forested valley dotted with wild Arctic flowers. Or you can take a super-Jeep tour or amphibious bus to Þórsmörk, and head out on day hikes around the valley. Those who are tighter on time can trek along the glacial tongue of **Sólheimajökull** instead.

On your way back west, roam the **Þjórsárdalur**, a broad volcanic river valley with a handful of disparate sights, including a Settlement Era farmstead, hidden waterfalls, and the foothills of Hekla volcano. Or, swing up to the gushing cascades at **Gullfoss**, the spurting **Geysir** from which all others got their name, and the rift valley and ancient parliament site **Þingvellir National Park** – the classic Golden Circle route.

Wrap up your minibreak with a night in **Reykjavík**. Iceland's capital bustles with an all-star assortment of design boutiques, interesting museums and galleries, scrumptious restaurants and lively bars, plus there's easy access to whale-watching trips from the Old Harbour.

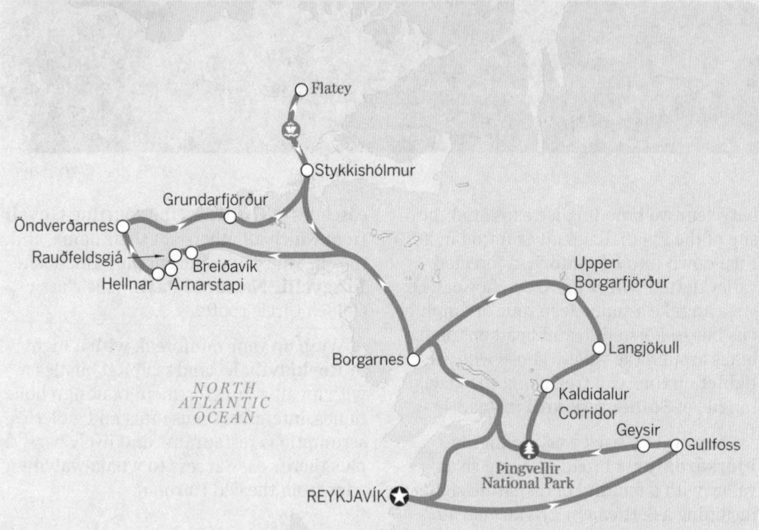
Flatey
Stykkishólmur
Grundarfjörður
Öndverðarnes
Rauðfeldsgjá
Breiðavík
Hellnar
Arnarstapi
Upper
Borgarfjörður
Langjökull
Borgarnes
NORTH
ATLANTIC
OCEAN
Kaldidalur
Corridor
Geysir
Gullfoss
Þingvellir
National Park
REYKJAVÍK

RAMIRO TORRENTS/GETTY IMAGES ©

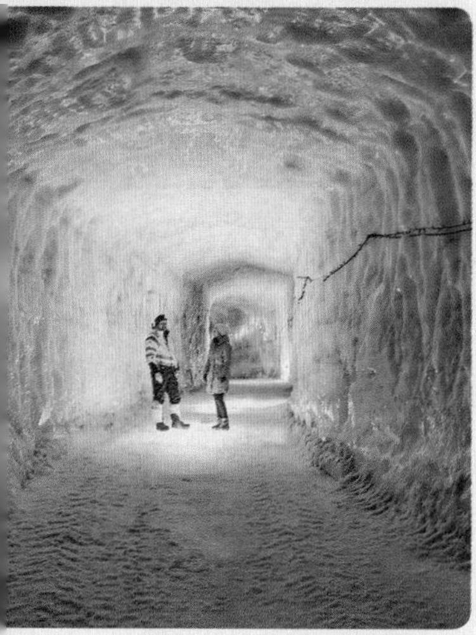

CULTURA EXCLUSIVE/TIM E WHITE/GETTY IMAGES ©

Top: Arnarstapi (p191)
Bottom: Langjökull (p180)

1 WEEK Best of the West

With one week to spend, you'll be able to roam further than the popular Golden Circle and the busy southwest. We like heading northwest from Reykjavík to lesser-travelled west Iceland, which is chock-a-block with history and boasts landscapes ranging from lava fields to broad fjords and ice caps, and gives a sense of the wonderful solitude that Iceland offers.

Start in **Reykjavík**, enjoying the city's museums, cafes and bars while getting acclimatised. Then complete the day-long Golden Circle with stops at glittering **Gullfoss**, surging **Geysir**, and historic **Þingvellir National Park**, where you'll witness the tearing apart of the continental plates. If you're feeling adventurous, go inland and bump along the rutted **Kaldidalur Corridor** for stunning vistas through the pinnacles of several ice caps. Stop in at **Langjökull** for exploration of its glistening tunnel and caves, or a taste of icy activities such as snowmobiling or dog sledding. You'll emerge at **Upper Borgarfjörður**, where you can sleep in the quiet countryside and explore enormous lava tubes. If you're not up for the back-country aspects of the Kaldidalur Corridor, instead head to **Borgarnes** along the coastal route, and learn about the sagas at its excellent Settlement Centre.

Next up, explore the wonderful Snæfellsnes Peninsula. Start by horse riding around the bay of **Breiðavík** or creeping into the bizarre gorge, **Rauðfeldsgjá**. Then head west to **Arnarstapi**, where you can hike the coastal trail to **Hellnar** or pick up a Snæfellsjökull glacier tour, exploring Jules Verne's fabled centre of the earth. The area is part of Snæfellsjökull National Park and offers a multitude of hikes, taking in bird cliffs, volcanic craters, lava tubes and protected native flower terrain.

On the tip of the peninsula near **Öndverðarnes** look for pods of orca whales, or catch a whale-watching or puffin-viewing tour near **Grundarfjörður**. Then alight in charming **Stykkishólmur**, where you can take in interesting museums and sup on tasty mussels. If time permits, hop aboard the *Baldur* ferry for a day trip to quaint **Flatey** island; it's a great way to really disconnect from the world before returning to the capital.

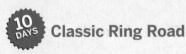

10 DAYS Classic Ring Road

For such a wild, wonderful land, much of Iceland is surprisingly compact; the classic Ring Road trip loops you near the most popular sights. With extra time, you can add on myriad other adventures along the way.

Start in **Reykjavík**, enjoying the city's creature comforts, before heading out in a clockwise fashion. Stop in **Borgarnes** for its fascinating Settlement Centre, historical sights and tasty restaurants. Then zip up to **Stykkishólmur**, an adorable village overlooking a bay studded by islets. With extra time, from here you could detour to the Snæfellsnes Peninsula. Either way, rejoin the Ring Road, breaking free of it once more to explore the quaint townships and coastal vistas of the **Tröllaskagi Peninsula** before gliding through **Akureyri**, Iceland's unofficial northern capital. Head to the geological treasure chest of the **Mývatn** region next, with a stop at **Dettifoss** to experience nature's awesome power firsthand. Push eastwards, detouring to **Borgarfjörður Eystri** for summer puffins galore. Take a break in **Seyðisfjörður**, then tackle the long journey through the rest of the east as the road curls along magical fjords.

Pause in **Höfn** for langoustine, then jump on a snowmobile to discover the vast ice cap at **Vatnajökull**. Don't miss the glacial lagoon at **Jökulsárlón**, or neighbouring Fjallsárlón, where giant bergs break off glaciers and float out to sea. You can warm up your hiking legs in **Skaftafell**, then head south across mossy lava fields and enormous river deltas to **Vík**, which has a fantastical basalt-columned beach and puffin cliffs. Still feeling spry? Tackle the awesome trek from **Skógar** to **Þórsmörk**, a verdant interior valley. Or continue west along the Ring Road, passing enormous waterfalls at **Skógafoss** and **Seljalandsfoss**, then veer away one last time to check out the Golden Circle: **Gullfoss**, **Geysir** and the yawning continental divide and ancient governmental seat at **Þingvellir National Park**. Roll back into **Reykjavík** to spend the remainder of your holiday chatting with the locals, whether in the city's geothermal pools or during late-night pub crawls.

ALEXEY STIOP/SHUTTERSTOCK ©

JUSTIN FOULKES/LONELY PLANET ©

Top: Stykkishólmur (p181)
Bottom: Dettifoss (p280)

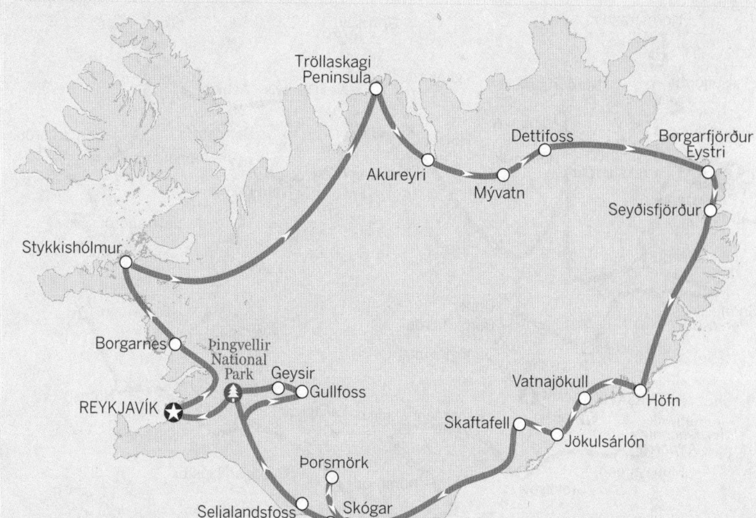

Tröllaskagi Peninsula
Akureyri
Dettifoss
Mývatn
Borgarfjörður Eystri
Seyðisfjörður
Stykkishólmur
Borgarnes
Þingvellir National Park
Geysir
Gullfoss
REYKJAVÍK
Vatnajökull
Höfn
Skaftafell
Jökulsárlón
Þorsmörk
Seljalandsfoss
Skógar
Skógafoss
Vík

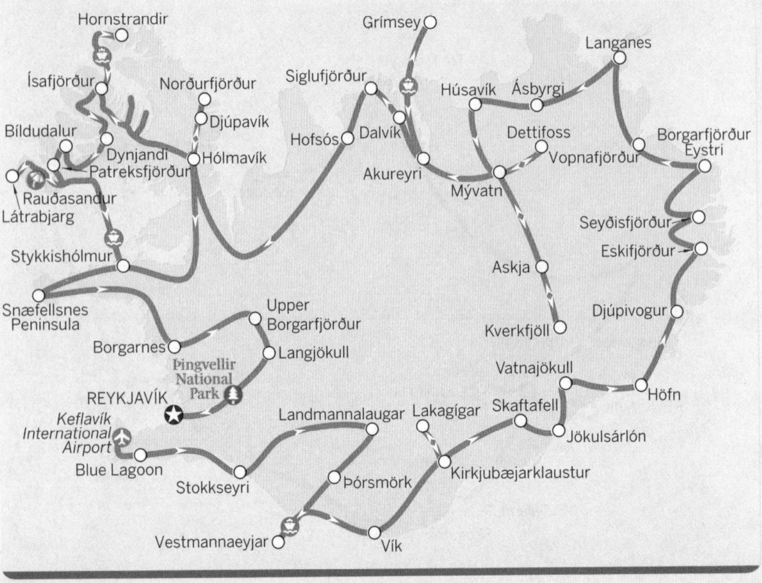
Hornstrandir
Ísafjörður
Norðurfjörður
Djúpavík
Bíldudalur
Dynjandi
Hólmavík
Patreksfjörður
Rauðasandur
Látrabjarg
Stykkishólmur
Snæfellsnes Peninsula
Borgarnes
Upper Borgarfjörður
Langjökull
Þingvellir National Park
REYKJAVÍK
Keflavík International Airport
Blue Lagoon
Stokkseyri
Vestmannaeyjar
Þórsmörk
Vík
Landmannalaugar
Lakagígar
Kirkjubæjarklaustur
Skaftafell
Jökulsárlón
Vatnajökull
Höfn
Djúpivogur
Eskifjörður
Seyðisfjörður
Borgarfjörður Eystri
Vopnafjörður
Langanes
Ásbyrgi
Húsavík
Dettifoss
Mývatn
Askja
Kverkfjöll
Grímsey
Siglufjörður
Dalvík
Hofsós
Akureyri

STANDRET/SHUTTERSTOCK ©

MENNO SCHAEFER/SHUTTERSTOCK ©

Top: Búðir (p192), Southern Snæfellsnes
Bottom: Puffins, Látrabjarg Peninsula (p200)

4 WEEKS The Grand Tour

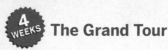

On an extended stay in addition to seeing major sights you can venture further from the Ring Road into the gorgeous Westfjords, or four-wheel-drive the Highlands.

From **Keflavík**, rent wheels and head to the **Blue Lagoon** to unwind. Follow the coastal road to arty **Stokkseyri**, then ditch the car to hike from **Landmannalaugar** to verdant **Þórsmörk**. Next, catch the boat to **Vestmannaeyjar**, where puffins flip-flap over fresh lava. Then sojourn near **Vík**, with its black basalt beach.

At **Kirkjubæjarklaustur** venture up to **Lakagígar** to learn about the devastating effects of Laki's eruptions. **Skaftafell** offers hiking and glacier walking. Don't miss a boat ride with icebergs at **Jökulsárlón** and a snowmobile safari on **Vatnajökull**, Europe's largest ice cap. Pause in **Höfn** for legendary langoustine, then relax in hushed **Breiðdalsvík** before negotiating hairpin fjord roads to peaceful **Eskifjörður** and inspiring **Seyðisfjörður**. Follow the rhyolite cliffs down to **Borgarfjörður Eystri** to photograph puffins, then climb through **Vopnafjörður** to the grassy plains of **Langanes**. The quiet northeastern circuit rolls through **Ásbyrgi** to charming **Húsavík**, perfect for whale watching. Scenic **Mývatn** makes a great base for exploring the pounding waterfall, **Dettifoss**, and Iceland's Highland treasures such as the mammoth caldera at **Askja** and silent ice caves at **Kverkfjöll**. Stop for a slice of civilisation in **Akureyri** before touching the Arctic Circle in **Grímsey**. Wander up through **Dalvík**, check out **Siglufjörður**, then treat yourself to a relaxing swim in **Hofsós**.

Next, head to the Westfjords to learn about ancient witchcraft in **Hólmavík**, sleep fjordside in **Djúpavík** and bathe in the **Norðurfjörður** geothermal spring. Use spunky **Ísafjörður** as a launch pad to **Hornstrandir**, Iceland's majestic hiking reserve. Enter the incredible heart of the Westfjords, to find the gushing waters of **Dynjandi**, and use **Bíldudalur** or Þingeyri as a base for exploring jaw-dropping fjords. Head down to **Patreksfjörður** for a square meal and to visit the bird cliffs at **Látrabjarg** and the mind-blowing pink-red beach at **Rauðasandur**.

Ferry over to charming **Stykkishólmur** and discover the treasures of the **Snæfellsnes Peninsula**. **Borgarnes** and **Upper Borgarfjörður** blend saga sites and hidden caves, then **Langjökull** presents some human handiwork in its ice tunnel. Finish the history lesson at **Þingvellir National Park**. Then end the epic journey in **Reykjavík**, the ebullient capital.

Plan Your Trip

Ring Road Planner

Unless you've visited Iceland before, you'll likely struggle to name an Icelandic town besides Reykjavík. You may worry about planning your visit when so much of the country is vast and unknown. Fear not, the path is clear: take the Ring Road.

Best Ring Road Detours

Snæfellsnes Peninsula

A veritable ring road unto itself that takes in lava fields, wild coastline and an infamous ice cap; 200km detour.

Tröllaskagi Peninsula

Follow Rte 76/Rte 82 as it climbs up towards the Arctic – hair-raising road tunnels and scenic panoramas await; 90km detour.

Borgarfjörður Eystri

Take Rte 94 through rhyolite cliffs and down into this quiet hamlet where there are visiting puffins and superb hiking trails; 150km detour.

Vestmannaeyjar

Hop on the ferry at Landeyjahöfn to discover a rugged archipelago of islets; 30km detour plus a 30-minute boat ride each way.

Þórsmörk

Park at Seljalandsfoss and take the bus into a forested kingdom rife with scenic walks; 50km detour along a rutty road accessible only by certified vehicles; hiking also an option.

The 'Diamond Circle'

Dreamed up by marketers, the Diamond Circle barrels north from Mývatn to take in the whale-filled bay of Húsavík; the grand canyon and trails of Ásbyrgi; and the roaring falls at Dettifoss; 180km detour.

Route 1

Route 1 (Þjóðvegur 1), known as the Ring Road, is the country's main thoroughfare, comprising a super-scenic 1330km (830 miles) of mostly paved highway. It's rarely more than one lane in either direction. Countless gems line its path, while secondary roads lead off it to further adventures.

When to Go

The Ring Road is generally accessible year-round (there may be exceptions during winter storms); many of the secondary roads are closed during the colder months. Check out www.road.is for details of road closures, and www.vedur.is for weather forecasts.

Clockwise or Anticlockwise

It doesn't matter which way you tackle the Ring Road – the landscape reveals itself in an equally cinematic fashion from both directions.

If you're travelling during the latter part of summer (August into September), we recommend driving the loop in a clockwise manner – check off your northern must-sees first as warmer weather sticks around a tad longer in the south.

How Long Do I Need?

Driving the Ring Road without stopping (or breaking the speed limit) would take about 16 hours. Thus, a week-long trip around the country means an average of about 2½ hours of driving per day. While this might seem a bit full-on, remember that the drive is extraordinarily scenic and in summer there's plenty of daylight.

We recommend a minimum of 10 days to do justice to the Ring Road (two weeks is better). For travellers planning an itinerary that's less than a week, we suggest committing to one or two regions in detail (eg Reykjavík and the south or west; or a week in the north), rather than trying to hoof it around the island.

By Car

Discovering Iceland by private vehicle is by far the most convenient way to go though it is the most expensive option.

Renting a Car

It's best to start planning early if searching for low rates. The internet is your best resource, but take care to ensure that the name of your rental service appears on your booking, and to double-check that all fees are included in the quoted price.

Book early for summer hires – companies sometimes run out of vehicles.

2WD or 4WD?

A 2WD vehicle is fine if you're planning to drive just the Ring Road and major secondary roads. If you want to explore the interior (driving on 'F' mountain roads), you'll need a 4WD – alternatively, hire a 2WD and book bus trips or super-Jeep tours to less-accessible areas.

For winter, we don't recommend small 2WDs; consider a 4WD for safety (rental prices are considerably lower in winter). Snow tyres are fitted to winter rentals.

Breaking Up the Journey

When travelling the Ring Road use it as a conduit to explore memorable detours. We recommend choosing five mini-bases along the journey to break up the drive. Try selecting one stop in each region through which the Ring Road passes: the west, north, east, southeast and southwest. You could spend several nights at each base, engaging in the area's best activities and detours before moving on.

RING ROAD ADVICE

➡ Don't confuse the Ring Road, which loops the country, with the Golden Circle (a tourist route in the country's southwest).

➡ The Ring Road doesn't traverse Iceland's interior – if you're keen to see more, two highland routes cut through the centre. These roads are only open in summer, and only to 4WDs; happily, all-terrain buses traverse the routes in summer.

By Bus

Far less convenient than car rental, Iceland's limited bus service is the most cost-effective option for solo travellers. You should budget double the time of a private vehicle to loop around, lest you spend the majority of the trip staring at the countryside through a window.

For comparison, a bus pass that carries two travellers around the island roughly equals the price (excluding petrol) of a small rental car for a week.

By Bicycle

We don't want to dash your dreams, but cyclists will have a tougher time than expected travelling the Ring Road. The changeable weather makes for tough going, and although the path is mostly paved, there is hardly any room on the shoulder of the road to provide a comfortable distance from vehicular traffic. Cycling can be a great way to explore more-rural regions.

By Hitching & Ridesharing

The most cost-effective way to venture around the Ring Road is to stick out your thumb. In summer it's quite easy to hitch all the way around the Ring Road but be aware of the potential risks involved.

Many hostels have ride-share posterboards in their lobbies. A great resource is www.samferda.is, an online ride-share messageboard.

Landmannalaugar, the start of the Laugavegurinn hike (p151

Plan Your Trip

Outdoor Adventures

Iceland's spectacular natural beauty encompasses Western Europe's largest national park and the mightiest ice cap outside the poles, plus a whale-filled ocean and the world's biggest puffin colonies. Prepare to greet soaring mountains, hidden valleys, dark canyons, roaring waterfalls, twisting rivers and fjord-riven coastlines. Getting among it is easy, and utterly exhilarating.

KOJIN/SHUTTERSTOCK ©

Best Time to Go

For multiday hiking Wait for spring thaw; hiking is at its best from July to mid-September.

For highlands exploration Mountain roads open sometime from mid-June to early July, and close again by late September or early October.

For midnight sun Around the summer solstice (21 June) the daylight is endless (especially in the north).

For Northern Lights You'll need dark, clear nights; viewings can occur any time between about mid-September and April.

For skiing The season runs from December to April, with best conditions (and increasing daylight) in February and March.

For whale watching Tours operate year-round, with peak viewing from June to August.

For puffin viewing Peak puffin time is from mid-May to early or mid-August.

For icy endeavours Glacier hikes and snowmobile trips can generally be done year-round (conditions permitting). Boat trips are scheduled on Jökulsárlón from April to October. Mid-November to March is best for ice caving.

For horse riding Multiday treks are great in the shoulder season (May and September to early October) when the weather is cool but mild, and visitor numbers are fewer.

Activities

Hiking

Opportunities for hiking are endless, from leisurely hour-long strolls to multiday wilderness treks. Setting off on foot will open up vast reaches of unspoilt nature; however, the unpredictable weather is always a consideration, and rain, fog and mist can turn an uplifting hike into a miserable trudge. Always be prepared.

Ferðafélag Íslands (www.fi.is) runs huts, campgrounds and hiking trips throughout the country. Offers solid advice on hikes – especially Laugavegurinn.

Top Short Walks

➡ **Skaftafell** Everyone's favourite part of Vatnajökull National Park; offers a slew of short walks around glinting glaciers and brooding waterfalls.

➡ **Þórsmörk** An emerald kingdom tucked between the unforgiving hills of the interior; moderate-to-difficult walks abound.

➡ **Skógar** Hike up into the interior for a parade of waterfalls; continue on to Fimmvörðuháls and down into Þórsmörk for one of Iceland's most rewarding day-long hikes.

➡ **Snæfellsnes Peninsula** Half-day hikes galore through crunchy lava fields; don't miss the coastal walk from Hellnar to Arnarstapi.

➡ **Mývatn** Flat and easy, the marshy Mývatn lakeshore hosts a variety of geological wonders as well as prolific bird life.

➡ **Borgarfjörður Eystri** Superb trails among the rhyolite cliffs, and hikes up to the fjordhead for views.

Best Multiday Treks

➡ **Laugavegurinn** Iceland's classic walk takes you through caramel-coloured dunes, smoking earth and devastating desert. Duration: two to five days.

➡ **Ásbyrgi to Dettifoss** A sampler of Iceland's geological phenomena starts at the northern end of Jökulsárgljúfur (in Vatnajökull National Park) and works its way down the gorge to Europe's most powerful waterfall. Duration: two days.

➡ **Royal Horn** Words can't do justice to Hornstrandir's fan-favourite route and the views of lonely fjords, emerald-green bluffs and swooping gulls. Duration: two to four days.

➡ **Fimmvörðuháls** A parade of waterfalls turns into desert as you pass between hulking glaciers. Then, the steaming stones from the 2010 eruption appear before the path leads down into flower-filled Þórsmörk. Duration: one to two days.

➡ **Kerlingarfjöll Loop** Largely untouched, this remote interior circuit unveils postcard-worthy vistas that rival those of well-trodden Laugavegurinn. Duration: three days.

Wildlife Watching

Iceland's range of wildlife is small but bewitchingly beautiful.

Arctic Foxes

Loveable like a dog but skittish like a rodent, the Arctic fox is Iceland's only native

HIKING CHECKLIST

The specifics of gear required in Iceland will vary, depending on your activity, the time of year, the remoteness of the trail, and how long you'll be exploring (day hike versus multiday trek; staying in a hut versus camping). One constant: the changeability of the weather, and the risk it poses.

Some of the following may be obvious to experienced hikers, but there are many newbies who may feel inspired by the wondrous Icelandic landscapes to get out onto trails...

Essentials

- Take proper navigation tools; topo map and GPS are vital.
- Dress in layers. This is essential. First base layer: thermal underwear (wool or synthetic). Second layer: light wool or fleece top; quick-drying trousers. Third layer: waterproof and windproof jacket (eg Gore-Tex). You'll need a breathable rain shell, including waterproof overtrousers. Your daypack should also be waterproof.
- Avoid cotton clothes such as jeans, T-shirts and socks – these lose insulation properties when wet and take hours to dry. Polypropylene, which is quick-drying (but can be flammable) or merino wool, which warms even when wet (but dries slowly), are recommended.
- Take gloves, hat, sunglasses and sunscreen. Woollen or synthetic socks, and waterproof, broken-in hiking boots or shoes.

For Longer Trips

- Packs need a waterproof cover or a plastic liner to keep things dry. A dry set of clothes is essential.
- Always carry a first-aid kit, a headlamp/torch and a survival kit (survival blanket, whistle etc).
- Sleeping bags should be capable of handling negative Celsius temperatures. Campers will need a tent (wind- and weatherproof), stove and cooking utensils (hut users may or may not need the latter).
- Pack a swimsuit (for hot springs), lightweight sandals (for river crossings, to keep your boots dry), and hiking poles for steep descents and river crossings.
- Take plastic bags, which are handy for separating wet and dry gear, and for carrying out rubbish.

Buying or Hiring Gear

You can buy hiking and camping gear in larger towns – Reykjavík is best for this; Akureyri also has options. Note that prices in Iceland aren't cheap – consider bringing what you need from home, and/or hiring gear.

A few car-rental places offer camping equipment for rent (this is particularly true of campervan-hire companies). Otherwise, two good rental places in Reykjavík are **Gangleri Outfitters** (www.outfitters.is) and **Iceland Camping Equipment** (www.iceland-camping-equipment.com).

mammal. Sightings are rare, but these are the best spots to try your luck:

- **Hornstrandir** The fox's main domain – join the team of researchers who set up camp here each summer.
- **Suðavík** Home of the Arctic Fox Center – there are often orphaned foxes living in a small habitat on-site.
- **Breiðamerkursandur** One of the main breeding grounds for skuas, the area has drawn a rising number of Arctic foxes hungry for a snack.

Puffins & Seabirds

On coastal cliffs right around the country you can see huge numbers of seabirds, often in massive colonies. The best time for birdwatching is between June and mid-August, when puffins, gannets, guillemots, razorbills, kittiwakes and fulmars get twitchers excited.

Seal, Jökulsárlón (p327)

The best bird cliffs and colonies:

➡ **Vestmannaeyjar** Puffins swarm like frantic bees as you sail into the harbour at Heimaey. Birds nest on virtually every turret of stone emerging from the southern sea.

➡ **Hornstrandir** This preserve offers an endless wall of stone that shoots down from the verdant bluffs straight into the waves – countless birds have built temporary homes within.

➡ **Borgarfjörður Eystri** This hamlet offers one of the best places in Iceland to spot puffins, who build their intricate homes just metres from the viewing platform.

➡ **Látrabjarg** Famous in the Westfjords for the eponymous bird cliffs.

➡ **Mývatn** A different ecosystem than towering coastal bird cliffs, Mývatn's swampy landscape is a haven for migratory avians.

➡ **Langanes** Remote windswept cliffs are home to prolific bird life; there's a new viewing platform above a colony of northern gannets.

➡ **Ingólfshöfði** Take a tractor ride to this dramatic promontory, where skuas swoop and puffins pose.

➡ **Grímsey** Visit for the treat of crossing the Arctic Circle, and to admire hardy locals outnumbered by countless puffins and Arctic terns.

➡ **Drangey** Climbing to the top of this storied Skagafjörður islet involves ropes, ladders and close-ups with puffins, guillemots, gannets and more.

Seals

Seals aren't as ubiquitous as Iceland's birds, but they're fun to spot.

➡ **Hvammstangi & Vatnsnes Peninsula** A seal museum, boat tours and a peninsula studded with basking pinnipeds.

➡ **Ísafjarðardjúp** Curling coastline and rock-strewn beaches offer good seal spotting.

➡ **Jökulsárlón** As if the ice lagoon wasn't photogenic enough – look out for seals swimming among the bergs.

➡ **Húsey** This remote, panoramic farm encourages you to do your seal spotting on horseback.

Whales

Iceland is one of the best places in the world to see whales and dolphins. The most common sightings are of minke and humpback whales, but you can also spot fin, sei and blue whales, among others.

Iceland's best spots for whale watching:

➡ **Húsavík** Iceland's classic whale-watching destination, complete with an excellent whale museum; 99% success rate during summer.

➡ **Eyjafjörður** Whale-watching cruises ply the scenic waters of Iceland's longest fjord from Akureyri, Dalvík and Hauganes.

➡ **Reykjavík** Easy viewing for visitors to the capital; boats depart from the old harbour downtown.

Horse Riding

Horses are an integral part of Icelandic life and many farms around the country offer short rides, including a handful of stables within a stone's throw of Reykjavík. Reckon on around 7000kr or 10,000kr for a one- or two-hour ride.

Best Horse-Riding Regions

➡ **Southern Snæfellsnes** The wild beaches under the shadow of a glinting glacier are perfect places for a ride. Several award-winning stables are located here.

➡ **Hella** The flatlands around Hella that roll under brooding Hekla host many horse ranches offering multiday rides and short sessions.

➡ **Skagafjörður** The only county in Iceland where horses outnumber people has a proud tradition of breeding and training.

Swimming & Spas

Thanks to Iceland's abundance of geothermal heat, swimming is a national institution, and nearly every town has at least one *sundlaug* (heated swimming pool – generally outdoors). Most pools also offer *heitir pottar* (hot-pots; small heated pools for soaking, with the water around 40°C), saunas and jacuzzis. Admission is usually around 800kr (half-price for children).

The clean, chemical-free swimming pools and natural hot springs require a strict hygiene regimen, which involves a thorough shower without swimsuit before you enter the swimming area. Instructions are posted in a number of languages. Not following these rules is a sure-fire way to offend the locals.

Best Resources

➡ **Swimming in Iceland** (www.swimminginiceland.com) Info on Iceland's thermal pools.

➡ **Thermal Pools in Iceland** – by Jón G Snæland and Þóra Sigurbjörnsdóttir. Comprehensive guide to Iceland's naturally occurring springs; sold in most bookstores.

➡ **Blue Lagoon** (www.bluelagoon.com) Iceland's favourite soaking venue and undisputed top attraction.

➡ **Visit Reykjavík** (www.visitreykjavik.is) Click through to 'What to Do' for pools in the region.

Glacier Walks & Snowmobiling

Trekking across an icy white expanse can be one of the most ethereal experiences of your Iceland visit. The island has several options that offer a taste of winter even on the warmest of days.

Common-sense safety rules apply: don't get too close to glaciers or walk on them without the proper equipment and guiding.

Best Glaciers & Ice Caps to Explore

➡ **Vatnajökull** Europe's biggest ice cap is perfect for snowmobile rides; it also has dozens of offshoot glaciers primed for guided hikes and ice climbs – arrange these from Skaftafell and points east towards Höfn.

➡ **Eyjafjallajökull** The site of a volcanic eruption in 2010; take a super-Jeep to discover the icy surface then wander over to Magni, nearby, to see the still-steaming earth.

➡ **Snæfellsjökull** Jules Verne's *Journey to the Centre of the Earth* starts here; try the snowcat tour from Arnarstapi.

➡ **Langjökull** Close to Reykjavík; draws icy crowds thanks to its new 'Into the Glacier' ice-cave experience.

➡ **Sólheimajökull** An icy tongue unfurling from Mýrdalsjökull ice cap, ideal for an afternoon trek.

Boating, Kayaking & Rafting

A new perspective on Iceland's natural treasures is offered from the water.

Best Boating Hot Spots

➡ **Heimaey** Zip across the Vestmannaeyjar archipelago, taking in the craggy cliffs and swooping birds.

➡ **Stykkishólmur** Wind through the islands of silent Breiðafjörður.

➡ **Húsavík** Traditional wooden ships or high-speed zodiacs sail through whale-filled waters.

Best Kayaking

➡ **Hornstrandir, Ísafjörður & Ísafjarðardjúp** Sea kayaking at its finest; try multiday tours or a one-day adventure to Vigur, an offshore islet.

Top: Horse riding, Snæfellsnes Peninsula (p181)

Bottom: Hiker near Þórsmörk (p152)

SUSTAINABLE TRAVEL

We can't stress this enough: the fast and furious boom in tourism to Iceland is placing enormous pressure on the local population, the fragile environment, and the at-times-inadequate infrastructure. Your actions have consequences, so please endeavour to travel safely and tread lightly.

➡ **Heed local warnings and advice** No one is trying to spoil your holiday – when a local tells you that your car isn't suitable for a particular road, or an area is off-limits due to fear of a glacial outburst flood, it's because they know this country and what it's capable of. Be flexible, and change your plans when necessary.

➡ **Recognise your impact** The numbers speak for themselves: 330,000 locals versus 1.3 million tourists in 2015, and an estimated 1.7 million in 2016. You may think that staying overnight in your campervan by a roadside isn't a problem. But it is when thousands of people do it – that's why there are new laws (p391) banning it.

➡ **Plan properly** Check weather-forecast and road-condition websites (p19). Pack a good map, the appropriate gear, common sense and a degree of flexibility. No hiking in jeans, no attempting to cross rivers in small cars, no striding out onto glaciers without proper guiding and equipment (p40).

➡ **Respect nature** Subglacial volcanoes, geothermal areas and vast lava fields are big draws. That's why you're visiting Iceland, no? So take care not to damage them. If you've hired a 4WD, whatever you do, stick to marked trails; off-roading is illegal and causes irreparable damage to the fragile landscape.

➡ **Travel green** Check out www.nature.is – it's chock-full of amazing tips on travelling sustainably in Iceland, and has an online map and apps with a goal of making ecofriendly choices easier for everyone.

➡ **Seyðisfjörður** The charismatic tour guide will leave you wondering what's more charming – the fjord or him.

➡ **Heinabergslón** Paddle among icebergs on this spectacular, silent glacier lagoon.

Best River Trips

➡ **Varmahlíð** Northern Iceland's white-water rafting base, with two glacial rivers to choose from (family-friendly rapids or full throttle).

➡ **Reykholt** White-water rafting thrills on the Hvítá; you can also get your adrenaline pumping on Iceland's only jetboat rides.

Cycling

Short cycling excursions can be a fun, healthy way to explore. In Reykjavík you'll find a couple of biking outlets, some offering day trips to nearby attractions such as the Golden Circle. Bike hire is possible in many other towns around the country.

Travelling around Iceland by bicycle can be more of a challenge than it might seem – shifting weather patterns mean that you'll often encounter heavy winds, and you'll be forced to ride closely alongside traffic on the Ring Road (there are no hard shoulders to the roads).

Scuba Diving & Snorkelling

Little-known but incredibly rewarding, diving in Iceland is becoming increasingly popular. The clear water (100m visibility!), great wildlife, spectacular lava ravines, wrecks and thermal chimneys make it a dive destination like no other. The best dive sites are Silfra at Þingvellir and the geothermal chimneys in Eyjafjörður.

A PADI Dry Suit Diver certificate is recommended – you can obtain this in Iceland, through a handful of diving companies. The unique PADI Tectonic Plate Awareness course (designed by Dive.is – www.dive.is) gives you an understanding of plate tectonics and what it means to dive between them.

Tours

Joining an organised tour may not be your idea of an independent holiday, but Iceland's rugged terrain and high costs can make it an appealing option. Tours can save you time and money, and can get you into some stunning but isolated locations where your hire car will never go. Many tours are by bus, others are by 4WD or

Diving at Silfra (p113)

super-Jeep, and some are by snowmobile, quad bikes or light aircraft. Most tours give you the option of tacking on adventure activities such as white-water rafting, horse riding and glacier hiking.

If you're planning to base yourself in Reykjavík and use day-long tours to explore the countryside, it's vital to note that you will spend (dare we say waste) a significant amount of time being transported from the capital out to the island's natural treasures. If a series of short tours is what you're after, you are better off choosing a base in the countryside closer to the attractions that pique your interest. Another advantage of this approach: sometimes the best and most personalised tours are offered by small-scale local operators who have grown up exploring the ice caves, glaciers, mountains and/or trails in their backyards, and can give you a real local insight (as opposed to large city-based companies that shuttle busloads to popular destinations).

There are hundreds of tour operators in Iceland, ranging from small scale to large. The following list represents some of the largest, most reputable tour operators; check their websites to get a sense of what is on offer. And don't forget to look out for the little guys, too.

- **Air Iceland** (www.airiceland.is) Iceland's largest domestic airline runs a range of combination air, bus, hiking and 4WD day tours around Iceland from Reykjavík and Akureyri. Also runs tours to Greenland from Reykjavík.
- **Arctic Adventures** (www.adventures.is) Specialises in action-filled tours – from straight-up sightseeing to mountain biking, sea kayaking and even surfing.
- **Grayline Iceland** (www.grayline.is) A bus-tour operator offering comprehensive day trips and plenty of activities.
- **Icelandic Mountain Guides** (www.mountainguides.is) Offers an incredibly diverse range of activities, plus multiday hiking, mountain climbing, biking and skiing tours. Hard-core expeditions, too.
- **Reykjavík Excursions** (www.re.is) Reykjavík's most popular day-tour agency, with a comprehensive range of year-round tours.
- **Saga Travel** (www.sagatravel.is) A company with strong ties to north Iceland, and a diverse, innovative year-round program of tours from Reykjavík, Akureyri and Mývatn.

Outdoor Activities

PATREKSFJÖRÐUR
A laid-back base for exploring the Westfjords' southern peninsulas: crowded bird cliffs at Látrabjarg, beaches like rosy Rauðasandur and the bike-friendly Þingeyri Peninsula. (p201)
ÍSAFJÖRÐUR
Stay in or around the Westfjords' largest town to access Hornstrandir, the kayak-friendly fjords of Ísafjarðardjúp and the rugged central peninsulas. (p207)
SNÆFELLSNES PENINSULA
A gorgeous sampler of all that Iceland has to offer: hiking trails, horse riding, hot springs, boat trips, puffins and whales, plus the peninsula's namesake glacier. (p181)
KERLINGARFJÖLL
The highlands region is all about 4WD trails to remote hiking; this mountain range is a hiker's paradise of geothermal wonders and multihued rhyolite mountains. (p343)
REYKJAVÍK
The hub of countless tours and adventure trips into the hinterlands, with a focus on the south and west, and of course, the Golden Circle. (p52)
Arctic Circle
Denmark Strait
Hornstrandir
Bolungarvík
Suðureyri
Ísafjörður
Drangajökull
Norðurfjörður
Þingeyri
Bíldudalur
Patreksfjörður
Brjánslækur
Hólmavík
Húnaflói
Skagaströnd
Skagafjörður
Drangey
Sauðárkrókur
Blönduós
Hóp
Varmahlíð
Hvammstangi
Flatey
Breiðafjörður
Stykkishólmur
Búðardalur
Hellissandur-Rif
Ólafsvík
Snæfellsnes
Grundarfjörður
Eiríksjökull (1675m)
Langjökull
Kerlingarfjöll
Borgarnes
Akranes
ÞINGVELLIR NATIONAL PARK
Geysir
Gullfoss
REYKJAVÍK
Þingvallavatn
Kópavogur
Keflavík
Njarðvík
Hafnarfjörður
Hveragerði
Landmannalaugar
Selfoss
Hella
Grindavík
Þorlákshöfn
Selvogsgrunn
Eyrarbakkabugur
Hvolsvöllur
NORTH ATLANTIC OCEAN
Mýrdalsjökull
Eyjafjallajökull (1450m)
Skógar
Heimaey
VESTMANNAEYJAR
Surtsey
Vík

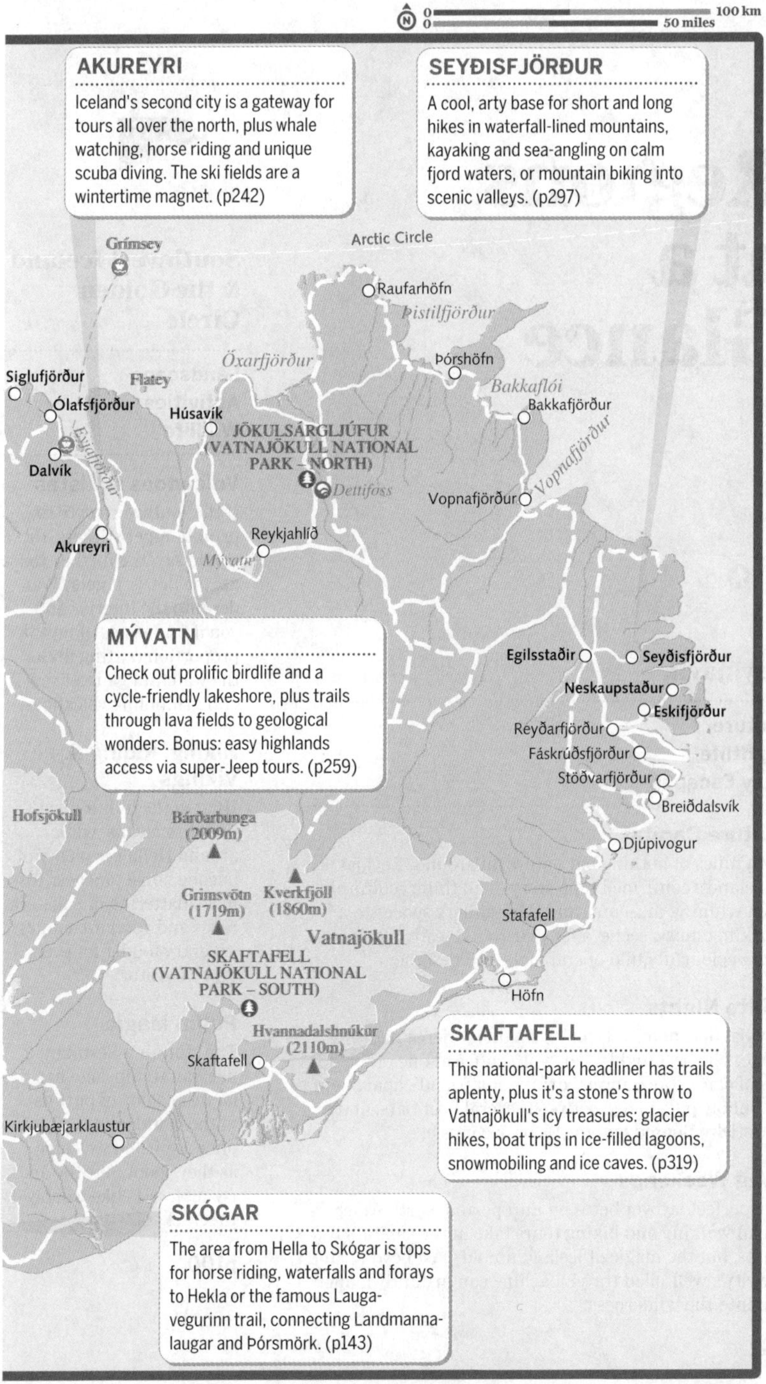
0 100 km
0 50 miles
AKUREYRI
Iceland's second city is a gateway for tours all over the north, plus whale watching, horse riding and unique scuba diving. The ski fields are a wintertime magnet. (p242)
SEYÐISFJÖRÐUR
A cool, arty base for short and long hikes in waterfall-lined mountains, kayaking and sea-angling on calm fjord waters, or mountain biking into scenic valleys. (p297)
Grímsey
Arctic Circle
Raufarhöfn
Þistilfjörður
Öxarfjörður
Þórshöfn
Bakkaflói
Siglufjörður
Flatey
Ólafsfjörður
Húsavík
Bakkafjörður
Eyjafjörður
JÖKULSÁRGLJÚFUR (VATNAJÖKULL NATIONAL PARK – NORTH)
Dalvík
Dettifoss
Vopnafjörður
Vopnafjörður
Reykjahlíð
Akureyri
Mývatn
MÝVATN
Check out prolific birdlife and a cycle-friendly lakeshore, plus trails through lava fields to geological wonders. Bonus: easy highlands access via super-Jeep tours. (p259)
Egilsstaðir
Seyðisfjörður
Neskaupstaður
Eskifjörður
Reyðarfjörður
Fáskrúðsfjörður
Stöðvarfjörður
Breiðdalsvík
Hofsjökull
Bárðarbunga (2009m)
Djúpivogur
Grímsvötn (1719m)
Kverkfjöll (1860m)
Stafafell
Vatnajökull
SKAFTAFELL (VATNAJÖKULL NATIONAL PARK – SOUTH)
Höfn
Hvannadalshnúkur (2110m)
SKAFTAFELL
This national-park headliner has trails aplenty, plus it's a stone's throw to Vatnajökull's icy treasures: glacier hikes, boat trips in ice-filled lagoons, snowmobiling and ice caves. (p319)
Skaftafell
Kirkjubæjarklaustur
SKÓGAR
The area from Hella to Skógar is tops for horse riding, waterfalls and forays to Hekla or the famous Laugavegurinn trail, connecting Landmannalaugar and Þórsmörk. (p143)

Regions at a Glance

Reykjavík

Culture
Nightlife
Easy Escapes

Culture Capital

With miles of nothing but nature all around, Reykjavík is Iceland's confirmed repository of all things cultural, from winning museums and sleek gallery spaces to a sparkling music scene, a fat year-round festival calendar and a colourful guild of craftsfolk and designers.

White Nights

Reykjavík is notorious for its small but fierce nightlife scene. The best nights start with coffee at one of the dozens of cafes, 'pre-gaming' drinks at a friend's apartment, an unholy pilgrimage between several beer bars, and a late sticky-floored jam to DJs or live music.

Long Weekends

The perfect layover between Europe and North America: urban walking and biking tours take in the capital's top sights, but the magic of Iceland unfolds just beyond, and the city's well-oiled travel machine can instantly launch you into the wilderness.

p52

Southwest Iceland & the Golden Circle

Landscape
Activities
Wildlife

Volcanoes & Vistas

If the southwest were to print bumper stickers, these would say 'the further you go, the better it gets'. Wander into the interior and you'll find vistas of mythic proportions sitting under the watchful glare of several grumbling volcanoes.

Hiking, Riding & Vikings

High in the hills a hiker's paradise awaits, while around Hella are plenty of bucolic horse ranches. Toss in a smattering of Saga-era relics and you have endless itinerary fodder for every type of visitor.

Puffin Magic

The stunning Vestmannaeyjar archipelago has the largest colony of puffins in the world, and the birds offer a spirited welcome as they shoot over the arriving ferries like wobbly firecrackers.

p100

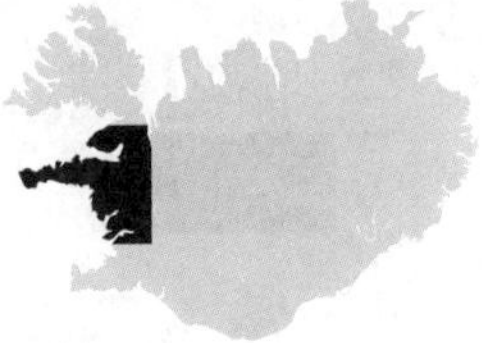

West Iceland

Landscape
History
Activities

Infinite Islets

The Snæfellsnes Peninsula is a technicolour realm composed of exotic splashes of sere lava, green waterfall-cut meadows, Arctic-blue water, and a dazzling ice cap. One of its most impressive vistas is Breiðafjörður – a bay reflecting cloud-filled skies and speckled with thousands of isles.

Viking Sagas

History buffs can take a trip back in time: the west is often dubbed Sagaland for its rich Viking history. Make a beeline for the Settlement Museum in buzzy Borgarnes to let the stories unfold.

Horseback Exploring

The southern shores of the Snæfellsnes Peninsula are among the best places to ride the small, tough Icelandic horse – follow the crests of sand or trot into the hills to find hidden geothermal sources.

p170

The Westfjords

Landscape
Activities
Wildlife

The End of the Line

On maps, the undulating coastline of the Westfjords makes the region resemble giant lobster claws snipping away at the Arctic Circle. The landscapes of this dramatic enclave of sea and stone inspire fables of magical, faraway lands.

Explore the Subarctic

Sitting at the edge of the Arctic, its jagged peninsulas stretching north, Iceland's final frontier is the perfect setting for rugged mountain biking, sea kayaking, sailing and springtime skiing. Hornstrandir hiking reserve is the jewel in the crown.

Foxy Friends

Wild-maned horses rove throughout, but the main draws are the impressive bird cliffs dotting the region and the fleet Arctic foxes scurrying between grassy hillocks. With preplanning, you can volunteer to monitor Iceland's only native mammal.

p196

North Iceland

Landscape
Wildlife
Activities

A Land with the Lot

What landscape *doesn't* north Iceland offer? There are offshore islands, lonely peninsulas, icy peaks, pastoral horse farms, belching mudpots, sleepy fishing villages, epic waterfalls, shattered lava fields, breaching whales…

Whale Wonderland

Seals inhabit Vatnsnes Peninsula; puffins and seabirds nest all over. Waterbirds take to Mývatn like, well, ducks to water. The biggest draw lurks beneath: Húsavík is the whale-watching hub and towns along western Eyjafjörður, including Akureyri, are its apprentice.

The Active North

Horse riding is best in the northwest. Birdwatching around Lake Mývatn is world-class, but remote Langanes and Arctic Grímsey hold their own. Hike the northern reaches of Vatnajökull National Park, or ski the Tröllaskagi Peninsula.

p221

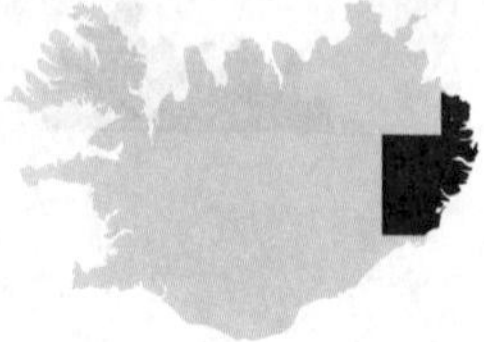

East Iceland

Landscape
Activities
Wildlife

Fan-fjord-tastic

The Eastfjords' scenery is particularly dramatic around the northern fjord villages, backed by sheer-sided mountains etched with waterfalls. Inland, scenic lake Lagarfljót (and the forest on its eastern shore) is ripe for exploration, as is the 1833m mountain Snæfell, part of Vatnajökull National Park.

On Land & Water

Kayaking the waters of Seyðisfjörður is a breathtaking highlight; mountain biking here is good for landlubbers; and seal spotting on horseback at Húsey is a unique treat. Trails in and around the fjords offer peak panoramas and hiking delights – Borgarfjörður Eystri is a local favourite.

Creatures of the East

Wild reindeer roam the mountains, and Iceland's version of the Loch Ness monster calls Lagarfljót home. Bird life is prolific, at the remote farms of Húsey and Skálanes, or the perfectly placed puffin-viewing platform at Borgarfjörður Eystri.

p285

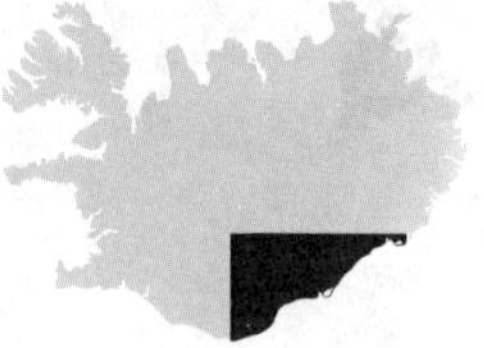

Southeast Iceland

Landscape
Wildlife
Activities

Glacial Glory

Home to glittering glaciers, toppling waterfalls, the iceberg-filled Jökulsárlón lagoon and Iceland's favourite walking area of Skaftafell, it's little wonder the southeast is among Iceland's most visited regions. Contrasting this beauty is the stark grey sands of the sandar (sand deltas).

Scene-Stealing Wildlife

Seals are a photogenic addition to the camera-friendly waters of Jökulsárlón, while great skuas make their homes in the sandar and harass visitors. Ingólfshöfði has nesting puffins and other seabirds – getting there in a tractor-drawn cart is a blast.

Ice-Cap Endeavours

Icy activities include glacier walks, snowmobiling and winter ice-cave visits. Boat and kayaking trips among glacial lagoon bergs are in demand. There's ace mountain biking from Kirkjubæjarklaustur and then finish by cracking langoustine claws in Höfn.

p311

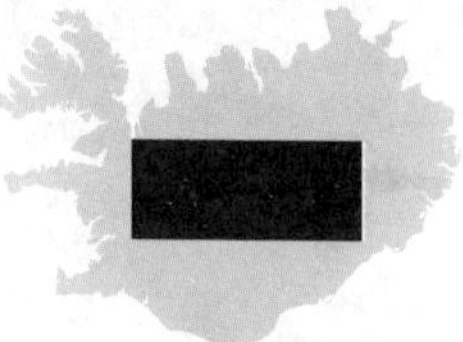

The Highlands

Landscape
Solitude
Activities

Lunar Landscapes

This region is practically uninhabited – there are no towns or villages, only summertime huts and accommodation. NASA astronauts once trained here, and the recent Holuhraun eruption has added a whole new dimension to ancient lava fields.

Barren Beauty

Touring the highlands will give you a new understanding of the word 'desolation'. The solitude is exhilarating, the views are vast. Some travellers are disappointed by the interior's ultra-bleakness and endless grey-sand desert, others are humbled by the sight of nature in its rawest form.

Remote Hiking

It's immensely tough but equally rewarding to hike, bike or horse ride along interior routes. Kerlingarfjöll and the Askja region have first-class hiking; Hveravellir lures with hot springs. Many visitors may be happiest touring the sights from the comfort of a super-Jeep tour!

p338

On the Road

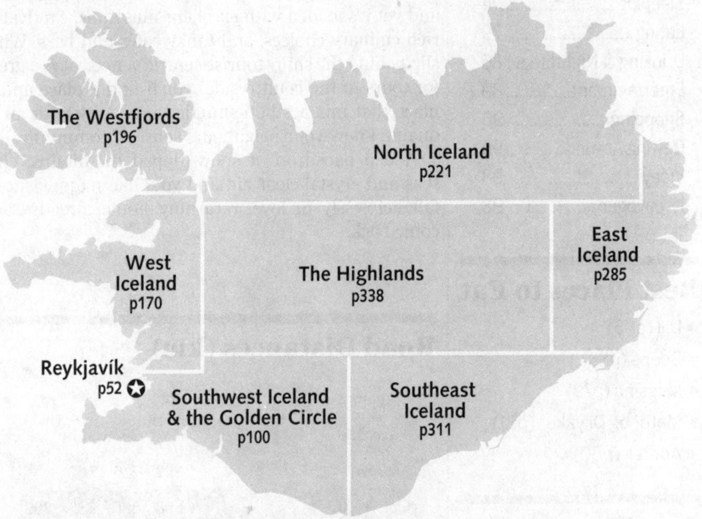

The Westfjords
p196
North Iceland
p221
West
Iceland
p170
The Highlands
p338
East
Iceland
p285
Reykjavík
p52
Southwest Iceland
& the Golden Circle
p100
Southeast
Iceland
p311

Reykjavík

POP 209,500

Includes ➡

Best Places to Eat

- Dill (p85)
- Snaps (p84)
- Messinn (p79)
- Matur og Drykkur (p81)
- Apotek (p80)

Best Places to Stay

- Kvosin Downtown Hotel (p74)
- Black Pearl (p74)
- Reykjavík Residence (p77)
- Alda Hotel (p77)

Why Go?

The world's most northerly capital combines colourful buildings, quirky, creative people, eye-popping design, wild nightlife and a capricious soul to devastating effect.

In many ways Reykjavík is strikingly cosmopolitan for its size. After all, it's merely a town by international standards, and yet it's loaded with excellent museums, captivating art, rich culinary choices, and funky cafes and bars. When you slip behind the shiny tourist-centric veneer (it *is* a great base for tours to the countryside) you'll find a place and a populace that mix aesthetic-minded ingenuity with an almost quaint, know-your-neighbours sense of community.

Add a backdrop of snow-topped mountains, churning seas and crystal-clear air, and you, like many visitors, may fall helplessly in love, returning home already saving to come back.

Road Distances (km)

	Reykjavík	Borgarnes	Ísafjörður	Akureyri	Egilsstaðir	Höfn
Borgarnes	74					
Ísafjörður	457	384				
Akureyri	389	315	567			
Egilsstaðir	698	580	832	265		
Höfn	459	519	902	512	247	
Vík	187	246	630	561	511	273

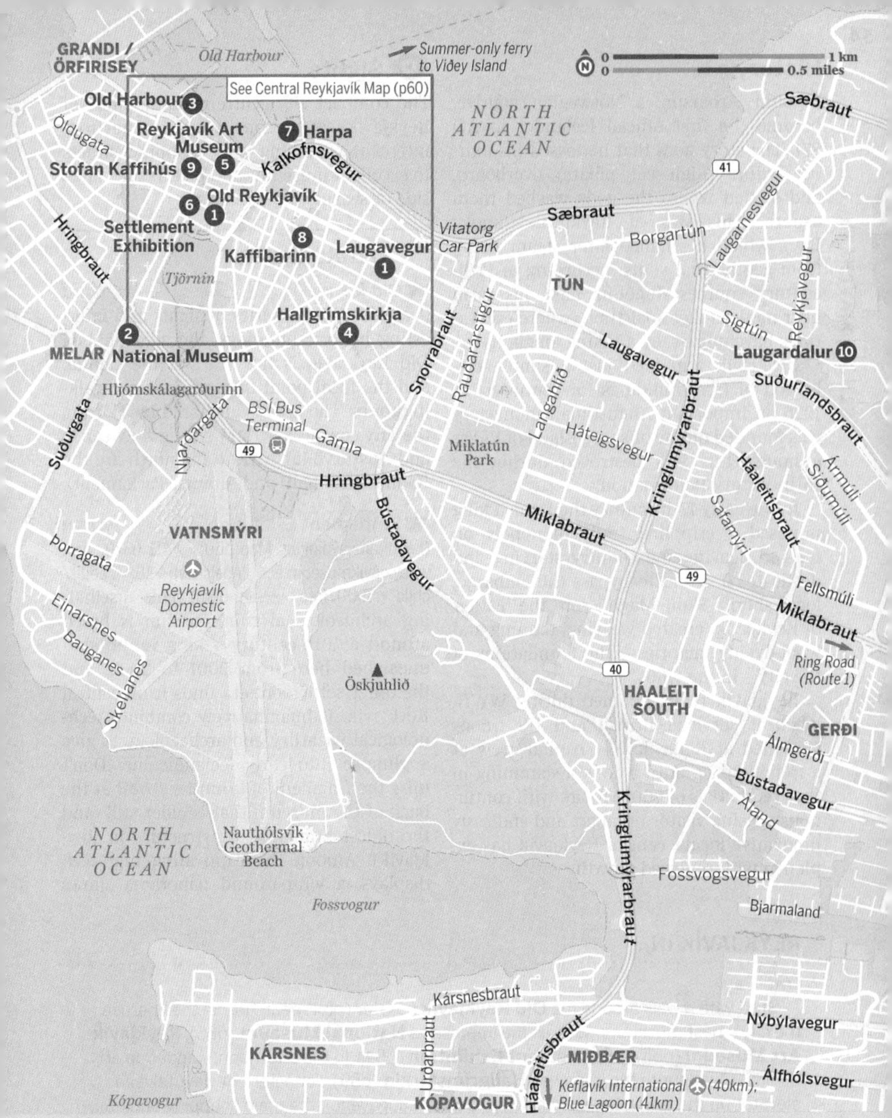

Reykjavík Highlights

❶ **Old Reykjavík** (p54) Exploring this historic quarter and shopping in Laugavegur.

❷ **National Museum** (p65) Learning about Iceland's fascinating history.

❸ **Old Harbour** (p58) Hitting the museums, microbrewery and restaurants.

❹ **Hallgrímskirkja** (p59) Scaling the heights of this landmark's modernist steeple.

❺ **Reykjavík Art Museum** (p55) Immersing yourself at these stand-out museums.

❻ **Settlement Exhibition** (p54) Perusing a Viking longhouse and artefacts from Reykjavík's first days.

❼ **Harpa** (p59) Enjoying a performance at the capital's twinkling concert hall.

❽ **Partying** (p87) Joining a wild pub crawl at nightspots, such as Kaffibarinn or Kiki.

❾ **Cafes** (p83) Sipping coffee at quirky cafes like Stofan Kaffihús.

❿ **Laugardalur** (p66) Soaking at the geothermal pool or strolling through botanical gardens.

History

Ingólfur Arnarson, a Norwegian fugitive, became the first official Icelander in AD 871. The story goes that he tossed his *öndvegissúlur* (high-seat pillars) overboard, and settled where the gods washed them ashore. This was at Reykjavík (Smoky Bay), which he named after steam rising from geothermal vents. According to 12th-century sources, Ingólfur built his farm near modern-day Aðalstræti (where excavations have unearthed a Viking longhouse).

Reykjavík remained just a simple collection of farm buildings for centuries. In 1225 an important Augustinian monastery was founded on the offshore island of Viðey, although this was destroyed during the 16th-century Reformation.

In the early 17th century the Danish king imposed a crippling trade monopoly on Iceland, leaving the country starving and destitute. In a bid to bypass the embargo, local sheriff Skúli Magnússon, the 'Father of Reykjavík', created weaving, tanning and wool-dyeing factories – the foundations of the city – in the 1750s.

Reykjavík really boomed during WWII, when it serviced British and US troops stationed at Keflavík. The capital grew at a frenetic pace until it took a slamming in the credit crisis of 2008. Today, with continuously rising visitor numbers and endlessly innovative locals, central Reykjavík has exploded with renewed growth.

Sights

The compact city centre contains most of Reykjavík's attractions, which range from interesting walking and shopping streets to excellent museums and picturesque lakeside or seaside promenades.

Old Reykjavík

★Old Reykjavík AREA

(Map p60) With a series of sights and interesting historic buildings, the area dubbed Old Reykjavík is the heart of the capital, and the focal point of many historic walking tours. The area is anchored by Tjörnin, the city-centre lake, and sitting between it and Austurvöllur park to the north are the Raðhús (city hall) and Alþingi (Parliament).

★Settlement Exhibition MUSEUM

(Landnámssýningin; Map p60; ☎411 6370; www.reykjavikmuseum.is; Aðalstræti 16; adult/child kr1500/free; ⏲9am-6pm) This fascinating archaeological ruin/museum is based around a 10th-century **Viking longhouse** unearthed here from 2001 to 2002, and the other settlement-era finds from central Reykjavík. It imaginatively combines technological wizardry and archaeology to give a glimpse into early Icelandic life. Don't miss the fragment of **boundary wall** at the back of the museum that is older still (and the oldest human-made structure in Reykjavík). Among the captivating high-tech displays, a wraparound panorama shows

REYKJAVÍK IN...

One Day

Start with a walk around the **Old Reykjavík** quarter (p54) near Tjörnin then peruse the city's best museums, such as the impressive **National Museum** (p65), **Reykjavík Art Museum** (p55)or **Settlement Exhibition** (p54). In the afternoon, wander up arty Skólavörðustígur to the immense **Hallgrímskirkja** (p59). For a perfect view, take an elevator up the tower, then circle down to stroll Laugavegur, the main shopping drag. Sit for people-watching and drinks at **Bravó** (p88) then head to dinner. Many of the more lively restaurants – including **Vegamót** (p84) and **KEX** (p88) – turn into party hangouts at night. On weekends, join Reykjavík's notorious pub crawl. Start at perennial favourite **Kaffibarinn** (p87) or beer-lovers' **Kaldi** (p87), then tag along with locals to the latest drinking holes, or dance at **Kiki** (p88).

Two Days

After a late night out, enjoy brunch at **Bergsson Mathús** (p79), **Grái Kötturinn** (p82) or **Laundromat Café** (p79). Then head down to the **Old Harbour** (p58) for a wander, museums or a whale-watching tour. For hot springs, gardens, **Café Flóra** (p86) and cool art, head to Laugardalur in the afternoon. Book ahead if you'd like a swanky evening at one of Reykjavík's top Icelandic restaurants, such as **Dill** (p85) or **Matur og Drykkur** (p81), then party late at places like **Paloma** (p86), **Húrra** (p90) or **Prikið** (p89). Alternatively, catch a show at **Harpa** (p59) or a movie at **Bió Paradís** (p89).

how things would have looked at the time of the longhouse.

Interactive multimedia tables explain the area's excavations, and a space-age-feeling panel allows you to steer through different layers of the longhouse construction. Artefacts range from great awk bones to fish-oil lamps and an iron axe. The latest finds from ancient workshops near the current Alþingi include a spindle whorl inscribed with runes.

★Reykjavík Art Museum – Hafnarhús ART MUSEUM

(Map p60; ☎411 6400; www.artmuseum.is; Tryggvagata 17; adult/child kr1500/free; ⊙10am-5pm Fri-Wed, to 10pm Thu) Reykjavík Art Museum's Hafnarhús is a marvelously restored warehouse converted into a soaring steel-and-concrete exhibition space. Though the well-curated exhibitions of cutting-edge contemporary Icelandic art change frequently (think installations, videos, paintings and sculpture), you can always count on an area with the comic-book-style paintings of Erró (Guðmundur Guðmundsson), a political artist who has donated several thousand works to the museum. The **cafe**, run by Frú Lauga (p85) farmers market, has great harbour views.

★Tjörnin LAKE

(Map p60) This placid lake at the centre of the city is sometimes locally called the Pond. It echoes with the honks and squawks of over 40 species of visiting birds, including swans, geese and Arctic terns; feeding the ducks is a popular pastime for the under-fives. Pretty sculpture-dotted parks like Hljómskálagarður (p57) line the southern shores, and their paths are much used by cyclists and joggers. In winter hardy souls strap on ice skates and turn the lake into an outdoor rink.

Austurvöllur PARK

(Map p60) Grassy Austurvöllur was once part of first-settler Ingólfur Arnarson's hay fields. Today it's a favourite spot for cafe lounging or lunchtime picnics and summer sunbathing next to the Alþingi, and is sometimes used for open-air concerts and political demonstrations. The **statue** (Map p60) in the centre is of Jón Sigurðsson, who led the campaign for Icelandic independence.

Alþingi HISTORIC BUILDING

(Parliament; Map p60; ☎563 0500; www.althingi.is; Kirkjustraeti) FREE Iceland's first parliament, the Alþingi, was created at Þingvellir in AD 930. After losing its independence in the 13th century, the country gradually won back its autonomy, and the modern Alþingi moved into this current basalt building in 1881; a stylish glass-and-stone annexe was completed in 2002. Visitors can attend sessions (four times weekly mid-September to early June; see website for details) when parliament is sitting.

REYKJAVIK ART MUSEUM

This excellent museum (Listasafn Reykjavíkur; www.artmuseum.is; adult/child kr1500/free) is split over three well-done sites: the large, modern downtown Hafnarhús (p55) focusing on contemporary art; Kjarvalsstaðir (p64), in a park just east of Snorrabraut, and displaying rotating exhibits of modern art; and Ásmundarsafn (p66), a peaceful haven near Laugardalur for viewing sculptures by Ásmundur Sveinsson.

One ticket is good at all three sites, and if you buy after 3pm you get a 50% discount should you want a ticket the next day.

Ráðhús NOTABLE BUILDING

(Map p60; Vonarstræti; ⊙8am-4pm Mon-Fri) FREE Reykjavík's waterside Ráðhús is a beautifully positioned postmodern construction of concrete stilts, tinted windows and mossy walls rising from Tjörnin. Inside there's a 3D topographical map of Iceland.

Reykjavík Museum of Photography MUSEUM

(Ljósmyndasafn Reykjavíkur; Map p60; ☎411 6390; www.photomuseum.is; 6th fl, Tryggvagata 15, Grófarhús; ⊙noon-7pm Mon-Thu, to 6pm Fri, 1-5pm Sat & Sun) FREE This gallery room above Reykjavík City Library is worth a visit for its top-notch exhibitions of regional photographers. If you take the lift up, descend by the stairs, which are lined with vintage black-and-white photos.

Volcano House FILM

(Map p60; ☎555 1900; www.volcanohouse.is; Tryggvagata 11; adult/child kr1990/free; ⊙9am-10pm) This modern theatre with a hands-on lava exhibit in the foyer screens a 55-minute pair of films (hourly) about the Vestmannaeyjar volcanoes and Eyjafjallajökull.

Reykjavík

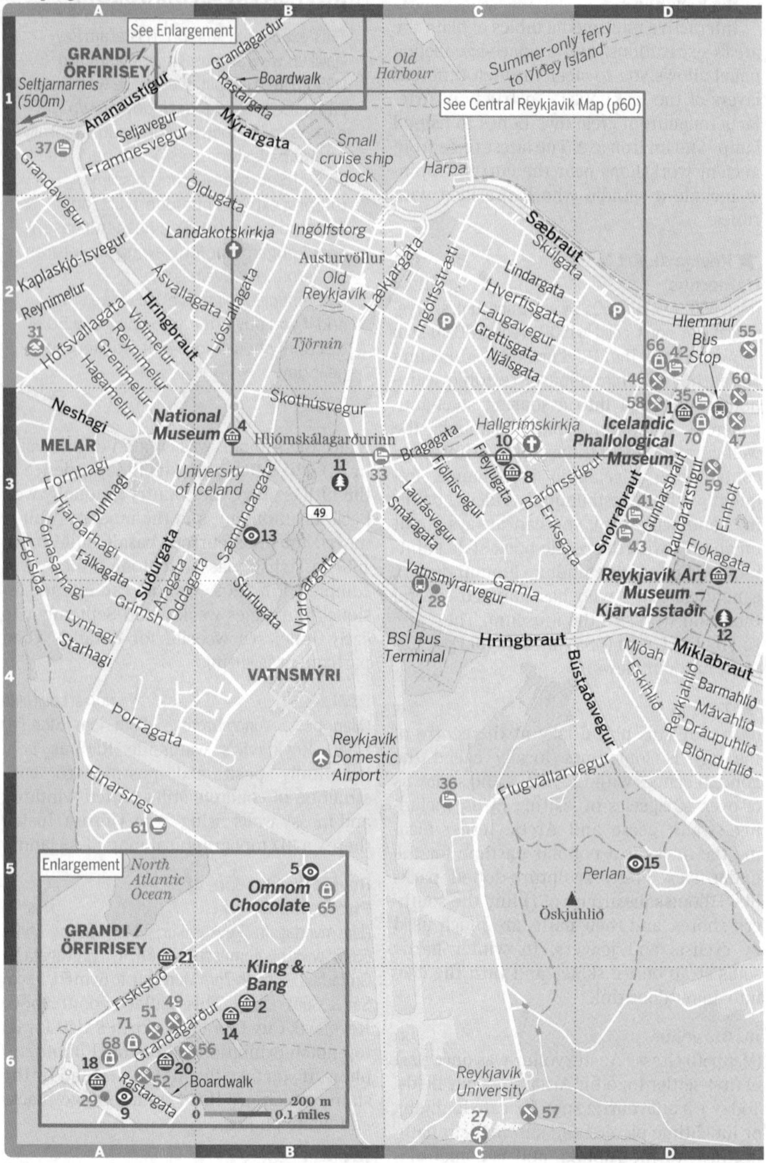

Dómkirkja CHURCH

(Map p60; www.domkirkjan.is; Kirkjustræti; ⏲10am-4.30pm Mon-Fri, Mass 11am Sun) Iceland's main cathedral, Dómkirkja is a modest affair, but it played a vital role in the country's conversion to Lutheranism. The current building (built in the 18th century and enlarged in 1848) is small and perfectly proportioned, with a plain wooden interior animated by glints of gold.

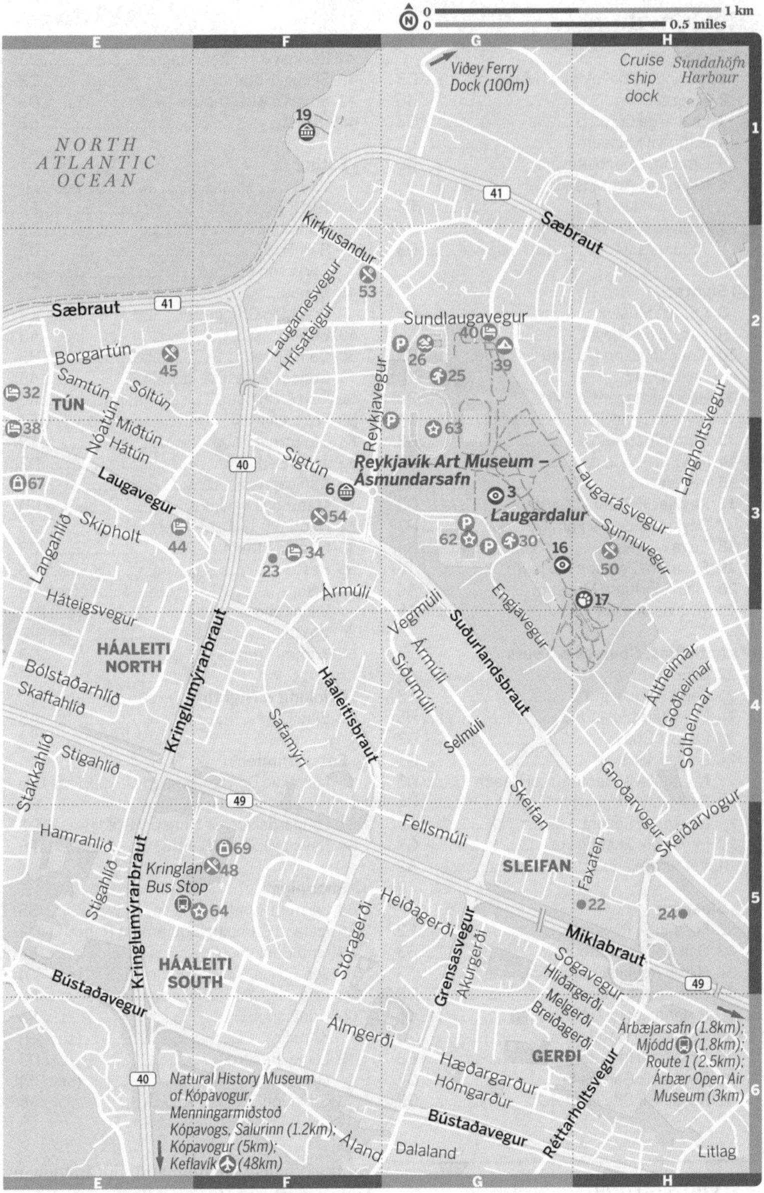

Hljómskálagarður Park PARK

(Map p56) FREE Hljómskálagarður Park sits on Tjörnin's southeast corner and has a section dedicated to sculptures by five Icelandic women: Gunnfríður Jónsdóttir (1889–1968), Nína Sæmundson (1892–1962), Þorbjörg Pálsdóttir (1919–2009), Ólöf Pálsdóttir (b 1920) and Gerður Helgadóttir (1928–75); and one Dane: Tove Ólafsson (1909–92).

Reykjavík

Old Harbour

★ Old Harbour AREA

(Map p60; Geirsgata; 🚌 1, 3, 6, 11, 12, 13, 14) Largely a service harbour until recently, the Old Harbour has blossomed into a hot spot for tourists, with several museums, volcano and Northern Lights films, and excellent restaurants. Whale-watching and puffin-viewing trips depart from the pier. Photo ops abound with views of fishing boats, Harpa concert hall and snowcapped mountains beyond. On the western edge of the harbour, the Grandi area, named after the fish factory there, has burgeoned with eateries and shops as well.

★Omnom Chocolate FACTORY

(Map p56; ☎519 5959; www.omnomchocolate.com; Hólmaslóð 4, Grandi; adult/child kr3000/1500; ⏲8am-5pm Mon-Fri) Reserve ahead for a tour at this full-service chocolate factory where you'll see how cocoa beans are transformed into high-end scrumptious delights. The shop also sells its bonbons and stylish bars, with specially designed labels and myriad sophisticated flavours. You'll also find the bars in shops throughout Iceland.

Whales of Iceland MUSEUM

(Map p56; ☎571 0077; www.whalesoficeland.is; Fiskislóð 23-25; adult/child kr2900/1500; ⏲10am-6pm Jun-Aug, to 5pm Sep-May; 🚌14) Ever stroll beneath a blue whale? This museum houses full-sized models of the 23 whales found off Iceland's coast. The largest museum of this type in Europe, it also displays models of whale skeletons, and has good audio guides and multimedia screens to explain what you're seeing. It has a cafe and gift shop, online ticket discounts and family tickets (kr5800).

Víkin Maritime Museum MUSEUM

(Víkin Sjóminjasafnið; Map p56; ☎517 9400; www.maritimemuseum.is; Grandagarður 8; adult/child kr1500/free; ⏲10am-5pm; 🚌14) Based appropriately in a former fish-freezing plant, this museum celebrates the country's seafaring heritage, focusing on the trawlers that transformed Iceland's economy. Guided tours go aboard coastguard ship *Óðinn* (kr1200, or joint ticket with museum kr2200; check website for times).

Saga Museum MUSEUM

(Map p56; ☎511 1517; www.sagamuseum.is; Grandagarður 2; adult/child kr2100/800; ⏲10am-6pm; 🚌14) The endearingly bloodthirsty Saga Museum is where Icelandic history is brought to life by eerie silicon models and a multi-language soundtrack with thudding axes and hair-raising screams. Don't be surprised if you see some of the characters wandering around town, as moulds were taken from Reykjavík residents (the owner's daughters are the Irish princess and the little slave gnawing a fish!).

Aurora Reykjavík EXHIBITION

(Northern Lights Centre; Map p56; ☎780 4500; www.aurorareykjavik.is; Grandagarður 2; adult/child kr1600/1000; ⏲9am-9pm; 🚌14) Learn about the classical tales explaining the Northern Lights, and the scientific explanation, then watch a 35-minute surround-sound panoramic high-definition recreation of Icelandic auroras.

LOCAL RESOURCES

Visit Reykjavík (www.visitreykjavik.is) Official tourism site.

Grapevine (www.grapevine.is) Excellent English-language content.

Iceland Review (www.icelandreview.com) Daily Icelandic news with current affairs, entertainment and more.

I Heart Reykjavík (www.iheartreykjavik.com) Fun local blog.

Iceland Design Centre (Hönnunarmiðstöð; ☎771 2200; www.icelanddesign.is; Aðalstræti 2; ⏲10am-6pm Mon-Sat) Promotes Iceland's designers and architects. Check online for the latest news, exhibitions and events, as well as a Reykjavík Design Guide and lists of designers (from architects to ceramicists). It also has a design shop.

Laugavegur & Skólavörðustígur

★Hallgrímskirkja CHURCH

(Map p60; ☎510 1000; www.hallgrimskirkja.is; Skólavörðustígur; tower adult/child kr900/100; ⏲9am-9pm Jun-Sep, to 5pm Oct-May) Reykjavík's immense white-concrete church (1945–86), star of a thousand postcards, dominates the skyline, and is visible from up to 20km away. Get an unmissable view of the city by taking an elevator trip up the 74.5m-high tower. In contrast to the high drama outside, the Lutheran church's interior is quite plain. The most eye-catching feature is the vast 5275-pipe organ installed in 1992. The church's size and radical design caused controversy, and its architect, Guðjón Samúelsson (1887–1950), never saw its completion.

★Harpa CULTURAL BUILDING

(Map p60; ☎box office 528 5050; www.harpa.is; Austurbakki 2; ⏲8am-midnight, box office 10am-6pm) With its ever-changing facets glistening on the water's edge, Reykjavík's sparkling Harpa concert hall and cultural centre is a beauty to behold. In addition to a season of top-notch shows (some free), it's worth stopping by to explore the

Central Reykjavík

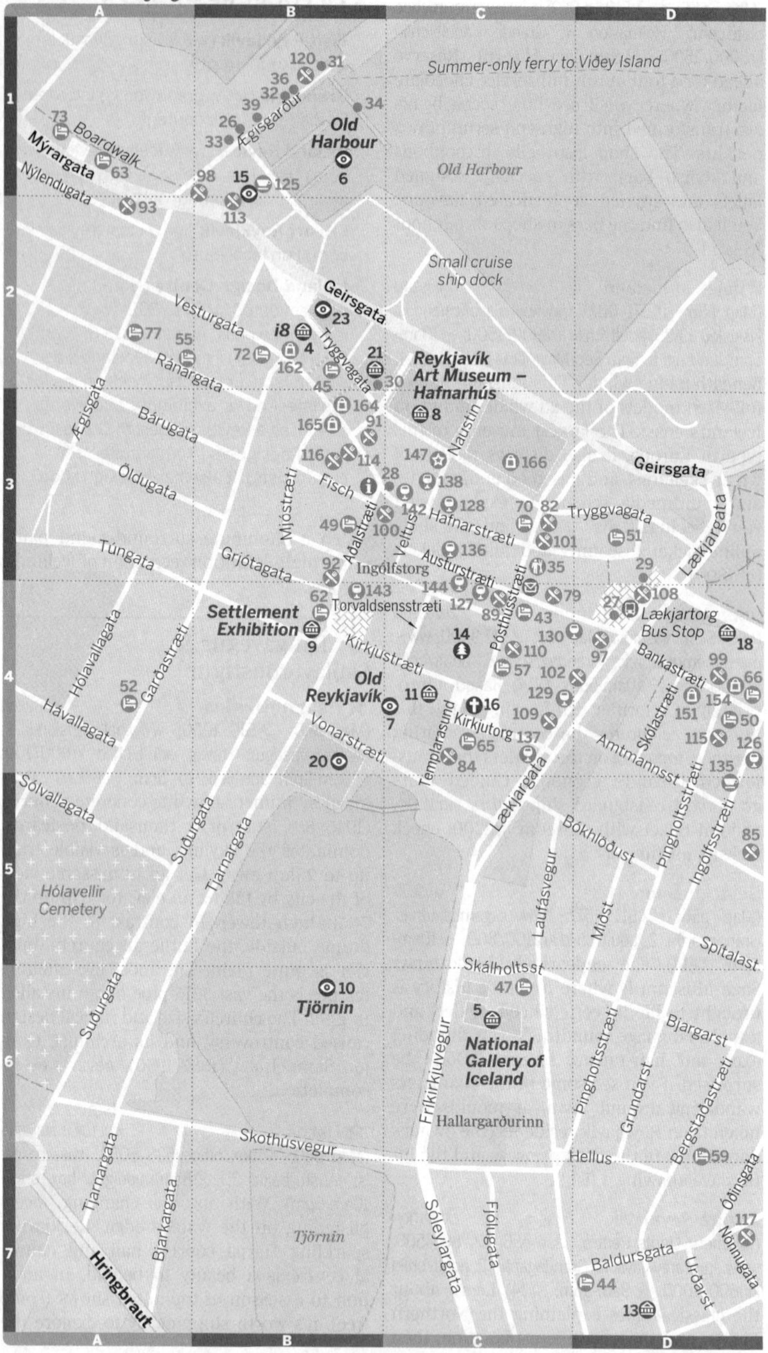

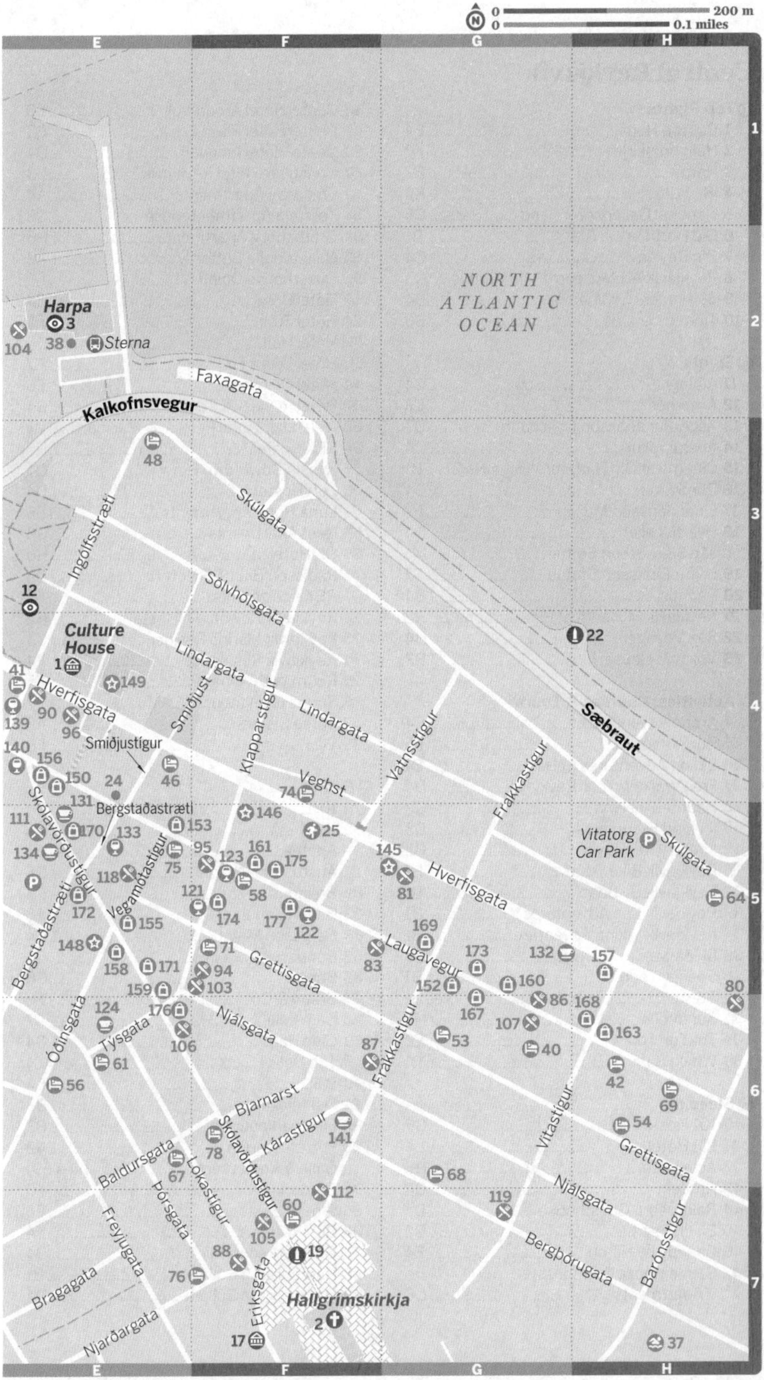
0 200 m
0 0.1 miles
E
F
G
H
1
2
3
4
5
6
7
NORTH ATLANTIC OCEAN
Harpa
3
38
104
Sterna
Faxagata
Kalkofnsvegur
48
Skúlagata
Ingólfsstræti
Sölvhólsgata
12
Culture House
1
41
149
Lindargata
Hverfisgata
90
139
96
Smiðjust
Klapparstígur
Lindargata
Vatnsstígur
22
Sæbraut
Frakkastígur
Smiðjustígur
140
156
150
24
46
74
Veghst
131
Bergstaðastræti
153
146
25
111
170
133
Skólavörðustígur
134
95
123
161
175
145
Vitatorg Car Park
Skúlagata
Vegamótastígur
75
118
121
58
81
Hverfisgata
64
172
174
177
122
Bergstaðastræti
155
169
148
71
Laugavegur
83
173
132
157
158
171
94
Grettisgata
152
160
159
103
167
86
168
80
124
176
Njálsgata
107
163
Týsgata
106
53
40
Óðinsgata
61
87
Frakkastígur
42
56
69
Bjarnarst
Vitastígur
54
141
Kárastígur
78
Skólavörðustígur
Grettisgata
Baldursgata
67
Lokastígur
68
Njálsgata
Þórsgata
112
119
60
Freyjugata
105
88
19
Bergþórugata
Barónsstígur
76
Bragagata
Hallgrímskirkja
2
Eiríksgata
Njarðargata
17
37

Central Reykjavík

Top Sights

1 Culture House ... E4
2 Hallgrímskirkja ... F7
3 Harpa ... E2
4 i8 ... B2
5 National Gallery of Iceland ... C6
6 Old Harbour ... B1
7 Old Reykjavík ... C4
8 Reykjavík Art Museum – Hafnarhús ... C3
9 Settlement Exhibition ... B4
10 Tjörnin ... B6

Sights

11 Alþingi ... C4
12 Árnarhóll ... E3
13 Ásgrímur Jónsson Collection ... D7
14 Austurvöllur ... C4
15 Cinema at Old Harbour Village No 2 ... B1
16 Dómkirkja ... C4
17 Einar Jónsson Museum ... F7
18 Hverfisgallerí ... D4
Jón Sigurðsson Statue ... (see 14)
19 Leifur Eiríksson Statue ... F7
20 Ráðhús ... B4
21 Reykjavík Museum of Photography ... B2
22 Sun Voyager ... H4
23 Volcano House ... B2

Activities, Courses & Tours

24 Arctic Adventures ... E4
25 Borgarhjól ... F5
26 Elding Adventures at Sea ... B1
27 Free Walking Tour Reykjavik ... D4
28 Haunted Iceland ... C3
29 Iceland Excursions ... D3
30 Literary Reykjavík ... B2
31 Reykjavík Bike Tours ... B1
32 Reykjavík By Boat ... B1
33 Reykjavík Sea Adventures ... B1
34 Reykjavík Viking Adventure ... B1
35 Skíðasvæði ... C3
36 Special Tours ... B1
Sterna ... (see 3)
37 Sundhöllin ... H7
38 TukTuk Tours ... E2
39 Whale Safari ... B1

Sleeping

40 101 Hostel ... G6
41 101 Hotel ... E4
42 Alda Hotel ... H6
43 Apotek ... C4
44 Baldursbrá Guesthouse ... D7
45 Black Pearl ... B2
46 Canopy by Hilton ... E4
47 Castle House & Embassy Apartments ... C6
48 CenterHótel Arnarhvoll ... E3
49 CenterHótel Plaza ... B3
50 CenterHótel Þingholt ... D4
51 Consulate Hotel Reykjavík ... D3
52 Embassy Apartments ... A4
53 Forsæla Apartmenthouse ... G6
54 Grettisborg Apartments ... H6
55 Guesthouse Butterfly ... A2
56 Guesthouse Óðinn ... E6
57 Hótel Borg ... C4
58 Hótel Frón ... F5
59 Hótel Holt ... D6
60 Hótel Leifur Eiríksson ... F7
61 Hótel Óðinsvé ... E6
62 Hótel Reykjavík Centrum ... B4
63 Icelandair Hotel Reykjavík Marina ... A1
64 KEX Hostel ... H5
65 Kvosin Downtown Hotel ... C4
66 Loft Hostel ... D4
67 Luna Hotel Apartments ... E6
68 Nest Apartments ... G6
69 OK Hotel ... H6
70 Radisson Blu 1919 Hotel ... C3
71 REY Apartments ... F5
72 Reykjavík Downtown Hostel ... B2
73 Reykjavík Marina Residence ... A1
74 Reykjavík Residence ... F4
75 Room With A View ... E5
76 Sunna Guesthouse ... F7
77 Three Sisters ... A2
78 Villa ... F6

Eating

79 10-11 ... C4
80 10-11 ... H6
Apotek ... (see 43)
81 Austur Indíafélagið ... G5
82 Bæjarins Beztu ... C3
83 Bakarí Sandholt ... F5
84 Bergsson Mathús ... C4
85 Bónus ... D5
86 Bónus ... G6
87 Brauð & Co ... F6
88 Café Loki ... F7
89 Café Paris ... C4
The Deli ... (see 140)
90 Dill ... E4
91 Fiskfélagið ... B3
92 Fiskmarkaðurinn ... B3
93 Forréttabarinn ... A2
Gallery Restaurant ... (see 59)
94 Garðurinn ... F5
95 Gló ... F5
96 Grái Kötturinn ... E4
97 Grillmarkaðurinn ... D4
98 Hamborgara Búllan ... B1
99 Hamborgara Búllan ... D4

100 Hlölla Bátar C3
101 Hornið C3
Hverfisgata 12 .... (see 90)
Icelandic Fish & Chips .... (see 23)
102 Jómfrúin D4
103 Joylato F5
K-Bar .... (see 69)
104 Kolabrautin E2
105 Krambúð F7
106 Krua Thai E6
Laundromat Café .... (see 136)
107 Lemon G6
108 Lobster Hut D4
109 Messinn C4
110 Nora Magasin C4
111 Ostabúðin E5
Public House .... (see 58)
112 ROK F7
113 Sægreifinn B2
Snaps .... (see 61)
114 Stofan Kaffihús B3
115 Sushisamba D4
116 Tapas Barinn B3
117 Þrír Frakkar D7
118 Vegamót E5
119 Vitabar G7
120 Walk the Plank B1

Drinking & Nightlife

B5 .... (see 99)
121 Bar Ananas F5
122 Boston F5
123 Bravó F5
124 C is for Cookie E6
125 Café Haiti B1
126 Den Danske Kro D4
Dillon .... (see 154)
127 English Pub C4
128 Frederiksen Ale House C3
129 Græna Herbergið C4
130 Hressingarskálinn D4
131 Kaffi Mokka E5
132 Kaffi Vínyl G5
133 Kaffibarinn E5
134 Kaffifélagið E5
Kaldi .... (see 95)
KEX Bar .... (see 64)
135 Kigali Kaffi D5
Kiki .... (see 123)
Lebowski Bar .... (see 95)
Loft Hostel Bar .... (see 66)
136 Loftið C3
Micro Bar .... (see 28)
Mikkeller & Friends .... (see 90)
137 Ölsmiðjan C4
138 Paloma C3
139 Petersen Svítan E4
140 Prikið E4
141 Reykjavík Roasters F6
142 Sæta Svínið Gastropub C3
143 Skúli Craft Bar B4
Slippbarinn .... (see 63)
144 Vínbúðin - Austurstræti C4

Entertainment

145 Bíó Paradís G5
146 Café Rosenberg F5
147 Gaukurinn C3
Húrra .... (see 147)
148 Mengi E5
149 National Theatre E4

Shopping

12 Tónar .... (see 171)
66° North .... (see 99)
150 Álafoss E4
151 Aurum D4
152 Beautiful Stories G5
153 Blue Lagoon Shop E5
154 Cintamani D4
Dogma .... (see 154)
155 Eymundsson E5
Eymundsson .... (see 43)
Fjallakofinn .... (see 24)
156 Fóa E4
157 Gangleri Outfitters H5
158 Geysir E5
159 Handknitting Association of Iceland E5
160 Handknitting Association of Iceland G5
Heilsuhúsið .... (see 95)
161 Hrím F5
162 Kickstart B2
163 Kiosk H6
164 Kirsuberjatréð B3
165 Kogga B3
166 Kolaportið Flea Market C3
Kraum .... (see 154)
167 Kron G6
168 KronKron H6
Mál og Menning .... (see 75)
169 My Concept Store G5
170 Ófeigur Björnsson E5
171 Orrifinn E5
172 Rammagerðin – Iceland Gift Store E5
173 Reykjavík Foto G5
174 Reykjavík Record Shop F5
175 Reykjavík's Cutest F5
176 Skúmaskot E6
177 Spúútnik F5
Stígur .... (see 171)

shimmering interior with harbour vistas, or take a 45-minute tour of the hall (kr1950; 11am, 1.30pm, 3.30pm and 5.30pm daily mid-May to mid-September, 3.30pm Monday to Friday, 11am and 3.30pm Saturday and Sunday rest of the year).

★**Culture House** ART MUSEUM

(Þjóðmenningarhúsið; Map p60; ☎530 2210; www.culturehouse.is; Hverfisgata 15; adult/child kr1200/free; ⊙10am-5pm May–mid-Sep, closed Mon mid-Sep–Apr) This fantastic collaboration between the National Museum, National Gallery and four other organisations creates a superbly curated exhibition covering the artistic and cultural heritage of Iceland from settlement to today. Priceless artefacts are arranged by theme, and highlights include 14th-century manuscripts, contemporary art and items including the skeleton of a great auk (now extinct). The renovated 1908 building is beautiful, with great views of the harbour, and a cafe on the ground floor. Check website for free guided tours.

★**Reykjavík Art Museum – Kjarvalsstaðir** ART MUSEUM

(Map p56; ☎411 6420; www.artmuseum.is; Flókagata 24, Miklatún Park; adult/child kr1300/free; ⊙10am-5pm) The angular glass-and-wood Kjarvalsstaðir, which looks out onto **Miklatún Park** (Map p56), is named for Jóhannes Kjarval (1885–1972), one of Iceland's most popular classical artists. He was a fisherman until his crew paid for him to study at the Academy of Fine Arts in Copenhagen, and his wonderfully evocative landscapes share space alongside changing installations of mostly Icelandic 20th-century paintings.

★**Icelandic Phallological Museum** MUSEUM

(Hið Íslenzka Reðasafn; Map p56; ☎561 6663; www.phallus.is; Laugavegur 116; adult/child kr1250/free; ⊙10am-6pm) Oh, the jokes are endless here, but though this unique museum houses a huge collection of penises, it's actually very well done. From pickled pickles to petrified wood, there are 286 different members on display, representing all Icelandic mammals and beyond. Featured items include contributions from sperm whales and a polar bear, minuscule mouse bits, silver castings of each member of the Icelandic handball team and a single human sample – from deceased mountaineer Páll Arason.

★**National Gallery of Iceland** MUSEUM

(Listasafn Íslands; Map p60; ☎515 9600; www.listasafn.is; Fríkirkjuvegur 7; adult/child kr1500/free; ⊙10am-5pm mid-May–mid-Sep, 11am-5pm Tue-Sun mid-Sep–mid-May) This pretty stack of marble atriums and spacious galleries overlooking Tjörnin offers ever-changing exhibits drawn from the 10,000-piece collection. The museum can only exhibit a small sample at any time; shows range from 19th- and 20th-century paintings by Iceland's favourite sons and daughters (including Jóhannes Kjarval and Nína Sæmundsson) to sculptures by Sigurjón Ólafsson and others. The museum ticket also covers entry to

REYKJAVÍK'S ART GALLERIES

Kling & Bang (Map p56; ☎691 4243; http://this.is/klingandbang/; Grandagarður 20, Marshall Húsið, Grandi; ⊙2-6pm Thu-Sun) FREE Perennially cutting-edge young artists' exhibitions in a new gallery space; a favourite with locals.

i8 (Map p60; ☎551 3666; www.i8.is; Tryggvagata 16; ⊙11am-5pm Tue-Fri, 1-5pm Sat) FREE This gallery represents some of the country's top modern artists, many of whom show overseas as well.

Hverfisgallerí (Map p60; ☎537 4007; www.hverfisgalleri.is; Hverfisgata 4; ⊙1-5pm Tue-Fri, 2-5pm Sat) Browse contemporary Icelandic art in a large, central space.

Gallerí Fold (Map p56; ☎551 0400; www.myndlist.is; Rauðarárstígur 12-14; ⊙10am-6pm Mon-Sat) FREE Large Icelandic art dealer and auction house.

ASÍ Art Museum (Map p56; ☎511 5353; www.listasafnasi.is; Freyjugata 41; ⊙1-5pm Tue-Sun) FREE Showing 20th-century Icelandic art as well as rotating contemporary art.

NÝLO (Nýlistasafnið – The Living Art Museum; Map p56; ☎551 4350; www.nylo.is; Grandagarður 20, Marshall Húsið, Grandi; ⊙10am-6pm Tue-Fri, to 9pm Thu, noon-5pm Sat & Sun) FREE Emerging and established contemporary artists. Also holds occasional live music or theatre.

the Ásgrímur Jónsson Collection (p65) and Sigurjón Ólafsson Museum (p66).

Ásgrímur Jónsson Collection ART MUSEUM
(Map p60; ☎515 9625; www.listasafn.is; Bergstaðastræti 74; adult/child kr1000/free; ⏲2-5pm Tue, Thu & Sun mid-May–mid-Sep, 2-5pm Sun mid-Sep–Nov & Feb–mid-May) Iceland's first professional painter, Ásgrímur Jónsson (1876–1958) lived and worked here, and you can visit his former atelier to see his work incorporating folk tales and Icelandic nature.

Einar Jónsson Museum ART MUSEUM
(Map p60; ☎551 3797; www.lej.is; Eriksgata 3; adult/child kr1000/free; ⏲10am-5pm Tue-Sun) Einar Jónsson (1874–1954) is one of Iceland's foremost sculptors, famous for intense symbolist works. Chiselled representations of Hope, Earth and Death burst from basalt cliffs, weep over naked women and slay dragons. Jónsson designed the building, which was built between 1916 and 1923, when this empty hill was the outskirts of town. It also contains his austere penthouse flat and studio, with views over the city.

The **sculpture garden** (Map p56; www.lej.is; Freyjugata; ⏲24hr) FREE behind the museum contains 26 bronzes, in the shadow of Hallgrímskirkja.

Árnarhóll LANDMARK
(Map p60) A statue of Iceland's first settler, Ingólfur Arnarson, takes pride of place at Árnarhóll, a greensward that is also a central gathering place for parades and demonstrations.

Sun Voyager SCULPTURE
(Sólfar; Map p60; Sæbraut) Reykjavík is adorned with fascinating sculptures, but it's Jón Gunnar Árnason's shiplike *Sun Voyager (Sólfar)* sculpture that seems to catch visitors' imaginations. Scooping in a skeletal arc along the seaside, it offers a photo shoot with snow-capped mountains in the distance.

South of the Centre

★**National Museum** MUSEUM
(Þjóðminjasafn Íslands; Map p56; ☎530 2200; www.nationalmuseum.is; Suðurgata 41; adult/child kr1500/free; ⏲10am-5pm May–mid-Sep, closed Mon mid-Sep–Apr; 🚌1, 3, 6, 12, 14) This superb museum displays artefacts from settlement to the modern age. Exhibits give an excellent overview of Iceland's history and culture, and the audio guide (kr300) adds loads of detail. The strongest section describes the Settlement Era – including how the chieftains ruled and the introduction of Christianity – and features swords, drinking horns, silver hoards and a powerful little bronze figure of Thor. The priceless 13th-century Valþjófsstaðir church door is carved with the story of a knight, his faithful lion and a passel of dragons.

Nordic House CULTURAL CENTRE
(Norræna Húsið; Map p56; ☎551 7030; www.nordichouse.is; Sturlugata 5; ⏲9am-5pm Mon-Fri, 11am-5pm Sat; 🚌1, 3, 6, 12, 14) This cultural centre fosters connections between Iceland and its Nordic neighbours with a rich program of events, a library, exhibition space (11am to 5pm) and bistro.

Perlan NOTABLE BUILDING
(Map p56; www.perlan.is; ⏲10am-10pm, cafe to 9pm; 🚌18) FREE The mirrored dome of Perlan, designed by Ingimundur Sveinsson, covers huge geothermal-water tanks on Öskjuhlíð hill, about 2km from the city centre. The wrap-around viewing deck offers a tremendous 360-degree panorama of Reykjavík and the mountains. There's a cafe (often busy with tour groups), so in a downpour you can admire the same views over coffee. The top of the dome contains the high-end Perlan dinner restaurant.

Two artificial geysers keep small children enthralled. Numerous walking and cycling trails criss-cross the hillside; one path leads down to Nauthólsvík geothermal beach (p67).

DISCOUNT CARDS

- The Reykjavík Art Museum ticket covers all three of its sites.
- A joint ticket for National Gallery, nearby Ásgrímur Jónsson Collection and further-afield Sigurjón Ólafsson Museum costs kr1500.
- **Reykjavík City Card** (www.citycard.is; 24/48/72hr kr3500/4700/5500) offers admission to Reykjavík's municipal swimming/thermal pools and to most of the main galleries and museums, plus free travel on the city's Strætó buses and on the ferry to Viðey. The cards are available at the Main Tourist Office, some travel agencies, 10-11 supermarkets, HI hostels and some hotels.

⊙ Laugardalur

★ Laugardalur NEIGHBOURHOOD, PARK
(Map p56; ⌂ 2, 5, 14, 15, 17) Laugardalur encompasses a verdant stretch of land 4km east of the city centre. It was once the main source of Reykjavík's hot-water supply: it translates as 'Hot-Springs Valley', and in the park's centre you'll find relics from the old wash house. The park is a favourite with locals for its huge swimming complex (p67), fed by the geothermal spring, alongside a spa, cafe (p86), skating rink, botanical gardens, sporting and concert arenas, and a kids' zoo/entertainment park.

★ Reykjavík Art Museum – Ásmundarsafn ART MUSEUM
(Ásmundur Sveinsson Museum; Map p56; ☑ 411 6430; www.artmuseum.is; Sigtún; adult/child kr1500/free; ⊙ 10am-5pm May-Sep, 1-5pm Oct-Apr; ⌂ 2, 5, 15, 17) There's something immensely playful about Ásmundur Sveinsson's (1893–1982) vast collection of sculptures housed in the studio and museum he designed: the rounded, white Ásmundarsafn. Monumental concrete creations fill the garden outside, while the peaceful haven of the interlocking cupolas showcases works in wood, clay and metals, some of them mobile, exploring themes as diverse as folklore and physics. Soaring skylights and white marble give way to a fun dome, where the acoustics create the museum's strict 'must-sing policy'.

Reykjavík Botanic Gardens GARDENS
(Grasagarður; Map p56; ☑ 411 8650; www.grasagardur.is; Laugardalur; ⊙ 10am-10pm May-Sep, to 3pm Oct-Apr; ⌂ 2, 5, 14, 15, 17) **FREE** These gardens contain over 5000 varieties of subarctic plant species, colourful seasonal flowers, the wonderful in-season Café Flóra (p86), and lots of bird life (particularly grey geese and their fluffy little goslings).

Reykjavík Zoo & Family Park ZOO
(Fjölskyldu og Húsdýragarðurinn; Map p56; ☑ 411 5900; www.mu.is; Laugardalur; adult/child kr840/620,1-/10-/20-ride ticket kr310/2500/4650, multi-ride pass kr2150; ⊙ 10am-6pm Jun–mid-Aug, to 5pm mid-Aug–May; ⟶; ⌂ 2, 5, 15, 17) This childrens' park in Laugardalur gets packed with happy local families on sunny days. Don't expect lions and tigers; think seals, foxes and farm animals in simple enclosures, and tanks of cold-water fish. The family park section is jolly, with a mini-racetrack, child-size

bulldozers, a giant trampoline, boats and kids' fairground rides.

Sigurjón Ólafsson Museum ART MUSEUM
(Listasafn Sigurjóns Ólafssonar; Map p56; ☑ 553 2906; www.lso.is; Laugarnestanga 70; adult/child kr1000/free; ⊙ 2-5pm Tue-Sun Jun-Aug, 2-5pm Sat & Sun Sep-Nov & Feb-May; ⌂ 12, 16) Sculptor Sigurjón Ólafsson (1908–82) used this peaceful seafront building as a studio. Now it showcases his varied, powerful work: portrait busts, driftwood totem poles and abstract pillars. A salty ocean breeze blows through the modern rooms, and the area is interlaced with waterfront paths with clear views back to Reykjavík. There are classical concerts (kr2500) on Tuesdays in July at 8.30pm. The museum is a branch of the National Gallery; the same ticket covers both.

⊙ Outskirts

Seltjarnarnes AREA
(www.seltjarnarnes.is; ⌂ 11) Seltjarnarnes, 5km west of central Reykjavík, is a coastal area that feels a world away. With 106 visiting species recorded, the offshore island of **Grótta** is a haven for birdwatching and boasts a red-and-white lighthouse. It is accessible at low tide, but is closed May to mid-July to protect nests. Get here along the pretty coastal path, popular with walkers, joggers and cyclists. Waves rush in to the lava-strewn beach, the air has that salt-sea tang, fish-drying racks sit by the shore and Arctic terns scream overhead. There are also super views across the fjord to Mt Esja (909m).

Árbær Open Air Museum MUSEUM
(Árbæjarsafn; www.reykjavikmuseum.is; Kistuhylur 4, Ártúnsholt; adult/child kr1500/free; ⊙ 10am-5pm Jun-Aug, by tour only 1pm Mon-Fri Sep-May; ⟶; ⌂ 12, 24) About 20 quaint old buildings have been transported from their original sites to open-air Árbæjarsafn, 4km southeast of the city centre beyond Laugardalur. Alongside 19th-century homes are a turf-roofed church and various stables, smithies, barns and boathouses – all very picturesque. There are summer arts-and-crafts demonstrations and domestic animals, and it's a great place for kids to let off steam. Tours are at 1pm, and there is a cafe.

Heiðmörk Nature Reserve PARK
(⌂ 5, 28) A nature reserve since 1950, this suburban open space 15km southeast of the city centre is great for walking among Sitka spruce and the Rauðhólar (Red Hills), a

volcanic area that's part of the Elliðaárhraun lava field.

Activities

Locally you can tour the city, rent bikes to zoom along lake or seaside trails, or pop into hot-pots all over town. Reykjavík is also the main hub for activity tours to all regions.

★Laugardalslaug GEOTHERMAL POOL, HOT-POT
(Map p56; ☎411 5100; Sundlaugavegur 30a, Laugardalur; adult/child kr900/140, suit/towel rental kr850/570; ⊙6.30am-10pm Mon-Fri, 8am-10pm Sat & Sun;) One of the largest pools in Iceland, with the best facilities: Olympic-sized indoor pool and outdoor pools, seven hot-pots, a saltwater tub, steam bath and a curling 86m water slide.

★Laugar Spa SPA, GYM
(Map p56; ☎553 0000; www.laugarspa.com; Sundlaugavegur 30a, Laugardalur; day pass kr5490; ⊙6am-11.30pm Mon-Fri, 8am-10pm Sat, to 8pm Sun) Super-duper Laugar Spa, next door to the Laugardalslaug geothermal pool, offers myriad ways to pamper yourself. There are six themed saunas and steam rooms, a sea-water tub, a vast and well-equipped gym, fitness classes, and beauty and massage clinics with detox wraps, facials and hot-stone therapies. The spa is open to visitors over 18 years of age, and entry includes access to Laugardalslaug.

There's a cafe (dishes kr1200 to kr2400) and Icelandic-language child care.

Sundhöllin GEOTHERMAL POOL, HOT-POT
(Map p60; ☎411 5350; Barónsstígur 16; adult/child kr900/140; ⊙6.30am-10pm Mon-Thu, to 8pm Fri, 8am-4pm Sat, 10am-6pm Sun;) Reykjavík's oldest swimming pool (1937), designed in art deco style by architect Guðjón Samúelsson, is smack in the city centre and offers the only indoor pool within the city, plus Hallgrímskirkja views from the decks.

Nauthólsvík Geothermal Beach BEACH
(Map p56; ☎511 6630; www.nautholsvik.is; summer/winter free/kr600, towel/swimsuit rental kr600/300; ⊙10am-7pm mid-May–mid-Aug, 11am-1pm Mon-Fri, also 5-7.30pm Mon & Wed, 11am-3pm Sat mid-Aug–mid-May; ; 5) The small sandy arc of Nauthólsvík Geothermal Beach, on the edge of the Atlantic, gets packed on sunny summer days. During opening hours in summer only, geothermal water is routed in to keep the lagoon between 15°C and 19°C. There is also a busy hot-pot (38°C year-round), a snack bar and changing rooms.

Vesturbæjarlaug GEOTHERMAL POOL, HOT-POT
(Map p56; ☎411 5150; Hofsvallagata; adult/child kr900/140; ⊙6.30am-10pm Mon-Thu, to 8pm Fri, 9am-6pm Sat & Sun; ; 11, 13, 15) Within walking distance of the city centre, Vesturbæjarlaug has a 25m pool, steam, sauna, three hot-pots and one cold plunge.

Árbæjarlaug GEOTHERMAL POOL, HOT-POT
(☎411 5200; Fylkisvegur 9, Elliðaárdalur; adult/child kr900/140; ⊙6.30am-10pm Mon-Thu, to 8pm Fri, 9am-6pm Sat & Sun; ; 19) Ten kilometres southeast of the city centre, slickly designed Árbæjarlaug is known as the best family pool: it's half inside and half outside, and lots of watery amusements (slides and waterfalls) keep kids entertained.

Borgarhjól CYCLING
(Map p60; ☎551 5653; www.borgarhjol.is; Hverfisgata 50; per 4/24hr kr2600/4200; ⊙8am-6pm Mon-Fri, 10am-2pm Sat) Rents and repairs bikes.

Reykjavík Skating Hall SKATING
(Skautahöllin; Map p56; ☎588 9705; www.skautaholl.is; Múlavegur 1, Laugardalur; adult/child kr950/650, skate hire kr450; ⊙noon-3pm Mon-Wed, noon-3pm & 5-7.30pm Thu, 1-7.30pm Fri, 1-6pm Sat & Sun Sep–mid-May) The Reykjavík Skating Hall throws open its doors from September to mid-May.

THE LOW-DOWN ON REYKJAVÍK'S POOLS

Reykjavík's naturally hot water is the heart of the city's social life (as in many Icelandic towns); children play, teenagers flirt, business deals are made and everyone catches up on the latest gossip at the baths. Volcanic heat keeps the temperature at a mellow 29°C, and most baths have *heitir pottar* (hot-pots): jacuzzi-like pools kept a toasty 37°C to 42°C. Bring towels and bathing suits or rent them on-site. For further information and more locations, see www.spacity.is.

To avoid causing huge offence to the locals, you must wash thoroughly with soap and without a swimsuit before hopping in.

Courses

★Creative Iceland CRAFT

(615 3500; www.creativeiceland.is) Get involved with graphic design, cooking, arts, crafts, music...you name it. This service hooks you up with local creative people offering workshops in their art or craft.

Icelandic Culture & Craft Workshops CRAFT

(869 9913; www.cultureandcraft.com; courses from kr15,900) Half-day knitting workshops using Icelandic wool.

Tours

City Tours

The tourist office has loads of free maps and self-guided walking-tour brochures, from *Literary Reykjavík* to *The Neighbourhood of the Gods,* and info on guided walking tours. The hard core can buy the more in-depth *Reykjavík Walks* (2014) by Guðjón Friðriksson at local bookshops.

There are downloadable smartphone apps, including several by Locatify (Smartguide) and Reykjavík Sightseeing.

★Literary Reykjavík WALKING TOUR

(Map p60; www.bokmenntaborgin.is; Tryggvagata 15; 3pm Thu Jun-Aug) FREE Part of the Unesco City of Literature initiative, free literary walking tours of the city centre start at the main library and include the Dark Deeds tour focusing on crime fiction. There is also a downloadable *Culture Walks* app with several themes.

Free Walking Tour Reykjavik WALKING TOUR

(Map p60; www.freewalkingtour.is; noon & 2pm Jun-Aug, reduced hours winter) FREE One-hour, 1.5km walking tour of the city centre, starting at the little clock tower on Lækjartorg Sq.

Haunted Iceland WALKING TOUR

(Map p60; www.hauntedwalk.is; adult/child kr2500/free; 8pm Sat-Thu Jun-early Sep) Ninety-minute tour, including folklore and ghost spotting, departing from the Main Tourist Office.

TukTuk Tours TOURS

(Map p60; 788 5500; www.tuktuktours.is; 30min adult/child kr4500/2500, 75min adult/child kr7500/3500) Zip around town on a *tuk tuk* tour, including a pub tour; they leave from Harpa.

City Sightseeing Reykjavík BUS TOUR

(580 5400; www.city-sightseeing.com; adult/child kr3500/free; half-hourly 9.30am-4.30pm mid-May–mid-Sep) Hop-on-hop-off bus taking in all the major sights around town; starts at Harpa.

Reykjavík Sightseeing BUS TOUR

(497 5000; www.reykjaviksightseeing.is) Reykjavík city tours (eg walking/cycling kr7000/10,000, food and beer tour kr9000) and regional trips (Golden Circle from kr9000).

Cycling Tours

Reykjavík Bike Tours CYCLING TOUR

(Reykjavík Segway Tours; Map p60; bike 694 8956, segway 897 2790; www.icelandbike.com; Ægisgarður 7, Old Harbour; bike rental per 4hr from kr3500, tours from kr6500; 9am-5pm Jun-Aug, reduced hours Sep-May; 14) This outfitter rents bikes and offers tours of Reykjavík and the countryside, eg Classic Reykjavík (2½ hours, 7km); Coast of Reykjavík (2½ hours, 18km); and Golden Circle and Bike (eight hours, 25km of cycling in 1½ hours). It also offers Reykjavík Segway (kr12,500) and walking (from kr20,000) tours. Most convenient place to rent a bike before catching the ferry to Viðey island.

Bike Company CYCLING TOUR

(Map p56; 590 8550; http://bikecompany.is; Faxafen 8) Bicycle tours (from kr20,000) throughout the region.

Whale-Watching, Fishing & Boating Tours

Although the northern waters near Akureyri and Húsavík are known for whale watching, Reykjavík is still a great option.

Tours generally run all year with more departures in the warmest months, which is also prime viewing season. If you don't spot whales, many outfits offer vouchers to come back and try again.

Several companies also offer sea-angling and puffin-viewing trips, though you'll often see puffins on small islets while whale watching.

Elding Adventures at Sea WHALE WATCHING

(Map p60; 519 5000; www.whalewatching.is; Ægisgarður 5; adult/child kr9900/4950; harbour kiosk 8am-9pm; 14) The city's most established and ecofriendly outfit, with an included whale exhibition and refreshments sold on board. Elding also offers angling (adult/child kr13,800/6900) and puffin-watching

CHOOSING YOUR DAY TRIP

If you have more than a day in Reykjavík, get out into Iceland's incredible natural beauty. Popular day-tour destinations get swamped in high season, but if you have the luxury of a rental car you can visit outside peak hours or head to lesser-stomped grounds. You can also use the Straetó, Sterna and Trex buses (p96) or Reykjavík Excursions (p70) for transport.

Golden Circle (p111) With three beloved attractions – **Þingvellir** (beautiful site of the original outdoor parliament and the continental rift), **Geysir** (huge eponymous geyser area) and **Gullfoss** (enormous waterfalls) – the Golden Circle is the ultimate and much-marketed taste of Icelandic countryside. You can combine a Golden Circle tour with virtually any activity from quad-biking to caving and rafting. Full-day trips generally depart around 8.30am and return around 6pm; shorter trips leave around noon, returning at 7pm. In summer there are evening trips (7pm to midnight). In your own car it takes about four hours.

Blue Lagoon (p101) Hugely popular, with crowds to match. Many day trips from Reykjavík tie in a visit to the lagoon. It's also seamless to visit on your journey to/from Keflavík International Airport. In high season it's best at night; you should always book ahead or risk being turned away.

Snæfellsnes Peninsula (p181) Less-travelled, gorgeous portion of the country that you can add to the popular Golden Circle loop or visit on its own. Expect short hikes along crunchy lava fields, snowmobiling on the glacier, seaside villages, and whale-watching or boat tours to offshore puffin-inhabited islets.

South Coast (p197) A wild assortment of geological wonders, including active volcanoes, glorious hikes and shivery ice caps. Tours run year-round from Reykjavík and regional hubs.

Þórsmörk (p152) Though beautiful back-country volcanic valley Þórsmörk has loads of hiking routes that take more time, you should be able to squeeze in one short walk on a day trip by super-Jeep or bus.

Landmannalaugar (p146) For day trippers, a (very short) visit to the geothermal Landmannalaugar region can only be done on a super-Jeep tour or bus, and you'll spend most of the day on the road. Jeep stops along the way, though, often include Hekla. Beware: Landmannalaugar is packed in summer.

Jökulsárlón (p327) This incredible glacial lagoon is quite far from the capital, making it one of the longest day trips. You'll arrive when the lagoon is at its most crowded. If possible, it'd be better to overnight on the south coast and go to the lagoon in the off-peak hours.

(adult/child from kr6500/3250) trips and combo tours, and runs the ferry to Viðey.

Special Tours WILDLIFE TOUR
(Map p60; ☎560 8800; www.specialtours.is; Ægisgarður 13; adult/child kr9900/4950; ⌚harbour kiosk 8am-8pm; 🚌14) One of the smallest, fastest boats used for sea angling and whale watching (20 minutes to reach the prime viewing spot). It uses a smaller vessel for puffin tours (adult/child kr5500/2250), and offers multiple combo tours.

Reykjavík Sailors WHALE WATCHING
(Map p56; ☎571 2222; www.reykjavik sailors.is; Mýrargata 26, Old Harbour; adult/child kr9900/4950; 🚌14) Whale-watching tickets also include admission to nearby Whales of Iceland (p59). Puffins, Northern Lights tours and more.

Whale Safari WHALE WATCHING
(Mr Puffin; Map p60; ☎497 0000; www.whale safari.is; Ægisgarður 7; adult/child kr9900/4950; ⌚harbour kiosk 8am-8pm mid-Apr–Oct; 🚌14) Small, fast Zodiac boats go in search of whales and puffins (kr11,900).

Reykjavík Viking Adventure BOAT TOUR
(Map p60; ☎842 6660; www.reykjavikviking adventure.is; Old Harbour; adult/child kr11,900/6900; ⌚Jun-Aug; 🚌14) Sail in a reconstruction of Viking ship *Gaukstad* from the Old Harbour.

FAROE FORAY

Flights and ferries give Arctic adventurers three or four days to explore the truly magical Faroe Islands. A half-week is just enough time to see the following highlights:

Tórshavn The first thing you'll notice are striking turf roofs adorning almost every bright-coloured building in the marina. Although light on sights, Tórshavn makes a great base if you're planning a series of day trips.

Gjógv It may be hard to pronounce (say 'jaykf'), but Gjógv is oh so easy to love. Tiny turf-roofed cottages cluster around a harbour that looks as though a lightning bolt ripped straight through the terrain. There's good hiking and an inn.

Mykines Marking the western limits of the island chain, Mykines (*mee*-chi-ness) offers innumerable bird colonies (puffins!), haunting basalt sea-stacks and solitary cliffs. Considered remote by Faroes standards (11 inhabitants), it is connected to Vágar by helicopter and ferry.

Hestir Just south of Streymoy, Hestir is best known for hollow grottoes carved into the cliffs by pounding waves.

Fish Partner FISHING TOUR
(☎571 4545; www.fishpartner.com; day tours per person from kr23,900 , plus guide fee kr29,900) Offers fishing day tours and a huge array of custom and multi-day possibilities: sea angling, trout fishing, volcano fishing, heli-fishing.

Reykjavík By Boat BOAT TOUR
(Map p60; ☎841 2030; www.reykjavikbyboat.is; Ægisgarður 11; adult/child kr4500/2200; 🚌14) Offers a 1½-hour boat trip on a small wooden boat from the Old Harbour, around Engey islet (with a puffin colony), to Viðey and back.

Reykjavík Sea Adventures BIRDWATCHING TOUR, FISHING TOUR
(Map p60; ☎775 5777; www.seaadventures.is; Ægisgarður 3; 🚌14) Sea-angling (adult/child kr11,500/6000, mid-April to mid-September) and puffin tours (adult/child kr4900/2500, mid-May to mid-September).

Iceland Angling Travel FISHING TOUR
(☎867 5200; www.icelandangling.com) Day trips and custom holidays for fishing of all sorts around Iceland. Loads of info online.

Bus & Activity Tours

A day-long bus tour from Reykjavík is one of the most cost-effective, efficient ways to see spectacular natural wonders if you're on a short holiday. They're also good if you want to combine sightseeing with activities like snowmobiling, horse riding, rafting or scuba diving.

Reykjavík Excursions BUS TOUR
(Kynnisferðir; Map p56; ☎580 5400; www.re.is; BSÍ Bus Terminal, Vatnsmýrarvegur 10) The largest and most popular bus-tour operator (with large groups) has an enormous booklet full of summer and winter programs (tours from kr9000 to kr47,900). Extras include horse riding, snowmobiling and themed tours tying in with festivals. Also offers 'Iceland on Your Own' bus tickets and passports for transport, and operates the Flybus to the Keflavík International Airport.

Iceland Excursions BUS TOUR
(Gray Line Iceland; Map p60; ☎540 1313; www.grayline.is; Hafnarstræti 20) Bus-tour operator with comprehensive day trips (Golden Circle kr8700) that often combine destinations and activities such as white-water rafting and horse riding. Book online for the best prices; expect large groups.

Sterna BUS TOUR
(Map p60; ☎551 1166; www.sterna.is; Harpa concert hall, Austurbakki 2; ⌚7am-midnight Jun-Aug, 8am-10pm Sep-May) Straight-up bus tours all around Iceland (eg Golden Circle and Green Energy kr9200), with transport passports for independent travellers.

Saga Travel ADVENTURE TOUR
(☎558 8888; www.sagatravel.is) Small groups with wide range of tours (eg Kjölur Route kr59,900). Some larger tours, in partnership with other local operators.

Arctic Adventures ADVENTURE TOUR
(Map p60; ☎562 7000; www.adventures.is; Laugavegur 11; ⌚8am-10pm) With young and

enthusiastic staff, this company specialises in action-filled tours: kayaking (kr20,000), rafting (from kr14,000), horse riding, quad-biking, glacier walking (kr11,000) and so on. It has a booking office with gear shop Fjallakofinn (p93) in central Reykjavík.

Icelandic Mountain Guides ADVENTURE TOUR
(Iceland Rovers; ☎587 9999; www.mountainguides.is; Stórhöfði 33) This full-action outfit specialises in mountaineering, trekking, ice climbing (from kr23,900) and the like. It also markets itself as 'Iceland Rovers' for its super-Jeep tours (Essential Iceland tour kr42,900).

Gateway to Iceland BUS TOUR
(☎534 4446; www.gtice.is) Gets great reviews from independent travellers because its minibus tours (eg Golden Circle kr13,500, South Iceland kr15,900) are smaller than the mass-market ones, and for its interesting guides.

Bustravel BUS TOUR
(☎511 2600; www.bustravel.is) Very popular among the hostelling crowd for informative driver-guides. Groups are large, prices low (Golden Circle from kr8500).

Go Green BUS TOUR
(☎694 9890, 551 9854; www.gogreen.is; tours kr45,500) Small, high-end operator that uses methane-powered vehicles and follows environmentally conscious practices.

Reykjavík Hiking HIKING TOUR
(☎893 2200; www.reykjavikhiking.is) Climb Mt Esja (kr15,000), or have an easier trek through lava-rich Búrfellsgjá canyon (kr12,000), both near Reykjavík.

Dog Sledding ADVENTURE TOUR
(☎863 6733; www.dogsledding.is; tours from kr17,900) Runs dog-sledding tours; visitors sit on the rig but do not drive the team. Check website: when there is snow tours operate from Skálafell ski area near Reykjavík, when there's no snow they operate on dry land at Hólmasel in the Southwest, and usually mid-May to mid-July they are on Langjökull glacier in West Iceland.

Ferðafélag Íslands HIKING TOUR
(Iceland Touring Association; Map p56; ☎568 2533; www.fi.is; Mörkin 6) Iceland Touring Association operates huts throughout Iceland's back country and offers some tours.

Icelandic Knitter CULTURAL TOUR
(www.icelandicknitter.com) Designer Hélène Magnússon offers multi-day knitting tours (six days from kr245,000) that take in spinning, wool work, design, folklore and hiking/sightseeing, in partnership with Icelandic Mountain Guides.

Extreme Iceland ADVENTURE TOUR
(☎588 1300; www.extremeiceland.is) Host of bus (Golden Circle kr12,900, Snæfellsnes Peninsula kr19,000), super-Jeep, caving, quad-bike and Northern Lights tours.

Iceland Horizons BUS TOUR
(☎866 7237; www.icelandhorizon.is) Small minibus operator with only 14 seats; readers have rated its three tours highly (Golden Circle kr10,900, South Shore kr13,900, Snæfellsnes Peninsula kr17,500).

Green Energy Travel BUS TOUR
(☎453 6000; www.get.is; tours from kr17,900) Small-group operator; hopes to switch to methane gas or biodiesel fuels once more established.

Super-Jeep & Supertruck Tours

Super-Jeep tours offer small groups (four to six people) a more customised experience. You'll reach your destinations a lot faster, and you can get out further into wild terrain. Prices are correspondingly higher than bus trips.

Icelandic Mountain Guides and Southcoast Adventure (www.southadventure.is) also offer super-Jeep trips. The tourist office has brochures for loads more.

Mountaineers of Iceland ADVENTURE TOUR
(☎580 9900; www.mountaineers.is) Excellent, knowledgeable guides, many with experience on the national rescue team. Lots of supertruck (from kr29,900) and snowmobiling tours (from kr25,500), with an emphasis on Langjökull, where it has several base camps.

Superjeep.is JEEP TOUR
(☎660 1499; www.superjeep.is; tours from kr36,900) Full range of super-Jeep trips with all the add-ons (snowmobiling, quad-biking).

Into the Wild JEEP TOUR
(☎866 3301; www.intothewild.is) Full roster of super-Jeep excursions, from the Golden Circle (kr34,900) to Eyjafjallajökull and Landmannalaugar (kr37,900).

Caving & Lava-Tunnel Tours

Exploring the wild underground world of Iceland's volcanic terrain is a wonderful way to experience the geology of the island. Many lava tubes and caverns are seen by tour only. Main sites from Reykjavík include Reykjanes Peninsula and upper Borgarfjörður. Arctic Adventures (p70), Icelandic Mountain Guides (p71) and many bus and super-Jeep tour operators lead caving expeditions.

Inside the Volcano ADVENTURE TOUR

(☎863 6640; www.insidethevolcano.com; tours kr42,000; ⊙mid-May–mid-Oct) This one-of-a-kind experience takes adventure-seekers into a perfectly intact 4000-year-old magma chamber. Hike 3km (about 50 minutes; or via helicopter kr86,900) to the Thrihnukagigur crater and an elevator lowers groups of six 120m into the bottom of a vase-shaped chasm that once gurgled with hot lava. Lights are dim and time inside is limited. Participants must be over 12 years old.

Iceland Expeditions ADVENTURE TOUR

(☎777 0708; www.icelandexpeditions.is) Adventure tours include lava-tube caving (kr12,900).

Horse-Riding Tours

Trotting through lava fields on an Icelandic horse under the midnight sun is an unforgettable experience. Stables offer everything from 90-minute outings to multi-day tours, and you can combine riding with other activities, such as visiting the Golden Circle or Blue Lagoon.

Eldhestar HORSE RIDING

(☎480 4800; www.eldhestar.is; Vellir, Hveragerði) Located near Hveragerði, Eldhestar is one of the most established riding outfits in Iceland. Trots take place on the surrounding grasslands (one hour kr7700, half-day from kr14,900) and throughout the region. It also has newly built accommodation.

Íshestar HORSE RIDING

(☎555 7000; www.ishestar.is; Sörlaskeið 26, Hafnarfjörður) One of the largest, oldest stables in the country with well-organised trots and multi-day tours through crumbling lava fields (half-hour/two hours from kr6600/11,400).

Laxnes HORSE RIDING

(☎566 6179; www.laxnes.is; Mosfellsbær) Small, family-owned Laxnes takes newbies out for relaxed trots (two-hour ride kr12,000). On the way out to Þingvellir. Also offers combo tours and pick-up.

Íslenski Hesturinn HORSE RIDING

(Icelandic Horse; ☎434 7979; www.theicelandichorse.is; Surtlugata 3; from kr14,500) With experienced local guides, this outfit near the capital takes care to match you with a horse that suits your capabilities; small groups.

Viking Horses HORSE RIDING

(☎660 9590; www.vikinghorses.is; Almannadalsgata 19) Run by a family, this stable is popular for its higher-end (from kr18,900) small-group rides around Hólmsheiði hill and surrounding lakes.

Reykjavík Riding Center HORSE RIDING

(☎477 2222; www.reykjavikridingcenter.is; Brekknaás 9; half-/full day kr13,900/23,900) Located near Reykjavík's main equestrian centre, this outfit takes small groups (no more than 10) of all levels around the Rauðholar (Red Hills), and offers a midnight sun tour.

Glacier Walks & Ice-Climbing Tours

Crunching across a rugged glacier is a thrill. Tours take visitors to Sólheimajökull, the most accessible glacial tongue of massive Mýrdalsjökull. Glacier walks run year-round; ice climbing runs September to April. For ice climbing you have to be able to pull your own weight (literally, up). Prices are significantly lower if you base yourself near the glacier and go with local guides.

Reykjavík-based operators are Arctic Adventures (p70) and Icelandic Mountain Guides (p71).

Asgard Beyond ADVENTURE TOUR

(☎779 6000; www.asgardbeyond.com) Glacier hikes (kr35,000), rock climbing (from kr72,900) and other outdoor activities.

Quad-Biking Tours

Quad-biking tours explore the lava fields of Reykjanes Peninsula. Many of the main bus/activity tour operators, such as Arctic Adventures (p70) and Reykjavík Excursions (p70), offer quad-bike options.

ATV Reykjavík QUAD-BIKE TOUR

(☎861 0006; www.atvreykjavik.is) All-terrain vehicle (ATV) tours around Hafrafell mountain (kr14,900, solo supplement kr3900) and beyond.

Safari Quads QUAD-BIKE TOUR

(Safari Buggy; ☎414 1533; www.quad.is; Lambhagavegur; 2hr kr19,900, single rider supplement kr6000) ATV and buggy outings in the hills near Mosfellsbær. Evening rides give sunset and city light views.

Rafting & Speedboating Tours

Fun for the family, these trips run from Reykholt with Arctic Rafting (p118) or Iceland Riverjet (p118), and offer Reykjavík pick-ups.

Scuba-Diving & Snorkelling Tours

Iceland has some of the most unique snorkelling and scuba diving in the world. Operators offer dives at Silfra, a fissure filled with crystalline water near Þingvellir on the Golden Circle, and a more technical one in the nearby lake. Advance booking is essential; outfitters can pick you up in town or meet you on-site. In summer it's possible to do a midnight dive.

Some of the bigger activity-tour companies, such as Arctic Adventures and Dive Silfra (www.divesilfra.is), also offer dive options.

PADI certification is required for scuba diving.

Dive.is DIVING

(☎578 6200; www.dive.is; 2 dives at Þingvellir kr45,000) The oldest and most established operator in Iceland, with snorkelling (kr20,000), diving and combo tours.

Scuba Iceland DIVING

(☎892 1923; www.scuba.is; Silfra dive tour with 2 dives kr39,900) Good reputation for small groups, and offers dives at Silfra, Kleifarvatn lake and in the ocean. Snorkelling too (kr17,900).

Snowmobiling Tours

Though most opportunities to jump on a snowmobile lie far beyond the capital, there are several operators that go to nearby Langjökull. (There are no day trips to Mýrdalsjökull proper, and day trips to Vatnajökull are done by air.) One hour with two riders costs about kr29,000 per rider; for solo riders it's kr35,000. The best operators in Reykjavík are Mountaineers of Iceland (p71) and Snowmobile.is (☎562 7000; www.snowmobile.is).

Northern Lights Tours

During winter, most bus and activity companies offer Northern Lights trips going into the countryside to escape urban light interference when viewing the aurora borealis. Trips last around four hours, usually starting at 9pm or 10pm. Since there's no guarantee when you'll see these magnificent curtains of light, or where they'll be, we recommend spending a night or two in the countryside to maximise viewing possibilities.

If you're not in Iceland during aurora season, you can have a multimedia immersion at Aurora Reykjavík (p59).

DAY TRIP TO GREENLAND

You can grab a day tour to Greenland from Reykjavík since it takes just under two hours to fly there. In summer Air Iceland (www.airiceland.is) offers regular tours to Kulusuk in east Greenland (about €1100). Hidden in a tapestry of icy whites and cool blues, on a mountainous island, Kulusuk has only 250 inhabitants. The village of brightly coloured wood-box houses and its icy bay reveal themselves to day trippers during the stunning walk over from the airport. Although the traditional Greenlandic drum dance demo is a tad kitsch, the rest of the experience is like one giant dream sequence. **Greenland Travel** (www.greenland-travel.com) offers multi-day tours.

Air Tours

Larger budgets offer the possibility of day trips and tours by air to far-flung or remote destinations like Lake Mývatn, the Westfjords, the steaming earth of the south coast and highlands, Vestmannaeyjar and even Greenland.

Atlantsflug FLIGHT TOUR

(☎854 4105; www.flightseeing.is; Reykjavík Domestic Airport) Offers flightseeing tours from Reykjavík, Bakki Airport and Skaftafell. From Reykjavík Domestic Airport you can overfly Eyjafjallajökull crater or Reykjanes Peninsula, or take a day trip with tours around Skaftafell and Jökulsárlón glacial lagoon. Also scheduled flights to Vestmannaeyjar.

Eagle Air Iceland FLIGHT TOUR

(Map p56; ☎562 4200; www.eagleair.is; Reykjavík Domestic Airport) Eagle Air Iceland offers sightseeing flights over volcanoes (€420) and glaciers and many combo tours. Also five set routes from Reykjavík: Vestmannaeyjar (€310); Höfn (€580); Húsavík; and in the Westfjords, Bíldudalur and Gjögur.

Reykjavík Helicopters FLIGHT TOUR
(☎589 1000; www.reykjavikhelicopters.com; Reykjavík Domestic Airport; tours from kr47,000, Reykjavík tour kr27,000) Helicopter trips all over, including Glymur (Iceland's tallest waterfall; kr77,000) and volcanoes like Eyjafjallajökull and Hekla.

Norðurflug FLIGHT TOUR
(☎562 2500; www.helicopter.is; tours from kr32,000, Reykjavík tour kr27,900) Helicopters fly over Reykjavík, or zip to craters, waterfalls, glaciers and beyond. Its multitude of trips go as far as the Westfjords, Mývatn (kr439,900) and Askja.

Sleeping

June through August accommodation books out entirely; reservations are essential. Prices are high. Plan for hostels, camping or short-term apartment rentals to save money. Most places open year-round and many offer discounts or variable pricing online.

Old Reykjavík

CenterHótel Plaza HOTEL €€
(Map p60; ☎595 8550; www.plaza.is; Aðalstræti 4; d incl breakfast from kr28,300; @) A full-service hotel in an enviably central spot in the Old Reykjavík quarter, this bland member of the CenterHótel chain has business-oriented rooms with polished wooden floors, and great views from the higher levels.

★**Black Pearl** APARTMENT €€€
(Map p60; ☎527 9600; www.blackpearlreykjavik.com; Tryggvagata 18 & 18c; apt kr54,600-144,000; P @) These 10 fully kitted-out apartments fill several black towers just back from the waterfront. Full-service reception provides personal attention (maid service, laundry, child care), but spacious, cleanly decorated apartments that sleep two to six offer independence. Think king-sized beds, designer furniture and balconies, some with water views.

★**Kvosin Downtown Hotel** APARTMENT €€€
(Map p60; ☎415 2400; www.kvosinhotel.is; Kirkjutorg 4; apt incl breakfast from kr46,200) Firmly a part of the luxury-apartment wave, these superbly located mod pads range from 'Big' and 'Bigger' to 'Mountain Suite'. Nespresso machines adorn the kitchenettes and all the mod cons are standard. The Mountain Suite has amazing balconies.

★**Apotek** BOUTIQUE HOTEL €€€
(Map p60; ☎512 9000; www.keahotels.is; Austurstræti 16; d incl breakfast from kr44,100) This new hotel in a well-renovated 1917 Guðjón Samúelsson building, a former pharmacy, smack in the centre of Old Reykjavík offers slick contemporary rooms in muted tones and a popular ground-floor tapas-style restaurant-bar (p80) as well.

Consulate Hotel Reykjavík LUXURY HOTEL €€€
(Map p60; www.curiocollection3.hilton.com; btwn Tryggvagata & Hafnarstræti; @) This brand-new Curio hotel by Hilton (in partnership with Icelandair Hotels) is in the heart of central Reykjavík, just across from the Harpa concert hall. The hotel uses renovated historic buildings and new construction to create 50 tastefully kitted-out rooms based on Icelandic culture. In 2018 Hilton will also open Iceland Parliament Hotel on Thorvaldsensstræti on Austurvöllur Sq, across from the Alþingi.

Hótel Borg LUXURY HOTEL €€€
(Map p60; ☎551 1440; www.hotelborg.is; Pósthússtræti 9-11; d from kr41,500; @) This historic hotel dates from 1930 and is now tricked out with super-smart beige, black and cream decor, parquet floors, leather headboards and flat-screen Bang & Olufsen TVs. The tower suite is two storeys of opulence with panoramic views.

Hótel Reykjavík Centrum HOTEL €€€
(Map p60; ☎514 6000; www.hotelcentrum.is; Aðalstræti 16; d/apt from kr34,600/51,400; P) Mezzanines and a glass roof unite two historic central buildings, giving this hotel a spry, light feel. Its 89 neatly proportioned rooms and apartments all have mini-fridges, satellite TV and coffee-making gear. Prices vary wildly online depending on date.

Radisson Blu 1919 Hotel HOTEL €€€
(Map p60; ☎599 1000; www.radissonblu.com; Pósthússtræti 2; d from kr43,600; @) Although part of a large chain, this is a decent place with a sense of style. Attractive rooms sport large beds and flat-screen TVs, and up the carved iron stairwells lie large, comfy suites.

Old Harbour

★**Reykjavík Downtown Hostel** HOSTEL €
(Map p60; ☎553 8120; www.hostel.is; Vesturgata 17; dm 4-/10-bed kr9100/6450, d with/without bathroom kr27,800/23,800; @) Squeaky clean and well run, this charming hostel gets such good reviews that it regularly lures large groups and the non-backpacker set. Enjoy friendly service, guest kitchen and excellent rooms. Discount kr700 for HI members.

Oddsson Hostel HOSTEL €
(Map p56; ☎511 3579; www.oddsson.is; Hringbraut 121; dm/pod kr5600/7500, d with/without bathroom kr35,000/22,000; 🚌14) You can't miss this large, quirky new hostel near the Old Harbour neighbourhood with its brightly colored facade. There are dorm rooms, tiny private pods and hotel rooms with shared or private bathrooms, some with excellent sea views. Everyone shares a kitchen, hot tub, rooftop, and yoga and karaoke rooms. A good restaurant-bar called Bazaar rounds it out.

Guesthouse Butterfly GUESTHOUSE €€
(Map p60; ☎894 1864; www.butterfly.is; Ránargata 8a; d with/without bathroom incl breakfast kr24,500/18,250) On a quiet, central residential street, you can't miss Butterfly's flamboyant mural. Neat, simply furnished rooms, a guest kitchen and friendly Icelandic-Norwegian owners make you feel right at home. Self-contained apartments (from kr27,000) with kitchen and some with balcony are great for the family.

Three Sisters APARTMENT €€
(Þrjár Systur; Map p60; ☎565 2181; www.threesisters.is; Ránargata 16; apt from kr25,700; ⊙mid-May–Aug; @) A twinkly-eyed former fisherman runs the Three Sisters, a corner town house in old Reykjavík, now divided into eight studio apartments. Comfy beds are flanked by homey decor and flat-screen TVs. Each studio has a kitchen.

★**Icelandair Hotel Reykjavík Marina** BOUTIQUE HOTEL €€€
(Map p60; ☎560 8000; www.icelandairhotels.is; Mýrargata 2; d kr38,900-49,900; @) This large design hotel on the Old Harbour is decked out in captivating art, cool nautical-chic decor elements and up-to-the-second mod cons. Clever ways to conserve space make small rooms winners overall. Attic rooms on the harbour side have excellent sea views. The lively lobby sports a live satellite feed to sights all over Iceland, and the happening Slippbarinn (p87).

> **SHORT-TERM RENTALS**
>
> Reykjavík's sky-high summertime accommodation prices have led enterprising locals in the capital's prized neighbourhoods to rent their apartments (or rooms) to short-stay visitors. Prices often beat commercial rates, though of course there's no maid, concierge etc. Aim for a Reykjavík 101 postal code to be centrally located.

Reykjavík Marina Residence SUITES €€€
(Map p60; ☎560 8500; www.reykjavikmarinaresidence.is; Mýrargata 14-16; ste kr150,000-300,000; @; 🚌14) Seven refined suites in two restored historical houses. Concierge service, access to facilities at the Icelandair Hotel Reykjavík Marina, and top-quality furnishings make them very comfortable, and some suites have harbour views. The Aðalbjörg Suite is the largest, spanning two floors.

Laugavegur & Skólavörðustígur

★**Loft Hostel** HOSTEL €
(Map p60; ☎553 8140; www.lofthostel.is; Bankastræti 7; dm kr7600-8700, d/q kr27,800/37,600; @) Perched high above the action on bustling Bankastræti, this modern hostel attracts a decidedly young crowd, including locals who come for its trendy bar and cafe terrace. This sociable spot comes with prim dorms, linen included and en suite bathrooms in each. HI members discount kr700/2800 for a dorm/double.

101 Hostel HOSTEL €
(Map p60; ☎661 4767; Laugarvegur 58b; dm kr8700) This tiny new yellow hostel is tucked back behind Laugavegur on an internal courtyard. There is a shared deck and grassy area, plus six simple dorm rooms. Book on Booking.com.

KEX Hostel HOSTEL €
(Map p60; ☎561 6060; www.kexhostel.is; Skúlagata 28; dm 4-/16-bed kr7900/4900, d with/without bathroom kr39,700/25,500; @) An unofficial headquarters of backpackerdom and popular local gathering place, KEX is a mega-hostel with heaps of style (think retro vaudeville meets rodeo) and sociability. Overall

it's not as prim as the other hostels – and bathrooms are shared by many – but KEX is a favourite for its lively restaurant-bar with water views and interior courtyard.

Reykjavík Hostel Village HOSTEL €
(Map p56; ☎552 1155; www.hostelvillage.is; Flókagata 1; dm/d/q without bathroom from kr5200/23,800/26,600) Pick between dorms, singles, doubles or quads, with refrigerators and kettles in any one of five area houses. A few apartments, too. Linen for dorms kr1500.

★**Nest Apartments** APARTMENT €€
(Map p60; ☎893 0280; http://nestapartments.is; Bergthorugata 15; apt from kr21,100) Four thoroughly modern apartments with neat antique touches make a superb home away from home on a peaceful residential street just north of Hallgrímskirkja. In a tall town house, each apartment has a different layout, and the largest sleeps four people. Two-night minimum.

★**Forsæla Apartmenthouse** GUESTHOUSE, APARTMENT €€
(Map p60; ☎551 6046; www.apartmenthouse.is; Grettisgata 33b; d/tr without bathroom incl breakfast kr22,700/30,800, apt/house from kr38,200/74,000) This lovely option in Reykjavík's centre stars a 100-year-old wood-and-tin house for four to eight people, which comes with all the old beams and tasteful mod cons you could want. Three apartments have small, cosy bedrooms and sitting rooms, kitchens and washing machines. Plus there's B&B lodging with shared bathrooms. Minimum three-night stay in apartments and the house.

★**REY Apartments** APARTMENT €€
(Map p60; ☎771 4600; www.rey.is; Grettisgata 2a; apt kr23,000-49,800) For those leaning towards private digs rather than hotel stays, REY is a very handy choice with a huge cache of modern apartments scattered across several Escher-like stairwells. They're well maintained and stylishly decorated.

★**Grettisborg Apartments** APARTMENT €€
(Map p60; ☎666 0655; www.grettisborg.is; Grettisgata 51; apt kr21,200-51,500) Like sleeping in a magazine for Scandinavian home design, these thoroughly modern studios and apartments sport fine furnishings and sleek built-ins. The largest sleeps six or seven.

★**Galtafell Guesthouse** GUESTHOUSE €€
(Map p56; ☎551 4344; www.galtafell.com; Laufásvegur 46; d with/without bathroom from kr25,300/22,100, apt from kr26,000) In a quiet lakeside neighbourhood within easy walking distance of the city centre, the four one-bedroom apartments in this converted historic mansion contain fully equipped kitchens and cosy seating areas. Three doubles share a guest kitchen. The garden and entry spaces feel suitably lovely.

Villa GUESTHOUSE €€
(Map p60; ☎823 1268; www.villa.is; Skólavörðustígur 30; d from kr23,700) Famous Icelandic architect Guðjón Samúelsson designed this mansion located on the fun shopping street leading to another of his creations: Hallgrímskirkja. The well-renovated rooms offers white furnishings with splashes of colour, and an unbeatable address.

Baldursbrá Guesthouse GUESTHOUSE €€
(Map p60; ☎552 6646; www.baldursbra.com; Laufásvegur 41; s/d without bathroom incl breakfast from kr11,900/18,500) This little guesthouse, on a quiet street near Tjörnin, is popular for decent-sized, comfy rooms with washbasins. Additional facilities include a sitting room–TV lounge, garden with hot-pot and barbecue. Some laud the kindness of its owners, others say they could be more organised.

Hótel Leifur Eiríksson HOTEL €€
(Map p60; ☎562 0800; www.hotelleifur.is; Skólavörðustígur 45; s/d incl breakfast from kr19,000/22,000) This hotel glories in one of the best locations in Reykjavík: arty Skólavörðustígur just in front of Hallgrímskirkja, and more than half of the 47 rooms have excellent church views. Rooms are fairly small and basic, but you're paying for the hotel's location not its interior design.

Castle House & Embassy Apartments APARTMENT €€
(Map p60; ☎511 2166; www.hotelsiceland.net) Pleasant self-contained apartments are satisfyingly central and commendably quiet. More personal than a hotel, they still come with room service: fresh towels appear daily and washing up seems to magically look after itself. Of the four locations, **Embassy Apartments** (Garðastræti 40; apt from kr19,700) is on the northwest side of Tjörnin, **Castle House** (Skálholtsstígur 2a; apt from kr22,000) on the east.

Sunna Guesthouse GUESTHOUSE €€
(Map p60; ☎511 5570; www.sunna.is; Þórsgata 26; d with/without bathroom incl breakfast kr29,700/23,900, apt incl breakfast from kr35,200; P @) The various room and apartment configurations are simple and sunny with honey-coloured parquet floors. Several at the front have good views of Hallgrímskirkja. Choose between studios or spacious apartments with room for eight. Limited free parking.

Hlemmur Square HOSTEL, HOTEL €€
(Map p56; ☎415 1600; www.hlemmursquare.com; Laugavegur 105; dm/d/apt from kr4750/25,000/39,000; @) Pick your poison at this hostel and hotel: big dorm rooms come with crisp linens and in various configurations; spacious doubles come with king-sized beds, some have balconies and sea views. Bathrooms are modern, the vibe is upbeat and there's a spacious downstairs lobby-cafe.

Guesthouse Óðinn GUESTHOUSE €€
(Map p60; ☎561 3400; www.odinnreykjavik.com; Óðinsgata 9; s/d without bathroom incl breakfast kr16,000/21,600, d/apt from 26,900/39,600) This family-run guesthouse has simple white rooms with bright, fun artwork. The buffet breakfast (included in room rate from June to August) is served in a handsome room with sea views. Also has one- and two-bedroom apartments.

Snorri's Guesthouse GUESTHOUSE €€
(Map p56; ☎552 0598; www.guesthousereykjavik.com; Snorrabraut 61; d with/without bathroom kr25,800/18,700) On the corner of large Snorrabraut, this pebble-dashed building has impeccably maintained rooms in muted shades. The more expensive 'family' rooms (kr31,800) and friendly owner make it a good base.

★**Reykjavík Residence** APARTMENT €€€
(Map p60; ☎561 1200; www.rrhotel.is; Hverfisgata 45; apt from kr33,300-70,200; @) Plush city-centre living feels just right in these two converted historic mansions. Linens are crisp, service attentive and the light a glowing gold. They come in loads of configurations from suites and studios with kitchenettes to two- and three-bedroom apartments.

★**Alda Hotel** BOUTIQUE HOTEL €€€
(Map p60; ☎553 9366; www.aldahotel.is; Laugavegur 66-68; d from kr34,300) This smart player on Reykjavík's city-centre hotel scene offers sleek rooms with all the mod cons, including a spa and fitness centre and a spacious lounge. All of the deluxe 4th-floor rooms have balconies, suites often have two bathrooms, and some rooms have ocean views.

Luna Hotel Apartments APARTMENT €€€
(Map p60; ☎511 2800; www.luna.is; Baldursgata 36; apt from kr29,000) A strong entry on Reykjavík's luxury-apartment scene, Luna maintains 15 excellent apartments near Skólavörðustígur. The streets are relatively quiet, and the apartments are bright and cheerful, ranging from small studios up to four-bedroom pads that sleep eight.

Canopy by Hilton BOUTIQUE HOTEL €€€
(Map p60; ☎528 7000; www.canopybyhilton.com; Smiðjustígur 4; d from kr43,000; @) The first in a new 'lifestyle brand' by Hilton, this hotel has comfortable rooms, the best of which have sea or mountain views. There are loan bikes, wholesome breakfasts, afternoon beer tastings and a gym.

Hótel Holt LUXURY HOTEL €€€
(Map p60; ☎552 5700; www.holt.is; Bergstaðastræti 37; d from kr39,000; @) Expect a totally cool blast to the luxurious past. Built in the 1960s as one of Reykjavík's first hotels, Holt is decked out with original paintings, drawings and sculptures (it boasts the largest private art collection in Iceland), set off by warm-toned decor. Downstairs, a handsome amber-hued library bar with a huge selection of single-malt whiskeys abuts top-notch Gallery Restaurant (p85).

OK Hotel BOUTIQUE HOTEL €€€
(Map p60; ☎578 9850; Laugavegur 74; studios from kr26,400) A creatively funky vibe pervades rooms kitted out in individual style, like the Mona Lisa with cool mismatched furniture and La Giaconda art. Two- to six-person studios have kitchenettes, and the downstairs K-Bar (p85) is a hit. It gets dinged by guests occasionally for unattentive service. Book on Booking.com.

Skuggi Hotel BOUTIQUE HOTEL €€€
(Map p56; ☎590 7000; www.keahotels.is; Hverfisgata 103; d incl breakfast from kr37,700; P) King-sized beds, sleek furnishings, satellite TV and an excellent location just off Laugavegur make this a good bet. Plus there's free parking.

Room With A View APARTMENT €€€
(Map p60; ☎552 7262; www.roomwithaview.is; Laugavegur 18; apt kr36,000-76,300) This central apartment hotel offers swanky studios and one- to four-bedroom apartments (that sleep 10!), decorated in luxe-Scandinavian style, including kitchenettes, CD players, TVs and washing machines. They have those eponymous sea or city views, plus access to a sundeck and jacuzzi. Each apartment varies: check online for details. The downside is nightlife noise.

101 Hotel BOUTIQUE HOTEL €€€
(Map p60; ☎580 0101; www.101hotel.is; Hverfisgata 10; d from kr59,900; @) The 101 aims to tickle the senses – with yielding downy beds, a stark black-and-white colour scheme, iPod sound systems and glass-walled showers. A spa, small gym and glitterati restaurant-bar add to the opulence.

CenterHótel Arnarhvoll HOTEL €€€
(Map p60; ☎595 8540; www.centerhotels.com; Ingólfsstræti 1; d incl breakfast from kr40,300; @) A glossy hotel on the waterfront, Arnarhvoll offers unimpeded views of the bay and Mt Esja. Cool, Scandinavian-designed rooms with clean lines and large windows let in lovely Nordic light; it's definitely worth paying for a sea view. Rooms are a bit small, but extremely comfortable beds compensate. The small sauna and steam room, and the Ský bar, add flair.

Hótel Óðinsvé HOTEL €€€
(Map p60; ☎511 6200; www.hotelodinsve.is; Þórsgata 1; d/ste from kr39,800/52,000; @) A solid hotel with personality, Oðinsvé contains 50 sunny rooms with wooden floors, original artworks and classic furnishings. They're all very different – some are split-level, some have balconies and many sport bath tubs.

Fosshotel Reykjavík HOTEL €€€
(Map p56; ☎531 9000; www.fosshotel.is; Þórunnartún 1; ⏰d/f incl breakfast from kr32,500/42,400) This 320-room behemoth is one of the new breed of high-rise hotels, especially centred around the Tün neighbourhood east of the city centre. Modern rooms with all the normal mod cons (flatscreen TV, hairdryer) get better, bigger and more expensive as you get higher in the tower. Smaller, older Fosshotels dot the capital.

Hótel Frón HOTEL €€€
(Map p60; ☎511 4666; www.hotelfron.is; Laugavegur 22a; d/studios incl breakfast from kr30,000/32,000; @) This hotel is excellently located overlooking Laugavegur (although rooms at the front can be noisy at weekends). The newer wing has good doubles, large studios with kitchenettes and a family apartment; older rooms are less inspiring.

CenterHótel Þingholt BOUTIQUE HOTEL €€€
(Map p60; ☎595 8530; www.centerhotels.com; Þingholtsstræti 3-5; d/ste from kr53,300/66,800; @) Full of character, Þingholt was designed by architect Gulla Jónsdóttir, using natural materials to create one of Reykjavík's more distinctive hotels. Compact rooms feel cosy with atmospheric lighting, stylish grey flooring, and black-leather headboards and furniture. Some have sleek tubs in the bedrooms.

Opal Apartments APARTMENT €€€
(Map p56; ☎860 1300; www.opalapartments.is; Laugavegur 151; apt from kr57,300) Eight cheerful apartments on the Hlemmur Sq end of Laugavegur are kept immaculately and are fully equipped with all the cooking equipment and comforts you could need.

Laugardalur

Reykjavík City Hostel HOSTEL €
(Map p56; ☎553 8110; www.hostel.is; Sundlaugavegur 34; dm from kr4750, d with/without bathroom kr17,900/12,900; P @) Reykjavík's original hostel is a large, ecofriendly complex with a fun backpacker vibe. Two kilometres east of the city centre in Laugardalur, it abuts the campground and swimming pool, and is served by the Flybus and many tour operators. It boasts bike rental, three guest kitchens and a spacious deck. Discounts are kr700 for HI members and kr1500 for kids four to 12 years.

Reykjavík Campsite CAMPGROUND €
(Map p56; ☎568 6944; www.reykjavikcampsite.is; Sundlaugavegur 32; sites per adult/child kr2100/free, cabin kr14,000; ⏰May-Sep; P @) Reykjavík's only campground (2km east of the city centre in Laugardalur, next to the swimming pool and City Hostel) is popular in summer with campers. There's space for 650 people in three fields, so you're likely to find a spot. Extensive, modern facilities include small cabins (three-night minimum), free showers, bike hire (five hours kr3500), kitchens and barbecue areas.

Hilton Reykjavík Nordica HOTEL €€€
(Map p56; ☎444 5000; www.hilton.com; Suðurlandsbraut 2; d from kr35,500; @) Spacious, easy-going Scandinavian chic makes this Hilton an effortless stay: amenities include 24-hour room service, gym, spa and gourmet restaurant Vox (p86). Light-filled rooms in subtle shades of cream and mocha have enormous beds; those on the upper floors have super sea views. It's about 2km from the city centre, near Laugardalur.

South of the Centre

Icelandair Hotel Natura HOTEL €€
(Map p56; ☎444 4500; www.icelandairhotels.com; Nauthólsvegur 52; d from kr28,400; P @) A bit out of the way, Natura is best for those using the domestic airport. Large with modern rooms, and local art.

Eating

Loads of seafood and Icelandic or 'New Nordic' restaurants serve tried-and-true variations on local fish and lamb, but the capital is also the main spot for finding international eats.

Kolaportið Flea Market (p91) also has a section with traditional Icelandic foods.

Old Reykjavík

Bæjarins Beztu HOT DOGS €
(Map p60; www.bbp.is; Tryggvagata; hot dogs kr420; ⏲10am-2am Sun-Thu, to 4.30am Fri & Sat; 🚸) Icelanders swear the city's best hot dogs are at this truck near the harbour (patronised by Bill Clinton and late-night barhoppers). Use the vital sentence *Eina með öllu* ('one with everything') to get the quintessential favourite with sweet mustard, ketchup and crunchy onions.

Jómfrúin SANDWICH SHOP €
(Map p60; ☎551 0100; www.jomfruin.is; Lækjargata 4; sandwiches from kr1700; ⏲11am-10pm) Wayward Danes seek out this no-frills joint specialising in *smørrebrød:* traditonal Danish open-face sandwiches with any number of Nordic toppings.

10-11 SUPERMARKET €
(Map p60; Austurstræti 17; ⏲24hr) Ever-present 10-11 are similar to 7-Elevens in other countries. Open all night, with inflated prices. Other locations include **Barónsstígur** (p83), **Borgartún** (Map p56; Borgartún 26; ⏲24hr) and **Laugalækur** (Map p56; Laugalækur 9; ⏲24hr).

Hlölla Bátar FAST FOOD €
(Map p60; www.hlollabatar.is; Ingólfstorg; subs kr950-1700; ⏲10am-2am Sun-Thu, to 5.30am Fri & Sat) Keep it local with a greasy sub sandwich in Ingólfstorg Sq.

★**Messinn** SEAFOOD €€
(Map p60; ☎546 0095; www.messinn.com; Lækjargata 6b; lunch mains kr1900-2100, dinner mains kr2500-3800; ⏲11.30am-3pm & 5-10pm) Make a beeline to Messinn for the best seafood that Reykjavík has to offer. The speciality is amazing pan-fries where your pick of fish is served up in a sizzling cast-iron skillet accompanied by buttery potatoes and salad. The mood is upbeat and comfortable, and the staff friendly.

Nora Magasin BISTRO €€
(Map p60; ☎578 2010; Pósthússtræti 9; mains kr1700-2500; ⏲11.30am-1am Sun-Thu, to 3am Fri & Sat) Hip and open plan, this buzzy bistro-bar serves up a tasty selection of pub food, from creative small plates to burgers and fresh fish. Coffee and cocktails run all night, but the kitchen closes at 10pm or 11pm.

Bergsson Mathús CAFE €€
(Map p60; ☎571 1822; www.bergsson.is; Templarasund 3; mains kr2000-2400; ⏲7am-9pm Mon-Fri, to 5pm Sat & Sun; 🖉) This popular, no-nonsense cafe features homemade breads, fresh produce and filling lunch specials. Stop by on weekends when locals flip through magazines, gossip and devour scrumptious brunch plates. After 4pm there is two-for-one takeaway.

Icelandic Fish & Chips SEAFOOD €€
(Map p60; ☎511 1118; www.fishandchips.is; Tryggvagata 11; mains kr1400-3000; ⏲11.30am-9pm Mon-Thu, to 10pm Fri-Sun) 🍃 Pick your fish, and voila, spelt-batter fried it becomes. Pair it with local beer, organic salads (kr900) and 'Skyronnaises' – *skyr*-based sauces (eg basil and garlic; kr290) that add a zing to this most traditional of dishes.

Lobster Hut SEAFOOD €€
(Map p60; mains kr1700-2500; ⏲11am-2am Mon-Thu, to 6am Fri & Sat) What's it gonna be? Lobster soup? Lobster salad? Sandwich? This little food truck dishes it all out, for fine diners on the run. By day it's at Hlemmur Sq and after 9pm it's on Lækergata in the city centre.

Laundromat Café INTERNATIONAL €€
(Map p60; www.thelaundromatcafe.com; Austurstæti 9; mains kr2000-2800; ⏲8am-11pm

Mon-Wed & Sun, 9am-midnight Thu-Sat;) This popular Danish import attracts both locals and travellers who devour heaps of hearty mains in a cheery environment surrounded by tattered paperbacks. Go for the 'Dirty Breakfast' (kr2390) to sop up the previous night's booze. Oh, and yes, there are (busy) washers and dryers in the basement (per wash/15-minute dry kr750/750). Kids' play area, too.

Café Paris INTERNATIONAL €€
(Map p60; 551 1020; www.cafeparis.is; Austurstræti 14; mains kr2800-6000; 8am-midnight Sun-Thu, to 1am Fri & Sat) This is one of the city's prime people-watching spots, particularly in summer, when outdoor seating spills onto Austurvöllur Sq, and at night, when the leather-upholstered interior fills with tunes and tinkling wine glasses. The mediocre selection of sandwiches, salads and burgers is secondary to the scene.

Hornið ITALIAN €€
(Map p60; 551 3340; www.hornid.is; Hafnarstræti 15; mains kr1700-5000; 11am-11.30pm) There's an easy-going air at this bright art deco cafe-restaurant. Pizzas are freshly made before your eyes, the prettily presented pasta meals will set you up for the day, and there are also seafood and meat options.

★ **Apotek** FUSION €€€
(Map p60; 551 0011; www.apotekrestaurant.is; Austurstræti 16; mains kr3000-8000; 11.30am-1am) This beautiful restaurant and bar with shining glass fixtures and a cool ambience is equally known for its delicious menu of small plates, perfect for sharing, and its top-flight cocktails. It's on the ground floor of the hotel of the same name.

★ **Grillmarkaðurinn** FUSION €€€
(Grill Market; Map p60; 571 7777; www.grillmarkadurinn.is; Lækargata 2a; mains kr4600-7000; 11.30am-2pm Mon-Fri, 6-10.30pm Sun-Thu, to 11.30pm Fri & Sat) Tippety-top dining is the order of the day here, from the moment you enter the glass atrium with the golden-globe lights to your first snazzy cocktail, and on through the meal. Service is impeccable, and locals and visitors alike rave about the food: locally sourced Icelandic ingredients prepared with culinary imagination by master chefs.

The tasting menu (kr10,400) is an extravaganza of its best dishes.

EATING THE LOCALS: WHALE, SHARK & PUFFIN

Many restaurants and tour operators in Iceland tout their more unusual delicacies: whale (*hvál/hvalur*), shark (fermented and called *hákarl*) and puffin (*lundi*). Before you dig in, consider that what may have been sustainable with 332,000 Icelanders becomes taxing on species and delicate ecosystems when 1,300,000 tourists annually get involved. Be aware:

➡ It's estimated 40% to 60% of the whale meat consumed in Iceland is eaten by tourists. About 82% of Icelanders never eat whale meat and only 3% of Icelanders eat whale regularly.

➡ Between 75% and 85% of a minke whale is thrown away after killing.

➡ Fin whales are classified as endangered globally; their status in the North Atlantic is hotly debated.

➡ Iceland's Ministry of Industries and Innovation maintains the whale catch is sustainable, at less than 1% of local stock, despite international protest.

➡ The Greenland shark, which is used for *hákarl*, has a conservation status of 'near threatened' globally.

➡ In 2002 there were an estimated seven million puffins in Iceland, in 2015 there were about four million – a 43% drop.

➡ At the time of writing, Icelandic puffins were experiencing an enormous breeding failure in their largest colonies, in the Vestmannaeyjar.

While we do not exclude restaurants that serve these meats from our listings, we leave it to you whether you wish to order these dishes. You can easily find whale-free spots at www.icewhale.is/whale-friendly-restaurants.

★Fiskfélagið SEAFOOD €€€
(Map p60; ☎552 5300; www.fishcompany.is; Vesturgata 2a; mains lunch kr2400-3000, dinner kr4900-6000; ⏰11.30am-2.30pm Mon-Sat, 5.30-11pm Sun-Thu, to 11.30pm Fri & Sat) The 'Fish Company' takes Icelandic seafood recipes and spins them through a variety of far-flung inspirations from Fiji coconut to Spanish chorizo. Dine in an intimate-feeling stone-and-timber room with copper light fittings and quirky furnishings or out on the terrace.

★Fiskmarkaðurinn SEAFOOD €€€
(Fishmarket; Map p60; ☎578 8877; www.fiskmarkadurinn.is; Aðalstræti 12; mains kr5100-5700; ⏰6-11.30pm) This restaurant excels in infusing Icelandic seafood and local produce with unique flavours like lotus root. The tasting menu (kr11,900) is tops, and it is renowned for its excellent sushi bar (kr3600 to kr4600).

Tapas Barinn TAPAS €€€
(Map p60; ☎551 2344; www.tapas.is; Vesturgata 3b; tapas kr1600-2400; ⏰5-11.30pm Sun-Thu, to 1am Fri & Sat) A great place to hang with friends, this outstanding tapas bar serves over 50 different dishes – thousands of possible combinations! Alongside familiar Spanish nibbles, such as mixed olives and *patatas bravas,* you'll find Icelandic ingredients turned into tasty titbits – saltfish or pan-fried lobster tails. Book ahead for a spot.

Old Harbour

★Sægreifinn SEAFOOD €
(Seabaron; Map p60; ☎553 1500; www.saegreifinn.is; Geirsgata 8; mains kr1350-1900; ⏰11.30am-11pm mid-May–Aug, to 10pm Sep–mid-May) Sidle into this green harbourside shack for the most famous lobster soup (kr1350) in the capital, or to choose from a fridge full of fresh fish skewers to be grilled on the spot. Though the original sea baron sold the restaurant some years ago, the place retains a homey, laid-back feel.

★Hamborgara Búllan BURGERS €
(Hamborgarabúlla Tómasar; Map p60; ☎511 1888; www.bullan.is; Geirsgata 1; mains kr1200-1800; ⏰11.30am-9pm; 👪) The Old Harbour's outpost of burgerdom and Americana proffers savoury patties that are perennial local favourites. Russell Crowe was spotted here while filming in 2012.

★Valdi's ICE CREAM €
(Map p56; ☎586 8088; www.valdis.is; Grandagarður 21; scoops kr450; ⏰11.30am-11pm May-Aug; 👪) Throughout summer happy families flock here, take a number and join the crush waiting for a scoop chosen from the huge array of homemade ice creams. Totally casual, totally fun.

Fish & Chips SEAFOOD €
(Map p56; Old Harbour; mains kr1200-2000; ⏰11am-9pm; 🚌14) Delicious, piping-hot fish and chips are on offer at this simple food truck near the Víkin Maritime Museum.

Burið CHEESE €
(Map p56; ☎551 8400; http://blog.burid.is; Grandagarður 35; ⏰11am-6pm Mon-Fri, noon-5pm Sat; 🚌14) Select from a broad range of Icelandic cheeses and *skyr* (yoghurt-like dessert), and other deli and sweet treats.

Walk the Plank SEAFOOD €
(Map p60; ww.facebook.com/walktheplankiceland/; Ægisgarður; mains kr1500-1900; ⏰10am-8pm) On decent-weather days and around whale-watching departures, this tiny food truck opens its window and dishes up yummy crab-cake sliders on the quay.

Víkin Cafe CAFE €
(Map p56; Víkin Maritime Museum, Grandagarður 8; snacks kr800-2200; ⏰10am-5pm; 🚌14) The Víkin Maritime Museum's on-site cafe offers relaxing views of the boat-filled harbour, and has a great sunny-weather terrace.

★Matur og Drykkur ICELANDIC €€
(Map p56; ☎571 8877; www.maturogdrykkur.is; Grandagarður 2; lunch mains kr1900-3200, dinner menus kr3000-5000; ⏰11.30am-3pm Mon-Sat, 6-10.30pm Tue-Sat; 🚌14) One of Reykjavík's top high-concept restaurants, Matur Og Drykkur means 'Food and Drink', and you surely will be plied with the best of both. The brainchild of brilliant chef Gísli Matthías Auðunsson, who also owns excellent Slippurinn (p169) in the Vestmannaeyjar, creates inventive versions of traditional Icelandic fare. Book ahead in high season and for dinner.

★Coocoo's Nest CAFE €€
(Map p56; ☎552 5454; www.coocoosnest.is; Grandagarður 23; mains kr1700-4500; ⏰11am-10pm Tue-Sat, to 4pm Sun) Pop into this cool eatery tucked behind the Old Harbour for popular weekend brunches (dishes kr1700 to kr2200; 11am to 4pm Friday to Sunday)

paired with decadent cocktails (kr1300). Casual, small and groovy, with mosaic plywood tables; the menu changes and there are nightly themes, but it's always scrumptious.

★ **Bryggjan Brugghús** BREWPUB €€
(Map p56; ☎456 4040; www.bryggjanbrugghus.is; Grandagarður 8; mains kr2300-5000; ⌚11am-midnight Sun-Thu, to 1am Sat & Sun, kitchen 11.30am-11pm) This enormous, golden-lit microbrewery and bistro is a welcome respite for one of it's home-brewed beers (start with IPA, lager and seasonal beers, from 12 taps) or for an extensive menu of seafood and meat dishes, and occasional DJs. You've also got great harbour views out the back windows. Settle in for a while.

Bergsson RE SEAFOOD €€
(Map p56; ☎571 0822; www.bergsson.net; Grandagarður 16; mains kr1400-2400; ⌚9am-5pm Mon-Fri; 🚌14) This long-time restaurant-operating family has opened this new seafood spot in the Grandi neighbourhood of the Old Harbour. It's got great harbour views and the lunch menu changes daily, but always features the freshest catch.

Forréttabarinn TAPAS €€
(Starter Bar; Map p60; ☎517 1800; www.forrettabarinn.is; Nýlendugata 14, entrance from Mýrargata; plates kr1700-2600; ⌚4-10pm, bar to 11pm) Tapas restaurants are popular in the capital, and this hip joint near the harbour is a favourite for its menu of creative plates like cod and pork belly with white beans. There is also an airy and relaxed bar area, with weathered wood tables and broad couches.

Kaffivagninn DINER €€
(Map p56; ☎551 5932; www.kaffivagninn.is; Grandagarður 10; mains kr2300-2700; ⌚7.30am-6pm Mon-Fri, from 9.30am Sat & Sun) This harbourside eatery has broad windows looking onto the bobbing boats, and serves good breakfasts and hearty seafood-based lunches.

Laugavegur & Skólavörðustígur

★ **Bakarí Sandholt** BAKERY €
(Map p60; ☎551 3524; www.sandholt.is; Laugavegur 36; snacks kr600-1200; ⌚7am-9pm) Reykjavík's favourite bakery is usually crammed with folks hoovering up the generous assortment of fresh baguettes, croissants, pastries and sandwiches. The soup of the day (kr1540) comes with delicious sourdough bread.

★ **Brauð & Co** BAKERY €
(Map p60; www.braudogco.is; Frakkastígur 16; ⌚6am-6pm Mon-Fri, to 5pm Sat & Sun) Queue for some of the city's best home-baked breads and pastries at this tiny new bakery where you can watch Viking hipsters make the goodies while you wait.

Grái Kötturinn CAFE €
(Map p60; ☎551 1544; Hverfisgata 16a; mains kr1000-2300; ⌚7.15am-2pm Mon-Fri, 8am-2pm Sat & Sun) Blink and you'll miss this tiny six-table cafe (a favourite of Björk's). It looks like a cross between an eccentric bookshop and an underground art gallery, and dishes up delicious breakfasts of toast, bagels, pancakes, or bacon and eggs served on thick, buttery slabs of freshly baked bread.

Garðurinn VEGETARIAN €
(Map p60; www.kaffigardurinn.is; Klapparstígur 37; mains kr1300-2000; ⌚11am-6.30pm Mon-Tue & Thu-Fri, to 5pm Wed, noon-5pm Sat; 🌿) This small, friendly restaurant serves up ever-changing vegetarian and vegan soups and dishes of the day.

Joylato ICE CREAM €
(Map p60; www.joylato.is; Njálsgata 1; scoops kr850; ⌚3-10pm Thu-Tue, to 5.30pm Wed) Scoops of high-end homemade ice cream and sorbets in delectable flavours. Some are made from cashew or coconut milk.

Hamborgara Búllan BURGERS €
(Map p60; www.bullan.is; Bankastræti 5; mains kr1200-1800; ⌚11am-9pm Sun-Wed, to 10pm Thu-Sat) This tiny burger booth, part of the famous local chain, is tucked back inside and behind the B5 nightclub and serves up tasty patties.

Johansen Deli DELI €
(Map p56; ☎517 0102; www.facebook.com/johansendeli/; Þórunnartún 2; lunch mains kr1400; ⌚8am-6pm Mon-Fri) This new family-run deli in the heart of the high-rise hotel district is a great pit-stop for fresh picnic supplies or a weekday breakfast or ready-made lunch.

Vitabar BURGERS €
(Map p60; Bergþórugata 21; mains kr800-3100; ⌚11.30am-11pm, bar to 1am or 2am Fri & Sat) Sidle up to the bar to order your short-order burger with all the fixings. It's got barbecue burgers and some of the best hand-cut fries you'll find. This is a tile-and-formica kind

REYKJAVÍK'S COFFEE CULTURE

Reykjavikers take their coffee seriously, and there are many sweet corners in which to dwell and sip your joe, or grab it on the go.

Reykjavík Roasters (Map p60; www.reykjavikroasters.is; Kárastígur 1; ⏲8am-6pm Mon-Fri, 9am-5pm Sat & Sun) These folks take their coffee seriously. Swig a perfect latte with a flaky croissant. They have a new branch at Brautarholt 2 in the Hlemmur area.

Kaffi Mokka (Map p60; ☎552 1174; www.mokka.is; Skólavörðustígur 3a; ⏲9am-6.30pm) The decor here has changed little since the 1950s, and its original mosaic pillars and copper lights either look retro-cool or dead tatty, depending on your mood.

Kaffi Vínyl (Map p60; ☎537 1332; www.facebook.com/vinilrvk/; Hverfisgata 76; ⏲9am-11pm Mon-Fri, 10am-11pm Sat, noon-11pm Sun) This new entry is popular for its chill vibe, great music and delicious vegan and vegetarian food.

Stofan Kaffihús (Map p60; ☎546 1842; www.facebook.com/stofan.cafe/; Vesturgata 3; dishes kr1500-1600; ⏲9am-11pm Mon-Wed, to midnight Thu-Sat, 10am-10pm Sun) Spacious and relaxed, this new coffee house fills a character-laden historic building in the city centre.

Café Haiti (Map p60; ☎588 8484; www.cafehaiti.is; Geirsgata 7c; ⏲8am-10pm Sun-Thu, to midnight Fri & Sat) Owner Elda buys her beans from her home country Haiti, and roasts and grinds them on-site, producing what regulars swear are the best cups of coffee in the country.

C is for Cookie (Map p60; Týsgata 8; ⏲7.30am-6pm Mon-Fri, 11am-5pm Sat, noon-5pm Sun) Named in honour of *Sesame Street's* Cookie Monster, this cheerful spot has super coffee, plus great homemade cakes, salad, soup and grilled sandwiches.

Kaffifélagið (Map p60; www.kaffifelagid.is; Skólavörðustígur 10; ⏲7.30am-6pm Mon-Fri, 10am-4pm Sat) A popular hole-in-the-wall for a quick cuppa on the run. It has a couple of outdoor tables, too.

Kigali Kaffi (Map p60; www.facebook.com/kigali.kaffi; Ingólfsstræti 8; ⏲10am-6pm Mon-Fri, 11am-8pm Sat) Rwandan fair-trade coffee in a small, welcoming coffee shop.

of joint, with American rock on the stereo and locals quaffing pints of cold Einstök and Viking.

Noodle Station THAI €
(Map p56; ☎551 3198; www.noodlestation.is; Laugavegur 86; mains kr890-1540; ⏲11am-10pm Mon-Fri, noon-10pm Sat & Sun) No-frills but delicious Thai noodle soups are dished out by the bowlful at this trusty popular establishment.

Lemon HEALTH FOOD €
(Map p60; Laugavegur 56; juices kr900-1100, sandwiches kr800-1400; ⏲8am-9pm Mon-Fri, from 10am Sat, from noon Sun) Lemon is tops for smoothies and healthy sandwiches to eat on the go.

The Deli PIZZERIA €
(Map p60; www.deli.is; Bankastræti 14; slices kr500; ⏲10am-9pm Mon-Wed, 11am-5am or 6am Thu-Sat) Reykjavík's best pizza by the slice.

Yummi Yummi THAI €
(Map p56; ☎588 2121; www.yummy.is; Hverfisgata 123; mains kr1600; ⏲11.30am-9pm Mon-Fri, 5-9pm Sat & Sun) Quick and easy Thai noodles and mains take away.

Bónus SUPERMARKET €
(Map p60; Laugavegur 59; ⏲11am-6.30pm Mon-Thu, 10am-7.30pm Fri, noon-6pm Sat) The best-value supermarket in the city centre. Also at **Hallveigarstígur** (Map p60; Hallveigarstígur 1), Grandi near the Old Harbour and **Kringlan shopping centre** (Map p56; Kringlunni 4; ⏲11am-6.30pm Mon-Thu, 10am-7.30pm Fri, 10am-6pm Sat, noon-6pm Sun).

Krambúð SUPERMARKET €
(Map p60; Skólavörðustígur 42; ⏲8am-11.30pm Mon-Fri, 10am-11.30pm Sat & Sun) Pricey but central and open late.

10-11 SUPERMARKET €
(Map p60; Barónsstígur 4; ⏲24hr) Part of the ubiquitous 24-hour chain.

BUYING BOOZE

- Alcohol is pricey in bars and restaurants, with happy hours bringing the best deals. Download the smartphone app *Reykjavík Appy Hour*.
- The only shops licensed to sell alcohol are government-owned liquor stores called Vínbúðin (www.vinbudin.is), with five branches around central Reykjavík.
- Buy when you arrive at Keflavík International Airport's duty-free store for the steepest discounts.

★Snaps FRENCH €€
(Map p60; ☎511 6677; www2.snaps.is; Þórsgata 1; dinner mains kr3800-5000; ⏰7-10am daily, 11.30am-11pm Sun-Thu, to midnight Fri & Sat) Reserve ahead for this French bistro that's a mega-hit with locals. Snaps' secret is simple: serve scrumptious seafood and classic bistro mains – think steak or *moules frites* – at surprisingly decent prices. Lunch specials (11.30am to 2pm; kr1990) and scrummy brunches (11.30am to 4pm Saturday and Sunday; kr1300 to kr4000) are a big draw, too. Seats fill a lively glassed-in porch and have views of the open kitchen.

★Ostabúðin DELI €€
(Cheese Shop; Map p60; ☎562 2772; www.facebook.com/Ostabudin/; Skólavörðustígur 8; mains kr3600-5000; ⏰restaurant 11.30am-9pm Mon-Fri, noon-9pm Sat & Sun, deli 10am-6pm Mon-Thu, to 7pm Fri, 11am-4pm Sat) Head to this gourmet cheese shop and deli, with a large dining room for the friendly owner's cheese and meat platters (from kr1900 to kr4000), or the catch of the day, accompanied by homemade bread. You can pick up other local goods, like terrines and duck confit, on the way out.

★Gló ORGANIC, VEGETARIAN €€
(Map p60; ☎553 1111; www.glo.is; Laugavegur 20b; mains kr1200-2000; ⏰11am-10pm Mon-Fri, 11.30am-10pm Sat & Sun; 🅥) Join the cool cats in this upstairs, airy restaurant serving fresh, large daily specials loaded with Asian-influenced herbs and spices. Though not exclusively vegetarian, it's a wonderland of raw and organic foods with your choice from a broad bar of elaborate salads, from root veggies to Greek. It also has branches in Laugardalur (p86) and Kópavogur (p99).

★Hverfisgata 12 PIZZERIA €€
(Map p60; ☎437 0203; www.hverfisgata12.is; Hverfisgata 12; pizzas kr2450-3400; ⏰5pm-1am Mon-Thu, 11.30am-1am Fri-Sun; 👪) There's no sign, but those in the know come to this cream-coloured converted corner house for some of the city's best pizzas with fabulous family-style ambience. Cheerful staff work behind the copper bar, and round tables fill bay windows. Weekend brunches are a big draw, too.

★Restó SEAFOOD €€
(Map p56; ☎546 9550; www.resto.is; Rauðarárstígur 27-29; mains kr3600-5000; ⏰5.30-10pm Sun-Thu, to 10.30pm Fri & Sat) This homey little restaurant is over by Hlemmur Sq but it's worth the trek for delicious changing menus of seafood, and the friendly family who runs the place. The owner-chef Jóhann Helgi Jóhannesson was the chef at celebrated seafood joint Ostabúðin, and he and his wife, Ragnheiður Helena Eðvarðsdóttir, have created a new anchor in this up-and-coming district.

Public House FUSION, TAPAS €€
(Map p60; ☎555 7333; www.publichouse.is; Laugavegur 24; small plates kr1300-2000; ⏰11.30am-1am) Excellent Asian-style tapas and great local draught beers and cocktails are only part of the draw to this new central gastropub. It's also just a fun place to hang out, with its bustling dining room and tables spilling out onto Laugavegur. A place to see and be seen.

Vegamót INTERNATIONAL €€
(Map p60; ☎511 3040; www.vegamot.is; Vegamótastígur 4; lunch mains kr1500-2900, dinner mains kr1500-4500; ⏰11am-10pm Sun-Wed, to 11pm Thu, to 11.30pm Fri & Sat, bar to 1am Sun-Thu, to 4am Fri & Sat) A long-running bistro-bar-club, with a name that means 'crossroads', this is a perennially popular place to eat, drink, see and be seen at night (it's favoured by families during the day). The 'global' menu ranges all over: from Mexican salad to Louisiana chicken. Weekend brunches (kr1500 to kr3000) are a hit, too.

ROK ICELANDIC €€
(Map p60; ☎544 4443; www.rokrestaurant.is; Frakkstígur 26a; dishes kr1400-1700; ⏰11.30am-11pm) Dive into the small timber house with a turf roof and sunny terrace across from Hallgrímskirkja for high-concept small plates and good beer and wine. Book ahead in summer and on weekends.

Ban Thai THAI €€
(Map p56; www.banthai.is; Laugavegur 130; mains kr1990-2800; ⏲6-10pm Sun-Thu, to 11.30pm Fri & Sat) Ban Thai is by far the local favourite for Thai food. Find it just east of Hlemmur Sq; it also has a cheaper takeaway outlet, Yummi Yummi (p83) across the street.

Austur Indíafélagið INDIAN €€
(East India Company; Map p60; ☎552 1630; www.austurindia.is; Hverfisgata 56; mains kr4000-5500; ⏲6-10pm Sun-Thu, to 11pm Fri & Sat) The northernmost Indian restaurant in the world is a refined, upmarket experience, with a choice of sublime dishes (a favourite: tandoori salmon). One of its finest features, though, is its lack of pretension – the atmosphere is relaxed and the service warm.

Krua Thai THAI €€
(Map p60; ☎552 2525; www.kruathai.is; Skólavörðustígur 21a; mains kr1500-2400; ⏲11.30am-9.30pm Mon-Fri, from noon Sat, from 5pm Sun) Tasty Thai curries, noodles and spring rolls are convenient for a quick bite in this small storefront.

K-Bar FUSION €€
(Map p60; ☎571 6666; Laugavegur 74; mains kr2800-5600; ⏲5-10pm Sun-Thu, to 11pm Fri & Sat) Leather banquettes and hammered copper tables at this cool bar-restaurant fill up with lively locals digging into creative California-Korean-style cuisine from tempura cod sliders to barbecue beef. Cocktails are delish, as are local tap beers.

Café Loki CAFE €€
(Map p60; www.loki.is; Lokastígur 28; mains kr1900-2600; ⏲9am-9pm Mon-Sat, 11am-9pm Sun) Near Hallgrímskirkja, you can duck in here for a bite to eat and a cup of coffee in a pinch, but there are more exciting places within 500m. Best seats are upstairs with a view.

★ **Dill** ICELANDIC €€€
(Map p60; ☎552 1522; www.dillrestaurant.is; Hverfisgata 12; 5-course meal from kr11,900; ⏲6-10pm Wed-Sat) Top 'New Nordic' cuisine is the major drawcard at this elegant yet simple bistro. The focus is very much on the food – locally sourced produce served as a parade of courses. The owners are friends with Copenhagen's famous Noma clan, and take Icelandic cuisine to similarly heady heights. Popular with locals and visitors alike, a reservation is a must.

★ **Þrír Frakkar** ICELANDIC, SEAFOOD €€€
(Map p60; ☎552 3939; www.3frakkar.com; Baldursgata 14; mains kr4000-6000; ⏲11.30am-2.30pm & 6-10pm Mon-Fri, 6-11pm Sat & Sun) Owner-chef Úlfar Eysteinsson has built up a consistently excellent reputation at this snug little restaurant – apparently a favourite of Jamie Oliver's. Specialities range throughout the aquatic world from salt cod and halibut to *plokkfiskur* (fish stew) with black bread. Non-fish items run towards guillemot, horse, lamb and whale.

Gallery Restaurant INTERNATIONAL €€€
(Map p60; ☎552 5700; www.holt.is; Hótel Holt, Bergstaðastræti 37; dinner mains kr 4850-7000; ⏲noon-2pm & 6-9pm Tue-Sat) One of the capital's top high-end restaurants, the Gallery lives up to its name, with original artwork lining the walls, making it feel like a smart friend's refined drawing room. A combination of Icelandic and French, expect to eat lavishly. The daytime brasserie menu (mains kr2900 to kr7000) is a tad simpler.

Kolabrautin ITALIAN €€€
(Map p60; ☎519 9700; www.kolabrautin.is; Harpa concert hall, Austurbakki 2; mains kr5500; ⏲5.30-11pm) Kolabrautin, high up on the top of the Harpa concert hall, creatively uses Icelandic ingredients with Mediterranean techniques. Start with a splashy cocktail before digging into dishes like cod with lobster cream.

Sushisamba FUSION €€€
(Map p60; ☎568 6600; www.sushisamba.is; Þingholtsstræti 5; sushi kr1300-4000, multicourse menus kr8000-9000; ⏲5-11pm Sun-Thu, to midnight Fri & Sat) Sushisamba is a perennial capital favourite for sushi, and puts an international spin on straight-up sushi, alongside meat and seafood mains.

Argentína STEAKHOUSE €€€
(Map p56; ☎551 9555; www.argentina.is; Barónsstígur 11a; mains kr4200-7500; ⏲6-10.30pm Sun-Thu, 5.30-11.30pm Fri & Sat) This dark steakhouse rightly prides itself on its succulent locally raised beef and fresh grilled fish, with a wine list to match. The bar stays open to midnight or 1am.

Laugardalur

★ **Frú Lauga** MARKET €
(Map p56; ☎534 7165; www.frulauga.is; Laugalækur 6; ⏲11am-6pm Mon-Fri, to 4pm Sat; 📶) Reykjavík's trailblazing farmers market sources its ingredients from all over the countryside,

featuring treats like *skyr* (yoghurt-like dessert) from Erpsstaðir (p195), organic vegetables, rhubarb conserves, meats, honey, and a range of carefully curated international pastas, chocolates, wine and the like. It also operates a cafe at Reykjavík Art Museum – Hafnarhús (p55).

★Café Flóra CAFE €€
(Flóran; Map p56; 553 8872; www.floran.is; Botanic Gardens; cakes kr950, mains kr1400-3000; 10am-10pm May-Sep;) Sun-dappled tables fill a greenhouse in the Botanic Gardens and spill onto a flower-lined terrace at this lovely cafe that specialises in wholesome local ingredients – some grown in the gardens themselves! Soups come with fantastic sourdough bread, and snacks range from cheese platters with nuts and honey to pulled-pork sandwiches. Weekend brunch, good coffee and homemade cakes round it all out.

Gló Street Food ORGANIC, VEGETARIAN €€
(Map p56; 553 1111; www.glo.is; Engjateigur 19; mains kr1200-2000; 11am-9pm Mon-Fri;) Branch of the tasty, popular organic restaurant, near the Hilton.

Vox ICELANDIC €€€
(Map p56; 444 5050; www.vox.is; Suðurlandsbraut 2; mains kr4200-7000, lunch buffet kr3650, brunch kr3950; 11.30am-10.30pm) The Hilton's five-star restaurant has a contemporary but welcoming vibe and continues to pack 'em in for New Nordic cuisine and a famous weekend brunch.

South of the Centre

Nauthóll ICELANDIC €€
(Map p56; 599 6660; www.nautholl.is; Nauthólsvegur 106; mains kr2700-6300; 11am-10pm) Out of the city centre beside Nauthólsvík Geothermal Beach, this reliable option for Icelandic faves sits in a delicate glass box with views out to the waterway. It's casual by day.

Drinking & Nightlife

Sometimes it's hard to distinguish between cafes, restaurants and bars in Reykjavík, because when night rolls around (whether light or dark out) many coffee shops and bistros turn lights down and volume up, swapping cappuccinos for cocktails. Craft-beer bars, high-end cocktail bars and music and dance venues flesh out the scene. Some hotels and hostels also have trendy bars.

Old Reykjavík

★Micro Bar BAR
(Map p60; www.facebook.com/MicroBarIceland/; Vesturgata 2; 2pm-12.30am Sun-Thu, to 2am Fri & Sat) Boutique brews are the name of the game at this low-key spot that's in the heart of the action. Bottled beers represent a slew of brands and countries, but more importantly you'll discover 10 local draughts on tap from the island's top microbreweries: one of the best selections in Reykjavík. Happy hour (5pm to 7pm) offers kr850 beers.

★Paloma CLUB
(Map p60; www.facebook.com/BarPaloma/; Naustin 1-3; 8pm-1am Thu & Sun, to 4.30am Fri & Sat;) One of Reykjavík's best late-night dance clubs, with DJs upstairs laying down reggae, electronica and pop, and a dark deep house dance scene in the basement.

★Loftið COCKTAIL BAR
(Map p60; 551 9400; www.loftidbar.is; 2nd fl, Austurstræti 9; 2pm-1am Sun-Thu, 4pm-3am Fri & Sat) Loftið is all about high-end cocktails and good living. Dress up to join the fray at this airy upstairs lounge with a zinc bar, retro tailor-shop-inspired decor, vintage tiles and a swank, older crowd. The well booze here is the top-shelf liquor elsewhere, and jazzy bands play from time to time.

Skúli Craft Bar CRAFT BEER
(Map p60; 519 6455; Aðalstræti 9; 2-11pm Sun-Thu, to 1am Fri & Sat) Loads of draught and bottled beers (130 at last count) served with a smile in a welcoming brick and beam sort of place. Six-beer flight costs kr3100.

Frederiksen Ale House PUB
(Map p60; 571 0055; www.frederiksen.is; Hafnarstræti 5) A modest selection of draught beers (happy hour is two-for-one; 4pm to 7pm) meets lots of bottled offerings and a good pub food menu, including brunch.

Sæta Svínið Gastropub PUB
(Map p60; www.saetasvinid.is; Hafnarstræti 1; 11.30am-11.30pm) Tuck into meaty and creative pub food while quaffing a litre of the local ale at this three-storey new entry on Reykjavík's gastropub scene.

Hressingarskálinn PUB
(Hressó; Map p60; www.hresso.is; Austurstræti 20; 9am-1am Sun-Thu, 10am-4.30am Fri & Sat) Known as Hressó, this large cafe-bar serves a diverse menu until 10pm – everything

DJAMMIÐ: HOW TO PARTY IN REYKJAVÍK

Reykjavík is renowned for its weekend party scene that goes strong into the wee hours, and even spills over onto some of the weekdays (especially in summer). *Djammið* in the capital means going out on the town, or you could say *pöbbarölt* for a 'pub stroll'.

Thanks to the high price of alcohol, things generally don't get going until late. Icelanders brave the melee at the government alcohol store Vínbúðin (www.vinbudin.is), then toddle home for a prepub party. People hit town around midnight, party until 5am, queue for a hot dog, then topple into bed.

Rather than settling into one venue for the evening, Icelanders like to cruise from bar to bar, getting progressively louder and less inhibited as the evening goes on. 'In' clubs may have long queues, but they tend to move quickly with the constant circulation of revellers.

Most of the action is concentrated near Laugavegur and Austurstræti. Places usually stay open until 1am Sunday to Thursday and 4am or 5am on Friday and Saturday. You'll pay around kr1000 to kr1600 per pint of beer, and cocktails hit the kr1800 to kr2600 mark. Some venues have cover charges (around kr1000) after midnight.

The legal drinking age is 20 years.

from porridge to *plokkfiskur* (fish stew); mains kr2800 to kr5000 – then at weekends it loses its civilised veneer and concentrates on drinks and dancing for the younger set.

English Pub PUB
(Enski Barinn; Map p60; www.enskibarinn.is; Austurstræti 12a; ⏲noon-1am Sun-Thu, to 4.30am Fri & Sat) Reliable pub for catching football matches.

Græna Herbergið CLUB
(Map p60; www.greenroom.is; Lækjargata 6; ⏲4pm-1am Tue-Thu & Sun, to 3am Fri & Sat) DJs and live music alternate in this large, two-storey bar.

Ölsmiðjan BAR
(Map p60; Lækjargata 10; ⏲3pm-1am) An Icelandic dive bar with low beer prices and decent ambience.

Old Harbour

Slippbarinn COCKTAIL BAR
(Map p60; ☎560 8080; www.slippbarinn.is; Mýrargata 2; ⏲noon-midnight Sun-Thu, to 1am Fri & Sat) Jet setters unite at this buzzy restaurant (mains kr2900 to kr5000) and bar at the Old Harbour in the Icelandair Hotel Reykjavík Marina (p75). It's bedecked with vintage record players and chatting locals sipping some of the best cocktails in town.

Laugavegur & Skólavörðustígur

★**Kaldi** BAR
(Map p60; www.kaldibar.is; Laugavegur 20b; ⏲noon-1am Sun-Thu, to 3am Fri & Sat) Effortlessly cool with mismatched seats and teal banquettes, plus a popular smoking courtyard, Kaldi is awesome for its full range of Kaldi microbrews, not available elsewhere. Happy hour (4pm to 7pm) gets you one for kr700. Anyone can play the in-house piano.

★**Kaffibarinn** BAR
(Map p60; www.kaffibarinn.is; Bergstaðastræti 1; ⏲3pm-1am Sun-Thu, to 4.30am Fri & Sat) This old house with the London Underground symbol over the door contains one of Reykjavík's coolest bars; it even had a starring role in the cult movie *101 Reykjavík* (2000). At weekends you'll feel like you need a famous face or a battering ram to get in. At other times it's a place for artistic types to chill with their Macs.

★**Mikkeller & Friends** CRAFT BEER
(Map p60; www.mikkeller.dk; Hverfisgata 12; ⏲5pm-1am Sun-Thu, 2pm-1am Fri & Sat) Climb to the top floor of the building shared by excellent pizzeria Hverfisgata 12 and you'll find this Danish craft-beer pub; It's 20 taps rotate through Mikkeller's own offerings and local Icelandic craft beers. The vibe is laid-back and colourful.

ICELANDIC BOOZE: WHAT TO CHOOSE

Spirits

Icelanders have a lot of time in winter to perfect their crafts. It's no wonder then that a slew of good local distilleries and breweries have sprung up. Here's a quick cheat sheet for your next bar-room order:

64° Reykjavík Microdistillery producing Katla vodka, aquavit, herbal liqueurs and schnapps (think juniper or blueberry).

Brennivín Caraway-flavoured 'black death' schnapps, nicely neon green (80 proof).

Flóki Icelandic single malt whisky.

Opal Flavoured vodka in several menthol and licorice varieties (52 proof).

Reyka Iceland's first distillery, in Borgarnes, with crystalline vodka.

Beer

Egils, Gull, Thule and Viking are the most common beers (typically lagers) in Iceland. But craft breweries are taking the scene by storm and you can ask for them in most Reykjavík and larger city bars.

Borg Brugghús (www.borgbrugghus.is) Award-winning craft brewery with scrumptious beers from Bríó pilsner to Úlfur IPA and Garún stout, all whimsically named. Its sheep-dung-smoked IPA Fenrir is an acquired taste.

Bryggjan Brugghús (www.bryggjanbrugghus.is) Microbrewery at Reykjavík's Old Harbour.

Einstök Brewing Company (www.einstokbeer.com) Akureyri-based craft brewery with a fab Viking label and equally distinctive Icelandic Pale Ale, among other ales and porters.

Kaldi (www.bruggsmidjan.is) Produced using Czech techniques, Kaldi's popular microbrews are widely available, and its cool bar **Kaldi** (p87) offers seasonal draught beers on offer nowhere else.

Ölvisholt Brugghús (www.brugghus.is) Solid range of microbrews from South Iceland, including eye-catching Lava beer.

Steðji Brugghús (www.stedji.com) This little, family-run Borgarnes brewhouse crafts good seasonal beers, from strawberry beer to lager.

Loft Hostel Bar BAR

(Map p60; www.lofthostel.is; Bankastræti 7) This lively patio bar, at the hostel of the same name, draws visitors and locals alike, especially for its happy hour (4pm to 7pm).

Kiki GAY

(Map p60; www.kiki.is; Laugavegur 22; ⏲9pm-1am Thu, to 4.30am Fri & Sat) Ostensibly a queer bar, Kiki is also *the* place to get your dance on (with pop and electronica the mainstays), since much of Reyjavík's nightlife centres around the booze, not the groove.

Bravó BAR

(Map p60; Laugavegur 22; ⏲11am-1am Mon-Thu, to 3am Fri & Sat) Friendly, knowledgeable bartenders, a laid-back corner-bar vibe with great people-watching, cool tunes on the sound system and happy-hour (11am to 8pm) draught local beers for kr650 – what's not to love?

KEX Bar BAR

(Map p60; www.kexhostel.is; Skúlagata 28; ⏲11.30am-11pm) Locals like this hostel bar-restaurant (mains kr1800 to kr2600) in an old cookie factory (*kex* means 'cookie') for its broad windows facing the sea, an inner courtyard and kids' play area. Happy hipsters soak up the 1920s Vegas vibe: saloon doors, old-school barber station, scuffed floors and happy chatter.

Boston BAR

(Map p60; www.facebook.com/boston.reykjavik/; Laugavegur 28b; ⏲4pm-1am Sun-Thu, to 3am Fri & Sat) Boston is cool, arty and found up through a doorway on Laugavegur that leads to its laid-back lounge and interior deck with sofas; DJs spin from time to time.

Prikið PUB

(Map p60; ☎551 2866; www.prikid.is; Bankastræti 12; ⊗8am-1am Mon-Thu, to 4.30am Fri, 11am-4.30am Sat, 11am-midnight Sun) Being one of Reykjavík's oldest joints, Prikið feels somewhere between diner and saloon: great if you're up for greasy eats (mains kr2000 to kr3500) and socialising. Things get hip-hop dancey in the wee hours, and if you survive the night, it's popular for its next-day 'hangover killer' breakfast (kr2590).

Dillon BAR

(Map p60; ☎578 2424; Laugavegur 30; ⊗2pm-1am Sun-Thu, to 3am Fri & Sat) Beer, beards and the odd flying bottle…atmospheric Dillon is a RRRRROCK pub with a great beer garden out the back. Loud live bands hit its tiny corner stage.

Petersen Svítan LOUNGE

(Gamla Bíó; Map p60; ☎563 4000; http://gamlabio.tji.li; Ingólfsstræti 2a; ⊗11.30am-1am Sun-Thu, to 3am Fri & Sat) Get wide open views from this lounge bar on the roof of a restored old theatre (which occasionally hosts events).

Den Danske Kro BAR

(Danski Barinn; Map p60; www.danski.is; Ingólfsstræti 3; ⊗noon-1am Sun-Thu, to 4.30am Fri & Sat) This popular new bar is 'the Danish bar', and offers good cocktails and a buzzy front deck.

Bar Ananas BAR

(Map p60; Klapparstígur 38; ⊗5pm-1am Sun-Thu, to 3am Fri & Sat) This tropical-themed bar is a good bet for warming up for a night out.

B5 CLUB

(Map p60; www.b5.is; Bankastræti 5; ⊗7pm-2am) Top 40 and bottle service pack this joint with a partying blinged-out crowd.

Lebowski Bar BAR

(Map p60; www.lebowskibar.is; Laugavegur 20a; ⊗11am-1am Sun-Thu, to 4am Fri & Sat) Named after the eponymous 'Dude' of moviedom, the grungy Lebowski Bar is smack in the middle of the action, with Americana smothering the walls and loads of white Russians – a favourite from the film.

Outskirts

Bike Cave CAFE

(Map p56; ☎770 3113; www.bikecave.is; Einarsnes 36; ⊗9am-11pm; 🚌12) This unusual cafe (dishes kr900 to kr3000) caters to cyclists, with coffee, beer, wine, a shower, laundry and workshop for DIY repairs.

☆ Entertainment

For the latest in Icelandic music and performing arts, and to see who's playing, consult free English-language newspaper *Grapevine* (www.grapevine.is; with events listing app *Appening*); websites Visit Reykjavík (www.visitreykjavik.is), What's On in Reykjavík (www.whatson.is/magazine) and Musik.is (www.musik.is); or city music shops.

Some tickets are sold online at Midi (www.midi.is).

Cinema at Old Harbour Village No 2 CINEMA

(Map p60; ☎898 6628; www.thecinema.is; Geirsgata 7b; adult/child kr1800/900; 🚌1, 3, 6, 11, 12, 13, 14) A tiny theatre perches in the top of one of the rehabbed Old Harbour warehouses. Nature films include volcanoes (Eyjafjallajökull, Westmann Islands), the creation of Iceland, and the Northern Lights, and are mostly shown in English with occasional German screenings. See schedule online.

★ **Bíó Paradís** CINEMA

(Map p60; www.bioparadis.is; Hverfisgata 54; adult kr1600) This totally cool cinema, decked out in movie posters and vintage officeware, screens specially curated Icelandic films with English subtitles. It's a chance to see movies that you may not find elsewhere. Plus there's a happy hour from 5pm to 7.30pm.

★ **Húrra** LIVE MUSIC

(Map p60; Tryggvagata 22; ⊗5pm-1am Sun-Thu, to 4.30am Fri & Sat) Dark and raw, this large bar opens up its back room to make a concert venue, with live music or DJs most nights, and is one of the best places in town to close out the night. Run by the same folks as Bravó (p88), it's got a range of beers on tap and happy hour runs till 9pm (beer or wine kr700).

Café Rosenberg LIVE MUSIC

(Map p60; ☎551 2442; Klapparstígur 25-27; ⊗3pm-1am Mon-Thu, 4pm-3am Fri & Sat) This big, booklined shopfront is dotted with couches and cocktail tables, and hosts all manner of live acts, from local singer-songwriters to jazz groups, with broad-paned windows looking onto the street.

LGBTI REYKJAVÍK

Reykjavík is very gay friendly; the annual **Reykjavík Pride** (www.hinsegindagar.is; ⌚Aug) festival and parade is one of Iceland's most attended events, with a quarter of the country's population parading in 2014. Visit Gayice (www.gayice.is) and Gay Iceland (www.gayiceland.is) for LGBTI tips and news. for a queer night out, head to **Kiki** (p88) dance club.

Literary Reykjavík (p68) Has a *Culture Walks* app with a Queer Literature feature.

Samtökin '78 (☎552 7878; www.samtokin78.is; Suðurgata 3; ⌚office 1-4pm Mon-Fri, Queer Centre 8-11pm Thu, closed Jul) This LGBT organisation provides information during office hours and operates a community centre on Thursday nights.

Pink Iceland (☎562 1919; www.pinkiceland.is; Hverfisgata 39; ⌚9am-5pm Mon-Fri) Iceland's first gay-and-lesbian owned-and-focused travel agency and welcomes all. It arranges all manner of travel, events and weddings and offers tours, including a two-hour walking tour of Reykjavík (kr5500).

National Theatre THEATRE
(Þjóðleikhúsið; Map p60; ☎551 1200; www.leikhusid.is; Hverfisgata 19; ⌚closed Jul) The National Theatre has three separate stages and puts on plays, musicals and operas, from modern Icelandic works to Shakespeare.

Mengi LIVE PERFORMANCE
(Map p60; ☎588 3644; www.mengi.net; Óðinsgata 2; ⌚noon-6pm Tue-Sat & for performances) This new entry on the gallery and performance art scene may be small, but it offers an innovative program of music and performing arts.

Gaukurinn LIVE MUSIC
(Map p60; www.gaukurinn.is; Tryggvagata 22; ⌚from 2pm daily) Grungy and glorious, it's a solid stop for live music, comedy, karaoke and open mikes. Happy hour is 7pm to 10pm (beer/wine kr600/750).

Reykjavík City Theatre THEATRE, DANCE
(Borgarleikhúsið; Map p56; ☎568 8000; www.borgarleikhus.is; Listabraut 3, Kringlan; ⌚closed Jul & Aug) Stages plays and musicals, and is home to the **Icelandic Dance Company** (☎588 0900; www.id.is).

Laugardalshöllin CONCERT VENUE
(Map p56; www.ish.is; Engjavegur 8, Laugardalur) Huge venue for major international acts.

Laugardalsvöllur National Stadium STADIUM
(Map p56; ☎510 2914; Laugardalur) Iceland's football (soccer) passion is huge. Cup and international matches are played at this national stadium in Laugardalur. See the sports sections of Reykjavík's newspapers or **Football Association of Iceland** (Knattspyrnusamband Íslands – KSÍ; ☎510 2900; www.ksi.is), and buy tickets directly from the stadium.

Smárabíó CINEMA
(www.smarabio.is; Smáralind; 🚌2) Iceland's biggest cinema, in Smáralind (p99) shopping centre. In summer a free shuttle connects Smáralind with Reykjavík's Main Tourist Office.

Shopping

Reykjavík's vibrant design culture makes for great shopping: from sleek, fish-skin purses and knitted *lopapeysur* (Icelandic woollen sweaters) to unique music or Icelandic schnapps *brennivín*. Laugavegur is the most dense shopping street. You'll find interesting shops all over town, but fashion concentrates near the Frakkastígur and Vitastígur end of Laugavegur. Skólavörðustígur is strong for arts and jewellery. Bankastræti and Austurstræti have touristy shops.

Don't forget – all visitors are eligible for a 15% tax refund on their shopping, under certain conditions.

Old Reykjavík

★**Kirsuberjatréð** ARTS & CRAFTS
(Cherry Tree; Map p60; ☎562 8990; www.kirs.is; Vesturgata 4; ⌚10am-7pm & 8-10pm Mon-Fri, to 5pm Sat, to 4pm Sun) This women's art-and-design collective in an interesting 1882 former bookshop sells weird and wonderful fish-skin handbags, music boxes made from string, and, our favourite, beautiful coloured bowls made from radish slices. It's been around for 25 years and now has 11 designers.

★ **Kolaportið Flea Market** MARKET
(Map p60; www.kolaportid.is; Tryggvagata 19; ⏲11am-5pm Sat & Sun) Held in a huge industrial building by the harbour, this weekend market is a Reykjavík institution. There's a huge tumble of secondhand clothes and old toys, plus cheap imports. There's also a food section that sells traditional eats like *rúgbrauð* (geothermally baked rye bread), *brauðterta* ('sandwich cake', a layering of bread with mayonnaise-based fillings) and *hákarl* (fermented shark).

Eymundsson BOOKS
(Map p60; www.eymundsson.is; Austurstræti 18; ⏲9am-10pm Mon-Fri, 10am-10pm Sat & Sun) This big central bookshop has a superb choice of English-language books, newspapers, magazines and maps, along with a great cafe. A second branch can be found on **Skólavörðustígur** (Map p60; Skólavörðustígur 11; ⏲9am-10pm Mon-Fri, 10am-10pm Sat & Sun).

Kogga CERAMICS
(Map p60; ☎552 6036; www.kogga.is; Vesturgata 5; ⏲9am-6pm Mon-Fri, 11am-3pm Sat) This tiny ceramics studio in the lower level of an old Reykjavík house offers imaginative pottery.

Kickstart CLOTHING
(Map p60; ☎568 0809; www.kickstart.is; Vesturgata 12; ⏲noon-6pm Mon-Fri) This tiny but inviting men's store stocks ties, gloves, motorcycle gear and other manly accoutrements.

Vínbúðin - Austurstræti ALCOHOL
(Map p60; www.vinbudin.is; Austurstræti 10a; ⏲11am-6pm Mon-Thu & Sat, to 7pm Fri) The most central branch of the national liquor-store chain. There's another store on the way towards Laugardalur at Borgartún 26.

Old Harbour

Farmers Market CLOTHING
(Map p56; ☎552 1960; www.farmersmarket.is; Hólmaslóð 2; ⏲10am-6pm Mon-Fri, 11am-4pm Sat, noon-4pm Sun) This design company run by a local couple is not about food, but rather sustainably designed and created clothing, accessories and housewares with an emphasis on natural fabrics and materials.

Steinunn CLOTHING
(Map p56; ☎588 6649; www.steinunn.com; Grandagarður 17; ⏲11am-6pm Mon-Fri, 1-4pm Sat) Browse the couture collection of celebrated Icelandic designer Steinunn Sigurðardóttir, featuring innovative knitwear.

Krínolín CLOTHING
(Map p56; www.krinolin.is; Grandagarður 37) Sigrún Einarsdóttir creates clothing out of natural fabrics like wool, lambskin and fish skin.

Kría BICYCLE
(Map p56; www.kriacycles.com; Grandagarður 5; ⏲10am-6pm Mon-Fri, 11am-1pm Sat) Full-service bike sales and repair shop (closed Saturday).

Laugavegur & Skólavörðustígur

★ **Kraum** ARTS & CRAFTS
(Map p60; www.kraum.is; Bankastræti 7; ⏲9am-7pm Mon-Fri, 10am-6pm Sat, 11am-6pm Sun) The brainchild of a band of local artists, Kraum literally means 'simmering', like the island's quaking earth and the inventive minds of its citizens. Expect a fascinating assortment of unique designer wares, like fish-skin apparel and driftwood furniture. Find it downstairs in the large Cintamani store.

★ **Skúmaskot** ARTS & CRAFTS
(Map p60; ☎663 1013; www.facebook.com/skumaskot.art.design/; Skólavörðustígur 21a; ⏲10am-6pm Mon-Fri, to 5pm Sat, noon-4pm Sun) Ten local designers create these unique handmade porcelain items, women's and kids' clothing, paintings and cards. It's in a recently renovated large gallery beautifully showcasing their creative Icelandic crafts.

★ **Kiosk** CLOTHING
(Map p60; ☎445 3269; www.kioskreykjavik.com; Laugavegur 65; ⏲11am-6pm Mon-Fri, to 5pm Sat) This wonderful designers' cooperative is lined with creative women's fashion in a glass-fronted boutique. Designers take turns (wo)manning the store.

★ **Orrifinn** JEWELLERY
(Map p60; ☎789 7616; www.facebook.com/OrrifinnJewels/; Skólavörðustíg 17a; ⏲10am-6pm Mon-Fri, to 4pm Sat) Subtle, beautiful jewellery captures the natural wonder of Iceland and its Viking history. Delicate anchors, axes and pen nibs dangle from understated matte chains.

★ **Geysir** CLOTHING
(Map p60; ☎519 6000; www.geysir.com; Skólavörðustígur 16; ⏲9am-10pm) For traditional Icelandic clothing and unique modern

designs, Geysir boasts an elegant selection of sweaters, blankets, and men's and women's clothes, shoes and bags. There's also a branch down the street at Skólavörðustígur 7.

★Beautiful Stories CLOTHING
(Map p60; www.beautifulstoriesclothes.com; Laugavegur 46; ⏲10am-6pm Mon-Fri, to 5pm Sat, 1-5pm Sun) Dreamy, feminine designs beg for browsing. Hip lace, silk and swingy little dresses are the order of the day.

★KronKron CLOTHING
(Map p60; ☎562 8388; www.kronkron.com; Laugavegur 63b; ⏲10am-6pm Mon-Thu, to 6.30pm Fri, to 5pm Sat) This is where Reykjavík goes high fashion, with the likes of Marc Jacobs and Vivienne Westwood. We really enjoy its Scandinavian designers (including Kron by KronKron) offering silk dresses, knit capes, scarves and even wool underwear. Its handmade shoes are off the charts; the shoes are also sold down the street at **Kron** (Map p60; ☎551 8388; www.kron.is; Laugavegur 48; ⏲10am-6pm Mon-Thu, to 6.30pm Fri, to 5pm Sat).

★Mál og Menning BOOKS
(Map p60; ☎580 5000; www.bmm.is; Laugavegur 18; ⏲9am-10pm Mon-Fri, 10am-10pm Sat) This friendly, popular and well-stocked independent bookshop carries great English-language books for getting under the skin of Iceland. Check out *Thermal Pools in Iceland* by Jón G Snæland and Þóra Sigurbjörnsdóttir; you can browse it in the lively cafe. Also sells CDs, games and newspapers.

★Rammagerðin – Iceland Gift Store SOUVENIRS
(Map p60; ☎535 6690; www.icelandgiftstore.com; Skólavörðustígur 12; ⏲9am-10pm) One of the city's better souvenir shops, Rammagerðin offers loads of woollens, crafts and collectibles. It also has locations at Skólavörðustígur 12, Bankastræti 9 and Keflavík International Airport.

★12 Tónar MUSIC
(Map p60; www.12tonar.is; Skolavörðustígur 15; ⏲10am-6pm Mon-Sat, from noon Sun) A very cool place to hang out, 12 Tónar is responsible for launching some of Iceland's favourite bands. In the two-storey shop you can listen to CDs, drink coffee and sometimes catch a live performance.

Lucky Records MUSIC
(Map p56; ☎551 1195; www.luckyrecords.is; Rauðarárstígur 10; ⏲10am-6pm Mon-Fri, 11am-5pm Sat & Sun) This deep den of musical goodness holds loads of modern Icelandic music, but plenty of vintage vinyl, too. The huge collection spans hip hop to jazz and electronica. Occasional live music.

Reykjavík Record Shop MUSIC
(Map p60; ☎561 2299; www.facebook.com/reykjavikrecordshop; Klapparstígur 35; ⏲11am-6pm Mon-Fri, to 5pm Sat, 1-5pm Sun) Scratch your vinyl itch at this hole-in-the-wall record store in the city centre.

Jör CLOTHING
(Map p56; ☎546 1303; www.jorstore.com; Laugavegur 89; ⏲10am-6pm Mon-Sat, 1-5pm Sun) Chic clothing is the order of the day at the trendy boutique of Guðmundur Jörundsson, who designs everything from strappy lingerie to sleek menswear.

Hrím DESIGN
(Map p60; www.hrim.is; Laugavegur 25; ⏲10am-8pm Mon-Thu, to 6.30pm Fri, to 6pm Sat, 1-6pm Sun) With one large high-concept design store, and one smaller kitchenware store (Laugavegur 32), Hrim stands out for its creative Scandinavian and high-end *tchotchkes*, linens and other eminently take-home-able gear.

Reykjavík's Cutest ARTS & CRAFTS
(Map p60; Laugavegur 27; ⏲10am-8pm May-Sep, to 6pm Oct-Apr) Follow the painted path to the polka-dotted house just back from Laugavegur for a great selection of handmade souvenirs and crafts.

Blue Lagoon Shop COSMETICS
(Map p60; ☎420 8849; www.bluelagoon.com; Laugavegur 15; ⏲10am-6pm Mon-Fri, to 4pm Sat, 1-5pm Sun) Forgot to stock up on facial masks and unguents at the Blue Lagoon? Here's your chance! You'll also find its line of beauty products at Lyfa pharmacies, Hagkaup and Keflavík International Airport dutyfree.

Cintamani CLOTHING
(Map p60; ☎533 3390; www.cintamani.is; Bankastræti 7; ⏲9am-10pm) One of Iceland's premier outdoor designwear companies. Clothes tend towards the stylish (and pricey) and are not always so practical for hard-core camping. It also has shops at Aðalstræti 10, Kringlan and Smáralind shopping centres, and an outlet store (☎533 3811; Austurhraun 3, Garðabær; ⏲10am-6pm) in Garðabær.

OUTDOOR OUTFITTERS

For outdoor wear turned stylish, costly streetwear – jackets, fleeces, hats and the like – try **66° North** (p92) or **Cintamani** (p92).

If you're looking to outfit for hiking or camping, your best bet is **Gangleri Outfitters** (Map p60; ☎583 2222; www.outfitters.is; Hverfisgata 82; ⏰10am-7pm Mon-Fri, 11am-5pm Sat & Sun), with camping gear sales and rentals: tents, sleeping bags, stoves, backpacks, boots, climbing gear, GPS etc. **Fjallakofinn** (Map p60; ☎510 9505; www.fjallakofinn.is; Laugavegur 11; ⏰9am-7pm Mon-Fri, 10am-5pm Sat, noon-6pm Sun) offers (pricey) brand-name camping and climbing gear, GoPros and more, plus equipment rental. Or check **Iceland Camping Equipment Rental** (Map p56; ☎647 0569; www.iceland-camping-equipment.com; Barónsstígur 5; ⏰9am-5pm May-Oct, by appt Nov-Apr).

66° North CLOTHING

(Map p60; ☎535 6680; www.66north.is; Bankastræti 5; ⏰9am-10pm) Iceland's premier outdoor-clothing company began by making all-weather wear for Arctic fishermen. This metamorphosed into costly, fashionable streetwear: jackets, fleeces, hats and gloves. It has another city-centre store at Laugavegur 17, and there are boutiques in Kringlan and Smáralind shopping centers, Keflavík International Airport duty free, and an outlet at Faxafen 12.

Ófeigur Björnsson FASHION & ACCESSORIES

(Map p60; ☎551 1161; www.ofeigur.is; Skólavörðustígur 5; ⏰10am-6pm Mon-Fri, 11am-4pm Sat) Ófeigur Björnsson and other local goldsmiths make jewellery with lava and other natural materials. Hildur Bolladóttir is a master dressmaker and also shows modern bags and felted hats. There's an art gallery upstairs.

Stígur ARTS & CRAFTS

(Map p60; ☎551 5675; Skólavörðustígur 17b; ⏰10am-6pm Mon-Sat, to 4pm Sun) Seven local artists work in textiles, graphics, ceramics, glass and paint. We're particularly fond of the vases. This is one of the few craft galleries open on Sundays.

Aurum JEWELLERY

(Map p60; ☎551 2770; www.aurum.is; Bankastræti 4; ⏰10am-7pm Mon-Fri, to 6pm Sat, noon-5pm Sun Jun-Aug, reduced hours Sep-May) Guðbjörg at Aurum is one of Reykjavík's more interesting designers; her whisper-thin silver jewellery is sophisticated stuff, its shapes often inspired by leaves and flowers. Collectibles fill the other side of the shop.

Orr JEWELLERY

(Map p56; www.orr.is; Lauagavegur 101; ⏰10am-6pm Jun-Aug, closed Sun Sep-May) A creative couple craft delicate, nature-inspired jewellery using pearls, semi-precious stones and lustrous metals.

Fóa ARTS & CRAFTS

(Map p60; ☎571 1433; www.facebook.com/foaiceland/; Laugavegur 2; ⏰10am-6pm Mon-Thu, to 7pm Fri-Sun) Cool handmade objects, from stationary to jewellery and ceramics.

Spúútnik VINTAGE

(Map p60; ☎533 2023; www.facebook.com/Spuutnik/; Laugavegur 28; ⏰9am-7pm Mon-Fri, to 6pm Sat & Sun Jun-Aug, reduced hours Sep-May) This jam-packed secondhand store offers a less expensive way to pick up that Icelandic sweater you've been hankering for.

My Concept Store DESIGN

(Map p60; ☎519 6699; www.myconceptstore.is; Laugavegur 45; ⏰10am-8pm Mon-Fri, to 6pm Sat, 1-5pm Sun May-Sep, reduced hours Oct-Apr) High-end cool collectibles include leather goods, jewellery and clothing. Some are designed by the owners.

Dogma CLOTHING

(Map p60; ☎562 6600; www.dogma.is; Laugavegur 32; ⏰10am-10pm Jun-Sep, to 6pm Oct-May) This quirky T-shirt specialist is the go-to spot for scouting out funky local designs with a cartoonish appeal, and zombie horse masks.

Reykjavík Foto ELECTRONICS

(Map p60; ☎577 5900; www.reykjavikfoto.is; Laugavegur 51; ⏰10am-6pm Mon-Fri, 11am-4pm Sat) Loads of cameras, tripods and water-resistant bags, with helpful service.

Heilsuhúsið FOOD

(Map p60; ☎552 2966; www.heilsuhusid.is; Laugavegur 20; ⏰10am-6pm Mon-Fri, 11am-4pm Sat, noon-4pm Sun) Stop by to shop with the locals for health food, smoothies and supplements beneath the equally organic and

WOOLLY JUMPERS: LOPAPEYSUR

Lopapeysur are the ubiquitous Icelandic woolly jumpers you will see worn by locals and visitors alike. Made from naturally water-repellant Icelandic wool, they are thick and cosy, with simple geometric patterns or regional motifs. They are no longer the bargain they were in the 1960s, so when shopping, be sure to make the distinction: do you want hand-knit or machine made? You'll notice the price difference (some cost well over €200), but either way these beautiful but practical items (and their associated hats, gloves and scarves) are exceptionally wearable souvenirs.

Handknitting Association of Iceland (Handprjónasamband Íslands; Map p60; ☎552 1890; www.handknit.is; Skólavörðustígur 19; ⏰9am-10pm Mon-Fri, to 6pm Sat, 10am-6pm Sun) Traditional handmade hats, socks and sweaters are sold at this knitting collective, or you can buy yarn, needles and knitting patterns and do it yourself. The association's smaller **branch** (Map p60; ☎562 1890; Laugavegur 53b; ⏰9am-7pm Mon-Fri. 10am-5pm Sat) sells made-up items only.

Álafoss (Map p60; ☎562 6303; www.alafoss.is; Laugavegur 8; ⏰10am-6pm) Loads of hand- or machine-made *lopapeysur* and other wool products. Its **outlet store** (☎566 6303; www.alafoss.is; Álafossvegur 23, Mosfellsbær; ⏰9am-6pm Mon-Fri, to 4pm Sat; 🚌15) in Mosfellsbær also sells yarn, patterns and needles.

health-conscious Gló restaurant. It carries the excellent local organic line of Sóley bath products.

Iðnú Bookshop MAPS
(Map p56; ☎517 7200; www.ferdakort.is; Brautarholt 8; ⏰10am-5pm Mon-Thu, to 4pm Fri) You'll find the largest selection of road and hiking maps is available from the specialist Ferðakort map department at Iðnú bookshop.

Outskirts

Páll Kristjánsson GIFTS & SOUVENIRS
(☎899 6903; www.knifemaker.is; Álafossvegur 29, Mosfellsbær) Páll Kristjánsson makes unique, handmade bone-handled knives. Find him at his studio in Mosfellsbær.

Kringlan SHOPPING CENTRE
(Map p56; ☎517 9000; www.kringlan.is; Kringlunni 4-12; 🚌1, 3, 4, 6, 13, 14) Reykjavík's main shopping centre, 1km from town, has 150 shops.

Orientation

The city is spread out along a small peninsula, with Reykjavík Domestic Airport and long-distance bus terminals BSÍ and Mjódd in the south, and the picturesque city centre and harbour occupying the north. The international airport is 48km away at Keflavík.

The city centre's social and commercial main street is Laugavegur, which is packed with shops, restaurants and bars. It changes its name to Bankastræti, then to Austurstræti as it runs across the centre. Running uphill off Bankastræti at a jaunty diagonal, artists' street Skólavörðustígur ends at spectacular modernist church, Hallgrímskirkja.

Busy boulevard Lækjargata cuts straight across Bankastræti/Austurstræti. To its west is Old Reykjavík. To the northwest lies Reykjavík's old harbour and to the southwest Tjörnin lake.

Information

EMERGENCY

Police Station (☎emergency 112, non-emergency 444 1000; Hverfisgata 113) Central police station.

INTERNET ACCESS

Almost all accommodation and many cafes have wi-fi. You can use terminals at libraries (free) and the tourist office (small fee).

Aðalbókasafn (Reykjavík City Library; www.borgarbokasafn.is; Tryggvagata 15; ⏰10am-7pm Mon-Thu, 11am-7pm Fri, 1-5pm Sat & Sun) Excellent main library.

LAUNDRY

Laundry is a perennial (pricey) problem in Iceland if you don't have lodging that offers it. In Reykjavík, you can head to **Laundromat Café** (p79) for its downstairs machines.

Úðafoss (☎551 2301; www.udafoss.is; Vitastígur 13; per 5kg kr4500; ⏰8am-6pm Mon-Fri) One of Reykjavík's only central laundries; same-day service available.

MEDICAL SERVICES

Dentist (☎575 0505)

Health Centre (☎585 2600; Vesturgata 7; ⏲call to arrange appointment).

Læknavaktin (☎doctor on duty 1770; ⏲5-11.30pm Mon-Fri, 8am-11.30pm Sat & Sun) Off-hours medical advice.

Landspítali University Hospital (☎543 1000, doctor on duty 1770; www.landspitali.is; Fossvogur) Casualty department open 24/7.

MONEY

Credit cards are accepted everywhere (except municipal buses); ATMs are ubiquitous. Currency-exchange fees at hotels or private bureaus can be obscenely high.

POST

Main Post Office (Map p60; www.postur.is; Pósthússtræti 5; ⏲9am-6pm Mon-Fri) Has poste restante.

TELEPHONE

Public phones are rare in mobile-crazy Reykjavík. Try the Main Tourist Office, post office, by the southwestern corner of Austurvöllur, on Lækjargata, or at Kringlan shopping centre.

TOURIST INFORMATION

Main Tourist Office (Upplýsingamiðstöð Ferðamanna; Map p60; ☎590 1550; www.visitreykjavik.is; Aðalstræti 2; ⏲8am-8pm) Friendly staff and mountains of free brochures, plus maps, Reykjavík City Card and Strætó city bus tickets. Books accommodation, tours and activities.

Visit Iceland (☎511 4000; www.visiticeland.com; Borgartún 35) offers Iceland-wide information.

TRAVEL AGENCIES

Icelandic Travel Market (ITM; ☎522 4979; www.icelandictravelmarket.is; Bankastræti 2; ⏲8am-9pm Jun-Aug, 9am-7pm Sep-May) Information and tour bookings.

Trip (☎433 8747; www.trip.is; Laugavegur 54; ⏲9am-9pm) Books tours as well lodging, and rents cars.

Getting There & Away

AIR

Keflavík International Airport

Iceland's primary international airport, **Keflavík International Airport** (KEF; ☎525 6000; www.kefairport.is) is 48km west of Reykjavík, on the Reykjanes Peninsula. The airport has ATMs, money exchange, car hire, an **information desk** (☎425 0330, booking service 570 7799; www.visitreykjanes.is; ⏲6am-8pm Mon-Fri, noon-5pm Sat & Sun) and cafes. The duty-free shops in the arrival area sell liquor at far better prices than you'll find in town. There's also a desk for collecting duty-free cash back from eligible purchases in Iceland. The 10-11 convenience store sells SIM cards, and major tour companies like Reykjavík Excursions and Grey Line have desks.

Reykjavík Domestic Airport

Reykjavík Domestic Airport (Reykjavíkurflugvöllur; Map p56; www.reykjavikairport.is; Innanlandsflug) is in central Reykjavík, just south of Tjörnin. Sightseeing services, domestic flights and those to/from Greenland and the Faroe Islands fly here.

Air Iceland (☎570 3030; www.airiceland.is) has a desk at the airport and serves Akureyri, Egilsstaðir, Ísafjörður and Greenland; but you can usually save money by booking online.

Atlantic Airways (☎in Faroe Islands 298 34 10 00; www.atlantic.fo) flies to the Faroe Islands.

Eagle Air Iceland (☎562 4200; www.eagleair.is) operates sightseeing services and five set routes from Reykjavík: Vestmannaeyjar Islands; Höfn; Húsavík; and in the Westfjords, Bíldudalur and Gjögur.

BUS

You can travel from Reykjavík by day tour (many of which offer hotel pick-up), or use Strætó and several of the tour companies for transport, getting on and off their scheduled buses. They also offer a multitude of bus transport passes. Things are changing rapidly in Iceland. The free *Public Transport in Iceland* map (www.publictransport.is) has a good overview of routes.

The bus network operates frequently from around mid-May to mid-September. Outside these months services are less frequent (or nonexistent).

For destinations on the northern and eastern sides of Iceland (eg Egilsstaðir, Mývatn and Húsavík), you usually change in Höfn or Akureyri; for the West and Westfjords change in Borgarnes.

Strætó (☎540 2700; www.bus.is) Operates Reykjavík long-distance buses from Mjódd bus terminal (p96), 8km southeast of the city centre, which is served by local buses 3, 4, 11, 12, 17, 21, 24 and 28. Strætó also operates city buses and has a smartphone app. For long-distance buses only you can use cash, credit/debit card with PIN or (wads of) bus tickets.

BSÍ bus terminal (Map p56; ☎562 1011; www.bsi.is; Vatnsmýrarvegur 10) Reykjavík Excursions (and its Flybus) uses the BSÍ bus terminal (pronounced 'bee-ess-ee'), south of the city centre. There's a ticketing desk, tourist brochures, lockers, luggage storage (www.luggagelockers.is), Budget car hire and a cafeteria with wi-fi. The terminal is served by Reykjavík buses 1, 3, 5, 6, 14 and 15. Reykjavík Excursions offers prebooked hotel pick-up to bring you to the terminal. Some Gray Line buses also stop here.

Sterna (Map p60; ☎551 1166; www.sterna.is) Sales and departures from the Harpa concert hall. Buses around the Ring Road and to tourist highlights.

Trex (☎587 6000; www.trex.is) Departs from the Main Tourist Office, Kringlan's Shell petrol station or Reykjavík Campsite. Buses to Þórsmörk and Landmannalaugar in the South.

Getting Around

TO/FROM THE AIRPORT

Keflavík International Airport

The journey from Keflavík International Airport to Reykjavík takes about 50 minutes. Three easy bus services connect Reykjavík and the airport and are the best transport option; kids get discounted fares.

Flybus (☎580 5400; www.re.is) Operated by Reykjavík Excursions, Flybus meets all international flights. One-way tickets cost kr2200. Pay kr2800 for hotel pickup/drop off (which shuttles you from/to the Flybus at the BSÍ bus terminal); you must schedule hotel pick-up a day ahead. A separate service runs to the Blue Lagoon (from where you can continue to the city centre or the airport; kr3900). Tickets online, at many hotels, or at the airport booth. Flybus will also drop off/pickup in Garðabær and Hafnarfjörður, just south of Reykjavík.

Airport Express (☎540 1313; www.airportexpress.is) Operated by Gray Line Tours between Keflavík International Airport and Lækjartorg Sq in central Reykjavík (kr2100) or Mjódd bus terminal, or via hotel pickup/drop off (kr2700; book ahead). Has connections to Borgarnes and points north, including Akureyri.

Airport Direct (☎497 5000; www.reykjaviksightseeing.is/airport-direct) Minibuses operated by Reykjavík Sightseeing shuttle between hotels and the airport (kr4500, return kr8000).

Strætó bus 55 also connects the BSÍ bus terminal and the airport (kr1680, nine daily Monday to Friday in summer).

Taxis cost around kr15,000.

Reykjavík Domestic Airport

From the Reykjavík Domestic Airport it's a 2km walk into town, there's a taxi rank, or bus 15 stops near the Air Iceland terminal and bus 19 stops near the Eagle Air terminal. Both go to the city centre and the Hlemmur bus stop.

BICYCLE

Reykjavík has a steadily improving network of cycle lanes; ask the Main Tourist Office for a map. You are allowed to cycle on pavements as long as you don't cause pedestrians problems.

At the Old Harbour, rent bikes at **Reykjavík Bike Tours** (p68) and get service at **Kría** (p91) bicycle shop, or do your own repairs at **Bike Cave** (p89) cafe.

BUS

Strætó (www.bus.is) operates regular, easy buses around Reykjavík and its suburbs (Seltjarnarnes, Kópavogur, Garðabær, Hafnarfjörður and Mosfellsbær); it also operates long-distance buses. It has online schedules, a smartphone app and a printed map. Many free maps like *Welcome to Reykjavík City Map* also include bus-route maps.

Buses run from 7am until 11pm or midnight daily (from 11am on Sunday). Services depart at 20-minute or 30-minute intervals. A limited night-bus service runs until 2am on Friday and Saturday. Buses only stop at designated bus stops, marked with a yellow letter 'S'.

Bus Tickets & Fares

The fare is kr420; you can buy tickets at the bus terminal, pay on board (though no change is given) or by using its app. Buy one-/three-day passes (kr1500/3500) at Mjódd bus terminal, the Main Tourist Office, 10-11 convenience stores, many hotels, **Kringlan** (Map p56) and Smáralind shopping malls, and bigger swimming pools. If you need to take two buses to reach your destination, get a *skiptimiði* (transfer ticket, good for 75 minutes in the city, 120 minutes in the countryside) from the driver.

The **Reykjavík City Card** (p65) also acts as a Strætó bus pass.

Bus Stations & Lines

Two central Strætó stops are at **Hlemmur** (Map p56), at the eastern end of Laugavegur, and **Lækjartorg Sq** (Map p60), in the centre of town. **Mjódd** (☎557 7854; www.bus.is; ⏲ticket office 7am-6pm Mon-Fri, 10am-6pm Sat, 12.30-6pm Sun), 8km southeast of the city centre, is the main bus terminal, and where you'll catch long-distance Strætó buses. Many buses make a loop around Tjörnin lake and serve the city centre, the National Museum and BSÍ bus terminal before heading onwards.

CAR & MOTORCYCLE

A car is unnecessary in Reykjavík as it's so easy to explore on foot and by bus. Car and camper hire for the countryside are available at both airports, the BSÍ bus terminal and some city locations.

Parking

Street parking in the city centre is limited and costs kr250 per hour in the 'Red Zone', kr125 per hour in the 'Blue Zone' and kr90 per two hours in the 'Green Zone' (coins and ATM or credit cards with PIN only); you must pay between 9am and 6pm from Monday to Friday and from 10am to 4pm Saturday; outside those hours it's free. Parking outside the city centre is free.

Vitatorg Car Park (1st hour kr80, subsequent hours kr50; ⏲7am-midnight) Covered parking area.

TAXI

Taxi prices are high. Flagfall starts at around kr680. Tipping is not required. From BSÍ bus terminal to Harpa concert hall costs about kr2000. From Mjódd bus termimal it's about kr4100.

There are usually taxis outside bus stations, airports and bars on weekend nights (huge queues for the latter), plus on Bankastræti near Lækjargata.

BSR (☎561 0000; www.taxireykjavik.is)

Hreyfill (☎588 5522; www.hreyfill.is)

BUS SERVICES FROM REYKJAVÍK

Below are sample routes and fares; check bus companies for current rates. Strætó usually offers the lowest fares. Private companies like Reykjavík Excursions (RE) and Sterna also ply these routes, and may offer pick-up, but usually cost more unless you buy a bus passport.

DESTINATION	COMPANY & LINE	PRICE (KR)	DURATION	FREQUENCY	YEAR-ROUND
Akureyri	Strætó 57	9240	6½hr	daily	Yes
Blue Lagoon	RE	3900	45min	daily	Yes
Borgarnes	Strætó 57/ Sterna/RE 320	1680/7200/3500	1½hr	daily	Yes/summer/ summer
Geysir/Gullfoss	RE 6 & 610	4500	2½hr	daily	Mid-Jun–mid-Sep
Höfn	Strætó 51/ Sterna 12a	12,180/11,600	7¼/10¼hr	daily	Yes/summer
Hólmavík	Strætó 59 via Borgarnes	6300	3½hr	2-5 weekly	Yes
Keflavík	RE	1680	1¼hr	several daily	Yes
Kirkjubæ-jarklaustur	Strætó 51/ Sterna 12a	7140/6800	4¼hr	daily	Yes/summer
Landmannal-augar	Trex/RE/ Sterna	7900/8000/8000	5½hr	daily	Mid-Jun–early Sep
Mývatn	RE	20,500	12hr	daily	Jul-Aug
Selfoss	Strætó 51/52, also Sterna, Trex & RE	1680	1hr	many daily	Yes
Skaftafell	Strætó 51/ Sterna/RE	9240/8800/11,000	5¼/6¾/7hr	daily	Yes/summer/ summer
Skógar	Strætó 51/ Sterna/RE	5040/4800/6000	2½/3/3½hr	daily	Yes/summer/ summer
Stykkishólmur	Strætó 57 to 58	4200	3hr	2 daily	Yes
Landeyjarhöfn port for Vest-mannaeyjar	Strætó 52	4200	2¼hr	daily	Yes
Vík í Mýrdal	Strætó 51/ Sterna/RE	5850/5600/7500	3/4¼/4hr	2 daily	Yes/summer/ summer
Þingvellir	RE	2500	45min	daily	Mid-Jun–mid-Sep
Þórsmörk	Trex/RE/ Sterna	7500/7500/6650	4½/4/4½hr	daily	May–mid-Oct

GREATER REYKJAVÍK

The area around the capital encompasses Mosfellsbær to the north, Kópavogur, Garðabær and Hafnarfjörður to the south.

Viðey

On fine-weather days, the tiny uninhabited island of Viðey (www.reykjavikmuseum.is) makes a wonderful day trip. Just 1km north of Reykjavík's Sundahöfn Harbour, it feels a world away. Well-preserved historic buildings, surprising modern art, an abandoned village and great birdwatching add to its remote spell. The only sounds are the wind, the waves and the golden bumblebees.

Little Viðey was settled around 900 and was farmed until the 1950s. It was home to a powerful monastery from 1225, but in 1539 it was wiped out by Danish soldiers during the Reformation. In the 18th and 19th century several significant Icelandic leaders lived here.

Sights & Activities

Just above the harbour, you'll find Iceland's oldest stone house, **Viðeyarstofa**. Icelandic Treasurer Skúli Magnússon was given the island in 1751 and he built Viðeyarstofa as his residence. It now houses a cafe (mains kr2300-3700; 11.30am-5pm mid-May–Sep, 1.30-4pm Sat & Sun Oct–mid-May). There's also an interesting 18th-century wooden church, the second oldest in Iceland, with some original decor and Skúli's tomb (he died here in 1794). Excavations of the old monastery foundations unearthed 15th-century wax tablets and a runic love letter, now in the National Museum.

Just northwest along the coast, Yoko Ono's **Imagine Peace Tower** (2007) is a 'wishing well' that blasts a dazzling column of light into the sky every night between 9 October (John Lennon's birthday) and 8 December (the anniversary of his death). See Viðey's website for Peace Tower tours from Reykjavík. Further along, Viðeyjarnaust day-hut has a barbecue for use if you bring all your own supplies.

In summer there are free guided walks.

Island Paths

The whole island is criss-crossed with walking paths. Some you can bicycle, others are more precarious. When boats are running from the Old Harbour, you can hire a bike there at Reykjavík Bike Tours (p68) and bring it to the island.

The island is great for birdwatching (30 species breed here) and botany (over one-third of all Icelandic plants grow on the island). In late August, some Reykjavikers come to pick wild caraway, which was originally planted here by Skúli Magnússon.

From the harbour, trails to the southeast lead past the natural sheep fold **Réttin**, the tiny grotto **Paradíshellir** (Paradise Cave) and then to the abandoned fishing village at Sundbakki.

Trails leading to the northwest take you to Vesturey, the northern tip of the island. You'll pass low ponds, monuments to several shipwrecks, and the low cliffs of Eiðisbjarg. Richard Serra's **Áfangar** (Standing Stones; 1990) sculptures, made from huge pairs of basalt pillars, dot this part of the island.

Sleeping & Eating

There is no lodging or camping on Viðey. There is one mediocre cafe on the island, but it's in a beautiful historic building. You can bring supplies to picnic or barbecue at the Viðeyjarnaust day-hut.

Getting There & Away

Viðey Ferry (533 5055; www.videy.com; return adult/child kr1200/600; from Skarfabakki hourly 10.15am-5.15pm mid-May–Sep, weekends only Oct–mid-May) The ferry takes five minutes from Skarfabakki, 4.5km east of the city centre. During summer, two boats a day start from Elding at the Old Harbour and the Harpa concert hall. Bus 16 stops closest to Skarfabakki, and it's a point on the Reykjavík hop-on-hop-off tour bus.

Kópavogur

Kópavogur (www.kopavogur.is), the first suburb south of Reykjavík, is just a short bus ride away but feels far from the tourist trail. There are a few sights in the cultural complex **Menningarmiðstoð Kópavogs** (next door to the distinctive arched church) and a huge shopping mall.

Sights

Gerðarsafn Art Museum ART MUSEUM
(570 0440; www.gerdarsafn.is; Hamraborg 4; adult/child kr500/free; 11am-5pm Tue-Sun) Next door to Kópavogur's concert hall, this beautifully designed museum dedicated to Icelandic stained-glass artist and sculptor

HAFNARFJÖRÐUR'S HIDDEN WORLDS

Many Icelanders believe that their country is populated by hidden races – *jarðvergar* (gnomes), *álfar* (elves), *ljósálfar* (fairies), *dvergar* (dwarves), *ljúflingar* (lovelings), *tívar* (mountain spirits), *englar* (angels) and *huldufólk* (hidden people). Although some are embarrassed to say they believe, most refuse to say hand on heart that they *don't* believe. You'll see many Icelandic gardens feature small wooden *álfhól* (elf houses).

Hafnarfjörður, 12km south of Reykjavík, is believed to lie at the confluence of several strong ley lines (mystical lines of energy) and rests on a 7300-year-old flow that, according to locals, hides a parallel elfin universe. Visitors walk through **Hellisgerði** FREE, a peaceful park filled with lava grottoes and apparently one of the favourite places of the hidden people. A 90-minute pricey **Hidden Worlds tour** (☑694 2785; www.alfar.is; per person kr4500; ⊙2.30pm Tue & Fri) leaves from the **tourist office** (☑585 5500; www. visithafnarfjordur.is; Strandgata 6; ⊙8am-4pm Mon-Fri), which also sells elf maps. On weekends get info at Pakkhúsið.

Hafnarfjörður Museum (☑585 5780; http://museum.hafnarfjordur.is) FREE, the town's other main attraction, is divided over several old tin-clad houses near the harbour, exploring local history. Start at **Pakkhúsið** (Vesturgata 6; ⊙11am-5pm Jun-Aug, Sat & Sun Sep-May) FREE, the primary site. There are hot springs and mud pools and vibrant mineral lakes south of town in **Krýsuvík**.

In a pinch, overnight at **Lava Hostel & Campsite** (☑565 0900; www.lavahostel.is; Hjallabraut 51; campsites per adult/child kr1700/free, dm from kr5400, d without bathroom kr14,200). Find good eats at popular cafe **Súfistinn** (☑565 3740; www.sufistinn.is; Strandgata 9; dishes kr1200-1600; ⊙8.15am-11.30pm Mon-Fri, 10am-11.30pm Sat, 11am-11.30pm Sun).

Get here on Strætó (www.bus.is) bus 1 (30 minutes from Reykjavík). Other Strætó lines circulate within the town. The **Flybus** (☑562 1011; www.re.is) to Keflavík International Airport will stop in Hafnarfjörður if prearranged.

Gerður Helgadóttir hosts excellent rotating modern-art exhibitions, and has a notable permanent collection of 20th-century Icelandic art.

Salurinn　　　　　　　　　CULTURAL BUILDING
(☑441 7500; www.salurinn.is; Hamraborg 6) Iceland's first specially designed concert hall is built entirely from local materials (driftwood, spruce and crushed stone) and has fantastic acoustics. See the website for its (mostly classical) concert program.

Natural History Museum of Kópavogur　　　　　　　　MUSEUM
(Náttúrufræðistofa Kópavogs; ☑441 7200; www. natkop.is; Hamraborg 6a; ⊙10am-7pm Mon-Thu, 11am-5pm Fri, 1-5pm Sat) FREE This museum explores Iceland's unique geology and wildlife. There's an orca skeleton, a good collection of taxidermied animals, geological specimens and some of Mývatn lake's unusual *Marimo* balls.

 Eating

Gló　　　　　　　　　HEALTH FOOD €€
(www.glo.is; Hæðasmári 6; mains kr1200-2000; ⊙11am-9pm Mon-Fri, 11.30am-9pm Sat & Sun;

☑) 🍴 This popular local restaurant serves fresh, large daily specials loaded with Asian-influenced herbs and spices. Though not exclusively vegetarian, it's a wonderland of raw and organic foods with your choice from a broad bar of elaborate salads, from root veggies to Greek. There are also branches on Laugavegur (p84) and Engjateigur (p86).

🛍 Shopping

Smáralind　　　　　　　　SHOPPING CENTRE
(☑528 8000; www.smaralind.is; Hagasmára 1, Kópavogur; ⊙11am-7pm Mon-Wed & Fri, to 9pm Thu, to 6pm Sat, 1-6pm Sun; 🚌2) Iceland's largest mall. Take bus 2 or its free shuttle May through August, which leaves from Reykjavík's Main Tourist Office and stops off at Kópavogur museums (see schedule online).

ℹ Getting There & Away

Strætó (www.bus.is) buses 1 and 2 leave from Hlemmur or Lækjartorg in central Reykjavík, and bus 4 from Hlemmur, stopping at the Hamraborg stop in Kópavogur (look for the church). It takes about 15 minutes.

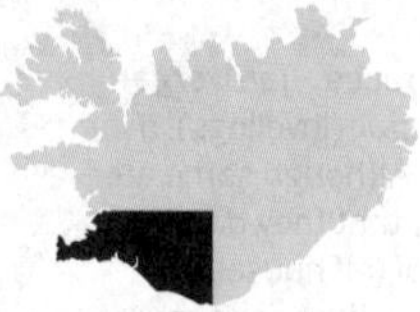

Southwest Iceland & the Golden Circle

Includes ➡

Best Places to Eat

- Slippurinn (p169)
- Við Fjöruborðið (p125)
- Lindin (p115)
- Efstidalur II (p115)

Best Places to Stay

- River Hotel (p136)
- Julia's Guesthouse (p125)
- Fljótsdalur HI Hostel (p141)
- Hótel Rangá (p137)

Why Go?

Black beaches stretch along the Atlantic, geysers spout from geothermal fields and waterfalls glide across escarpments while brooding volcanoes and glittering ice caps score the inland horizon. The beautiful Southwest has many of Iceland's most legendary natural wonders, so it's a relatively crowded and increasingly developed area. The Golden Circle (a tourist route comprising three famous sights: Þingvellir, Geysir and Gullfoss) draws by far the largest crowds outside of Reykjavík, but visit during off-hours or venture further afield and you'll find awe-inspiring splendour.

The further you go the better it gets. Tourist faves such as the silica-filled Blue Lagoon and the rift valley and ancient parliament at Þingvellir are just beyond the capital. Churning seas lead to the Vestmannaeyjar archipelago offshore. At the region's far reaches lie the powerful Hekla and Eyjafjallajökull volcanoes, busy Skógar and Vík, and the hidden valleys of Þórsmörk and Landmannalaugar.

Road Distances (km)

	Keflavík	Selfoss	Gullfoss	Landmannalaugar	Vík
Selfoss	100				
Gullfoss	156	71			
Landmannalaugar	230	130	147		
Vík	226	130	177	218	
Reykjavík	51	57	113	185	186

Reykjanes Peninsula

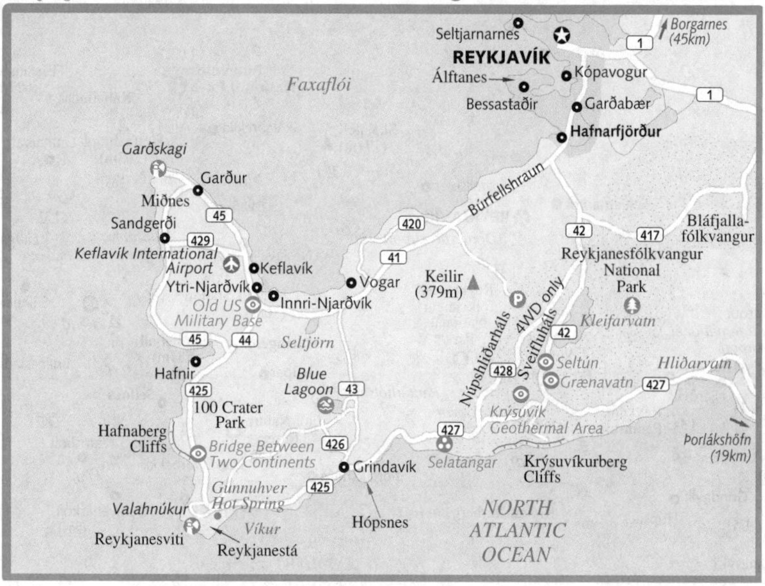

REYKJANES PENINSULA

The Reykjanes Peninsula expands in drama as you move away from the highway between Reykjavík and Keflavík International Airport. You'll find not only the Blue Lagoon, Iceland's most famous attraction, but numerous other gorgeous and interesting sights, many of them based around active volcanoes. The busiest towns are no-frills Keflavík and nearby Njarðvík, but the sweet, windswept fishing hamlets of Garður and Sandgerði – great for whale watching – are just minutes to the west of the airport on a small northwestern spur. The rest of the Reykjanes, from dramatic Reykjanestá in the southwest to the Reykjanesfólkvangur wilderness reserve in the east, is an untamed landscape of multihued volcanic craters, mineral lakes, bubbling hot springs, rugged mountains and coastal lava fields.

The Reykjanes Peninsula is a Unesco Global Geopark (www.reykjanesgeopark.is), formed to research and protect the region's unusual geology (pillow lava! oceanic ridge! meeting of tectonic plates! four volcanic systems!) and local culture.

Getting There & Away

Public transport to Keflavík and the Blue Lagoon is fast and frequent from Reykjavík. There is limited public bus service to other villages, but you'll do best with private transport to reach the more remote parts of the peninsula.

Blue Lagoon

As the Eiffel Tower is to Paris, so the Blue Lagoon is to Iceland...with all the positive and negative connotations implied. Those who say it's too commercial and too crowded aren't wrong, but you'll be missing something special if you don't go.

Activities

★Blue Lagoon GEOTHERMAL POOL

(Bláa Lónið; ☎420 8800; www.bluelagoon.com; adult/child Jun-Aug from €50/free, Sep-May from €40/free; ⏲8am-midnight Jun–mid-Aug, reduced hours mid-Aug–May) In a magnificent black-lava field, the milky-teal Blue Lagoon spa is fed water from the futuristic Svartsengi geothermal plant; with its silver towers, roiling clouds of steam, and people daubed

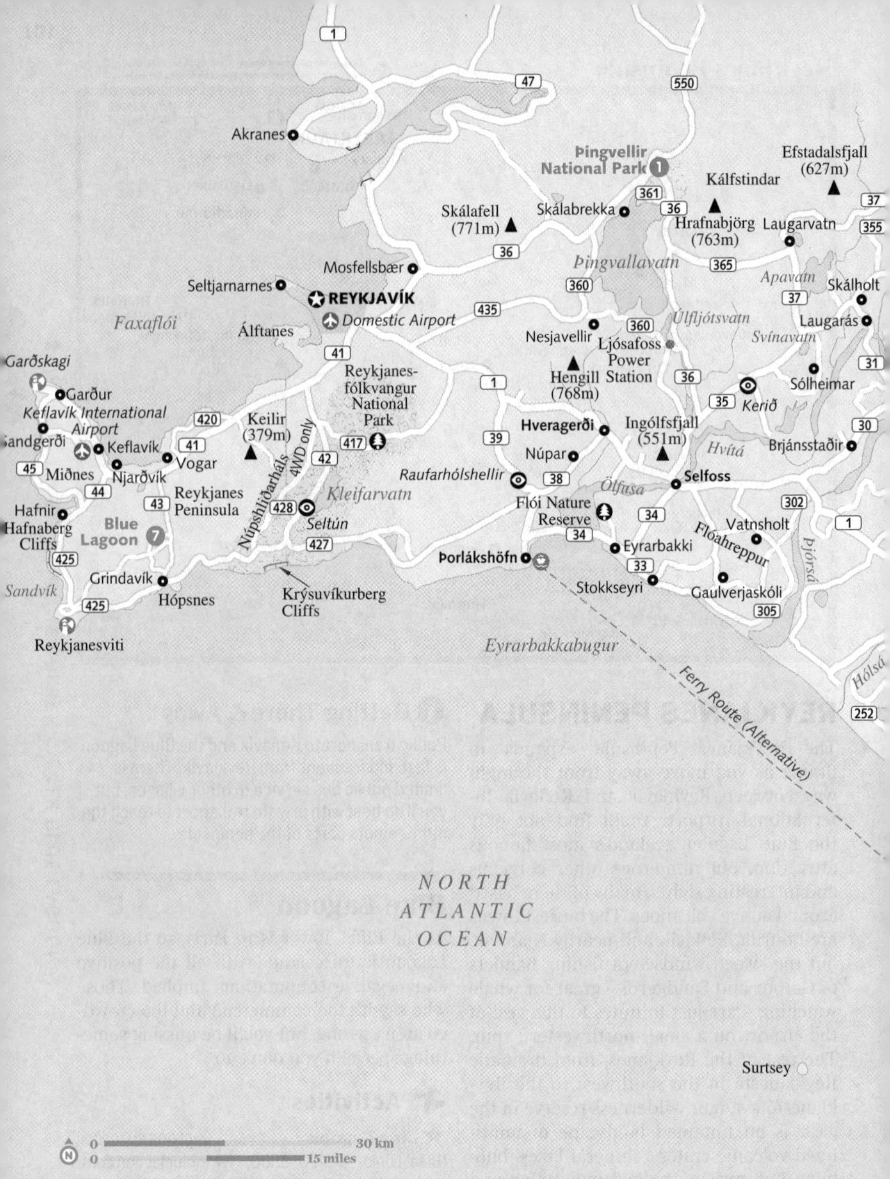

Southwest Iceland & Golden Circle Highlights

1. **Þingvellir** (p111) Seeing the continental plates part at historic Þingvellir National Park.
2. **Reynisfjara** (p155) Marvelling at black basalt columns, sea stacks and rocky buttes near buzzy Vík.
3. **Þórsmörk** (p152) Camping in a lush kingdom surrounded by brooding glaciers.
4. **Vestmannaeyjar** (p163) Setting sail to see zippy puffins and a small town tucked between lava flows.
5. **Þjórsárdalur** (p134) Exploring a volcanic valley

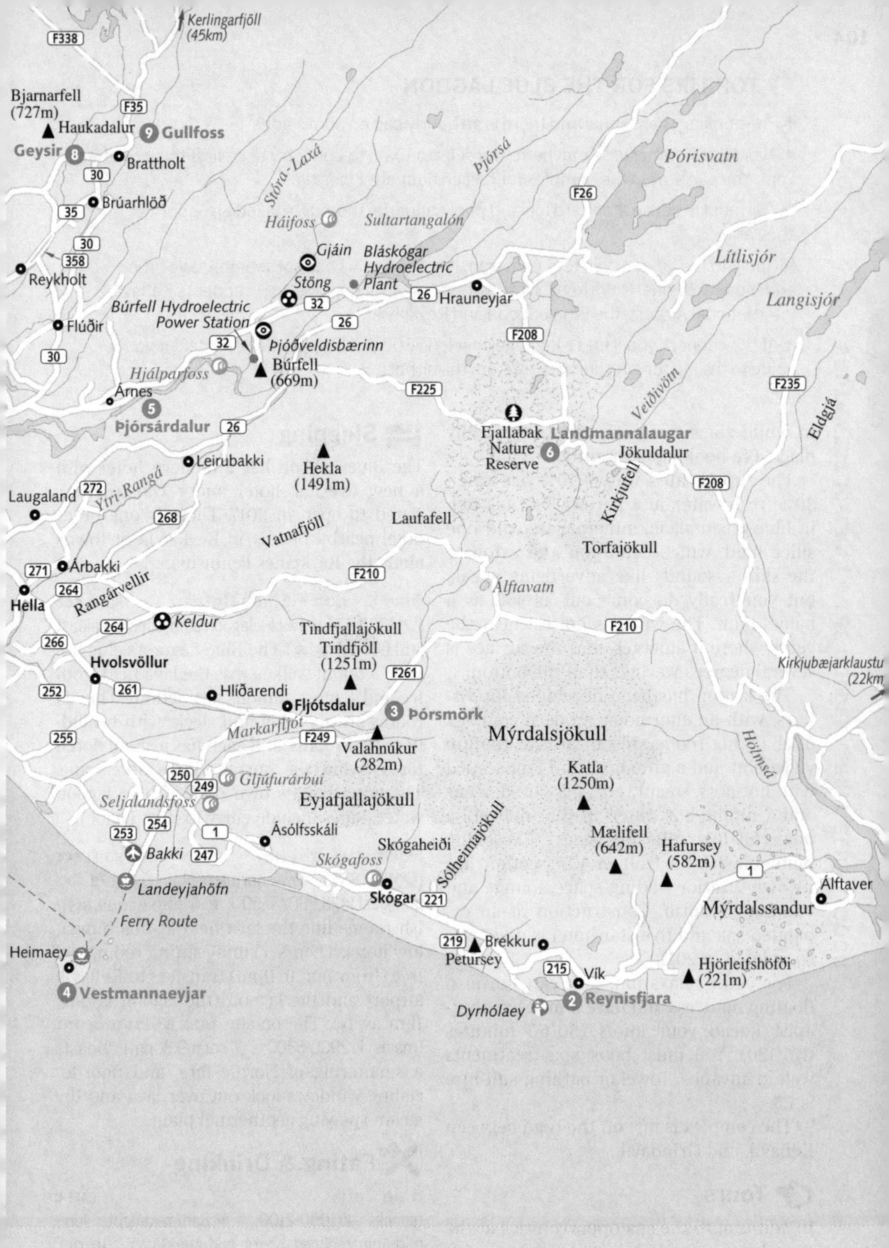

of raw terrain carved by the powerful Þjórsá river.

6 **Landmannalaugar** (p146) Traversing multicoloured peaks past pristine lakes, then hiking the Laugavegurinn.

7 **Blue Lagoon** (p101) Washing away your cares at the Vegas version of Icelandic hot-pots.

8 **Geysir** (p116) Waiting for water to shoot skywards at Geysir, which gave its name to geysers the world over.

9 **Waterfalls** (p117) Tracking brilliant cascades from Háifoss, Seljalandsfoss and Skógafoss to the most famous of them all, Gullfoss.

TOP TIPS FOR THE BLUE LAGOON

- Pre-booking is essential and there is an hourly cap on admissions.
- Avoid the summertime mayhem (worst from 10am to 2pm); try to go first thing or after 7pm. You can stay in the complex for half an hour after closing.
- You must practise standard Iceland pool etiquette: thorough naked pre-pool showering.
- Going to the lagoon on a tour or in transit to the airport can sometimes save time and money. By bus, **Reykjavík Excursions** (☎580 5400; www.re.is) connects Keflavík International Airport, the Blue Lagoon and Reykjavík.
- At the car park you'll find a luggage check (kr600 per bag, per day); perfect if you're going to the lagoon on your way to/from the airport.

in white silica mud, it's an other-worldly place. Pre-booking is essential.

The superheated water (70% sea water, 30% fresh water, at a perfect 38°C) is rich in blue-green algae, mineral salts and fine silica mud, which condition and exfoliate the skin – sounds like advertising speak, but you really do come out as soft as a baby's bum. The water is hottest near the vents where it emerges, and the surface is several degrees warmer than the bottom.

The lagoon has been developed for visitors, with an enormous, modern complex of changing rooms, restaurants, a rooftop viewpoint and a gift shop, and landscaped with hot-pots, steam rooms, a sauna, a bar and a piping-hot waterfall that delivers a powerful hydraulic massage – like being pummelled by a troll. A VIP section has its own interior wading space, lounge and viewing platform. Construction of an expanded spa and five-star hotel is due to be completed in 2017.

For extra relaxation, you can lie on a floating mattress and have a massage therapist knead your knots (30/60 minutes €75/120). You must book spa treatments well in advance. Towel or bathing-suit hire is €5.

The complex is just off the road between Keflavík and Grindavík.

Tours

In addition to the spa opportunities at the Blue Lagoon, you can combine your visit with package tours, or hook up with nearby ATV Adventures (p109) for quad-bike or cycling tours (kr9900 from the Blue Lagoon through the lava fields) or bicycle rental. The company can pick you up and drop you off at the lagoon.

Sleeping

The Blue Lagoon has a modern hotel with a new five-star hotel under construction, slated to open in 2017. There is one other hotel nearby, or stay in Reykjavík or towns along the Reykjanes Peninsula.

Blue Lagoon – Silica Hotel HOTEL €€€
(☎420 8806; www.bluelagoon.com; d incl breakfast kr51,600; P @ ≋) The Blue Lagoon's chic hotel is a 600m walk across the lava field from Iceland's most famous attraction. The 35 rooms are soothing and sleek, with heated-floor bathrooms, and each has a small porch for viewing the surrounding moonscape. The hotel has its own pool of blue lagoon water. Rates include entry to Blue Lagoon.

Northern Light Inn HOTEL €€€
(☎426 8650; www.northernlightinn.is; s/d incl breakfast kr28,500/37,500; P @) Spacious, stylish rooms line the lava field at this bungalow hotel. There's a sunny sitting room, and free (from 7am to 9pm) transfers to Keflavík airport and the lagoon (the lagoon is only 1km away). The on-site **Max's Restaurant** (mains kr2900-5300; ⌚noon-9.30pm) boasts a smattering of Nordic fare, and floor-to-ceiling windows look out over lava and the steam-spewing geothermal plant.

Eating & Drinking

Blue Café CAFE €
(snacks kr1000-2100; ⌚8am-midnight Jun–mid-Aug, reduced hours mid-Aug–May) Simple, cafeteria-style eating at the Blue Lagoon, with smoothies, sandwiches and pre-made sushi.

LAVA Restaurant ICELANDIC €€€
(☎420 8800; www.bluelagoon.com; mains lunch/dinner kr4500/5900; ⌚11.30am-9.30pm Jun-Aug, to 8.30pm Sep-May) The Blue Lagoon's cavern-

ous dining room can feel like a function hall, but views to the lagoon are serene, the waitstaff are excellent and the menu features Iceland's favourite dishes.

Getting There & Away

The lagoon is 47km southwest of Reykjavík and 23km southeast of Keflavík International Airport. The complex is just off the road between Keflavík and Grindavík. Bus services run year-round, as do tours (which sometimes offer better deals than a bus ticket plus lagoon admission). You must book in advance. If your bus or tour does not include lagoon entry, you must pre-book at www.bluelagoon.com.

Blue Lagoon partners with **Reykjavík Excursions** (www.re.is), which runs buses to the lagoon from/to Reyjavík and from/to the airport. With frequent buses (10 to 16 daily June to August; see www.bluelagoon.com for details), you can do a round trip from either Reykjavík or the airport, or stop off at the lagoon on your way between the two. These bus tickets can be booked when you book lagoon entry.

Bustravel (☎511 2600; www.bustravel.is) also runs transfers from the airport or Reykjavík (kr3900).

Keflavík & Njarðvík (Reykjanesbær)

POP 15,240

The twin towns of Keflavík and Njarðvík, on the coast about 47km southwest of Reykjavík, are both rather ungainly expanses of suburban boxes and fast-food outlets. Together they're known as 'Reykjanesbær'. Don't stay here unless you've an early flight; it's worth the 40-minute ride into Reykjavík.

Sights

Keflavík

The waterfront strip in Keflavík has most of the town's hotels and restaurants, and also the museum Duushús. To the east on the seashore is an impressive **Ásmundur Sveinsson sculpture**, used as a climbing frame by the local kids. Just beyond, on the edge of the little harbour, find a black cave where a larger-than-life **Giantess** (Skessa; Gróf small boat harbour; ⏲1-5pm Sat & Sun) FREE, a character from Herdís Egilsdóttir's children's books, sits in a rocking chair.

★Duushús MUSEUM
(☎421 3796; Duusgata 2-8; adult/child kr1500/free; ⏲noon-5pm) In a long red warehouse by the harbour, Duushús is Keflavík's historic cultural centre. There's a permanent exhibition of around 60 of Grímur Karlsson's many hundreds of miniature ships, made over a lifetime, as well as Reykjanes Art Museum galleries with international art exhibitions, and a changing local-history display.

Icelandic Museum of Rock 'n' Roll MUSEUM
(Rokksafn Íslands; ☎420 1030; www.rokksafn.is; Hjallavegur 2; admission kr1500; ⏲11am-6pm Mon-Sat) This museum delves into the history of the awesome Icelandic music scene, from Björk to Sigur Rós and Of Monsters and Men. Admission includes an audio guide with music. There's also the Music Hall of Fame, instruments for you to jam on, a cafe, and a shop where you can stock up on local tunes.

Njarðvík

★Víkingaheimar MUSEUM
(Viking World; ☎422 2000; www.vikingaheimar.is; Víkingabraut 1; adult/child kr1500/free; ⏲7am-6pm) At the eastern end of Njarðvík's waterfront, the spectacular Víkingaheimar is a Norse exhibition centre built in one beautiful, sweeping architectural gesture. The centrepiece is the 23m-long *Íslendingur,* an exact reconstruction of the Viking Age *Gokstad* longship. It was built almost single-handedly by Gunnar Marel Eggertsson, who then sailed it from Iceland to New York in 2000 to commemorate the 1000th anniversary of Leif the Lucky's journey to America.

Stekkjarkot HISTORIC BUILDING
(⏲1-5pm Tue-Sun Jun-Aug, by appointment Sep-May) FREE On the point near Víkingaheimar, tiny folk museum Stekkjarkot is a restored turf house, abandoned in 1924, with parts dating to the 19th century.

Activities

Swimming Pool SWIMMING
(☎420 1500; Sunnubraut 31; adult/child kr700/free; ⏲6.30am-8pm Mon-Thu, to 7pm Fri, 9am-5pm Sat & Sun) Keflavík has a good 25m outdoor swimming pool with hot tubs, a sauna and a 50m indoor pool.

Keflavík

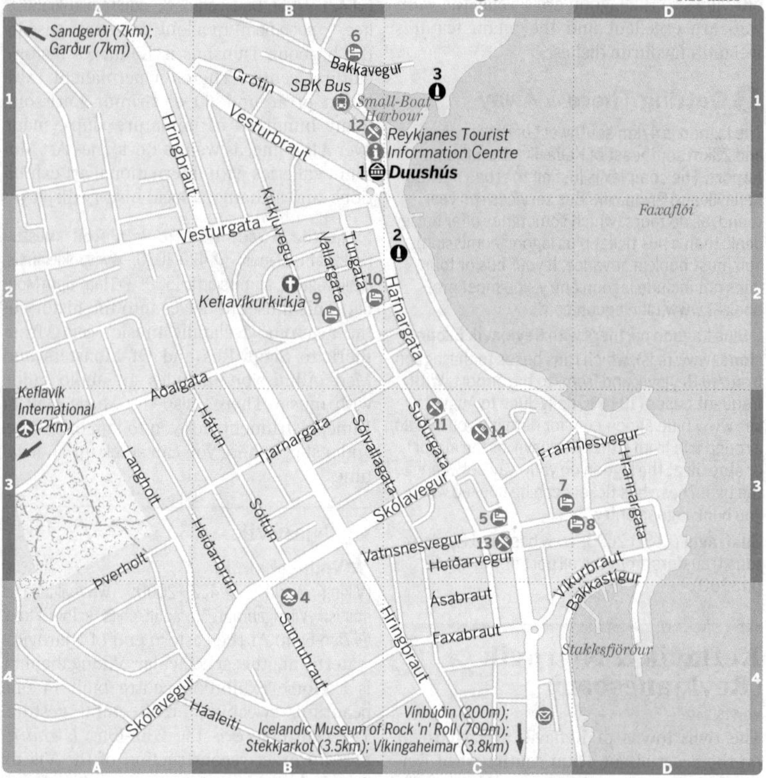

Keflavík

Top Sights

1 Duushús ... B1

Sights

2 Ásmundur Sveinsson Sculpture ... C2
3 Giantess ... C1

Activities, Courses & Tours

4 Swimming Pool ... B4

Sleeping

5 CB Guesthouse ... C3
6 Hótel Berg ... B1
7 Hótel Keflavík ... C3
8 Hótel Keflavík Guesthouse ... D3
9 Nupan Deluxe ... B2
10 Svítan Guesthouse & Apartments ... B2

Eating

11 Fernando's ... C3
12 Kaffi Duus ... B1
13 Olsen Olsen ... C3
14 Thai Keflavík ... C3

Drinking & Nightlife

Paddy's ... (see 11)

Festivals & Events

Night of Lights CULTURAL

(Ljósanótt í Reykjanesbæ; www.ljosanott.is; Sep) If you're around at the beginning of September, the well-attended Night of Lights festival is worth seeing, particularly its grand finale, when waterfalls of fireworks pour over the Bergið cliffs.

Sleeping

Check www.visitreykjanes.is for accommodation; many hotels in the area provide free airport transfers.

Svítan Guesthouse & Apartments APARTMENT €
(☎663 1269; www.svitan.is; Túngata 10; d incl breakfast kr12,000, apt from kr16,200) Choose from simple guest rooms or fully furnished apartments at this centrally located (and recently renovated) historic building. Rooms have kitchen and terrace access, and some have private bathrooms.

CB Guesthouse GUESTHOUSE €
(☎786 0577; Hafnargata 56; s/d without bathroom from kr9300/12,000; P) CB Guesthouse offers straightforward, tidy rooms on the main street in Keflavík, as well as kitchen and terrace access.

Hótel Keflavík Guesthouse GUESTHOUSE €
(www.hotelkeflavik.is; Vatnsnesvegur 9; d without bathroom kr12,600) This small guesthouse is a basic annexe to the Hótel Keflavík and offers very simple rooms with shared bathrooms. There's a microwave available.

Hótel Berg B&B €€
(☎422 7922; www.hotelberg.is; Bakkavegur 17; d incl breakfast from kr27,600; @) This homey guesthouse overlooking a little inlet harbour has common spaces with charming touches, and modern rooms with flat-screen TVs and original photography on the walls. It's located at the northern (and most charming) end of Keflavík, and is a wonderfully welcoming place to stay.

Nupan Deluxe B&B €€
(☎565 3333; www.hotelnupan.com; Aðalgata 10; s without bathroom incl breakfast kr12,200, d/tr incl breakfast kr25,200/28,800) Sleek, clean and simple is the order of the day at this residential-area B&B on the main drag out of town. It has a hot tub.

Hótel Keflavík HOTEL €€
(☎420 7000; www.hotelkeflavik.is; Vatnsnesvegur 12-14; d/f incl breakfast kr24,500/41,600; @) Serviceable, central rooms, some with ocean views; rates vary wildly online. The hotel also runs a small guesthouse (p107) across the street, with simple rooms and shared bathrooms.

Airport Hotel Aurora Star HOTEL €€€
(☎595 1900; www.hotelairport.is; Blikavöllur 2, Keflavík International Airport; s/d/tr incl breakfast kr30,500/33,000/39,000; P @) The only hotel actually at the airport, Hotel Aurora Star is about 100m from the terminal and offers a tower of solid business-style rooms with flat-screen TVs. Superior rooms are bigger, with two double beds.

ℹ SOUTHWEST RESOURCES

South Iceland Tourist Information (www.south.is) Has a thorough print booklet and excellent free detailed maps for each sub-region. Get them at local tourist offices.

Visit Reykjanes (www.visitreykjanes.is) Information on the Reykjanes Peninsula.

Eating & Drinking

Fernando's PIZZERIA €
(☎557 1007; www.facebook.com/fernandospizza; Hafnargata 36; pizzas kr1300-2900; ⏰11am-10pm Mon-Wed, to 11pm Thu & Fri, 2-11pm Sat, 4-10pm Sun) This simple eatery is the local favourite for wood-fired pizza. There's also a basic burger, salad and pasta menu.

Olsen Olsen FAST FOOD €
(☎421 4457; www.olsenolsendiner.com; Hafnargata 62; mains kr1000-2700; ⏰11am-10pm) In the 1950s, thanks to American-introduced rock and roll, Keflavík was the coolest place in Iceland. This US-style diner transports locals back to the glory days, with shiny silver tables, red plastic seats and pictures of Elvis.

Kaffi Duus SEAFOOD, INDIAN €€
(☎421 7080; www.duus.is; Duusgata 10, Duushús; mains kr2750-5000; ⏰11am-11pm) This friendly, nautical-themed cafe-restaurant-bar, decorated with walrus tusks, overlooks the small-boat harbour. It serves generous platefuls of fresh fish, plus pasta, salads, burgers and, incongruously, Indian food. It's a popular evening hang-out.

Thai Keflavík THAI €€
(☎421 8666; www.thaikeflavik.is; Hafnargata 39; mains kr1900-2800; ⏰11.30am-10pm Mon-Fri, 4-10pm Sat & Sun) With authentic Thai dishes, this restaurant is a great choice if you're up to your eyeballs with fish and lamb. There's outdoor seating during warm weather.

Paddy's BAR
(☎421 8900; Hafnargata 38; ⏰6pm-1am Mon-Thu, to 4.30am Fri, noon-4.30am Sat, noon-1am Sun) A hole-in-the-wall that can get raucous at weekends and has occasional live music.

Shopping

Vínbúðin ALCOHOL
(☎421 5699; Krossmói 4; ⊙11am-6pm Mon-Thu, to 7pm Fri, to 4pm Sat) National liquor chain.

Information

Reykjanes Tourist Information Centre (☎420 3246; www.visitreykjanes.is; Duusgata 2-8, Keflavík; ⊙9am-5pm Mon-Fri, 10am-2pm Sat & Sun) Reykjanes Peninsula information, maps and brochures; inside the **Duushús** (p105).

Getting There & Away

AIR

Apart from flights to Greenland and the Faroes, all of Iceland's international flights use **Keflavík International Airport** (p400).

To/From the Airport

Most of Reykjanesbær's lodgings offer free transfers to/from Keflavík International Airport for guests. A taxi costs about kr5000; call **Airport Taxi** (☎420 1212; www.airporttaxi.is) or **Hreyfill Taxi** (☎588 5522; www.hreyfill.is).

BUS

Strætó (www.bus.is) services:

- Bus 55 goes between Keflavík airport and BSÍ bus terminal in Reykjavík (adult/child kr1680/840, 1¼ hours, nine daily Monday to Friday). On Saturday (nine daily) and Sunday (seven daily) buses only go as far east as Hafnarfjörður.
- Bus 88 goes from Keflavík to Grindavík (kr420, two daily, 20 minutes). On weekends it only goes from Grindavík to the crossroads where you can connect to bus 55.
- Bus 89 goes from Keflavík to Garður and Sandgerði (both services kr420, 11 daily Monday to Friday, four Saturday, three Sunday).

Airport buses can also drop you near the town limits.

Getting Around

SBK Bus (☎420 6000; www.sbk.is; Grófin 2-4, Keflavík) SBK runs local buses around Keflavík.

Northwestern Reykjanes

The western edge of the Reykjanes Peninsula is rugged and exposed – perfect if you love wild rain-lashed cliffs and beaches. There are several fishing villages and some sights among the lava fields.

To best see the countryside around Northwestern Reykjanes bring your own wheels. Strætó bus 89 goes from Keflavík to Garður and Sandgerði.

Garður

POP 1430

From Keflavík, if you follow Rte 41 for 9km, through the village of Garður (www.svgardur.is), you'll reach beautiful wind-battered **Garðskagi headland**, one of the best places in Iceland for birdwatchers. It's a big breeding ground for seabirds, and it's often the place where migratory species first touch down. It's also possible to see seals (and maybe whales) from here, as well as offering superb views over the ocean to Snæfellsjökull.

Two splendid **lighthouses**, one tall and one tiny, add drama, and you can get near-360-degree sea views from the tall one. The small **folk museum** (Byggdasafn; ☎422 7220; www.svgardur.is; Skagabraut 100; ⊙1-5pm Apr-Oct) is filled with a pleasing mishmash of fishing boats, birds' eggs and sewing machines.

There's a tranquil, free camping area by the lighthouse, with toilets and fresh water, plus several guesthouses in town.

There is occasionally a cafe open at the lighthouses, but Sandgerði, Keflavík and Grindavík offer more choice.

Sandgerði & Around

POP 1540

Sandgerði is an industrious fishing village, 5 km south of Garður. There are pleasant beaches on the coast south of Sandgerði, and the surrounding marshes are frequented by more than 190 species of birds.

Sights

Sudurnes Science & Learning Center MUSEUM
(☎423 7551; www.thekkingarsetur.is; Gerðavegur 1; adult/child kr600/300; ⊙10am-4pm Mon-Fri, 1-5pm Sat & Sun May-Sep, 10am-2pm Mon-Fri Oct-Apr) This scientific learning centre has a fascinating exhibit about Polar explorer Jean-Baptiste Charcot, whose ship *Pourquoi Pas?* wrecked near here in 1936 (all but one sailor perished). There are original artefacts from the wreck and memorabilia. Other displays include stuffed and jarred Icelandic creatures (look out for the walrus) and a small aquarium.

Eating

★Vitinn SEAFOOD €€

(☎423 7755; www.vitinn.is; Vitatorg 7; mains kr2000-4300; ⊙11.30am-2pm & 6-9pm Mon-Sat) Vitinn is not to be missed. A friendly team serves heaps of seafood (stored in tanks out back in the courtyard) in marine-fancy surrounds. The crab and shellfish bisque is delicious.

Southwestern Reykjanes

The southwestern tip of the Reykjanes Peninsula is a wild and interesting landscape of volcanic terrain surrounding the rift between the North American and European tectonic plates.

Visit the area with your own wheels. There is no public transport.

Sights

If you turn off Rte 41 onto Rte 44 just outside Keflavík, you'll reach the bird cliffs at **Hafnaberg**, then the **Bridge Between Two Continents**, where a teeny footbridge spans a sand-filled gulf between the North American and European plates.

In the far southwest of the peninsula the landscape alternates between lava fields and wild volcanic crags and craters, thus it's been named **100 Crater Park**. Several power plants here exploit geothermal heat to produce salt from seawater and to provide electricity for the national grid. **Power Plant Earth** (Orkuverið Jörð; ☎436 1000; www.hsorka.is; Reykjanesvirkjun Power Plant; adult/child kr1500/1000; ⊙9am-4pm May-Aug) is an interactive exhibition about energy. You also get a glimpse into the vast, spotless turbine hall, and there are scaled representations of the planets positioned around the peninsula.

One of the most wild and wonderful spots on the peninsula is **Valahnúkur**, where a winding road leads off Rte 425 through 13th-century lava fields. Turn right at the T-intersection and go 900m on an unpaved road to dramatic, climb-able cliffs and **Reykjanesviti lighthouse** (1878), the oldest in Iceland.

From Valahnúkur and the nearby coast you can see the flat-topped rocky islet Eldey, 14km offshore, home to the world's largest gannet colony and a protected bird reserve.

If you take the left branch of the aforementioned T-intersection, in 500m you reach a steaming multicoloured geothermal area. This includes the hot spring **Gunnuhver**, named after the witch-ghost Gunna, who was trapped by magic and lured into the boiling water to her death.

Grindavík

POP 3130

The only settlement on the south coast of Reykjanes, Grindavík is one of Iceland's most important fishing centres. Here, all flimflam is rejected in favour of working jetties, cranes and warehouses, though its proximity to the Blue Lagoon has drawn more tourism in recent years.

Sights

Kvíkan MUSEUM

(Magma; ☎420 1190; www.visitgrindavik.is; Hafnargata 12a; adult/child kr1200/free; ⊙10am-5pm) Grindavík's only tourist attraction is Kvíkan, a museum with two exhibits: a well-curated one on the fish-salting industry, and another about the earth's energy.

Tours

ATV Adventures QUAD-BIKE TOUR

(☎857 3001; www.atv4x4.is) The major provider for quad-bike rides around the peninsula: explore lava fields and see shipwrecks (from kr13,000 per seat for a two-person self-drive buggy; driver's licence required). Also runs cycling tours from Blue Lagoon (kr9900) and has bicycle rental (four/24 hours kr4900/6900 or kr5900 for four hours with Blue Lagoon delivery).

Arctic Horses HORSE RIDING

(☎848 0143; www.arctichorses.is; Hópsheiði 16) Small, family-run outfit with horse rides along the peninsula. The popular lighthouse tour (adult/child kr8000/5000) lasts one to 1½ hours.

Salty Tours TOURS

(☎820 5750; www.saltytours.is) Day tours of Reykjanes (kr10,900) and beyond. Picks up at the airport or from Reykjavík.

Sleeping

Grindavík has good lodging, and is a quick drive to the Blue Lagoon, so it's an increasingly popular place to sleep over.

Mar Guesthouse GUESTHOUSE €

(☎856 5792; www.marguesthouse.is; Hafnargata 28; d without bathroom kr13,000, studios from kr21,000) Some of these modern, newly built guest rooms with shared bathrooms, and studios with kitchenettes, have harbour views. Everything is tidy, staff are helpful, and there's kitchen and laundry access for all.

Guesthouse Borg GUESTHOUSE €
(☎895 8686; www.guesthouseborg.com; Borgarhraun 2; s/d without bathroom incl breakfast kr9500/14,500; @) Borg is an older home in the centre of town with the cosiness of 'grandma's place'. Kitchen and laundry access.

Campsite CAMPGROUND €
(☎660 7323; www.visitgrindavik.is; Austurvegur 26; sites per adult/child k1289/free; ⏲mid-May–Sep) Grindavík's fresh-faced campsite near the harbour is a patch of green with good amenities, including barbecues and a playground.

Eating

★Bryggjan CAFE €
(☎426 7100; Miðgarður 2; cakes kr850, soup kr1600-2000; ⏲8am-11pm) Facing the harbour front, in a block of warehouses, this adorable cafe serves up homemade cakes and light meals amid framed photos, old fishing buoys and locals relaxing in the sunshine.

Papa's SEAFOOD €€
(☎426 9955; Hafnargata 7; mains kr1600-3200; ⏲11.30am-9pm) Fish and chips at Papa's are a treat, although you'll also find locals crowding in for pizza and burgers.

Salthúsið SEAFOOD €€
(☎426 9700; www.salthusid.is; Stamphólsvegur 2; mains kr3300-4900; ⏲noon-10pm mid-May–mid-Sep) The classy wooden Salthúsið specialises in local *saltfiskur* (saltfish), which is prepared in different ways, plus there's salmon, lobster, chicken and lamb.

Information

Tourist Information Centre (☎420 1190; www.visitgrindavik.is; ⏲10am-5pm mid-May–mid-Sep) In **Kvíkan museum** (p109); has an internet terminal.

Getting There & Away

Strætó (www.bus.is) bus 88 goes to Keflavík (kr420, two daily, 20 minutes). On weekends it only goes from Grindavík to the crossroads where you can connect to bus 55.

Reykjanesfólkvangur National Park

For a taste of Iceland's raw countryside, visit this 300-sq-km wilderness reserve, a mere 40km from Reykjavík. Established in 1975, the reserve protects the elaborate lava formations created by the dramatic Reykjanes ridge volcanoes. Its three show pieces are Kleifarvatn, a deep mineral lake with submerged hot springs and black-sand beaches; the spitting, bubbling Krýsuvík geothermal zone at Seltún; and the Southwest's largest bird cliffs, the epic Krýsuvíkurberg. The whole area is criss-crossed by walking trails. Get good maps at Keflavík, Grindavík or Hafnarfjörður tourist offices. You'll see parking turnouts at the head of the most popular walks, including the loop around Kleifarvatn, and the tracks along the craggy Sveifluháls and Núpshliðarháls ridges.

There is no public transport within the wilds of the park, so either come with your own wheels, or on one of the many guided tours on offer.

Sights & Activities

Kleifarvatn LAKE
This deep, brooding lake sits in a volcanic fissure, surrounded by wind-warped lava cliffs and black-sand shores. A walking trail runs around the edge, offering dramatic views and the crunch of volcanic cinders underfoot. Legend has it that a wormlike monster the size of a whale lurks below the surface – but the poor creature is running out of room, as the lake has been shrinking ever since two major earthquakes shook the area in 2000.

Seltún HOT SPRINGS
The volatile geothermal field Austurengjar, about 2km south of Kleifarvatn, is often called Krýsuvík after the nearby abandoned farm. At the main sight, Seltún, boardwalks meander round a cluster of seething hot springs. The mud pots and steaming sulphuric solfataras (volcanic vents) shimmer with rainbow colours from the minerals in the earth.

Grænavatn LAKE
Just to the south of the Seltún hot springs, this lake is an old explosion crater filled with gorgeous teal water – caused by a combination of minerals and warmth-loving algae.

Krýsuvíkurberg Cliffs BIRDWATCHING
About 3km south of Seltún across the Krýsuvíkurhraun lava fields, a dirt track leads down to the coast at Krýsuvíkurberg (marked on the main road as Krýsuvíkurbjarg). These sweeping black cliffs stretch for 4km and are packed with some 57,000 seabird breeding pairs in summer, from guillemots to occasional puffins. A walking path runs the length of the cliffs.

THE GOLDEN CIRCLE

The Golden Circle – not to be confused with the Ring Road, which wraps around the entire country and takes a week or more – takes in three popular attractions within 100km of the capital, all in one doable-in-a-day loop: Þingvellir (a meeting point of the continental plates and site of the ancient Icelandic parliament), Geysir (a spouting hot spring) and Gullfoss (a roaring waterfall). Visiting under your own steam allows you to visit at off-hours and explore exciting attractions further afield. Almost every tour company in the Reykjavík area offers a Golden Circle excursion (from bus to bike to super-Jeep), often combinable with other sights as well.

Þingvellir National Park

Þingvellir National Park (www.thingvellir.is), 40km northeast of central Reykjavík, is Iceland's most important historical site and a place of vivid beauty. The Vikings established the world's first democratic parliament, the Alþingi (pronounced *ál-thingk-ee,* also called Alþing), here in AD 930. The meetings were conducted outdoors and, as with many Saga sites, there are only the stone foundations of ancient encampments. The site has a superb natural setting, in an immense, fissured rift valley, caused by the meeting of the North American and Eurasian tectonic plates, with rivers and waterfalls. The country's first national park, Þingvellir was made a Unesco World Heritage Site in 2004.

History

Many of Iceland's first settlers had run-ins with royalty back in mainland Scandinavia. These chancers and outlaws decided that they could live happily without kings in the new country, and instead created district *þings* (assemblies) where justice could be served by and among local chieftains *(goðar)*.

Eventually, a nationwide *þing* became necessary. Bláskógur – now Þingvellir (Parliament Fields) – lay at a crossroads by a huge fish-filled lake. It had plenty of firewood and a setting that would make even the most tedious orator dramatic, so it fitted the bill perfectly. Every important decision affecting Iceland was argued out on this plain – new laws were passed, marriage contracts were made and even the country's religion was decided here. The annual parliament was also a great social occasion, thronging with traders and entertainers.

Over the following centuries, escalating violence between Iceland's most powerful groups led to the breakdown of law and order. Governance was surrendered to the Norwegian crown and the Alþingi was stripped of its legislative powers in 1271. It functioned solely as a courtroom until 1798, before being dissolved entirely. When it regained its powers in 1843, members voted to move the meeting place to Reykjavík.

Sights

From the Park Service Centre on Rte 36, follow the path from the outlook down to the Lögberg (Law Rock), and the only standing structures in the great rift. You can also approach the waterfall Öxarárfoss from a parking area on Rte 36, and hike down into the rift valley from there. Or, come in on Rte 361 on the eastern edge of the site, and park there. Get a good map at www.thingvellir.is.

WORTH A TRIP

HALLDÓR LAXNESS' HOU

Nobel Prize–winning author Hall Laxness (1902–98) lived in Mosf all his life. His riverside home is now the **Gljúfrasteinn Laxness Museum** (☎586 8066; www.gljufrasteinn.is; Mosfellsbær; adult/child kr900/free; ⏲9am-5pm daily Jun-Aug, 10am-5pm Tue-Sun Mar-May, Sep, Oct & Dec, 10am-5pm Tue-Fri Jan, Feb & Nov), easy to visit on the road from Reykjavík to Þingvellir (Rte 36). The author built this upper-class 1950s house and it remains intact with original furniture, writing room and Laxness' fine-art collection (needlework, sweetly, by his wife Auður). An audio tour leads you round. Look for his beloved Jaguar parked out the front.

ree one-hour guided tours run most days June to August; check the website or visitors centre for the schedule.

★Tectonic Plates CANYONS, WATERFALLS

The Þingvellir plain is situated on a tectonic-plate boundary where North America and Europe are tearing away from each other at a rate of 1mm to 18mm per year. As a result, the plain is scarred by dramatic fissures, ponds and rivers, including the great rift **Almannagjá**. A path runs along the fault between the clifftop visitors centre and the Alþingi site.

The river **Öxará** cuts the western plate, tumbling off its edge in a series of pretty cascades. The most impressive is **Öxarárfoss**, on the northern edge of the Alþingi site. The pool **Drekkingarhylur** was used to drown women found guilty of infanticide, adultery or other serious crimes.

There are other smaller fissures on the eastern edge of the site. During the 17th century nine men accused of witchcraft were burnt at the stake in **Brennugjá** (Burning Chasm). Nearby are the fissures of **Flosagjá** (named after a slave who jumped his way to freedom) and **Nikulásargjá** (after a drunken sheriff discovered dead in the water). The southern end of Nikulásargjá is known as **Peningagjá** (Chasm of Coins) for the thousands of coins tossed into it by visitors (an act forbidden these days).

★Alþingi Site LANDMARK

Near the dramatic Almannagjá fault and fronted by a boardwalk is the **Lögberg** (Law Rock), where the Alþingi convened annually. This was where the *lögsögumaður* (law speaker) recited the existing laws to the assembled parliament (one third each year). After Iceland's conversion to Christianity, the site shifted to the very foot of the Almannagjá cliffs, which acted as a natural amplifier, broadcasting the voices of the speakers

DIY GOLDEN CIRCLE

It's very easy to tour the Golden Circle on your own (by bike or car) – plus, it's fun to tack on additional elements that suit your interests. In the Golden Circle area, signs are well marked, roads well paved and the distances relatively short (it takes about four hours to drive the loop without any add-on stops). You can also cobble some of it together by bus (and buses do go into highlands not accessible by 2WD). The excellent, free *Uppsveitir Árnessýslu* map details the region; find it at tourist offices.

The primary points of the Golden Circle are Þingvellir, Geysir and Gullfoss. DIYers can add the following elements to their tour:

Laugarvatn (p114) Located between Þingvellir and Geysir, this small lakeside town has two must-tries: Lindin, an excellent restaurant, and Fontana, an upmarket geothermal spa.

Þjórsárdalur (p128) Largely untouristed, the quiet valley along the Þjórsá river is dotted with ancient Viking ruins and mysterious natural wonders such as Gjáin. Ultimately it leads up into the highlands (a main route to Landmannalaugar, the starting point of the famous Laugavegurinn hike).

Reykholt (p117) & Flúðir (p119) On your way south from Gullfoss, you can go river-rafting on the Hvítá river from Reykholt or swing through the geothermal area of Flúðir, for its beautiful natural spa and to pick up fresh veggies for your evening meal.

Eyrarbakki (p123) & **Stokkseyri** (p124) South of Selfoss, these two seaside townships are strikingly different than others nearby. Feast on seafood, peruse seasonal local galleries and birdwatch in nearby marshes.

Kaldidalur Corridor (p181) Not all rentals are allowed to drive this bumpy dirt track (Rte 550), but if you have a sanctioned vehicle, you can explore this isolated road that curves around hulking glaciers. It starts near Þingvellir and ends near Húsafell, so if you have time, do the traditional Golden Circle in reverse, then head westward, where many more adventures await.

Kerlingarfjöll (p343) You'll need a 4WD (or to go by bus) to travel beyond Gullfoss, but if you have one, it's worth continuing on to this highland reserve, a hiker haven, about two hours beyond the falls.

across the assembled crowds. That site is marked by the Icelandic flag.

Þingvallakirkja CHURCH
(⏲9am-5pm Jun-Aug) Behind the Þingvallabær farmhouse, Þingvallakirkja is one of Iceland's first churches. The original was consecrated in the 11th century, but the current wooden building only dates from 1859. Inside are several bells from earlier churches, a 17th-century wooden pulpit, and a painted altarpiece from 1834. The independence-era poets Jónas Hallgrímsson and Einar Benediktsson are interred in the small cemetery behind the church.

Þingvallabær HISTORIC BUILDING
The little farmhouse in the bottom of the rift, Þingvallabær was built for the 1000th anniversary of the Alþing in 1930 by state architect Guðjón Samúelsson. It's now used as the park warden's office and prime minister's summer house.

Búðir RUIN
Straddling both sides of the Öxará river are the ruins of various temporary camps called *búðir* (literally 'booths'). These stone foundations were covered during sessions and were where parliament-goers camped. They also acted like stalls at today's music festivals, selling beer, food and vellum to the assembled crowds. Most of the remains date from the 17th and 18th centuries; the largest, and one of the oldest, is **Biskupabúð**, which belonged to the bishops of Iceland and is located north of the church.

Þingvallavatn LAKE
Filling much of the rift plain, Þingvallavatn is Iceland's largest lake, at 84 sq km. Pure glacial water from Langjökull filters through bedrock for 40km before emerging here. It's joined by the hot spring **Vellankatla**, which spouts from beneath the lava field on the northeastern shore. Þingvallavatn is an important refuelling stop for migrating birds (including the great northern diver, barrow's golden-eye and harlequin duck).

Weirdly, its waters are full of *bleikja* (Arctic char) that have been isolated for so long that they've evolved into four subspecies.

Ljósafoss Power Station EXHIBITION
(Ljósafossstöð; ☎896 7407; www.landsvirkjun.com; Ljósafoss; ⏲10am-5pm Jun-Aug, reduced hours Sep-May) FREE The 1937 Ljósafoss Power Station catches the outflow of lake Úlfljótsvatn and turns it into power. In 2016 an elaborate, state-of-the-art, multimedia exhibition called Powering the Future opened, bringing principles of electricity, hydropower, and geothermal and renewable energy to life. Free at the time of writing, a fee may be instituted; check the website for updates on opening hours and costs.

The power station is 5km south of Þingvallavatn.

Activities

Check in with park centres for lake fishing rules (some areas are off limits, and any imported equipment must be disinfected), and get a permit (kr2000 per pole per day; May to mid-September). The fishing card (www.veidikortid.is) also covers part of Þingvallavatn.

Tours

Diving & Snorkelling

One of the most other-worldly activities in Iceland is strapping on a scuba mask (or snorkel) and wetsuit and exploring the crystalline **Silfra fissure**, one of the cracks in the rift valley. There's also a rift, **Davíðsgjá**, out in Þingvallavatn lake, which is harder to reach. You must book ahead with a Reykjavík dive operator. People with their own equipment must have licences, dive in groups of at least two, and buy the permit (kr1000) from the visitors centre.

Horse Riding

In the valley on the Rte 36 approach from Reykjavík, you can go horse riding with Laxnes (p72).

Sleeping

There is camping in Þingvellir National Park, and other accommodation around the southern part of Þingvallavatn lake.

Þingvellir Campsites CAMPGROUND €
(www.thingvellir.is; sites per adult/child/tent kr1300/free/100; ⏲Jun-Sep) Overseen by the park information centre, the best two areas are at Leirar, near the cafe: Syðri-Leirar is the biggest and Nyrðri-Leirar has laundry facilities. Fagrabrekka and Hvannabrekka are for campers only (no cars). Vatnskot is down by the lake and has toilets and cold water (no electricity).

Ljósafossskóli Hostel GUESTHOUSE €
(☎695 4099; www.ljosafossskoli.is; Brúarási 1, Úlfljótsvatn; d without bathroom from kr12,000; P) Many of the good, simple rooms in this

modern, converted schoolhouse have excellent lake and mountain views. Find it 28km south of Þingvellir and 21km north of Selfoss, on the edge of Úlfljótsvatn lake.

Útilífsmiðstöð Skáta Úlfljótsvatni CAMPGROUND €
(☎482 2674; www.ulfljotsvatn.is; Úlfljótsvatn; sites per adult/child kr1500/free, dm incl breakfast kr5000; P) This scouts' centre has camping in summer and basic dorm huts in winter. It offers a full program of lakefront activities and extensive playgrounds. Find it on the south side of Þingvellir's lake, Þingvallavatn.

Lake Thingvellir Cottages COTTAGE €€
(☎892 7110; www.lakethingvellir.is; Heiðarás; cottages kr18,500, plus per person per night kr2400; P) Four modern pine cottages with views to the lake sit near the national-park entrance along Rte 36.

Ion Luxury Adventure Hotel BOUTIQUE HOTEL €€€
(☎482 3415; www.ioniceland.is; Nesjavellir vid Þingvallavatn; d kr50,100; P@) A leader in a new breed of deluxe countryside hotels, Ion is all about hip, modern rooms and sustainable practices. Its geothermal pool, organic spa, **restaurant** (mains lunch kr2500-6000, dinner kr5000-7000; 11.30am-10pm) with slow-food local ingredients and bar with floor-to-ceiling plate-glass windows are all sumptuous. Rooms are a tad smallish, but kitted out impeccably, with fun touches such as horse portraits on the walls.

Hótel Grimsborgir HOTEL €€€
(☎555 7878; www.grimsborgir.com; d incl breakfast kr49,200, 2-bedroom apt kr66,000) Hótel Grimsborgir offers fully kitted-out luxury hotel suites and apartments. Find it on Rte 36, 5.5km south of Ljósafossstöð, and 5km north of the junction with Rte 35.

Hótel Borealis HOTEL €€€
(☎561 3661; www.hotelborealis.is; Bruarholt, Úlfljótsvatn; cottage/d incl breakfast from kr31,000/33,500) Rooms and cottages on the south side of Þingvellir's lake Þingvallavatn are relatively plain.

Eating

There is a **small cafe/mini-mart** (soup kr990; 9am-10pm Apr-Oct, reduced hours Nov-Mar) at the Þingvellir Information Centre serving hot dogs and soup, but the closest proper restaurant is at Ion Luxury Adventure Hotel.

Information

Þingvellir Visitors Centre (Gestastofa; ☎482 3613; 9am-6:30pm Apr-Oct, to 5pm Nov-Mar) At the top of the Almannagjá rift is a simple visitors centre with a video on the area's nature and history, and a shop. The adjacent boardwalk offers great valley views. Toilets cost kr200. You can park here and walk down, or walk up from the Alþingi site.

Þingvellir Information Centre (Leirar Þjónustumiðstöð; ☎482 2660; www.thingvellir.is; 9am-8pm May-Sep, to 5pm Oct-Apr) On Rte 36, on the north side of the lake, the information centre has details about the national park, as well as a cafe.

Getting There & Away

The easiest way to get here is on a Golden Circle tour or in a hire car. Parking per car/jeep costs kr500/750.

Reykjavík Excursions (www.re.is) services:

- Bus 6/6a Reykjavík–Gullfoss (Reykjavík BSÍ Bus Station–Þingvellir kr2500, one daily mid-June to mid-September, stopping at various points around Þingvellir for 75 minutes, then continuing to Laugarvatn, Geysir, Gullfoss and back).
- Bus 320 Reykjavík–Borgarnes–Húsafell–Þingvellir–Reykjavík (kr12,500, one daily mid-June to August, stops for around 15 minutes).

Laugarvatn

POP 160

Laugarvatn (Hot Springs Lake) is fed not only by streams running from the misty fells behind it, but by the hot spring Vígðalaug, famous since medieval times. A village, also called Laugarvatn, sits on the lake's western shore in the lap of the foothills. It is one of the better places to base yourself in the Golden Circle area.

Activities & Tours

★Fontana GEOTHERMAL POOL
(☎486 1400; www.fontana.is; Hverabraut 1; adult/child kr3800/2000; 10am-11pm early Jun-late Aug, 11am-10pm late Aug-early Jun) This swanky lakeside soaking spot boasts three mod wading pools, and a cedar-lined steam room that's fed by a naturally occurring vent below. The cool cafe (buffet lunch/dinner kr2950/4500) has lake views. You can rent towels or swimsuits (kr800 each) if you left yours at home.

Laugarvatn Swimming Pool GEOTHERMAL POOL
(☎486 1251; Hverabraut 2; adult/child kr500/250; ⊙10am-10pm Mon-Fri, to 6pm Sat & Sun Jun–mid-Aug, reduced hours mid-Aug–May) If you want skip the Fontana hot-pot hoopla, there's a regular geothermal swimming pool, hot-pots and sauna next door that costs a fraction of the price, with none of the glitz.

Laugarvatn Adventures ROCK CLIMBING, CAVING
(☎862 5614; www.caving.is) Runs two- to three-hour caving and rock-climbing trips (from kr12,300) in the hills around town.

Sleeping & Eating

Laugarvatn HI Hostel HOSTEL €
(☎486 1215; www.laugarvatnhostel.is; dm/s/d without bathroom kr4100/7000/10,900, s/d kr13,400/16,650; P @) This large hostel, spread over several buildings along the village's main street, is professional and comfortable. There's a newly renovated two-storey building with plenty of kitchen space (great lake views while washing up or from the dining room). Some buildings are much smaller and house-like. There's a kr700 discount for HI members.

Laugarvatn Campsite CAMPGROUND €
(☎771 6869; Háholt 2c; sites per adult/child kr1100/500; ⊙late May–mid-Sep; P) By the highway just outside the village, this campground is a plain grassy expanse with some tree protection.

★**Héraðsskólinn** HOSTEL, GUESTHOUSE €€
(☎537 8060; www.heradsskolinn.is; dm/s/d/q without bathroom from kr5400/14,000/15,300/30,100, d with bathroom kr25,400; P) This sparkling hostel and guesthouse fills an enormous renovated historical landmark school, built in 1928 by Guðjón Samúelsson. The beautiful lakeside building with peaked roofs offers both private rooms with shared bathrooms (some sleep up to six) and dorms, plus a spacious library/living room and a cafe (open 7.30am to 10pm).

★**Efstidalur II** GUESTHOUSE €€
(☎486 1186; www.efstidalur.is; Efstidalur 2, Bláskógabyggð; d/tr incl breakfast from kr26,200/29,700; P) Located 12km northeast of Laugarvatn on a working dairy farm, Efstidalur offers wonderfully welcoming digs, tasty meals and amazing ice cream. Adorable semidetached cottages have brilliant views of hulking Hekla, and the **restaurant** (mains kr2250-5500; ⊙7.30am-9.30am, 11.30am-9pm; P) serves beef from the farm and trout from the lake. The ice-cream bar scoops farm ice cream (kr400 per scoop) and has windows looking into the dairy barn.

Golden Circle Apartments APARTMENTS €€
(☎487 1212; www.goldencircleapartments.is; Laugarbraut 1; 1-/2-bedroom apt kr18,800/26,700; P) Several bland, white block buildings stepping up the slope next to Laugarvatn lake contain spacious, modern apartments with full kitchens, convenient for staying over in the Golden Circle area, as the name suggests.

Hótel Edda HOTEL €€
(☎444 4000; www.hoteledda.is; ⊙early Jun–mid-Aug; P @) Laugarvatn's two big schools become Edda hotels in summer. The 101-room **ML Laugarvatn** (d with/without bathroom from kr24,700/15,700, tr kr27,900) has serviceable college-like rooms. **ÍKÍ Laugarvatn** (d/tr from kr22,300/19,900) is better positioned: its 28 rooms all have private bathrooms, half with beautiful panoramic lake views. Its in-house restaurant has great Hekla views as well.

★**Lindin** ICELANDIC €€
(☎486 1262; www.laugarvatn.is; Lindarbraut 2; restaurant mains kr3800-6300, bistro mains kr2200-5600; ⊙noon-10pm May-Sep, reduced hours Oct-Apr; P) Owned by Baldur, an affable, celebrated chef, Lindin is the best restaurant for miles. In a sweet little silver house, the restaurant faces the lake and is purely gourmet, with high-concept Icelandic fare featuring local or wild-caught ingredients. The casual, modern bistro serves a more informal menu, from soups to an amazing reindeer burger. Book ahead for dinner in high season.

Shopping

Gallerí Laugarvatn ARTS & CRAFTS
(☎847 0805; www.gallerilaugarvatn.is; Háholt 1; ⊙1-6pm mid-May–mid-Sep, 1-6pm Sat & Sun mid-Sep–mid-May) Local handicrafts, from ironwork to ceramics and woollens. Also operates a small B&B and offers courses.

Getting There & Away

Strætó (www.bus.is) services:

- Bus 73 Selfoss–Flúðir–Reykholt–Laugarvatn–Selfoss (Selfoss–Laugarvatn kr1680, 1¼ hours, one daily).

Reykjavík Excursions (www.re.is) services:

- Bus 6/6a Reykjavík–Gullfoss (Reykjavík–Laugarvatn kr4000, one daily mid-June to mid-September, 2¼ hours, continues to Geysir, Gullfoss and back).

➡ Bus 610/610a Reykjavík–Akureyri (one daily mid-June to early September, 1½ hours, continues to Geysir, Gulfoss, Kjölur Highlands and Kerlingarfjöll to Akureyri). This same bus ticket is also sold by Sterna (www.icelandbybus.is) and starts at Harpa.

Geysir

One of Iceland's most famous tourist attractions, **Geysir** FREE (*gay*-zeer; literally 'gusher') is the original hot-water spout after which all other geysers are named. Discovered in the **Haukadalur geothermal region**, the Great Geysir has been active for perhaps 800 years, and once gushed water up to 80m into the air. But the geyser goes through periods of lessened activity, which seems to have been the case since 1916. Earthquakes can stimulate activity, though eruptions are rare. Luckily for visitors, the very reliable **Strokkur** geyser sits alongside. You rarely have to wait more than five to 10 minutes for the hot spring to shoot an impressive 15m to 30m plume before vanishing down its enormous hole. Stand downwind only if you want a shower.

The undulating, hissing geothermal area containing Geysir and Strokkur were free to enter at the time of writing, though there is discussion of instituting a fee.

Tours

Geysir Hestar HORSE RIDING
(☎847 1046; www.geysirhestar.com; Kjóastaðir 2) Four kilometres east of Geysir at Kjóastaðir horse farm, this outfit offers horse riding in the area (one-/two-/three-hour rides kr9500/12,500/17,000) as well as along Hvítá river canyon to Gullfoss, with trips for all skill levels. It also has great lodging in private cabins (kr33,000) or a guesthouse (double with shared bathroom kr15,000).

Iceland Safari JEEP TOURS
(☎544 5454; www.icelandsafari.com) Super-Jeep tours around the southwest (from kr25,000), with a base 1km south of Geysir.

Sleeping

Gljasteinn Skálinn CABIN, GUESTHOUSE €
(☎486 8757; www.gljasteinn.is; Myrkholt; dm adult/child kr6500/4000, d without bathroom kr11,000) This beautiful farm in the widening sweep of the valley between Geysir and Gullfoss has a clutch of tidy houses, one of which has dorms and doubles with shared bathrooms, a kitchen and living room. A nearby three-bedroom cabin (from kr25,500) is a great bargain. It also has cabins with dorm beds in the highlands on the Kjölur route (F35).

Skjól Camping HOSTEL, CAMPGROUND €
(☎899 4541; www.skjolcamping.com; Kjóastaðir; sites per adult/child kr1200/free, dm/d without bathroom kr5400/14,000; ⊙mid-May–mid-Sep) Simple dorms and field camping with a summertime bar, 3.5km northeast of Geysir, next to Kjóastaðir horse farm.

Mengi GUESTHOUSE €€
(☎780 1414; www.mengi-kjarnholt.com; Kjarnholt; d/f without bathroom from kr18,400/25,000; P) This freshly renovated farmhouse in the countryside 10km south of Geysir has 10 rooms with sweeping pastoral views and a shared geothermal hot tub.

Litli Geysir HOTEL €€
(☎480 6800; www.geysircenter.is; Geysir Center; s/d incl breakfast 25,100/29,400; P) This simple, modern hotel is a part of the vast Geysir complex and offers tidy rooms, some with good countryside and Geysir views. There's also a hot tub, sauna and lounge.

Hótel Geysir HOTEL, CAMPGROUND €€
(☎480 6800; www.geysircenter.is; Geysir Center; s/d incl breakfast kr18,000/22,900; P @) The restaurant (three-course meal kr7900) at this alpine-style hotel across the street from Geysir can be completely overrun with tour-bus visitors during summer. The hotel's studio rooms offer good countryside views, and the company also operates the small Litli Geysir hotel and a nearby campground (sites per adult/child kr1700/500; open mid-May to mid-September).

Construction is under way for a 77-room high-end hotel and spa to be completed in 2017.

Eating

Geysir Center INTERNATIONAL €€
(☎480 6800; www.geysircenter.com; ⊙10am-10pm Jun-Aug, to 6pm Sep-May; P 🚸) This large centre has been erected to corral the masses across the street from the geysers. Here you'll find a massive restaurant (mains kr2500 to kr5400), a cafe (mains kr1600 to kr3000), a fast-food joint (kr990 to kr1990), and a souvenir shop of mall-like proportions with Icelandic name brands.

Getting There & Away

Reykjavík Excursions (www.re.is) services:

- Bus 6/6a Reykjavík–Þingvellir–Gullfoss (Reykjavík BSÍ Terminal–Geysir kr4500, three hours, one daily mid-June to mid-September, stops for 1½ hours then continues to Gullfoss and back).
- Bus 610/610a Reykjavík–Akureyri (kr4600, two hours, one daily mid-June to early September, continues to Gullfoss, Kjölur Highlands and Kerlingarfjöll to Akureyri). This same bus service is also sold by Sterna (www.icelandbybus.is) and starts at Harpa.

Gullfoss

Iceland's most famous waterfall, **Gullfoss** (Golden Falls; www.gullfoss.is) FREE is a spectacular double cascade. It drops 32m, kicking up tiered walls of spray before thundering away down a narrow ravine. On sunny days the mist creates shimmering rainbows, and it's also magical in winter when the falls glitter with ice. On grey, drizzly days, mist can envelop the second drop, making Gullfoss slightly underwhelming.

A tarmac path suitable for wheelchairs leads from the tourist information centre to a lookout over the falls, and stairs continue down to the edge. There is also an access road down to the falls.

History

Visited since 1875, the falls came within a hair's breadth of destruction during the 1920s, when a team of foreign investors wanted to dam the Hvítá river for a hydroelectric project. The landowner, Tómas Tómasson, refused to sell to them, but the developers went behind his back and obtained permission directly from the government. Tómasson's daughter, Sigríður, walked (barefoot!) to Reykjavík to protest, even threatening to throw herself into the waterfall if the development went ahead. Thankfully, the investors failed to pay the lease, the agreement was nullified, and the falls escaped destruction. Gullfoss was donated to the nation in 1975 and has been a nature reserve ever since.

Sleeping & Eating

Hótel Gullfoss HOTEL €€

(☎486 8979; www.hotelgullfoss.is; d incl breakfast kr20,000) A few kilometres south of the falls, Hótel Gullfoss is a modern bungalow hotel. Its clean en suite rooms overlook the moors (get one facing the valley), and th[e] hot-pots and a restaurant (mains [...] kr5000) with sweeping views.

Tourist Information Centre, Shop & Cafe CAFE €

(www.gullfoss.is; mains kr1250-1950; ⊙9am-9pm Jun-Aug, to 6.30pm Sep-May) Above Gullfoss, the small tourist information centre boasts a large shop and a simple cafe.

Getting There & Away

Gullfoss is the final attraction on the traditional Golden Circle tour. You can continue along Rte F35 beyond the falls (the Kjölur route) for 14.8km while it's paved, after which you need to have 4WD as it heads deep into the highlands.

Reykjavík Excursions (www.re.is) services:

- Bus 6/6a (Reykjavík–Þingvellir–Geysir–Gullfoss, kr5000, five hours, one daily mid-June to mid-September; stops at the falls for an hour).
- Bus 610/610a (Reykjavík–Akureyri, Reykjavík–Gullfoss kr4800, one daily mid-June to early September; stops at the falls for 30 minutes). This same bus service is also sold by Sterna (www.icelandbybus.is) and starts at Harpa.

Gullfoss to Selfoss (Route 35)

If you're completing the Golden Circle in the traditional direction, then the route from Gullfoss back to the Ring Road at Selfoss will be the final stage of your trip. Along the way you'll find plenty to lure you to stop. Most people follow surfaced Rte 35, which passes through Reykholt, with its river rafting. You can also detour slightly to Flúðir with its geothermal greenhouses and hot spring, and Skálholt, once Iceland's religious powerhouse.

If you'd like to continue east rather than return to Reykjavík, the western Þjórsárdalur area is the next valley of interesting sights.

Reykholt

POP 260

The rural township of Reykholt – one of several Reykholts around the country – is centred on the hot spring Reykjahver and has a geothermal pool. For visitors, however, the main attraction is the nearby Hvítá river – south Iceland's centre for white-water rafting.

Tours

Arctic Rafting RAFTING TOUR
(☎571 2200; www.arcticrafting.com; ⊙mid-May–mid-Sep) Full range of Hvítá river rafting and combination (horse-riding, quad-bike) tours. Three- to four-hour trips start at kr13,990 per adult; Reykjavík pick-up costs kr5000. Children are half-price. The company's base is near Reykholt at Drumboddsstaðir, and its Reykjavík office is at Arctic Adventures (p70).

Iceland Riverjet BOAT TOUR
(☎863 4506; www.icelandriverjet.com; Skólabraut 4; ⊙mid-Apr–Sep) Forty-minute jet-boat rides (adult/child kr14,900/8900) zip along the Hvítá. Based in the same complex as Café Mika, the company also offers pick-up and combo tours with the Golden Circle.

Sleeping

Fellskot Guesthouse GUESTHOUSE €
(☎899 8616; www.fellskot.com; Fellskot 2 Farm; d/f without bathroom kr12,200/16,500; P) This sweet farmhouse 2.5km north of Reykholt, just off Rte 35, makes a cosy base, with three comfortable rooms with country views, and shared kitchen space. Guests are welcome to pat the horses.

Húsið B&B €
(☎486 8680; Bjarkarbraut 26; d without bathroom incl breakfast kr12,800; P) Friendly Húsið is a small guesthouse on a quiet residential cul-de-sac. There's a hot tub, barbecue and kitchen.

★**Buubble Hotel** TENTED CAMP €€
(www.buubble.com; Blaskogabyggd, near Reykholt; bubbles from kr27,900) This once-in-a-lifetime sleeping experience offers you a clear bubble tent in the countryside near the Golden Circle. Recline and watch the midnight sun or, in winter, look for the aurora borealis. A small, modern hut holds bathrooms and a kitchen. Each bubble can accommodate two adults and one child under 12. Prices are high, but the experience is unique.

★**Fagrilundur Guesthouse** B&B €€
(☎486 8701; www.fagrilundur.is; Skólabraut 1; d with/without bathroom incl breakfast kr23,000/17,000) A flower-pot-lined walk through the forest leads to a fairy-tale wooden cottage. Cosy rooms have patterned quilts and there's a shared porch. The attentive owners offer a warm welcome, celebrated breakfasts and loads of local advice.

Eating

There's a supermarket and restaurant in Reykholt, as well as occasional farm stands for produce.

Café Mika INTERNATIONAL €€
(☎896 6450; Skólabraut 4; mains kr1900-6000; ⊙noon-9pm) Café Mika is popular with locals for its huge menu, outdoor pizza oven, sandwiches and Icelandic mains.

Friðheimar CAFE
(☎897 1915; www.fridheimar.is; Rte 35; lunch kr2000; ⊙noon-4pm) This farm has big greenhouses from which staff sell produce and offer a good buffet lunch of tomato soup, cucumber salsa and fresh bread. It also has reservation-only horse shows for groups of 15 or more.

Getting There & Away

Strætó (www.bus.is) services:

- Bus 73 Selfoss–Flúðir–Reykholt–Laugarvatn–Selfoss (Selfoss–Reykholt kr2100, 45 minutes, two daily Monday to Friday, one daily Saturday).
- Bus 72 Selfoss–Flúðir–Reykholt–Laugarás–Selfoss (Selfoss–Reykholt kr2100, 45 minutes, two daily Monday to Friday).

Skálholt

An important religious centre, Skálholt was one of two bishoprics (the other was Hólar in the north) that ruled Iceland's souls from the 11th to the 18th centuries.

Unfortunately, the great cathedral that once stood at Skálholt was destroyed by a major earthquake in the 18th century. Today there's a modern Protestant theological centre with a **visitor centre** (☎486 8870; www.skalholt.is; museum admission kr500; ⊙9am-7pm Jun-Aug, reduced hours Sep-May), a turf-house re-creation of Þorlagsbúð, and a prim church with a museum in the basement containing the stone sarcophagus of Bishop Páll Jónsson (bishop from 1195 to 1211). According to *Páls Saga*, an Old Norse account of the bishop's life, the earth was wracked by storms and earthquakes when he died. Spookily, a huge storm broke at the exact moment that his coffin was reopened in 1956.

The centre also hosts summertime concerts.

Sleeping & Eating

The Skálholt centre has peaceful accommodation in rooms with private or shared bathroom, as well as camping and several cottages.

Skálholt has a restaurant, and the neighbouring village, Laugarás, is essentially a community of farms, some of which sell their produce on-site. Visit **Engi** (☎486 8913; www.engi.is; Laugarás; ⏰noon-6pm Jun-Aug) for greenhouse-grown fruit and vegetables, as well as cute souvenirs. It's marked at the entrance to Laugarás when arriving from Skálholt.

Sólheimar Eco-Village GUESTHOUSE €€
(☎422 6080; www.solheimar.is; Rte 354, Sólheimar; d with/without bathroom from kr18,600/10,600, apt kr24,000; P) Sólheimar Eco-Village is a collection of homes and greenhouses utilising ecologically sound practices. The two guesthouses in the village offer clean rooms with private or shared bathrooms and one apartment suitable for four people. There are shared kitchens and living areas, as well as a nice pool and hot tub. There is a cafe and shop in the village as well.

Find it 15km southwest of Skálholt, just south off of Rte 35 on Rte 354.

Getting There & Away

There is no public transport to Skálholt. Laugarás (3km from Skálholt) is served by **Strætó** (www.bus.is) buses 72 (two daily Monday to Friday) and 73 (two daily Monday to Friday, one daily Saturday) from Selfoss (kr2100, 40 minutes), Flúðir and Reykholt.

Kerið

Around 15.5km north of Selfoss on Rte 35, **Kerið** (adult/child kr400/free; ⏰8.30am-9pm Jun-Aug, daylight hours Sep-May) is a 6500-year-old explosion crater with vivid red and sienna earth and containing an ethereal green lake. Björk once performed a concert from a raft floating in the middle.

Flúðir

POP 450

The approaches to little agrarian Flúðir become increasingly dramatic, with interesting rock buttes rising from the rolling green plains. Flúðir is known throughout Iceland for its geothermal greenhouses that grow the majority of the country's mushrooms, and it's also a popular weekend getaway for Reykjavikers with private cottages. More recently it's a super stop not only for good food, but also for its beautifully refurbished hot springs.

Activities

★**Gamla Laugin** GEOTHERMAL POOL
(Secret Lagoon; ☎555 3351; www.secretlagoon.is; adult/child kr2800/free; ⏰10am-10pm May-Sep, noon-8pm Oct-Apr) Soak in this broad, calm geothermal pool, mist rising and ringed by natural rocks. The walking trail along the edge of this lovely hot spring passes the local river and a series of sizzling vents and geysers. Surrounding meadows fill with wildflowers in summer. Increasingly popular, the lagoon gets packed with tour bus crowds in mid-afternoon, so come earlier or later.

Sleeping

The local camping site along the Litla-Laxá river is usually crammed on summer weekends.

Grund – Guesthouse Flúðir GUESTHOUSE €€
(Gistiheimilið Flúðum; ☎565 9196; www.gistingfludir.is; d with/without bathroom incl breakfast kr25,000/20,000; P) This adorable guesthouse has five homey rooms filled with antiques, and a new wing of rooms opened in 2016 with private bathrooms and decks with mountain views. The popular restaurant prides itself on offering fresh local food.

Icelandair Hótel Flúðir HOTEL €€€
(☎486 6630; www.hotelfludir.is; Vesturbrún 1; d kr33,500; @) These two silver motel-style strands of rooms are comfortable, with en suite bathrooms and a restaurant, but it's pricey for what you get.

Eating

There's a farm stand at Melar on the western edge of town on Rte 311 and a **Samkaup-Strax** (⏰9am-10pm Mon-Sat, 10am-10pm Sun) supermarket.

★**Minilik Ethiopian Restaurant** ETHIOPIAN €€
(☎846 9798; www.minilik.is; mains kr2000-3000; ⏰noon-9pm Jun-Aug, 6-9pm Sep-May) Azeb cooks up traditional Ethiopian specialities in this welcoming, unpretentious spot. There are loads of vegetarian options, but also lamb dishes such as *awaze tibs* or chicken *(doro kitfo)*. As far as we know, this is the only Ethiopian restaurant in Iceland, and it should beckon all lovers of spice.

Grund Restaurant ICELANDIC €€
(☎565 9196; www.gistingfludir.is; mains kr2600-4900; ⊙11.30am-9pm Jun–mid-Aug) This popular restaurant serves fresh local food in a large, cheerful dining room.

ℹ Getting There & Away

Strætó (www.bus.is) buses 72 and 73 from Selfoss (kr2100, 40 to 60 minutes, two daily) serve Flúðir. Bus 76 links up to those routes to reach Árnes.

THE SOUTH

As you work your way east from Reykjavík, Rte 1 (the Ring Road) emerges into austere volcanic foothills punctuated by surreal steam vents, around Hveragerði, then swoops through a flat, wide coastal plain, full of verdant horse farms and greenhouses, before the landscape suddenly begins to grow wonderfully jagged, after Hella and Hvolsvöllur. Mountains thrust upwards on the inland side, some of them volcanoes wreathed by mist (Eyjafjallajökull, site of the 2010 eruption), and the first of the awesome glaciers appears, as enormous rivers such as the Þjórsá cut their way to the black-sand beaches rimming the Atlantic.

Throughout the region, roads pierce deep inland, to realms of lush waterfall-doused valleys such as Þjórsárdalur and Fljótshlíð, and awe-inspiring volcanoes such as Hekla. Two of the most renowned inland spots are Landmannalaugar, where vibrantly coloured rhyolite peaks meet bubbling hot springs; and Þórsmörk, a forested valley tucked safely away from the brutal northern elements under a series of wind-foiling ice caps. They are linked by the famous Laugavegurinn hike, Iceland's most popular trek. Though these areas lie inland on roads that are sometimes impassable by standard vehicles, most visitors access them on tours or amphibious buses from the southern Ring Road. Þórsmörk, one of Iceland's most popular hiking destinations, can be done as a day trip.

Public transport (and traffic) is solid along the Ring Road, which is studded with interesting settlements: Hveragerði, famous for its geothermal fields and hot springs; Skógar, the leaping-off point for Þórsmörk; and Vík, surrounded by glaciers, vertiginous cliffs and black-sand beaches. South of the Ring Road the tiny fishing villages of Stokkseyri and Eyrarbakki feel refreshingly local. The south coast is also filled with family farms, some rich with Saga heritage, offering lovely rural guesthouses.

ℹ SLEEPING IN THE SOUTH

The south is the most developed region outside of Reykjavík, with lodging in all of the towns along the Ring Road, plus many farms with guesthouses. Increasingly, hotels are staying open year-round.

It is absolutely essential to book well ahead for summer and holidays, especially in the far south, as visitor numbers often exceed beds.

Camping is easy, with municipal campgrounds in each town. Wild camping is discouraged (and illegal for campervans).

Hveragerði & Around

POP 2500

The grid of boxy buildings that is Hveragerði (www.hveragerdi.is) emerge from other-worldly lava fields and hills pierced, surreally, by natural steaming vents. You're not here for the architecture, you're here for Hveragerði's highly active geothermal field, which heats hundreds of greenhouses. Nationally, the town is famous for its horticultural college and naturopathic clinic. There are also some fantastic hikes in the area, though routes are sometimes overly packed in summer.

Pick up the handy *Hveragerði, The Capital of Hot Springs and Flowers* map, which details all of the sights, activities and dining options in the area.

⊙ Sights

★**Geothermal Park** HOT SPRINGS
(Hveragarðurinn; ☎483 4601; Hveramörk 13; adult/child kr300/free; ⊙9am-6pm Mon-Sat, 10am-4pm Sun Jun-Aug, reduced hours Apr, May & Sep, closed Oct-Mar) The geothermal park Hverasvæðið, in the centre of town, has mud pots and steaming pools where visitors can dip their feet (but no more). You can book ahead for a guided walk to learn about the area's unique geology and greenhouse power. Or they'll give you an egg and apparatus (kr100) for boiling it in the steaming vents. There's also a small cafe with geothermally baked bread.

Hveragerði

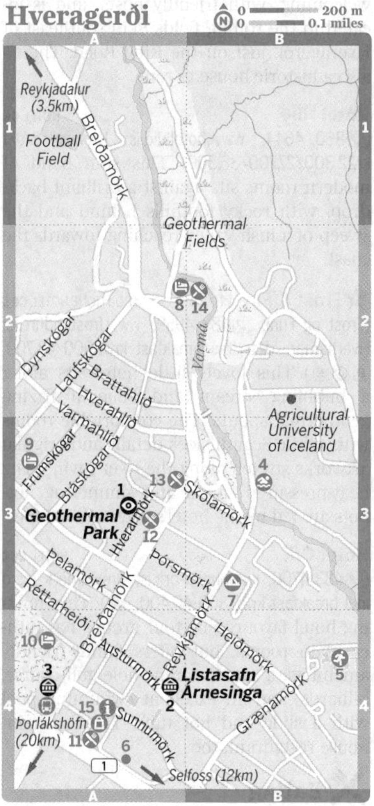

Hveragerði

Top Sights

1 Geothermal Park

2 Listasafn Árnesinga

Sights

3 Hveragerði Stone & Geology Exhibition A4

Activities, Courses & Tours

4 Geothermal Swimming Pool B3

5 HNLFÍ Health Clinic & Spa B4

6 Iceland Activities A4

Sleeping

7 Campsite B3

8 Frost & Fire Hotel A2

9 Gistiheimilið Frumskógar A3

10 Hótel Örk A4

Eating

11 Almar A4

12 Kjöt og Kúnst A3

13 Skyrgerðin A3

14 Varmá B2

Shopping

15 Vínbúðin A4

★ **Listasafn Árnesinga** ART MUSEUM
(☎483 1727; www.listasafnarnesinga.is; Austurmörk 21; ⏱noon-6pm May-Sep, noon-6pm Thu-Sun Oct–mid-Dec & mid-Jan–Apr) FREE This airy modern-art gallery puts on great exhibitions and also has a fine cafe.

Hveragerði Stone & Geology Exhibition MUSEUM
(Ljósbrá Stone Exhibition; www.ljosbra.is; Breiðamörk 1b; adult/child kr1000/free; ⏱8am-8pm Jun-Aug, 8am-5pm Mon-Fri, 10am-5pm Sat & Sun Sep-May) One of Iceland's largest private collections of stones, crystals and geological artefacts opened in 2016 in the same building as the N1 petrol station.

Hellisheiði Geothermal Power Plant EXHIBITION
(☎412 5800; www.onpower.is; adult/child kr950/free; ⏱9am-5pm) Seventeen kilometres west of Hveragerði, just north of the Ring Road, you'll see the sleek shell of Hellisheiði Geothermal Power Plant, one of the few that provide 30% of Iceland's electricity. ON Power, which operates the plant, has a multimedia exhibition laying out the details of harnessing the earth's hot-water power.

Raufarhólshellir LAVA TUBE
FREE This 11th-century lava tube is 1360m long (Iceland's third largest), and contains wonderful lava columns. You'll need a helmet, torch (flashlight) and sturdy boots, but even so the going is treacherous from earlier cave-ins. In winter cold air is funnelled down and trapped inside, producing amazing ice formations. If in doubt, go with a local tour operator.

You'll find the tube southwest of Hveragerði off Rte 39, which passes right over it; park on the north side.

Activities

★ **Reykjadalur** GEOTHERMAL POOL
(Hot River Valley) Reykjadalur is a delightful geothermal valley where there's a hot river you can bathe in; bring your swimsuit. There are maps at the tourist office to find the trail; from the trailhead car park, it's a 3km hike through fields of sulphur-belching plains. Stick to marked paths, lest you melt your shoes, and leave no rubbish.

..FÍ Health Clinic & Spa SPA
(..eilsustofnun Náttúrulækningafélags Íslands; ☎483 0300; www.heilsustofnun.is; Grænumörk 10; ⊙by appointment) Iceland's most famous clinic treats both prescription-bearing patients and visitors seeking relaxing massages (kr7500 to kr12,000), deep-heat mud baths (kr6500) and more. They offer many packages and have excellent facilities, including indoor and outdoor pools, hot-pots, a sauna, a steam bath and modest accommodation (apartments kr48,000).

Geothermal Swimming Pool SWIMMING
(☎483 4113; Laugaskarði; adult/child kr700/300; ⊙6.45am-9.15pm Mon-Fri, 10am-5.15pm Sat & Sun Jun-Aug, reduced hours Sep-May) Hveragerði's open-air geothermal swimming pool, beside the Varmá river just north of town, is among Iceland's favourites. Goodies include a massaging hot-pot and a steam room built directly over a natural hot spring.

Tours

Iceland Activities ADVENTURE TOUR
(☎777 6263; www.icelandactivities.is; Mánamörk 3-5; ⊙8am-5pm Mon-Fri, 9am-4pm Sat) This family-run adventure company specialises in biking, surfing and hiking tours (from kr15,600) in the Southwest.

Sólhestar HORSE RIDING
(☎892 3066; www.solhestar.is; Borgargerði, Ölfus) Various half-day and full-day riding tours through the volcanic wilds or down on the beach (one-/three-hour tours from kr8000/11,000). It's 8km south of Hveragerði on the Ring Road; go 500m north on Rte 374.

Sleeping

Gistiheimilið Frumskógar GUESTHOUSE €
(☎896 2780; www.frumskogar.is; Frumskógar 3; d/apt without bathroom incl breakfast from kr16,200/21,000) This cosy apartment-style guesthouse accommodation also boasts a hot-pot and steam bath.

Campsite CAMPGROUND €
(hveracamping@gmail.com; Reykjamörk 1; sites per adult/child kr1400/free) This campsite lies just east of the centre, and has toilets, showers, a cooking area and a laundry.

Hjarðarból Guesthouse GUESTHOUSE €€
(☎567 0045; www.hjardarbol.is; d/q kr18,500/24,500, d without bathroom kr11,000; P) This buttercup-yellow set of cottages and guesthouse buildings is pastoral and welcoming, with friendly hosts, and is located in the rolling fields 8km southeast of Hveragerði, just off the Ring Road. There's also a historic house to rent.

Hótel Hlíð HOTEL €€
(☎860 4644; www.hotelhlid.is; Krókur; s/d/f kr22,300/27,700/36,300) This slim band of modern rooms sits against a brilliant backdrop, with rocky foothills behind and the sweep of a lush valley reaching towards the coast.

★ **Frost & Fire Hotel** BOUTIQUE HOTEL €€€
(Frost og Funi; ☎483 4959; www.frostandfire.is; Hverhamar; d/tr incl breakfast kr31,000/42,700; P@≋) This lovely little hotel sits along a bubbling stream and beneath fizzing geothermal spouts. The comfortable rooms with subtle Scandi-sleek details and original artworks stretch along the river ravine. The heat-pressured sauna and simmering hot-pots are fed by the hotel's private borehole.

Hótel Örk HOTEL €€€
(☎483 4700; www.hotel-ork.is; Breiðamörk 1c; d incl breakfast kr29,800-40,400; @) This hulking hotel favoured by tour groups has rather plain rooms, but offers family-friendly amenities: a sauna, a nine-hole golf course, billiards, and an excellent swimming pool with a slide and hot tubs. There's an in-house restaurant, too.

Eating

The town has several busy bakeries, fast-food joints and supermarkets. Some restaurants offer bread cooked using geothermal heat.

★ **Almar** BAKERY €
(Sunnumörk 2; soup kr950; ⊙7am-6pm Mon-Fri, 8am-5pm Sat, 9am-5pm Sun) A large, bustling bakery that also serves sandwiches and soup of the day with fresh bread. In the complex with the tourist office.

Skyrgerðin CAFE €€
(☎481 1010; Breiðamörk 25; mains kr2000-2500; ⊙11am-10pm Mon-Thu, to 11pm Fri-Sun) This chilled-out new cafe incorporates rough wood furniture, antiques and vintage photos to create an interesting environment for dining on creative meals crafted from fresh Icelandic ingredients. The menu ranges from fresh *skyr*-based smoothies and drinks to sliders, lasagne and fish. There are also pretty little rooms (doubles with/without bathrooms from kr35,000/24,500) upstairs.

Kjöt og Kúnst INTERNATIONAL €€
(☎483 5010; www.kjotogkunst.com; Breiðamörk 21; mains kr2200-4000; ⏰noon-9pm Mon-Sat Jun-Aug, reduced hours Sep-May) On the touristy side, but there are Icelandic dishes (soup, fish and lamb) in among the sandwiches and pizzas. Loads of cakes and geothermal bread, too.

★**Varmá** ICELANDIC €€€
(☎483 4959; www.frostogfuni.is; Hverhamar; mains kr4300-6000; ⏰8am-10pm; P) At the Frost & Fire Hotel, this wonderfully scenic restaurant boasts floor-to-ceiling windows looking over the stream and gorge. Dishes are Icelandic, using fresh, local ingredients and herbs and often geothermal cooking techniques. Book ahead in summer.

Entertainment

Icelandic Horse Park Fákasel LIVE PERFORMANCE
(☎483 5050; www.icelandichorsepark.com; Ingolfshvoll, Ölfus) Performances at Fákasel combine people, horses and multimedia lights and music. Quick daytime shows start at kr1800, more elaborate 45-minute evening shows with a backstage visit cost kr4800, and there's an occasional Northern Lights show (kr2000). There are also combo tours including riding or meals (restaurant open 10am to 10pm), and Reykjavík pick-up.

Shopping

Vínbúðin ALCOHOL
(☎481 3932; Sunnumörk 2; ⏰11am-6pm Mon-Thu, to 7pm Fri, to 4pm Sat) National liquor chain.

Getting There & Away

The **bus stop** is at the petrol stations on the main road into town (check whether your stop is the Shell or N1).

Strætó (www.bus.is) services:

- Buses 51 & 52 Reykjavík–Vík/Höfn & Reykjavík–Landeyjahöfn (Reykjavík–Hveragerði kr1260, 35 minutes, 11 daily Monday to Friday, eight daily Saturday and Sunday).

Sterna (www.sterna.is) services:

- Bus 12/12A Reykjavík–Höfn stops in Hveragerði.

Reykjavík Excursions (www.re.is) services:

- Buses 9/9A Reykjavík–Þórsmörk, 11/11a Reykjavík–Landmannalaugar, 17/17a Reykjavík–Mývatn, 18 Reykjavík–Álftavatn–Emstrur, 20/20a Reykjavík–Skaftafell, 21/21a Reykjavík–Vík and 610/610a Reykjavík–Kjölur–Akureyri all stop in Hveragerði.

SOUTH ICELAND VISITOR CENTRE

Hveragerði has the regional tourist office for the entire south: The **Tourist Information Centre** (Upplýsingamiðstöð Suðurlands; ☎483 4601; www.southiceland.is; Sunnumörk 2-4; ⏰8.30am-6pm Mon-Fri, 9am-3pm Sat, to 1pm Sun Jun-Aug, reduced hours Sep-May) is *the* spot to stock up on free subregional maps and brochures. It shares space with the post office and a small exhibit about the earthquake that ripped through in 2008; there's a freaky earthquake simulator (kr300).

Trex (www.trex.is) services:

- Buses T21 Reykjavík–Landmannalaugar and T11 Reykjavík–Þórsmörk can stop with pre-booking.

Þorlákshöfn

In the past, most people came to the fishing town of Þorlákshöfn, 20km south of Hveragerði, to catch the ferry to the Vestmannaeyjar. Now the ferry departs from Landeyjahöfn on the southwest coast near Hvolsvöllur. When it's stormy, the ferry does leave from here, though. There's little other reason to come.

Þorlákshöfn is served by Strætó bus 74 from Selfoss (kr1260, 45 minutes, three daily Monday to Friday).

Eyrarbakki

POP 520

It's hard to believe, but tiny Eyrarbakki was Iceland's main port and a thriving trading town well into the 20th century. Today the seaside town is known for its prison – the largest in Iceland – and its good museums and nearby nature reserve.

Sights

★**Flói Nature Reserve** NATURE RESERVE
Birdwatchers should head 3km northwest of Eyrarbakki to Flói Nature Reserve, an important estuary and marshland on the eastern bank of the Ölfusá. It's visited by many wetland birds (common species include red-throated divers and various kinds of ducks and geese) most present during nesting season (May to July). There's a 2km

circular hiking trail through the marshes. For more information, contact the **Icelandic Society for the Protection of Birds** (☎562 0477; www.fuglavernd.is).

★**Húsið á Eyrarbakka** MUSEUM
(House at Eyrarbakki; ☎483 1504; www.husid.com; Hafnarbrú 3; adult/child incl Sjöminjasafnið á Eyrarbakka kr1000/free; ⏲11am-6pm mid-May–mid-Sep) One of Iceland's oldest houses, built by Danish traders in 1765, Húsið á Eyrarbakka has glass display cabinets explaining the town's history, interesting rooms restored with original furniture, and a stuffed bird collection. Keep an eye out for Ólöf Sveinsdóttir's shawl, hat and cuffs, knitted from her own hair.

Sjöminjasafnið á Eyrarbakka MUSEUM
(☎483 1082; Túngata 59; adult/child incl Húsið á Eyrarbakka kr100/free; ⏲11am-6pm May-Sep) Just behind Húsið á Eyrarbakka, this small maritime museum has displays on the local fishing community. Its main exhibit is the beautiful 12-oared fishing boat, *Farsæll*.

Sleeping & Eating

Eyrarbakki is a fishing port, and the restaurants do a great job with seafood.

Bakki Hostel & Apartments HOSTEL, APARTMENTS €
(☎788 8200; www.bakkihostel.is; Eyrargata 51-53; dm/studio kr5300/24,000; P) This broad building offers 6-bed dorms that share a living area and kitchen, and studio or one-bedroom self-catering apartments, some with sea views.

★**Sea Side Cottages** COTTAGE €€
(☎898 1197; www.seasidecottages.is; Eyrargata 37a; cottages from kr22,800) Living up to their name, these two quaint cottages are just metres away from the pounding Atlantic, behind a protective berm. Each is tricked out in fine fashion, with thoughtful antiques, flat-screen TVs, fully equipped kitchens and outdoor seating.

★**Rauða Húsið** SEAFOOD €€
(☎483 3330; www.raudahusid.is; Búðarstígur 4; mains kr3000-6000; ⏲11.30am-10pm Jun-Aug, reduced hours Sep-May) This elegant white-linen restaurant fills a red house (hence the name), and has cheery staff and great fresh seafood, though the menu is broad, with plenty to choose from.

★**Hafið Bláa** SEAFOOD €€
(☎483 1000; www.hafidblaa.is; Óseyri; mains kr2500-6000; ⏲11am-9pm Jun-Aug, reduced hours Sep-May) Three kilometres west of Eyrarbakki on Rte 34, this seafood restaurant sits on the water's edge in an ovoid building, with a beautiful arcing-wood interior. Even if you don't get a table overlooking the ocean, the sweeping estuary views on the opposite side are equally impressive. The menu offers a small range of seafood and lamb.

Getting There & Away

Strætó (www.bus.is) services:

- Bus 74 Selfoss–Stokkseyri–Eyrarbakki–Þorlákshöfn (kr420, 30 minutes, three daily Monday to Friday).
- Bus 75 Selfoss–Eyrarbakki (kr420, 30 minutes, six daily Monday to Friday, four Saturday).

Stokkseyri

POP 460

Stokkseyri can seem like Eyrarbakki's twin to the east, but it actually quietly asserts its own unique character. Although it, too, is a small fishing village, it has a fun dose of quirky sites and summer art galleries that make it an entertaining high-season stop.

Sights & Activities

Veiðisafnið MUSEUM
(☎483 1558; www.hunting.is; Eyrarbraut 49; adult/child kr1500/750; ⏲11am-6pm Apr-Sep, 11am-6pm Sat & Sun Feb, Mar, Oct & Nov) You may be snagged by the roadside sign: 'Have you seen a giraffe today?' Here a local hunter displays his collection of prey from all around the world. It's very professionally done, with dozens of well-lit taxidermied animals accompanied by info on where they were killed and how. We're talking zebras, boars and two full-sized lions, among many others (yes, a giraffe). A chat with the friendly owner brings fascinating stories, but this museum plainly won't appeal to everyone.

Draugasetrið EXHIBITION
(Ghost Centre; ☎483 1202; www.draugasetrid.is; Hafnargata 9; adult/child kr2000/1000, incl Icelandic Wonders kr3500/1500; ⏲1-6pm Jun-Aug) Draugasetrið, on the top floor of a huge maroon-and-black warehouse in the centre, is a veritable haunted house run by a gaggle of blood-thirsty teens. A 50-minute iPod guide (in many languages) recites 24 spooky

stories in a series of dry-ice-filled stations. Not recommended for small fry. There's a water-view cafe, too. On the other side of the building, the accompanying **Icelandic Wonders** (☎483 1202; www.icelandicwonders.com; adult/child kr1500/990; ⌚10am-6pm Mon-Fri, noon-6pm Sat & Sun Jun-Aug) involves trolls, elves and Northern Lights (so is a better bet for youngsters).

Orgelsmiðjan ORGAN WORKSHOP
(☎566 8130; www.orgel.is; Hafnargata 9; adult/child kr700/free; ⌚10am-5pm Mon-Fri, by appointment Sat & Sun) Iceland's only organ builder, Björgvin Tómasson, built a gamelan-celesta instrument for Björk, and allows visitors to his workshop, with exhibits and occasional concerts. Find it on the seashore side of Draugasetrið's warehouse.

Sundlaug Stokkseyrar SWIMMING
(☎480 3260; adult/child kr900/150; ⌚1-9pm Mon-Fri, 10am-5pm Sat & Sun Jun–mid-Aug, reduced hours mid-Aug–May) The town's swimming pool and hot-pots.

Tours

Kajakferðir Stokkseyri KAYAKING TOUR
(☎868 9046; www.kajak.is; Heiðarbrún 24; ⌚Apr-Oct) Explore the nearby lagoon by kayak or get out on the ocean (tours kr4950 to kr9600). Based at the town pool, Sundlaug Stokkseyrar.

Sleeping & Eating

For cheap meals, there's a grill at the Shell petrol station.

Art Hostel HOSTEL, APARTMENTS €
(☎854 4510; www.arthostel.is; Hafnargata 9; dm kr4500, d with/without bathroom kr20,000/14,000) On the 2nd floor of the central culture complex and warehouse, above mosaic, painting and photography galleries, you'll find a 15-person dorm, small twins, and larger studios with microwaves and bathrooms. There's a cafe-bar, too (open 1pm to 5pm June to August).

Kvöldstjarnan GUESTHOUSE €€
(Evening Star; ☎483 1800; www.kvoldstjarnan.is; Stjörnusteinum 7; d without bathroom incl breakfast kr16,500, 3-bedroom apt kr31,400) The five bright, white rooms here come with washbasins and fluffy feathery duvets. There's a small lounge area, a hot-pot, a barbecue and a sparkling kitchen. There's also an apartment.

Freyja B&B B&B €€
(☎567 1060; www.bbfreyja.com; Blomsturvellir 2; s/d without bathroom incl breakfast kr11,700/15,300; ⌚May-Sep) Tina and Tofi welcome guests to an immaculate ranch house in the village of Stokkseyri. The only downside is there's no shared kitchen.

★**Við Fjöruborðið** SEAFOOD €€
(☎483 1550; www.fjorubordid.is; Eyrabraut 3a; mains kr3200-6000; ⌚noon-9pm Jun-Aug, 5-9pm Sep-May) This large seafood restaurant sits on the shore, just behind the ocean berm, and is known for making some of the best lobster bisque in Iceland. Slurp your bisque amid chatting locals, glass fishing buoys and marine memorabilia. Reserve for dinner.

Getting There & Away

Strætó (www.bus.is) services:
- Bus 74 Selfoss–Stokkseyri–Eyrarbakki–Þorlákshöfn (kr420, 20 minutes, three daily Monday to Friday).
- Bus 75 Selfoss–Eyrarbakki (kr420, 20 minutes, six daily Monday to Friday, four Saturday).

Flóahreppur

For being so close to the most travelled portion of the Ring Road, it's a wonder you can feel like you've fallen into a rural region of rolling pastures leading to the ocean. Bordered by the Ring Road in the north, Rte 34 in the west, the Þjórsá river in the east, and the Atlantic Ocean in the south, this small agricultural area has a few laid-back farms with accommodation.

Sleeping & Eating

Head to Selfoss or Stokkseyri for food – Flóahreppur is quite rural.

★**Julia's Guesthouse** B&B €
(☎856 4788; www.julias-guesthouse.com; Hnaus; d/tr without bathroom incl breakfast kr10,400/12,200; P) Friendly Julia from Switzerland runs this charming guesthouse in the countryside to perfection. A menagerie including birds, cats and a bunny fill this immaculate house with life, and Julia and her husband Mike have decorated with great love, plus they create a sumptuous homemade breakfast. Some rooms have wonderful views, and the triple room has its own toilet. Cash only.

Gaulverjaskóli HI Hostel HOSTEL €
(☎551 0654; www.south-hostel.is; Gaulverjaskóli; sites per person kr1000, dm/s/d/f without bathroom kr4700/7100/13,500/25,500; ⊙Feb-Oct; P) Friendly owners have poured their hearts into renovating this former school; today it's a clean, quiet hostel and campground with a welcoming common space in the attic and a spacious kitchen. It's based in a tiny hamlet marooned in a vast expanse of flat agricultural land, 9km from Stokkseyri along the coastal road leading back towards Selfoss. HI members get a kr700 discount.

Vatnsholt GUESTHOUSE €€
(☎482 4829; www.hotelvatnsholt.is; Vatnsholti 2; d with/without bathroom kr23,700/19,500, cottages from kr24,400; ⊙mid-Feb–mid-Dec; @) A wonderful place if you have the kids in tow, Vatnsholt is located about 16km southeast of Selfoss, just 8km off the Ring Road. Here you'll find over 30 sun-filled bedrooms and cottages scattered throughout a sweeping farmstead with views to Eyjafjallajökull, Hekla and Vestmannaeyjar. It does buffet meals, too.

Bike rentals, a restaurant, a menagerie of animals (including Elvis the dancing goat) and an elaborate playground could have you staying longer than you expect.

Selfoss

POP 6940

Selfoss is the largest town in southern Iceland, an important centre for getting business done, and relatively ugly unless you get into the neighbourhoods. Iceland's Ring Road is its main street, so the primary reason to stop is to transfer buses or to load up on groceries.

Sights & Activities

Bobby Fischer Center MUSEUM
(☎894 1275; www.fischersetur.is; Austurvegur 21; adult/child kr1000/free; ⊙1-4pm mid-May–mid-Sep) This little museum houses the memorabilia of chess champion Bobby Fischer, who is buried 2km northeast in Laugardælirkirkja's cemetery.

Sundhöll Selfoss GEOTHERMAL POOL, HOT-POT
(☎480 1960; Tryggvagata 15; adult/child kr900/150; ⊙6.30am-9.30pm Mon-Fri, 9am-7pm Sat & Sun) Selfoss has a fine geothermal swimming pool, with hot-pots, water slides and a kids' play pool.

Tours

Iceland South Coast Travel TOURS
(☎777 0705; www.isct.is) Bundle of tours include the south coast (from kr39,000), Golden Circle, Vestmannaeyjar or Jökulsárlón. Based in Selfoss, but can do Reykjavík and various south-coast pick-ups.

Sleeping

There are loads of accommodation options in and around Selfoss, so it can be a convenient base for taking day trips around the south.

★**Geirakot** GUESTHOUSE €
(☎482 1020; geirakot@simnet.is; Geirakot farm; s/d without bathroom incl breakfast kr8400/14,000; ⊙Feb-Oct) Sweet Geirakot is a nice alternative to Selfoss town. A friendly family on a dairy farm has renovated the grandparents' small farmhouse into a homey guesthouse. Breakfast is lovely, local and served on china. Sleeping-bag space is kr8300. Book through Icelandic Farm Holidays (www.farmholidays.is).

Selfoss HI Hostel HOSTEL €
(☎482 1600; www.hostel.is; Austurvegur 28; dm/s/d without bathroom kr5400/10,700/14,600) There's plenty of common space and comfortable lounge chairs, plus a hot tub. HI members get a kr700 discount.

Gesthús CAMPGROUND, GUESTHOUSE €€
(☎482 3585; www.gesthus.is; Engjavegur 56; sites per person kr1400, d/tr kr16,200/19,400; P) At this friendly place by the park, choose between camping, doubles in two-room cabins with shared kitchen and bathroom, or a full summer house with kitchenette and TV. Hot-pots cost kr300 for campers, but are free for other guests.

★**Icelandic Cottages** COTTAGES €€€
(☎898 0728; www.icelandiccottages.is; Hraunmörk; cottage kr33,000) These ubercool modern cottages dot the lava fields 18km east of Selfoss, just north of the Ring Road on Rte 30. They're beautifully kitted out, have terraces and barbecues, and sleep up to six people. Two-night minimum.

★**Bella Apartments & Rooms** APARTMENT €€€
(☎859 6162; www.bellaguesthouse.is; Austurvegur 33-35; d/apt kr29,200/46,300) This brand-new property on the main street combines comfortable double rooms and luxury two-bedroom apartments, complete with bal-

Selfoss

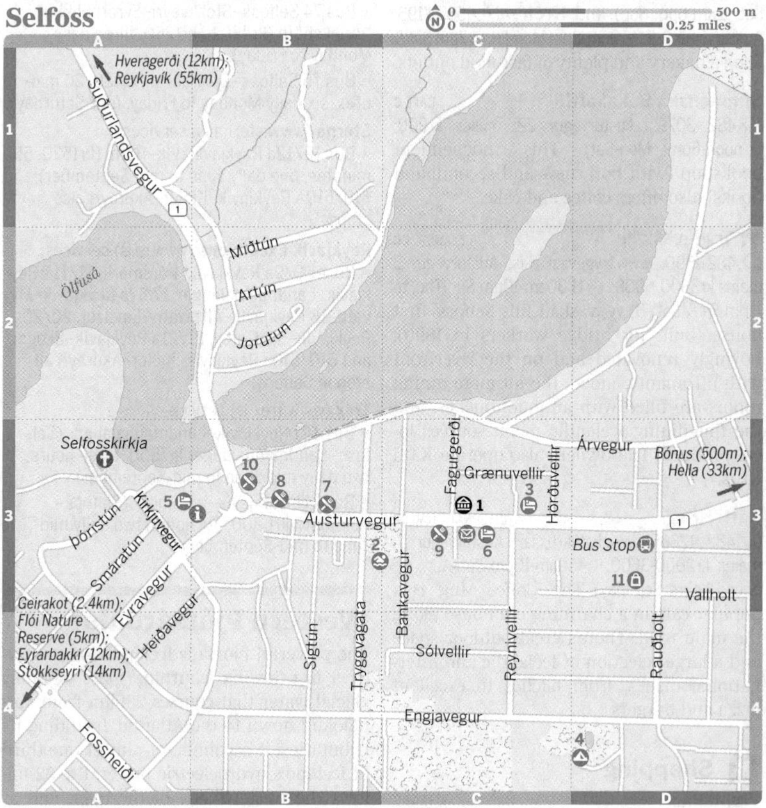

Selfoss

Sights

1 Bobby Fischer Center C3

Activities, Courses & Tours

2 Sundhöll Selfoss B3

Sleeping

3 Bella Apartments & Rooms C3
4 Gesthús D4
5 Hótel Selfoss A3
6 Selfoss HI Hostel C3

Eating

7 Kaffi Krús B3
8 Krónan B3
9 Sunnlenska Bókakaffið C3
10 Tryggvaskáli B3

Shopping

11 Vínbúðin D3

conies and furnished kitchens. The apartments can sleep up to seven people, and there are washer/dryer facilities for all.

Hótel Selfoss HOTEL €€€
(☎480 2500; www.hotelselfoss.is; Eyravegur 2; s/d from kr30,000/42,300; @) This 99-room behemoth near the bridge looks horrendous from the outside, but it has a calm interior with snappy business-style rooms and great facilities, including a large spa and a good in-house restaurant. Get a room overlooking the lovely river, not the dire car park.

Eating

Selfoss is the best place in the south to stock up on groceries before setting off for remote areas. It has most major supermarkets, including **Bónus** (☎481 3710; Larsenstræti 5; ⏰11am-6.30pm Mon-Thu, 10am-7.30pm Fri, to 6pm

Sat, 11am-6pm Sun) and **Krónan** (☎585 7195; Austurvegur 3-5; ⏱9am-8pm Mon-Fri, to 7pm Sat & Sun), a bakery and plenty of fast-food outlets.

Sunnlenska Bókakaffið CAFE €
(☎482 3079; Austurvegur 22; cakes kr900; ⏱noon-6pm Mon-Sat) This independent bookshop (with both new and secondhand books) also offers coffee and cake.

★ **Tryggvaskáli** ICELANDIC €€
(☎482 1390; www.tryggvaskali.is; Austurvegur 1; mains kr3300-6000; ⏱11.30am-10pm Sun-Thu, to 11pm Fri & Sat) Tryggvaskáli fills Selfoss' first house (built for bridge workers in 1890). Lovingly renovated and on the riverfront with a romantic mood, the intimate dining rooms are filled with antique touches, and the fine-dining Icelandic menu sources local produce. The owners also operate Kaffi Krús.

Kaffi Krús INTERNATIONAL €€
(☎482 1266; www.kaffikrus.is; Austurvegur 7; mains kr2000-3600; ⏱10am-10pm Jun-Aug, reduced hours Sep-May) The 'Coffee Mug' is a popular cafe in a charming old house along the main road. There's great outdoor space and a large selection of Icelandic and international dishes, from nachos to excellent pizza and burgers.

Shopping

Vínbúðin ALCOHOL
(☎482 2011; Vallholt 19; ⏱11am-6pm Mon-Thu, to 7pm Fri, to 4pm Sat) National liquor chain.

Information

Árborg Tourist Information Centre (☎480 1990; http://tourinfo.arborg.is; Eyravegur 2; ⏱9am-4pm Mon-Fri May-Aug) In the same building as **Hótel Selfoss** (p127); the tourist office in Hveragerði is better.

Getting There & Away

Most buses between Reykjavík and Höfn, Skaftafell, Fjallabak, Þórsmörk, Flúðir, Gullfoss, Laugarvatn and Vík stop at the **N1 station** in Selfoss.

Strætó (www.bus.is) services:

- Buses 51 & 52 Reykjavík–Vík/Höfn & Reykjavík–Landeyjahöfn (kr1680, 50 minutes, 11 daily Monday to Friday, eight daily Saturday and Sunday).
- Buses 72 & 73 Selfoss–Flúðir (kr2100, 40 to 60 minutes, two daily).
- Bus 74 Selfoss–Stokkseyri–Eyrarbakki–Þorlákshöfn (kr420 to kr1260, three daily Monday to Friday).
- Bus 75 Selfoss–Eyrarbakki (kr420, 20 minutes, six daily Monday to Friday, four Saturday).

Sterna (www.sterna.is) services:

- Bus 12/12a Reykjavík–Vík–Höfn, (kr1520, 55 minutes, one daily June to mid-September); 610/610A Reykjavík–Kjölur–Akureyri also stops.

Reykjavík Excursions (www.re.is) services:

- Buses 9/9a Reykjavík–Þórsmörk, 11/11A Reykjavík–Landmannalaugar, 17/17a Reykjavík–Mývatn, 18 Reykjavík–Álftavatn–Emstrur, 20/20a Reykjavík–Skaftafell, 21/21a Reykjavík–Skógar and 610/610a Reykjavík–Kjölur–Akureyri all stop in Selfoss.

Trex (www.trex.is) services:

- Bus T21 Reykjavík–Landmannalaugar (Selfoss–Landmannalaugar kr7500, three hours, two daily mid-June to mid-September).
- Bus T11 Reykjavík–Þórsmörk (Selfoss–Þórsmörk kr6300, 3¼ hours, two daily mid-June to mid-September).

Western Þjórsárdalur

The powerful Þjórsá is Iceland's longest river, a fast-flowing, churning mass of milky glacial water that courses 230km from Vatnajökull down to the Atlantic. Including its tributaries, it accounts for almost one-third of Iceland's hydroelectric power. Rte 32 follows the western side of the river, and as it moves upstream and into the highlands you'll traverse broad plains, split by the enormous river, that lead to volcanic fields and finally the foothills of the mountains beyond. It is a relatively untouristed area, with Viking ruins, hidden waterfalls and river landscapes that feel prehistoric.

Rte 32 is one of the preferred ways to reach Landmannalaugar (the starting point for the famous Laugavegurinn hike) by vehicle (via the 4WD-only Rte F26). It's also possible (if you don't have a 4WD) to make a day's loop up this side of the valley, cross over the river after the Búrfell Hydroelectric Plant and return down the other side of the valley to Hella on Rte 26.

There are also horse riding companies peppering the journey along Rte 32.

There is no public transport beyond Árnes. Bring your own wheels or come with a local tour operator.

Árnes

Stop in the tiny settlement of Árnes, near the junction of Rtes 30 and 32, where a large white building houses the informative **Þjórsárstofa** (Þjórsá Visitor Centre; ☎486 6115; www.thjorsarstofa.is; ⏲10am-6pm Jun-Aug) FREE. It has an excellent 10-minute surround-sound-style film about the river valley and what you will see further along, and a film about the aurora borealis, as well as multimedia displays and a good restaurant.

Tours

Núphestar HORSE RIDING
(☎852 5930; www.nupshestar.is; Breiðanes) This friendly, family-run horse farm offers short rides (one-/two-hour ride kr6000/8500) and multiday tours. It's near the junction of Rtes 30 and 32.

Steinsholt HORSE RIDING
(☎486 6069; www.steinsholt.is; Steinsholt II) This tidy horse farm offers multiday riding trips, hourly tours (one-/two-hour rides kr6500/11,000) and cosy accommodation (doubles with/without bathroom including breakfast kr15,400/18,700). Find it at the end of Rte 326, just north of Árnes.

Sleeping & Eating

Árnes HI Hostel HOSTEL €
(☎486 6048; www.hostel.is; dm kr4750; ⏲Apr-Sep) This hostel isn't the cosiest place on earth, but it has serviceable twin rooms and dorm space, a guest kitchen, and a small pool nearby (kr1000; open June to August).

Guesthouse Denami FARMSTAY €€
(☎698 7090; www.tolt.nu/denami; d with/without bathroom incl breakfast kr19,500/14,000) Stay on a lovely family-run horse farm in the lush rolling countryside on the north edge of Árnes. Rooms are simple but tidy, and views of the nearby volcanoes can be magnificent.

Fosshotel Hekla HOTEL €€
(☎486 5540; www.hotelhekla.is; Brjánsstaðir; d/q incl breakfast from kr29,000/32,000; @) As you head up the Þjórsá valley, this hotel complex sits just off Rte 30, 17km before Árnes. Large, modern doubles have flat-screen TVs; excellent family rooms are bigger still. The lounge feels like a warm library, and the restaurant serves up good Icelandic staples using local produce. A hot-pot and sauna add to the fun.

WORTH A TRIP

TRAUSTHOLTSHÓLMI PRIVATE ISLAND

Go with Hákon to check his salmon fishing nets and explore his grass-covered **private island** (☎699 4256; www.thh.is; tour per person kr22,000; ⏲by reservation) in the Þjórsá river before settling down to a dinner of fresh-caught fish and island-grown herbs, and perhaps a campfire. You can book to stay over in his yurt, and he may have a guesthouse in 2017. Check online for current offerings.

Þjórsárstofa Restaurant ICELANDIC €€
(Matstofan; ☎664 6555; www.arnesferdamenn.is; mains kr1800-3200; ⏲10am-9pm Jun-Aug, to 7pm Sep-May) The Þjórsárstofa has a good restaurant with an ever-changing menu of regional cuisine and local beers. It also operates the nearby campground (sites per adult/child kr1300/free).

Getting There & Away

From the junction of Rtes 30 and 32, **Strætó** buses 72 and 73 connect to bus 76 (two daily Monday to Friday) to Árnes. (Buses to Landmannalaugar follow a route further east.)

Búrfell & Around

As the Þjórsá's valley gets more remote inland, the drama and unusual sights increase. The austere black-stone river delta around Búrfell Hydroelectric Power Station leads to jagged mountains and hidden valleys.

There is no public transport. Come with your own wheels or with a local tour operator.

Sights

The following sights are arranged in the order you'll encounter them driving northeast on Rte 32.

Hjálparfoss WATERFALL
Twenty-six kilometres northeast of Árnes along Rte 32, take a short (1km) detour along a signposted track to this delightful waterfall. The azure falls tumble in two chutes over twisted basalt columns and into a deep pool.

(Continued on page 134)

GIEDRIIUS/SHUTTERSTOCK ©

1. Arctic fox **2.** Seal pup **3.** Humpback whale
4. Puffins

2

EMKA74/SHUTTERSTOCK ©

Wildlife Watching

Iceland's magical natural realm is the playground for some headlining acts, including breaching whales, basking seals, elusive Arctic foxes and bumper bird life (the scene stealer: cute, clownish puffins, of course). The support cast of wandering sheep and wild-maned horses are still impossibly photogenic against a cinematic, mountainous backdrop.

The bird life in Iceland is abundant, especially during the warmest months when migrating species arrive to nest. On coastal cliffs and islands around the country, you can see a mind-boggling array of seabirds. Posted coastal hikes offer access to some of the most populous bird cliffs in the world – don't miss a chance to cavort with puffins (p40).

Whale watching has become one of Iceland's most cherished pastimes – boats depart throughout the year (limited service in the colder months) to catch a glimpse of these lurking beasts as they wave their fins and spray the air. The northern waters around Húsavík and Akureyri are a haven for feeding creatures (usually minke and fin species); travellers who are short on time can hop on a boat that departs directly from downtown Reykjavík (p68). In winter, it's possible to see orcas crash through the frigid waters – the best point of departure is the Snæfellsnes Peninsula (p181).

4

BEST WILDLIFE-WATCHING SPOTS

Vestmannaeyjar (p163) Zoom between islets as you snap photos of a Peterson Field Guide's worth of bird life.

Borgarfjörður Eystri (p295) It's like you've died and gone to puffin heaven, where encounters with these clumsy birds are up close and personal.

Húsavík (p270) Sample Iceland's original flavour of whale watching at this charming fishing village. There are tours aplenty, especially in summer.

1

SIMON DANNHAUER / GETTY IMAGES ©

2

4

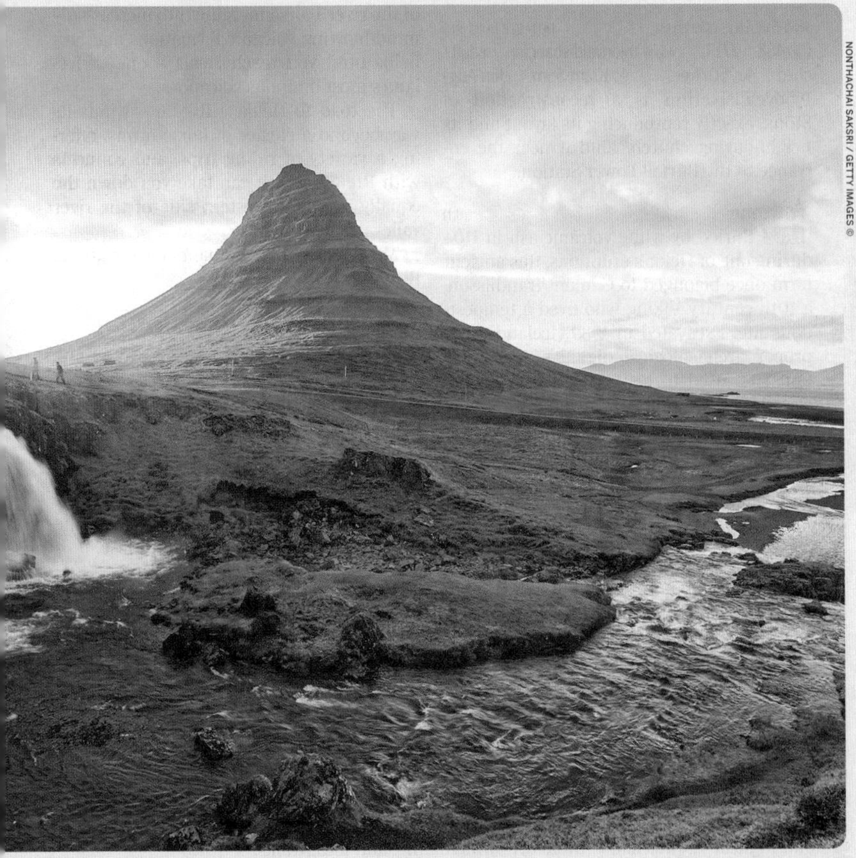

1. Þingvellir National Park (p111)
The location of Iceland's original outdoor parliament, dramatically situated in a fissured rift valley.

2. Kirkjufell (p186)
The distinctive symmetrical shape of Kirkjufell makes it one of the most photographed spots in Iceland.

3. Whale watching
Eleven species of whale are regulary spotted around the coast of Iceland. Húsavík (p270) is the top spot for whale-watching tours.

4. Northern Lights
The result of solar wind, the Northern Lights or aurora borealis, are best seen between mid-September and mid-April.

 (Continued from page 129)

Þjóðveldisbærinn NOTABLE BUILDING
(☎488 7713; www.thjodveldisbaer.is; adult/child kr750/free; ⏲10am-5pm Jun-Aug) Þjóðveldisbærinn is a reconstruction of Stöng, exactly reproducing its layout and its neighbouring church. Find it near the entrance to the Búrfell Power Station.

★Stöng RUIN
FREE Buried by white volcanic ash in 1104 during one of Hekla's eruptions, this ancient farm once belonged to Gaukur Trandilsson, a 10th-century Viking who lived a tempestuous life. Excavated in 1939 (Iceland's first proper archaeological dig), it's an important site, used to help date Viking houses elsewhere. The ruins are covered by a large wooden shelter at the end of a rough 5km dirt road that branches off Rte 32 about 26km northeast of Árnes. The site has toilets and water.

★Gjáin CANYON
A walking path from Stöng farm takes you a couple of kilometres to a lovely lush little valley, Gjáin, full of twisting lava, otherworldly caves and spectacular waterfalls. The dirt road from Stöng also continues on to the upper ridge of the valley. Gjáin simply means 'rift', and it was a filming location in *Game of Thrones*.

★Háifoss WATERFALL
From Stöng you can walk 9km northeast along a 4WD track to Iceland's second-highest waterfall, Háifoss, which plunges 122m off the edge of a plateau into an undulating lava canyon. You can also get most of the way there by 4WD.

Sleeping & Eating

There are no grocery stores or restaurants anywhere nearby, so provision or eat before arriving.

Sandartunga Camping CAMPGROUND €
(asolfsstadir@simnet.is; sites per adult/child kr1000/free; ⏲mid-May–Aug) This simple campground has water and toilets. The blessing is its grand setting in the broad lava fields and river valley of the Þjórsá.

Eastern Þjórsárdalur

Between the township of Hella to the southwest and Landmannalaugar to the northeast, you'll find the sweeping seaside floodplains of the river Þjórsá merging into increasingly mind-blowing volcanic formations and lava fields until you reach Hekla – one of Iceland's most ominous volcanoes.

The road to Hekla – Rte 26 – winds its way beyond a cluster of horse farms, offering a variety of riding trips, and connects with Rte 32, which can take you down the equally dramatic western side of the river valley.

Most buses to Landmannalaugar go via Rte 26.

Sights

Hellnahellir CAVE
(☎847 5015; www.hellar.is; adult/child kr1000/free; ⏲by appointment) This austere human-made cave built into the earth beneath Skarðsfjall on the farm Hellar in Landsveit dates to 700 to 1100 years ago. In 2016 it was opened to the public for the first time. Find it on Rte 26 about 5km northeast of the turn-off for the Heimaland guesthouse.

Hekla Center EXHIBITION
(Heklusetrið; ☎487 8700; www.leirubakki.is; Leirubakki; adult/child kr900/450; ⏲9am-10pm Jun-Aug, 10am-10pm Sep-May; P) The Hekla Center is part of the Leirubakki compound (camping, hotel, restaurant, petrol). It details the explosive history of Hekla in a deliberately dark building with flashing lights and multimedia exhibits. You'll learn that the volcano is long overdue to erupt. The centre also has regional information, and offers horse riding, and local walks.

Tours

The many horse farms around the Þjórsárdalur offer rides, and most have high-quality guesthouse accommodation.

Skeiðvellir HORSE RIDING
(Icelandic HorseWorld; ☎487 6572, horse riding 899 5619; www.skeidvellir.is; Skeiðvellir farm) This well-regarded horse-breeding farm offers rides (one-/two-hour ride kr8000/15,000) and excellent accommodation (studio/cottage kr14,000/28,700). Find it on Rte 26 about 9km north of Rte 1.

Hekluhestar HORSE RIDING
(☎487 6598; www.hekluhestar.is; Austvaðsholt) Hidden along Rtes 271 and 272, 9km northeast of Hella, a friendly French-Icelandic family specialises in six- to eight-day highland rides (from kr227,000). Sleeping-bag accommodation is available (kr4500, linen

kr2000) in a cosy dorm. Book ahead for tours.

Kálfholt HORSE RIDING
(487 5176; www.kalfholt.is; Kálfholt 2, Ásahreppi;) This family-run farm offers one of the best ranges of hourly rides, day trips and two- to eight-day treks for every skill level (two-hour ride kr11,500, children's ride kr3,900). On Rte 288, 17km west of Hella and south of the Ring Road. Comfy lodging is in two little cabins (per person kr7000).

Hestheimar HORSE RIDING
(487 6666; www.hestheimar.is) Take family-run riding trips (two-hour/one-day ride kr12,000/20,000), rent horses, or bunk in a variety of comfortable accommodation (double from kr11,900) at this horse farm above a bubbling stream. On Rte 281, 7km northwest of Hella.

Herríðarhóll HORSE RIDING
(487 5252; www.herridarholl.is; Herríðarhóli) Multiday horse tours (from kr227,000) and short rides (one hour kr7000), plus a warm welcome to those who simply want a farmstay (double with shared bathroom, including breakfast kr16,000). West of Hella, then 6km north of the Ring Road on Rte 284.

Sleeping & Eating

Most of the horse farms in the plains around Hella have good accommodation options for their riders and welcome other travellers as well.

You'll find most eating options are part of hotel and guesthouse complexes.

HEKLA

The name of Iceland's most famous and active volcano means 'Hooded One', as its 1491m-high summit is almost always shrouded in ominous-looking clouds. Hekla has vented its fury numerous times throughout history, and during the Middle Ages it was commonly believed to be the gateway to hell.

Viking-era settlers built farms on the rich volcanic soils around Hekla, only to be wiped out by the eruption of 1104, which buried everything within a radius of 50km. Since then there have been 15 major eruptions; the 1300 eruption covered more than 83,000 sq km in ash.

In recent years hellish Hekla has been belching out ash in steady 10-year intervals. This ash has a high fluorine content and has poisoned thousands of sheep. The most recent eruption (in 2000) produced a small pyroclastic flow (a high-speed and highly destructive torrent of rock particles and gas, which typically travels at over 130km per hour and can reach temperatures of 800°C). As you travel the region, look for grey pumice…it's probably from Hekla.

Locals live with the knowledge that the mighty mound could erupt at any time; it is long overdue.

For more on Hekla, check out the exhibition at the Hekla Center.

Climbing Hekla

You can climb Hekla, but there's never much warning before eruptions, usually indicated by multiple small earthquakes 30 to 80 minutes before it blows. Stick to days when the summit is free of heavy clouds, and carry plenty of water – the area's ash makes you thirsty. Most climbs are done June to September.

There's a small car park where mountain road F225 branches off Rte 26 (about 45km northeast of Hella). Most hire cars aren't allowed on F roads and need to be parked here, but it's a long and dusty walk (16km) to the foot of the volcano (or try your luck at hitching).

With a large 4WD you can continue along F225 to the trailhead at the bottom of Hekla (about 14.7km); the largest vehicles can continue a few kilometres further, but most have to park here. From this lower trailhead, a well-marked path climbs steadily up to the ridge on the northeastern flank of the mountain, then onto the summit crater; expect snow walking at altitude. Although the peak is often covered in snow, the floor of the crater is still hot. The trip to the summit takes about 3½ hours.

Alternatively, you can organise bespoke super-Jeep tours from anywhere in the region.

Laugaland CAMPGROUND €
(☎895 6543; www.tjalda.is/en/laugaland; sites per adult/child kr1100/free) Family camping complex northwest of Hella on Rte 26. There's also a swimming pool and hot-pots (adult/child kr700/300).

Rjúpnavellir COTTAGE, CAMPGROUND €
(☎892 0409; www.rjupnavellir.is; Landsveit; sites per person kr1500) Just where the paved road ends, and the closest accommodation to the Rte 26–F225 junction, you'll find these two large cabins with sleeping-bag space (kr4900; showers kr400) and cooking facilities, camping, and a six-person cottage (kr24,000). Linen kr1800.

Hótel Leirubakki HOTEL €€
(☎487 8700; www.leirubakki.is; Leirubakki; sites per adult kr1000, d with/without bathroom incl breakfast kr28,800/23,400; @) This large farmstead is one of the last outposts before you hit volcanoes and highlands. The well-run house and more modern hotel block are a good base for Hekla climbers. The restaurant serves Icelandic faves like lamb and trout (from a nearby stream). There's a great hot-pot in the lava field, an N1 petrol pump and sleeping-bag accommodation (kr6100).

Hrauneyjar Highland Center HOTEL €€
(Hotel Highland; ☎487 7782; www.hrauneyjar.is; Hrauneyjar; guesthouse s/d incl breakfast from kr19,900/22,500, hotel s/d incl breakfast kr32,050/36,250; P) This simple hotel-restaurant complex is the last outpost (and last petrol) before heading into the Highlands. Rooms are austere for the high prices, but it's in the middle of nowhere, so you're lucky to get anything! Sleeping-bag accommodation starts at kr9600. The restaurant (mains kr1500 to kr4900) serves burgers and sandwiches all day, and more elaborate lamb and fish dishes at night.

Northeast of Hrauneyjar, Rte F26 continues across the interior highlands as the Sprengisandur route.

Getting There & Away

Landmannalaugar buses stop in Leirubakki and/or Hrauneyjar.

Reykjavík Excursions (www.re.is) services:

- Bus 11/11a Reykjavík–Landmannalaugar (Reykjavík–Leirubakki kr5500, 2½ hours, three to four daily mid-June to mid-September).
- Bus 17/17a Reykjavík–Mývatn (Reykjavík–Hrauneyjar kr7500, three hours, one daily late June to August).

Sterna (www.sterna.is) services:

- Bus 13/13a Reykjavík–Landmannalaugar (Reykjavík–Leirubakki kr6000, 2½ hours, one daily late June to early September).

Trex (www.trex.is) services:

- Bus T21 Reykjavík–Landmannalaugar (Reykjavík–Leirubakki kr5400, 2½ hours, two daily mid-June to mid-September).

Hella & Around

POP 820

This small agricultural community sits on the banks of the pretty Ytri-Rangá river in an important horse-breeding area in the plains around the Þjórsá river. The nearest town to shadow-wreathed volcano Hekla, 35km north, it remains relatively sleepy despite the arrival of new hotels in the area.

Activities & Tours

Sundlaugin Hellu GEOTHERMAL POOL, HOT-POT
(☎487 5334; Útskálum 4; adult/child kr700/300; ⏲6.30am-9pm Mon-Fri, 10am-7pm Sat & Sun Jun–mid-Aug, reduced hours mid-Aug–May) Hella's top attraction might be its geothermal swimming pool, with hot-pots, sauna and a cool water slide (April to October) to keep the kids happy.

Mud Shark FISHING TOUR, JEEP TOUR
(☎691 1849; www.mudshark.is) Offerings include beach-fishing trips (kr31,000) and south-coast tours (from kr42,000).

Sleeping

Árhús CAMPGROUND €
(South Door; ☎487 5577; www.arhus.is; Rangárbakkar 6; sites per tent kr2500, cottages with/without bathroom from kr20,500/13,000) Set along the river, just south of the Ring Road, Árhús has a cluster of cottages (from a simple room to a complete cabin with kitchenette and bathroom), ample camping space, a guest kitchen, and a top town restaurant (open noon to 10pm; mains kr2000 to 5000) with a great riverside deck.

★**River Hotel** HOTEL €€
(☎487 5004; www.riverhotel.is; Þykkvabæjarvegur (Rte 25); d/f kr22,000/30,000; P) Relax and watch the river glide by through giant plate-glass windows in the lounge areas of this immaculate new hotel on the banks of the Ytri-Rangá river. Contemporary rooms and a separate cottage are super-comfortable and there's an on-site restaurant for dinner. It's

THE EDDAS

The medieval monastery at **Oddi**, in Rangárvellir about 8km south of Hella on Rte 266, was the source of the Norse Eddas, the most important surviving books of Viking poetry. The *Prose Edda* was written by the poet and historian Snorri Sturluson around 1222. It was intended to be a textbook for poets, with detailed descriptions of the language and meters used by the Norse *skalds* (court poets). It also includes the epic poem 'Gylfaginning', which describes the visit of Gylfi, the king of Sweden, to Ásgard, the citadel of the gods. In the process, the poem reveals Norse creation myths, stories about the gods, and the fate in store for men at Ragnarök, when this world ends.

The *Poetic Edda* was written later in the 13th century by Sæmundur Sigfússon. It's a compilation of works by unknown Viking poets, some predating the settlement of Iceland. The first poem, 'Voluspá' (Sibyl's Prophecy), is like a Norse version of Genesis and Revelations: it covers the beginning and end of the world. Later poems deal with the story of how Óðinn discovered the power of runes, and the legend of Siegfried and the Nibelungs, recounted in Wagner's *Ring Cycle*. The most popular poem is probably 'Þrymskviða', about the giant Thrym, who stole Þór's hammer and demanded the goddess Freyja in marriage in exchange for its return. To get his hammer back, Þór disguised himself as the bride-to-be and went to the wedding in her place. Much of the poem is devoted to his appalling table manners at the wedding feast, during which he consumes an entire ox, eight salmon and three skins of mead.

Today Oddi is simply a church and farmsteads.

ideal for Northern Lights watching as well, and the owners are avid anglers.

Guesthouse Brenna HOUSE €€
(☎487 5532; www.guesthousebrenna.wordpress.com; Þrúðvangur 37; house kr27,000) This adorable riverside house sleeps eight and has a little kitchen, a washing machine and a comfy sitting room. Linen costs kr1400 per bed. Prices drop with additional nights. No individual rooms rented.

Guesthouse Nonni GUESTHOUSE €€
(☎894 9953; www.bbiceland.com; Arnarsandur 3; s/d without bathroom incl breakfast kr16,000/14,700) Run by friendly Nonni, who loves cooking a large breakfast (fresh bread and flower-shaped waffles) for his guests, this small guesthouse on a residential street has four wooden-walled rooms tucked up a cork stairwell.

★**Hótel Rangá** HOTEL €€€
(☎487 5700; www.hotelranga.is; Suðurlandsvegur; d/ste incl breakfast from kr42,000/65,400; @) Just south of the Ring Road 8km east of Hella, Hótel Rangá looks like a log cabin but caters to Iceland's high-end travellers. Service is top-notch, and the wood-panelled rooms and luxurious common areas are cosy. The restaurant (lunch mains kr2600 to kr3900, dinner mains kr4800 to kr7200) has broad windows looking across open pastures. To splash out, go for a 'World Pavilion' suite.

Stracta Hótel HOTEL €€€
(☎531 8010; www.stractahotels.is; Rangárflatir 4; d with/without bathroom incl breakfast from kr30,200/22,000, 3-/6-person studios incl breakfast from kr47,000/71,300) Stracta is one of the new breed of higher-end tourist hotels. Rooms range from modern, comfortable doubles to studios with microwaves and refrigerators, on up to family-friendly apartments. The upstairs restaurant has sweeping views of Vestmannaeyjar and volcanoes, but the food is rather lacklustre.

Eating

Hella has a few restaurants, and a small bakery next door to the supermarket.

Kjarval SUPERMARKET €
(☎585 7585; Suðurlandsvegur 1; ⏲9am-9pm) Local supermarket.

Information

Hekla Handverkshús (☎864 5531; Þrúðvangur 35; ⏲1-5pm May-Sep, 1-5pm Sat & Sun Oct-Apr) This handicrafts cooperative doubles as an informal tourist information desk.

Getting There & Away

BUS

Buses stop at the Olís petrol station.

Strætó (www.bus.is) services:

➡ Buses 51 & 52 Reykjavík–Vík–Höfn and Reykjavík–Landeyjahöfn (Reykjavík–Hella kr2940, 1½ hours, five daily).

Sterna (www.sterna.is) services:

➡ Bus 12/12a Reykjavík–Vík–Höfn (Reykjavík–Hella kr3040, 1½ hours, one daily June to mid-September).

Reykjavík Excursions (www.re.is) services:

➡ Buses 9/9a Reykjavík–Þórsmörk, 11/11a Reykjavík–Landmannalaugar, 17/17a Reykjavík–Mývatn, 18 Reykjavík–Álftavatn–Emstrur, 20/20a Reykjavík–Skaftafell and 21/21a Reykjavík–Skógar all stop in Hella (kr4500).

Trex (www.trex.is) services:

➡ Bus T21 Reykjavík–Landmannalaugar (Hella–Landmannalaugar kr6000, 2¼ hours, two daily mid-June to mid-September).

➡ Bus T11 Reykjavík–Þórsmörk (Hella–Þórsmörk kr4600, two hours, two daily mid-June to mid-September).

TAXI

Mountain Taxi (☎862 1864) Jón Pálsson offers a taxi service into the mountains and Highlands. He is based in Hella but can pick up anywhere.

Hvolsvöllur & Around

POP 950

The farms around Hvolsvöllur were the setting for the bloody events of *Njál's Saga*, one of Iceland's favourites; today, though, the Saga sites exist mainly as place names, peaceful grassed-over ruins or modern agricultural buildings. Hvolsvöllur itself had not been much more than a pit stop, with a couple of petrol stations and a cluster of houses, but the advent of the new LAVA Centre and numerous guesthouses make it an increasingly popular base.

Sights

★Sögusetrið — MUSEUM

(Saga Centre; ☎487 8781; www.njala.is; Hliðarvegur 14, Hvolsvöllur; adult/child kr900/free; ⏲9am-6pm mid-May–mid-Sep, 10am-5pm Sat & Sun mid-Sep–mid-May) Hvolsvöllur's Saga Centre is devoted to the dramatic events of *Njál's Saga*, which took place in the surrounding hills. Interactive displays explain the many highlights of the story. In 2013 an intricate 90m embroidery called **Njál's Saga Tapestry** was begun; visitors can pay to add stitches to the enormous collaborative project (kr1000; check www.njalurefill.is for the sewing schedule), or just observe. There's also an art exhibition, a longhouse coffee shop and tourist information (brochures, maps and helpful staff).

LAVA – Iceland Volcano & Earthquake Center — EXHIBITION

(www.lavacentre.is; Austurvegur 14, Hvolsvöllur; adult/child kr2600/free, cinema only kr1200/free; ⏲exhibition 10am-7pm, LAVA house 9am-10pm) The new LAVA Center opens in summer 2017 with a full-blown multimedia experience immersing you in Iceland's volcanic and seismic life, and includes a 12m-high model of Iceland's volcanic core, an earthquake simulator and a cinema. Its LAVA House is an information centre for the region with a shop and restaurant.

Keldur — RUIN

(☎530 2200; www.thjodminjasafn.is; kr750; ⏲10am-5pm mid-Jun–mid-Aug) About 5km west of Hvolsvöllur, unsurfaced Rte 264 winds about 8km north along the Rangárvellir valley to the medieval turf-roofed farm at Keldur. This historic settlement once belonged to Ingjaldur Höskuldsson, a character in *Njál's Saga*. The structure is managed by the National Museum Historic Buildings Collection and has interesting historical exhibits and a pastoral setting.

Tours

★Midgard Adventure — HIKING TOUR, ADVENTURE TOUR

(☎770 2030; www.midgardadventure.is; Dufþaksbraut 14) One of south Iceland's best bespoke adventure operators; founder Siggi Bjarni and the other guide-owners know the area incredibly well and are tops for guided hikes along Fimmvörðuháls or Laugavegurinn and beyond (from kr19,900). They offer loads of day tours with pick-up, including super-Jeep trips (from kr37,900) canyoning and ice climbing. Midgard also has a hostel due to open in 2017.

Sleeping

There are excellent sleeping options in the village of Hvolsvöllur and the verdant countryside nearby, such as Fljótshlíð. The municipal campsite is just off the Ring Road in the heart of town, and Midgard Adventure is opening a hostel in 2017.

Asgarður — COTTAGES €

(☎487 1440; www.asgardurinn.is; d without bathroom kr13,200) These cute picket-lined individual cottages cluster under a stand of

WORTH A TRIP

FJALLABAK ROUTE

In summer the Fjallabak (pronounced *fiat*-la-back; Fjallabaksleið Nyrðri) Rte (F208) makes a spectacular alternative to the coast road between Hella, in southwest Iceland, and Kirkjubæjarklaustur, if you have a large 4WD. Its name translates as 'Behind the Mountains', and that's exactly where it goes.

Leave the Ring Road west of Hella on Rte 26 (the east side of the Þjorsá), then take Rte F208 from near the Sigölduvirkjun power plant until you reach Landmannalaugar. From there, F208 continues east past the **Kirkjufell** marshes and beyond **Jökuldalur**, before coursing through the icy veins of a riverbed for 10km, climbing up to the **Hörðubreið lookout**, then descending down into **Eldgjá**. Rte F235 to **Langisjór** lake turns off from Rte F208 about 3km west of Eldgjá. You can camp or sleep in a hut in **Hólaskjól** (www.holaskjol.com).

The 40km stretch of Rte F208 from Eldgjá to **Búland** is in reasonable shape, but there are some rivers to ford before the road turns into Rte 208 and emerges back along the Ring Road southwest of Kirkjubæjarklaustur.

Note that a 2WD vehicle wouldn't have a hope of completing even a small portion of the route and car-hire companies prohibit taking 2WD vehicles on F roads. Since much of the Fjallabak Rte is along rivers (or rather, in rivers!), it's not ideally suited to mountain bikes either. People attempt it, but it's not casual cycling by any stretch.

You can follow the entire route by bus by leaving Reykjavík on an early bus and switching to Skaftafell-bound Reykjavík Excursions bus 10A in Landmannalaugar. The journey takes about 13 hours. You can break it up by spending nights at the Landmannalaugar base and exploring the area before taking the second leg of the bus journey.

Well-established trekking company **Fjallabak** (☎511 3070; www.fjallabak.is) leads multiday guided treks and assisted backpacking tours throughout the southern back country, with a speciality in the Fjallabak Nature Reserve area, which the Fjallabak Rte passes through. **Midgard Adventure** (p138) is another great option.

trees. They have two bedrooms and private bathrooms and kitchenettes. A quaint restored 1927 schoolhouse sits in the centre. Made-up beds cost kr6600 and sleeping-bag accommodation is kr4900. Camping is also available.

Spói Guesthouse B&B €€
(☎861 8687; www.spoiguesthouse.is; Hlíðarvegur 15; d without bathroom kr17,000; Ⓟ) This impeccable family-run guesthouse has a collection of pristine rooms grouped around a large dining room with a broad wooden table for the lavish breakfast. The owners offer a wealth of local knowledge.

Hótel Hvolsvöllur HOTEL €€
(☎487 8050; www.hotelhvolsvollur.is; Hlíðarvegur 7; s/d incl breakfast from kr12,000/14,600; @) This large bland-looking hotel is slightly better than it appears. The 64 rooms are often being updated, so you could get lucky.

Eating

Eating options in town aren't brilliant. Both petrol stations have grills and there's a Kjarval supermarket.

★**Eldstó Art Café** CAFE €€
(☎482 1011; www.eldsto.is; Austurvegur 2, Hvolsvöllur; mains kr2000-4000; ⏲11am-9.30pm Jun-Aug; Ⓟ) Eldstó offers fresh-brewed coffee, homemade daily specials (such as coconut curry soup), and a couple of outdoor Ring Road-side tables. Friendly owners are ceramicists with a small on-site gallery, and also offer simple accommodation upstairs (doubles from kr28,000).

Gallerí Pizza FAST FOOD €€
(☎487 8440; www.gallerypizza.weebly.com; Hvolsvegur 29; mains kr1800-3000; ⏲11.30am-10pm) The town pizzeria, one street back from the main road, is a busy, no-frills place with vinyl booths and munching locals. The Béarnaise burger is a favourite.

Shopping

Una Local Products ARTS & CRAFTS
(Sveitabúðin Una; ☎544 5455; Austurvegur 4, Hvolsvöllur; ⏲10am-6pm) This large hangar on the Ring Road is loaded with all manner of handmade Icelandic crafts, from fish-skin purses to woolly jumpers, jewellery and leather goods.

NJÁL'S SAGA

One of Iceland's best-loved (and longest) sagas is also one of the most complicated. The story involves two friends and neighbours, Gunnar Hámundarson and Njál Þorgeirsson. A petty squabble between their wives is a prelude to the feuds and battles that ultimately leave almost every character dead. Written in the 13th century, it recounts 10th-century events that took place in the hills around Hvolsvöllur.

Doomed hero Gunnar of Hlíðarendi (near Fljótsdalur) falls for and marries the beautiful, hot-tempered Hallgerður, who has long legs but – ominously – a 'thief's eyes'. Hallgerður has a falling-out with Bergþóra, wife of Njál. Things become increasingly strained between Gunnar and Njál as Hallgerður and Bergþóra begin murdering each other's servants.

In one important episode, Hallgerður sends a servant to burgle food from a man named Otkell. When Gunnar comes home and sees Hallgerður's stolen feast, his temper snaps. 'It's bad news indeed if I've become a thief's accomplice', he says, and slaps his wife – an act that later comes back to haunt him. (Spoiler alert: each of Hallgerður's two previous husbands was killed as a result of slapping her.)

Through more unfortunate circumstances, Gunnar ends up killing Otkell and is sentenced to exile. As he rides away from home, his horse stumbles. Fatally, he takes one last glance back at his beloved farm Hlíðarendi and is unable to leave the valley after all. His enemies gather their forces and lay siege to the farm, but Gunnar manages to hold off the attackers until his bowstring breaks. When he asks Hallgerður for a lock of her hair to repair it, she refuses, reminding him of the slap she received (years earlier) – and Gunnar is killed.

The feud continues as Gunnar and Njál's clan members try to avenge their slaughtered kin. Njál himself acts as a peace broker, forming treaties between the two families, but in the end, the complicated peacemaking is all for naught. Njál and his wife are besieged in their farm. Tucking themselves in bed with their little grandson between them, the couple allow themselves to be burnt alive.

The only survivor of the fire is Njál's son-in-law Kári, who launches a legal case against the arsonists, commits a bit of extrajudicial killing himself and is finally reconciled with his arch-enemy, Flosi, who ordered the burning of the Njál family.

Vínbúðin ALCOHOL
(☎486 1886; Austurvegur 1; ⊙11am-6pm Mon-Thu, to 7pm Fri, to 4pm Sat) National liquor chain.

Getting There & Away

Buses to Þórsmörk stop in Hvolsvöllur.

Strætó (www.bus.is) services:

➡ Buses 51 & 52 Reykjavík–Vík–Höfn & Reykjavík–Landeyjahöfn (Reykjavík–Hvolsvöllur kr3360, 1¾ hours, five daily).

Sterna (www.sterna.is) services:

➡ Bus 12/12a Reykjavík–Vík–Höfn (Reykjavík–Hvolsvöllur kr3420, 1¾ hours, one daily June to mid-September).

Reykjavík Excursions (www.re.is) services:

➡ Buses 9/9a Reykjavík–Þórsmörk, 18 Álftavatn–Reykjavík, 20/20a Reykjavík–Skaftafell and 21/21a Reykjavík–Skógar all stop in Hvolsvöllur (Reykjavík–Hvolsvöllur kr4500).

Trex (www.trex.is) services:

➡ Buses T11 Reykjavík–Þórsmörk (Hvolsvöllur–Þórsmörk kr4600, two hours, two daily mid-June to mid-September).

Hvolsvöllur to Skógar

After Hvolsvöllur, the Ring Road loops east toward Skógar with three important side roads. The first is Fljótshlíð (Rte 261), just at the eastern end of Hvolsvöllur; the second is Rte 254, which shoots south 12km to Landeyjahöfn where the ferry leaves for Vestmannaeyjar; and the third is Rte 249 north to Þórsmörk passing Seljalandsfoss. Staying on the Ring Road, will bring you along the base of hulking Eyjafjallajökull, made famous with its ashy 2010 explosion.

Fljótshlíð

Rte 261 follows the mossy green edge of the lush Fljótshlíð hills, offering great views of their waterfalls, such as **Gluggafoss**, on one side, and the Markarfljót river delta and Eyjafjallajökull on the other.

The surfaced section of the road ends soon after the farm and church at **Hlíðarendi**, once the home of Gunnar Hámundarson from *Njál's Saga*. With a 4WD you can continue along road F261 towards Landmannalaugar and **Tindfjöll** – a hiker's paradise. Though it seems tantalisingly close, Þórsmörk can only be reached via Rte F249.

Tours

Midgard Adventure (p138) and Southcoast Adventure (p141) run hiking and canyoning tours in Tindfjöll and around the region.

Óbyggðaferðir QUAD-BIKE TOURS
(☎661 2503; www.atvtravel.is; Lambalæk) Quad-bike tours around Eyjafjallajökull, Þórsmörk and beyond. A day trip per single/double rider costs kr69,500/55,000.

Sleeping & Eating

Along the length of the valley there is a series of good guesthouses and hotels, some with camping.

Some of the region's hotels have dining options, or head into Hvolsvöllur for restaurants.

★**Fljótsdalur HI Hostel** HOSTEL €
(☎487 8498; www.hostel.is; dm kr4750; ⊙Apr-Oct) It's very basic and not for everyone, but if you're looking for a peaceful, remote base for highland walks, with a beautiful garden, homey kitchen, cosy sitting room, and mountain views that make your knees tremble, then you'll find it here. There are only seven bare mattresses in the attic and two four-bed rooms on the main floor. Book ahead. HI members get a kr750 discount.

Find it 27km east of Hvolsvöllur; the road gets rough toward the end. Bring all supplies.

★**Hótel Fljótshlíð** HOTEL €€
(Guesthouse Smáratún; ☎487 1416; www.smaratun.is; Smáratún; sites per adult/child kr1350/670, d with/without bathroom kr24,800/12,400, chalets/cottages from kr16,400/24,600; P) This attractive white farm with a blue-tin roof has four- to six-person summerhouses, smart hotel-style rooms, cheaper guesthouse rooms (with shared facilities), sleeping-bag places (kr4700; linen kr1660) and spots for tents. Unwind in the hot tub, or let the kids loose on the playground. It's 12.5km east of Hvolsvöllur.

Fagrahlíd Guesthouse B&B €€
(☎863 6669; www.fagrahlid.is; Fagrahlíd farm; d without bathroom incl breakfast kr22,500, studio incl breakfast kr32,430; P) This pretty clutch of butter-yellow buildings clusters on a slope with sweeping views of the valley and the volcanoes in the distance. The friendly owner keeps everything tip-top, and comfortable rooms or the self-catering studio share a hot tub. Find it 6.5km east of Hvolsvöllur on Rte 261.

Hótel Eyjafjallajökull B&B, CAMPGROUND €€
(☎487 8360; www.hoteleyjafjallajokull.is; Hellishólar; s/d incl breakfast kr18,300/26,500; P) This long, narrow, wooden hotel is newly built and accompanied by a high-quality campground with hot tubs and laundry. Hotel rooms have en suite bathrooms and flat-screen TVs. Kids can romp on the playground. Find it 11km east of Hvolsvöllur on Rte 261.

Rte 249 to Þórsmörk

You'll see glistening Seljalandsfoss thundering off the lower escarpments of Eyjafjallajökull volcano from miles away. It's a popular stop on the Ring Road and a pick-up point for Þórsmörk-bound buses (Þórsmörk is impossible to reach by regular vehicles due to big rivers).

The road to Þórsmörk (Rte 249/F249) begins just east of the Markarfljót river and alongside Seljalandsfoss, and leads north off the Ring Road. It quickly turns into a spectacular 4WD-only road.

Sights

★**Seljalandsfoss & Gljúfurárbui** WATERFALL
From the Ring Road you'll see the beautiful high falls at Seljalandsfoss, which tumble over a rocky scarp into a deep, green pool. A (slippery) path runs around the back of the waterfall. A few hundred metres further down the Þórsmörk road, Gljúfurárbui gushes into a hidden canyon.

Tours

★**Southcoast Adventure** ADVENTURE TOUR
(☎867 3535; www.southadventure.is) South Coast Adventure is a small tour operator run by enthusiastic locals with loads of regional knowledge and excellent reputations. Book tailor-made super-Jeep tours (two-/five-hour

FLIGHTSEEING THE VOLCANOES

From Bakki Airport, on the coast 5km northwest of Landeyjahöfn, **Atlantsflug** (☎854 4105; www.flightseeing.is) offers overflights (kr26,900 to kr52,900) of Eyjafjallajökull, glaciers and highlands. Flights also run to Heimaey, Vestmannaeyjar (Westman Islands; one-way kr8500).

tours from kr19,900/32,900) from Þórsmörk to Landmannaulagar and longer hikes such as Fimmvörðuháls or Laugavegurinn. Also offers snowmobiling, volcano tours, glacier walks and winter trips. Info desk is at Hamragarðar (p142) on 2WD-friendly Rte 249, next to Seljalandsfoss.

Sleeping & Eating

Head to Hvolsvöllur or Skógar for eating options.

★**Hamragarðar** CAMPGROUND €
(☎867 3535; sites per adult/child kr1300/free; ⊙May-Sep) Camp right next to the hidden waterfall at Gljúfurárbui at the start of Rte 249. There's a small cafe (9am to 11pm June to August) that sells cake and coffee, plus a laundry (kr500), showers (kr300), a shared kitchen and an info area for Southcoast Adventure (p141).

★**Stóra-Mörk III** GUESTHOUSE, COTTAGES €€
(☎487 8903; www.storamork.com; d with/without bathroom incl breakfast kr17,000/12,000) About 5km along Rte 249 beyond the cluster of traffic at Seljalandsfoss falls, a dirt track leads to historic Stóra-Mörk III farmhouse (mentioned, of course, in *Njál's Saga*), which offers large, homey rooms. The main house has some rooms with private bathrooms, a large kitchen and a dining room with excellent mountain-to-sea views. Sleeping-bag accommodation with/without bathroom costs kr4500/3800.

Getting There & Away

Strætó, Sterna, Trex and Reykjavík Excursions buses from Reykjavík to Skógar and beyond, or to Þórsmörk, stop at Seljalandsfoss.

South of Eyjafjallajökull

The Ring Road (Rte 1) goes directly through the flood zone south of Eyjafjallajökull (*ay-ya-fiat*-la-yo-gootl) volcano that was inundated with muddy ash during the infamous eruption in 2010. The gorgeous area skirts its lower cliffs and foothills, and is scored by waterfalls and dotted with farms.

Sights & Activities

Eyjafjallajökull Visitor Centre EXHIBITION
(Þorvaldseyri Visitor Center – Iceland Erupts; ☎487 8815; www.icelanderupts.is; Þorvaldseyri; adult/child kr800/free; ⊙9am-6pm Jun-Aug, 10am-4pm May & Sep, 11am-4pm Mon-Fri Oct-Apr) This centre, about 7km west of Skógar on the Ring Road, is on a farm on the southern flanks of Eyjafjallajökull that was impacted by the 2010 eruption. A 20-minute film (usually in English) tells the family's story, from the ominous warnings to the devastating aftermath of the flooding ash. Movie snippets include tender family moments and highlights from the team of local rescuers that dug the farm out.

Seljavallalaug GEOTHERMAL POOL
FREE Seljavallalaug, a peaceful 1923 pool, is filled by a natural hot spring and has become very popular with tourists. From Edinborg (7km west of Skógar) follow Rte 242 and signs 2km to Seljavellir; park by the farm, and walk up the beautiful river valley for about 10 minutes.

Tours

Skálakot HORSE RIDING
(☎487 8953; www.skalakot.com) Horse farm Skálakot (15km west of Skógar on Rte 246) offers an array of shorter rides (one hour kr6500), longer treks (day-long glacier and beach ride kr29,500) and hiking tours. Also offers a range of accommodation (p142).

Sleeping

There's a loose string of guesthouses and farmsteads along the Ring Road.

Skálakot GUESTHOUSE, FARMSTAY €
(☎487 8953; www.skalakot.com; dm kr5500, d/f without bathroom kr13,000/19,500, farmstay with full board kr18,500; P) The fresh-faced Skálakot horse farm offers dorms, guesthouse rooms and sleeping bag accommodation (kr3800), plus full farmstay experiences. It's 15km west of Skógar on Rte 246.

Hótel Lambafell HOTEL €€
(☎487 1212; www.lambafell.is; Rte 242, Lambafell; d/q incl breakfast from kr24,800/34,300) This big, recently built log-cabin-style hotel offers spacious rooms with private bathrooms.

Guesthouse Edinborg GUESTHOUSE €€
(☎487 1212; www.greatsouth.is; Rte 242, Lambafell; d incl breakfast kr20,500; @) Formerly named Hótel Edinborg (and still signposted that way on the main road), this tall, tin-clad farmhouse has inviting wood-floored rooms with comfy beds and private bathrooms, and an attic seating area with glacier views. It feels out in the remote countryside despite being just off the Ring Road. It also operates the nearby Hótel Lambafell (p143).

Country Hotel Anna HOTEL €€
(☎487 8950; www.hotelanna.is; Rte 246, Moldnúpur; s/d incl breakfast kr19,900/28,900) This inn's namesake, Anna, wrote books about her worldwide voyages – and her descendants' country hotel upholds her passion for travel, with seven sweetly old-fashioned rooms furnished with antiques and embroidered bedspreads. The hotel and its little restaurant (open 6.30pm to 9pm; mains kr4200 to kr5200) sit at the foot of Eyjafjallajökull volcano on Rte 246.

Eating

Heimamenn Cafe & Minimart CAFE €
(Rte 1, Skarðshlíð 2; snacks kr390-1790; 11am-7pm Jun-Aug) This small cafe with burgers, hot dogs and soup, and a teeny mini-mart selection opened in 2016, and it may remain open in winters. It's 2km west of Skógar.

★ **Gamla Fjósið** ICELANDIC €€
(Old Cowhouse; ☎487 7788; www.gamlafjosid.is; Hvassafell; mains kr1900-6500; 11am-9pm Jun-Aug, reduced hours Sep-May) Built in a former cowshed that was in use until 1999, this charming eatery's focus is on farm-fresh and grass-fed meaty mains, from burgers to Volcano Soup, a spicy meat stew. The hardwood floor and low beams are cheered with polished dining tables, large wooden hutches and friendly staff.

It also operates the basic **South Iceland Guesthouse** (d without bathroom, incl breakfast, kr17,000) across the street.

Getting There & Away

Strætó, Sterna and Reykjavík Excursions buses from Reykjavík to Skógar and beyond, pass through here, but you'll need to arrange for them to stop.

Skógar

POP 20

Skógar nestles under the Eyjafjallajökull ice cap just off the Ring Road. This little tourist settlement is the start (or occasionally end) of the hike over the Fimmvörðuháls Pass to Þórsmörk, and is one of the activities centres of the Southwest. At its western edge, you'll see the dizzyingly high waterfall, Skógafoss, and on the eastern side you'll find a fantastic folk museum.

Sights

★ **Skógafoss** WATERFALL
This 62m-high waterfall topples over a rocky cliff at the western edge of Skógar in dramatic style. Climb the steep staircase alongside for giddy views, or walk to the foot of the falls, shrouded in sheets of mist and rainbows. Legend has it that a settler named Þrasi hid a chest of gold behind Skógafoss...

★ **Skógar Folk Museum** MUSEUM
(Skógasafn; ☎487 8845; www.skogasafn.is; adult/child kr2000/free; 9am-6pm Jun-Aug, 10am-5pm Sep-May) The highlight of little Skógar is the wonderful Skógar Folk Museum, which covers all aspects of Icelandic life. The vast collection was put together by 95-year-old Þórður Tómasson over more than 75 years. There are also restored buildings – a church, a turf-roofed farmhouse, cowsheds – and a huge, modern building that houses an interesting transport and communication museum, the basic cafe **Skógakaffi** (www.skogasafn.is; soup kr1600; 10am-5pm) and a shop.

BOOK AHEAD

Moving west from Hella all the way to Vík, many local farms have pretty, rural guesthouses. It's a beautiful, but incredibly popular place to stay, so they get booked solid in summer. Reservations are essential.

The excellent, free regional maps available at tourist offices show all lodging. Look on Icelandic Farm Holidays (www.farmholidays.is) and booking.com for more choices; we review but a top sample.

FIMMVÖRÐUHÁLS TREK

Fimmvörðuháls (www.fimmvorduhals.is) – named for a pass between two brooding glaciers – dazzles the eye with a parade of wild inland vistas. Linking Skógar and Þórsmörk, the awesome hike is 23.4km long, and can be divided into three distinct sections of somewhat equal length. Figure around 10 hours to complete the trek, which includes stops to rest, and to check out the steaming remnants of the Eyjafjallajökull eruption. It's best to tackle the hike from late June to early September, but get local advice on conditions, and check www.safetravel.is and log your trip. Pack wisely; you can experience all four season over the course of this hike. If in doubt, go with a guide, as there are two treacherous passes, and tours here are great.

Part 1: Waterfall Way From Skógafoss to the 'bridge'. Starting on the right side of splashy Skógafoss, the path zooms up and over the falls quickly, revealing a series of waterfalls just behind. Stay close to the tumbling water as you climb over small stones and twisting trees – there are 22 chutes in all, each one magnificent. The path flattens out as the trees turn to windswept shrubs, then set your sights on the 'bridge', which is a crude walkway over the gushing river below. It's imperative that you make the crossing on the walkway otherwise you won't make it over and down into Þórsmörk later on.

Part 2: The Ashtray From the 'bridge' to the eruption site. After crossing the crude bridge onto the left side of the moving water you start to enter the gloomy heart of the pass between two glaciers: Eyjafjallajökull and Mýrdalsjökull. The weather can be quite variable here – it could be raining in the pass when there is sunshine in Skógar. Expect to bundle up at this point as you move through icy rifts in the earlier parts of summer; from August on the region feels like some kind of giant ashtray. If you want to break up the hike over two days, book ahead for either the 12-person **Baldvinsskáli** (p153) hut, or the 20-person **Fimmvörðuháls** (p153) hut. The latter is positioned 600m away from the main trail about halfway through the walk (it can be difficult to find in bad weather). There's no campsite. Continuing on, the initial eruption site from the Eyjafjallajökull eruption reveals itself; here you'll find steaming earth and the world's newest mountains – Magni and Móði. Climb up to the top of Magni and roast some sausages over one of the sizzling vents.

Part 3: Goðaland From the eruption site down into Þórsmörk. After climbing down from Magni, the last part of the hike begins. The barren ashiness continues for a while, then an other-worldly kingdom reveals itself – a place ripped straight from the pages of a fairy tale. Here in Goðaland – the aptly named 'Land of the Gods' – wild Arctic flowers bloom as stone cathedrals emerge in the distance. Vistas of green continue as you descend into Þórsmörk to complete the journey.

GPS markers Although the hike is relatively short compared to some of Iceland's famous multiday treks, it's important to bring a GPS along – especially for the second portion of the hike when the way isn't always obvious. The following nine GPS markers can keep DIYers on track:

1 N 63°31.765, W 19°30.756 (start)

2 N 63°32.693, W 19°30.015

3 N 63°33.741, W 19°29.223

4 N 63°34.623, W 19°26.794 (the 'bridge')

5 N 63°36.105, W 19°26.095

6 N 63°38.208, W 19°26.616 (beginning of eruption site)

7 N 63°39.118, W 19°25.747

8 N 63°40.561, W 19°27.631

9 N 63°40.721, W 19°28.323 (terminus at Básar)

Tours

Several major operators have their base in or around Skógar and offer tours to natural wonders, from glaciers to volcanoes and beyond. Excellent operators near Skógar include Southcoast Adventure (p141), which offers guided hikes of Fimmvörðuháls, among many other adventure tours, and Midgard Adventure (p138) in Hvolsvöllur, again tops for treks, super-Jeeps, ice climbing etc. Both can pick up from Skógar. Arctic Adventures (www.adventures.is) has a small booking table at Fossbúð (p145).

Icelandic Mountain Guides ADVENTURE TOUR
(587 9999, Skógar desk 894 2956; www.mountainguides.is; 9am-6pm) One of the largest and best operators in Iceland, Icelandic Mountain Guides has a downtown Reykjavík office and this Skógar branch, located at Hótel Skógafoss (p145). Locally, it runs glacier walks and ice climbs on Sólheimajökull (kr8900 to lkr25,900), guided Fimmvörðuháls hikes (kr26,900) and many tours further afield. Offers Reykjavík pick-up.

Sleeping

Although Skógar is set up for tourists, with various places to stay, it's essential to book well ahead in high season.

★ **Skógar Campsite** CAMPGROUND €
(sites per adult/child kr1200/800; May-Sep) Basic grassy lot with a great location, right by Skógafoss; the sound of falling water makes a soothing lullaby. There's a no-frills toilet block (shower kr300); pay at the hostel nearby.

Skógar HI Hostel HOSTEL €
(487 8780; www.hostel.is; dm/d kr4750/12,900) A solid link in the HI chain, this spot is located a stone's throw from Skógafoss in an old school with utilitarian rooms. There's a guest kitchen and a laundry.

★ **Skógar Guesthouse** GUESTHOUSE €€
(894 5464; www.skogarguesthouse.is; d/tr without bathroom incl breakfast kr21,000/30,000) This charming white farmhouse is tucked back inside the trees, beyond the Hótel Edda, almost to the cliff face. A friendly family offers quaint, impeccably maintained rooms with crisp linens and cosy quilts, a large immaculate kitchen and bathrooms, and a hot tub on a wood deck beneath the maples. It feels well out of the tourist fray despite being in central Skógar.

Hótel Skógafoss HOTEL €€
(487 8780; www.hotelskogafoss.is; d incl breakfast with/without waterfall view kr27,000/25,000) This hotel opened in 2014 and offers simple, modern rooms (half of which have views of Skógafoss) with good bathrooms. The bistro-bar (p145) is one of the best eating and drinking spots in town, with plate-glass windows looking onto the falls and local beer on tap.

Hótel Edda Skógar HOTEL €€
(444 4000; www.hoteledda.is; d without bathroom kr18,000; early Jun-late Aug; P) Perfectly serviceable but rather bland and worn, this summer inn in the local school close to the museum is split over two buildings. All rooms have shared bathrooms.

Hótel Skógar HOTEL €€€
(487 4880; www.hotelskogar.is; s/d/tr incl breakfast kr38,300/41,100/51,400) This architecturally interesting hotel has small, eclectic rooms with quirky antiques, some with hill views. One upstairs room has a king-size bed and waterfall views, a downstairs room is uninhabitable due to noise – check carefully. A hot tub and sauna plus an elegant restaurant (open noon to 3pm and 6pm to 10pm; mains kr3000 to kr4900) round it out.

The hotel also has a nearby house for rent.

Eating

Hótel Skógafoss Bistro-Bar ICELANDIC €€
(487 8780; www.hotelskogafoss.is; Skógar; mains kr1600-2500; 8am-11pm Jun-Sep, to 10pm Oct-May) The bistro-bar at Hótel Skógafoss is one of the best eating and drinking spots in town, with plate-glass windows looking onto the falls and local beer on tap.

Fossbúð FAST FOOD €€
(487 4880; mains kr1200-3000; 9am-9pm Jun-Aug) Advertised as a restaurant, Fossbúð is really a convenience store and place for quick snacks: soup, hamburgers, sandwiches, bagged chips and chocolate bars. Arctic Adventures has a small tour desk here.

Getting There & Away

Strætó (www.bus.is) services:

- Bus 51 Reykjavík–Vík–Höfn (Reykjavík–Skógar kr5040, 2½ hours, two daily).

Sterna (www.sterna.is) services:

- Bus 12/12a Reykjavík–Vík–Höfn (Reykjavík–Skógar kr4800, three hours, one daily June to mid-September).

Reykjavík Excursions (www.re.is) services:
➡ Bus 20/20a Reykjavík–Skaftafell (Reykjavík–Skógar kr6000, four hours, one daily June to early September).
➡ Bus 21/21a Reykjavík–Skógar (kr6000, 3¼ hours, two daily June to August).

Landmannalaugar

Mind-blowing multicoloured mountains, soothing hot springs, rambling lava flows and clear blue lakes make Landmannalaugar one of Iceland's most unique destinations, and a must for explorers of the interior. It's a favourite with Icelanders and visitors alike… as long as the weather cooperates.

Part of the Fjallabak Nature Reserve, Landmannalaugar (600m above sea level) includes the largest geothermal field in Iceland outside the Grímsvötn caldera in Vatnajökull. Its multihued peaks are made of rhyolite – a mineral-filled lava that cooled unusually slowly, causing those amazing colours.

The area is the official starting point for the famous Laugavegurinn hike, and there's some excellent day hiking as well. The day-use fee for the facilities at Landmannalaugar is kr500.

Activities

There's plenty to do in and around Landmannalaugar, though many hikers skip the area's wonders and set off right away for their Laugavegurinn hike. If you plan to stick around you'll be happy to know that the crowds dwindle in the evenings and, despite the base's chaotic appearance, you'll find peace in the hills above.

Hot Springs

Follow the wooden boardwalk just 200m from the Landmannalaugar hut, to find a steaming river filled with bathers. Both hot and cold water flow out from beneath Laugahraun and combine in a natural pool to form an ideal hot bath. Landmannalaugar could be translated as the People's Pools… and here they are.

Hiking

If you're day hiking in the Landmannalaugar area, stop by the information hut to purchase the useful day-trip map (kr300), which details all of the best hikes in the region. Guided hikes (through operators from Hvolsvöllur to Skógar areas) can also be a great way to explore the area.

The start of the Laugavegurinn hike (p148) is behind the Landmannalaugar hut, marked in red.

★ Ljótipollur HIKING

Day-hike to the ill-named Ljótipollur (Ugly Puddle), an incredible magenta crater filled with bright-blue water. The intense, fiery red comes from iron-ore deposits. Oddly enough, although it was formed by a volcanic explosion, the lake is rich in brown trout. The walk to the Puddle offers plenty of eye candy, from tephra desert and lava flow to marsh and braided glacial valleys.

To get there from Landmannalaugar you can climb over the 786m-high peak **Norðurnámur** or just traverse its western base to emerge on the Ljótipollur road (a 10km to 13.3km return trip, depending on the route).

Brennisteinsalda HIKING

When the weather is clear, opt for a walk that takes in the region's spectacular views. From Landmannalaugar climb to the summit of rainbow-streaked Brennisteinsalda – covered in steaming vents and sulphur deposits – for a good view across the rugged and variegated landscape (it's a 6.5km round trip from Landmannalaugar). From Brennisteinsalda it's another 90 minutes along the Þórsmörk route to the impressive **Stórihver** geothermal field.

Frostastaðavatn HIKING

This blue lake lies behind the rhyolite ridge immediately north of the Landmannalaugar hut. Walk over the ridge and you'll be rewarded with far-ranging views as well as close-ups of the interesting rock formations and moss-covered lava flows flanking the lake. If you walk at least one way on the road and spend some time exploring around the lake, the return trip takes two to three hours.

Fishing

Buy fishing licences (kr3500) for local lakes from the Mountain Mall at Landmannalaugar or at Landmannahellir (p147).

Tours

Landmannalaugar has on-site **horse-riding tours** (☎868 5577; www.hnakkur.is; 1/2hr tour kr9000/12,500) from July to mid-August. The horse farms in the plains around Hella also offer riding (usually longer trips) in and around the Landmannalaugar area.

Sleeping

Landmannalaugar has a large base with camping and hut facilities. The camp opens for the season depending on when the roads are clear, usually sometime in June. It closes for sure by mid-October, but it can be earlier if there's loads of snow or the water has to be turned off.

Landmannalaugar Hut & Camping Complex HUTS, CAMPGROUND €

(☎ booking 568 2533, huts Jul-Sep 860 3335; www.fi.is; sites/huts per person kr1800/7500) In the middle of summer this campground can look surprisingly raggle-taggle, with hundreds of tents, several structures inundated with hikers, and laundry dangling throughout. The hut accommodates 78 people in close quarters; it is essential to book ahead. There's a kitchen area and showers (kr500 for five minutes of hot water). Day use costs kr500.

Campers pitch a tent in the designated areas and have access to the toilet and shower facilities as well. Wild camping is strictly prohibited, as the entire area is in the protected Fjallabak Nature Reserve. There are several wardens on-site. At the time of writing there was no limit on the number of campers at Landmannalaugar, and you cannot reserve.

The base – simply known as Landmannalaugar – is operated by Ferðafélag Íslands (Icelandic Touring Association), like the huts on the Laugavegurinn hike, and its website is loaded with information.

Landmannahellir CAMPGROUND €

(☎ 893 8407; www.landmannahellir.is; sites per adult/tent kr1300/110; ⏲ mid-Jun–early Sep) This remote campsite has basic facilities (shower and toilets), and there is hut lodging (sleeping bag accommodation kr5600), and a few summer houses for rent. It also sells fishing licences. Trex (www.trex.is) bus T21 Reykjavík–Landmannalaugar can stop at Landmannahellir (kr8400, 3¾ hours, two daily mid-June to early September) if arranged in advance.

Eating

There are no restaurants at Landmannalaugar; bring all of your own food. The Mountain Mall shop sells some basic food supplies at a premium, and the huts have cooking facilities for guests.

Shopping

Mountain Mall FOOD & DRINKS, CLOTHING

(www.landmannalaugar.info) The Mountain Mall on the Landmannalaugar grounds is set up inside two buses, selling basic supplies from hats, long johns, hot tea and maps to beer (kr1000), soup (kr1000) and fresh fish from the nearby lakes. It also sell fishing licences.

Information

The Landmannalaugar hut wardens can answer questions and provide directions and advice on hiking routes. They also sell a map of day hikes (kr300) and the Laugavegurinn hike (kr1700), as well as a booklet in English and Icelandic on the hike (kr3000). Note that wardens do not know if it will rain (yes, this is the most frequently asked question here). At the time of writing there was no wi-fi, but there was some mobile-phone reception.

Getting There & Away

BUS

Landmannalaugar can be reached by rugged, semi-amphibious buses from three different directions. They run when the roads are open to Landmannalaugar (check www.road.is).

From Reykjavík Buses travel along the western part of the Fjallabak Rte, which first follows Rte 26 east of the Þjorsá to F225.

From Skaftafell Buses follow the Fjallabak Rte (F208).

From Mývatn Buses cut across the highlands via Nýidalur on the Sprengisandur Rte (F26).

It's possible to travel from Reykjavík and be in Landmannalaugar for two to 10 hours before returning to Reykjavík, or three to five hours before going on to Skaftafell. That's about enough time to take a dip in the springs and/or a short walk. Schedules change, but morning buses usually reach Landmannalaugar by midday. Alternatively, stay overnight and catch a bus out when you're done exploring.

Reykjavík Excursions (www.re.is) services:

- Bus 10/10a Skaftafell–Landmannalaugar (kr9000, five hours, one daily late June to early September).
- Bus 11/11a Reykjavík–Landmannalaugar (kr8000, 4¼ hours, three to four daily mid-June to mid-September).
- Bus 14/14a Mývatn–Landmannalaugar (kr16,500, 10 hours, one daily late June to early September).

Sterna (www.sterna.is) services:

- Bus 13/13a Reykjavík–Landmannalaugar (kr8000, four hours, one daily late June to early September).

Trex (www.trex.is) services:
➜ Bus T21 Reykjavík–Landmannalaugar (kr7900, 4¼ hours, two daily mid-June to early September).

CAR

Roads to Landmannalaugar are open in summer only (approximately late June to September) depending on weather and road conditions (check www.safetravel.is and www.road.is). There are three routes to Landmannalaugar from the Ring Road, all requiring a minimum of a 4WD. Driving from Mývatn to Landmannalaugar takes all day along the Sprengisandur Rte route (4WD only). If you have a small 4WD, you will have to leave your vehicle about 1km before Landmannalaugar, as the river crossing here is too perilous for little cars, and cross by footbridge. Two-wheel-drive rentals are not allowed to drive on F roads to Landmannalaugar.

There's no petrol at Landmannalaugar. The nearest petrol pumps are 40km north at **Hrauneyjar** (p136), close to the beginning of the F208 and also in the Fjallabak Reserve; and 90km southeast at Kirkjubæjarklaustur, but to be on the safe side you should fill up along the Ring Road if approaching from the west or the north.

F208 Northwest You can follow the west side of the Þjorsá (Rte 32), passing Árnes, then take Rte F208 down into Landmannalaugar from the north. This is the easiest path to follow for small 4WDs. After passing the power plant, the road from Hrauneyjar becomes horribly bumpy and swerves between power lines all the way to Ljótipollur ('Ugly Puddle').

F225 On the east side of the Þjorsá, follow Rte 26 inland through the low plains behind Hella, loop around Hekla, then take Rte F225 west until you reach the base. This route is harder to tackle (rougher roads).

F208 Southeast The hardest route comes from the Ring Road between Vík and Kirkjubæjarklaustur. This is the Skaftafell–Landmannalaugar bus route.

You can also take a super-Jeep tour with local tour operators, which will take you out to Landmannalaugar from Reykjavík, or from anywhere in the south.

Laugavegurinn Hike: Landmannalaugar to Þórsmörk

The hike from Landmannalaugar to Þórsmörk – commonly known as Laugavegurinn – is where backpackers earn their stripes in Iceland. It means 'Hot Spring Road', and it's easy to understand why. The harsh, other-worldly beauty of the landscape morphs in myriad ways as you traipse straight through the island's interior, with much of the earth steaming and bubbling from the intense activity below its surface. Expect wildly coloured mountainsides, glacial rivers and the glaciers themselves, and then you'll finally emerge at a verdant nature reserve in Þórsmörk. It is the most popular hike in Iceland and infrastructure is sound, with well positioned huts along the zigzag 55km route. But it is essential that you book months in advance if you intend to use them. Campers do not need to reserve.

Check www.safetravel.is before setting out (and log your plan with them), and be sure to register at the information hut in Landmannalaugar. It is imperative not to attempt the hike out of season (opening dates vary according to weather, but tend to be early July to early September), as the conditions can be lethal and there will be no services on the route. Even in summer there will be snow and fog along the way, and rivers to cross; prepare accordingly.

Sleeping & Eating

As the Laugavegurinn trail is very well travelled, you'll find a constellation of carefully positioned huts along the way, all owned and maintained by Ferðafélag Íslands (www.fi.is). These huts sleep dozens of people, but must be booked (and prepaid) months in advance – you can get on a waiting list the year before, and bookings officially open in October or November prior to the summer. We cannot stress enough that these beds go quickly. Also note that bunk beds at most huts sleep four people each – two (side by side) on each level. If you are alone, expect to be paired with a stranger.

Huts usually have a solar panel for wardens to charge their communications equipment and perhaps lights for the hut, but there is no electricity for hikers. There is a strict quiet rule from midnight to 7am.

There is camping in designated areas around the huts, though with the increasing popularity of the hike, these can become full as well (no numbers cap was in place at the time of writing). Note that campers *do not* have access to hut kitchens or facilities and must bring all their own camping and cooking equipment. Campers can use bathrooms and running water. Camping areas are often exposed to the elements – streamline your tent with the wind, then pin it down with extra boulders. All camping costs kr1800 per person, and does not need to be reserved. Wardens accept cash and credit cards.

Huts are usually open late June to early September, but this is weather dependent; check ahead. Huts are locked in winter. Wild camping is strictly forbidden along the whole trail, as these are protected nature reserves.

There is no food for sale along the trail; bring everything.

Hrafntinnusker HUT, CAMPGROUND €
(Höskuldsskáli; ☎568 2533; www.fi.is; N 63°56.014', W 19°10.109'; sites/huts per person kr1800/7500) This hut holds 52 people (around 22 of whom sleep on mattresses on the floor in a converted attic space). It is at an elevation of 1027m – be prepared for particularly inhospitable conditions if you are camping – and it's the barest-bones of the huts. There's an outhouse and geothermal heating, but no refuse facilities and no showers – you must carry your rubbish to Hvangil.

Some campers cook their food on the natural steam vents nearby; ask the warden (July and August only) to tell you where. When there is no warden, water must be sourced from a stream or snow.

Álftavatn HUT, CAMPGROUND €
(☎568 2533; www.fi.is; N 63°51.470', W 19°13.640'; sites/huts per person kr1800/7500) Two huts here hold 72 people in total; both have drinking water and mattresses. Kitchen facilities have gas stoves. Showers cost kr500. Opening coincides with the opening of local F roads (anywhere from early to late June, depending on weather), and it closes in mid-September.

Hvanngil HUT, CAMPGROUND €
(☎568 2533; www.fi.is; sites/huts per person kr1800/7500) This hut is on an alternative path on the Laugavegurinn hike, 5km south of Álftavatn. It holds 60 people, and has a kitchen and shower (kr500). It's a good choice for people tackling Laugavegurinn in two days. It's usually quieter than Álftavatn.

Emstrur HUT, CAMPGROUND €
(Botnar; ☎568 2533; www.fi.is; N 63°45.980', W 19°22.450'; sites/huts per person kr1800/7500) Emstrur has 60 beds divided into three huts. There are two showers (kr500 for five minutes of hot water), toilets and a gas stove. There are no garbage facilities or power outlets. Although it's located under the glacier, the other huts have a more striking position along the trail. Note that mobile-phone reception is particularly spotty here.

ℹ Information

Ferðafélag Íslands (Iceland Touring Association; ☎568 2533; www.fi.is) runs the facilities in the area and its website is loaded with information, including details on the hike. It publishes (and sells at Landmannalaugar) a small booklet (kr3000) about the hike in English and Icelandic offering detailed information about the landscape, sights and path, and also sells a map (kr1700).

Most adventure operators throughout south Iceland offer Laugavegurinn guiding. In addition to the traditional hike, some do longer variations off the beaten track (literally), to hiker-free mountains that run parallel to the main trail.

Most hikers walk from north to south to take advantage of the net altitude loss and the facilities at Þórsmörk. From Þórsmörk you can catch a bus or continue hiking to Skógar on the Fimmvörðuháls trek (p144), which takes an extra day or two (about an additional 20km).

WEATHER & GEAR

We highly recommend taking a map and GPS if you plan on tackling the walk without a guide.

The track is almost always passable for hiking from early July through to mid-September. Early in the season (late June to early July) there can be icy patches or deep snow that are difficult to navigate – projected hut openings offer a good gauge of conditions. In summer some of the rivers can be too deep to cross. Huts are locked out of season, so hiking the trail out of season is decidedly discouraged (and dangerous).

At any time of the year the Landmannalaugar to Þórsmörk hike is not to be undertaken lightly. It is imperative that you pack appropriate warm and waterproof clothing and gear, as weather conditions change dramatically in an instant. You will be fording rivers, and fog and rain can come up at any time. That means no jeans or cotton clothes next to your skin at all. If you are not a seasoned hiker and don't know what to bring, do your research first. Wardens have reported a huge upswing in unprepared hikers needing intervention. Don't be one of them.

You must carry sufficient food and water.

LUGGAGE TRANSPORT

You don't have to schlep all your bags along the Laugavegurinn hike. Going with a tour company, staff will usually transport your extra bags from the start to the end of the trail, and even, sometimes, between huts.

ALTERNATIVE ACCESS POINTS

Improbable though it may seem, Reykjavík Excursions (www.re.is) bus 18 goes from Reykjavík to Álftavatn, Hvanngil and Emstrur daily from late June through August (Reykjavík–Álftavatn kr9000, four hours) with short stops to get out and walk around.

Laugavegurinn Hike

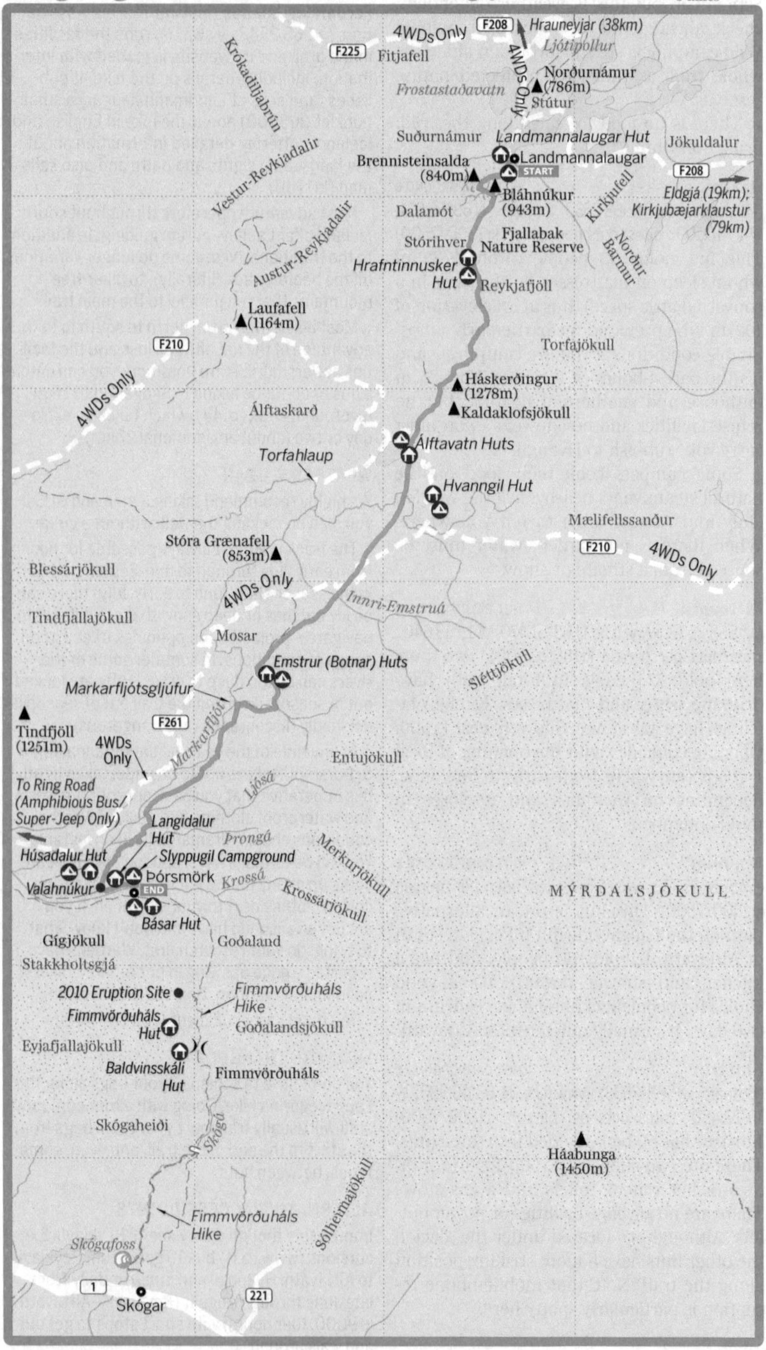

HIKING LAUGAVEGURINN

Laugavegurinn in Four Days

Ferðafélag Íslands (www.fi.is) breaks Laugavegurinn into four sections (see the website for a detailed description), and many hikers opt to tackle one section each day for four days, as carefully positioned sleeping huts (and adjoining campsites) punctuate the start and end point of each leg.

Part 1: Landmannalaugar to Hrafntinnusker (12km; four to five hours) A relatively easy start to your adventure, the walk to the first hut passes the boiling earth at Stórihver and sweeping fields of glittering obsidian. If you want to extend the walk, start at Landmannalaugar and hike to Hrafntinnusker via Skalli; the information hut in Landmannalaugar has a handout that details this quieter route. You'll need to fill up on fresh water before you depart as there's no source until you reach the first hut. About 2km before Hrafntinnusker there's a memorial to a solo Israeli hiker who died on the trail in 2005 after ignoring a warden's warning – a reminder to properly prepare for your hike and always keep your ear to the ground.

Part 2: Hrafntinnusker to Álftavatn (12km; four to five hours) At Hrafntinnusker you can try a couple of short local hikes without your pack before setting off. There are views at Södull (20 minutes return) and Reykjafjöll (one hour return), and a hidden geothermal area behind the ice caves (three hours return); ask the warden for walking tips. Views aplenty are found on the walk to Álftavatn as well – hike across the northern spur of the Kaldaklofsfjöll ice cap for vistas from the summit. Walking into Álftavatn you'll see looming Tindfjallajökull, Mýrdalsjökull and the infamous Eyjafjallajökull before reaching the serenely beautiful lake where you'll spend the night.

Part 3: Álftavatn to Emstrur-Botnar (15km; six to seven hours) To reach Emstrur you'll need to ford at least one large stream – you can take your shoes off and get wet or wait at the edge of the river for a 4WD to give you a lift over. Not to be missed is the detour to spectacular Markarfljótsgljúfur – a gigantic multihued canyon. It's well marked from Emstrur, and takes about an hour to reach (you come back the same way).

Part 4: Emstrur-Botnar to Þórsmörk (15km; six to seven hours) Barrenness turns to brilliantly verdant lands dotted with lush Arctic flowers. If you're not planning on staying in Þórsmörk, you need to arrive before the last bus leaves.

Laugavegurinn in Three Days

If you're fit, it's within your reach to complete the hike in three days instead of four. Cover Part 1 and Part 2 in one day, arriving at Álftavatn after a full eight to 10 hours of hiking. Hike to Emstrur on your second day, and arrive in Þórsmörk on the evening of your third.

Laugavegurinn in Two Days

If you're a fleet, avid hiker, you can complete all 55km of the hike in two long days. On your first day hike all the way to Álftavatn, or better yet, continue the additional 5km to reach Hvanngil. It's possible to combine Part 3 and Part 4 on your second day, as these 30km are relatively flat. There's an overall 100m decline.

Laugavegurinn in Five Hours

Wanna get nuts? Join the endurance race **Laugavegur Ultra Marathon** (Laugavegshlaupið; www.marathon.is; ⏲Jul), when Iceland's toughest runners complete the entire hike in under five hours. The latest record: Þorbergur Ingi Jónsson at 3:59:13.

Laugavegurinn Extended

If weather conditions are favourable, there's no reason to rush. You can use the huts as hiking bases, and explore paths that veer away from the main Laugavegurinn trail. You can also spend time based in Landmannalaugar before setting off, though we prefer Þórsmörk.

Þórsmörk

A nature reserve, Þórsmörk is a verdant realm of forest and flower-filled lees that looks onto curling gorges, icy rivers and three looming glaciers (Tindfjallajökull, Eyjafjallajökull and Mýrdalsjökull). The glaciers protect this quiet spot from some of the region's harsher weather; it is often warmer or drier in Þórsmörk than nearby. Be warned, though: Þórsmörk's lovely setting and proximity to Reykjavík (130km) make it a popular spot in summer.

The higher, northeastern reaches of the area are known as **Goðaland** (Land of the Gods), which is – as the name suggests – divine. Rock formations twist skyward like the stone arches of an ancient cathedral. Fluorescent Arctic flowers burst forth from spongy moss bringing brilliant slashes of colour. At its higher altitudes, Goðaland often has rougher weather than Þórsmörk.

Þórsmörk may seem relatively close to the Ring Road on a map, but you'll need to take a bus or go by high-clearance 4WD (super-Jeep tour) to ford the rivers on the way to the reserve (or hike in from Skógar or Landmannalaugar). As you get close, coming from the south, you must cross the dangerous Krossá river. Regular 4WDs cannot make it. You'll see that they are parked where people have hitched rides with buses or super-Jeeps.

Goðaland is the endpoint for the glorious Fimmvörðuháls trek (p144), which starts in Skógar. The main camping area in Goðaland is Básar (p153); to go between it and Þórsmörk by car you must make the dangerous Krossá river crossing mentioned above. Walkers use footbridges.

Húsadalur – Volcano Huts Þórsmörk (p153) is open year-round, but buses tend to run May to mid-October. The rest of the year you'll need to come on a private super-Jeep tour to reach Þórsmörk.

Activities

Although Þórsmörk is the terminus for the uber-popular Laugavegurinn hike (p148), many tired trekkers catch a bus out of the reserve immediately, missing spectacular day hiking (sans backpack). Some continue along the Fimmvörðuháls trek (p144) into Skógar, a truly incredible walk, but better approached in the opposite direction (departing from Skógar).

It's possible to volunteer to help with trail maintenance with Þórsmörk Trail Volunteers (www.trailteam.is), an Iceland Forest Service initiative.

★Stakkholtsgjá Canyon — HIKING

Stakkholtsgjá is a wonderful alternately rocky and mossy gorge with a hidden waterfall. Walk along the river bed, hop across the river, and when it splits in two veer left down a narrower canyon. Scamper over boulders and you'll spot a crashing cascade (or dramatic icicles in winter). The walk takes around 90 minutes. Reykjavík Excursions buses stop here.

★Valahnúkur Circle — HIKING

A 2½-hour loop takes you up to the brilliant viewpoint at Valahnúkur, which takes in canyons, glaciers and sightlines all the way to the ocean. From Húsadalur, follow the trail up to the viewpoint then down into Langidalur. From there pass along the ridge between the valleys back to your starting point. Or, do it in reverse.

You can hike one way and connect with buses on either side as well.

Tindfjöll Circle — HIKING

The longest of the most popular 'short hikes' in the area takes around 4½ hours from Langidalur and around six hours from Húsadalur. It will take you along the Tindfjöll gorge and ridge. Húsadalur – Volcano Huts Þórsmörk (p153) sells maps.

Wander through the **Slyppugil Valley** (or follow the like-named ridge), then hike across moraine along the side of a second ridge. You'll then pass through **Tröllakirkja** (Trolls' Church) with its sweeping stone arches. A lush green field appears next before revealing a postcard-worthy viewpoint to the Þórsmörk valley. Follow the top of the sandstone ridge until you find yourself at the coursing Krossá river, which leads you back to Langidalur, or further on to Húsadalur.

Tours

Coming by guided super-Jeep tour can be a lovely treat, revealing more than what you'll find on your own.

Guides throughout the south, such as Southcoast Adventure (p141), Midgard Adventure (p138) and Icelandic Mountain Guides (p145) are a great value-add as not only do they get you to the region, but they can take you to hidden valleys, waterfalls and glacier approaches that the buses do not reach, while sharing local geological and cultural insights. For example, **Gígjökull** glacial tongue, with its formerly enormous moraine, was one of the main sites of flooding when Eyjafjallajökull erupted; you can get close enough to lick it.

Sleeping

There are three lodging areas in Þórsmörk: Langidalur, with huts as well at nearby Slyppugil; Básar (technically in Goðaland); and Húsadalur. All have huts and campsites, cooking facilities and running water. They get rammed during summer months, so it's crucial to book space in the huts in advance. We recommend bringing a sleeping bag and your own food. Note that wild camping is forbidden in the area.

Langidalur HUT, CAMPGROUND €
(Þórsmörk, Skagfjörðsskáli; ☎893 1191, booking 568 2533; www.fi.is; N 63°40.960', W 19°30.890'; sites/huts per person kr1800/7500; ⏲May-Sep) Langidalur – also referred to simply as Þórsmörk, or Skagfjörðsskáli – is the most rustic option of the four in Þórsmörk, but is well-maintained. It sleeps 75 and has two kitchens. Campers do not have access to the hut or its facilities (kitchens), so must bring their own stoves etc. The well-tended camping space has access to a dining hut and large shower block.

A small shop offers hot coffee and tea, plus basic provisions: camping gas, wool socks, soup, jam, light beer etc and is open variable hours from May to September. Operated by Ferðafélag Íslands, which manages the Laugavegurinn huts.

Básar HUT, CAMPGROUND €
(☎893 2910, booking 562 1000; www.utivist.is; Goðaland, N 63°40,559', W 19°29,014'; sites/huts per person kr1500/5500) Básar is the choice base for Icelanders, largely due to its beautiful position in the trees. Space is very cramped, but there's hut accommodation for 83 people, which can be booked through Útivist. Grass and wooden planks lead around the private camping space, which gets extremely crowded on summer weekends. Showers cost kr500.

Slyppugil Campsite CAMPGROUND €
(☎575 6700; www.hostel.is; sites per person kr1200; ⏲mid-Jun–mid-Aug) This campground run by Hostelling International sits within sight (about 500m) from Langidalur and has showers, toilets and barbecues. The warden can help with information on day hikes. Discounts available when buying a bus ticket from Reykjavík Campsite (p78).

Baldvinsskáli HUT €
(☎568 2533; www.fi.is; N 63°36.622', W 19°26.477'; dm kr6000; ⏲mid-Jun–mid-Sep) This tiny 12-person A-frame hut run by Ferðafélags Íslands is about halfway along the Fimmvörðuháls trek and has a small kitchen and outhouse, but no running water. Book well ahead.

Fimmvörðuháls HUT €
(☎893 4910, booking 562 1000; www.utivist.is; N 63°37.320', W 19°27.093'; per person kr6000; ⏲mid-Jun–Aug) The 20-bed hut at Fimmvörðuskáli at 1000m altitude on the pass between Eyjafjallajökull and Mýrdalsjökull lies 600m west of the main trail and is easy to miss in poor weather. Útivist tour groups have priority here, so it's often booked out. There's no campsite or running water.

Húsadalur – Volcano Huts Þórsmörk HUT, CAMPGROUND €€
(☎552 8300; www.volcanohuts.com; Húsadalur; sites per person kr2000, dm/s/d & cottages without bathroom kr7500/16,000/25,000) Busy Volcano Huts Þórsmörk fills the Húsadalur area with basic dorm-style huts, private rooms, five-person cottages (sleeping-bag accommodation with kitchenettes) and a campground, all with shared bathrooms and sauna. There's a cooking area, but you must bring your own stove and utensils. Linen costs kr3000.

The good restaurant (breakfast/lunch/dinner costs kr2200/2700/4500) offers a lunch of soup, fresh bread, coffee and cake, and a buffet dinner, and has wi-fi. It also sells trail maps and box lunches (kr2500).

Eating

There is a basic buffet-style restaurant at Húsadalur – Volcano Huts Þórsmörk. Otherwise bring your own food.

Getting There & Away

BUS

Special all-terrain buses reach all the way to Þórsmörk when the roads are open (see www.road.is). Reykjavík buses to/from Þórsmörk stop in Hveragerði, Selfoss, Hella, Hvolsvöllur and Seljalandsfoss en route. The Reykjavík Excursions schedule is particularly helpful in hopping around the sites within Þórsmörk. Note that buses are special amphibiously equipped rigs for fording rivers.

Reykjavík Excursions (www.re.is) services:

- Buses 9/9a Reykjavík–Þórsmörk (kr7500, four hours, one daily May to mid-October stopping at Húsadalur, Stakkholtsgjá Canyon, Básar, Langidalur; plus two additional services June to August). Returning 9a buses have a slightly simplified route heading back towards Reykjavík; if you want the bus to stop at Básar or Langidalur, you must request it with the hut supervisor before noon. Other sample prices: from Hella or Hvolsvöllur kr5000, from Seljalandsfoss kr4000, from the impassable Krossá river crossroads kr2000.

Sterna (www.sterna.is) services:

- Bus 14/14a Reykjavík–Þórsmörk (kr6650, 4½ hours, one daily late June to early September). There's also an afternoon bus to/from Seljalandsfoss.

Trex (www.trex.is) services:

- Bus T11 Reykjavík–Þórsmörk (kr7500, 4½ hours, two daily mid-June to mid-September; stops at Gígjökull, Básar and Langidalur). Other sample prices: from Hveragerði or Selfoss kr6300, from Hella, Hvolsvöllur or Seljalandsfoss kr4600.

CAR

You cannot drive all the way into Þórsmörk with your rental vehicle. End of story. If you have your own 4WD with excellent clearance, you can plough down Rtes 249 and F249 until you reach the crossroads for Húsadalur and Básar at the Krossá river. It's there that you must leave your vehicle – you will not be able to ford the gushing river unless you're driving a super-Jeep and know what you're doing. The buses that serve Þórsmörk are special amphibious vehicles outfitted to pass the deep river and boulder-littered ravines. If you park at the crossroads, you can hitch with the bus (kr2000 per person) or a super-Jeep. Super-Jeeps can get there in winter.

HIKING

Þórsmörk is usually the terminus of the popular Laugavegurinn hike, with the beginning at Landmannalaugar. It's also popular to reach Þórsmörk from Skógar on the beautiful Fimmvörðuháls hike. If you are planning to reach Þórsmörk by foot we recommend one of these; walking along Rtes 249 and F249 from Seljalandsfoss is far less scenic.

It takes around 30 minutes to walk between Langidalur and Húsadalur on the shortest path.

Skógar to Vík

As the Ring Road arcs east from Skógar to Vík the haunches of the foothills rise to the glaciers, mountain tops and volcanoes inland, while rivers descend from mysterious gorges and course across the broad sweep of pastures to black-sand beaches and the crashing ocean. This rural area may be dotted with farmhouses (many of which have guesthouses), but considering the volume of summertime visitors, it still feels alternately dramatic and pastoral.

Sights

The following landmarks are listed from west to east.

★Sólheimajökull GLACIER

One of the easiest glacial tongues to reach is Sólheimajökull. This icy outlet glacier unfurls from the main Mýrdalsjökull ice cap and is a favourite spot for glacial walks and ice climbing. Rte 221 leads 4.2km off the Ring Road to a small car park and the Arcanum Glacier Café (p160), from where you can walk the 800m to the ice along a wide track edging the glacial lagoon. Don't attempt to climb onto the glacier unguided.

Mýrdalsjökull ICE CAP

This gorgeous glacier is Iceland's fourth-largest ice cap, covering 700 sq km and reaching a thickness of almost 750m in places. The volcano Katla snoozes beneath, periodically blasting up through the ice to drown the coastal plain in a deluge of melt water, sand and tephra. Local operators run tours along the glacial crown as part of longer trips. Don't explore the area on your own; the ice is unstable and the track to the caldera can be impossible to navigate.

Sólheimasandur BEACH

On 21 November, 1973, a US Navy aeroplane was forced to crash-land at Sólheimasandur. The crew all survived, but the wreckage of the militarised Douglas DC-3 remains on the black-sand beach. It's east of the Sólheimajökull/Rte 221 turn-off and south down a farm lane to the beach. The road was closed due to abuse by visitors, so now you must walk from a basic car park. There is talk of paving a road to the site.

★Dyrhólaey WILDLIFE RESERVE

One of the south coast's most recognisable natural formations is the rocky plateau and huge stone sea arch at Dyrhólaey (*deer-lay*), which rises dramatically from the surrounding plain 10km west of Vík, at the end of Rte 218. Visit its crashing black beaches and get awesome views from atop the promontory. The islet is a nature reserve that's rich in bird life, including puffins; some or all of it can be closed during nesting season (15 May to 25 June).

★ **Reynisfjara** BEACH

On the west side of Reynisfjall, the high ridge above Vík, Rte 215 leads 5km down to black-sand beach Reynisfjara. It's backed by an incredible stack of **basalt columns** that look like a magical church organ, and there are outstanding views west to Dyrhólaey. Surrounding cliffs are pocked with caves formed from twisted basalt, and puffins belly flop into the crashing sea during summer. Immediately offshore are the towering Reynisdrangur (p161) sea stacks. Watch for rogue waves: people are often swept away.

Tours

Arcanum ADVENTURE TOUR

(☎487 1500; www.arcanum.is) This popular tour operator runs daily Sólheimajökull glacier walks (kr12,990), plus snowmobile (from kr24,990), quad-bike and other tours geared toward all ages. Based on Ytri-Sólheimar I farm 11km east of Skógar. Offers Reykjavík pick up and local accommodation.

Mountain Excursion ADVENTURE TOUR

(☎897 7737; www.mountainexcursion.is) A small outfit offering two-hour Sólheimajökull glacier hikes (kr14,900) and a volcano super-Jeep tour (kr23,900). Based at Volcano Hotel (p160).

Sleeping & Eating

Note that camping is prohibited on Dyrhólaey.

★ **Garðar** GUESTHOUSE €

(☎487 1260; www.reynisfjara-guesthouses.com; Reynisfjara; cottages kr12,000-18,000) Garðar, at the end of Rte 215, to the west of Vík, is a magical, view-blessed place. Friendly farmer Ragnar rents out self-contained beachside huts: one stone cottage sleeps four, other timber cottages sleep two to four. Linen costs kr1500 per person.

★ **Grand Guesthouse Garðakot** B&B €€

(☎487 1441; www.ggg.is; Garðakot farm; d kr26,000) Set on a pastoral sheep farm, this small tidy house holds four beautiful rooms, two with private bathrooms. Heated hardwood floors, sweeping views of volcanoes and sea and friendly proprietors, pretty decor, serenity and flat-screen TVs for all. It's 14km west of Vík, south of the Ring Road on Rte 218.

Giljur Gistihús GUESTHOUSE €€

(☎866 0176; s/d without bathroom incl breakfast kr15,000/20,200, d/tr incl breakfast kr25,700/38,600; ⏲Jun–mid-Sep) Just 7km west of Vík and tucked back off the Ring Road at the foot of lush cliffs creased by a waterfall and dotted with grazing horses, this small farm guesthouse offers rooms with shared or private bathroom and a hearty breakfast. Book via Icelandic Farm Holidays (www.farmholidays.is).

Gistiheimlilið Reynir GUESTHOUSE €€

(☎894 9788; www.reyni.is; Reynisfjara; d without bathroom kr14,000, f with/without bathroom kr24,100/22,000) This family-owned silver strip of rooms looks out over the ocean at Dyrhólaey. The twin bedrooms and six-person family rooms share bathrooms and a kitchen. Older mini-cottages have their own sinks and toilets.

Sólheimahjáleiga Guesthouse B&B €€

(☎864 2919; www.solheimahjaleiga.is; Sólheimahjáleiga farm; d with/without bathroom kr27,500/23,400, tr with/without bathroom kr38,400/33,300, q kr49,300; P) A series of cosy renovated farm buildings house rooms with shared bathrooms and a kitchen, and family rooms upstairs with private bathrooms. A newly built silver building has ten cosy rooms with private bathrooms. Find it 11km east of Skógar, just north of the Ring Road.

Farmhouse Lodge B&B €€

(☎571 5879; www.farmhouse.is; Skeiðflöt; d with/without bathroom incl breakfast kr39,500/37,000, apt kr39,500) Surprisingly sleek and contemporary designer rooms fill this low-key farm lodge on the Ring Road 14km west of Vík. Bedside tables are made from hewn tree trunks, public spaces are tastefully decorated and the buffet breakfast is generous.

Mið-Hvoll Cottages COTTAGES €€

(☎863 3238; www.hvoll.com; cottages kr21,000) This stand of seven cosy wooden cottages sits within sight of Dyrhólaey in a pastoral area south of the Ring Road, with mountain and ocean views. Each kitchen-equipped cottage sleeps five; linen and towels cost kr1500 per person. The owners also offer horse riding on nearby beaches and pastures for all ages and skill levels (from kr6000).

Find it about 12km west of Vík, 3km down tiny Rte 216, just west of the turn-off for Dyrhólaey (Rte 218).

(Continued on page 160)

The Northern Lights

Topping countless bucket lists and filling Instagram feeds, the Northern Lights (or aurora borealis) are a magnet drawing countless cool-weather visitors, who arrive with fingers crossed for good viewing conditions, their necks craned skywards.

What Are They?

The Inuit thought the Northern Lights were the souls of the dead; Scandinavian folklore described them as the spirits of unmarried women; and the Japanese believed that a child conceived under the dancing rays would be fortunate in life. Modern science, however, has a different take on the aurora borealis.

The magical curtains of colour that streak across the northern night sky are the result of solar wind – a stream of particles from the sun that collides with oxygen, nitrogen and hydrogen in the upper atmosphere. These collisions produce the haunting greens and magentas as the earth's magnetic field draws the wind towards the polar regions.

Where & How to See Them

Catching a glimpse of the Northern Lights requires nothing more than a dark, partly clear night (ie few clouds) and a pinch of luck. It's as simple as that.

Many tour companies offer 'Northern Lights tours' (by boat, jeep or bus) – they are essentially taking you to an area with less light pollution and cloud cover to increase your viewing odds. You can do this yourself, too, though we don't recommend inexperienced winter drivers chase clear skies in remote, snowy areas.

KRISSANAPONG WONGSAWARNG/SHUTTERSTOCK ©

KRISSANAPONG WONGSAWARNG/SHUTTERSTOCK ©

1. Jökulsárlón (p327)
2. Kirkjufell (p186)
3. Skaftafell (p319)

COOLKENGZZ/SHUTTERSTOCK ©

Head to recommended viewing spots on the outskirts of Reykjavík (these include Grótta lighthouse at Seltjarnarnes, or Öskjuhlíð hill), or book a few nights at a rural inn and wait for the light show in the evening. Many hotels offer viewing wake-up calls should the lights appear in the middle of the night while you're asleep.

Recent winters have been excellent for Northern Lights, with viewings beginning as early as late August. Mid-September to mid-April is the 'official' season, but it can be longer, in the right conditions. Peak winter months enjoy the most darkness (an important factor for viewing), but also heavier weather conditions, storms and cloud cover.

And note you don't always need to be away from the city to enjoy a show – when the aurora is strong, even the lights of Reykjavík can't hide them.

Predicting Activity

Predicting the likelihood of an aurora is close to impossible, but there are various tools, apps and alerts that report factors such as solar activity and therefore the likelihood of seeing one in the short term.

The comprehensive website of the Icelandic Met Office details aurora activity, cloud cover, sunlight and moonlight, in order to provide an aurora forecast (generally for the week ahead, from September to mid-April). Check it out at http://en.vedur.is/weather/forecasts/aurora. More resources are outlined at www.easyaurora.com.

1

GAVIN QUIRKE/GETTY IMAGES ©

KELLY CHENG/GETTY IMAGES ©

1. Seljalandsfoss (p141)
Pick your way along a slippery path to stand behind the cascade as it thunders into the pool below.

2. Blue Lagoon (p101)
Ringed by a black-lava field, these geothermal pools are rich in skin-softening minerals, mud and algae.

3. Þórsmörk (p152)
Three glaciers surround this nature reserve, site of some spectacular hiking.

4. Icelandic horses
Icelandic horses – brought to Iceland by the Vikings – have an unusual gait, the *tölt*, a smooth running walk.

WANDERLUSTER/GETTY IMAGES ©

 (Continued from page 155)

KATLA GEOPARK

In 2011 Iceland formed its first 'geopark' to protect a region of great geological importance, promote local culture and sustainable development, and educate visitors. The **Katla Geopark** (☎560 2043; www.katlageopark.is) extends from Hvolsvöllur northeast to the great Vatnajökull and down to the volcanic black-sand beaches. It includes its namesake Katla volcano, the infamous Eyjafjallajökull and the tortured earth at Lakagígar. All told, that's about 9% of Iceland. There is no park office, but the geopark website offers information.

Of all the volcanoes in Iceland, it is thought that Katla may cause the most trouble to Icelanders over the next few years. This highly active 30km-long volcano, buried deep under the Mýrdalsjökull glacier, has erupted roughly twice per century in the past. Since the last eruption was in 1918, it's now several decades overdue.

It's expected that when Katla does blow, days of ash fall, tephra clouds and lightning strikes will follow the initial explosion, with flash floods caused by the sudden melting of glacial ice. The geological record shows that past eruptions have created tidal waves, which have boomeranged off the Vestmannaeyjar and deluged the area where the town of Vík stands today.

Local residents receive regular evacuation training for the day when Katla erupts. In the event of an eruption, all mobile phones within range of a tower (including yours) will receive a warning. After the alert, farmers must hang a notice on their front doors to show that they have evacuated, before unplugging their electric fences, opening cattle sheds so that their animals can flee to higher ground, and heading for one of the evacuation centres in Hvolsvöllur, Vík and Kirkjubæjarklaustur.

Hótel Dyrhólaey HOTEL €€
(☎487 1333; www.dyrholaey.is; d kr27,100-33,100; @) On a bluff 10km west of Vík, this 88-room hotel is popular with tour groups. Large rooms with basic mod cons sprout off three wings with wide, carpeted hallways, and new additions continue being added. The restaurant is open from 7pm to 9pm from May to October, and also occasionally for lunch.

Guesthouse Steig GUESTHOUSE €€€
(☎487 1324; www.guesthousesteig.is; d with/without bathroom incl breakfast kr32,890/23,000; @) Sixteen kilometres west of Vík and 1.5km north of the Ring Road on a dirt track, sweet Guesthouse Steig is a simple farm building filled with surprisingly spacious, modern and bright rooms. There's a shared kitchen, the staff are friendly, and it feels like a real rural homestay.

Volcano Hotel HOTEL €€€
(☎486 1200; www.volcanohotel.is; Ketilsstaðaskóli; s/d/f incl breakfast from kr27,200/31,900/40,500) This seven-room hotel, 11.5km west of Vík, plays with a volcano motif in its decor: floors are made from a mosaic of pebbles, and candles glow throughout. It's a top hotel option in the area, so books up early. Mountain Excursion, a small tour operator, is based here.

Arcanum Glacier Café CAFE €
(Café Solheimajökull; ☎547 1500; www.arcanum.is; snacks kr750-1375; ⏲9.30am-5pm May-Sep, reduced hours Oct-Apr) This welcoming oasis at the foot of the Solheimajökull glacier tongue offers a range of simple snacks such as pizza, sandwiches and cakes.

Svarta Fjaran CAFE €€
(Black Beach Restaurant; ☎571 2718; www.svartafjaran.com; Reynisfjara; snacks kr990, dinner mains kr2500-6000; ⏲11am-10pm) Black volcanic cubes, meant to mimic the nearby black beach Reynisfjara with its famous basalt columns, house this contemporary restaurant that serves homemade cakes and snacks during the day and a full dinner menu at night. Plate-glass windows give views to the ocean and Dyrhólaey beyond.

Vík

POP 320

The welcoming little community of Vík (aka Vík í Mýrdal) has become a booming hub for a very beautiful portion of the south coast. Iceland's southernmost town, it's also the rainiest, but that doesn't stop the madhouse atmosphere in summer, when every room within 100km is booked solid. With loads of services, Vík is a convenient base for the beautiful basalt beach Reynisfjara and its puffin cliffs, and the rocky plateau Dyrhólaey (both just to the west) and for the volcanoes running from Skógar to Jökulsárlón glacier lagoon and beyond. Along the coast, white-capped waves wash up on black sands and the cliffs glow green from all that rain. Put simply, it's gorgeous.

⊙ Sights

Reynisdrangur LANDMARK
Vík's most iconic cluster of sea stacks is known as Reynisdrangur, which rise from the ocean like ebony towers at the western end of Vík's black-sand beach. Tradition says they're masts of a ship that trolls were stealing when they got caught in the sun. The nearby cliffs are good for puffin watching. A bracing walk up from Vík's western end takes you to the top of **Reynisfjall** ridge (340m), offering superb views.

Víkurkirkja CHURCH
(Hátún) High above town, Vík's 1930s church has stained-glass windows in spiky geometrical shapes, but we like it most for its village views.

Brydebúð MUSEUM
(☑ 487 1395; http://brydebud.vik.is; Víkurbraut 28; museum adult/child kr500/free; ⊙ 11am-8pm Mon-Fri, to 5pm Sat & Sun Jun-Aug) In town, the tin-clad house Brydebúð was built in Vestmannaeyjar in 1831 and moved to Vík in 1895. Today it houses the tourist office, the Halldórskaffi restaurant and a small museum with displays on local fishing, as well as explanations of what it's like to live under the volcano Katla.

☞ Tours

Skógar (33km west of Vík) and Hvolsvöllur are the hubs for activity tours on the south coast. In Vík, you can check with the hostel for tours to Mýrdalsjökull. Many Reykjavík tour companies also make the long haul out here.

Katla Track JEEP TOUR
(☑ 849 4404; www.katlatrack.is) Katla Track runs tours of the area (kr29,900, from Reykjavík kr44,900) that take in local landmarks and get to the edge of Mýrdalsjökull.

🛏 Sleeping

Vík HI Hostel HOSTEL €
(Norður-Vík Hostel; ☑ 487 1106; www.hostel. is; Suðurvíkurvegur 5; dm/d without bathroom kr4750/12,900, cottages from kr32,800; @) ⌖

Vík's small, homey, year-round hostel is in the beige house on the hill behind the village centre. Good facilities include a guest kitchen and bike hire (per half-/full day kr2000/3000), plus several stand-alone cottages sleeping up to eight people. Staff also arrange local tours (from kr9000) and paragliding (kr35,000; May to September). There's a kr750 discount for HI members. Green-certified.

Vík Campsite CAMPGROUND €
(Tjaldsvæðið Vík; ☑ 487 1345; www.vikcamping.is; Klettsvegur 7; sites per adult kr1500; ⊙ Jun-Sep) The campsite sits under a grassy ridge at the eastern end of town, just beyond the Hótel Edda. An octagonal building houses cooking facilities, a washing machine, toilets and showers (kr200), and a new one should open in 2017. There are also four little cottages (kr10,000).

★**Guesthouse Carina** B&B €€
(☑ 699 0961; www.guesthousecarina.is; Mýrarbraut 13; s/d/q without bathroom incl breakfast from kr16,900/21,900/31,500; P) Friendly Carina and her husband Ingvar run one of the best lodging options in Vík. Neat-as-a-pin, spacious rooms with good light and clean shared bathrooms fill a large converted house near the centre of town.

Heimagisting Erika B&B €€
(☑ 487 1117; www.erika.is; Sigtún 5; d without bathroom incl breakfast kr21,000) German Erika is a warm hostess with a lovely panorama-filled house and a couple of guest rooms. Her highly praised breakfasts feature homemade jams, syrups and herbal teas (many for sale). Bookings essential; cash only.

Hótel Edda Vík HOTEL €€
(☑ 444 4840; www.hoteledda.is; Klettsvegur 1-5; d incl breakfast kr27,000; P @) This motel-style place on a busy spot just in front of the Icelandair Hotel and near the N1 petrol station has unmemorable but decent rooms, 31 of which have phone, TV and bathroom, and 10 of which are cottages with en suite bathrooms. It shares a reception desk with Icelandair Hotel; breakfasts are sumptuous.

★**Icelandair Hótel Vík** HOTEL €€€
(☑ 487 1480, booking 444 4000; www.icelandair hotels.com; Klettsvegur 1-5; d/tr/f from kr24,500/29,000/50,000; P) This sleek black-window-fronted hotel is improbably tucked just behind the Hótel Edda, on the eastern edge of town, near the campground.

The hotels share a lobby (and have the same friendly owners), but that's where the resemblance ends. The Icelandair hotel has suitably swanky rooms, some with views to the rear cliffs or the sea. The light, natural decor is inspired by the local environment.

Puffin Hotel HOTEL €€€
(☎467 1212; www.puffinhotelvik.is; Víkurbraut 24-26; d/tr incl breakfast from kr29,400/36,000; @) This busy complex of bare-bones and small rooms is packed in high season, often by tour groups. Prices are stiff for what you get. It also has a small hostel (single/double without bathroom from kr11,000/13,400) and apartments to rent (from kr50,100). New owners hope to improve the standards.

Eating

Víkurskáli INTERNATIONAL €
(☎487 1230; Austurvegur 18; mains kr1400-3000; ⏲11am-9pm) Grab a booth and a burger at the old-school grill inside the N1 with a view of Reynisdrangur. Daily specials from casserole to lamb stew.

★**Suður-Vík** ICELANDIC, ASIAN €€
(☎487 1515; www.facebook.com/Sudurvik; Suðurvíkurvegur 1, Vík; mains kr2100-5000; ⏲noon-10pm) The friendly ambience, from hardwood floors and interesting artwork to smiling staff, helps elevate this restaurant beyond the competition. Food is Icelandic hearty, and ranges from heaping steak sandwiches with bacon and Béarnaise sauce to Asian (think Thai satay with rice). In a warmly lit silver building atop town. Book ahead in summer.

Halldórskaffi INTERNATIONAL €€
(☎487 1202; www.halldorskaffi.is; Víkurbraut 28, Vík; mains kr2000-5000; ⏲11am-10pm Jun-Aug, reduced hours Sep-May) Inside Brydebúð museum, this lively timber-lined all-rounder is very popular in high season for its crowd-pleasing menu ranging from burgers and pizza to lamb fillet. Be prepared to wait in summer sinceit doesn't take reservations. Weekend nights it stays open later as a bar.

Ströndin Bistro INTERNATIONAL €€
(☎487 1230; www.strondin.is; Austurvegur 18, Vík; mains kr2000-5000; ⏲6-10pm) Behind the N1 petrol station is this semi-smart wood-panelled option enjoying sea-stack vistas. Go local with lamb soup or fish stew, or global with pizzas and burgers.

Kjarval SUPERMARKET
(☎487 1325; Víkurbraut 4; ⏲9am-9pm) Groceries.

Shopping

Víkurprjón GIFTS & SOUVENIRS
(☎487 1250; www.vikwool.is; Austurvegur 20, Vík; ⏲8am-7pm) The big Icewear souvenir and knitwear shop next to the N1 station is a coach-tour hit. You can peek inside the factory portion to see woollens being made.

Vínbúðin ALCOHOL
(Ránarbraut 1; ⏲4-6pm Mon-Thu, 2-6pm Fri) National liquor chain with limited hours.

Information

Tourist Information Centre (☎487 1395; www.visitvik.is; Víkurbraut 28; ⏲10am-8pm Mon-Fri, 11am-5pm Sat & Sun Jun-Aug) Inside Brydebúð.

Getting There & Away

Vík is a major stop for all Reykjavík–Höfn bus routes; buses stop at the N1 petrol station.

Strætó (www.bus.is) services:

- Bus 51 Reykjavík–Vík–Höfn (Reykjavík–Vík kr5880, 2¾ hours, two daily) If you take the early bus you can stop in Vík then continue on to Höfn on the later bus; however, from Sep-

RESPECTING NATURE

Tantalising as the sights of Iceland may be, with its black-sand beaches and glaciers glinting along the roadside, it is paramount to realise that there are real dangers involved. For example, the famous beach Reynisfjara near Vík is known for rogue waves, and tourists are regularly rescued or drowned there. As for glaciers, no one should go onto them without experienced, local guidance. Crevasses form suddenly and are often invisible (beneath snow), gasses can be emitted by volcanic activity, and flooding (sometimes invisible from above) can destabilise the ice even further.

With the growing popularity of tourism in Iceland, the foolhardy behaviour of inexperienced visitors regularly makes the news (one man drove his family onto a glacier in a rental car). Don't be one of them. Always check on local conditions, change your plan if it's not safe, and log your treks with www.safetravel.is.

tember to May service is reduced and you can't count on that connection.

Sterna (www.sterna.i) services:

- Bus 12/12a Reykjavík–Vík–Höfn (Reykjavík–Vík kr5600, 4¼ hours, one daily June to mid-September).

Reykjavík Excursions (www.re.is) services:

- Bus 20/20a Reykjavík–Skaftafell (Reykjavík–Vík kr7500, four hours, one daily June to early September).
- Bus 21/21a Reykjavík–Skógar (Reykjavík–Vík kr7500, 3¾ hours, one daily June to August) One of the two services to Skógar goes as far as Vík each day.

East of Vík

Mælifell

On the edge of the Mýrdalsjökull glacier, the 642m-high Mælifell ridge and the countryside around it are spectacular. The simple, idyllic cottages and campsite at **Þakgil** (☎893 4889; www.thakgil.is; Höfðarbrekkuafrétti; sites per person kr1500, cabins kr25,000; ⊙Jun–mid-Sep), a green bowl among stark mountains and dramatic rock formations, make a convenient base for explorations. You can walk up Mælifell or to the nunatak (hill or mountain completely surrounded by a glacier) Huldufjöll, if you are properly equipped. There are also easier walks around the nearby rivers. Check on weather and route conditions before leaving.

You can drive to Þakgil, 15km along an extremely rough dirt road (Rte 214) that branches off Rte 1 about 5km east of Vík, or there is a hiking trail from Vík.

Sleeping & Eating

Buy groceries and food in Vík – there are no facilities in the isolated Mælifell ridge area.

Hótel Katla – Höfðabrekka HOTEL €€€
(☎487 1208; www.hotelkatla.is; Höfðabrekka; d incl breakfast from kr31,000; @) At the start of Rte 214, 5.5km east of Vík, Hótel Katla – Höfðabrekka is a large country hotel with 72 comfy rooms with en suite bathrooms in annexes of varying vintage. Four hot-pots and a good restaurant, too.

Mýrdalssandur

The vast black-lava sand flats of Mýrdalssandur, east of Vík, are formed from material washed out from underneath Mýrdalsjökull during Katla eruptions. This 700-sq-km desert is bleak and desolate (some say haunted), but rather awe-inspiring. It looks lifeless, but Arctic foxes and seabirds are common sights.

South of Rte 1, the small peak of **Hjörleifshöfði** (221m) rises above the sands and offers good views towards Vestmannaeyjar. On the other side of Rte 1, the green hill of **Hafursey** (582m) is another option for walks from Vík.

VESTMANNAEYJAR

Jagged and black, the Vestmannaeyjar (sometimes called the Westman Islands) form 15 eye-catching silhouettes off the southern shore. The islands were formed by submarine volcanoes around 11,000 years ago, except for Surtsey, the archipelago's newest addition, which rose from the waves in 1963. Surtsey was made a Unesco World Heritage Site in 2008, but its unique scientific status means that it is not possible to land there, except for scientific study.

Heimaey is the only inhabited island. Its little town and sheltered harbour lie between dramatic *klettur* (escarpments) and two ominous volcanoes – blood-red Eldfell and conical Helgafell. These days Heimaey is famous for its puffins (around 10 million birds come here to breed); Þjóðhátíð, Iceland's biggest outdoor festival, held in August; and its state-of-the-art volcano museum.

Heimaey

POP 4290

The small town of Heimaey (*hey*-my) is encased in a fortress of jagged lava; its port sits at the end of a contorted waterway that carves a path between towering cliffs dotted with bird nests. Although only a few kilometres from the mainland, Heimaey feels light years away, lost amid the frigid waters of the North Atlantic.

The volcanoes that formed Heimaey have come close to destroying the island on several occasions. The most famous eruption in modern times began unexpectedly at 1.45am on 23 January 1973, when a vast fissure burst open, gradually mutating into the volcano Eldfell, and prompting the island's evacuation.

History

Over the centuries the island of Heimaey was a marauders' favourite. The English raided the island throughout the 15th century, building the stone fort Skansinn as their HQ. In 1627 Heimaey suffered its most violent attack at the hands of Algerian pirates, who went on a killing spree, murdering 36 islanders and kidnapping 242 more (almost three-quarters of the population). The rest managed to escape by abseiling down cliffs or hiding in caves along the west coast. Those who were kidnapped were taken as slaves to north Africa; years later, 27 islanders had their freedom bought for them…and had a long journey home.

Sights

The island's sights cluster in the main village, on the point around Skalinn, and in the fascinating fresh lava fields and volcano, plus along puffin-viewing cliffs outside of town. You can download an iPhone or iPad guide with treasure hunt by searching 'Vestmannaeyjar' in the App Store.

A museum pass for Sæheimar, Sagnheimar and Eldheimar costs kr3200 for one person, or kr8700 for a family.

Town Centre

★Eldheimar MUSEUM
(488 2700; www.eldheimar.is; Gerðisbraut 10; adult/child kr2300/1200; 10.30am-6pm May-mid-Oct, 1-5pm Wed-Sun mid-Oct–Apr) More than 400 buildings lie buried under lava from the 1973 eruption, and on the edge of the flow 'Pompei of the North' is a new museum revolving around one house excavated from 50m of pumice, along what was formerly Suðurvegur. The modern volcanic-stone building allows a glimpse into the home with its crumbling walls and intact but toppled knick-knacks, and is filled with multimedia exhibits on the eruption and its aftermath, from compelling footage and eyewitness accounts to the home-owners' story.

★Skansinn FORT, HISTORIC SITE
This lovely green area by the sea has several unique historical sights. The oldest structure on the island was Skansinn, a 15th-century fort built to defend the harbour (not too successfully – when Algerian pirates arrived in 1627, they simply landed on the other side of the island). Its walls were swallowed up by the 1973 lava, but some have been rebuilt. Above them, you can see the remains of the town's **old water tanks**, also crushed by molten rock.

Landlyst MUSEUM
(11am-5pm mid-May–mid-Sep) FREE A shocking 80% of Heimaey's babies once died at birth, until in the 1840s an island woman, Sólveig, was sent abroad to be trained as a midwife. The tiny wooden house Landlyst was Sólveig's maternity hospital (and is the second oldest building on the island). Today it contains a small display of her blood-letting equipment and other 19th-century medical paraphernalia.

Stafkirkjan CHURCH
(11am-5pm mid-May–mid-Sep) The bitumen-coated Stafkirkjan is a reconstruction of a medieval wooden stave church. It was presented by the Norwegian government in 2000 to celebrate 1000 years of Christianity.

★Sæheimar AQUARIUM
(481 1997; www.saeheimar.is; Heiðarvegur 12; adult/child kr1200/500; 10am-5pm May-Sep, 1-4pm Sat Oct-Apr) The Aquarium and Natural History Museum has an interesting collection of stuffed birds and animals, videos on puffins and catfish, and fish tanks of Icelandic fish. It's great fun for the family, and there's often a teenage puffin wobbling about – the museum is an informal bird hospital as well.

Sagnheimar Byggðasafn MUSEUM
(Folk Museum; 488 2045; www.sagnheimar.is; Raðhústræti; adult/child kr1000/free; 11am-5pm mid-May–mid-Sep, 1-4pm Sat mid-Sep–mid-May) Housed in the city library, this interactive folk museum tells the story of Heimaey from the era of marauding pirates up to the 1973 eruptions and beyond. Displays also shed light on local sports heroes and native birds.

Stóraklif & Heimaklettur VIEWPOINT
The top of the craggy precipice Stóraklif is a treacherous 30-minute climb from behind the N1 petrol station at the harbour. The trail starts on the obvious 4WD track; as it gets steeper you're 'assisted' by ropes and chains (don't trust them completely). If you can bear the terror, you'll get outstanding views. Further out on the pier, Heimaklettur is more perilous, with wild rickety ladders. Both are top puffin-breeding grounds. When it's rainy or slick, neither is a good idea.

Heimaey

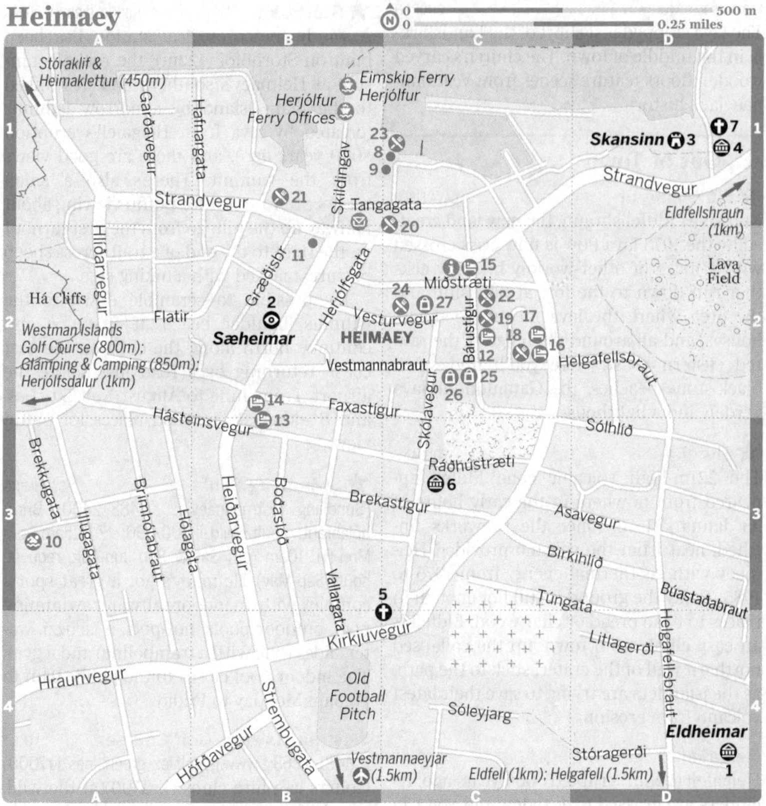

Heimaey

Top Sights
1 Eldheimar ... D4
2 Sæheimar ... B2
3 Skansinn ... D1

Sights
4 Landlyst ... D1
5 Landskirkja ... C4
6 Sagnheimar Byggðasafn ... C3
7 Stafkirkjan ... D1

Activities, Courses & Tours
8 Eyja Tours ... C1
9 Ribsafari ... C1
Segway Tours ... (see 11)
10 Swimming Pool ... A3
11 Viking Tours ... B2

Sleeping
12 Aska Hostel ... C2
13 B&B Hrafnabjörg ... B3
14 Gistiheimilið Hreiðrið ... B2
15 Hótel Eyjar ... C2
16 Hótel Vestmannaeyjar ... C2
17 Sunnuhöll HI Hostel ... C2

Eating
18 Einsi Kaldi ... C2
19 Gott ... C2
20 Krónan ... C1
21 Slippurinn ... B1
22 Stofan Bakhús ... C2
23 Tanginn ... C1
24 Vöruval ... C2

Shopping
25 Nostra ... C2
26 Útgerðin ... C2
27 Vínbúðin ... C2

Landskirkja CHURCH

The lava stopped just short of the Landskirkja in the middle of town. The church's carved wooden doors feature scenes from Vestmannaeyjar's history.

Out of Town

★Eldfellshraun LAVA FIELD

Known as Eldfellshraun, the new land created by the 1973 lava flow is now criss-crossed with a maze of other-worldly hiking tracks that run down to the fort at Skansinn and the area where the lava meets the town's houses, and all around the bulge of the raw, red eastern coast. Here you'll find small black-stone beaches, the Gaujulundur lava garden and a lighthouse.

★Eldfell VOLCANO

The 221m-high volcanic cone Eldfell appeared from nowhere in the early hours of 23 January 1973. Once the fireworks finished, heat from the volcano provided Heimaey with geothermal energy from 1976 to 1985. Today the ground is still hot enough in places to bake bread or char wood. Eldfell is an easy climb from town, up the collapsed northern wall of the crater; stick to the path, as the islanders are trying to save their latest volcano from erosion.

Helgafell VOLCANO

Helgafell (226m) erupted 5000 years ago. Its cinders are grassed over today, and you can scramble up here easily from the football pitch on the road to the airport.

Herjólfsdalur LANDMARK

FREE Sheltered by an extinct volcano, green and grassy Herjólfsdalur was the home of Vestmannaeyjar's first settler, Herjólfur Barðursson. Excavations have revealed remains of a Norse house where a replica now stands. The island's campsite is also here.

On the cliffs west of the golf course, there's a little monument to the 200 people who converted to Mormonism and departed for Utah in the 19th century.

Activities

Ask at the tourist office for a detailed walking and cycling map of Heimaey. Walks through the lava fields, along puffin-nesting areas and on the island's western shores are particularly ethereal. Hotel Eyjar has bicycle rental.

★Stórhöfði HIKING, BIRDWATCHING

A windy meteorological station has been built on Stórhöfði (122m), the rocky peninsula at Heimaey's southern end. It's linked to the main island by a narrow isthmus (created by lava from Helgafell's eruption 5000 years ago), and there are good views from the summit. There's also a small **bird-watching hut** for puffin viewing about halfway up the hill; go from the first turnout on the right to the end of a trail across sheep pasture, marked with a hiking sign.

It's possible to scramble down to the isthmus' boulder beach at **Brimurð** and continue north along the cliffs on the east coast, returning by a road just before the airport. From June to August **Kervíkurfjall** and **Stakkabót** are good places for puffin viewing.

★Swimming Pool SWIMMING

(Sundlaug Vestmannaeyja; ☎488 2400; Brimhólabraut; adult/child Ik600/190; ⏲6.15am-9pm Mon-Fri, 10am-7pm Sat & Sun Jun-Aug, reduced hours Sep-May) Heimaey's got a great sports complex with an indoor saltwater swimming pool, outdoor pools, hot-pots, a jacuzzi, water slides (one with a trampoline) and a gym. The indoor pool closes to the public 9am to 11.15am Monday to Friday.

Westman Islands Golf Course GOLF

(☎481 2363; www.gvgolf.is; green fees kr7000) Golfers can hire clubs (kr3500) at the wild, wonderful 18-hole seaside golf course in Herjólfsdalur.

West Coast HIKING, BIRDWATCHING

Several perilous tracks climb the steep slopes around Herjólfsdalur, running along the top of Norðklettur to **Stafnsnes**, one of the prime puffin-breeding areas. The ascent is exhilarating, but there are some sheer drops. A gentler walk runs south along the western coast of the island, passing above numerous lava caves where local people hid from the pirates in 1627. At **Ofanleitishamar**, hundreds of puffins nest in the cliffs.

Tours

Most boat tours coincide with ferry departures, making them convenient for day trippers.

★Ribsafari BOATING

(☎661 1810, 846 2798; www.ribsafari.is; Básaskersbryggja 8, Harbour; 1hr tour per adult/child kr8000/4500, Surtsey tour kr16,500/9500;

THE 1973 ERUPTION

Without warning, at 1.45am on 23 January 1973 a mighty explosion blasted through the winter's night as a 1.5km-long volcanic fissure split the eastern side of the island. The eruption area gradually became concentrated into a growing crater cone, which fountained lava and ash into the sky.

Normally the island's fishing boats would have been out at sea, but a force-12 gale had prevented them from sailing the previous afternoon. Now calm weather and a harbourful of boats allowed all but two to three hundred of the island's 5273 inhabitants to be evacuated to the mainland. Incredibly, there was just a single fatality (from toxic gases).

Over the next five months more than 30 million tonnes of lava poured over Heimaey, destroying 360 houses and creating a brand-new mountain, the red cinder cone Eldfell. One-third of the town was buried beneath the lava flow, and the island increased in size by 2.5 sq km.

As the eruption continued, advancing lava threatened to close the harbour and make the evacuation permanent – without a fishing industry, there would have been little way to survive on the island. In an attempt to slow down the inexorable flow of molten rock, firefighters hosed the lava with over six million tonnes of cold sea water. The lava halted just 175m short of the harbour mouth – actually improving the harbour by creating extra shelter!

The islanders were billeted with friends and family on the mainland, watching the fireworks and waiting to see if they could ever go home. Finally, the eruption finished, five months after it started, at the end of June. Two-thirds of the islanders returned to face a mighty clean-up operation. The fantastic **Eldheimar** (p164) museum gives a view into the dramatic occurrence.

⏲mid-Apr–Oct) High adrenaline one-hour tours run daily in a souped-up Zodiac that jets through the archipelago. The small boat allows the captain to navigate through little caves and between rocky outcrops for up-close views of bird colonies. Trips to Surtsey (note: you cannot get off the boat) require a minimum of five people. Check online for schedules and longer tours.

Circumnavigate the entire cluster of islands for kr11,500/6500 per adult/child (100 minutes).

Viking Tours BOAT TOUR, BUS TOUR
(☎488 4884; www.vikingtours.is; Strandvegur 65; ⏲10am-6pm May–mid-Sep) Boat trips (adult/child from kr6900/5900) take in the big bird-nesting sites on the south coast, and sail into the sea cave Klettshellir. Bus trips (adult/child kr5900/4900) tour the island. Children under nine are free.

Eyja Tours BUS
(☎852 6939; www.eyjatours.com; Básaskersbryggja, Harbour) Bus tours cover the island's highlights, such as the puffin colonies (adult/child kr7000/3500).

Lyngfell HORSE RIDING
(☎898 1809; www.lyngfell.123.is) Lyngfell, on the road to Stórhöfði, offers horse riding (one hour kr6000) along black-sand beaches.

Segway Tours SEGWAY TOUR
(☎891 6818; www.segwaytours.is; Strandvegur 65, Viking Tours; per hour kr6000) Zip around town.

Festivals & Events

★**Þjóðhátíð** MUSIC
(National Festival Þjódhátíð Vestmannaeyjar; www.dalurinn.is; kr22,900) Three-day Þjóðhátíð is the country's biggest outdoor festival. Held at Herjólfsdalur festival ground over the last weekend in July or the first weekend in August, it involves music, dancing, fireworks, a big bonfire, gallons of alcohol and, as the night progresses, lots of drunken sex (it's something of a teen rite of passage), with upwards of 17,000 people attending.

A song is written for each festival.

Extra flights are laid on from Reykjavík, but you must book transport and accommodation months in advance.

Historically, the festival was first celebrated when bad weather prevented Vestmannaeyjar people from joining the mainland celebrations of Iceland's first constitution (1 July 1874). The islanders held their own festival a month later, and it's been an annual tradition ever since.

Sleeping

The 30-minute ferry ride from the mainland means many people visit Vestmannaeyjar as a day trip, though we highly recommend spending the night. Out of festival season it's not hard to find lodging. Visit www.vestmannaeyjar.is for a full list of accommodation.

B&B Hrafnabjörg B&B €
(☎858 7727; www.facebook.com/BogBGuesthouse; Hásteinsvegur 40; s/d without bathroom incl breakfast kr8800/13,400; ⏲Apr-Nov) This cosy B&B has tidy rooms and a large breakfast room (perfect for the generous breakfast, including homemade waffles).

Aska Hostel HOSTEL €
(☎662 7266; www.askahostel.is; Bárustigur 11; dm/d/q without bathroom kr5400/12,900/27,100) This cheery yellow historic building is home to a good hostel in the village centre with bright, modern rooms and welcoming staff.

Sunnuhöll HI Hostel HOSTEL €
(☎481 2900; www.hotelvestmannaeyjar.is; Vestmannabraut 28; dm kr4750) Dorms are rarely full, and there's generally a quiet and laid-back vibe here. Reception is at Hótel Vestmannaeyjar. HI members get a discount of kr750.

Glamping & Camping CAMPGROUND €
(☎846 9111; www.glampingandcamping.is; sites per adult/child kr1300/free, huts & barrels kr7900-9900; ⏲mid-May–mid-Sep) Cupped in an extinct volcano, the **Herjólfsdalur** campsite has hot showers, a laundry and cooking facilities. You can also pitch a tent inland and across the street next to the football field at **Þórsheimili**, which is less windy. There are also A-frame huts and barrel houses to rent. Linen is kr1600 per person.

Gistiheimilið Hreiðrið GUESTHOUSE €
(☎481 1045; http://tourist.eyjar.is; Faxastígur 33; s/d/q without bathroom kr7900/12,500/18,700) This guesthouse looks a little worse for wear on the outside, but friendly Ruth ensures it feels like home. Features include a well-stocked kitchen and a cosy TV lounge, and it also runs walking tours in summer. Sleeping-bag accommodation costs kr4300.

Hótel Eyjar HOTEL €€
(☎481 3636; www.hoteleyjar.is; Bárustígur 2; d/studio kr23,000/24,000) Spacious, basic rooms are well-lit and have private bathrooms; some are extra-large with kitchenettes.

Hótel Vestmannaeyjar HOTEL €€
(☎481 2900; www.hotelvestmannaeyjar.is; Vestmannabraut 28; s/d incl breakfast from kr14,600/20,500; @) Iceland's first cinema is now a pleasant hotel, with modern rooms (some with good town and harbour views), friendly staff and the top restaurant Einsi Kaldi downstairs. Book ahead in summer.

Eating

Heimaey has a surprisingly robust food scene for such a remote-feeling isle, and has one of Iceland's best restaurants: Slippurinn. There is a nice selection of cafes and eateries on and around Bárustigur.

Stofan Bakhús BAKERY €
(Bárustígur 7; baked goods kr300-990; ⏲9am-5pm Mon-Fri, to 3.30pm Sat & Sun) Delicious baked goodies and pastries with top-notch coffee drinks.

SURTSEY

In November 1963 the crew on the fishing boat *Ísleifi II* noticed something odd – the sea south of Heimaey appeared to be on fire. Rather than flee, the boat drew up for a closer look – and its crew were the first to set eyes on the world's newest island.

The incredible subsea eruption lasted for 4½ years, throwing up cinders and ash to form a 2.7 sq km piece of real estate (since eroded to 1.4 sq km). What else could it be called but Surtsey (Surtur's Island), after the Norse fire giant who will burn the world to ashes at Ragnarök.

It was decided that the sterile island would make a perfect laboratory, giving a unique insight into how plants and animals colonise new territory. Surtsey (www.surtsey.is) is therefore totally off limits to visitors. Just so you know: in the race for the new land, the blue-green algae *Anabaena variabilis* got there first. Another discovery? Fossils were carried up by lava during the eruption and are now part of the island.

Both **Ribsafari** (p166) and **Viking Tours** (p167) run boat trips (no entry on the island). You can get a vicarious view of Surtsey's thunderous birth by visiting the display at the museum **Eldheimar** (p164).

★Slippurinn
ICELANDIC €€

(☎481 1515; www.slippurinn.com; Strandvegur 76; lunch kr 2200-3000, dinner kr3500-4000; ⏰noon-2.30pm & 5-10pm early May–mid-Sep) Lively Slippurinn fills the upper storey of a beautifully remodelled old machine workshop that once serviced the ships in the harbour. The food is delicious Icelandic with a level of creativity that sets it above most restaurants in the country. Ingredients are exquisite and combinations of fish, local produce and locally sourced meats divine.

★Gott
ORGANIC €€

(☎481 3060; www.gott.is; Bárustigur 11; mains kr1900-2600; 🅥) Fresh fusion food is done with care, using organic, healthy ingredients in this jolly corner dining room. Think cod fillet with cauliflower puree or spelt-wrapped grilled chicken.

Tanginn
ICELANDIC €€

(☎414 4420; www.tanginn.is; Básaskersbryggja 8; mains kr1600-5800) Giant windows looking onto the harbour and comfortable, modern decor in slate and wood, make for a fun stop for fresh fish, burgers, creative salads and the like. Dishes are beautifully presented and there's Icelandic beer on tap.

Einsi Kaldi
SEAFOOD €€€

(☎481 1415; www.einsikaldi.is; Vestmannabraut 28; mains kr3300-6000; ⏰noon-10pm Jun–mid-Sep, reduced hours mid-Sep–May) On the ground floor of Hótel Vestmannaeyjar, Einsi Kaldi is Heimaey's highest-end dining experience, with well-crafted seafood recipes.

Self-Catering

Krónan
SUPERMARKET

(Strandvegur 48; ⏰9am-9pm Mon-Fri, 10am-7pm Sat & Sun) Groceries.

Vöruval
SUPERMARKET

(Vesturvegur 18; ⏰7.30am-9pm Mon-Fri, 10am-9pm Sat, 11am-9pm Sun) Groceries in a geodesic dome.

Shopping

Nostra
ARTS & CRAFTS

(☎571 0550; www.nostraverzlun.is; Vestmannabraut 33; ⏰10am-6pm Mon-Fri, 11am-3pm Sat) Three local artists create interesting embroidery, clothing, textiles and homewares.

Útgerðin
CLOTHING, ARTS & CRAFTS

(☎891 9060; www.facebook.com/utgerdin; Vestmannabraut 37; ⏰11am-6pm Mon-Sat) This large, modern shop is a good bet for Icelandic crafts and design.

Vínbúðin
ALCOHOL

(☎481 1301; Vesturvegur 50; ⏰11am-6pm Mon-Thu, to 7pm Fri, to 4pm Sat) National liquor chain.

Information

Tourist Information Centre (☎488 2555; www.vestmannaeyjar.is; Strandvegur; ⏰9am-6pm Mon-Fri, 10am-5pm Sat, 1-5pm Sun) The summer tourist office is staffed by local teens at a cafe-bookstore.

Getting There & Around

AIR

Vestmannaeyjar Airport (Vestmannaeyjaflugvöllur; VEY; ☎481 1969; www.isavia.is) is about 3km south of central Heimaey; a **taxi** (p169) costs about kr2500, or you can walk. **Atlantsflug** (p73) runs scheduled flights from Bakki (near the ferry port at Landeyjahöfn; one-way adult/child kr8500/5950).

There are two daily flights between Reykjavík's domestic airport and Vestmannaeyjar on **Eagle Air** (www.eagleair.is); approximately kr17,000 one way.

BOAT

Eimskip's ferry Herjólfur (☎481 2800; www.eimskip.is; adult/child/bicycle/car kr1320/660/660/2120) sails from Landeyjahöfn (about 12km off the Ring Road between Hvolsvöllur and Skógar) to **Heimaey** year-round. The journey takes about 30 minutes. Always reserve ahead for cars, and passengers should book ahead in high season, especially at peak day-tripper hours: the morning to Vestmannaeyjar and the afternoon back. You must arrive at least 30 minutes before departure. Landeyjahöfn ferry terminal has vending machines, bathrooms and water, but no other services.

From 15 May to 14 September five boats depart daily (on Tuesdays there are four). Low-season boats function on a reduced schedule.

In really foul weather (summer or winter), the port at Landeyjahöfn can fill with sand, in which case the ferry sails to/from Þorlákshöfn instead on a reduced schedule of two per day. The sail takes 2¾ hours, and the fare is substantially more. Changes are posted on the website and Facebook page, and you need to check on your rebooking. It takes roughly two hours to drive from Landeyjahöfn west to Þorlákshöfn.

Getting to or from Landeyjahöfn, Strætó bus 52 runs from Reykjavík (Mjódd terminal)–Hveragerði–Selfoss–Hella–Hvolsvöllur–Landeyjahöfn (kr4200, 2¼ hours, three daily in summer); plus there's a Landeyjahöfn **taxi** (p138).

TAXI

Heimaey Taxi (☎698 2038, 897 1190)

West Iceland

Includes ➡

Best Places to Eat

- Bjargarsteinn Mathús (p187)
- Settlement Centre Restaurant (p176)
- Gamla Rif (p189)
- Narfeyrarstofa (p184)

Best Places to Stay

- Hótel Egilsen (p183)
- Hótel Flatey (p186)
- Hótel Húsafell (p180)
- Egils's Guesthouse & Apartments (p176)

Why Go?

Geographically close to Reykjavík, yet far, far away in sentiment, West Iceland (known as Vesturland) West Iceland offers everything from windswept beaches to historic villages and awe-inspiring terrain in one neat little package. Yet many tourists have missed the memo, and you're likely to have remote parts of this wonderful region to yourself.

The long arm of Snæfellsnes Peninsula is a favourite for its glacier, Snæfellsjökull, and the area around its national park is tops for birding, whale watching, lava-field hikes and horse riding. Inland beyond Reykholt you'll encounter lava tubes and remote highland glaciers, including enormous Langjökull with its unusual ice cave. Icelanders honour West Iceland for its local sagas: two of the best known, *Laxdæla Saga* and *Egil's Saga,* took place along the region's brooding waters, marked today by haunting cairns and an exceptional museum in lively Borgarnes.

Road Distances (km)

	Borgarnes	Húsafell	Stykkishólmur	Hellnar	Búðardalur
Húsafell	65				
Stykkishólmur	99	158			
Hellnar	122	179	90		
Búðardalur	79	103	86	145	
Reykjavík	74	129	173	194	152

HVALFJÖRÐUR

Hvalfjörður and the surrounding area feels suddenly pastoral despite being a mere 30-minute drive from the capital. Although lacking the majesty of the Snæfellsnes Peninsula further on, the sparkling fjord offers excellent day-trip fodder. Those in a hurry to get to Borgarnes and beyond should instead head straight through the 5.7km-long tunnel (kr1000) beneath the fjord. Cyclists aren't permitted in the tunnel.

Interestingly, during WWII the fjord contained a submarine station; over 20,000 American and British soldiers passed through.

Bring your own wheels. The buses between Reykjavík and points north bypass the fjord by taking the tunnel.

Sights & Activities

★Glymur WATERFALL
At the head of Hvalfjörður, Glymur, Iceland's highest waterfall (198m), can be reached by following the turn-off to Botnsdalur. From the end of the road, it'll take a couple of hours to reach the cascade on rough trails; a log is placed to bridge one river only in summer. Try to visit after heavy rains or snowmelt for full effect.

Saurbæjarkirkja CHURCH
(Hallgrímskirkja í Saurbæ; Rte 47) The church at the Saurbær farmstead is worth a look for its beautiful stained-glass work by Gerður Helgadóttir. It is named for Reverend Hallgrímur Pétursson, who served here from 1651 to 1669, and composed Iceland's most popular religious work, *Passion Hymns*.

Esja HIKING
On the southern side of Hvalfjörður you'll find dramatic mount Esja (914m), a great spot for wilderness hiking. The most popular trail to the summit begins at Esjuberg, just north of Mosfellsbær, and ascends via **Kerhólakambur** (850m) and **Kistufell** (830m).

Sleeping & Eating

Hvalfjörður has several places to stay and good campgrounds. There are no grocery stores

Hótel Glymur HOTEL €€€
(☎430 3100; www.hotelglymur.is; d incl breakfast from kr37,000; @) This hotel on the northern side of Hvalfjörður, near Saurbær, is a cache of contemporary amenities, from double-decker 'executive doubles' with giant picture windows, to a hot-pot named one of the 'top five hot tubs in the world' by the *New York Times*. There's also a good restaurant (two-course meal kr5900) with spectacular views.

Akranes

POP 6970

Set under striking **Akrafjall** (572m), the town of Akranes lies at the tip of the peninsula separating Hvalfjörður from Borgarfjörður. Largely an administrative and factory town, it's mainly worth a stop for its **lighthouse** and its sprawling **Folk Museum** (Byggðasafnið í Görðum Akranesi; ☎431 5566; www.museum.is; adult/child kr800/free; ⏲10am-5pm mid-May–mid-Sep, by appointment mid-Sep–mid-May), with a restored boathouse, drying shed, church and fishing boats.

BORGARBYGGÐ

Buzzy Borgarnes and its broad Borgarfjörður were the landing zone for several famous Icelandic settlers. Inland, up the river-twined valley, you'll find fecund farms with deep history leading to powerful stone-strewn lava tubes and highlands, the gateway to the ice caps beyond. This inland area is part of a proposed Unesco Geopark, called the **Saga Geopark**, celebrating the unique culture and landscape of the area.

Borgarnes

POP 1890

Unassuming Borgarnes has got it going on. For such a tiny place, it bubbles with local life. One of the original settlement areas for the first Icelanders, it's loaded with history, and sits on a scenic promontory along the broad waters of Borgarfjörður. Zip past the busy petrol stations and go into the old quarter to encounter the fun small-town vibe and one of Iceland's best museums.

Sights

★Settlement Centre MUSEUM
(Landnámssetur Íslands; ☎437 1600; www.settlementcentre.is; Brákarbraut 13-15; adult/child 1 exhibition kr1900/free, 2 exhibitions kr2500/free; ⏲10am-9pm) Housed in an imaginatively restored warehouse by the harbour, the must-see Settlement Centre offers fascinating insights into the history of Icelandic

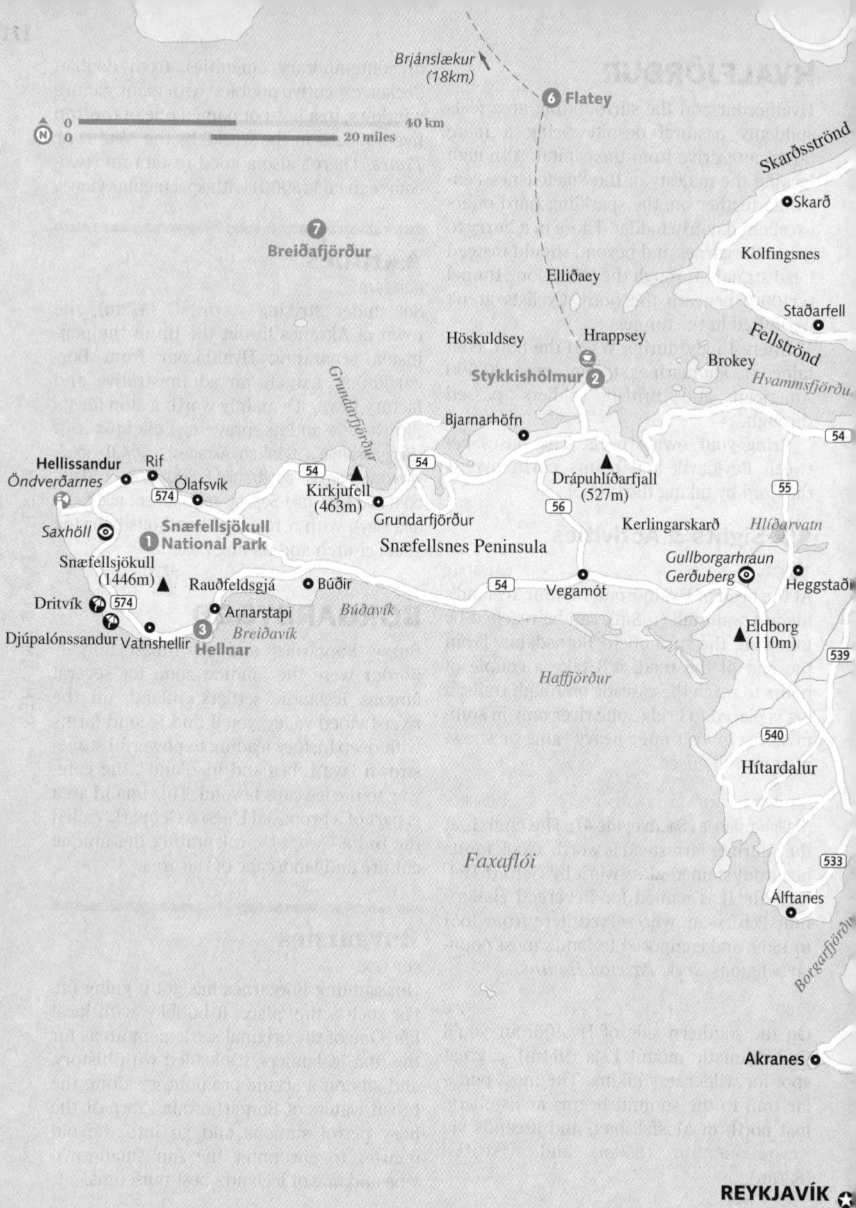

West Iceland Highlights

1 Snæfellsjökull National Park (p189) Tramping through crunchy lava fields, along windswept coastlines, and over Snæfellsjökull.

2 Stykkishólmur (p181) Wandering past charming chocolate-box houses in this buzzy harbour town.

3 Coastal walks (p192) Following seabirds past trailside crags on the slender trail east from Hellnar.

4 Langjökull Glacier (p180) Exploring deep inside this glacier's ice cave, or tracing its raw edges on the Kaldidalur Corridor.

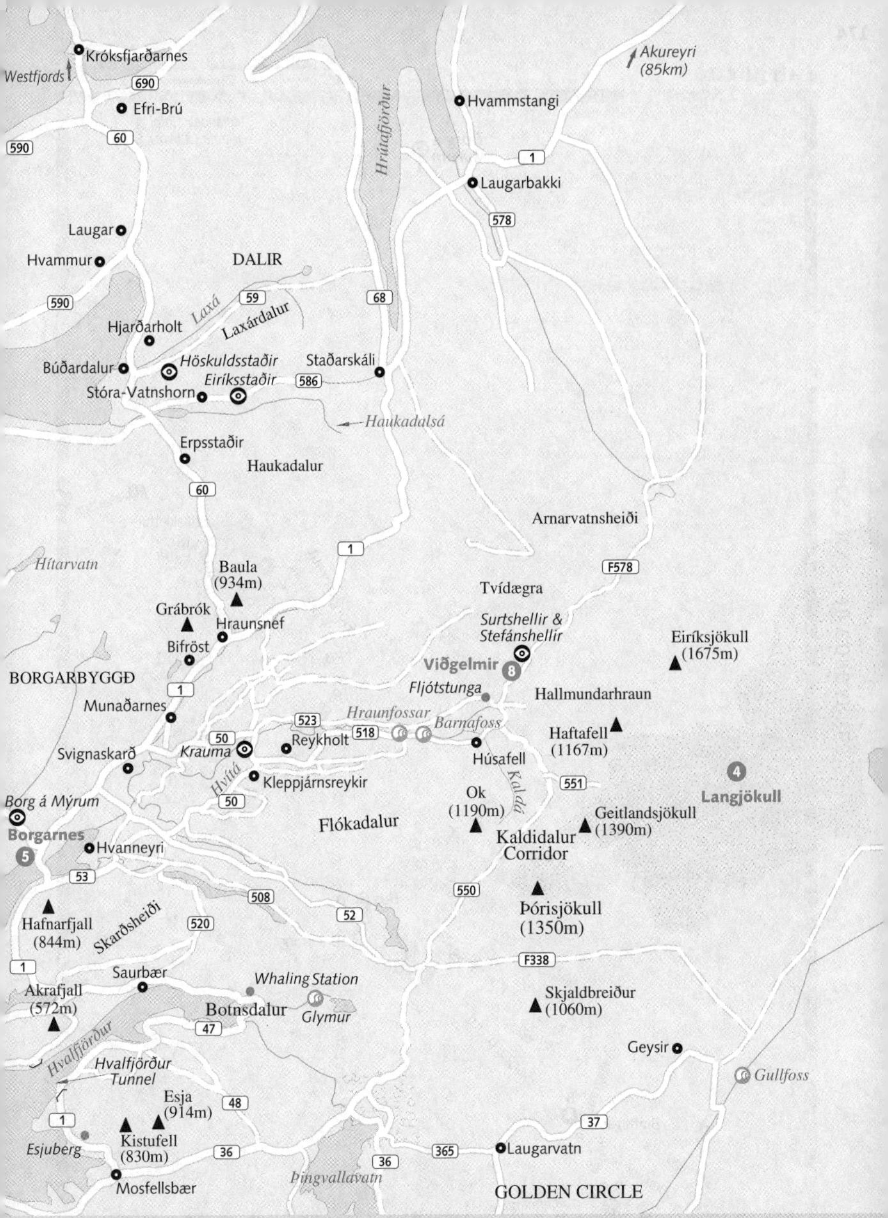

5 Borgarnes (p171) Stepping back into Saga times at the impressive Settlement Centre in this fun-loving town.

6 Flatey (p186) Casting away all of your cares and spending a night (or six) on this tiny island.

7 Breiðafjörður (p181) Sailing past swooping puffins and searching for whales on this beautiful fjord.

8 Viðgelmir (p180) Discovering the fascinating subterranean remains of a violent volcanic eruption in this huge lava tube.

Borgarnes

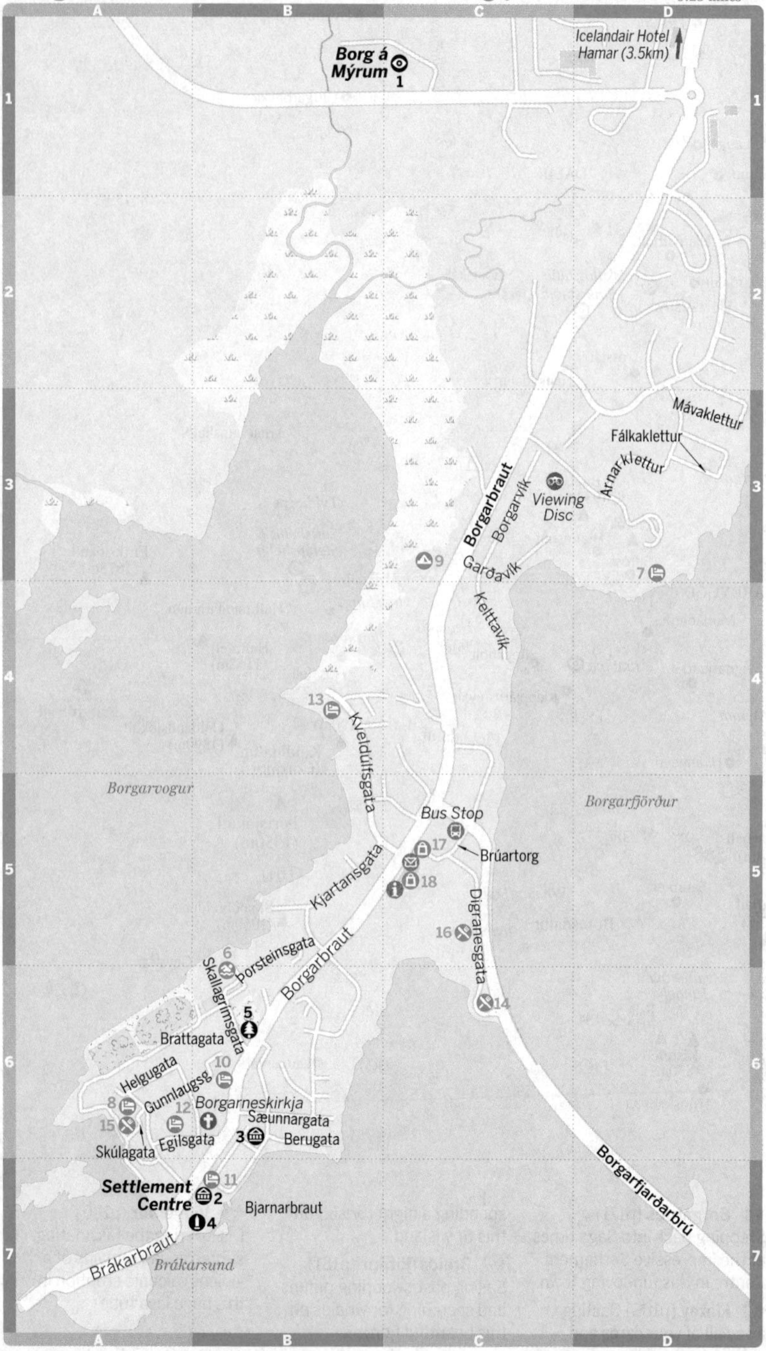
0
500 m
0
0.25 miles
A
B
C
D
1
2
3
4
5
6
7
Icelandair Hotel Hamar (3.5km)
Borg á Mýrum
1
Mávaklettur
Fálkaklettur
Arnarklettur
Borgarbraut
Borgarvík
Viewing Disc
9
Garðavík
7
Keittavík
13
Kveldúlfsgata
Borgarvogur
Bus Stop
Borgarfjörður
17
Brúartorg
Kjartansgata
18
Digranesgata
16
6
Þorsteinsgata
Borgarbraut
Skallagrímsgata
5
14
Brattagata
10
Helgugata
Gunnlaugsg
8
12
Borgarneskirkja
Sæunnargata
15
3
Berugata
Skúlagata
Egilsgata
11
Settlement Centre
2
Bjarnarbraut
4
Borgarfjarðarbrú
Brákarbraut
Brákarsund

Borgarnes

Top Sights

1 Borg á Mýrum C1
2 Settlement Centre B7

Sights

3 Borgarfjördur Museum B6
4 Brákin B7
5 Skallagrímsgarður B6

Activities, Courses & Tours

6 Swimming Pool B6

Sleeping

7 Bjarg D3
8 Borgarnes B&B A6
9 Borgarnes Campsite C3
10 Borgarnes HI Hostel B6
11 Egils's Guesthouse & Apartments B7
12 Hótel Borgarnes A6
13 Kría Guesthouse B4

Eating

14 Bónus C6
15 Englendingavík A6
16 Ok Bistro C5
Settlement Centre Restaurant ... (see 2)

Shopping

17 Ljómalind C5
18 Vínbúðin C5

settlement and the Saga era. The museum is divided into two exhibitions; each take about 30 minutes to visit. The Settlement Exhibition covers the discovery and settlement of Iceland. Egil's Saga Exhibition recounts the amazing adventures of Egill Skallagrímsson (the man behind *Egil's Saga*; p176) and his family. A detailed multilingual audio guide is included.

This is not your run-of-the-mill Icelandic folk museum: the Settlement Centre offers deep background into Iceland's history and flora and fauna, and a firm context in which to place your Icelandic visit; and *Egil's Saga* is one of the most nuanced and action packed of the sagas. The centre has placed cairns throughout town marking key sites from *Egil's Saga*. It also has a top-notch restaurant.

Borgarfjördur Museum MUSEUM
(Safnahús; ☎433 7200; www.safnahus.is; Bjarnarbraut 4-6; adult/child kr1000/free; ⏲1-5pm May-Aug, 1-4pm Mon-Fri Sep-Apr) This small municipal museum has an engaging exhibit on the story of children in Iceland over the last 100 years. It's told through myriad photographs and found items, and though it's accompanied by English translations, don't be shy about having museum staff show you through. The story behind each photograph is captivating; you'll be thinking about this exhibit long after you've left.

Brákin SCULPTURE
Þorgerður Brák was Egill's nursemaid, thought to be a Celtic slave. In one of the more dramatic moments in *Egil's Saga*, she heroically saves Egill's life (from an attempted crime of passion, by his own father, Skallagrímur Kveldúlfsson), and jumps into the sea to escape the enraged Skallagrímur. Today a sculpture marks a spot near where she leapt, ultimately to her death: Skallagrímur hit her with a stone, and she never emerged from the water again.

Skallagrímsgarður PARK
A cairn marks the burial mound of the father and son of saga hero Egill Skallagrímsson.

Activities & Tours

Swimming Pool GEOTHERMAL POOL
(www.borgarbyggd.is; Þorsteinsgata; adult/child kr600/250; ⏲6am-10pm Mon-Fri, 9am-6pm Sat & Sun) Borgarnes' beautiful pool, hot-pots and steam room are part of a large fjordside sports complex, and are a wonderful respite.

Oddsstaðir HORSE RIDING
(☎435 1413; www.oddsstadir.is; Oddsstaðir farm) Multiday riding tours throughout West Iceland with a large herd of horses.

Festivals & Events

Brákarhátíð CULTURAL
(www.brakarhatid.is; ⏲late Jun) A festival in honour of Þorgerður Brák, a heroine from *Egil's Saga*. Expect town decorations, parades, a concert and a lively, offshore, mud-football match.

Sleeping

Borgarnes HI Hostel HOSTEL €
(☎695 3366; www.hostel.is; Borgarbraut 11-13; dm kr4750, d with/without bathroom kr17,900/12,900; @) This no-frills sleeping spot gets the job done. Despite the murals and African masks on the cinder-block walls, it still feels a bit like a high-school dorm. There's a kr750 discount for HI members.

Borgarnes Campsite CAMPGROUND €
(Borgarbraut; sites per person kr1200) There's a basic fjordside campground on the main road running up the peninsula.

EGIL'S SAGA

Egil's Saga starts by recounting the tale of Kveldúlfur, grandfather of the warrior-poet Egill Skallagrímsson, who fled to Iceland during the 9th century after a falling out with the king of Norway. Kveldúlfur grew gravely ill on the journey, and instructed his son, Skallagrímur Kveldúlfsson, to throw his coffin overboard after he died and build the family farm wherever it washed ashore – this happened to be at **Borg á Mýrum** (p177). Egill Skallagrímsson grew up to be a fierce and creative individual who killed his first adversary at the age of seven, went on to carry out numerous raids on Ireland, England and Denmark, and saved his skin many a time by composing eloquent poetry. Learn about him at Borgarnes' excellent **Settlement Centre** (p171).

For those who'd like to go deep into how the saga ties to the landscape around Borgarnes, download the detailed Locatify SmartGuide smartphone or iPad app and load the 'Borg on the Moors' tour, which tells the stories of local landmarks from the tale. The Settlement Centre has marked eight of the sites with cairns, including **Brákin** (p175), Borg á Mýrum, and **Skallagrímsgarður** (p175), the burial mound of the father and son of saga hero Egill Skallagrímsson.

★ Egils's Guesthouse & Apartments GUESTHOUSE €€
(www.egilsguesthouse.is; Brákarbraut 11; d with/without bathroom incl breakfast kr20,000/17,000, studios from kr20,400; P) Choose from pristine tasteful guest rooms with fjord views in the Kaupangur Guesthouse to full studios and apartments nearby in the centre of town. The guesthouse also has a small cafe.

★ Bjarg GUESTHOUSE €€
(☎437 1925; bjarg@simnet.is; Bjarg farm; d with/without bathroom incl breakfast kr20,400/18,300) One of the most beautifully situated places to stay in the area, this attractive series of linked cottages 1.5km north of the centre overlooks the fjord with the mountains across the way. It has warm, cosy rooms with tasteful wood panelling and crisp white linens. There are shared guest kitchens, a good buffet breakfast, a BBQ, spotless bathrooms, and a turf-roofed cottage that sleeps four.

Borgarnes B&B B&B €€
(☎434 1566, 842 5866; www.borgarnesbb.is; Skúlagata 21; s/d/q without bathroom incl breakfast kr15,500/18,500/31,900, d with bathroom incl breakfast kr21,500; @) Go for one of the two rooms on the ground floor with antique wooden doors and modern fixtures (the rest are in the basement); they have fab views of the bay. Great buffet breakfast.

Kría Guesthouse GUESTHOUSE €€
(☎845 4126; www.kriaguesthouse.is; Kveldúlfsgata 27; s/d without bathroom incl breakfast kr13,000/18,000) Kría offers two rooms with great water views in a private home on a quiet residential street. There's a pleasant shared kitchen and a large wheelchair-accessible bathroom, plus outdoor seating with views and a hot-pot.

Hótel Borgarnes HOTEL €€
(☎437 1119; http://hotelborgarnes.is; Egilsgata 16; s/d incl breakfast kr20,100/23,700; ⏲Apr-Nov; @) Large and relatively characterless, Hótel Borgarnes has business-style rooms with good views that are largely the domain of package tourists.

Icelandair Hotel Hamar HOTEL, GUESTHOUSE €€€
(☎433 6600; www.icehotels.is; Rte 1, Golfvöllurinn; hotel d from kr26,100; @) Hotel Hamar sits on a popular golf course 4km north of town. We found the silver prefab exterior to be off-putting, but surprisingly sleek decor and mod cons hide within. On-site restaurants.

Eating

Bónus SUPERMARKET €
(Digranesgata 6; ⏲11am-6.30pm Mon-Thu, 10am-7.30pm Fri, to 6pm Sat, noon-6pm Sun) Bónus is at the edge of the fjord bridge coming into town.

★ Settlement Centre Restaurant INTERNATIONAL €€
(☎437 1600; www.landnam.is; Brákarbraut 13; lunch buffet kr2200, mains kr2200-5000; ⏲10am-9pm) The Settlement Centre's restaurant, in a light-filled room built into the rock face, is airy, upbeat and one of the region's best bets for food. Choose from traditional Icelandic and international eats (lamb, fish stew etc). The lunch buffet (noon to 3pm) is very popular. Book ahead for dinner.

Ok Bistro
ICELANDIC €€

(☑437 1200; www.okbistro.is; Digranesgata 2; small courses kr2000-3000, large courses kr3700-5000; ⊙11.30am-10pm) Make your way to the 3rd floor in a modern business building to this refined dining room with sweeping fjord and mountain views. The emphasis here is on locally sourced ingredients creatively prepared. Order tapas style and share or go for beautifully presented large mains. The restaurant is named after the 1200m mountain named Ok.

Englendingavík
CAFE €€

(☑555 1400; www.englendingavik.is; Skúlgata 17; mains kr2450-4500; ⊙11.30am-11pm May-Sep, reduced hours Oct-Apr; ☑) Casual and friendly, with a wonderful waterfront deck, Englendingavík serves good homemade dishes, from cakes to full meals of roast lamb or fresh fish. They have an attached guesthouse (doubles with shared bathroom from kr14,600) in a recently restored building.

🛍 Shopping

★Ljómalind
MARKET

(Farmers Market; ☑437 1400; www.ljomalind.is; Brúartorg 4; ⊙10am-6pm May-Aug, reduced hours Sep-Apr) ✔ A recent collaboration between local producers, this packed farmers market sits at the edge of town near the roundabout. It stocks everything from fresh dairy from Erpsstaðir (p195) and organic meat to locally made bath products, handmade wool sweaters, jewellery and all manner of imaginative collectables.

Vínbúðin
ALCOHOL

(Borgarbraut 58-60, Hyrnu Torg centre; ⊙11am-6pm Mon-Thu, to 7pm Fri, to 4pm Sat Jun-Aug, reduced hours Sep-May) National liquor-store chain.

ℹ Information

Tourist Information Centre (☑437 2214; www.west.is; Borgarbraut 58-60; ⊙9am-6pm Mon-Fri, 10am-4pm Sat, noon-4pm Sun Jun-Aug, 9am-5pm Mon-Fri Sep-May) West Iceland's main tourist information centre; in the big shopping centre.

ℹ Getting There & Away

Borgarnes is the major transfer point between Reykjavík and Akureyri, Snæfellsnes and the Westfjords. The **bus stop** (Borgarbraut) is at the cluster of petrol stations (N1, Orkan).

Strætó (www.bus.is) services:

➡ Bus 57 to Reykjavík (kr1680, 1½ hours, 12 Monday to Friday, six Saturday and Sunday).

➡ Bus 57 to Akureyri (kr7980, five hours, two daily Monday to Friday).

➡ Bus 58 to Stykkishólmur (kr2520, 1½ hours, two daily, can change to bus 82 at the Vatnaleið crossroads for buses to Hellissandur and Arnarstapi).

➡ Bus 59 to Holmavík (kr5040, 2¼ hours, one daily Monday, Wednesday, and Friday to Sunday).

➡ Bus 81 to Reykholt (kr840, one hour and 20 minutes, one daily Monday to Friday).

Reykjavík Excursions (www.re.is) services:

➡ Bus 320 loops from Reykjavík to Borgarnes, Kleppjárnsreykir, Deildartunguhver, Reykholt, Hraunfossar, Húsafell, Þingvellir (via the Kaldidalur Corridor) and back to Reykjavík (to Borgarnes kr3500, one daily mid-June to August).

Sterna (www.sterna.is) services:

➡ Bus 60 to Akureyri (kr7200, four hours, one daily late-June to August)

➡ Bus 60a to Reykjavík (kr1600, one hour, one daily late-June to August).

Around Borganes

There is lots of great-value accommodation around Borgarnes; the Borgarnes tourist information centre can supply information on more, as can Icelandic Farm Holidays (www.farmholidays.is).

◉ Sights & Activities

★Borg á Mýrum
LANDMARK

(Rock in the Marshes; Rte 54) **FREE** The farm, Borg á Mýrum, just northwest of Borgarnes on Rte 54, is the site where Skallagrímur Kveldúlfsson, Egill's father, made his farm at settlement. The farm is named for the large rock *(borg)* behind the farmstead (private property); you can walk up to the cairn for

BORGARNES' LOCAL LIQUORS

Crystalline **Reyka Vodka** (www.reyka.com), found across Iceland, is produced in Borgarnes at Iceland's first distillery.

A little family-run brewhouse, **Steðji Brugghús** (☑896 5001; www.stedji.com; tasting kr1500; ⊙1-5pm Mon-Sat) 25km north of Borgarnes off Rte 50 has a good range of local beers, from strawberry beer to lager and seasonal beers. Try them all in the brand-new tasting room.

views all around. You can also visit the small cemetery, which includes an ancient gravestone marked by runes.

Hafnarfjall HIKING

The dramatically sheer mountain Hafnarfjall (844m) rises south across the fjord from Borgarnes. You can climb it (7km) from the trailhead on Rte 1, near the southern base of the causeway into Borgarnes. Be careful of slippery scree cliffs once you ascend. You'll get sweeping views from the top.

Sleeping & Eating

Fossatún HOTEL €

(☎433 5800; www.fossatun.is; Rte 50; huts kr8000, d with/without bathroom kr18,600/12,500; @) This family-friendly spot has a guesthouse, hotel and huts next to a roaring waterfall. The spacious on-site restaurant (mains kr2000 to kr3800) overlooks the falls and walking paths. Located on the southern branch of Rte 50, about 23km east of Borgarnes and 18km southwest of Reykholt.

Ensku Húsin GUESTHOUSE €€

(☎437 1826; www.enskuhusin.is; Rte 54; d with/without bathroom incl breakfast kr20,400/16,700) Located 8km northwest of central Borgarnes off Rte 54, this former fishing lodge with a dramatic riverside setting has been refitted with generous coats of old-school charm. Upstairs rooms retain much of the long-ago feel, and there's a newer block with additional rooms. The owners also offer accommodation in a farmhouse 2km away.

Skemma Cafe CAFE €

(Skemman Kaffihús; ☎868 8626; www.facebook.com/skemmancafe; Agricultural Museum of Iceland complex, Havnneyri; snacks 890-1350; ⏲noon-5pm Jun–mid-Aug) Tucked away in the village of Havnneyri, in a renovated building that dates from 1896, this small cafe has a sunny deck and a range of soups, cakes and coffees.

Shopping

★**Ullarselið** CLOTHING, ARTS & CRAFTS

(☎437 0077; www.ull.is; Hvanneyri; ⏲11am-5pm Jun-Aug, 1-5pm Thu-Sat Sep-May) Find your way to off-the-beaten-path village Hvanneyri, 12km east of Borgarnes, and in among fjordside homes you'll find this fantastic wool centre. Handmade sweaters, scarves, hats and blankets share space with skeins of beautiful hand-spun yarn, and interesting bone and shell buttons. Plus there are needles and patterns to get you started.

Upper Borgarfjörður

Reykholt

Incredibly unassuming, Reykholt (www.reykholt.is) is a sleepy outpost (just a few farmsteads really) that on first glance offers few clues to its past as a major medieval settlement. It was home to one of the most important medieval chieftains and scholars, Snorri Sturluson (who was killed here) and today the main sights revolve around him.

Sights

Krauma HOT SPRINGS

(Deildartunguhver; ☎555 6066; www.krauma.is; Rte 50; adult/child kr4900/2900; ⏲10am-10pm) Find Europe's biggest hot spring, Deildartunguhver, about 5km west of Reykholt, just off Rte 50, near the junction with Rte 518. Look for billowing clouds of steam, which rise from scalding water bubbling from the ground (180L per second and 100°C!). A brand-new bathing complex called Krauma offers sleek hot pools, a cold pool and two steam rooms. The scalding spring water is mixed with cold water from nearby Rauðsgil ravine, and no chemicals are added. There's also a restaurant.

Snorrastofa MUSEUM

(☎433 8000; www.snorrastofa.is; kr1200; ⏲10am-6pm May-Aug, to 5pm Mon-Fri Sep-Apr) The interesting medieval study centre Snorrastofa is devoted to celebrated medieval poet, historian and statesman Snorri Sturluson, and is built on his old farm, where he was brutally slain. The centre houses displays explaining Snorri's life and accomplishments, including a 1599 edition of his *Heimskringla* (sagas of the Norse kings). There's also material on the laws, literature and society of medieval Iceland, and on the excavations of the site. You can ask to see the modern church and reading room upstairs.

Snorralaug SPRING

FREE The most important relic of Snorri's farm is Snorralaug (Snorri's Pool), a circular, stone-lined pool fed by a hot spring. The stones at the base of the pool are original (10th century), and it is believed that this is where Snorri bathed. A wood-panelled tunnel beside the spring (closed to the public) leads to the old farmhouse – the site of Snorri's gruesome murder. The pool may be the oldest handmade structure in Iceland.

Reykholt Old Church CHURCH

FREE Among the more modern buildings found on Snorri's ancient farm is a quaint church dating from 1896, which is open to the public. A 1040–1260 cistern for a smithy was found beneath it in 2001; look for the viewing glass in the floor.

Icelandic Goat Centre FARM

(435 1448; www.geitur.is; Rte 523, Háafell; tour per adult/child kr1500/750; 1-6pm Jun-Aug) Farm workers walk you through pretty fields with endangered Icelandic goats; coffee or tea included. The farm's most famous resident is Casanova, a bright-eyed goat who had a starring turn in *Game of Thrones* (running from a dragon). Find it on dirt-road Rte 523, northeast of Reykholt.

Sleeping & Eating

Reykholt has a simple restaurant at its hotel. Head to Borgarnes for much better choice and to stock up on groceries.

Steindórsstaðir GUESTHOUSE €

(435 1227; www.steindorsstadir.is; Rte 517, Reykholtsdalur; s/d/tr without bathroom kr10,000/14,500/18,000) Set on a farm in the rolling fields about 2km from Reykholt proper, this sweet guesthouse offers clean, cosy rooms with countryside views. There's a shared kitchen, a hot tub (with views, too!) and friendly owners. Some sleeping-bag accommodation (kr5000).

Fosshótel Reykholt HOTEL €€

(562 4000, 435 1260; www.fosshotel.is; d incl breakfast from kr21,100; P @) The only hotel in Reykholt proper, the Fosshótel is a bland block with basic motel-style rooms, a couple of hot-pots and a restaurant.

Hverinn Restaurant INTERNATIONAL €

(571 4433; www.hverinn.is; Rte 50, Kleppjárnsreykir; mains kr1600-2500; 10.30am-9pm May-Oct) Simple eats from daily soups to burgers are on offer at this large roadside restaurant with friendly staff. Also has basic groceries and a campground (kr1500 per adult) and guesthouse (double with shared bathroom kr14,500). Find it about 5km west of Reykholt near the junction of Rtes 518 and 50.

Getting There & Away

Strætó (www.bus.is) services:

- Bus 81 to Borgarnes (kr840, one hour and 20 minutes, one daily Monday to Friday).

A FOODIE TOUR OF THE WEST

Crisscross Food Tour (897 6140; www.crisscross.is) offers food tours across West Iceland, with farm stops, snacks and a meal (full day kr39,500) while taking in local natural sites, from waterfalls to lava fields. Pick-up in Reykjavík or Borgarnes.

Reykjavík Excursions (www.re.is) services:

- Bus 320 loops from Reykjavík to Borgarnes, Kleppjárnsreykir, Deildartunguhver, Reykholt, Hraunfossar, Húsafell, Þingvellir (via the Kaldidalur Corridor) and back to Reykjavík (to Reykholt kr7000, one daily mid-June to August).

Húsafell

Tucked into an emerald, river-crossed valley, with the river Kaldá on one side and a dramatic lava field on the other, Húsafell's, with its encampment of summer cottages and its chic hotel, is a popular outdoor retreat for Reykjavík residents, and the main access point for nearby Langjökull glacier.

Sights

Hraunfossar WATERFALL

(Rte 518) The name of this spectacular waterfall translates to 'Lava Field Waterfall' because the crystalline water streams out from below the lava field all around. Find the turn-off on the north side of Rte 518, 6.5km west of Húsafell.

Sleeping & Eating

The Húsafell complex has a simple bistro with a mini-mart and there's a gourmet restaurant in the hotel. Borgarnes is the largest nearby city for more choices.

Gamli Bær GUESTHOUSE €

(Old Farmhouse; 895 1342; sveitasetrid@simnet.is; Rte 518; d with/without bathroom from kr14,000/13,000; mid-May–Sep) Renovated 1908 farmhouse with shared or private bathrooms; just east up the valley from Húsafell, on Rte 518.

Húsafell CAMPGROUND €

(Ferðaþjónustan Húsafelli; 435 1556; www.husafell.is; sites per adult/child kr1500/800) The Húsafell vacation resort is a one-stop shop, with campsites and summer houses, plus a minimarket, bistro (mains kr2000 to kr2700; open 11am to 9pm) and outdoor geothermal swimming pool (adult/child kr1200/300; open 10am to 10pm daily June to September, reduced hours October to May).

★Hótel Húsafell HOTEL €€€
(☎435 1551; www.hotelhusafell.com; d incl breakfast from kr39,500; P) The star of the show in the Húsafell vacation village is this chic and contemporary new hotel, offering spacious, comfortable rooms. Art is the original work of local artist Páll Guðmundsson, and the outstanding **restaurant** (mains lunch kr2000 to kr4000, dinner kr4500 to kr7000) serves creative, Icelandic cuisine showcasing superb ingredients and refined presentation.

Getting There & Away

Reykjavík Excursions (www.re.is) services:
- Bus 320 loops from Reykjavík to Borgarnes, Kleppjárnsreykir, Deildartunguhver, Reykholt, Hraunfossar, Húsafell, Þingvellir (via the Kaldidalur Corridor) and back to Reykjavík (to Húsafell kr8000, one daily mid-June to August).

Hallmundarhraun

East of Húsafell, along Rte 518, the vast, barren lava flows of Hallmundarhraun make up a wonderful eerie landscape dotted with gigantic lava tubes. These long, tunnel-like caves are formed by flows of molten lava beneath a solid lava crust, and it's possible to visit several of them.

If you've got a 4WD, it's also possible to continue into the interior along Rte F578 beyond Surtshellir, through the lakes at **Arnarvatnsheiði**, and on to **Hvammstangi**. Note that Rte F578 is usually only open seven weeks a year; see www.road.is.

Sights

★Viðgelmir – the Cave LAVA TUBE
(☎783 3600; www.thecave.is; tour per adult/child from kr6500/free) The easiest lava tube to visit, and the largest in Iceland, 1100-year-old, 1.5km-long Viðgelmir is located on private property near the farmstead Fljótstunga. It sparkles with ever-changing rock formations and has a stable walkway within it on which tours are conducted. Check the website for tour times; helmet and torch included.

Surtshellir LAVA TUBE
FREE Just a bit to the southeast of Fljótstunga on Rte 518, a bright yellow sign marks the turn-off to Arnarvatnsheiði along Rte F578 (rental cars not allowed). Follow the bumpy track for 7km to reach Surtshellir, a dramatic, 2km-long lava tube connected to Stefánshellir, a second tunnel about half the size. You can explore Surtshellir on your own if you have caving gear (helmet, torch etc).

Langjökull & Kaldidalur Corridor

Southeast of Húsafell, the absolutely incredible Kaldidalur valley skirts the edge of a series of glaciers, offering incredible views of the Langjökull ice cap (the second largest glacier in Iceland) and, in clear weather, Eiríksjökull, Okjökull and Þórisjökull. The Kaldidalur Corridor, also simply known as unsurfaced Rte 550, is slow but dramatic going (mountain ice, barren rock), and often fogged in in summer. It links south to the Golden Circle, offering the option to create an extended loop from Reykjavík. The primary way to see the Kaldidalur Corridor is with your own wheels or on the Reykjavík Excursions bus, but tours are available.

Sights

★Langjökull GLACIER
The Langjökull ice cap is the second largest glacier in Iceland, and the closest major glacier to Reykjavík. It's accessed from the Kaldidalur or Kjölur tracks, and its closest access village in West Iceland is Húsafell. Do not attempt to drive up onto the glacier yourself. Tours depart from Reykjavík or Húsafell: Mountaineers of Iceland (p71) offers snowmobiling, and Dog Sledding (p71) has summertime dog-sledding tours.

★Into the Glacier ICE CAVE
(Langjökull Ice Cave; ☎578 2550; www.intotheglacier.is) This enormous (300m-long) man-made tunnel and series of caves head into Langjökull glacier at 1260m above sea level. The glistening, LED-lit tunnel and caves opened in 2015 and contain exhibitions, a cafe and even a small chapel for those who want to tie the knot inside a glacier. Tours can be had from Húsafell or the glacier edge (adult/child kr19,500/free), from Reykjavík (kr29,900), or on many combo tours, such as snowmobiling, by helicopter, or including the Golden Circle.

A maximum of 80 visitors at a time can travel up the glacier by monster truck, then have about 45 minutes touring the glacier.

Sleeping & Eating

Head to Húsafell, Reykholt or Borgarnes for accommodation.

You'll find food in Húsafell, Reykholt or Borgarnes; the Ice Cave base camp has just a tiny cafe.

Getting There & Away

Reykjavík Excursions (www.re.is) services:

- Bus 320 loops from Reykjavík to Borgarnes, Kleppjárnsreykir, Deildartunguhver, Reykholt, Hraunfossar, Húsafell, Þingvellir (via the Kaldidalur Corridor) and back to Reykjavík (one daily mid-June to August).

Otherwise, come on a tour. While you can drive the roads with a sanctioned vehicle (check with your rental company), you should never go up on the glacier without a guide.

SNÆFELLSNES PENINSULA

Sparkling fjords, dramatic volcanic peaks, sheer sea cliffs, sweeping golden beaches and crunchy lava flows make up the diverse and fascinating landscape of the 100km-long Snæfellsnes Peninsula. The area is crowned by the glistening ice cap Snæfellsjökull, immortalised in Jules Verne's *Journey to the Centre of the Earth*. Good roads and regular buses mean that it's an easy trip from Reykjavík, offering a cross section of the best Iceland has to offer in a very compact region.

Stykkishólmur, on the populated northern coast, is the region's largest town and a logical base. Moving west along the northern coast, you'll pass smaller townships. On the western part of the peninsula, Snæfellsjökull National Park encompasses not only its glacier but bird sanctuaries and lava fields. The quiet southern coast has several good horse farms beneath towering crags.

Stykkishólmur

POP 1110

The charming town of Stykkishólmur (www.visitstykkisholmur.is), the largest on the Snæfellsnes Peninsula, is built up around a natural harbour tipped by a basalt islet. It's a picturesque place with a laid-back attitude and a sprinkling of brightly coloured buildings from the late 19th century. With a comparatively good choice of accommodation and restaurants, and handy transport links, Stykkishólmur makes an excellent base for exploring the region. There's free wi-fi throughout the whole town.

Sights & Activities

★Breiðafjörður FJORD

Stykkishólmur's jagged peninsula pushes north into stunning Breiðafjörður, a broad waterway separating the Snæfellsnes from the looming cliffs of the distant Westfjords. According to local legend, there are only two things in the world that cannot be counted: the stars in the night sky and the craggy islets in the bay. You *can* count on epic vistas and a menagerie of wild birds (puffins, eagles, guillemots etc). Boat trips, including whale watching and puffin viewing, are available from Stykkishólmur, Grundarfjörður or Ólafsvík.

★Norska Húsið MUSEUM

(Norwegian House; ☎433 8114; www.norskahusid.is; Hafnargata 5; adult/child kr800/free; ⏲11am-6pm Jun-Aug, 2-5pm Tue-Thu Sep-May) Stykkishólmur's quaint maritime charm comes from the cluster of wooden warehouses, shops and homes orbiting the town's harbour. Most date back about 150 years. One of the most interesting (and oldest) is the Norska Húsið, now the regional museum. Built by trader and amateur astronomer Árni Thorlacius in 1832, the house has been skilfully restored and displays a wonderfully eclectic selection of local antiquities. On the 2nd floor you visit Árni's home, an upper-class 19th-century residence, decked out with his original wares.

★Súgandisey ISLAND

The basalt island Súgandisey features a scenic lighthouse and grand views across Breiðafjörður. Reach it via the stone causeway from Stykkishólmur harbour.

Volcano Museum MUSEUM

(Eldfjallasafn; ☎433 8154; www.eldfjallasafn.is; Aðalgata 8; adult/child kr1000/free; ⏲11am-5pm) The Volcano Museum, housed in the town's old cinema, is the brainchild of vulcanologist Haraldur Sigurðsson, and features art depicting volcanoes, plus a small collection of interesting lava ('magma bombs'!) and artefacts from eruptions.

Library of Water ART MUSEUM

(Vatnasafn; ☎857 1221; www.libraryofwater.is; Bókhlöðustígur 17; adult/child kr500/free; ⏲1-6pm Jun-Aug, by appointment Sep-May) For relaxing views of town and bay, head up the hill to the Library of Water. This window-lined space showcases an installation by American artist Roni Horn (b 1955). Light reflects

Snæfellsnes Peninsula

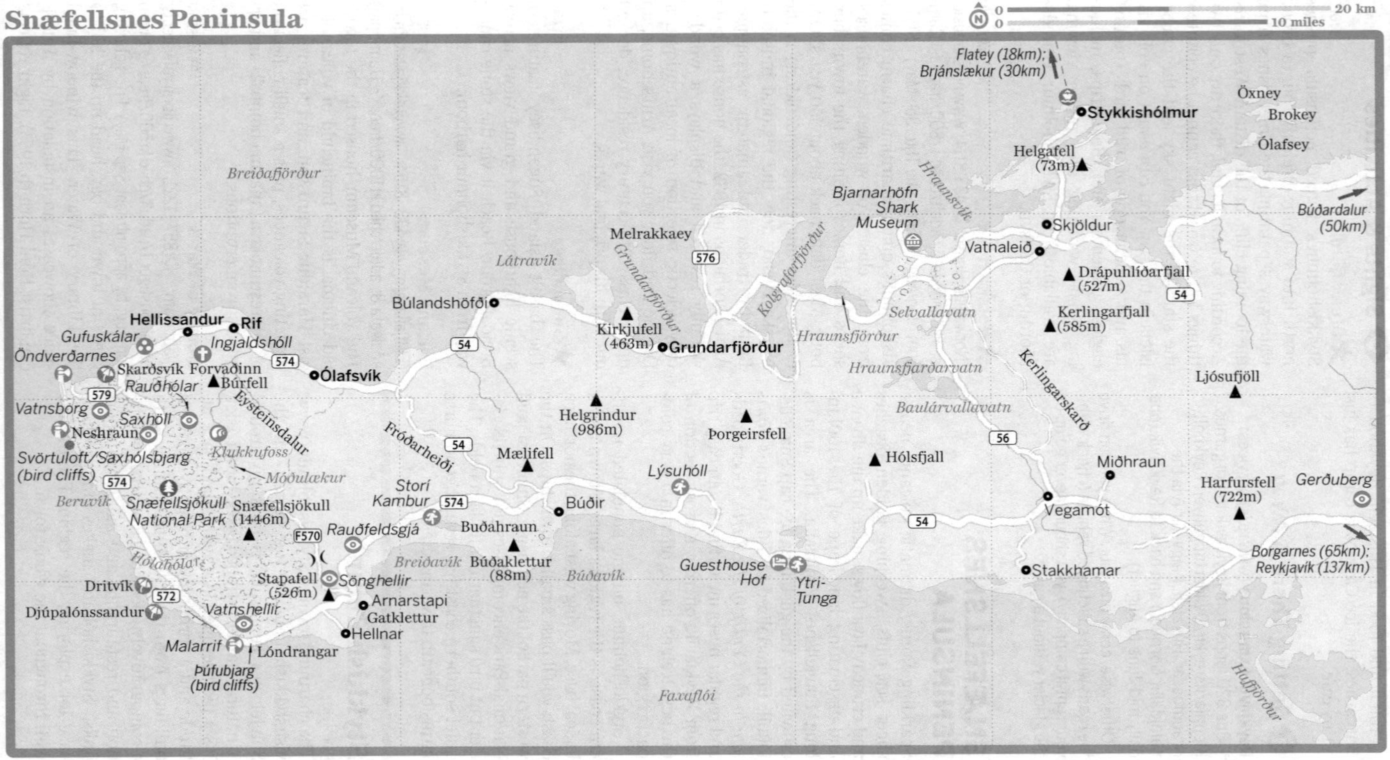

and refracts through 24 glass pillars filled with Icelandic glacier water.

Stykkishólmskirkja CHURCH
(☎438 1288; www.stykkisholmskirkja.is; ⏰10am-5pm) Stykkishólmur's futuristic church, designed by Jón Haraldsson, has a sweeping bell tower that looks like a whale vertebra. The interior features hundreds of suspended lights and a painting of the Madonna and child floating in the night sky.

Stykkishólmur Swimming Pool GEOTHERMAL POOL, HOT-POT
(Sundlaug Stykkishóms; ☎433 8150; Borgarbraut 4; adult/child kr800/220; ⏰7am-10pm Mon-Thu, to 7pm Fri, 10am-6pm Sat & Sun Jun-Aug, reduced hours Sep-May) Water slides and hot-pots are the highlights at the town's geothermal swimming pool, in the municipal sports complex.

Tours

Seatours BOATING
(Sæferðir; ☎433 2254; www.seatours.is; Smiðjustígur 3; ⏰8am-8pm mid-May–mid-Sep, 9am-5pm mid-Sep–mid-May) Various boat tours, including the much-touted 'Viking Sushi', a one- or two-hour boat ride (kr5900/7370) taking in islands, bird colonies (puffins until August) and basalt formations. A net brings up shellfish to devour raw. Also offers dinner cruises and runs the Baldur Ferry to Flatey. Partners with Reykjavík Excursions for Reykjavík pick-up. On-site shop and cafe. Children under 15 are free.

Sleeping

Harbour Hostel HOSTEL €
(☎517 5353; www.harbourhostel.is; Hafnargata 4; dm/q without bathroom from kr4400/23,000) This simple harbourside hostel offers some of the town's best cheap lodging, with dorm rooms (four-, eight- and 12-bed dorms), doubles and family rooms.

Campground CAMPGROUND €
(☎438 1075; mostri@stykk.is; Aðalgata 27; sites per adult/child kr1300/free; ⏰May-early Sep) Basic; managed by the golf course nearby.

Bænir og Brauð GUESTHOUSE €€
(☎820 5408; www.baenirogbraud.is; Laufásvegur 1; d kr19,600-29,900) This snug, immaculate house sits along the fjord, and some rooms have lovely views of the bay. Greta, the kindly owner, also owns Hótel Egilsen down the road. Breakfast costs kr2300; there is a shared refrigerator and coffee maker.

Fransiskus Hotel HOTEL €€
(☎422 1101; www.fransiskus.is; Austurgata 7; s with/without bathroom incl breakfast from kr17,900/12,900, d/f incl breakfast from kr29,100/34,400; P) This new hotel in a renovated wing of a Catholic monastery and hospital complex offers well-maintained modern rooms with private bathrooms and flat-screen TVs.

Höfðagata Guesthouse GUESTHOUSE €€
(☎694 6569; Höfðagata 11; d with/without bathroom incl breakfast from kr23,000/18,000, apt kr25,000) This tidy, well-run guesthouse offers five small but well-appointed double rooms with a shared refrigerator, and one fully equipped apartment.

★**Hótel Egilsen** BOUTIQUE HOTEL €€€
(☎554 7700; www.egilsen.is; Aðalgata 2; s/d kr24,000/30,000; @) One of our favourite little inns in Iceland, this boutique hotel fills a lovingly restored timber house that creaks when winds howl off the fjord. The friendly owner has outfitted cosy (tiny!) rooms with traditional woollen blankets and original artwork. Complimentary iPads and a homemade breakfast (kr2500) sweeten the deal.

Fosshotel Stykkishólmur HOTEL €€€
(☎430 2100; www.fosshotel.is; Borgarbraut 8; s/d/tr incl breakfast kr26,200/30,500/37,800; @) The best rooms in this jarring silver box up on a hill have super bay and island views. Rooms are motel-basic and not all have wi-fi.

Eating

Meistarinn FAST FOOD €
(www.facebook.com/meistarinnsth; Aðalgata; hot dogs kr540-600, sub sandwiches kr1400-1600; ⏰noon-8pm Jun-Aug) This friendly *pýlsuvagninn* (wiener wagon) has the best hot dogs in town. Each menu item is named after someone from Stykkishólmur.

Nesbrauð BAKERY €
(☎438 1830; Nesvegur 1; snacks kr400-1200; ⏰7.30am-9pm Mon-Fri, 8am-9pm Sat & Sun) On the road into town, this bakery is a good choice for a quick breakfast or lunch. Stock up on sugary confections such as *kleinur* (traditional twisty doughnuts) or *ástar pungur* ('love balls'; fried dough and raisins).

Bónus SUPERMARKET €
(Borgarbraut 1; ⏰11am-6.30pm Mon-Thu, 10am-7.30pm Fri, to 6pm Sat, noon-6pm Sun) Groceries; near the swimming pool.

Stykkishólmur

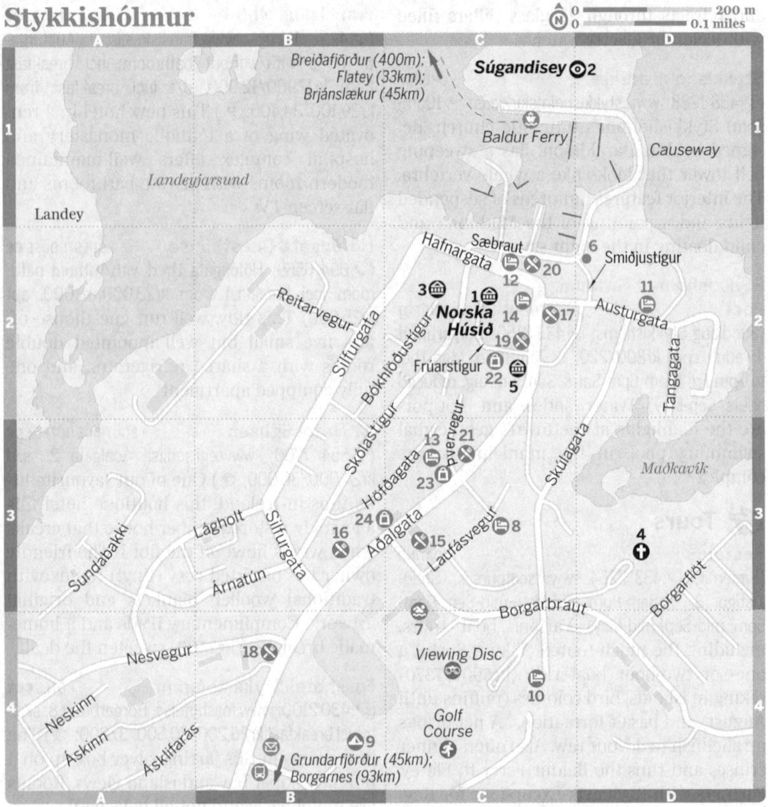

★Narfeyrarstofa ICELANDIC €€
(☎438 1119; www.narfeyrarstofa.is; Aðalgata 3; mains kr2000-5000; ⏲11.30am-midnight Mon-Thu, to 1am Fri-Sun May-Sep, reduced hours Oct-Apr; ✎) This charming restaurant is the Snæfellsnes' darling fine-dining destination. Book a table on the second floor for the romantic lighting of antique lamps and harbour views. Ask your waiter about the portraits on the wall; the building has an interesting history.

Plássið ICELANDIC €€
(☎436 1600; www.plassid.is; Frúarstígur 1; mains kr2500-5000; ⏲11.30am-10pm May-Sep; ✎👪) This bistro-style old-town building is a perfect family-friendly spot, with elegant touches (wine glasses, mod furnishings) and friendly service. Using local ingredients, it serves up a full run of regional specials, and the catch of the day is usually delicious, paired with salad or barley risotto. Local beers, too. New management took over in late 2016; we'll see if they can keep it going!

Sjávarpakkhúsið ICELANDIC €€
(☎438 1800; Hafnargata 2; mains kr2600-3500; ⏲noon-11pm Sun-Thu, to 3am Fri & Sat Jun-Aug, reduced hours Sep-May) This old fish-packing house has been transformed into a wood-lined cafe-bar with harbour-front outdoor seating. The speciality is blue-shell mussels straight from the bay, but it's also a great daytime hang-out. On weekend evenings it's a popular bar where locals come to jam.

Skúrinn INTERNATIONAL €€
(☎544 4004; Þvervegur 2; mains kr1700-2800; ⏲noon-11pm) Casual spot for grabbing a pizza, burger, nachos, fish and chips, and beer, with a nice deck for sunny days.

Shopping

Leir 7 ARTS & CRAFTS
(www.leir7.is; Aðalgata 20; ⏲2-5pm Mon-Fri, to 4pm Sat) Artist Sigríður Erla produces tableware from the fjord's dark clay at this pottery studio in the heart of town. There's also woodcraft.

Stykkishólmur

Top Sights	12 Harbour Hostel ... C2
1 Norska Húsið ... C2	13 Höfðagata Guesthouse ... C3
2 Súgandisey ... D1	14 Hótel Egilsen ... C2
Sights	**Eating**
3 Library of Water ... C2	15 Bónus ... C3
4 Stykkishólmskirkja ... D3	16 Meistarinn ... B3
5 Volcano Museum ... C2	17 Narfeyrarstofa ... C2
	18 Nesbrauð ... B4
Activities, Courses & Tours	19 Plássið ... C2
6 Seatours ... D2	20 Sjávarpakkhúsið ... C2
7 Stykkishólmur Swimming Pool ... C4	21 Skúrinn ... C3
Sleeping	**Shopping**
8 Bænir og Brauð ... C3	22 Gallerí Lundi ... C2
9 Campground ... B4	23 Leir 7 ... C3
10 Fosshotel Stykkishólmur ... C4	24 Vínbúðin ... B3
11 Fransiskus Hotel ... D2	

Gallerí Lundi ARTS & CRAFTS
(Aðalgata 4a; 12.30-6pm May-Sep) Local handicrafts sold by friendly villagers. Also offers coffee.

Vínbúðin ALCOHOL
(Aðalgata 24; 2-6pm Mon-Thu, 1-7pm Fri, 11am-2pm Sat Jun-Aug, reduced hours Sep-May) Across the main road from Bónus.

Getting There & Away

BOAT

Baldur Ferry (433 2254; www.seatours.is) Car ferry between Stykkishólmur and Brjánslækur in the Westfjords (2½ hours) via Flatey (1½ hours). From early June to late August there are daily departures from Stykkishólmur at 9am and 3.45pm, returning from Brjánslækur at 12.15pm and 7pm. During the rest of the year there is only one ferry per day, leaving Stykkishólmur at 3pm (no boats on Saturdays), returning at 6pm.

Adult/child fares to Brjánslækur are kr5460/free. Reserve ahead for vehicles (additional kr5460/7910 per car/camper). Round trip from Stykkishólmur to Flatey costs kr7480. Check online for concession and winter fares.

BUS

You can get to Reykjavík (2½ hours) by changing in Borgarnes. All service is greatly reduced in winter.

Strætó (www.bus.is) services from the bus stop (Aðalgata) at the Olís petrol station:

- Bus 58 to Borgarnes (kr2520, 1½ hours, two daily).
- Bus 82 to Arnarstapi via Grundarfjörður–Ólafsvík–Rif–Hellissandur (kr2100, 1¼ hours, two daily June to mid-September). The rest of the year it only goes from Stykkishólmur to Hellissandur four days per week.

Stykkishólmur to Grundarfjörður

The scenic stretch between Stykkishólmur and Grundarfjörður is filled with myth and mystique, from spiritual mountains to Saga-storied lava fields.

Sights

Helgafell MOUNTAIN
About 5km south of Stykkishólmur, the holy mountain Helgafell (73m) was once venerated by worshippers of the god Þór. Although quite small, the mountain was so sacred in Saga times that elderly Icelanders would seek it out near the time of their death. Today, locals believe that wishes are granted to those who climb the mount.

Berserkjahraun LAVA FIELD
About 15km west of the intersection of Rte 54 and Rte 56 lies the dramatic, spiky lava field at Berserkjahraun (Berserkers' lava field). Crowned by looming mountains, this lunar landscape gets its name from *Eyrbyggja Saga*.

Bjarnarhöfn Shark Museum MUSEUM
(438 1581; www.bjarnarhofn.is; Bjarnarhöfn farm; adult/child kr1100/free; 9am-6pm Jun-Aug, reduced hours Sep-May) The farmstead at Bjarnarhöfn is the region's leading producer of *hákarl* (fermented shark meat), a traditional Icelandic dish. The museum has exhibits on the history of this culinary curiosity, along with the family's fishing boats and processing tools. A video explains the butchering and fermenting procedure.

WORTH A TRIP

FLATEY

Of Breiðafjörður's innumerable islands, little Flatey (literally 'Flat Island') is the only one with year-round inhabitants. In the 11th century Flatey (www.flatey.com) was home to a monastery, and today the appealing island is a popular stopover for travellers heading to (or from) the Westfjords. Push the slow-mo button on life, and enjoy a windswept afternoon amid brightly coloured houses and swooping Arctic terns.

Sleeping & Eating

Læknishús (☎438 1476; s without bathroom kr9000; ⊙Jun-Aug) Læknishús is about 400m from the pier and offers simple farm accommodation in summer. Sleeping-bag accommodation kr4000.

Krákuvör (☎438 1451; sites per person kr1200; ⊙Jun-Aug) One of the island's farms, about 300m from the pier, Krákuvör offers camping.

Hótel Flatey (☎555 7788; www.hotelflatey.is; s/d/tr without bathroom incl breakfast kr23,900/27,500/36,900; ⊙Jun-Aug) Hótel Flatey has some of the most charming, nook-like rooms in Iceland, and the on-site **restaurant** (lunch mains kr2200 to kr3100, dinner mains kr5000, three-course menu kr9300 to kr9700; open noon to 9pm) is fantastic as well. On some weekends, slip down into the basement for live evening jam sessions with locals.

Getting There & Away

To cross Breiðafjörður aboard the Baldur Ferry (p185) and stop off in Flatey, you must take the first ferry of the day, disembark, and board the second daily ferry across, or one the next day (boats only pause on the island for around five minutes as they cross the fjord). No cars are allowed on Flatey, so for those taking a car to the Westfjords, it is possible to send it on across (no additional charge) while staying behind in Flatey.

To visit Flatey as a day trip from Stykkishólmur, take either boat during summer, disembark at Flatey and catch the ferry as it returns to Stykkishólmur. Note that the twice-per-day ferry service only runs in summer. You can also visit with local tour companies.

Find the museum off Rte 54 on a turnout from Rte 577, on the fjordside, northeastern edge of **Bjarnarhafnarfjall** (575m).

Greenland shark, which is used to make *hákarl,* is poisonous if eaten fresh; fermentation neutralises the toxin. Note that Greenland shark is classified as near threatened.

Each visit to the museum comes with a bracing nibble of *hákarl,* accompanied by Brennivín (aka 'black death') schnapps. Ask about the drying house out back. You might find hundreds of dangling shark slices drying; the last step in the process.

Grundarfjörður

POP 860

Spectacularly set on a dramatic bay, little Grundarfjörður is backed by waterfalls and surrounded by ice-capped peaks often shrouded in cottony fog. More prefab than wooden, the town feels like a typical Icelandic fishing community, but the tourist facilities are good and the surrounding landscape can't be beat, with its iconic Kirkjufell.

Sights

★Kirkjufell MOUNTAIN

Kirkjufell (463m), guardian of Grundarfjörður's northwestern vista, is said to be one of the most photographed spots in Iceland. You'll see Ben Stiller skateboarding past in *The Secret Life of Walter Mitty* (2013). Ask staff at the Saga Centre (p186) if you want to climb it, they may be able to get you a guide. Two spots involving a rope climb make it dangerous to scale when wet or without local knowledge.

Kirkjufell is backed by the roaring waterfalls, Kirkjufellsfoss; more camera fodder.

Saga Centre MUSEUM

(Eyrbyggja Heritage Centre; ☎438 1881; www.grundarfjordur.is; Grundargata 35; ⊙9am-5pm) The Saga Centre is a tourist information centre, cafe (p187), library, internet point and small museum rolled into one. The museum displays an old fishing boat and gear, plus a children's toy collection. It sells national park maps, and has a free walking map of the area.

Tours

★Láki Tours WHALE WATCHING, WILDLIFE
(☎546 6808; www.lakitours.com; Nesvegur 5) Láki Tours has excellent fishing, puffin-spotting and whale-watching trips from Grundarfjörður or Ólafsvík. The puffin tour (adult/child kr5900/free; June to August) from Grundarfjörður goes to wonderful basalt island, **Melrakkaey**, with colonies of puffins, kittiwakes and other seabirds, and super views of Kirkjufell. Whale-watching tours (adult/child kr9400/free) depend on the season, but cover the best whale terrain in the region; orca, fin, sperm, blue, minke and humpback whales are all possibilities.

Check online for tours and departure points. Its Grundarfjörður office has a cafe (mains kr1600 to kr2500; open 9am to 9pm) with a good buffet lunch, and a shop.

Snæfellsnes Excursions BUS TOUR
(☎616 9090; www.sfn.is; tours from kr10,000) Day trips around the major sites of Snæfellsnes Peninsula, from Stykkishólmur, Grundarfjörður and Ólafsvík. Offers Reykjavík pick-up (from kr17,000 including a boat trip).

Sleeping

Grundarfjörður has a good collection of guesthouses and rental apartments, as well as a campground; check www.grundarfjordur.is for a full list. See Icelandic Farm Holidays (www.farmholidays.is) for accommodation on nearby headlands, such as Suður-Bár.

Grund GUESTHOUSE €
(☎840 6100; www.resthouse.is; Rte 54; d without bathroom kr14,500) This well-renovated little family-run guesthouse sits 2.8km east of Grundarfjörður, and has cosy rooms, some with sea or mountain views. Guests share a kitchen, living room and laundry.

Grundarfjörður HI Hostel HOSTEL €
(☎562 6533; www.hostel.is; Hlíðarvegur 15; dm from kr4750, d with/without bathroom from kr17,900/12,900; @) This outfit features everything from prim dorm rooms to smart, apartment-style lodging. Reception is in the red house, while accommodation is spread across several buildings in town. HI members get a discount of kr750.

H5 Apartments APARTMENT €€
(☎898 0325; Hrannarstígur 5; apt kr23,700) Large modern apartments in the centre of town. Book via Airbnb or booking.com.

Hótel Framnes HOTEL €€
(☎438 6893; www.hotelframnes.is; Nesvegur 8; s/d incl breakfast from kr17,100/24,000; @) This basic dockside inn has a spacious lobby, and small rooms, some with views. A nearby building holds the least costly rooms.

Eating

Emil's Cafe CAFE €
(Grundargata 35, Saga Centre; mains kr1190-1950; ⏰9am-9pm) In the Saga Centre, this cheery cafe is tops for cappuccinos, hot soup and sandwiches.

Meistarinn FAST FOOD €
(hot dogs kr540-600, sandwiches kr700-1600; ⏰Jun-Sep) The Meistarinn hotdog wagon has menu items named after members of the Danish royal family.

Samkaup SUPERMARKET €
(Grundargata 38; ⏰9am-8pm Mon-Sat, 10am-8pm Sun Jun-Aug, reduced hours Sep-May) Small supermarket and N1 petrol station.ith a grill.

★Bjargarsteinn Mathús SEAFOOD €€
(☎438 6770; www.facebook.com/Bjargarsteinnrestaurant; Sólvellir 15; mains kr2900-4000; ⏰2-10pm Jun-Aug, 5-8pm Sep-May, closed mid-Dec–mid-Jan) This new restaurant is operated by seasoned restaurateurs who have created a lively menu of Icelandic dishes, with an emphasis on seafood and everything fresh. Desserts are delicious, and pretty, too. The seasonal menu is always changing, and views to Kirkjufell are stupendous.

RúBen INTERNATIONAL €€
(☎438 6446; Grundargata 59; mains kr2100-4900; ⏰10am-11pm Mon-Thu, to 1am Fri & Sat, noon-10pm Sun Jun-Aug, reduced hours Sep-May) This joint is popular with locals for its friendly staff, no-nonsense diner-style atmosphere, and broad menu: from pasta to soup, burgers, fish and chips or lamb.

Information

Saga Centre (p186) has tourist information and local maps.

Getting There & Away

Strætó (www.bus.is) services:

➡ Bus 82 Stykkishólmur–Arnarstapi (kr840 to Stykkishólmur, two daily June to mid-September, the rest of the year four days per week and only as far as Hellissandur). It runs via Vatnaleið (crossroads Rtes 54 and 56) and Ólafsvík–Rif–Hellissandur; stops at the N1 station in Grundarfjörður.

WISHING AT HELGAFELL

It is commonly believed that those who ascend humble Helgafell (p185) will be granted three wishes, provided that the requests are made with a pure heart. However, you must follow three important steps to make your wishes come true:

Step 1 Start at the grave of Guðrún Ósvífursdóttir, heroine of an ancient local saga.

Step 2 Walk up to the Tótt (the chapel ruins), not uttering a single word, and (like Orpheus leaving Hades), never looking back.

Step 3 Once at the chapel ruins, you must face east while wishing. And never tell your wishes to anyone, or they won't come true.

Ólafsvík

POP 960

Quiet, workaday Ólafsvík won't win any hearts with its fish-processing plant. Although it's the oldest trading town in the country (it was granted a trading licence in 1687), few of the original buildings survive. For visitors it's best as a jumping-off point for whale watching or a quick stop at Hraun for a meal.

Some Láki Tours (p187) whale-watching trips depart from here: the waters offshore and west to the tip of the peninsula are the region's best for whale sightings.

Sights

Steypa GALLERY
(☎866 8358; www.steypaphoto.com; Norðurtangi; ⊙10am-5pm Jun-Aug) FREE Peruse an interesting photography exhibition in the former Marine Museum (Sjávarsafn).

Ólafsvíkurkirkja CHURCH
(www.kirkjanokkar.is; ⊙8am-6pm) Ólafsvík's modern church is made entirely of triangular pieces.

Pakkhúsið MUSEUM
(Packhouse; ☎433 6930; Ólafsbraut; adult/child kr500/free; ⊙noon-5pm Jun–mid-Sep) Mildly interesting display telling the story of the town's development as a trading centre, and an on-site cafe (snacks kr250 to kr650).

Sleeping & Eating

Við Hafið Guesthouse GUESTHOUSE €
(☎436 1166; vid.hafid@hotmail.com; Ólafsbraut 55; dm/d without bathroom kr4100/14,600) Clean, simple rooms with shared bathrooms and kitchen facilities are the order of the day in this large guesthouse.

Campground CAMPGROUND €
(☎433 6929; www.snb.is; Dalbraut; sites per adult/child kr1000/free; ⊙Jun-Aug) Local campground with showers and playground.

Hringhótel Ólafsvík HOTEL €€
(☎436 1650; www.hringhotels.is; Ólafsbraut 20; d & studio kr29,100; @) This large hotel has merely functional rooms in its main building, but the annexe across the street has good studios with kitchenettes, some with sea views. Popular with tour groups.

Hraun INTERNATIONAL €€
(☎431 1030; Grundarbraut 2; mains kr2000-5000; ⊙noon-10pm Jun-Aug, some weekends Sep-May) This upbeat establishment on the main road cheerfully fills a blond-wood building with a broad front deck. The only gig in town besides fast food, it does excellent fresh mussels, burgers and fish, and has beer on tap.

Information

Ólafsvík is the largest settlement in the Snæfellsbær district – the region's **tourist information centre** (☎433 6929; www.snb.is; Kirkjutún 2; ⊙10am-5pm Jun-Aug, reduced hours Sep-May) is located in a white building behind Pakkhúsið.

Getting There & Away

Strætó (www.bus.is) services:

- Bus 82 Stykkishólmur–Arnarstapi (kr1260 to Stykkishólmur, two daily June to mid-September, four days per week in low season; stops at the petrol station).

To get to Reykjavík (kr4620, 3½ hours) you must change for bus 58 at the Vatnaleið crossroads, and then again in Borgarnes.

Rif

POP 160

Blink-and-you'll-miss-it Rif is a harbour village that makes Ólafsvík look like the big city. Dramatic waterfall Svödufoss, with its barrelling cascades and dramatic hexagonal basalt, can be seen in the distance.

Between Rif and Hellissandur, spot the lonely church (built 1903) at Ingjaldshóll, the setting of *Víglundar Saga*. If the church doors are open, you can see a painting depicting Christopher Columbus' possible visit to Iceland in 1477; it's thought he came with the merchant marine and inquired about Viking trips to Vinland.

Sleeping & Eating

Tiny Rif doesn't offer much in the way of accommodation, though there's a good hostel. Head to Grundarfjörður for more choice.

Freezer Hostel HOSTEL €
(☎865 9432; www.thefreezerhostel.com; Hafnargata 16; dm/apt from kr6100/28,500) This quirky joint in a former fish factory combines austere four-, six-, and eight-bed dorms with a cool theatre and live-music venue. In summer there's an active program of plays, storytelling and music. Check online for the schedule. It also lets two apartments.

★**Gamla Rif** CAFE €
(☎436 1001; Háarifi 3; cakes from kr850, fish soup kr1900; ⊙noon-8pm Jun-Aug) Gamla Rif is run by two fishermen's wives who have perfected a variety of traditional snacks. They dispense local travel tips with a smile, and serve tasty coffee and cakes. The show-stopper is their fish soup (from their husbands' daily catch) with fresh bread; don't miss it.

Getting There & Away

Strætó (www.bus.is) services:

- Bus 82 Stykkishólmur–Arnarstapi (kr1680 to Stykkishólmur, two daily June to mid-September, four days per week the rest of the year, when it only goes as far as Hellissandur).

Hellissandur

POP 380

Hellissandur is the original fishing village in its area. There's not much to it any more, except great views of the glacier and fjord.

Sights

Sjómannagarður MUSEUM
(Maritime Museum; ☎436 6619; Útnesvegur; adult/child kr800/free; ⊙9.30am-noon & 1-6pm Tue-Fri, 1-6pm Sat & Sun Jun-Aug) This small maritime museum houses *Bliki*, the oldest fishing boat in Iceland, and a cool replica of a fisher's turf house, plus loads of old photos and memorabilia. Look for the set of lifting stones once used to test the strength of prospective fishermen.

Sleeping & Eating

There's fast food at the petrol station. Otherwise, go east to Rif, Ólafsvík and Grundarfjörður for more choices.

Hellissandur Campground CAMPGROUND €
(☎433 6929; sites per adult/child kr1000/free; ⊙Jun–mid-Sep) This campground is one of our favourites, set right in the middle of spiky lava field Sandahraun, with showers and a small playground.

Hótel Hellissandur HOTEL €€
(☎430 8600; Klettsbuð 7; d incl breakfast kr26,400) This hotel has good, clean rooms with modern bathrooms, and some top-floor rooms have views to the glacier. But, under new management, the restaurant has closed and the lobby is generally unstaffed.

Getting There & Away

Strætó (www.bus.is) services:

- Bus 82 Stykkishólmur–Arnarstapi (kr1680 to Stykkishólmur, stops at the N1 petrol station).

Snæfellsjökull National Park

Encompassing much of the western tip of Snæfellsnes Peninsula **Snæfellsjökull National Park** (☎436 6860; www.snaefellsjokull.is) wraps around the rugged slopes of the glacier Snæfellsjökull, the icy fist at the end of the long Snæfellsnes arm. Around its flanks lie lava tubes, protected lava fields, which are home to native Icelandic fauna, and prime hiking and coastal bird- and whale-watching spots.

When the fog swirling around the glacier lifts, you'll see the mammoth ice cap, which was made famous when Jules Verne used it as the setting for *Journey to the Centre of the Earth*. In his book, a German geologist and his nephew embark on an epic journey into the crater of Snæfells, guided by a 16th-century Icelandic text:

Descend into the crater of Yocul of Sneffels, which the shade of Scartaris caresses, before the kalends of July, audacious traveller, and you will reach the centre of the earth.

Today, the park is criss-crossed with hiking trails, and during proper weather it is possible to visit the glacier with a tour or guide. Malarrif is home to the National Park Visitor Centre (p190), and area tourist offices sell maps and give advice, too. The park's online map is also excellent.

◎ Sights

★ Snæfellsjökull
GLACIER

It's easy to see why Jules Verne selected Snæfell for his adventure *Journey to the Centre of the Earth:* the peak was torn apart when the volcano beneath it exploded and then collapsed back into its own magma chamber, forming a huge caldera. Among certain New Age groups, Snæfellsjökull is considered one of the world's great 'power centres'. Today the crater is filled with the ice cap (highest point 1446m) and is a popular summer destination.

The best way to reach the glacial summit is to take a tour with Summit Adventure Guides, Snæfellsjökull Glacier Tours or Go West! (p191). These companies approach the peak from the south, on Rte F570; Rte F570's northern approach (near Ólafsvík) is frustratingly rutty (4WD needed) and frequently closed due to weather-inflicted damage. Even the well trained and outfitted are not allowed to ascend the glacier without a local guide; contact the National Park Visitor Centre in Malarrif for more information.

Saxhöll Crater
VOLCANO

Southeast of the Öndverðarnes area, on Rte 574, follow the marked turn-off to the roadside scoria crater Saxhöll, which was responsible for some of the lava in the area. There's a drivable track leading to the base, from where it's an uneven 300m climb for magnificent views over the enormous Neshraun lava flows.

★ Djúpalón Beach
BEACH

(Djúpalónssandur) On the southwest coast, Rte 572 leads off Rte 574 to the wild black-sand beach Djúpalónssandur. It's a dramatic place to walk, with rock formations (an elf church, and a kerling – a troll woman), two brackish pools (for which the beach was named), and the rock-arch Gatklettur. Some of the black sands are covered in pieces of rusted metal from the English trawler *Eding,* which was shipwrecked here in 1948. An asphalt car park and public toilets allow tour-bus access, and crowds.

Vatnshellir
LAVA TUBE

This 8000-year-old lava tube with multiple caverns lies 32m below the earth's surface, 1km north of Malarrif. The pull-out is visible from Rte 574, and the tube can only be visited by guided tour with Summit Adventure Guides.

Malarrif
LIGHTHOUSE

FREE About 2km south of Djúpalónssandur, a paved road leads down to the rocket-shaped lighthouse at Malarrif, from where you can walk 1km east along the cliffs to the rock pillars at Lóndrangar (an eroded crater), which surge up into the air in surprising pinnacles. Locals say that elves use the lava formations as a church. A bit further to the east lie the Þúfubjarg bird cliffs, also accessible from Rte 574.

⚐ Tours

★ Summit Adventure Guides
ADVENTURE

(☑787 0001; www.summitguides.is) Offers much-loved 45-minute tours of the Vatnshellir lava tube (adult/child kr3250/free). Guides shed light on the fascinating geological phenomena and region's troll-filled lore. Helmet and torch included. Dress warmly, wear hiking boots, and preferably gloves, too. They also run myriad Snæfellsjökull glacier tours (kr9900 to kr19900) with hiking (kr10900), skiing (kr13900), snowshoeing (kr9900) and ice-climbing (kr14900) options.

Snæfellsjökull Glacier Tours
SNOWMOBILE TOUR

(☑663 3371; www.theglacier.is; snowcat/snowmobile tours kr11,500/27,000; ⊙Mar-Jul) Two-hour snowcat (truck with chain wheels) and snowmobile tours ascend the glacier to about 1410m.

🛏 Sleeping & Eating

Most of the hamlets in the park have rental houses, campgrounds or guesthouses, and there are a few hotels throughout the park.

Stock up on groceries in Borgarnes or Stykkishólmur; provisions and restaurants are few and far between in the park.

ℹ Information

National Park Visitor Centre – Gestastofa (Snæfellsjökull National Park Visitor Centre; ☑436 6888, 591 2000; www.snaefellsjokull. is; Malarrif; ⊙10am-5pm Jun-Sep, 10am-4pm Mon-Fri Oct-May) This is the spot for information on Snæfellsjökull National Park: it's an information office in **Malarrif** with maps and brochures, as well as displays on local geology, history, flora, fauna and customs. Rangers have an active summer program of free park **guided tours**; check online or email. Note: the park office in Hellissandur is administrative only and not open to the public.

Getting There & Away

Strætó (www.bus.is) services:

Bus 82 Stykkishólmur–Anarstapi runs twice daily June to mid-September (four days per week in the rest of the year, when it only goes as far as Hellissandur).

Having your own wheels is the best way to see the park.

Southern Snæfellsnes

To the east of Snæfellsjökull National Park, coastal Rte 574 passes the hamlets of Hellnar and Arnarstapi, with their glacier tour companies and sea-sculpted rock formations. It continues east along the broad southern coastal plain, hugging huge sandy bays such as Breiðavík on one side, and towering peaks with waterfalls on the other. This stretch has some super horse riding.

Hellnar

Bárður, the subject of *Bárðar saga Snæfellsáss*, was part giant, part troll and part human. He chose an area near Hellnar, a picturesque spot overlooking a rocky bay, as his home (called Laugarbrekka). Toward the end of his intense saga, he became the guardian spirit of Snæfell. Today Hellnar is a tiny fishing village (once huge) where the shriek of seabirds fills the air and whales are regularly sighted.

Sights

Bárðarlaug, up near the main road, was supposedly Bárður's bathing pool, though the pond is no longer hot. Down on the shore, the cave **Baðstofa** is chock-a-block with nesting birds. Nearby is the head of the trail to Arnarstapi (p192). Ancient, velvety moss-cloaked lava flows tumble east through the **Hellnahraun**.

Sleeping & Eating

★**Fosshotel Hellnar** HOTEL €€

(435 6820; www.fosshotel.is; d incl breakfast from kr27,900; Mar-Oct; P) Fosshotel Hellnar, with its sun-filled, comfortable rooms, is the area's choice sleeping option (and thus often booked solid). Even if you're not overnighting, we highly recommend having dinner at the restaurant. It's all run with sustainability in mind.

Primus Café CAFE €

(865 6740; mains kr1500-2500; 10am-9pm May–mid-Sep, 11am-4pm mid-Sep–Apr) Welcoming spot for cakes, soups and simple meals.

★**Fjöruhúsið** SEAFOOD €€

(435 6844; cakes & quiches kr950, mains kr2500-2800; 11am-10pm Jun-Aug, reduced hours Mar-May & Sep-Nov) It's well worth following the stone path down to the ocean's edge for the renowned fish soup at beautifully situated, quaint Fjöruhúsið. Located by the bird cliffs at the trailhead of the scenic Hellnar–Arnarstapi path, it also serves coffee in sweet, old-fashioned china.

Fosshotel Hellnar Restaurant ICELANDIC €€

(435 6820; dinner mains kr3500-5600; 6-9.30pm Mar-Oct; P) Even if you're not overnighting at Hótel Hellnar, we highly recommend having dinner at its restaurant, which sources local organic produce for its Icelandic menu, plus offers heavenly *skyr* cake for dessert. Reserve ahead.

Getting There & Away

There's no public transport in Hellnar. You can catch Strætó bus 82 Stykkishólmur–Anarstapi (two daily June to mid-September, four days per week in winter) in nearby Arnarstapi.

Arnarstapi

Linked to Hellnar by both the main road and a wonderful coastal hike this hamlet of summer cottages is nestled between the churning Arctic waters and the gnarled pillars of two neighbouring lava fields. A monument pays tribute to Jules Verne and a comical signpost measures distances to major cities via the earth's core. A second, enormous troll-like monument stands as a tribute to Bárður, the region's guardian spirit, and the leading character in a local saga.

Tours to ascend the Snæfellsjökull glacial crown usually start from near Arnarstapi.

Tours

★**Go West!** ADVENTURE TOUR, CYCLING TOUR

(695 9995; www.gowest.is) Friendly couple Jon Joel and Maggy run ecofriendly cycling, hiking, boating, hot-spring and glacier

HIKING THE COAST BETWEEN ANARSTAPI & HELLNAR

Local maps detail myriad hiking trails connecting the sights of the Snæfellsnes Peninsula (online at www.snaefellsjokull.is). One of the most popular (and scenic!) is the 2.5km coastal walk (around 40 minutes) between Hellnar and Arnarstapi. This trail follows the jagged coastline through a nature reserve, passing lava flows and eroded stone caves. During tumultuous weather, waves spray through the rocky arches; when it's fine, look for nesting seabirds.

tours. Some focus on cultural aspects, others on landscape. Snæfellsjökull glacier tours (from kr14,000) are hikes, with crampons, ice axe etc included. Also runs tours in Southern Iceland, or with Reykjavík pick up.

Sleeping & Eating

Buy groceries in Borgarnes or Stykkishólmur before arriving; there are no shops in Arnarstapi and just one basic cafeteria.

Snjófell Guesthouse GUESTHOUSE, CAMPGROUND €€
(☎435 6783; www.hringhotels.is; sites per tent kr1600, d with/without bathroom kr25,100/15,700; ⊙May-Sep) Snjófell has basic accommodation and cafeteria dining (mains kr2000 to kr5000). Travellers pitch tents on grass outside (no showers), or bed down in the guesthouse or new cabins with private bathrooms. Wi-fi in reception area only.

Getting There & Away

There is no public transport going east. To get to Reykjavík, you can take bus 82 to the Vatnaleið crossroads (at Rtes 56 and 55) and change for bus 58 to Borgarnes, where you must change once more.

Strætó (p401) services:

- Bus 82 Stykkishólmur–Anarstapi (two daily June to mid-September, four days per week the rest of the year).

Rauðfeldsgjá

Rauðfeldsgjá CANYON
Just north of Arnarstapi and Stapafell, on Rte 574, a small track branches off to the stunning Rauðfeldsgjá, a steep, narrow cleft that mysteriously disappears into the cliff wall. Birds wheel overhead, a stream runs along the bottom of the gorge, and you can slink between the sheer walls for quite a distance. The gorge figures in a dramatic part of the local saga of Bárður, described on a sign at the parking area.

Breiðavík

East of Rauðfeldsgjá, Rte 574 skirts the edges of an enormous sandy bay at Breiðavík. The windswept coast, with its yellow expanse of sand, is wonderfully peaceful, though tricky to access. The pasture-filled region running along the coastal mountains from here east to Vegamót is considered one of the best places in Iceland for horse riding, and there are several stables of international repute.

On the eastern edge of Breiðavík, look for the placard telling the grisly tale of Axlar-Björn, Iceland's notorious 16th-century serial killer, who made his living in lean times by murdering travellers here.

Tours

Stóri Kambur HORSE RIDING
(☎852 7028; www.storikambur.is; ⊙Jun–mid-Sep) Family-run operation offering one-/two-hour rides on the beach (kr7500/13,000), with glacier views when it's clear.

Búðir & Búðahraun

Búðir has a lonely church and a hotel, but there is no sign of its former fishing village along its craggy, mossy inlets. A walking trail leads across the elf-infested nature preserve, Buðahraun lava field. The ancient lava field is protected; if you look down into its hollows and cracks you'll find flourishing flowers and ferns, many of them themselves protected native Icelandic species. The path also leads to the crater Búðaklettur. According to local legend, a lava tube beneath Buðahraun, paved with gold and precious stones, leads all the way to Surtshellir in upper Borgarfjörður. It takes about three hours to walk to the crater and back.

Sleeping & Eating

Hótel Buðir HOTEL €€€
(☎435 6700; www.hotelbudir.is; Buðir; d kr39,900-54,500; @) Windswept and on a gorgeous, remote coastline, Hótel Buðir tries to be stylish, though it's besieged by tour groups and prices are stiff for what you get. No 28

has the best views (and a teeny balcony). The restaurant (mains kr7900 to kr9900) is sometimes closed to those not in prebooked tour groups.

Lýsuhóll to Gerðuberg

Horse ranches dot this area, several offering accommodation. Grassy fields and sandy beaches alternate with lava fields and mountain backdrops, making for great riding country.

Sights & Activities

★Lýsuhólslaug GEOTHERMAL POOL
(☎433 9917; adult/child kr3000/1000; ⌚1.30-8.30pm Mon-Sat, to 6pm Sun Jul-Aug) The geothermal source for Lýsuhólslaug pumps carbonated, mineral-filled waters in at a perfect 37°C to 39°C. Don't be alarmed that the pool is a murky green: the iron-rich water attracts some serious algae. Find it just beyond the horse ranch at Lýsuhóll.

Gerðuberg LANDMARK
Just where Rte 54 curves between the Snæfellsnes Peninsula and the mainland, you'll find the dramatic basalt towers of Gerðuberg rising from the plain.

Ytri-Tunga WILDLIFE WATCHING
The deserted farmstead at Ytri-Tunga, just east of Hof, occasionally has a colony of seals offshore, best seen in June and July.

Tours

★Lýsuhóll HORSE RIDING, COTTAGES
(☎435 6716; www.lysuholl.is) Equine enthusiasts should look no further than this friendly horse farm. Even if you're not riding, the farm and its guesthouse and cottages (double/quad including breakfast kr20,000/32,000, cottage kr25,000) are a fun place to stay. Guides will show you around the stables, and there are both short excursions (one hour kr7000) and multiday tours (eight days €1850).

Sleeping & Eating

Traðir Guesthouse GUESTHOUSE €€
(☎431 5353; www.tradirguesthouse.net; Rte 54, Traðir farm; d without bathroom kr15,300, cottage kr21,200) Comfortable guest rooms and a private cottage are set on the shore of the southern Snæfellsnes Peninsula, and there's a small cafe serving simple meals. It also offers horse riding, and fishing licenses for the nearby Staðará river.

> **FROM ARNARSTAPI TOWARDS THE GLACIER**
>
> If you drive up the F570 from Arnarstapi, you'll pass **Stapafell** (526m), home to the local little people, and you'll see miniature house gables painted onto rocks in their honour. Further along you'll pass a collapsed crater, which created a series of lava caves about 1.5km from the main road. The largest cave is **Sönghellir** (Song Cave), which is full of 18th-century graffiti and is rumoured to resound with the songs of dwarfs. Bring a torch to read the various markings and don't be shy about belting out your favourite melody.

Hotel Rjúkandi HOTEL €€
(☎788 9100; www.rjukandi.com; cnr Rtes 54 & 56, Vegamót; d incl breakfast kr27,100; ⌚cafe 10am-6pm, restaurant 6-9.30pm) Vegamót means 'crossroads', and that's exactly where you'll find this sustainably operated hotel, cafe and restaurant. You'll probably spot its cafe, **Rjúkandi Kaffi** (snacks kr450-1600), first. It's next to the N1 station, and is loaded with homemade cakes, daily soups and happy locals. Simple, clean rooms have private bathrooms. The hotel's restaurant serves well-presented Icelandic fare.

Guesthouse Hof GUESTHOUSE, COTTAGE €€
(☎846 3897; www.gistihof.is; Rte 54, Hof farmstead; d with/without bathroom kr17,800/14,700, 2-bedroom houses kr26,000) Friendly Hof has a varied selection of basic apartment-style accommodation, each with their own hot tub and beautiful views, as well as free-standing cabins with private bathrooms, and their own shared kitchen cabin. There is also sleeping-bag accommodation. Wi-fi in public areas only.

Langaholt GUESTHOUSE €€
(☎435 6789; www.langaholt.is; Rte 54, Görðum; sites per person kr1000, d kr25,200) Langaholt is a family-run golf course, guesthouse, campground, and restaurant (open 8am to 9pm). Simple rooms often have great views, but the bathrooms could be better.

DALIR

The scenic corridor of rolling fields and craggy river-carved buttes between West Iceland and the Westfjords served as the setting for the *Laxdæla Saga*, the most popular of the Icelandic sagas. The story revolves around a love triangle between Guðrun Ósvífursdóttir, said to be the most beautiful woman in Iceland, and the foster brothers Kjartan Ólafsson and Bolli Þorleiksson. In typical saga fashion, Guðrun had both men wrapped around her little finger and schemed and connived until both were dead – Kjartan at the hands of Bolli, and Bolli at the hands of Kjartan's brothers. Most Icelanders know the stories and characters by heart and hold the area in which the story took place in great historic esteem.

Eiríksstaðir

Eiríksstaðir Reconstruction LANDMARK
(☎434 1118; www.leif.is; Rte 586; adult/child kr1250/free; ⌚9am-6pm Jun-Aug) The farm Eiríksstaðir was home to Eiríkur Rauðe (Erik the Red), father of Leifur Eiríksson, the first European to visit America. Although only a faint outline of the original farm remains, a reconstruction turf house was built using only the tools and materials available at the time. Period-dressed guides show visitors around and tell the story of Erik the Red, who went on to found the first European settlement in Greenland.

Find Eiríksstaðir 8km inland on gravel and paved Rte 586, east of Stóra-Vatnshorn's church, on Haukadalsá river.

Búðardalur

POP 270

Founded as a cargo depot in Saga times, this pin-sized town occupies a pleasant position looking out over Hvammsfjörður, at the mouth of the Laxá river. A current claim to fame is its dairy, which produces most of the cheese in Iceland. The local supermarket carries a good sampling.

Sights

Leifsbúð MUSEUM
(☎434 1441; www.dalir.is; Buðarbraut 1; ⌚11am-5pm Apr-Sep, reduced hours Oct-Mar) FREE There's a folk museum, **tourist information centre** and cafe-restaurant (p194) all rolled into one at Leifsbúð down by the harbour. Look out for the museum's Viking exhibit featuring Leifur Eiríksson and Erik the Red.

Sleeping

Búðardalur Campground CAMPGROUND €
(☎434 1644; sites per adult/child kr1200/free; ⌚mid-May–mid-Sep) This simple campsite has showers and laundry.

Dalakot GUESTHOUSE €€
(☎434 1644; www.dalakot.is; Dalbraut 2; d with/without bathroom kr21,900/15,900) Guesthouse Dalakot has simple rooms, and a restaurant (open noon to 9pm) with a broad menu (mains kr1600 to kr2600).

Eating & Drinking

Leifsbúð Café & Restaurant CAFE €
(☎434 1441; www.leifsbud.is; cafe noon-6pm, restaurant 6-10pm Mon-Fri Jun-Sep; ⌚snacks kr800-1800, mains kr2500-3000) Part of the Leifsbúð museum and tourist information centre, this little cafe offers cakes, pizza, soup and meatballs, and a dinner restaurant should be opening in 2017.

ÖNDVERÐARNES

At the westernmost tip of Snæfellsnes, Rte 574 cuts south, while Rte 579, a tiny gravel and occasionally surfaced track, heads further west across an ancient lava flow to the tip of the Öndverðarnes peninsula, which is great for whale watching.

As the paved road winds through charcoal lava cliffs you'll pass **Skarðsvík**, a golden beach with basalt cubes alongside. A Viking grave was discovered here in the 1960s and it's easy to understand why this stunning spot would have been a favoured final resting place.

After Skarðsvík the track is unpaved and bumpier (still manageable for a 2WD). Park at the turn-off (left side) to walk through craggy lava flows to the imposing volcanic crater **Vatnsborg**, or continue driving straight on until you reach a T-intersection. One kilometre to the left lie the dramatic **Svörtuloft bird cliffs** (Saxhólsbjarg), with excellent walkways, and a tall, orange **lighthouse**. To the right, a bumpy track runs parallel to the sea 1.9km to a squat, orange **lighthouse**. From its parking area, you can walk to the very tip of the peninsula, for **whale watching**, or walk 200m northeast to **Fálkí**, an ancient stone well which was thought to have three waters: fresh, holy and ale!

Blómalindin Kaffihornið CAFE
(☎434 1606; www.blomalindin.is; Vesturbraut 12a) Get a good cup of coffee at this coffee house-cum flower shop.

Shopping

Bolli Craft ARTS & CRAFTS
(☎434 1410; www.facebook.com/bollicraft; Vesturbraut 12; ⏰10am-6pm mid-May–Aug, noon-6pm late Apr–mid-May & Sep) Cool local arts and crafts include handmade sweaters, sheep-horn buttons and charming elves.

Getting There & Away

Strætó (www.bus.is) services:

➡ Bus 59 Borgarnes–Bifröst–Búðardalur–Skriðuland–Króksfjarðarnes–Hólmavík (to Hólmavík kr2940, five weekly mid-May to mid-September, two weekly mid-September to mid-May) stops in Búðardalur at the N1 petrol station).

Hjarðarholt & Around

Although the Dalir is central to several of the best-loved Icelandic sagas, little remains of the original farms. For example no trace remains of **Hjarðarholt**, the one-time home of Kjartan Ólafsson and his father, Ólaf the Peacock. Their farmstead was said to be one of the wonders of the Norse world, with scenes from the sagas carved into the walls, and a huge dining hall that could seat 1100. You will find, however, a beautiful **church** on the site with great views over the valley where the region's history unfurled.

Nearby, and also on the Laxá river, **Höskuldsstaðir** was the birthplace of Hallgerður Longlegs (also called Longtresses), wife of Gunnar of Hlíðarendi, who starred in *Njál's Saga*. Other important residents of the farm include Bolli and his foster brother Kjartan from *Laxdæla Saga*.

Laugar

Just north of the spot where Rte 590 heads west off Rte 60 you'll find the encampment at Laugar, the birthplace of *Laxdæla Saga* beauty Guðrun Ósvífursdóttir. Historians believe they've found **Guðrun's bathing pool (Guðrúnarlaug)**: the hot pool is well marked above the entrance to Hótel Edda, and has a small changing kiosk. **Tungustapi**, in the distance, is a large elf cathedral.

You'll need your own wheels to get here.

WORTH A TRIP

ERPSSTAÐIR DAIRY FARM

When the peanut gallery starts moaning, 'Are we there yet?', you know it's time to head to **Erpsstaðir** (☎868 0357; www.erpsstadir.is; Rte 60; cowshed adult/child kr650/free; ⏰1-5pm Jun–mid-Sep; 👪) the perfect place to stretch your legs. Like a mirage for sweet-toothed wanderers, this dairy farm on the gorgeous Rte 60 (between Búðardalur and the Ring Road; with high mountain valleys, streams and waterfalls) specialises in delicious homemade ice cream (kr400). You can tour the farm, greet the buxom bovines, chickens, rabbits and even guinea pigs, then gorge on a scoop.

The farm also sells *skyr* and cheese; try the rocket-shaped *skyr-konfekt* (meant to look like an udder), a delicious dessert made with a hard white chocolate shell encasing thick *skyr*. It'll blow you away.

Erpsstaðir also offers a rental cottage (from kr20,000; linen kr1000 per person) if you're contemplating ice cream for breakfast...

Sights

Dalir Heritage Museum MUSEUM
(☎434 1328; adult/child kr1000/free; ⏰10am-4pm Jun-Aug, by appointment Sep-May) This neat museum's curator is a wonderful character who knows a great deal about Dalir's brilliant history. There's an unexpected 1883 traditional baðstofa (living/sleeping room). The museum is in the basement of the Hótel Edda, of all places.

Sleeping & Eating

Hótel Edda HOTEL, CAMPGROUND €€
(☎444 4930; www.hoteledda.is; Sælingsdalur; sites per person kr1200, d with/without bathroom kr28,200/15,700; ⏰early Jun-late Aug; @🏊) The Hótel Edda has a newer wing with surprisingly modern rooms, an older hospital-style annexe with shared bathrooms, and sleeping-bag space in converted classrooms. The **restaurant** (☎444 4930; www.hoteledda.is; Sælingsdalur; mains kr2000-5000; ⏰6-9pm early Jun-late Aug) gets good reviews – it serves the delicious ice cream from Erpsstaðir, plus there's a large swimming pool.

The Westfjords

Includes ➡

Best Places to Eat

- Tjöruhúsið (p210)
- Litlibær (p212)
- Heimsendi Bistro (p202)
- Simbahöllin (p205)
- Stúkuhúsið (p202)

Best Places to Stay

- Guesthouse Kirkjuból í Bjarnardal (p206)
- Hótel Laugarhóll (p219)
- Urðartindur (p220)
- Camping in Hornstrandir Nature Reserve (p214)

Why Go?

The Westfjords is where Iceland's dramatic landscapes come to a riveting climax and where mass tourism disappears – only about 10% of Iceland's visitors ever see the region. Jagged bird cliffs and broad multihued dream beaches flank the south. Rutted dirt roads snake north along jaw-dropping coastal fjords and over immense central mountains, revealing tiny fishing villages embracing traditional ways of life. In the far north, the Hornstrandir hiking reserve crowns the quiet region, and is home to cairn-marked walking paths revealing bird life, Arctic foxes and ocean vistas. The Strandir coast is less visited still, with an end-of-the-line, mystical feel, geothermal springs and minuscule oceanside hamlets.

Leave plenty of time: unpaved roads weave around fjords and over pothole-pitted mountain passes, but the scenery is never short of breathtaking. Once you get used to it, you may not want to leave.

Road Distances (km)

	Patreksfjörður	Þingeyri	Ísafjörður	Hólmavík	Norðurfjörður
Þingeyri	129				
Ísafjörður	175	47			
Hólmavík	234	265	221		
Norðurfjörður	333	348	303	105	
Reykjavík	397	405	450	230	334

SOUTH COAST

The sparsely populated south coast of the Westfjords is a tiny version of what's to come on the wild and wonderful peninsulas further north. Remote fjords twist into the coastline, and though there's been a new road built to cut across their desolate isolation, it's still a bare and dramatic place. It's the primary breeding area for the endangered white-tailed eagle.

Reykhólar

Tiny Reykhólar sits on the southern edge of the Reykjanes Peninsula, a minor geothermal area and gateway to the southernmost Westfjords. Gilsfjörður is an eagle breeding ground, and west along the coast, the key inlets for eagle spotting are Þorskafjörður, Djúpifjörður and Vatnsfjörður.

Sights & Activities

Reykhólar Tourist Office Museum MUSEUM
(☎894 1011; www.visitreykholahreppur.is; kr750; ⏲11am-5pm Jun-Aug) The well-managed tourist office has a little museum with antique boats, stuffed birds and a movie of local life in the 1950s and '60s. There's a small on-site cafe (snacks kr500 to kr1200), plus lots of Westfjords information.

White-Tailed Eagle Centre MUSEUM
(☎894 1011; www.visitreykholahreppur.is; Króksfjarðarnes; adult/child kr500/free; ⏲11am-6pm mid-Jun–mid-Aug) The White-Tailed Eagle Centre highlights the attempts to increase the population of the struggling species, which peaked in 2011 at 66 nests. It also has a handicraft market. The centre is just north of the causeway on Rte 60 that crosses Gilsfjörður.

Norður Salt LANDMARK
(www.nordursalt.com) Norður Salt, on the point in Reykhólar, processes sea salt from the local salt bays. You can peek in its windows.

Reykhólar Sea Baths HOT-POT
(Sjávarsmiðjan; ☎577 4800; www.sjavarsmidjan.is; adult/child kr3900/free; ⏲1-7pm Jun-Aug) In windswept Reykhólar, the seaweed baths give you soft skin and a view of the coastal plain, rimmed by salt bays.

Sleeping & Eating

There are a couple of simple places to stay in Reykhólar plus a campground, and there is camping in Miðjanes (about 4km to the west of Reykhólar), where a guesthouse is also being added.

There are no restaurants or grocery stores in Reykhólar, just a minuscule minimart and cafe at the tourist office. Bring in your own supplies.

Reykhólar HI Hostel GUESTHOUSE €
(Álftaland; ☎892 7558, bookings 575 6700; www.hostel.is; dm kr4750) This hostel under new ownership has two simple eight-bed dorm rooms, two soothing hot-pots out back and a guest kitchen. Thre's a discount for HI members of kr750.

Hótel Bjarkalundur HOTEL €€
(☎434 7863; www.bjarkalundur.is; d with/without bathroom incl breakfast kr26,900/19,900, cottages kr24,500; ⏲May-Oct) On Rte 60, just north of the turn-off to Reykhólar, Hótel Bjarkalundur is a summer hotel with an impersonal motel feel. The cottages are quieter. There's a petrol station and a restaurant serving lacklustre grub (mains kr1700 to kr4500). Wi-fi is spotty.

Getting There & Away

Strætó (www.bus.is):

➡ Bus 59 Hólmavík–Búðardalur–Borgarnes stops at Króksfjarðarnes' White-Tailed Eagle Centre.

Flókalundur

Flókalundur, the junction between the road up to Arnarfjörður and Ísafjörður, and Rte 62 to the southwestern peninsulas, sits at the head of Vatnsfjörður. The two-house encampment at Flókalundur was named after the Viking explorer Hrafna-Flóki Vilgerðarson, who gave Iceland its name in AD 860.

Today, the most interesting thing in the area is **Hellulaug** (Rte 62; by donation) a natural hot-pot in among the rocks near the seashore. At high tide, do as the locals do and jump in the frigid sea, then run back to the pool to warm up (38°C). The **Vatnsfjörður Nature Reserve** was established to protect the area around Lake Vatnsdalsvatn, a nesting site for harlequin ducks and great northern divers (loons). Various hiking trails run around the lake and into the hills beyond. **Hótel Flókalundur**(☎456 2011; www.flokalundur.is; sites per person kr1400, d incl breakfast kr24,200; ⏲mid-May–mid-Sep) is a recently updated bungalow-style hotel with small, tidy wood-panelled rooms with renovated

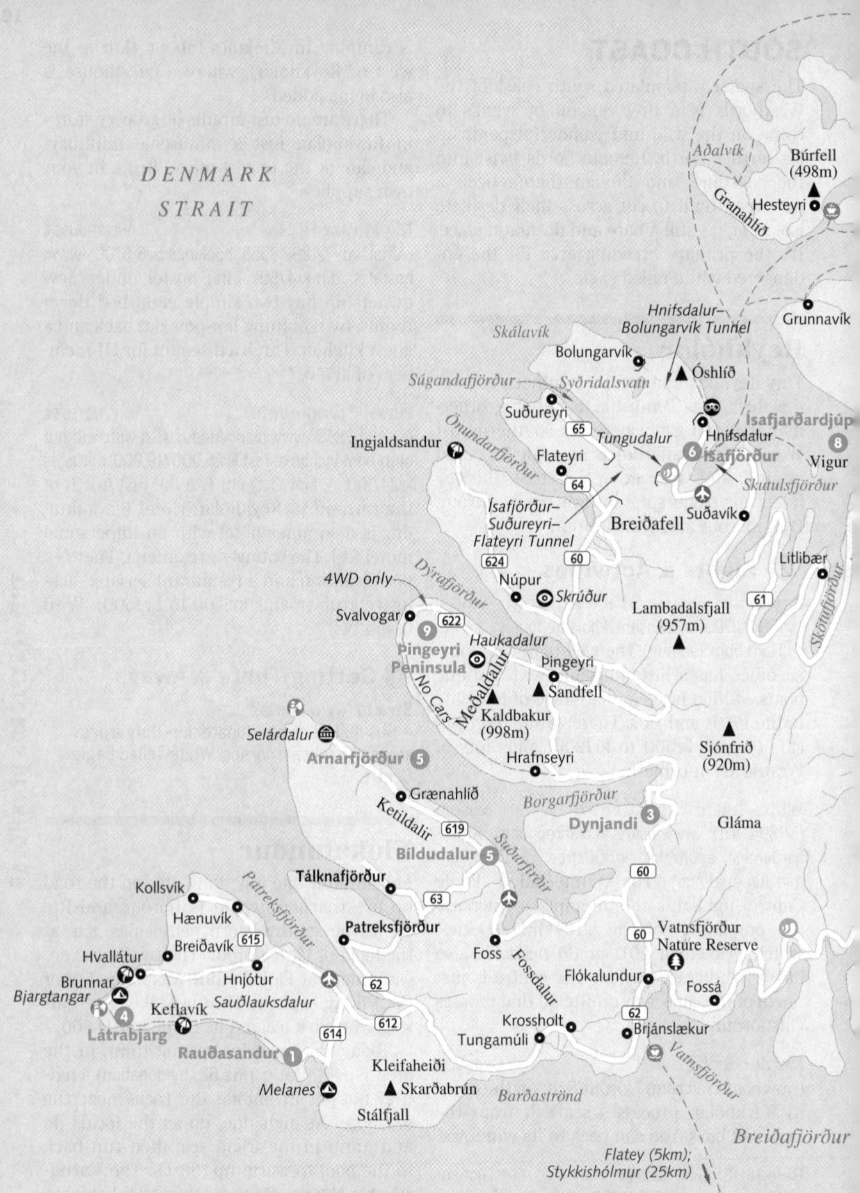

The Westfjords Highlights

1. **Rauðasandur** (p200) Exploring an ethereal rosy beach and azure lagoon while looking for basking seals.
2. **Hornstrandir Nature Reserve** (p214) Roving saw-toothed cliffs while spying on Arctic foxes.
3. **Dynjandi** (p204) Letting the mists of this majestic waterfall swirl around you as you climb its dizzying cascades.
4. **Látrabjarg** (p201) Watching puffins swoop around gigantic bird cliffs.
5. **Arnarfjörður** (p204) Spooking yourself with sea-monster lore in Bíldudalur

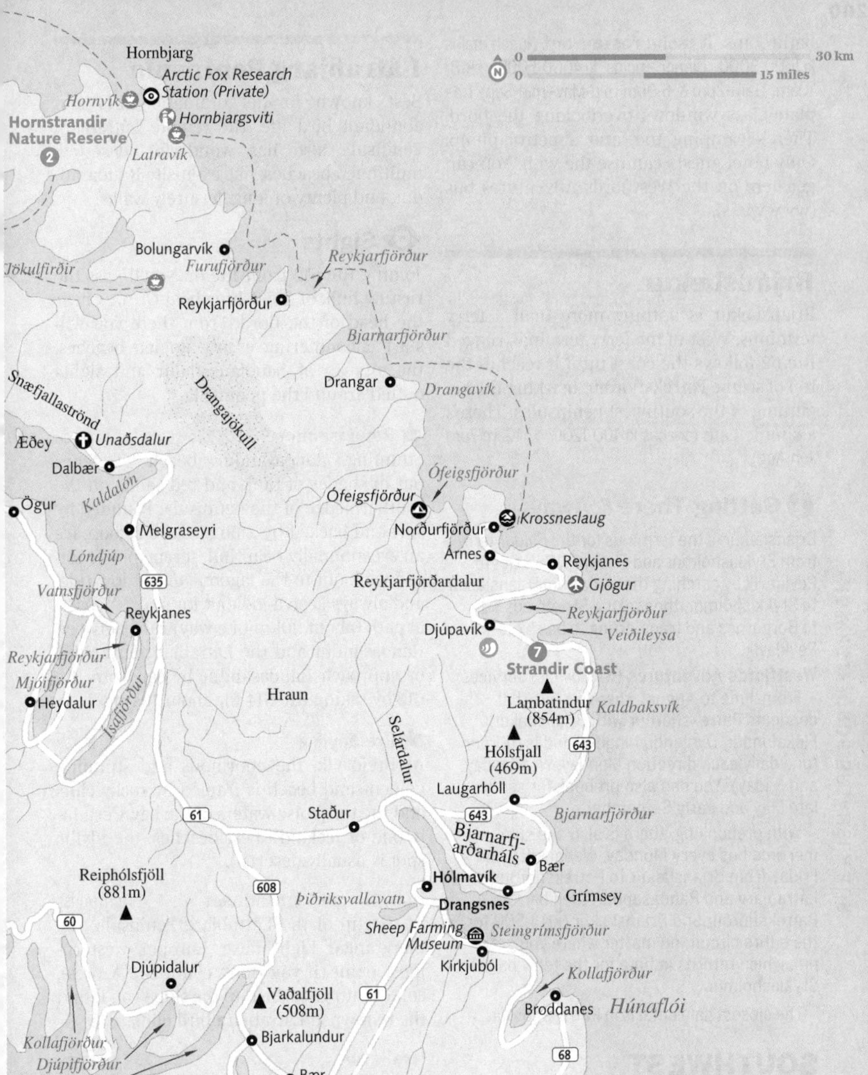

before heading out to the tip of breathtaking Arnarfjörður.

6 **Ísafjörður** (p207)
Kayaking the fjords, then tipping back a local beer.

7 **Strandir coast** (p217)
Taking in this windswept coast, stopping at charming Djúpavík before soaking in the waters at Krossneslaug.

8 **Ísafjarðardjúp** (p212)
Duelling with Arctic terns on Vigur island, learning about Arctic foxes, or kayaking past seals on this vast fjord.

9 **Þingeyri Peninsula**
(p204) Cycling remote coastal tracks to the lighthouse at Svalvogar.

bathrooms. Its solid **restaurant** (lunch mains kr1600-3000, dinner mains kr4000-5000; ⏲8-10am, 11am-2pm & 6-9pm mid-May–mid-Sep) has plate-glass windows overlooking the fjord. There's camping too, and a petrol pump. Only hotel guests can use the wi-fi. You can get here on the Westfjords Adventures bus (www.wa.is).

Brjánslækur

Brjánslækur is nothing more than a ferry terminus. West of the ferry terminal, rugged Rte 62 follows the coast until it reaches the top of scenic Patreksfjörður, marking the beginning of the southwest peninsulas. There's a simple cafe (snacks kr400-1200; ⏲10am-7pm Jun-Aug).

Getting There & Away

Brjánslækur is the terminus for the *Baldur* ferry from Stykkishólmur and Flatey (p185). Get to Reykjavík by catching the ferry from Brjánslækur to Stykkishólmur, then taking Strætó bus 58 to Borgarnes and transferring to bus 57 to Reykjavík.

Westfjords Adventures (www.wa.is) services:

- From June to August, there's a bus that connects Patreksfjörður with Brjánslækur, Flókalundur, Dynjandi, Þingeyri and Ísafjörður (one daily each direction Monday, Wednesday and Friday). You can also prebook for service in late May and early September.
- With prebooking, there is also one summertime bus every Monday, Wednesday and Friday from Brjánslækur to Patreksfjörður, Látrabjarg and Rauðasandur, then back to Patreksfjörður and Brjánslækur (kr14,500 for the entire circuit, no matter where you get on), which returns in time for the ferry back to Stykkishólmur.

The closest car rental is in Patreksfjörður.

SOUTHWEST PENINSULAS

The trident-shaped peninsulas in the southwest of the Westfjords are spectacularly scenic. It's a truly wild-feeling area, where white, black, red and pink beaches meet shimmering blue water, and towering cliffs and stunning mountains cleave the fjords. The region's most popular destination is Látrabjarg, a 12km stretch of cliffs that is home to thousands of nesting seabirds in summer. The roads in this sparsely populated region are rough and it's a slow drive

Látrabjarg Peninsula

Best known for its dramatic cliffs and abundant bird life, the remote Látrabjarg Peninsula also has wonderful, deserted, multihued beaches, like exquisite Rauðasandur, and plenty of long, leisurely walks.

Sights

Joining Rte 612 from Rte 62, you'll pass the rusting hulk of the fishing boat *Garðar* near the head of the fjord. From there you will start encountering empty, golden beaches, the airstrip at Sauðlauksdalur and sights dotted around the peninsula.

★Rauðasandur BEACH

Stunning Rauðasandur beach stretches out in shades of pink and red sands on the southern edge of the peninsula. Pounded by surf and backed by a huge azure lagoon, it's an exceptionally beautiful, serene place. You can walk out to the lagoon edge at low tide, and always keep a lookout for seals. A coastal path (about 20km one way) runs between Rauðasandur and the Látrabjarg bird cliffs, or approach Rauðasandur by car from Rte 612 by taking Rte 614 for about 10km.

★Breiðavík BEACH

At Breiðavík, the enormous and stunning golden-sand beach is framed by rocky cliffs and the turquoise waters of the bay. Certainly one of Iceland's best beaches, the idyllic spot is usually deserted.

Bjargtangar Lighthouse LIGHTHOUSE

At the tip of the Látrabjarg Peninsula, the Bjargtangar Lighthouse, Europe's westernmost point (if you don't count the Azores), comes into view. Just up the slope you'll find the renowned Látrabjarg bird cliffs.

Hvallátur BEACH

Eight kilometres west of Breiðavík the tiny hamlet of Hvallátur has a gorgeous white-sand beach, but no services.

Minjasafn Egils Ólafssonar Museum MUSEUM

(Hnjótur Museum; ☎456 1511; www.hnjotur.is; Hnjótur, Örlygshöfn; adult/child kr1000/free; ⏲10am-6pm May-Sep) In Hnjótur, about 10km west of Sauðlauksdalur, it's worth stopping to see this eclectic collection including salvaged fishing boats and displays on regional history, from whaling and farming to 1947 footage of a trawler wreck. There's a basic cafe (cake kr450).

Activities

★Látrabjarg Bird Cliffs BIRDWATCHING
Just up from Bjargtangar Lighthouse are these renowned bird cliffs. Extending for 12km along the coast and ranging from 40m to 400m, the dramatic cliffs are mobbed by nesting seabirds in early summer; it's a fascinating place even for the most reluctant of twitchers. Unbelievable numbers of puffins, razorbills, guillemots, cormorants, fulmars, gulls and kittiwakes nest here from June to mid-August.

On calm days, seals are often seen basking on the skerries around the lighthouse. It's best to go bird viewing in the evening when the birds return to their nests. Beware: there are no railings along the cliffs, so when winds are high, use extreme caution. There are no facilities; camping at the cliffs is prohibited.

Tours

Patreksfjörður tour operators offer hiking and guided trips to view birds and seals; they can meet you on the peninsula or take you out there.

Festivals & Events

Rauðasandur Festival MUSIC
(www.raudasandurfestival.is; early Jul) Popular three-day early-July music festival with camping on the beach at Melanes; check online to see if it's happening this year.

Sleeping & Eating

The few camping and accommodation options are remote, rather basic and usually in gorgeous settings.

★Melanes Camping CAMPGROUND €
(565 1041; melanes451@gmail.com; Rauðasandur; sites per adult/child kr1500/free; mid-May–mid-Sep) A simple campground at Melanes sits back on the grass behind the Rauðasandur cove, 4km from the turn-off from Rte 614 to Rauðasandur. The beachside setting is spectacular, and new amenities were recently added: running water, flush toilets, a shower, kitchen and laundry. There's also a small info centre with mini-mart.

Brunnar Camping CAMPGROUND
FREE You can camp at Brunnar, about 2km before (northeast of) the Látrabjarg bird cliffs. There are basic toilets but no reliable running water.

Hnjótur Guesthouse GUESTHOUSE, CAMPGROUND €€
(456 1596; www.hnjoturtravel.is; Hnjótur, Örlygshöfn; site per person kr2000, d with/without bathroom kr23,000/15,900, f kr24,000) This simple guesthouse and campground also has a shared kitchen, and the friendly owner runs the adjacent aviation museum (open daily 9am to 6pm May to September; kr2000).

Hótel Látrabjarg HOTEL €€
(456 1500; www.latrabjarg.com; Örlygshöfn; s/d/tr from kr11,900/23,900/26,700; mid-May–mid-Sep) This former boarding school has been converted into a simple hotel with tasteful rooms; dinner is served at night. To get to the hotel, turn right onto Rte 615 just after the museum at Hnjótur and go about 3km.

Hotel Breiðavík GUESTHOUSE €€€
(456 1575; www.breidavik.is; Breiðavík Bay; sites per adult/child kr2000/free, d with/without bathroom incl breakfast kr31,500/21,500; mid-May–mid-Sep) Hotel Breiðavík, located behind the incredible cream-coloured beach of the same name, has a bit of a lock on the accommodation market in this location. Prices are stiff for what is offered: basic rooms, sleeping-bag accommodation (kr11,500) and camping. But the setting is sublime, and it sure is nice to overnight on the peninsula. Facilities include a laundry, restaurant, guest kitchen and barbecue.

★French Café CAFE
(866 8129; Rauðasandur; snacks kr600-900; noon-5pm mid-Jun–Aug) This wonderful cafe serves delicious cake and coffee or beer and wine (kr1300) on a farm called Kirkjuhvammur, just back from Rauðasandur. At low tide you can walk right down to the reef.

Getting There & Away

Use the **Westfjords Adventures** bus (p200). If you get on at Breiðavík it costs kr8000 to the bird cliffs and back.

Two-wheel-drive cars can traverse the rutted tracks slowly, but there is no petrol on the peninsula. Fuel up in Patreksfjörður.

Patreksfjörður

POP 683

The largest village in this part of the Westfjords, zippy little Patreksfjörður on the fjord of the same name is a convenient jumping-off point for visits to the Látrabjarg Peninsula. The no-frills town has dramatic views to the bluffs and good services for

PETROL & DRIVING

It's important to gas up when you have the chance throughout the Westfjords, because petrol stations can be few and far between.

- The Westfjords official tourist map shows the N1 petrol stations.
- Many of the stations have unmanned pumps; using these requires a credit card with a PIN.
- You can also buy N1 cards stocked with credit when you do find someone manning a full-service station. We recommend it, just in case your own credit card does not work in a pinch.
- Expect lots of unpaved, often rugged, but universally beautiful roads; most are accessible with a 2WD.
- For ride-sharing, consult www.samferda.net and www.bilfar.is.

those preparing to head out to more remote fjords. The town was named after St Patrick of Ireland, who was the spiritual guide of Örlygur Hrappson, the first settler in the area.

Tours

★Westfjords Adventures HIKING TOUR, JEEP TOUR
(☎456 5006; www.wa.is; Aðalstræti 62) The area's top tour provider offers everything from birdwatching and hikes on the Látrabjarg Peninsula (eight hours kr30,000) to day-long jeep tours around the fjords (kr34,000) or along the remote Kjaran's Ave (kr34,900), a rough gravel track hewn into the fjord. There's a menu of boat, whale-watching and fishing tours (from kr9900) on Patreksfjörður, as well as tours further afield.

Sleeping

Patreksfjörður Camping CAMPGROUND €
(Aðalstræti 107; sites per adult/child kr1450/free; ⊙Jun–mid-Sep) Municipal campground in a grassy field. Has excellent new showers, laundry (per load kr1100) and kitchen.

Ráðagerði Guesthouse GUESTHOUSE €€
(☎456 0181; www.radagerdi.com; Aðalstræti 31; s with/without bathroom kr16,200/12,000, d with/without bathroom kr23,000/16,200, incl breakfast) Many of the rooms at this guesthouse have sweeping fjord views. Owners are friendly and breakfast is hearty. Sleeping-bag accommodation kr5500, linen kr1000.

Hotel West HOTEL €€
(☎456 5020; www.hotelwest.is; Aðalstræti 62; s/d kr15,900/23,900) Opened in 2014, this hotel has bright, sunny rooms, some with fjord views, and private bathrooms in a renovated former co-op building.

Fosshótel Westfjords HOTEL €€€
(Fosshótel Vestfirðir; ☎456 2004; www.fosshotel.is; Aðalstræti 100; s/d incl breakfast from kr29,050/30,900; ⊙May-Sep) A historic buildings has been well-renovated into this hotel with modern rooms offering private baths, flat-screen TVs and views to either the fjord or the mountain. There's a restaurant too.

Eating

Patreksfjörður is the best place to stock up on groceries or eat out before heading to more remote fjords.

★Stúkuhúsið CAFE €€
(☎456 1404; www.stukuhusid.is; Aðalstræti 50; mains kr1200-4500; ⊙11am-11pm Jun-Aug, noon-4pm Wed-Sat Sep-May; ☑) This cool spot in an adorable, sunny little house with fjord views perches on the street running parallel to and above the water. There are daily specials, soups, sandwiches and decadent pastries. Also makes a mean cappuccino.

★Heimsendi Bistro INTERNATIONAL €€
(☎456 5150; Eyrargata 5; lunch mains kr1300-1900, dinner mains kr1700-4800; ⊙5.30-10pm Jun–mid-Sep; ☑) This cool eatery in a mod, refurbished red-sided building down by the docks whips up creative Icelandic dishes. The mood is fresh and open, with pallets for stairs and other found objects for decorations; the food is exceptional. It can get lively on summer nights.

Shopping

Vínbúðin ALCOHOL
(☎456 2244; Þórsgata 10; ⊙2-6pm Mon-Thu, 1-7pm Fri, 11am-2pm Sat Jun-Aug, reduced hours Sep-May) National liquor-store chain.

Getting There & Around

Use the **Westfjords Adventures** bus (p200) to move around the region.

Flybus runs by request from Patreksfjörður to meet flights into **Bíldudalur Airport** (p204). Check www.westfjords.is for detailed schedules.

Westfjords Adventures is also a Europcar rental outlet and rents bikes (four hours kr4200).

Tálknafjörður

POP 251

Set amid rolling green hills, rocky peaks and a wide fjord, sleepy Tálknafjörður village is a bit bland, but it's surrounded by truly magnificent scenery.

In summer swimming pool staff administer the local campground and provide tourist information: get the detailed hiking map *Vestfirðir & Dalir 4* and try the gorgeous 10km cairn-marked hike to Bíldudalur.

Activities

★Pollurinn GEOTHERMAL POOL, HOT-POT

FREE The cement-lined natural hot-pots (46°C) at Pollurinn (literally, 'The Puddle'), 3.8km along Rte 617, are signposted with a tiny white sign with black lettering. Backed by the mountains, the shallow pools look out on the broad sweep of the fjord.

Tálknafjörður Swimming Pool GEOTHERMAL POOL, HOT-POT

(456 2639; www.talknafjordur.is; adult/child kr650/300; 9am-9pm Jun-Aug, reduced hours Sep-May) Fed by one of the few geothermal fields in the area, this is the town's main hang-out.

Sleeping & Eating

Tálknafjörður Campground CAMPGROUND €

(sites per adult/child kr1400/free; Jun-Aug) This campground beside the swimming pool has laundry, cooking facilities and showers.

★Guesthouse Bjarmaland GUESTHOUSE €€

(891 8038; www.guesthousebjarmaland.is; Bugatún 8; d with/without bathroom kr17,800/15,000; P) Spotless accommodation awaits here where the five friendly sisters also offer sleeping-bag space (kr4300).

★Dunhagi CAFE €

(662 0463; www.cafedunhagi.is; Sveinseyri; mains kr1200-3900; 11am-10pm Jun-Aug) This lovely, newly renovated historic building has rough-hewn wood floors, comfy booths and vintage photographs. Delicious local cuisine such as pan-seared trout is served, along with rich chocolate cake.

Hópið INTERNATIONAL €

(456 2777; Hrafnardalsvegur; mains kr1200-4400; noon-11pm Mon-Fri, 2-11pm Sat & Sun Jun-Aug, reduced hours Sep-May) Hópið is a low-key joint with a pool table. It serves burgers and basic Icelandic mains.

Shopping

★Villimey COSMETICS

(892 8273; www.villimey.is; Strandagata 44) This renowned Icelandic company is family run, and makes a line of excellent organic balms and ointments from wild-gathered Icelandic herbs. There are no set opening hours, so call if the shop is closed and someone from the family will come open it up.

Getting There & Away

The Patreksfjörður–Bíldudalur **Flybus** (p204) stops in Tálknafjörður, but it only runs in conjunction with flights. Ask at the town's swimming pool for details.

Bíldudalur

POP 207

Set on a gloriously calm bay on grand Arnarfjörður, and surrounded by towering peaks, the attractive fishing village Bíldudalur (www.bildudalur.is) has one of the finest fjordside positions in the country. Arriving by road from either direction, you're treated to spectacular views. Bíldudalur was founded in the 16th century and today is a major supplier of prawns and salmon.

Sights

★Skrímslasetur Icelandic Sea Monster Museum MUSEUM

(456 6666; www.skrimsli.is; Strandgata 7; adult/child kr1000/free; 10am-6pm mid-May–mid-Sep) This museum across from the church, has moody, fun, impressively elaborate and dramatic multimedia exhibits about local and foreign monster legends. The interactive multimedia table tells 180 stories of sightings around Arnarfjörður. While it's great for larger kids, wee ones might get freaked out (especially by the giant-sized models). It also has a small cafe.

Sleeping & Eating

Bíldudalur has a campsite down by its swimming pool.

★Bíldudalur HI Hostel HOSTEL €

(456 2100; www.hostel.is; Hafnarbraut 2; dm/s/d without bathroom kr4750/8100/12,900) This hostel provides super, immaculate accommodation. The inviting little spot has basic but squeaky-clean rooms and a nice kitchen. There's a discount of kr750 for HI members.

DON'T MISS

NATURAL SPRINGS

At the head of tiny Reykjarfjörður, 23km southeast of Bíldudalur (17km west of the junction with Rte 60), plan to stop at the glorious geothermal pools of **Reykjarfjarðarlaug**. Up front there's a newly refinished concrete pool (32°C), in the back there's a natural, stone one (45°C), and all around are soaring seabirds, mountains and fjord views.

Stiklur-Steppin' Stones B&B B&B €
(☎456 5005; www.stiklur.is; Dalbraut 1; d without bathroom kr14,100) This excellent little B&B has seven cosy rooms with either fjord or mountain views.

Vegamót CAFE €
(☎456 2232; Tjarnarbraut 2; mains kr1350-4000; ⏰10am-10pm Mon-Fri, noon-10pm Sat & Sun) This welcoming small grill specializes in burgers, but also offers a few fish and lamb dishes, and has an excellent small minimarket. Located at the petrol station.

ℹ Getting There & Away

Eagle Air (☎562 4200; www.eagleair.is) runs flights to/from Reykjavík (from kr20,200, 45 minutes, one daily) and **Bíldudalur Airport** (BIU; ☎Eagle Air 456 2152), 8km south of town.

Flybus (☎893 0809, 456 2336, 893 2636; flat rate for all destinations kr2000) runs on request to/from Patreksfjörður via Tálknafjörður to connect with flights.

Hertz rents cars at Bíldudalur Airport; there are other car-hire outfits in Patreksfjörður and Ísafjörður.

CENTRAL PENINSULAS

The central peninsulas of the Westfjords range from Ísafjarðardjúp in the north, with its bustling city of Ísafjörður, south to the teeny fjord at Súgandafjörður, and the broad blue Önundarfjörður with its hamlet, Flateyri. These three fjords are connected by an elaborate tunnel.

Further south, spectacular Dýrafjörður is worth exploring from its village at Þingeyri. A rutted track leads over the mountains to the Westfjords' mightiest waterfall, Dynjandi, in a branch fjord off enormous Arnarfjörður.

Tumbling in a broad sweep over a 100m-rocky scarp at the head of Dynjandivogur bay, **Dynjandi** (Fjallfoss) is the most dramatic waterfall in the Westfjords. The bumpy drive to Dynjandi, from either direction, is famous in Iceland for its incredible views; you'll see how the falls are the catchment area for run-off from the peaks and inland valleys all around.

The Westfjords Adventures bus (p200) stops at Dynjandi.

From Dynjandi, rutted Rte 60 edges along the north side of Arnarfjörður and turns north and inland at farmstead **Hrafnseyri** the birthplace (on 17 June 1811) of Jón Sigurðsson, the architect of Iceland's independence. The **Jón Sigurðsson Memorial Museum** (☎456 8260; www.hrafnseyri.is; Hrafnseyri, Arnarfjörður; adult/child kr800/free; ⏰11am-6pm Jun–early Sep) outlines his life and has a reconstruction of his turf house, a 19th-century church and a small cafe. It's on a beautiful point with fjord views.

Rte 60 between Hrafnseyri and Þingeyri is closed for six to eight months in winter. Check www.road.is.

Þingeyri

The tiny village of **Þingeyri**, on the southern side of beautiful Dýrafjörður, was the first trading station in the Westfjords, but these days the world seems to have passed by. Although there's little to see here, the town is a good jumping-off point for hiking, cycling and horse riding on Þingeyri Peninsula, the area to the west of town.

The **Old Blacksmith's Workshop** (Gamla Smiðjan Þingeyri; ☎456 3294; www.nedsti.is; Hafnarstræti 14; adult/child kr900/free; ⏰9am-6pm mid-May–Aug) in Þingeyri is part of Ísafjörður's Westfjords Heritage Museum (p207); the ticket includes admission to both sights.

West of Þingeyri, the peninsula and its dramatic peaks offer spectacular hiking and cycling. You can rent mountain bikes at Simbahöllin cafe and follow the dirt road that runs northwest along the eastern edge of the peninsula and along Dýrafjörður to the scenic valley at **Haukadalur**, an important Viking site.

If landslides don't block the road, you can continue around the peninsula, passing cliffs where birds perch and the remote lighthouse at **Svalvogar**. Do not attempt this track with a 2WD car – you will not make it. Local tour operators, and those in Ísafjörður, also offer tours here.

Inland, the Westfjords' highest peak, **Kaldbakur** (998m), is a good hiking spot. The steep trail to the summit begins from the road about 2km west of Þingeyri town.

Tours

Eagle Fjord Tours TOURS
(☎894 1684; www.eaglefjord.is; ⊙Jun-Sep) This small company runs tours around the area (adult/child approximately kr18,500/9500), sea-angling excursions (kr13,500/6500) and boat outings.

Sleeping & Eating

Þingeyri Campsite CAMPGROUND €
(sites per tent kr1500; ⊙mid-May–mid-Sep) The Þingeyri campground is behind the swimming pool and has a laundry.

Hotel Sandafell HOTEL €€
(☎456 1600; www.hotelsandafell.com; Hafnarstræti 7; s without bathroom incl breakfast kr13,700, d with/without bathroom incl breakfast kr24,100/16,500; ⊙late May–early Sep; P) The straightforward hotel has immaculate rooms down in the village centre. The restaurant (mains kr2200 to kr3200) serves good Icelandic fare, and the breakfast buffet (kr1800) is open for all.

Við Fjörðinn GUESTHOUSE €€
(☎456 8172; www.vidfjordinn.is; Aðalstræti 26; s/d without bathroom kr9500/20,000, apt from kr20,000; ⊙mid-May–Sep) This bland guesthouse has old-fashioned rooms with homey decor. There's a good guest kitchen and a TV lounge. Wi-fi is patchy.

★**Simbahöllin** CAFE €
(☎899 6659; www.simbahollin.is; Fjarðargata 5; mains kr1400-3100; ⊙10am-10pm mid-Jun–Aug, noon-6pm late May–mid-Jun & early Sep) Simbahöllin is a cool cafe in a restored general store with friendly staff serving tasty Belgian waffles during the day and hearty lamb tagines at night. There's outdoor seating with fjord views, and the welcoming bolthole rents high-quality mountain bikes (kr10,000 per day) and arranges horse-riding tours (from kr9900 for two hours).

Information

Þingeyri Tourist Office (☎456 8304; www.thingeyri.is; Hafnarstræti 6; ⊙10am-6pm Mon-Fri, 11am-6pm Sat & Sun Jun-Aug) On the main road with basic brochures and a handicraft shop.

Getting There & Away

Municipal bus (www.isafjordur.is) services:
- Flateyri (kr350, 30 minutes, three daily Monday to Friday)
- Ísafjörður (kr350, one hour, three daily Monday to Friday)

Westfjords Adventures (www.wa.is) bus services also run to Þingeyri (p200).

Dýrafjörður

Sights

Skrúður GARDENS
(⊙24hr) FREE On Dýrafjörður's northern shore is one of Iceland's oldest botanic gardens, teeny Skrúður, which was established as a teaching garden in 1909. You'll see arched whalebones at one entrance, just off Rte 624.

Ingjaldsandur BEACH
West of Hótel Núpur on the northern edge of Dýrafjörður, Rte 624 turns into a dirt road and passes an abandoned farmhouse before swerving inland to head over the top of the rugged peninsula. It takes about 20 minutes to reach Ingjaldsandur at the mouth of Önundarfjörður. Set in a picturesque valley, this isolated beach is a fantastic spot to watch the midnight sun as it flirts with the sea before rising back up into the sky.

Sleeping & Eating

Hotel Núpur HOTEL €€
(☎456 8235; www.hotelnupur.is; Rte 624; sites per tent kr2500, d/tr without bathroom incl breakfast kr17,000/23,300; ⊙mid-May–mid-Sep) Brothers Siggi and Gummi have done their darnedest to turn this rumpled former schooling complex into desirable digs. All but two of the basic rooms share bathrooms and there are shared kitchens. Sleeping-bag accommodation costs kr4500. They also run a restaurant. Find it about 7km west of Rte 60 along Rte 624, just west of Skrúður (p205).

Önundarfjörður

Azure Önundarfjörður has sheer mountain walls on either side, with cod drying racks arranged along the shores. The tiny village of Flateyri looks across the fjord onto beautiful sand bars, and you'll notice an unusual avalanche-blocking wall above the town to keep it from being inundated with snow, built after a tragic avalanche in 1995.

Sleeping

Korpudalur HI Hostel GUESTHOUSE, HOSTEL €
(Korpudalur Kirkjuból; ☎456 7808; www.korpudalur.is; Rte 627; sites per tent kr1400, dm/d without bathroom from kr5700/13,000; ⊙mid-May–mid-Sep) At the head of Önundarfjörður, a turn-off marked Kirkjuból (not to be confused with a guesthouse of the same name) leads 5km down rough Rte 627 to this popular hostel. The stunning location and home-made bread make this 100-year-old farmhouse worth visiting. Only drawback: rooms are tiny. Sleeping-bag accommodation kr5000. HI members get a discount of kr750.

★**Guesthouse Kirkjuból í Bjarnardal** GUESTHOUSE €€
(☎456 7679; www.kirkjubol.is; Rte 60, Bjarnardalur; d with/without bathroom incl breakfast kr20,700/15,300; ⊙Jun-Aug) Just south of Önundarfjörður, lying on the east side of Rte 60, a marked turn-off for Kirkjuból leads to this lovely, remote white-and-green farmstead. It's squeaky-clean inside, with lovely rooms sporting antiques, a guest kitchen and a living room. It's a serene spot with friendly owners and good views.

Flateyri

POP 187

Once a support base for Norwegian whalers, Flateyri is now a quiet little place set on a striking gravel spit sticking out into sparkling Önundarfjörður. There are a couple of museums, and a geothermal pool, but the beautiful scenery is the main draw.

Sights & Activities

Old Bookstore in Flateyri MUSEUM
(Gamla Bókabúðin Flateyri; Hafnarstræti 3-5; by donation; ⊙11am-5pm Jun-Aug) Peruse a well-preserved historic bookshop and its attached apartment, which feel wonderfully trapped in amber. Coffee and cake (kr1200) on offer too.

Nonsense Museum MUSEUM
(Hafnarstræti 11; adult/child kr1000/free; ⊙1-5.30pm Mon-Fri, 1-4pm Sat & Sun Jun-Aug) Flateyri's Nonsense Museum contains the eclectic collections of several locals. You'll find hundreds of pens, matchboxes and model ships showcased in pathologically organised displays. Cafe downstairs.

Kayak Flateyri KAYAKING
(☎863 7662; www.kayakflateyri.com) Paddle out on gorgeous Önundarfjörður, with or without a guide. Also offers accommodation.

Iceland ProFishing FISHING
(☎456 6667; www.icelandprofishing.com; Hafnarstræti 9; ⊙Apr-Sep) Rents boats for angling trips around the fjords (guides can be hired), and offers week-long trips (from €960) with lodging in Flateyri and Suðureyri.

Sleeping & Eating

Síma Hostel GUESTHOUSE €
(☎897 8700; www.icelandwestfjords.com; Ránargata 1; d/f without bathroom from kr10,800/17,900; ⊙mid-May–early Sep) Many of these tidy, simple rooms have good fjord views.

Bryggjukaffi CAFE €
(Harbor Café; Hafnarstræti 4; soup kr1500; ⊙11.30am-6pm Jun-Sep, Sat & Sun Oct-May) A friendly local woman cooks up delicious daily soup (the fish stew is outstanding) with excellent fresh bread and cakes (kr800 to kr900). There are guest rooms upstairs (double/family with shared bathroom kr10,000/16,000).

Getting There & Away

Municipal buses (www.isafjordur.is) connect Þingeyri, Flateyri and Ísafjörður (kr350, three daily Monday to Friday).The bus stops in Flateyri at Ránargata 1 (in front of the Síma Hostel).

Suðureyri

POP 268

Perched on the tip of 13km-long Súgandafjörður, the fishing community of Suðureyri (www.sudureyri.is) was isolated for years by the forbidding mountains. Now connected with Ísafjörður and Flateyri by a 9km tunnel network, the village is a natural stop for anglers; its waters are the best place in Iceland to catch halibut.

Geothermal Swimming Pool GEOTHERMAL POOL, HOT-POT
(☎450 8490; Túngata 8; adult/child kr650/300; ⊙11am-7pm Jun-Aug, reduced hours Sep-May) Locals congregate at the geothermal swimming pool, sauna and hot-pots.

Tours

Iceland ProFishing in Flateyri also fishes from Suðureyri. The Fisherman hotel-restaurant complex promotes the life of the fishing village with fishing and seafood tours, including a visit to the local fish factory (kr5000) and tours further afield.

Sleeping & Eating

Fisherman Hotel HOTEL €€
(☎450 9000; www.fisherman.is; Aðalgata 14; sites per person kr1500, d with/without bathroom incl breakfast kr25,000/18,500; @) This friendly hotel has bright rooms, crisp linens and pine furniture. Its top seafood **restaurant** (mains kr3800-4900; ⊙6-9pm; ☎) has place mats and menu covers made from fish skins, setting the tone. Cuisine features locally sourced fresh fish, lamb and a veggie option. There's a simpler **cafe** (8am to 11pm mid-May to mid-September; dishes kr1400 to kr2800) across the street.

Shopping

Á Milli Fjalla ARTS & CRAFTS
(☎456 6163; Aðalgata; ⊙1-6pm Mon-Fri, 1-4pm Sat & Sun Jul & Aug) This teeny shop sells locally crafted knits, ceramics and unique trinkets.

Getting There & Away

Municipal buses (www.isafjordur.is) run to Ísafjörður (kr350, 25 minutes, three daily Monday to Friday)

Ísafjörður

POP 2559

Hub of Westfjords adventure tours, and by far the region's largest town, Ísafjörður (www.isafjordur.is) is a pleasant and prosperous place and an excellent base for travellers. The town is set on an arcing spit that extends out into Skutulsfjörður, and is hemmed in on all sides by towering peaks and the dark waters of the fjord.

The centre of Ísafjörður is a charming grid of old timber and tin-clad buildings, many unchanged since the 18th century, when the harbour was full of tall ships and Norwegian whaling crews. Today it is a surprisingly cosmopolitan place, and after some time spent travelling in the Westfjords, it'll feel like a bustling metropolis with its tempting cafes and fine choice of restaurants.

There's hiking in the hills around the town, skiing in winter, and regular summer boats ferry hikers across to the remote Hornstrandir Peninsula.

Sights & Activities

★ **Westfjords Heritage Museum** MUSEUM
(Byggðasafn Vestfjarða; ☎456 3293; www.nedsti.is; Neðstíkaupstaður; adult/child kr1000/free; ⊙9am-6pm mid-May–mid-Sep) Part of a cluster of historic wooden buildings by the harbour, the Westfjords Heritage Museum is in the Turnhús (1784), which was originally a warehouse. It is crammed with fishing and nautical exhibits, tools from the whaling days, fascinating old photos depicting town life over the centuries, and accordions. To the right is the Tjöruhús (1781), now an excellent seafood restaurant. The Faktorhús (1765), which housed the manager of the village shop, and the Krambúd (1757), originally a storehouse, are now private residences.

★ **Ísafjörður–Suðureyri–Flateyri Tunnel** LANDMARK
(Vestfjarðagöng) FREE Completed in 1996, this 9km-long tunnel network beneath the mountains becomes an unusual one-lane tunnel in parts of the 6km stretch from Ísafjörður to Flateyri. In the middle of the mountain it branches, and a 3km section of tunnel shoots off to Suðureyri. Worry not: pull-outs throughout allow oncoming traffic to alternate.

Seamen's Monument MONUMENT
Ísafjörður's enormous bronze Seaman's Monument commemorates fishermen who have died at sea.

Path Towards Óshlíð HIKING, CYCLING
A precarious path leads around the point from Ísafjörður towards Bolungarvík and the mountain Óshlíð. The teeny dangerous track, which is prone to rockfalls and avalanches, used to be the only route to Bolungarvík. If you use caution, you can walk or cycle along the bit nearest the tunnel to Bolungarvík and see Hornstrandir and Snæfjallaströnd in the distance.

Swimming Pool SWIMMING
(☎450 8480; Austurvegur 9; adult/child kr650/350; ⊙10am-9pm Mon-Fri, 10am-5pm Sat & Sun) Although plain by Icelandic standards, the town swimming pool makes a good retreat on a wet day.

Tours

★ **West Tours** ADVENTURE TOUR
(Vesturferðir; ☎456 5111; www.westtours.is; Aðalstræti 7; ⊙8am-6pm Mon-Fri, 8.30am-4.30pm Sat, 10am-3pm Sun Jun-Aug, 8am-4pm Mon-Fri

Ísafjörður

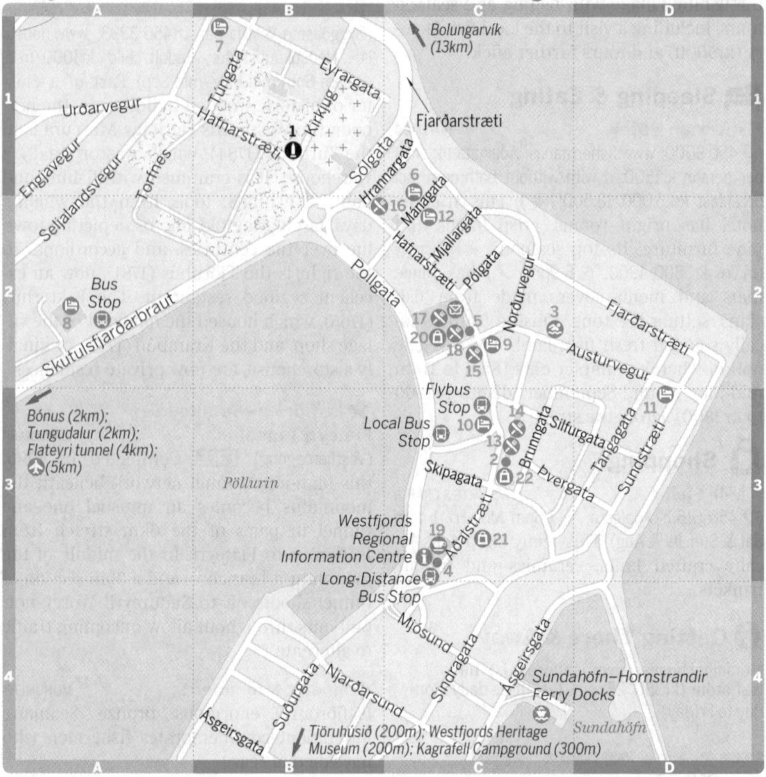

Sep-May) Popular, professional West Tours organises a mind-boggling array of trips throughout the Westfjords. There are tours of Vigur (kr10,800), hiking in Hornstrandir (kr13,900 to kr41,900) and kayaking trips (kr6600 to kr27,900). Cycling, horse riding, boat and angling tours, birdwatching and cultural excursions are but a few of the other activities on offer. Kids are half-price.

★ **Borea** OUTDOORS
(☎456 3322; www.borea.is; Aðalstræti 22b; ⏰9am-7pm Mon-Fri, to 6pm Sat & Sun Jun-Aug, reduced hours Sep-May) Adventure outfitter offering fjord kayaking (from kr9900), excellent hiking in Hornstrandir (from kr41,900) and cycling (from kr9900). It also runs ferry services to Hornstrandir and operates Kviar, its private cabin in the reserve.

Fosshestar HORSE RIDING
(☎842 6969; www.fosshestar.is) Short riding tours (from kr25,000) for all skill levels in the Engidalur Valley, or horse petting (per person kr5000). Prices drop for more people. Book ahead; cash only. Also has a couple of rental houses.

Wild Westfjords ADVENTURE TOUR
(☎456 3300; www.wildwestfjords.com; Hafnarstræti 9; ⏰9am-6pm Jun-Aug, reduced hours Sep-May) Operates multiday guided or self-drive tours around the fjords and Iceland, as well as day tours, such as to Dynjandi (kr20,000), kayaking trips (from kr9900) and hiking in Hornstrandir (from kr29,900).

Sleeping

Tungudalur Campground CAMPGROUND €
(☎864 8592; www.gih.is; sites per adult/child kr1700/free; ⏰mid-Jun–mid-Sep) This campground is almost 5km out of town and very scenic, set by a pretty waterfall, Bunarfoss, in Tungudalur. The last stop on the town bus will take you to within 1km of the site. Facilities include a kitchen and coin laundry.

Ísafjörður

Litla Guesthouse GUESTHOUSE €
(☎893 6993; www.guesthouselitla.is; Sundstræti 43; d without bathroom kr15,000) Basic rooms are a bit steep for what you get, but the owner is helpful and there's a guest kitchen, though it's not all that well-equipped.

Mánagisting Guesthouse GUESTHOUSE, APARTMENT €
(Gistiheimilið Mánagisting; ☎615 2014; www.simnet.is/managisting; Mánagata 4; dm/d without bathroom kr5300/12,000, studio kr15,000) Simple shared rooms line the halls of this no-frills guesthouse with kitchens and sitting rooms. Cleanliness is an issue, but the studios with bathroom and kitchen are a deal.

Kagrafell Campground CAMPGROUND €
(☎862 8623; Suðurtangi 2; ⏲mid-May–mid-Sep) Bare-bones campground with no facilities; use the WC at the nearby museum.

★**Gentle Space Guesthouse & Apartments** APARTMENT €€
(☎892 9282; www.gentlespace.is; Hlíðarvegur 14; r/apt from kr13,000/19,800) This family run outfit offers three rooms with kitchenettes and flat-screen TVs in a small, well-run guesthouse, and rents immaculate, fully equipped apartments in the centre.

Gamla Gistihúsið GUESTHOUSE €€
(☎456 4146; www.gistihus.is; Mánagata 5; dm kr5200, d/tr without bathroom incl breakfast kr20,600/27,000; @) Bright, cheerful and well kept Hótel Ísafjörður has simple but comfortable rooms with plenty of cosy touches. The bathrooms are shared, but each double room has telephone, washbasin and bathrobes. An annexe just down the road has a guest kitchen and more modern rooms.

Hótel Horn HOTEL €€
(☎456 4611; www.hotelhorn.is; Austurvegur 2; d incl breakfast kr24,500) This big hotel in the centre offers basic rooms with private bathrooms. Family rooms sleep five and also have a kitchenette.

Hótel Edda HOTEL, CAMPGROUND €€
(☎444 4960; www.hoteledda.is; Mantaskólinn; d with/without bathroom kr24,700/17,700; ⏲early Jun–mid-Aug) No-frills summer accommodation is available at the town's secondary school. Choose from basic sleeping-bag accommodation (kr2800) in the classrooms, or rooms with shared or private bathrooms. Camping costs kr1200, plus kr800 for each additional person in the tent.

Hótel Ísafjörður BUSINESS HOTEL €€€
(☎456 4111; www.hotelisafjordur.is; Silfurtorg 2; d incl breakfast from kr31,000; @) The rooms on the higher floors of this central, classic business hotel favoured by tour groups have great views over the tin-roofed town and the waters beyond.

Eating

★**Gamla Bakaríð** BAKERY €
(☎456 3226; Aðalstræti 24; ⏲7am-6pm Mon-Fri, to 4pm Sat, 8am-4pm Sun) For breakfast, lunch or a mid-morning sugar fix, there's a clutch of tempting bakeries in town. Gamla Bakaríð is usually packed for its full range of sweet treats (cookies, doughnuts and cakes) as well as fresh bread.

Bræðraborg CAFE €
(www.borea.is; Aðalstræti 22b; mains kr1190-1690; ⌚9am-7pm Mon-Fri, to 6pm Sat & Sun Jun-Aug, reduced hours Sep-May;) Bræðraborg is a comfy travellers' cafe where people munch on healthy snacks and chat with other visitors. The cafe is the headquarters for Borea tours.

Thai Koon THAI €
(Hafnarstræti 9, Neisti Centre; mains kr1790-1990; ⌚11.30am-8pm Mon-Fri, 5-8pm Sat & Sun) After a stretch of limited food options in remote Iceland, this small Thai canteen seems decidedly exotic. There's no grand ambience but the curries and noodles are reliably tasty and served up in heaping portions.

★ **Tjöruhúsið** SEAFOOD €€
(☎456 4419; www.facebook.com/tjoruhusid; Neðstakaupstaður 1; mains kr2500-5000; ⌚noon-2pm & 7-10pm Jun-Sep, reduced hours Oct-May) The warm and rustic restaurant next to the heritage museum offers some of the best seafood around. Go for the *plokkfiskur* – flaked fish, potatoes and onions – or try the various catches of the day, fresh off the boat from the harbour, all served up in hot skillets. There's outdoor seating on benches when it's sunny. Occasional live music.

★ **Húsið** INTERNATIONAL €€
(☎456 5555; Hrannargata 2; mains kr1600-3000; ⌚11am-10pm Sun-Thu, to 2am Fri & Sat) Sidle up to the varnished, rough-hewn wood tables inside this tin-clad house, or kick back on the sunny terrace for scrumptious, relaxed meals and local beer on tap. Groovy tunes play as hip staff sling soup, sandwiches, burgers, pizza and Icelandic staples like lamb. It's a fun hang-out and there are occasional DJs and live music.

Hamraborg FAST FOOD €€
(Hafnarstraeti 7; mains kr1000-2790; ⌚9am-11.30pm) Voted Iceland's best fast-food joint by national radio polls, this outpost attracts locals who gossip over Béarnaise burgers and pizza. Sport frequently plays on the TV.

Við Pollinn ICELANDIC, SEAFOOD €€€
(☎456 3360; www.vidpollinn.is; Silfurtorg 2; mains kr4400-5900; ⌚7am-9pm May-Sep, 11am-2pm Mon-Wed, 7-9pm Thu-Sat Oct-Apr, closed mid-Nov–early Jan) Although the decor feels a bit bland, the restaurant at Hótel Ísafjörður has an excellent selection of local cuisine prepared with flair. The windows offer great views over the fjord – you might even see your next meal being caught.

Self-Catering

Ísafjörður is the place to stock up before heading to remote areas.

Bónus SUPERMARKET €
(Skeiði 1; ⌚11am-6.30pm Mon-Thu, 10am-7.30pm Fri, 10am-6pm Sat, noon-6pm Sun) Moderately priced supermarket on the main road.

Samkaup SUPERMARKET €
(Hafnarstræti 9, Neisti Centre; ⌚10am-8pm Mon-Sat, noon-8pm Sun) In the Neisti Centre.

Drinking & Nightlife

Edinborg CAFE, BAR
(☎456 8335; Aðalstræti 7; mains kr2000-3500; ⌚restaurant noon-10pm, bar to 1am Mon-Fri, to 3am Sat & Sun Jun-Aug, noon-9pm Sep-May) In the same building as the tourist office this relaxed spot attracts travellers who stop by for beer or coffee on the sunny patio. The house bread is made with a special recipe that incorporates beer.

Shopping

Rammagerð Ísafjarðar ARTS & CRAFTS
(☎456 3041; Aðalstræti 16; ⌚1-5pm Mon-Fri, noon-2pm Sat) Rammagerð Ísafjarðar sells quality knitting and other local crafts.

Vínbúðin ALCOHOL
(☎456 3455; Aðalstræti 20; ⌚11am-6pm Mon-Thu, to 7pm Fri, to 4pm Sat Jun-Aug, reduced hours Sep-May) National liquor chain.

Neisti Centre SHOPPING CENTRE
(Hafnarstræti 9-13) Ísafjörður's central shopping centre houses the post office, a supermarket and various restaurants and shops.

Information

Hospital (Heilbrigðisstofnun Vestfjarða Ísafirði; ☎450 4500; www.fsi.is; Torfnes) Ísafjörður has a full-service hospital, which also operates clinics around the Westfjords.

Westfjords Regional Information Centre (☎450 8060; www.isafjordur.is; Aðalstræti 7, Edinborgarhús; ⌚8am-6pm Mon-Fri, 8am-3pm Sat & Sun Jun-Aug, reduced hours Sep-May) By the harbour in the Edinborgarhús (1907), helpful staff have loads of info on the Westfjords and Hornstrandir Nature Reserve. Internet terminal with free 10-minute session; luggage storage kr200 per day.

Getting There & Away

AIR

Air Iceland (☎456 3000; www.airiceland.is) flies between **Ísafjörður Airport** (IFJ; ☎570

WORTH A TRIP

VIGUR

With one farm and scads of puffins, charming **Vigur** is a popular destination for day trippers from Ísafjörður. The tiny island sits at the mouth of Hestfjörður, offering sweeping fjord views in every direction. There's not much to do on the island besides taking a stroll (grab a stick from the windmill and hold it over your head – the Arctic terns are fierce here!), visiting the eider ducks and savouring cakes at the cafe (look out for the interesting egg collection inside).

West Tours (p207) in Ísafjörður and **Ögur Travel** (p213) in Ögur run tours and boats to the island.

3000), 5km south on the fjord, and Reykjavík's domestic airport twice daily. It also offers day tours.

A **Flybus** (www.isafjordur.is; Hafnarstræti), timed to meet flights, runs between the airport and Bolungarvík (kr1500), and stops near the Hótel Ísafjörður (kr1000) about 45 minutes before departure.

BOAT

In summer, **West Tours** (p217) and **Borea** (p208) ferries to Hornstrandir depart from the Sundahöfn docks on the eastern side of the town promontory.

BUS

Ísafjörður is the major bus hub in the Westfjords. The **long-distance bus stop** (www.westfjords.is; Aðalstræti) is at the tourist information centre.

Westfjords Adventures (www.wa.is) services:

- From June to August there's a bus to Patreksfjörður (kr9900) and Brjánslækur (the terminal for the Stykkishólmur ferry; kr8400) via Þingeyri, Dynjandi and Flókalundur (one daily each direction Monday, Wednesday and Friday).
- You must prebook in late May and early September.
- There are no buses in the off season.

Hópferðamiðstöð Vestfjarða (vidfjordinn@vidfjordinn.is) operates buses mid-May to mid-September between Ísafjörður and Hólmavík, four times a week.

To get to Reykjavík, take a bus to Hólmavík or Brjánslækur then transfer. In Hólmavík, catch Strætó (www.bus.is) bus 59 to Borgarnes, where you transfer again. In Brjánslækur, take the ferry to Stykkishólmur then catch Strætó bus 58 to Borgarnes. To get to Akureyri, you also need to transfer in Borgarnes; alternatively you can transfer in Bifröst to the middle-of-the-night Sterna (www.sternatravel.com) bus 60, or stay overnight (no campground there, though) and catch the Strætó bus 57 to Akureyri in the morning.

Municipal buses (☎456 5518; www.isafjordur.is) stop at marked stops (Skutulsfjarðarbraut) along the waterfront:

- Flateyri and Þingeyri (kr350, three daily Monday to Friday)
- Suðureyri (kr350, 20 minutes, three daily Monday to Friday)
- A bus for Bolungarvík (kr1000, 15 minutes, three daily Monday to Friday) leaves from the kiosk at Hamraborg, near the **Samkaup** (p210) supermarket.

CAR

For ride-sharing check www.samferda.net and www.bilfar.is.

Avis (☎591 4000; www.avis.is; Ísafjörður Airport)

Europcar (☎461 6000, 840 6074; www.holdur.is; Ísafjörður Airport)

Hertz (☎522 4490; www.hertz.is; Ísafjörður Airport)

Getting Around

City buses (kr350) operate from 7.20am to 6.15pm and connect the town centre with Hnífsdalur and Holtahverfi on the town's edges; they **stop** (Pollgata) along the waterfront.

West Tours (p207) rents bikes.

Bolungarvík

POP 882

Despite its stunningly dramatic position at the end of the fjord, Bolungarvík is rather dull and uninspiring. It has a couple of cool sights, though. Bolungarvík used to be connected to Ísafjörður by a perilous track around the mountain Óshlíð, but now there is a 5.4km tunnel connecting the two, and the track is used only for walking (p207).

Sights

★**Ósvör Maritime Museum** MUSEUM

(Ósvör Sjóminjasafn; ☎892 5744; www.osvor.is; adult/child kr950/free; ⏲9am-5pm Mon-Fri, 10am-5pm Sat & Sun Jun–mid-Aug, by appointment Sep-May) Ósvör Maritime Museum, housed in a series of old turf-and-stone fishing shacks, down a turn-off just after the tunnel into town, is well worth a visit. A guide in a typical lambskin fishing outfit shows you around (his English isn't the best), explaining the history of the area and traditional seafaring life from the Settlement Era to the era of plastics. The cramped fishing hut is full of interesting relics. A traditional rowing boat is also on display.

Natural History Museum MUSEUM
(☎456 7507; www.nabo.is; Vitastígur 3; adult/child kr950/free; ⏱9am-5pm Mon-Fri, 10am-5pm Sat & Sun Jun–mid-Aug, 9am-4pm Mon-Fri mid-Aug–May) In the town's main shopping arcade, the Natural History Museum has a comprehensive collection of minerals (lignite from when Iceland was covered in forests) and taxidermied animals – including a giant blue whalebone more than 100 years old and a polar bear shot by local fishers while swimming off the Hornstrandir coast.

Sleeping & Eating

There's really only one eatery in Bolungarvík; head to Ísafjörður for more choices and large grocery stores.

Einarshúsið GUESTHOUSE €€
(☎456 7901; www.einarshusid.is; Hafnargata 41; d without bathroom incl breakfast kr18,500; ⏱May-Sep, restaurant 11.30am-9pm) Einarshúsið is a turn-of-the-century heritage home on the harbour, and the best place to eat and sleep rolled into one. The friendly owner dotes on guests, who gorge on seafood (mains kr1290 to kr2690; weekend seafood buffet kr4500) or sleep over in five lovely rooms upstairs, decorated in the house's original style (c 1902), but with modern bathrooms. Avoid the basement room.

Shopping

O-Design ARTS & CRAFTS
(www.facebook.com/odesigniceland; Aðalstræti 21; ⏱4-6.30pm Thu & Fri, noon-4pm Sat) This bright, small Icelandic-design arts and homewares shop opened in 2016; check ahead for opening times.

Getting There & Away

BOAT

Vaxon (☎862 2221; www.vaxon.is; Aðalstræti 9) boat charters can take you to Hornstrandir or around the fjords.

BUS

Buses (www.bolungarvik.is) serve Ísafjörður (kr1000, three daily Monday to Friday) and leave from the corner of Vitastígur and Aðalstræti.

Flybus (www.isafjordur.is) services to Ísafjörður Airport (kr1500) are timed to coincide with flights.

Ísafjarðardjúp

The largest of the fjords in the region, 75km-long Ísafjarðardjúp takes a massive swath out of the Westfjords' landmass. Circuitous Rte 61 winds in and out of a series of smaller fjords on the southern side, making the drive from the bustling city of Ísafjörður (the largest in the Westfjords) to Hólmavík on the Strandir coast like sliding along each tooth of a fine comb.

Across the fjord lies the enormous Drangajökull glacier. The remote Hornstrandir Nature Reserve lies further north still.

Súðavík

POP 151

Just east of Ísafjörður, the small fishing community of Súðavík (www.sudavik.is) commands an imposing view across the fjord to Snæfjallaströnd peninsula. Although the township is nothing more than a string of bright, box-shaped houses, it is definitely worth stopping to visit the Arctic Fox Center.

The Ísafjörður–Hólmavík bus stops in Súðavík (kr1000, 20 minutes, four weekly mid-May to mid-September); check www.westfjords.is for schedules.

Arctic Fox Center MUSEUM
(Melrakkasetur; ☎456 4922; www.arcticfoxcenter.com; adult/child kr1200/free; ⏱9am-6pm Jun-Aug, 10am-4pm Sep-May) The study of the Arctic fox has been underway on nearby Hornstrandir for years, and this locally loved exhibition centre details the life of the local fox and its relationship with humans and its habitat. The centre sits inside the renovated farmstead of **Eyrardalur** – one of the oldest buildings in the area.

Skötufjörður

★ **Litlibær** CAFE €
(☎456 4809; Skötufjörður; waffles & coffee kr1000; ⏱10am-5pm mid-May–mid-Sep) Litlibær is a charming cafe with interesting memorabilia in a historic 19th-century farmstead

VOLUNTEERING AT THE ARCTIC FOX RESEARCH STATION

Volunteers are welcomed at the Arctic Fox Research Station, situated on the northern cliffs of the jaw-dropping Hornstrandir Peninsula.

Each day from June to August, the team of researchers/volunteers sets off for six-hour viewing shifts, during which they monitor fox behaviours and changes in location. There are no requirements for becoming a volunteer, but applications are competitive and preference is given to those studying biology, conservation science or photography. Volunteers are asked to give at least one week of their time. You'll also need to pay for your own transport and provide your own tent and gear. The research centre will handle food and cooking equipment.

You can also volunteer at the Arctic Fox Center headquarters in Suðavík, near Ísafjörður. Staff working here must spend a minimum of two weeks, and run the coffee house plus care for any orphaned foxes on site.

on Skötufjörður. The owner was born and raised on the land, and these days his family dotes on weary tourists, offering tasty heart-shaped waffles with fresh jam and whipped cream, coffee and tips on spotting the seals and Celtic ruins nearby.

After filling your belly, scout out the picnic table about 200m north – there's a small box with binoculars for viewing the blubbery beasts.

Ögur

Ögur Travel TOURS

(☎857 1840; www.ogurtravel.com; Rte 61, Ögur; ⊙May-Sep) Book ahead to join Ögur Travel, run by seven siblings, on kayaking or hiking trips (from kr3500) for a few hours or a few days. A popular kayak is the four-hour tour of Vigur island (kr15,000), which takes in the incredible scenery and local bird life. Tours run from the family's cute, welcoming **cafe** (Rte 61, Ögur; snacks kr600-1400; ⊙10am-6pm Jun-Aug) on the point just east of Skötufjörður.

Mjóifjörður

Heydalur GUESTHOUSE €€

(☎456 4824; www.heydalur.is; Mjóifjörður; sites per adult kr1200, s/d/cabins from kr13,600/17,100/21,500) Heydalur is a good place to break up the journey along Rte 61 as it wiggles along the undulating coast. At the head of Mjóifjörður, 11km from the main road, Heydalur is run by affable Stella, who cooks up delicious meals in the restaurant (mains kr1800 to kr4000; 11.30am to 10pm June to August) in a restored barn.

Reykjarfjörður

Hótel Reykjanes HOTEL €€

(☎456 4844; www.hotelreykjanes.is; Reykjarfjörður; sites per tent kr2700, d/q without bathroom kr18,300/36,000; @) At the end of tiny Reykjarfjörður, well-weathered Hótel Reykjanes is housed in a huge white complex that was once the district's school. Best only if you can't drive any further: rooms are basic (most bathrooms shared), but there's a 50m outdoor geothermal pool (adult/child kr700/350) fed by a steamy spring. Sleeping bag accommodation costs kr5200. Simple meals cost kr1600 to kr4800.

Snæfjallaströnd

On the northeastern shore of Ísafjarðardjúp, the unsurfaced Rte 635 leads north to **Kaldalón**, where a beautiful green valley runs up to the receding **Drangajökull** ice cap. It's possible to hike up to the snow line, but don't venture any further without a local guide, as dangerous crevasses form in the ice and are often invisible under the snow.

Further northwest, **Snæfjallaströnd** was abandoned in 1995, but adventurous hikers can walk along the 'Postal Road' from the church at Unaðsdalur along the coast to the bunkhouse at **Grunnavík**, from where you can catch boats to Ísafjörður and Hesteyri.

Just before the church at Unaðsdalur, **Dalbær** (☎821 7121; www.snjafjallasetur.is/tourism.html; N 66° 6' 3.173" W 22° 34' 18.642", Snæfjallaströnd; ⊙mid-Jun–late-Aug) is a great wilderness outpost on the edge of Hornstrandir with sleeping-bag accommodation and camping.

Steinshús MUSEUM
(☎822 1508; www.steinnsteinarr.is; Rte 635, Nauteyri; ⊙10am-8pm Jun-Sep) This museum opened in 2015 at the homestead of Steinn Steinarr (1908–58), one of Iceland's most famous poets. It details, in Icelandic and English, his wretched childhood, during which his family was split up, and his discovery of poetry and blossoming as a writer. It's about 3km north of Rte 61 on unpaved Rte 635.

HORNSTRANDIR

Craggy mountains, precarious sea cliffs and plunging waterfalls ring the wonderful, barely inhabited Hornstrandir Peninsula, at the northern end of the Westfjords. **Hornstrandir Nature Reserve** (☎591 2000; www.ust.is/hornstrandir) is one of Europe's last true wilderness areas, covering some of the most extreme and inhospitable parts of the country. It's a fantastic destination for hiking, with challenging terrain and excellent opportunities for spotting Arctic foxes, seals, whales and teeming bird life.

Weather, Safety & Gear

There are no services available in Hornstrandir and hikers must be fully prepared to tackle all eventualities. The passes are steep, heavy rains will make rivers impassable, fog can be dense and you'll need to carry all your gear, so hiking can be slower than you might expect. In addition, most trails are unmarked, primitive and uneven, so it's essential to carry a good map (try *Vestfirðir & Dalir: 1*), a compass and a GPS. Rangers stress the need for high-quality, completely weatherproof gear as you will often be hiking in rain, without any way to get dry. Don't force a rescue operation due to ill preparation.

The best time to visit is in July. Outside the summer season (which runs from late June to mid-August; ferry boats run June to August) there are few people around and the weather is even more unpredictable. It is essential to plan ahead and get local advice, as vast snow drifts with near-vertical faces can develop on the mountain passes and rivers can be unfordable. Before 15 June it is mandatory to register with a ranger (p217). It's also always smart to register your plans with www.safetravel.is.

At various points in the park there are emergency huts with VHF radios preset to the Icelandic Coast Guard in case of emergency. Emergency huts are often located near campsites.

You always need to book your return boat in advance; this serves as a safety measure, in case you don't turn up for it. Ask local operators about current conditions before setting off. Guided trips can also be easily arranged with Ísafjörður operators.

Tours

The main operators running tours (boating, hiking, kayaking, skiing etc) into Hornstrandir are West Tours (p207), Borea (p208) and Wild Westfjords (p208), based in Ísafjörður.

Sleeping

Camping is the main way to stay in Hornstrandir. There are also three options for sleeping-bag accommodation in the main part of Hornstrandir: Hesteyri, Hornbjargsviti and Grunnavík. Two additional options are in the far-eastern part of the reserve at Reykjarfjörður and Bolungarvík.

Camping in Hornstrandir is free. Carry out all rubbish, and stick to designated campgrounds: wild camping is prohibited in the nature reserve. All campsites have dry latrines. Latrine doors are weighed down with heavy timber to prevent near-certain wind damage if they are left open, so be sure to secure the door after use.

Camping on private grounds with facilities costs around kr1800. Expect to pay upwards of kr6500 for sleeping-bag space, which must be reserved well in advance, especially in Hesteyri.

Old Doctor's House HOSTEL €
(☎845 5075, Hesteyri 899 7661; www.hesteyri.net; Hesteyri; dm kr9000; ⊙Jun-Aug) By far the most developed lodging in Hornstrandir, Hesteyri has accommodation for 16 at the Old Doctor's House, with breakfast (coffee and pancakes; kr2000) and dinner (kr5000) available, and a guest kitchen. Book well ahead for June and July.

Hornbjargsviti HOSTEL €
(☎Ferðafélag Íslands 568 2533; www.fi.is; sites per person kr1800, dm kr7500; ⊙Jul–early Aug) Run by Ferðafélag Íslands (FI), and attached to the lighthouse of the same name on the east coast, this hostel sleeps 50 and has a kitchen and coin-operated showers. Campers have access to WCs but not the hut kitchen.

Hornstrandir

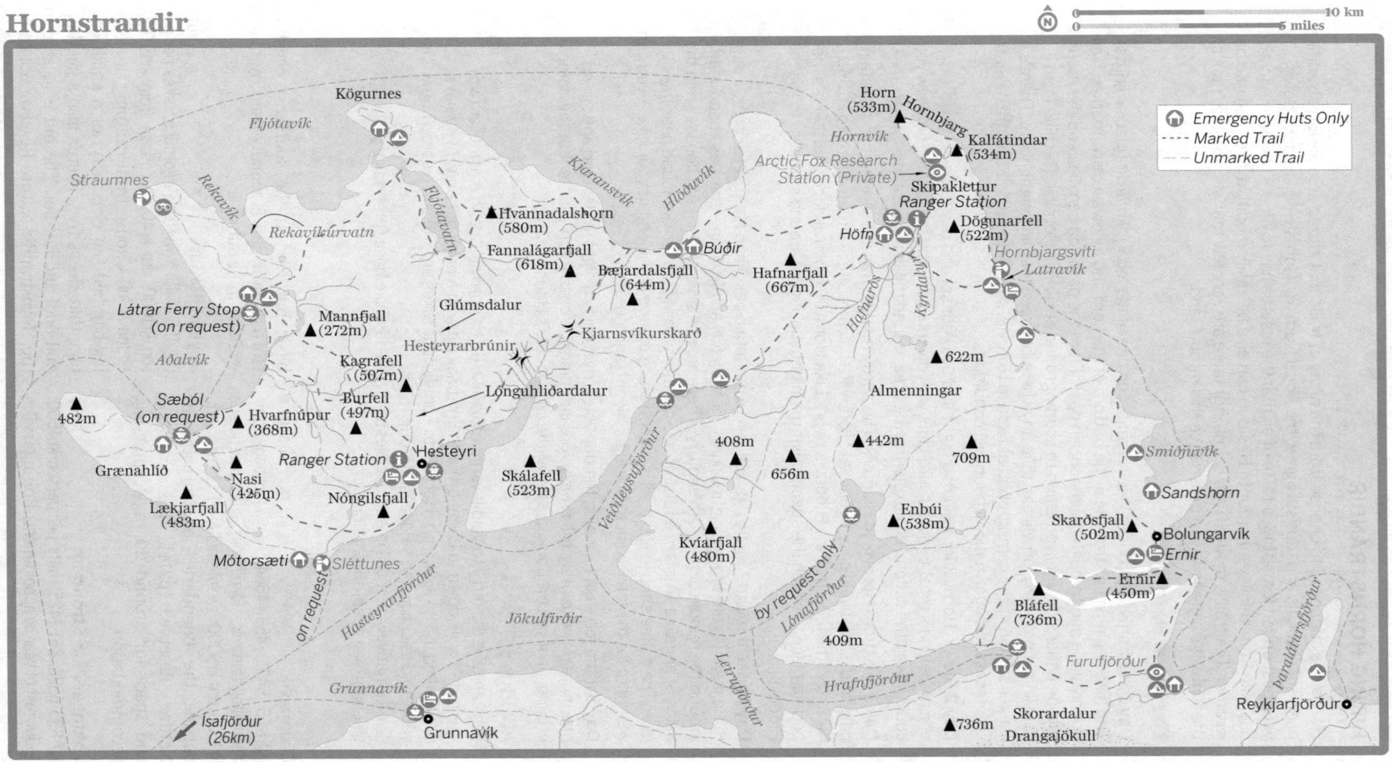

HIKING HORNSTRANDIR

How is one supposed to choose from the array of trails that zigzag across Hornstrandir's peninsula? Locals and tourists agree: the Royal Horn (or 'Hornsleið') is, hands down, your best option for getting a taste of all that the reserve has to offer. This four- to five-day hike from Veiðileysufjörður to Hesteyri can also be easily modified if you run into bad weather. The trail is marked with cairns, but there are very few tourists, so keep track of the route. It's a great way to experience this remote land.

The Royal Horn

Day 1 Sail from Ísafjörður to Veiðileysufjörður, one of the local *jökulfirðir* (glacier fjords). The hike begins on a street near the bottom of the fjord and follows a cairn-marked trail up the slope and through the mountain pass. From the pass you can descend the mountain on either side until you reach the campground at Höfn in Hornvík. The hike from Veiðileysufjörður to Hornvík can take anywhere between four and eight hours. There's a ranger station at the campground at Höfn in Hornvík, so feel free to get the latest weather forecast and information about trail conditions.

Day 2 Stay in Hornvík for a second night and use your second day to visit **Hornbjarg**, one of Iceland's most beautiful bird cliffs with diverse flora and fauna. Alternatively, you could spend the second day exploring the area around the lighthouse, **Hornbjargsviti**.

Day 3 Hike from Hornvík to Hlöðuvík. The partly marked trail goes through a mountain pass and is relatively easy to find. At Hlöðuvík, the campsite is situated next to **Hlöðuvíkurós** (the mouth of the Hlöðuvík river). Like Hornvík, Hlöðuvík faces north – it's the perfect place to watch the spectacular midnight sun. Figure around six hours to reach Hlöðuvík.

Day 4 Hike through **Kjarnsvíkurskarð** (a mountain pass) and **Hesteyrarbrúnir** pass to Hesteyri (figure around eight hours). **Hesteyri** is an old village that was abandoned around the middle of the 20th century. There are still several well-kept houses amid the fields of angelica. Ruins of a turn-of-the-century whaling station are found near the village. The coffee shop in Hesteyri is a good place to stop at the end of your hike – you can wait here for the ferry back to Bolungarvík or Ísafjörður.

Day 5 If the ferry isn't running the day you arrive, enjoy a night in Hesteyri and spend one more day exploring the area before catching the boat. Pitch your tent at the campground, or, if you prebooked, stay at the Old Doctor's House (p214).

Abridged Hike

You can take the ferry to Veiðileysufjörður, hike up to Hornvík, spend a night (or two) there, and walk down to Lónafjörður to link back up with a boat, *but only if you have prebooked it*. The walk from Hornvík to Lónafjörður takes around six to seven hours. Or you could backtrack to Veiðileysufjörður.

Alternatively, just sail in and use Hesteyri as a day-hike base (prebook if you want sleeping-bag accommodation).

Grunnavík HOSTEL €

(☎866 5491, 456 4664; www.facebook.com/thjonustagrunnavik; Jökulfjirðir; sites per person kr1500, dm kr5000; ⊙Jul–mid-Aug) Grunnavík, outside the boundaries of Hornstrandir Nature Reserve (p214), has camping and space for around 20 in sleeping-bag accommodation.

Bolungarvík á Ströndum HUT €

(☎893 6926, 861 1425; huts per person kr4500; ⊙Jul, rest of year by appointment) Bolungarvík's basic hut sits on the southeast coast of Hornstrandir and is usually used by hikers walking in or out.

Reykjarfjörður HUT €

(☎456 7545; www.reykjarfjordur.is; sites per person kr1000, dm kr4000, cottage from kr15,000; ⊙Jun & Jul) Choose from camping, a sleeping-bag bed (no electricity) or a small cottage that sleeps five. There's also a geothermal pool and hot-pot. The hut is located in the Hornstrandir Nature Reserve, not to be confused with Reykjarfjörður further south on the Strandir coast.

Eating

Besides the basic meals available at the Old Doctor's House (p214) in Hesteyri, you'll need to bring in all food and supplies.

Campfires are prohibited in the reserve, and cooking equipment should be used with caution.

Information

Hornstrandir Park Rangers (Environmental Agency of Iceland; ☎591 2000; www.ust.is/hornstrandir) When entering Hornstrandir Nature Reserve before 15 June it is mandatory to register with a ranger.

Getting There & Away

Take a ferry from Ísafjörður (at the **Sundahöfn** docks on the eastern side of the town promontory) or Norðurfjörður (on the Strandir Coast) to Hornstrandir from June to August. One-way rides cost kr9500 to kr15,500, depending on your destination; children are half-price. It is strongly advised to book your return boat ticket, for safety reasons. You can book all boats direct, or through **West Tours** (p207).

From Ísafjörður, West Tours runs **Sjóferðir** (☎bookings 456 5111; www.sjoferdir.is) boats to the following, among other destinations:

- Aðalvík (kr9900, two weekly)
- Grunnavík (kr9600, one weekly)
- Hesteyri (kr9500, six weekly)
- Hornvík (kr15,800, one weekly)
- Hrafnfjörður (kr14,800, one weekly)
- Veiðileysufjörður (kr11,900, two weekly)

Also from Ísafjörður, **Borea** (p208) runs **Bjarnarnes** boats to:

- Aðalvík (kr10,000, two weekly)
- Grunnavík (kr8500, three weekly)
- Hesteyri (kr9500, five weekly)
- Hornvík (kr14,500, one weekly)
- Veiðileysufjörður (kr11,000, five weekly)

Hornbjargsviti, Hlöðuvík, Fljótavík, Slétta (Sléttunes) and Lónafjörður are by request only. Early June and late August there is an eight-person minimum.

From Norðurfjörður on the Strandir coast, **Strandferðir** (☎849 4079, 859 9570, West Tours bookings 456 5111; www.strandferdir.is; Norðurfjörður, Hornstrandir) boats run on a schedule from June to mid-August or can be chartered to Drangar (kr8500), Reykjarfjörður (kr9500), Þaralátursfjörður/Furufjörður (kr12,500), Bolungarvík (in Hornstrandir, not the town of the same name west of Ísafjörður), Látravík/Hornbjargsviti (kr14,500) and Hornvík (kr15,500).

HIKING

It is possible to hike into the reserve from Norðurfjörður on the Strandir coast. It'll take three days to reach Reykjarfjörður hut; Bolungarvík hut is one more day beyond that. On days one and two you can camp at Ófeigsfjörður and Drangar.

There's a trail from Grunnavík as well.

STRANDIR COAST

Sparsely populated, magnificently peaceful and all but deserted by travellers, the Westfjords' eastern spine is one of the most dramatic places in all of Iceland. Indented by a series of bristle-like fjords and lined with towering crags, the drive north of Hólmavík, the region's only sizeable settlement, is rough, wild and incredibly rewarding. The end of the line in Iceland, Strandir was thought to be the home of the island's great, persecuted sorcerers. South of here, gently rolling hills stretch along the isolated coastline as far as Staðarskáli, where the sudden rush of traffic tells you that you've returned to the Ring Road and the travelling masses.

Staðarskáli to Hólmavík

Although lacking the natural drama on show further north, the long drive along Rte 68 from Staðarskáli (formerly Brú) to Hólmavík is pleasantly pastoral, with rolling hills dotted by small farmhouses and lonely churches, alongside the vast fjords. The small **Sheep Farming Museum** (Sauðfjársetur á Ströndum; ☎661 2213, 451 3324; www.strandir.is/saudfjarsetur; adult/child kr800/free; ⏲10am-6pm Jun-Aug), 12km south of Hólmavík, details the region's farming history through photos and artefacts. Chessboards, pie, ice cream and coffee in the cafe (snacks kr800 to kr1300) may keep you around longer than expected.

For lodging try **Kirkjuból** (☎451 3474; www.strandir.is/kirkjubol; Rte 68; s/d with shared bathroom incl breakfast kr9600/15,400) with basic guesthouse rooms and a guest kitchen, or **Broddanes HI Hostel** (☎618 1830; www.broddanes.is; dm/d with shared bathroom kr5000/13,200; ⏲mid-May–mid-Sep), on the point south of Kollafjörður.

There is no public transit on Rte 68, but Strætó (www.bus.is) bus 57 travels the routes Staðarskáli–Reykjavík (kr4200, two daily) and Staðarskáli–Akureyri (kr5600, two daily), and bus 59 connects Hólmavík with Borgarnes (kr6300, five weekly).

Hólmavík

POP 341

Fishing town Hólmavík offers sweeping views over the still waters of Steingrímsfjörður and has a quirky witchcraft museum. The no-frills village is the best place to stock up on supplies before venturing off into the more rugged territory further north.

Sights

★Museum of Icelandic Sorcery & Witchcraft MUSEUM
(Strandagaldur; ☎897 6525; www.galdrasyning.is; Höfðagata 8-10; adult/child kr950/free; ⊙9am-7pm) Unlike the witches of the infamous Salem trials in New England, almost all of Iceland's convicted witches were men. Most of their occult practices were simply old Viking traditions or superstitions, but hidden *grimoires* (magic books) full of puzzling runic designs were proof enough for the local witch hunters (the area's elite) to burn around 20 souls (mostly peasants) at the stake. Great multilingual descriptions detail their spells, and don't miss the 'necropants'.

Tours

Strandahestar HORSE RIDING
(☎862 3263; www.strandahestar.is; Víðidalsá) Horse riding for all levels. Book by phone or at the tourist information centre.

Sleeping & Eating

Iceland Visit Hostel HOSTEL €
(☎860 6670; www.icelandvisit.is; Hafnarbraut 25; dm kr6000) This spanking new hostel offers clean, cheerful dorms with TVs and a shared kitchen.

Holmavík Campsite CAMPGROUND €
(☎451 3560; www.strandabyggd.is; sites per adult/child kr1200/free; ⊙mid-May–mid-Sep) Near the N1 petrol station, with pay laundry.

Steinhúsið GUESTHOUSE, APARTMENT €€
(☎856 1911; www.steinhusid.is; Höfðagata 1; d with/without bathroom kr24,000/19,000, apt kr25,000) A pleasant option across from the witchcraft museum, Steinhúsið has a small collection of prim rooms with living space and a kitchen, and a basement apartment.

Finna Hótel HOTEL €€
(☎451 3136; www.finnahotel.is; Borgarbraut 4; s/d incl breakfast kr18,900/23,000, d without bathroom incl breakfast kr17,800) Finna sits up a hill, with basic and small but clean rooms, and a decent breakfast. Wi-fi is spotty.

Restaurant Galdur CAFE €€
(www.galdrasyning.is; Höfðagata 10; mains kr1600-3100; ⊙9am-9pm) The menu changes daily at this friendly restaurant: look for mussels fresh from the fjord and wild berries for dessert. Great outdoor tables when sunny.

Café Riis INTERNATIONAL €€
(☎451 3567; Hafnarbraut 39; mains kr1200-4300; ⊙11.30am-9pm Jun-Aug, bar to 10pm) The town's popular pub and restaurant is set in a historic wooden building with carved magic symbols on the bar. Roasted chicken breast and trout are delish.

Information

Tourist Information Centre (☎451 3111; www.holmavik.is/info; Höfðagata 8-10; ⊙9am-7pm) In the witchcraft museum, with internet access and lots of info, including hiking maps (kr1500).

Getting There & Away

Buses stop at the N1 petrol station.

Strætó (www.bus.is) services:

➡ Bus 59 Hólmavík–Búðardalur–Borgarnes (kr6300, five weekly mid-May to mid-September, two weekly mid-September to mid-May), with connections to Reykjavík.

You must connect in Bifröst (with an overnight stay; no campground in Bifröst) or Borgarnes for the bus 57 service to Akureyri. You can also catch a Sterna (www.sternatravel.com) night bus 60 in Bifröst to Akureyri.

Hópferðamiðstöð Vestfjarða (vidfjordinn@vidfjordinn.is) services:

➡ From mid-May to mid-September there are buses between Hólmavík and Ísafjörður (kr7000, three hours, four times weekly). Check www.westfjords.is for schedules.

Note that purchasing petrol in Hólmavík requires an N1 card (not available on site), chip card or card with PIN.

Drangsnes

POP 73

Across Steingrímsfjörður from Hólmavík, Drangsnes (*drowngs*-ness) is a remote little village with views across to North Iceland and the small uninhabited island of Grímsey, one of several Grímsey islands in Iceland. On Drangsnes' waterfront, rocky stack **Kerling** is believed to be the remains of a petrified troll. Uxi, her bull, is the formation out at sea near Grímsey. Malarhorn operates boats out to the island.

North of Drangsnes, a rough road winds around a series of gorgeous crumbling escarpments and tiny driftwood-filled bays. There are no services on this route, but if you've got your own vehicle, the utter tranquillity, incredible views and sheer sense of isolation are truly remarkable. For those interested in the sagas, you'll be keen to know that *Njál's Saga* starts here.

There's a card-operated petrol pump in Drangsnes but no public transport.

Activities

★Drangsnes Hot-Pot HOT-POT

(by donation) A favourite Drangsnes attraction is its free, waterfront, geothermal hot-pots built into the sea wall along the main road. Eagle eyes will have to spot a small swimming sign and white building with blue trim containing showers and WCs. Remember to do as Icelanders do and shower thoroughly before entering the hot-pots. There are three geometric jacuzzis directly across the street.

Drangsnes Sundlaug GEOTHERMAL POOL

(☎451 3201; Grundargata 15; adult/child kr300/free; ⊙10am-9pm Mon-Thu, to 6pm Fri-Sun Jun-Aug, reduced hours Sep-May) The town's swimming pool has two hot-pots – handy when the seaside weather is too tumultuous.

Sleeping & Eating

Malarhorn GUESTHOUSE €€

(☎853 6520; www.malarhorn.is; Grundargata 17; d with/without bathroom kr20,800/15,000, apt from kr29,500) Located next to the Kerling rock stack, Malarhorn has a variety of accommodation, including a peaceful row of crisp pine cabins that feel thoroughly modern yet remarkably cosy, plus apartments. There's a good **cafe** (mains kr2200-5900) that serves a super array of fish on its 2nd-storey verandah overlooking the fjord. It also runs boat tours to Grímsey (adult/child kr8000/4000), with its puffin-breeding ground, are offered.

Bjarnarfjörður

Bjarnarfjörður has a few attractions, and then north of the fjord the scenery becomes more rugged and there are fine views across to the Skagi Peninsula in North Iceland. This road often closes with the first snows in autumn and may not reopen until spring; ask locally for information on conditions.

At **Kaldbaksvík** the steep sides of a broad fjord sweep down to a small fishing lake that serenely reflects the surrounding mountains. Just beyond the lake, a 4km trail runs up to the summit of craggy **Lambatindur** (854m). You'll notice copious amounts of enormous driftwood piled up along the shore on this coast – most of it has arrived from Siberia across the Arctic Ocean.

There is no public transport to Bjarnarfjörður.

Sights & Activities

Sorcerer's Cottage MUSEUM

(www.galdrasyning.is; Bjarnarfjörður; ⊙8am-10pm Jun-Aug) FREE The three-room turf-roofed Sorcerer's Cottage is part of the Museum of Icelandic Sorcery & Witchcraft in Hólmavík and shows what living conditions were like for the purported sorcerers. Find it signposted behind Hótel Laugarhóll.

Gvenderlaug LANDMARK

FREE Gvenderlaug is a landmark, 42°C miracle pool (no bathing!) that was blessed by the bishop Gvendur the Good in the 13th century and is now a national monument. It's signposted behind Hótel Laugarhóll; Gvenderlaug feeds the hotel's pool.

Geothermal Pool GEOTHERMAL POOL

(adult/child kr500/250; ⊙8am-10pm May-Sep) Hótel Laugarhóll (p219) has a beautifully situated, hot geothermal pool.

Sleeping & Eating

★Hótel Laugarhóll HOTEL €€

(☎451 3380; www.laugarholl.is; d with/without bathroom incl breakfast kr24,500/19,000; ⊙May-Sep; @☒) Hótel Laugarhóll, at Bjarnarfjörður, is run by friendly former school teachers – in fact they once taught in this very building, which has now been turned into a welcoming hotel. Crisp white duvets lie neatly folded on every bed, some with original artwork hanging just above.

There's a yummy restaurant serving soups and sandwiches at lunch (kr1000 to kr1200) and an elaborate buffet at dinner (kr4000 to kr5000; 6.30pm to 8.30pm).

Reykjarfjörður

Tucked beneath a looming rock wall and an enormous waterfall at Reykjarfjörður, and approached by way of incredible mountain roads and fjord views, is the strangely enchanting factory at **Djúpavík**. Once a thriving centre for herring processing, the area was all but abandoned when the plant closed in 1950. The deserted factory (which has since been reclaimed) and a beached trawler dominate this hamlet of quaint dorms and houses, and create a magical, memorable mood on this enormous, remote, deep fjord.

Sleeping & Eating

Hótel Djúpavík INN €€
(☎451 4037; www.djupavik.com; d in inn/cottage without bathroom kr15,300/14,300) This charming inn decorated with antiques is set on one of the most stunning bays in Iceland in a defunct herring factory's former women's dormitory. The vibe is warmly welcoming from the moment you step into its bustling ground-floor restaurant (mains kr1800 to kr5000). Hotel bookings essential in summer. Rooms can be very noisy since walls are thin.

Norðurfjörður

As you drive north of Djúpavík to Norðurfjörður, there are two interesting churches at Árnes – one is a traditional wooden structure, and the other (virtually across the street) is dramatically futuristic. The small museum, Kört, has displays on fishing and farming, and sells handicrafts.

Kistan (meaning 'Coffin'), an area of craggy rocks, served as the region's main site for witch executions. Iceland's last documented case of witch burning took place here. It's marked on the main road, but is easier to find if you ask for directions.

Clinging to life at the end of the bumpy road up the Strandir coast is the tiny fishing hamlet Norðurfjörður (also the name of the fjord). The bustling hamlet has a cafe, a petrol pump and a few guesthouses, and it's the last place to stock up before heading off to Hornstrandir Nature Reserve (p214) on foot or by boat.

Activities

★**Krossneslaug** GEOTHERMAL POOL
(adult/child kr500/200) Krossneslaug is a geothermal (infinity) pool and hot-pot that shouldn't be missed! Up a dirt track about 3km beyond Norðurfjörður, you'll park, then walk down to where it sits at the edge of the universe on a wild black-pebble beach. It's an incredible place to watch the midnight sun flirt with the roaring waves.

Sleeping & Eating

There's one good restaurant and a tiny minimart near the petrol pump in Norðurfjörður.

Norðurfjörður Hut HUT €
(☎568 2533; www.fi.is; N 66°03.080', W -21°33.970'; dm kr6500; ⏰Jun-Sep) Run by Ferðafélag Íslands (FI), this simple hostel sleeps 22 and has a kitchen.

Bergistangi HOSTEL €
(☎451 4003; www.bergistangi.is; dm kr9000) Just behind the harbour, this friendly guesthouse has simple rooms and a guest kitchen.

★**Urðartindur** GUESTHOUSE €€
(☎843 8110; www.urdartindur.is; sites per adult/child kr1200/free, d kr17,100; ⏰May-Sep) These simple, modern guest rooms with private bathrooms and refrigerators are blessed with unobstructed fjord views and a balcony along a black-sand beach. Two cottages (from kr21,600) each sleep up to four; camping is possible here too. Ask Arinbjörn, the kindly owner, about a secret hiking path that leads to a hidden lake.

Kaffi Norðurfjörður INTERNATIONAL €€
(☎862 3944; www.nordurfjordur.is; mains kr2200-4900; ⏰noon-9pm mid-May–mid-Sep) A pair of friendly women home-cook all the food here, using fresh ingredients and incorporating creative Asian accents. The peaceful fjord and harbour views are lovely. You can also book ahead for a breakfast buffet (kr2400).

Getting There & Away

AIR

Eagle Air (www.eagleair.is) flies between Reykjavík's domestic airport and the airstrip at Gjögur (kr20,200, 50 minutes, one weekly), 16km southeast of Norðurfjörður.

BOAT

Strandferðir (www.strandferdir.is) boats to Hornstrandir Nature Reserve run on a schedule from June to mid-August or can be chartered from Norðurfjörður to Drangar (kr8500), Reykjarfjörður (kr9500), Þaralátursfjörður/Furufjörður (kr12,500), Bolungarvík (in Hornstrandir, not the town of the same name west of Ísafjörður), Látravík/Hornbjargsviti (kr14,500) and Hornvík (kr15,500). Children are half-price.

North Iceland

Includes ➜

Best Places to Eat

- Vogafjós (p265)
- Gísli, Eiríkur, Helgi (p241)
- Kaffi Kú (p258)
- Sjávarborg (p225)
- Naustið (p274)

Best Places to Stay

- Skjaldarvík (p248)
- Dalvík HI Hostel (p241)
- Kaldbaks-Kot (p274)
- Halllandsnes (p248)
- Apartment Hótel Hjalteyri (p242)

Why Go?

Iceland's mammoth and magnificent north is a geologist's heaven. A wonderland of moonlike lava fields, belching mudpots, epic waterfalls, snowcapped peaks and whale-filled bays – this is Iceland at its best. The region's top sights are variations on one theme: a grumbling, volcanically active earth.

There are endless treats to uncover: little Akureyri, with its surprising moments of big-city living; windy fjordside pastures full of stout Viking horses; fishing villages clinging tenaciously to life at the end of unsealed roads.

Prepare to be enticed by offshore islands populated by colonies of seabirds and a few hardy locals; lonely peninsulas stretching out towards the Arctic Circle; white-water rapids ready to deliver an adrenalin kick; national-park walking trails to reach unparalleled views; unhyped and underpopulated ski fields; and underwater marvels that woo divers into frigid depths.

Road Distances (km)

	Reykjavík	Akureyri	Siglufjörður	Húsavík	Reykjahlíð (Mývatn)
Akureyri	389				
Siglufjörður	384	76			
Húsavík	476	92	168		
Reykjahlíð (Mývatn)	478	100	176	54	
Þórshöfn	613	235	311	142	172

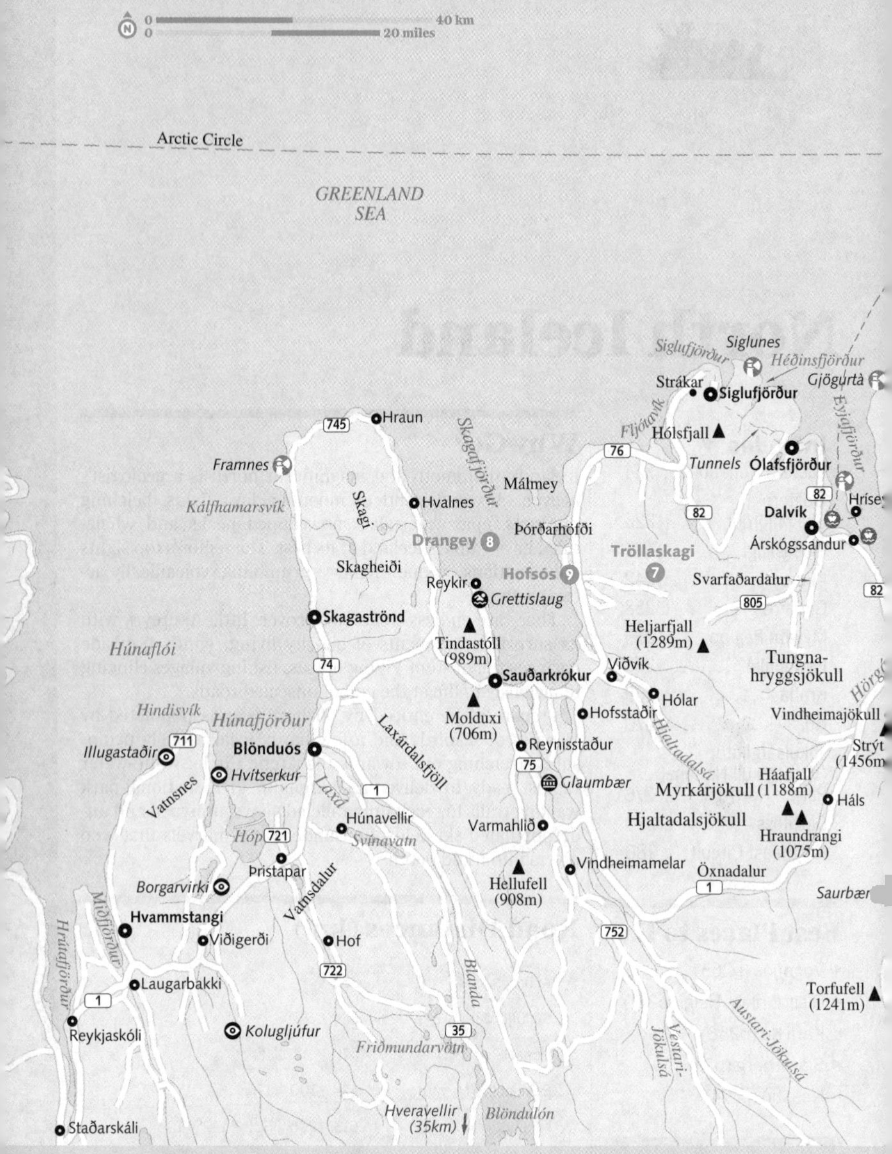

North Iceland Highlights

1 **Akureyri** (p242) Discovering northern Iceland's version of urban living in the country's second city.

2 **Grímsey** (p260) Crossing Iceland's only slice of the Arctic Circle on this bird-filled and troll-infested island.

3 **Mývatn** (p259) Wandering around lava castles and pseudo-craters before a soak at the Nature Baths.

4 **Húsavík** (p270) Holding your breath as whales emerge from the deep.

5 **Hverir** (p269) Stepping through stinky, other-worldly scenes in this lunar landscape.

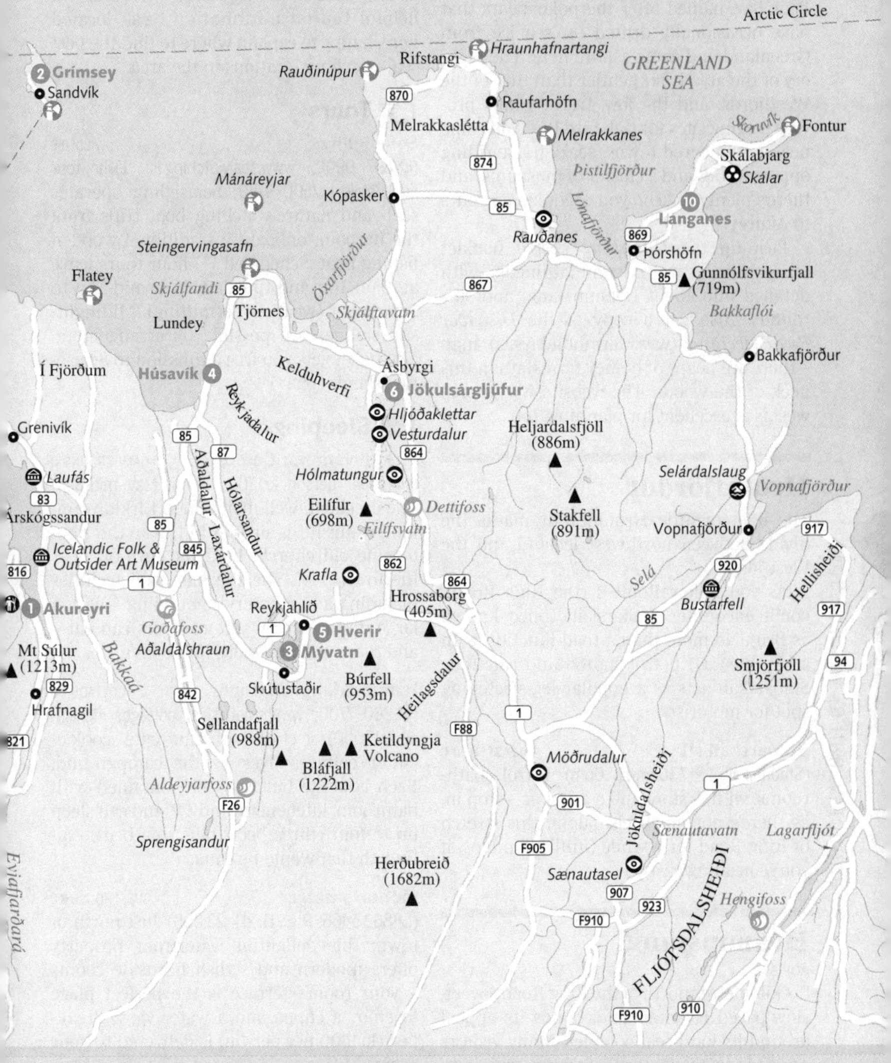

6 Jökulsárgljúfur (p276) Savouring hypnotic rock forms and a storied canyon in this national park zone.

7 Tröllaskagi (p231) Eyeballing vast vistas and rugged mountainscapes between perfect pit stops.

8 Drangey (p230) Summiting this tiny, puffin-filled outpost in Skagafjörður.

9 Hofsós (p231) Soaking up infinity views from Sundlaugin á Hofsósi, a perfect fjordside swimming pool.

10 Langanes (p283) Getting twitchy over bird-filled cliffs at Langanes.

EASTERN HÚNAFLÓI

Sparsely populated and scattered with only a handful of tiny settlements, the bay of Húnaflói is rich in wildlife. It's known as Bear Bay, named after the polar bears that have occasionally drifted on sea ice from Greenland and come ashore here. The scenery of the area is far gentler than that of the Westfjords, and the low, treeless hills provide nesting sites for rich bird life. Add some neatly manicured towns, seals, horse-riding opportunities and a cluster of museums, and there's plenty to keep you occupied en route to Akureyri.

Pick up the *Húnaþing vestra* booklet (also online at www.visithunathing.is), with detailed info about Hvammstangi and surrounds. Also get a copy of the *Discover Rural Iceland* (www.farmholidays.is) map – there are heaps of homey farmstays in this neck of the woods. The website www.northwest.is is excellent for planning, too.

Hrútafjörður

The inlet of little Hrútafjörður marks the divide between northwest Iceland and the Westfjords.

As you follow Route 1 (the Ring Road), you'll encounter Staðarskáli (once known as Brú). No more than a road junction with a big, busy N1 petrol station and cafeteria, Staðarskáli acts as a popular leg-stretching spot for motorists.

Staðarskáli N1 FAST FOOD €
(Staðarskáli; 7.30am-11.30pm) Petrol, bathrooms, wi-fi, a store and a grill bar – stop in, as there's not much else along this stretch of Ring Road for a while (until Blönduós, if you're heading east).

Hvammstangi

POP 580

Six kilometres north of the Ring Road, sweet, slow-paced Hvammstangi builds its appeal around its local seal colonies. Many visitors are here to take a seal-watching cruise, go horse riding in the area, or drive the scenic loop around the Vatnsnes Peninsula.

Sights

Selasetur Íslands MUSEUM
(451 2345; www.selasetur.is; Strandgata 1; adult/child kr950/free; 9am-7pm Jun-Aug, 9am-4pm May & Sep, noon-3pm Tue-Sat Apr & Oct) The town's prime attraction is the prominent Icelandic Seal Centre on the harbourfront, where you can learn about conservation of seals, historic seal products and traditional folk tales involving seals. There's also a helpful **tourist information desk** located here, happy to explain where to find the best seal-watching locations in the area.

Tours

Selasigling WILDLIFE
(897 9900; www.sealwatching.is; 1¾hr tour adult/child kr7500/3750) Selasigling operates seal- and nature-watching boat trips from the harbour, onboard a traditional wooden fishing boat. Scheduled 1¾-hour tours leave at 10am, 1pm and 4pm daily from mid-May to September (weather permitting). Midnight-sun sailings are possible by arrangement. The ticket gets you free admission to Selasetur Íslands (p224).

Sleeping

Kirkjuhvammur Campsite CAMPGROUND €
(sites per person kr1200; mid-May–mid-Sep) The excellent, well-maintained Kirkjuhvammur campsite is up the hill near the photogenic old church. Find the turn-off near the town pool. The site has good facilities including a handy service building – with a large dining area where campers can eat – and there are nice walks in the area.

Hvammstangi Cottages COTTAGE €€
(860 7700; www.smahysi.is; cottages incl linen kr17,000) A cluster of nine cute, cookie-cutter cottages lives by the campground. Each is petite but fully self-contained with bathroom, kitchenette and TV, and can sleep up to four (three beds, plus sofa bed) – although that would be snug.

Mörk Homestay GUESTHOUSE €€
(862 5466; Rte 711; d kr23,000) Just north of town, this delightful waterfront property offers modern and stylish fjordside rooms – your room's terrace is the perfect place to enjoy a cuppa and a water view. Breakfast (kr1500 per person) is delivered to your room.

Guesthouse Hanna Sigga GUESTHOUSE €€
(451 2407; www.facebook.com/hannasigg; Garðavegur 26; d/tr without bathroom from kr15,000/18,800) An excellent choice, this homey and welcoming guesthouse is on a residential street in the town centre. Rooms are well kept, and there's a guest kitchen,

but the real draw is the homemade breakfast (kr1700) served in a beautiful nook overlooking the water.

Eating

KVH Supermarket SUPERMARKET €
(Strandgata; 9am-6pm Mon-Thu, 9am-7pm Fri, 10am-6pm Sat, 11am-4pm Sun May-Sep, shorter hours Apr & Oct) For self-caterers.

★**Sjávarborg** ICELANDIC €€
(451 3131; www.sjavarborg-restaurant.is; Strandgata 1; mains kr2250-5550; 11.30am-10pm) Hats off to this stylish new restaurant above the Icelandic Seal Centre, with big picture windows offering fjord views, and a menu that roves from seared tuna to gourmet burgers to slow-cooked lamb shank. The homemade blueberry ice cream is a treat (and more than big enough to share).

Hlaðan Kaffihús CAFE €€
(Brekkugata 2; meals kr1400-3500; 9am-10pm Mon-Sat, 10am-10pm Sun May–mid-Sep) At the harbour is this sweet old-time cafe, luring customers with the usual suspects: soup, panini, quiche and cakes, plus heartier meals of lamb chops and trout.

Getting There & Away

The summer Sterna buses (60, 60a) that travel the Ring Road (Rte 1) between Reykjavík and Akureyri only service the Hvammstangi crossroads, 6km from town.

Strætó (www.straeto.is) services:

- Bus 57 to Reykjavík (kr5460, 3½ hours, two daily).
- Bus 57 to Akureyri (kr4200, three hours, two daily).

The Strætó bus 57 between Reykjavík and Akureyri stops at the crossroads. Strætó runs a separate service to/from the crossroads (bus 83; kr420) to link up with these services, but it must be prebooked with at least two hours' notice; call 540 2700.

Vatnsnes Peninsula

Poking out into Húnaflói, stubby Vatnsnes Peninsula is a starkly beautiful place with a ridge of craggy hills marching down its spine. Route 711, a rough gravel road, weaves along the coast and makes a splendid detour off the Ring Road (it's about 82km in total, from the Ring Road to Hvammstangi and around the peninsula on Rte 711).

Rte 711 is easily accessible to small cars in summer, but drive carefully. You'll need your own wheels to tour the peninsula.

Sights

Illugastaðir FARM
(Rte 711) On the west side of Vatnsnes Peninsula is Illugastaðir farm, with wonderful views of peaks along the Strandir coast in the Westfjords. A 10-minute walk through bird-filled fields leads from the car park to a popular site for sunbaking seals; at the trail's end there's a hut with binoculars for visitor use. Note that the farm is closed from 1 May to 20 June due to eider duck nesting. There are toilets and a small campground (sites per person kr1000) here.

★**Hvítserkur** LANDMARK
(Rte 711) On the Vatnsnes Peninsula's east coast there's a signed path leading to the splendidly photogenic 15m-high sea stack Hvítserkur. Legend has it that Hvítserkur was a troll caught by the sunrise while attempting to destroy the monastery at Þingeyrar; we think he looks like a huge stone beast drinking from the water.

If you're not circling the peninsula, you can reach Hvítserkur by driving 30km north of the Ring Road on Rte 711.

Sleeping & Eating

★**Ósar HI Hostel** HOSTEL €
(862 2778; www.hostel.is; Rte 711; dm/d without bathroom kr4700/12,400; Feb-Nov) Just south of Hvítserkur (or 30km north of the Ring Road on gravel) is Ósar, one of Iceland's nicest farm hostels thanks to friendly owner Knútur, sweeping views and the nearby wildlife. The simple accommodation is in various buildings on a working dairy farm, with rooms, cottages and a Mongolian yurt where breakfast is served!

★**Geitafell** ICELANDIC €€
(861 2503; www.geitafell.is; Rte 711; fish soup kr3200; 11am-10pm mid-May–Sep) Roughly 25km from Hvammstangi (3km past Illugastaðir) is the wonderfully unique Geitafell, a restaurant in a converted barn where fish soup is the star, served with salad and homebaked bread (*skyr* tart is another highlight on the short menu). The property owners, Sigrún and Robert, are long-time locals with fascinating stories.

Hvammstangi to Blönduós

If you're following the Ring Road (Rte 1) between Hvammstangi and Blönduós, you can be tempted off the main road with some nice little diversions, from horse farms to photogenic stone churches.

Kolugljúfur CANYON

(Rte 715) Take Rte 715 south off the Ring Road to reach the scenic waterfalls at Kolugljúfur, an enchanting canyon that was once home to a beautiful female troll. (It's a 6km drive if you take the turn-off 7km past Gauksmýri horse farm.)

Þingeyrar CHURCH

(http://thingeyraklausturskirkja.is/en; Rte 721; adult/child kr1000/free; ⏲10am-5pm Jun-Aug) Around 19km west of Blönduós, a 6km detour along Rte 721 leads you to a precious stone church, Þingeyrar, sitting quietly and photogenically beside Hóp lagoon. The current structure was erected in the 1860s, but 800 years earlier the site hosted a district *þing* (assembly) and a Benedictine monastery. There's a small visitor centre here too, with exhibits and a few refreshments for sale. The church's entrance fee gets you a guided tour.

Tours

Gauksmýri Lodge HORSE RIDING

(☎451 2927; www.gauksmyri.is; Rte 1) As well as its lovely accommodation and restaurant, Gauksmýri is well-known for its short, guided horse-riding tours. The most popular option is the 90-minute 'Country Tour' (adult/child kr9500/6000), which runs at 10am, 2pm, 4pm and 6pm daily from mid-May to mid-September (weather permitting). Bookings are advised. There are longer tours, midnight-sun tours, family-friendly options and, if you prefer, stable visits (kr800).

Sleeping & Eating

Gauksmýri Lodge COUNTRY HOTEL €€

(☎451 2927; www.gauksmyri.is; Rte 1; d with/without bathroom incl breakfast kr21,300/14,500; @) Horse-lovers will be in heaven at Gauksmýri, a highly regarded horse farm and lodge on the Ring Road 3.5km east of the turn-off to Hvammstangi. Rooms are comfy, with equine accents in the decor, and the lodge has lovely grounds, restaurant and lounge.

Blönduós

POP 880

A couple of museums and an unusual modern church – the underwhelming service town Blönduós is about as simple as that. Except for an incredible foodie retreat there isn't much to woo you off the road, but the town makes an OK place to refuel and stretch your legs.

The churning Blanda River divides the town in half; the N1 station marks the northern entrance (its grill bar is the liveliest place in town).

★ **Brimslóð Atelier** GUESTHOUSE €€

(☎820 0998; www.brimslod.is; Brimslóð 10; d/tr without bathroom incl breakfast kr22,000/30,500; ⏲Mar-Nov) This fabulous seaside guesthouse is hands down Blönduós' finest option. It's a stylish new retreat from welcoming locals with a fine food pedigree (including publishing cookbooks and running food workshops). Four rooms share two bathrooms and a chic lounge. As you might expect, breakfast is a highlight. With prior notice, guests can also enjoy a three-course dinner showcasing local ingredients (kr7500).

WESTERN SKAGAFJÖRÐUR

Skagafjörður is renowned for horse breeding and wild landscapes – this, plus its historic remains and adrenalin-infused activities, make it a rewarding destination.

Note that settlements on the western half of Tröllaskagi Peninsula (Hólar í Hjaltadalur, Hofsós, Lónkot) sit on the Skagafjörður shoreline, and there are a couple of fjord islands – Drangey (p230) in particular is well worth a visit.

For online information, see www.visitskagafjordur.is.

Varmahlíð

POP 140

This Ring Road service centre is slightly more than a road junction and yet not quite a town, and it's a great base for white-water rafting and horse riding. Access to most activity operators is along the sealed Rte 752, just west of the township.

Varmahlíð is also a convenient 'doorway' into the highlands: the Kjölur route (Rte

35) leaves the Ring Road about 25km west of town (note that 2WD rental cars are prohibited to drive it – you need a 4WD). A bus runs this route daily in summer.

Activities

Horse Shows & Exhibitions

Horse farms in the area often host hour-long horse shows that showcase the five gaits of the Icelandic horse, and detail the breed's history. Shows are usually scheduled for groups, and individuals can then attend. Ask at the tourist information centre (p228) if you're interested, or contact the farms directly.

We also like the weekly 'Horses & Heritage' evening program at Lýtingsstaðir, encompassing facts and stories in a beautifully crafted turf house known as the Old Stable; it's held weekly in summer (8.30pm Tuesday), or on request for groups; the price is kr2500 (or free for overnight guests at Lýtingsstaðir). You can also call at Lýtingsstaðir to check out its Old Stable exhibition (adult/child kr750/free, open daily May to September).

Tours

Horse Riding

There are half a dozen companies in and around Varmahlíð, offering shorter rides (one to two hours) for beginners, plus longer day outings. A few companies plan full week long expeditions into the highlands, or offer you the chance to participate in the annual sheep roundup (*réttir*) in September.

Hestasport HORSE RIDING
(☎453 8383; www.riding.is; Rte 752) One of Iceland's most respected horse-riding outfits, with its helpful office just off the Ring Road on Rte 752. It offers one-/two-hour tours along the Svartá river for kr6400/9400 (no experience required), and full-day rides for kr18,000. Longer trips are also available (book well in advance), including eight-day trips through the highlands (from €2585). Short winter rides are available (kr7800).

Lýtingsstaðir HORSE RIDING
(☎453 8064; www.lythorse.com; Rte 752; 1/2hr horse ride kr6000/7800) The lovely farm Lýtingsstaðir, 20km south of Varmahlíð, has a great program of short and long horse rides. There's a fantastic 'Stop and Ride' package that includes one night in a self-contained cottage and a two-hour ride for kr30,000 (two people, including linen).

> WORTH A TRIP
>
> **GLAUMBÆR**
>
> Following Rte 75 north from Varmahlíð leads to the 18th-century turf-farm museum at **Glaumbær** (www.glaumbaer.is; adult/child kr1500/free; ⏲9am-5pm May, 9am-6pm Jun–mid-Sep, 10am-4pm Mon-Fri mid-Sep–mid-Oct). It's the best museum of its type in northern Iceland and worth the easy 8km detour off the Ring Road.
>
> The traditional Icelandic turf farm was a complex of small separate buildings, connected by a central passageway. Here you can see this style of construction, with some building compartments stuffed full of period furniture, equipment and utensils. It gives a fascinating insight into the cramped living conditions of the era.

Multiday tours (from €1200 for six days) are also available, including a highlands expedition, or sheep roundup participation.

Rafting

The area around Varmahlíð is home to northern Iceland's best white-water rafting. Trips run from about May to September; drysuits are provided.

Trips run the high-octane Austari-Jökulsá (East Glacial River; Class IV+ rapids) and the more placid, family-friendly Vestari-Jökulsá (West Glacial River; Class II+ rapids).

Viking Rafting RAFTING
(☎823 8300; www.vikingrafting.com; Rte 752) Options include a family-friendly four-hour float on the Vestari-Jökulsá (adult/child kr14,990/9990; minimum age six); a challenging six-hour adventure on the Austari-Jökulsá (kr24,990); and the ultimate rafting expedition, a three-day trip (kr189,990) that starts from the Sprengisandur highlands. Also possible: guided white-water kayaking trips.

The company's base camp is at Hafgrímsstaðir, 15km south of Varmahlíð on Rte 752. Camping is possible here. Pick-ups for the longer trips can be arranged from Akureyri.

Bakkaflöt RAFTING
(☎453 8245; www.bakkaflot.com) South along Rte 752 (11km from the Ring Road), the farm Bakkaflöt offers three hours of rafting on the Vestari-Jökulsá (kr13,500), and six hours on the Austari-Jökulsá (kr24,400). The centre

also has a good range of accommodation, from camping to cottages.

Sleeping & Eating

There are plenty of rural places to crash in the area; ask at the information centre. If you're doing rafting or riding tours with Bakkaflöt (p227) or Lýtingsstaðir (p227), note that they both have sleeping options. These are open to all; see their websites for details.

Campsite CAMPGROUND €
(http://tjoldumiskagafirdi.is; sites per person kr1300; ⏲ mid-May–mid-Sep) Follow the signs from the hotel to reach this secluded, sheltered campground above the town.

★ **Hestasport Cottages** COTTAGE €€
(☎453 8383; www.riding.is/cottages; cottages for 2/4/6 kr20,800/28,600/35,100) Perched on the hill above Varmahlíð (follow the road past the town hotel, this cluster of seven high-quality self-contained timber cottages has good views, comfy rooms and a very inviting stone hot-pot. There are photos of the interiors on Hestasport's website; some sleep six, all include kitchen facilities and linen. They're excellent value, especially for families and groups.

Sauðárkróksbakarí BAKERY €
(Rte 1; ⏲9am-4pm Mon-Sat, 10am-4pm Sun) In summer 2016, a branch of Sauðárkrókur's fine bakery set up inside the old bank building next door to the N1 petrol station/supermarket complex – hopefully it's a permanent move. On offer are good sandwiches, pastries, snacks and coffee.

KS Supermarket SUPERMARKET €
(Rte 1; ⏲9am-11.30pm mid-Jun–mid-Aug, to 10pm rest of year) The supermarket by the N1 is open until late; also part of the complex is a grill-bar serving up burgers and hot food. The kitchen closes at 9pm.

Information

Tourist Information Centre (☎455 6161; www.visitskagafjordur.is; ⏲ daily year-round) Inside the N1 service station, this efficient centre is a room of brochures and maps, with an info desk staffed in summer (from 10am to 6pm daily). Ask here for directions to the hidden waterfall **Reykjafoss**.

Getting There & Away

All buses stop at the N1.

SBA-Norðurleið (www.sba.is) services:
- Bus 610a to Reykjavík via the Kjölur route (kr13,000, nine hours, one daily mid-June to mid-September).

Sterna (www.sterna.is) services:
- Bus 60a to Reykjavík (kr7400, 4¾ hours, one daily mid-June to early September).
- Bus 60 to Akureyri (kr1400, one hour, one daily mid-June to early September).

Strætó (www.bus.is) services:
- Bus 57 to Reykjavík (kr7140, 5¼ hours, two daily)
- Bus 57 to Akureyri (kr2520, 1¼ hours, two daily)
- Bus 57 to Sauðárkrókur (kr840, 20 minutes, two daily)

Öxnadalur

If you haven't the time to explore scenic Skagafjörður or magnificent Tröllaskagi, never fear: you'll still be treated to some incredible vistas courtesy of Öxnadalur, a narrow, 30km-long valley on the Ring Road between Varmahlíð and Akureyri. Stunning peaks and thin pinnacles of rock flank the mountain pass; the imposing 1075m spire of **Hraundrangi** and the surrounding peaks of **Háafjall** are among the most dramatic in Iceland.

Sauðárkrókur

POP 2640

As the winding Jókulsá river collides with the marshy delta of upper Skagafjörður, you'll find scenic Sauðárkrókur sitting quietly at the edge of the waterway.

Economically, Sauðárkrókur is doing quite nicely, thank you, with fishing, tanning and trading keeping the community afloat and the population vibrant. The town has all the services you'll need, plus good sleeping and eating options; tourist information is dispensed by the town museum. Sauðárkrókur is also the gateway to treasures around Tindastóll (p230), and brilliant excursions to offshore Drangey (p230).

Sights

Tannery Visitor Centre FACTORY
(Gestastofa Sútarans; ☎512 8025; www.sutarinn.is; Borgarmýri 5; ⏲8am-4pm Mon-Fri, 8am-noon Sat & Sun mid-May–mid-Sep, 11am-4pm Mon-Fri rest of year) At 10am and 2pm weekdays (from mid-May to mid-September) you can tour

Iceland's only tannery (kr500), or stop by the visitor centre anytime to admire (and purchase) the products: gorgeous long-hair sheepskins, colourful leather goods, and unique products made from fish skin processed at the tannery.

Minjahúsið MUSEUM
(Aðalgata 16b; ⏲noon-7pm Jun-Aug) FREE There's a quirky ensemble of exhibits at the excellent 'heritage house', including a series of restored craftsmen's workshops, a pristine A-model Ford from 1930, and a stuffed polar bear caught locally in 2008.

Sleeping

MicroBar & Bed GUESTHOUSE €
(☎467 3133; microbar2@outlook.com; Aðalgata 19; s/d without bathroom kr10,500/13,000) At the MicroBar on the main street, the '& Bed' part of the equation is 10 budget beds in five rooms in the building adjacent to the bar. There's a small guest kitchen and lounge, and decent-sized rooms.

Campsite CAMPGROUND €
(http://tjoldumiskagafirdi.is; sites per person kr1300; ⏲mid-May–mid-Sep) The campsite beside the swimming pool is a bit barren and treeless, but has decent facilities.

★ **Gamla Posthúsið** APARTMENT €€
(☎892 3375; www.ausis.is; Kirkjutorg 5; apt kr23,400-25,000) Australian Vicki moved to town in 2010 and took it upon herself to restore the old post office opposite the church. The two resulting one-bedroom apartments make a superb home away from home. Each boasts a full modern kitchen, a welcome pack of food, oodles of room and Scandi-chic decor. Winter prices drop by around 40%, making them a great bargain.

★ **Guesthouse Hofsstaðir** GUESTHOUSE €€
(☎453 7300; www.hofsstadir.is; Rte 76; s/d incl breakfast kr26,500/29,500) In a unique position at the head of Skagafjörður, roughly equidistant (20km to 25km) from Sauðárkrókur, Varmahlíð and Hofsós, this high-end guesthouse offers warm hospitality, first-class rooms and a cosy restaurant (open April to October). The panoramas are pretty cool, and easily enjoyed from your terrace.

Guesthouse Mikligarður GUESTHOUSE €€
(☎453 6880; www.arctichotels.is; Kirkjutorg 3; s/d without bathroom incl breakfast from kr11,500/15,000) This welcoming spot near the church has petite but comfortable rooms with TV and tasteful decor (most share bathrooms). There's also a spacious guest kitchen and TV lounge, and a good breakfast spread.

Hótel Tindastóll HOTEL €€
(☎453 5002; www.arctichotels.is; Lindargata 3; r incl breakfast from kr27,500) Legend has it that Marlene Dietrich once stayed at this charming boutique hotel, which dates from 1884. The individually decorated rooms blend period furniture and modern style. Outside there is an irresistible stone hot-pot, and in the basement there's a cosy bar. There is also a new annexe of modern rooms, but the period rooms have loads more character.

Eating & Drinking

Sauðárkróksbakarí BAKERY, CAFE €
(Aðalgata 5; ⏲7am-6pm Mon-Fri, 8am-4pm Sat, 9am-4pm Sun) This main-street bakery is the heartbeat of the town. Stop in to stock up on supplies for your drive – everything from fresh baked bread to soup to iced doughnuts, and some fine choc-chip cookies.

Skagfirðingabúð SUPERMARKET €
(Ástorg; ⏲9am-7pm Mon-Fri, 10am-4pm Sat) South of town, close to the N1.

Ólafshús ICELANDIC €€
(☎453 6454; www.olafshus.is; Aðalgata 15; lunch buffet kr1960, dinner mains kr1690-6750; ⏲11am-10.30pm; 👪) A bold blue paint job announces this quality year-round option, where you can go radical with pan-fried foal, fancy-pants with lobster tails, or safe and budget-oriented with pizza, pasta and burgers. The menu is big and the kitchen competent, shining a spotlight on local produce like Arctic char, lamb cutlets and vanilla *skyr* cake.

Kaffi Krókur ICELANDIC €€
(www.kaffikrokur.is; Aðalgata 16; mains kr1550-3790; ⏲11.30am-11pm Sun-Wed, to 1am Thu, to 3am Fri & Sat Jun-Aug) This cafe has an understated beige exterior and a crowd-pleasing menu. It's known for its lobster and shrimp sandwich, filled crêpes and warm rhubarb cake. In winter it's the local pub (with live music), open only on Thursday, Friday and Saturday nights.

MicroBar & Bed BAR
(Aðalgata 19; ⏲9-11.30pm Thu, 9pm-2.30am Fri & Sat) Cool mountain-peak graphics and vintage sofas set the scene at this end-of-week bar on Sauðárkrókur's main drag, where

DON'T MISS

DRANGEY

The tiny rocky islet of **Drangey** (*drown-gay*), in the middle of Skagafjörður, is a dramatic flat-topped mass of volcanic tuff with 180m-high sheer cliffsides rising abruptly from the water. The cliffs serve as nesting sites for around a million seabirds (puffins, guillemots, gannets, kittiwakes, fulmar, shear-waters), and have been used throughout Iceland's history as 'nature's grocery store' (for locals seeking birds and eggs). **Drangey Tours** offers fabulous three-hour boat trips to Drangey, departing from a small harbour beside Grettislaug, at Reykir.

Grettir's Saga recounts that both outlaw hero Grettir and his brother Illugi lived on the island for three years and were slain there. Brave (foolhardy?) saga fans come to the area to recreate Grettir's feat, swimming the 7km between Drangey and Reykir.

Note that puffins have usually departed Drangey by mid-August.

local brews are on tap, plus loads more in bottles. Gæðingur is the local draught pick: Indian Pale Ale, wheat beer or stout.

Vínbúðin ALCOHOL
(Smáragrund 2; ⏲noon-6pm Mon-Thu, 11am-7pm Fri, 11am-2pm Sat) Government-run liquor store.

Getting There & Away

The bus stop is at the N1, about 1.3km south of the town centre along Aðalgata.

Strætó (www.bus.is) services:

- Bus 57 to Reykjavík (kr7140, five hours, two daily).
- Bus 57 to Akureyri (kr2520, 1½ hours, two daily).
- Bus 57 to Varmahlíð (kr840, 20 minutes, two daily).
- Bus 85 to Hólar and Hofsós (kr840 to either destination, two daily Wednesday, Friday and Sunday) These services only operate if prebooked. Call Strætó at least two hours before departure.

North of Sauðárkrókur

North of Sauðárkrókur, Skagafjörður's western coast is a stunningly silent place capped by scenic mountains. Tindastóll is the most prominent peak, and at its northern end is a geothermal area and storied waterfront bathing pool known as Grettislaug.

Offshore, guarding the mouth of Skagafjörður, are the uninhabited islands of Drangey and Málmey, tranquil havens for nesting seabirds. Summertime boat tours of Drangey depart from a small harbour beside Grettislaug.

Sights

Tindastóll MOUNTAIN
Tindastóll (989m) is a prominent Skagafjörður landmark, extending for 18km along the coast. The mountain and its caves are believed to be inhabited by an array of sea monsters, trolls and giants. The summit of Tindastóll affords a spectacular view across all of Skagafjörður. The easiest way to the top is along the marked trail that starts from the high ground along Rte 745 west of the mountain (it's a strenuous hike). There's skiing here in winter (see http://skitindastoll.is).

Grettislaug GEOTHERMAL POOL
(Grettir's Bath; adult/child kr1000/free) At the northern end of Tindastóll is a geothermal area, Reykir, that was mentioned in *Grettir's Saga*. Grettir supposedly swam ashore from the island of Drangey and soothed his aching bones in an inviting spring. Today, Grettislaug is a popular natural bathing hole, alongside a second hot-pot.

Drivers beware: it's a rough, skiddy 15km on gravel from Sauðárkrókur north to Grettislaug on Rte 748 (the turn-off is on Rte 744, just north of town). You'll need your own transport.

In the immediate vicinity of Grettislaug are a small cafe, campground (per person kr1000) and guesthouse, plus great walks. Tours to Drangey leave from here.

Tours

Drangey Tours BOAT TOUR
(☎821 0090; www.drangey.net; tours adult/child kr11,900/6500) Drangey Tours offers fabulous three-hour boat trips to Drangey, departing from a small harbour beside Grettislaug at Reykir. Boats leave at 9.30am daily from mid-May to mid-August (conditions permitting); bookings required. The tour involves a boat trip and a guided hike up the steep cliff-face – this is challenging for people with

height phobias or mobility issues, as it involves ropes and ladders.

Sleeping & Eating

There's a simple campground at Grettislaug, and a small cafe serving drinks and snacks. Bring food supplies from Sauðárkrókur.

Reykir Guesthouse GUESTHOUSE €€
(☎841 7313; fagranesgisting@gmail.com; Rte 748, Reykir; per person with/without linen kr8000/4800) On the property at Reykir, not far from Grettislaug (p230) pool, this cosy timber house has decent rooms with shared bathrooms and kitchen.

TRÖLLASKAGI

Tröllaskagi (Troll Peninsula) rests its mountainous bulk between Skagafjörður and Eyjafjörður. Here, the craggy mountains, deep valleys and gushing rivers are more reminiscent of the Westfjords than the gentle hills that roll through most of northern Iceland. In great news for travellers seeking spectacular road trips, tunnels now link the northern Tröllaskagi townships of Siglufjörður and Ólafsfjörður, once dead-end towns that saw little tourist traffic.

Having your own wheels makes exploring this region easier. The journey from Varmahlið to Akureyri along the Ring Road (Rte 1) measures 95 very scenic kilometres, but if you have some time up your sleeve and a penchant for getting off the beaten track, the 186km journey between those two towns following the Tröllaskagi coastline (Rtes 76 and 82) conjures up some magical scenery, and plenty of excuses to pull over and explore.

Hólar í Hjaltadalur

With its prominent church dwarfed by the looming mountains, tiny Hólar (www.holar.is), in the scenic valley of Hjaltadalur, makes an interesting historical detour. The bishopric of Hólar was the ecumenical and educational capital of northern Iceland between 1106 and the Reformation, and it continued as a religious centre and the home of the northern bishops until 1798, when the bishop's seat was abolished.

Hólar then became a vicarage until 1861, when the vicarage was shifted west to Viðvík. In 1882 the present agricultural college was established – it's now known as Hólar University College, specialising in equine science, aquaculture and rural tourism. In 1952 the vicarage returned to Hólar.

There's some basic accommodation in the college buildings at Hólar, plus an appealing campground.

Hólar is 11km off Rte 76; the turn-off is signed 20km east of Sauðárkrókur, or 15km south of Hofsós.

Sights

A historical-trail brochure (available at the accommodation info desk) guides you round some of the buildings at Hólar. **Nýibær** is a historical turf farm dating from the mid-19th century and inhabited until 1945. Also worth seeing is **Auðunarstofa**, a replica of the 14th-century bishop's residence, built using traditional tools and methods.

Cathedral CHURCH
(⏲10am-6pm Jun–mid-Sep) Completed in 1763, Hólar's red-sandstone cathedral is the oldest stone church in Iceland and brimming with historical works of art, including a 1674 baptismal font carved from a piece of soapstone that washed in from Greenland on an ice floe.

Icelandic Horse History Centre MUSEUM
(Sögusetur Íslenska Hestsins; www.sogusetur.is; adult/child kr900/free; ⏲10am-6pm Jun-Aug) The admission price gets you a personalised tour around this comprehensive exhibit on Iceland's unique horse breed and its role in Iceland's history. It's fittingly located in an old stable at the heart of the Hólar estate.

Hofsós

POP 190

The sleepy fishing village of Hofsós has been a trading centre since the 1500s, but was recently put on the map with its designer swimming pool (p232).

Sights & Activities

Icelandic Emigration Center MUSEUM
(Vesturfarasetrið; ☎453 7935; www.hofsos.is; adult kr1000-1500, child free; ⏲11am-6pm Jun-Aug) Several restored harbourside buildings have been turned into a museum exploring the reasons behind Icelanders' emigration to North America, their hopes for a new life and the reality of conditions when they arrived. Incredibly, this small country lost 16,000 emigrants from 1870 to 1914, leaving behind a 1914 population of only 88,000.

The main exhibition, 'New Land, New Life', follows the lives of emigrating Icelanders through carefully curated photographs, letters and displays.

★ Sundlaugin á Hofsósi SWIMMING
(Suðurbraut; adult/child kr700/300; ⏲9am-9pm Jun-Aug, 7am-1pm & 5-8pm Mon-Fri, 11am-3pm Sat & Sun Sep-May) The village's magnificent outdoor swimming pool (with adjacent hotpot) has placed Hofsós firmly in the country's collective consciousness. It was opened in 2010 thanks to donations from two local women, and its fjordside design, integrated into the landscape and offering almost-infinity views, is close to perfect.

Infinity Blue (www.infinityblue.is) offers a relaxing late-night 'float therapy' session at the pool (kr3500), available nightly from 10pm to 1am (under midnight sun or even Northern Lights, if conditions are right). Bookings are essential.

Tours

Sailing in Skagafjörður BOAT TOUR
(☎861 9803; www.hafogland.is; tours kr7500; ⏲May-Oct) This operator runs boat trips from the small harbour (by the museum, taking in the scenery and bird life around the tiny island of **Málmey** and the bizarre promontory **Þórðarhöfði** (tethered to the mainland by a delicate spit). Tours generally leave at 9.30am, but you need to book. There's also the possibility of arranging sea-angling and birdwatching tours.

Sleeping & Eating

There are simple lodgings in town, a small and basic campsite on Skólagata (kr1300 per person) and a few options in the surrounds.

For somewhere quite special, consider driving 25km south to Guesthouse Hofsstaðir (p229).

Sunnuberg GUESTHOUSE €
(☎893 0220; www.sunnuberg.is; Suðurbraut 8; s/d kr10,600/14,500) Cosy rooms with bathroom are available at homey Sunnuberg, 200m past the pool, opposite the petrol pump and grocery store (note: no kitchen). The managers also arrange cheap sleeping-bag beds (kr5200) at the simple nearby Prestbakki cottage.

KS Hofsósi SUPERMARKET €
(Suðurbraut 9; ⏲9.30am-9.30pm Mon-Fri, 10am-8pm Sat, 11am-8pm Sun Jun-Aug, 9.30am-6pm Mon-Fri, 11am-4pm Sat Sep-May) If you're staying in town, you may need to self-cater. Pick up supplies here, where you can also get simple grill-bar food. There's a petrol pump out front.

Sólvík ICELANDIC €€
(mains kr1250-3400; ⏲10am-9pm mid-May–mid-Sep) Down at the small harbour among the museum buildings, Sólvík is a sweet country-style restaurant with a short, simple menu of local classics (cod, lamb, burgers, fish and chips). Traditional pancakes, too.

Getting There & Away

Hofsós is difficult to reach without your own wheels, but not impossible.

Strætó (www.bus.is) services:

- Bus 85 is a connecting service between Sauðárkrókur and Hofsós, which runs to meet bus 57 between Akureyri and Reykjavík. The catch? It only operates three days a week (Wednesday, Friday and Sunday) and must be prebooked at least two hours before departure.

Hofsós to Siglufjörður

The 60km stretch between Hofsós and Siglufjörður is full of scenic eye candy. Offshore the panorama is of the wee islet of **Málmey** and the promontory **Þórðarhöfði**, and lakes in the north. Inland are a few farms and fields dotted among valleys and peaks – the latter attract heliskiers in winter and spring. There are also rivers that lure fishers. The area is so scenic that the Fljót valley is home to Iceland's most exclusive accommodation, the ultra-luxe Deplar farm (www.elevenexperience.com), a secluded new hideout for celebs and tycoons.

You need your own transport to get here – there is no bus service covering this route.

Sleeping & Eating

★ Brúnastaðir COTTAGE €€
(☎467 1020; bruna@simnet.is; Rte 76; house from kr27,000) Brúnastaðir is run by a big friendly family, for big families (or groups). It has a newly built, fully equipped three-bedroom cottage (sleeps 10) on its farm. The views are stupendous, and there's a flower-filled garden, access to kayaks and boats, and loads of animals – kids will love it. Price excludes linen (kr2000 per person per stay).

Lónkot GUESTHOUSE €€€
(☎453 7432; www.lonkot.com; d with/without bathroom incl breakfast kr30,900/24,900; ⏲May-Dec)

Wonderfully blustery Lónkot is a gourmet pit stop along the rugged coast, 13km north of Hofsós, billed as a 'rural resort'. It has boutique accommodation (including a big family suite) with super sea views, and an indoor hot-pot. The output from its kitchen (open noon to 9.30pm; dinner mains kr4100 to kr5400) is inspired by local produce and slow-cooking principles.

Siglufjörður

POP 1200

Sigló (as the locals call it) sits precariously at the foot of a steep slope overlooking a beautiful fjord. In its heyday it was home to 10,000 workers, and fishing boats crammed into the small harbour to unload their catch for the waiting women to gut and salt.

After the herring abruptly disappeared from Iceland's north coast in the late 1960s, Siglufjörður declined and never fully recovered.

New tunnels now link the town with Ólafsfjörður and points further south, and these days Sigló is receiving warranted attention from travellers smitten by its hiking, marina and excellent diversions (and its role as the sordid small town in the 2015 Icelandic TV series *Trapped*, which was filmed here). Just reaching the town (from either direction) involves a journey that will take your breath away.

Sights

★Herring Era Museum MUSEUM
(Síldarminjasafnið; www.sild.is; Snorragata 10; adult/child kr1500/free; 10am-6pm Jun-Aug, 1-5pm May & Sep, by appointment Oct-Apr) Lovingly created over 16 years, this award-winning museum does a stunning job of recreating Siglufjörður's boom days between 1903 and 1968, when it was the herring-fishing capital of Iceland. Set in three buildings that were part of an old Norwegian herring station, the museum brings the work and lives of the town's inhabitants vividly to life. Start at the red building on the left, and move right.

Icelandic Folk Music Centre MUSEUM
(www.folkmusik.is; Norðurgata 1; adult/child kr800/free; noon-6pm Jun-Aug) Traditional-music enthusiasts may be interested in this sweet little museum, which displays 19th-century instruments and offers recordings of Icelandic songs and chants. It's free to enter if you have a ticket to the Herring Era Museum.

Activities

Siglufjörður is a great base for hikers, with a series of interesting hikes in the area. Some 19km of paths are marked along the avalanche-repelling fence above town, with numerous access points. There's a worthwhile information panel on the northern outskirts of town, beside a parking area, detailing these avalanche defences.

Another popular option is over the passes of Hólsskarð and Hestsskarð into the beautiful, uninhabited **Héðinsfjörður**, the next fjord to the east. This is where the tunnels connecting Siglufjörður and Ólafsfjörður see the light.

There's a large amount of hiking-trail info at www.fjallabyggd.is – go to About, then Hiking.

In winter ski lifts operate in the expanded, improved ski fields at **Skarðsdalur** (878 3399; www.skardsdalur.is) above the head of the fjord. A growing number of heliskiing operators work in Tröllaskagi over the winter; contact Viking Heliskiing (p239) based out of Ólafsfjörður for info.

In summer you can opt for an ultrascenic round of **golf** at the newly designed nine-hole course, which should be open by the time you read this.

Tours

Steini Vigg BOAT TOUR
(461 7730; Snorragata 3; tour adult/child kr8900/4450) Sigló Hótel operates a sightseeing and sea-angling boat tour (open to nonguests) onboard a 40-year-old fishing vessel that leaves from outside the hotel at 2pm daily in summer. Cruises last two to 2½ hours, and your catch can be cooked at the hotel's restaurant, should you wish.

Festivals & Events

Folk Music Festival MUSIC
(www.folkmusik.is; Jul) Folk-music aficionados will enjoy this relaxed five-day affair in early July.

Herring Festival CULTURAL
(Aug) Siglufjörður's biggest shindig takes place on the bank-holiday weekend in early August and recreates the gold-rush atmosphere of the town's glory days. The week leading up to it is full of events: singing, dancing, fishy feasting.

(Continued on page 238)

1

ARCTIC-IMAGES/GETTY IMAGES ©

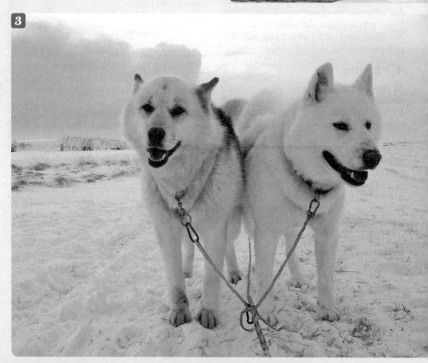

1. Ski slopes at Hlíðarfjall (p243) **2.** Skógafoss (p143)
3. Dog sledding **4.** Ice cave near Þórsmörk (p152)

3

Winter Travel

Winter travel to Iceland is surging in popularity, and it's not hard to figure out the appeal: Northern Lights dance across the sky, nature is at its most raw, and night-owls have the chance to experience crazy diurnal rhythms. It's also a great option if summer crowds don't appeal – but beware, those winter crowds are growing...

Tours from Reykjavík

Despite shortened daylight hours, city life goes on as normal in the capital, and opportunities for outdoor adventure are great: frozen waterfalls, snowy peaks, and skating, skiing and snowshoeing. Seek out the experts to travel safely during this time – day tours from Reykjavík (p69) are ideal, and locals know the best winter secrets.

Skiing & Snowsports

Bláfjoll outside Reykjavík draws skiers from November to April, but North Iceland is where serious snow bunnies should head: Akureyri is home to Hlíðarfjall (p243), Iceland's biggest ski field, while just north of here are smaller local ski fields and top-shelf heliskiing on the Tröllaskagi peninsula (p231). Time your visit for the Iceland Winter Games (p247) in Akureyri in late March.

Ice Caves

The southeast is a winter magnet, thanks to the frozen blue wonder of ice caves. The caves are accessible (usually at glacier edges) from around November to March. You'll need a guide: there are local experts leading the way from points between Skaftafell and Höfn. Bonus: the glaciated landscapes often take on a gleaming blue hue in the winter.

Snowshoeing & Dog Sledding

Snowmobiling, ice climbing, glacier hikes and even dog sledding can be done year-round in Iceland (those ice caps come in handy!), but if you're seeking the full fairy-tale experience, Mývatn makes a fine choice, for its snowshoe and cross-country ski tours, snowmobiling on the frozen lake, and dog sledding in the hills.

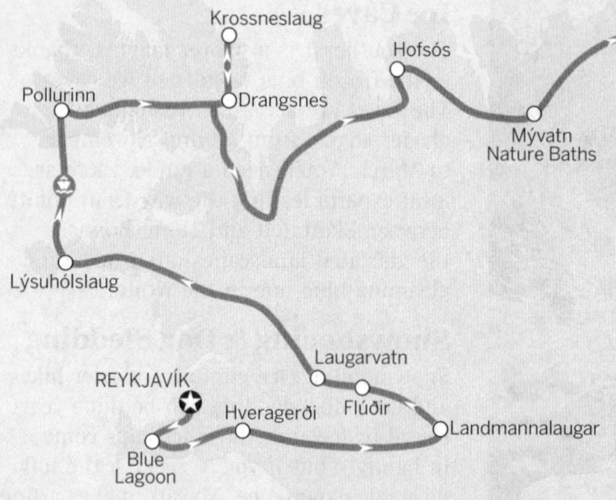
Krossneslaug
Hofsós
Selárdalslaug
Pollurinn
Drangsnes
Mývatn
Nature Baths
Egilsstaðir
Lýsuhólslaug
Laugarvatn
REYKJAVÍK
Hveragerði
Flúðir
Landmannalaugar
Blue
Lagoon

Top: Gamla Laugin, Flúðir
Bottom: Reykjadalur hot river, Hveragerði

2 WEEKS Hot-Pot Hop

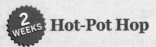

Slap on those swim trunks and enjoy Iceland's favourite pastime: wading in warm, mineral-rich hot springs that soothe both the body and the mind. Hop across this geothermic kingdom, dipping your toes in at each source.

Start in **Reykjavík** and do as the locals do – bring your backstroke and some gossip to share at the public pools.

Next, try the **Blue Lagoon**, the Disneyland of swimming spots, and slather rich silica over your face.

Pause in **Hveragerði**, one of Iceland's most geothermally active areas – bubbling water abounds.

Head to **Landmannalaugar**, where a steaming stream is the perfect cure-all after some serious hiking.

Cruise by **Flúðir** and see just who else is in on the secret of the natural, meadow-surrounded lagoon.

Swing through mod Fontana, in **Laugarvatn**, for its naturally occurring geyser-sauna (you'll see!).

Soak in **Lýsuhólslaug** and emerge from the algae soup with baby-soft skin.

Scout out **Pollurinn**, just outside of Tálknafjörður – a favourite local hang-out.

Blink and you'll miss the roadside hot-pots in **Drangsnes**, built into a sea wall.

Bask in the otherworldly beauty at **Krossneslaug**, set along the wild, pebble-strewn shore.

Check out stunning **Hofsós**, with near-infinity views from its fjordside pool, plus the chance to book a midnight float.

The north's mellower version of the Blue Lagoon is found at **Mývatn Nature Baths**.

Finish up at **Selárdalslaug**, tucked between two hillocks near Vopnafjörður. Then fly back to Reykjavík from **Egilsstaðir**.

…nued from page 233)

Sleeping

Campsite CAMPGROUND €
(Snorragata; sites per person kr1100; ⏲mid-May–mid-Sep) Oddly placed in the middle of town near the harbour, with a small block housing showers and a laundry. There's a second patch of grass beyond the city limits; follow Suðurgata (or take Norðurtún, signed off Snorragata).

★**Herring Guesthouse** GUESTHOUSE €€
(☎868 4200; www.theherringhouse.com; Hávegur 5; s/d without bathroom kr13,500/17,900, 4-person apt kr44,800) Þorir and Erla are charming, knowledgable hosts (he's a former town mayor) offering personalised service at their stylish, view-blessed guesthouse, now with two locations (the second is at Hlíðarvegur 1, behind the church). There is a guest kitchen at the main house, and a lovely (optional) breakfast spread (kr2000). Families will appreciate the two-bedroom apartment.

★**Siglunes Guesthouse** GUESTHOUSE €€
(☎467 1222; www.hotelsiglunes.is; Lækjargata 10; d with/without bathroom from kr19,400/15,900) Personality shines through in this cool guesthouse, where vintage furniture is paired with contemporary art and ultra-modern bathrooms in the hotel-standard wing. There are equally appealing guesthouse rooms (shared bathrooms, no kitchen), a big dining hall for breakfast (kr2000), and a cosy bar area celebrating happy hour from 5pm to 7pm. Nice touch: the free bikes for guests to use.

Siglo Harbour Hostel & Apartments GUESTHOUSE, APARTMENT €€
(☎897 1394; www.sigloharbourhostel.is; Tjarnargata 14; d without bathroom kr13,500, apt kr32,000) The 'hostel' element of this establishment is more like a decent-value guesthouse: five double rooms with linen, shared bathroom and kitchen access (and bonus: free laundry). The two spacious apartments each sleep six and are good for families and groups. There's a multinight discount.

Sigló Hótel HOTEL €€€
(☎461 7730; www.siglohotel.is; Snorragata 3; d incl breakfast kr37,000) The town's 'patron', a local man made good in the US, is behind the vibrant marina redevelopment; his latest project is this upmarket, 68-room harbourside hotel, which opened in mid-2015. Rooms are smart and well fitted-out, but it's the public areas that shine brightest: the elegant restaurant and bar, stylish lounge and waterside hot-pot.

Eating & Drinking

The street opposite the supermarket is Aðalgata; it's home to a busy bakery and pizzeria, but come mealtime many appetites are focused on the primary-coloured marina.

It's well worth investigating whether Siglunes Guesthouse has anything interesting cooking – it recently had a Moroccan chef preparing authentic Moroccan cuisine.

Aðalbakarinn BAKERY, CAFE €
(Aðalgata 28; soup buffet kr1590; ⏲7am-5pm Mon-Fri, 8am-5pm Sat, 9am-4pm Sun) A big space popular with locals and tourists alike. Stop by for coffee and cake, the lunchtime soup buffet, or sandwiches and picnic supplies.

Samkaup-Úrval SUPERMARKET €
(Aðalgata; ⏲10am-7pm Mon-Fri, 11am-7pm Sat, 1-5pm Sun) Well stocked for self-caterers. ATM inside.

Kaffi Rauðka ICELANDIC €€
(www.raudka.is; mains kr1690-2950; ⏲11.30am-9.30pm Jun-Aug; 👪) Ruby-red Rauðka has an informal atmosphere, with an all-day menu of sandwiches, salads and hearty mains such as barbecue ribs, burgers, and fish and chips. The open sandwich of local shrimp is delicious. At weekends, Rauðka often stages live music. Winter hours are intermittent.

Hannes Boy ICELANDIC €€€
(☎461 7734; www.hannesboy.is; Gránugata 23; buffet adult/child kr6490/3245; ⏲6-10pm Jun-Aug) Dressed in sunny yellow, this stylish, light-filled space is furnished with funky seats made from old herring barrels. It's under the same ownership as Sigló Hótel and offers a high-quality dinner buffet primarily visited by groups, but open to walk-ins too (for à la carte options, visit the hotel's restaurant). It's got a good selection of seafood, and an ice-cream dessert bar.

Vínbúðin ALCOHOL
(Eyrargata 25; ⏲2-6pm Mon-Thu, noon-7pm Fri, 11am-2pm Sat May-Aug, closed Sat Sep-Apr) Government-run liquor store.

Information

The town has services such as a bank, pharmacy, post office etc. The **Herring Era Museum** offers some tourist info.

There's also information on the website www.fjallabyggd.is (Fjallabyggð is the municipality covering Siglufjörður and Ólafsfjörður), and more at www.visittrollaskagi.is.

Tourist Information Centre (☎464 9120; Gránugata 24; ⏲9am-5pm Mon-Fri, 11am-3pm Sat & Sun Jun-Aug, shorter hours Sep-May) A helpful desk inside the Ráðhús (town hall) on Gránugata.

Getting There & Away

BUS

Strætó (www.bus.is) services:

- Bus 78 to Ólafsfjörður (kr840, 15 minutes, three daily Monday to Friday, one daily Sunday)
- Bus 78 to Akureyri (kr2520, 70 minutes, three daily Monday to Friday, one daily Sunday) Runs via Dalvík.

CAR

Prior to the tunnels opening in 2010, Siglufjörður and Ólafsfjörður were joined by the 62km mountain road over Lagheiði (the old Rte 82). This road was only accessible in summer; in winter the towns were 234km apart. Thanks to the new tunnels through the mountains, that connection now measures 16km.

Travelling east, there's a 4km tunnel that opens into beautiful Héðinsfjörður, before a second tunnel travels the remaining 7km to Ólafsfjörður.

Ólafsfjörður

POP 825

Beautifully locked between sheer mountain slopes and dark fjord waters, fishing town Ólafsfjörður still retains a sense of isolation, even with tunnels now linking it with Siglufjörður, its sister settlement further north.

From Akureyri, you have to pass through a thin 3km tunnel just to make your way into town, which makes for a cinematic entrance.

Activities

Ólafsfjörður receives good snow in winter, when the downhill ski slopes above town lurch into action. A few companies are ramping up winter activities in the pristine peaks of Tröllaskagi, with bases in and around Ólafsfjörður.

There's also an excellent swimming pool, and nine-hole golf course. Brimnes Hotel (p239) offers rental of boats and kayaks for exploration; check the hotel's website for a rundown of possible activities in the area.

Tours

Arctic Freeride ADVENTURE

(☎859 8800; www.arcticfreeride.com; 2hr tour adult/child kr9000/5500) A local father-son team operates tours aboard a snowcat from January to May. Take a sightseeing tour up the 984m peak Múlakolla, or a longer evening tour to view the Northern Lights (kr20,000). There's the option of a one-way ride, too (snowcat up, ski down).

Viking Heliskiing SKIING

(☎846 1674; www.vikingheliskiing.com) Expert local guides (former Winter Olympians) offer heliskiing trips exploring the peaks of the peninsula (vertical drop is up to 1500m), operating from about mid-March to mid-June (conditions permitting). There are package-tour options that include transfers from Akureyri and lodge accommodation with meals. A two-day, two-night guided heliskiing package costs from €4300.

Sleeping & Eating

At mealtimes, consider a jaunt up the road to Siglufjörður, where options are better.

Campsite CAMPGROUND €

(sites per person kr1100; ⏲mid-May–mid-Sep) Toilets, water and electricity are available; guests use the showers inside the neighbouring swimming-pool complex. Payments are made at Kaffi Klara (p240).

Brimnes Hotel & Bungalows HOTEL, COTTAGES €€

(☎660 3955; www.brimnes.is; Bylgjubyggð 2; s/d incl breakfast kr12,300/18,000, cottages from kr23,200) The real draws at the town's primary accommodation are the fabulous lakeshore log cabins (varying sizes, sleeping up to seven), with hot tubs built into the verandah and views over the water. There are also 11 bright, freshly renovated en suite rooms, plus a decent summertime restaurant serving the usual fare (soup, fish, burgers) but open somewhat intermittently (depending on group bookings).

Gistihús Jóa GUESTHOUSE €€

(Joe's Guesthouse; ☎847 4331; http://joesguesthouse.is; Strandgata 2; d without bathroom incl breakfast kr15,000-18,000) Joe's handsome six-room guesthouse is in a restored old post office next to the supermarket, with a sweet cafe downstairs (where breakfast is served). Compact rooms have hand basins, quirky flooring and modern chocolate-brown decor.

Kaffi Klara CAFE €
(www.kaffiklara.is; Strandgata 2; lunch buffet kr1850; ⊙10am-6pm) This sweet cafe has info about the area, plus a selection of soups, sandwiches and cakes. There are books and board games to help pass rainy days, plus our favourite feature: the old phone booths (this used to be the post office).

Information

Tourist Information Centre (☎464 9215; Ólafsvegur 4; ⊙1-5pm Mon-Fri, 11am-3pm Sat Jun-Aug, shorter hours Sep-May) Helpful desk inside the local library, just off the main road through town.

Getting There & Away

Strætó (www.bus.is) services:

- Bus 78 to Siglufjörður (kr840, 15 minutes, three daily Monday to Friday, one daily Sunday)
- Bus 78 to Akureyri (kr2100, 55 minutes, three daily Monday to Friday, one daily Sunday) Runs via Dalvík.

Dalvík

POP 1455

Sleepy Dalvík is in a snug, scenic spot between breezy Eyjafjörður and the rolling hills of Svarfaðardalur. Most tourists come here to catch the Grímsey ferry (p251), but if you've got some time there are plenty of reasons to linger, including great activities in the area, plus interesting museums and quality accommodation.

Byggðasafnið Hvoll MUSEUM
(www.dalvik.is/byggdasafn; Karlsbraut; adult/child kr700/free; ⊙11am-6pm Jun-Aug, 2-5pm Sat Sep-May) Dalvík's quality folk museum is high on oddball factor. Skip the usual taxidermic characters (yes, another polar bear!) and find the rooms dedicated to the poignant story of local giant Jóhan Pétursson. At 2.34m (almost 7ft 7in), Jóhan was Iceland's tallest man.

Tours

Arctic Sea Tours WHALE WATCHING
(☎771 7600; www.arcticseatours.is; Hafnarbraut 22; 3hr tour adult/child kr9900/4950; ⊙Mar-Nov) This professional outfit operates three-hour tours up to five times a day in high summer (it has scheduled whale-watching tours from March to November). All tours include a short sea-angling stint, and your catch is grilled on the barbecue as soon as the boat docks. Meet at its office on the main road through town, by the N1 petrol pumps.

Bergmenn Mountain Guides ADVENTURE
(☎858 3000; www.bergmenn.com) Based outside Dalvík, this pioneering company

WINTER WONDERS

You're probably aware that the number of visitors to Iceland has skyrocketed in recent years. You may well be asking: what if there was a way to experience Iceland's awesome outdoors, but with smaller crowds? There is: visit in winter. For the Northern Lights, yes, but so much more. And don't feel you need to be confined to Reykjavík and surrounds – domestic flights to Akureyri operate year-round, and there's a growing number of winter activities and operators in the country's north to help you experience the snowy-mountain magic.

Akureyri, the Tröllaskagi Peninsula and Mývatn are all winter wonderlands. Akureyri has winter festivals and easy access to Iceland's biggest ski field at **Hlíðarfjall** (p243). Tröllaskagi offers smaller ski fields (at Dalvík, Ólafsfjörður and Siglufjörður), plus great heliskiing (peak months: March and April); check out skiing info online at www.skiiceland.is. Mývatn has activities like snowshoe and cross-country ski tours, snowmobiling on the frozen lake and dog sledding in the hills. Packages can be arranged that cover a variety of activities plus transfers and accommodation. A good tip is to travel from around February, when daylight hours are increasing (but don't discount Christmas–New Year as a festive time to visit).

If you're not experienced in winter driving, it's a good idea to leave that to the kitted-out professionals with their super-Jeeps and local expertise. Operators such as **Saga Travel** (p245), based in Akureyri and Mývatn, are a sure bet – and do check out the websites of companies such as **Bergmenn Mountain Guides** (p240), **Viking Heliskiing** (p239), and Mývatn's **Hike&Bike** (p261) and **Sel-Hótel** (p267), to see what else appeals.

specialises in ski touring, ski mountaineering, heliskiing, ice climbing, alpine climbing and other mountain-related activities. Fun fact: the name of the company's owner, Jökull Bergmann, translates as 'Glacier Mountainman' – so you know he found his calling. The company runs Arctic Heli Skiing (www.arcticheliskiing.com) and has four lodges dotted around the peninsula.

Sleeping & Eating

★Dalvík HI Hostel HOSTEL €
(☎699 6616, 865 8391; www.dalvikhostel.com; Hafnarbraut 4; dm/d without bathroom kr4900/12,700) This is, for our money, one of Iceland's best hostels, and certainly its prettiest – it's more like a boutique guesthouse than a budgeteer's bunkhouse. Heiða, one of the friendly owners, has a creative streak put to good use in quirky, vintage-inspired decor. The seven-room hostel is in the town centre, in a white building called Gimli.

Campground CAMPGROUND €
(per campervan/tent kr2250/1750; ⏲Jun-Aug) Large camping area by the town pool; follow the signs to Fosshótel to access it (pay at the pool).

Vegamót COTTAGE €€
(☎699 6616, 865 8391; www.dalvikhostel.com; Skiðarbraut; cottages kr16,300-24,900) Heiða and Bjarni, the friendly owners of the town's excellent hostel (p241), have more accommodation options, including three wooden cabins and Gamli Bærinn (the 'Old Farmhouse'), a gorgeously romantic self-contained cottage. These are at their property opposite the Olís petrol station at the southern entrance to town. Check-in is done at Gísli, Eiríkur, Helgi, the great cafe under the same ownership.

★Gísli, Eiríkur, Helgi ICELANDIC €
(Kaffihús Bakkabræðra; Grundargata 1; soup & salad buffet kr1990; ⏲10am-10pm) Named after three brothers from a folk tale, this might just be the perfect small-town cafe. It's decked out in timber, full of vintage bric-a-brac and mismatched china (it's owned by the folks behind the town's retro-chic hostel), and serves delicious fish soup and homemade cakes. The locals love it (understandably), and there's a bar area and small theatre out the back.

Information

Tourist Information Desk (☎846 4908; www.dalvikurbyggd.is; Goðabraut; ⏲8am-6pm Mon-Fri, 1-5pm Sat) This helpful info desk is at Menningarhúsið Berg, the modern cultural centre that houses the library and a cafe. Staff can help with information on activities in the region, including horse riding, skiing, golf, hiking and birdwatching.

Getting There & Away

Dalvík is the jumping-off point for ferries to Grímsey (p260).

Strætó (www.bus.is) bus services:

- Bus 78 to Siglufjörður (kr1260, 35 minutes, three daily Monday to Friday, one daily Sunday).
- Bus 78 to Akureyri (kr1680, 40 minutes, three daily Monday to Friday, one daily Sunday).

Akureyri to Dalvík

A rich agricultural region runs north from Akureyri to Dalvík along Rte 82, punctuated by side roads to tiny fishing villages on the western shore of Eyjafjörður – from south to north these are Hjalteyri, Hauganes and Árskógssandur.

There are dramatic views across the water to the mountains opposite, and a handful of pit stops and activities. Árskógssandur is the main jumping-off point for those who want to explore little Hrísey island (p251), out in the middle of the fjord.

Sights & Activities

Hjalteyri VILLAGE
Hjalteyri (population 43) was once a major herring harbour, and its old fish factory was Iceland's largest herring-processing plant when it was built in 1937. The herring disappeared in the 1960s and the factory was closed. These days, it's a cool place to wander around, with a few surprises; summertime art exhibitions, craftspeople, a diving operator (p242), maybe some whale-watching tours. It's 20km from Akureyri.

Whale Watching Hauganes WHALE WATCHING
(☎867 0000; www.whales.is; Hafnargata 2, Hauganes; 3hr tour adult/child kr9400/4700; ⏲mid-May–mid-Sep) From the hamlet of Hauganes, climb aboard the former fishing boat *Níels Jónsson* for an adventure that includes fishing and whale watching (this is Iceland's oldest whale-watch operator).

DIVING IN EYJAFJÖRÐUR

Thoughts of scuba diving usually involve sun-kissed beaches and tropical fish, so perhaps it's surprising that some of the world's most fascinating diving lies within Iceland's frigid waters. Most divers flock to crystalline Silfra near Þingvellir in the south, but the real diving dynamo, known as **Strýtan**, lurks beneath Eyjafjörður.

Strýtan, a giant cone (55m) soaring up from the ocean floor, commands a striking presence as it spews out gushing hot water. This geothermal chimney – made from deposits of magnesium silicate – is truly an anomaly. The only other Strýtan-like structures ever discovered were found at depths of 2000m or more; Strýtan's peak is a mere 15m below the surface.

In addition to Strýtan, there are smaller steam cones on the other side of Eyjafjörður. Known as **Arnanesstrýtur**, these smaller formations aren't as spectacular, but the water bubbling out of the vents is estimated to be 11,000 years old. The water is completely devoid of salt, so you can put a thermos over a vent, bottle the boiling water, and use it to make hot chocolate when you get back to the surface!

Diving around the island of Grímsey (p260) is also memorable. The water is surprisingly clear here, but the main draw is the bird life: bazaars of guillemots swoop down deep as they search for food. Swimming with birds is definitely a strange experience – when the visibility is particularly good it can feel like you're flying!

If you're interested in checking out these and more underwater curiosities in the north (including fissures and geothermal rivers), contact Erlendur Bogason at his diving outfit, **Strytan Divecentre** (☎862 2949; www.strytan.is; Hjalteyri; 2 guided dives kr40,000), based at Hjalteyri, about 20km north of Akureyri. Erlendur discovered Strýtan in 1997, and now officially protects it. Check the website for the diving experience required; note that there is also the opportunity for drysuit snorkelling in some locales.

Bruggsmiðjan – Kaldi BREWERY
(Kaldi Beer; ☎466 2505; www.bruggsmidjan.is; Öldugata 22, Árskógssandur; tour kr2000; ⏲tours by appointment 11am-3pm) Árskógssandur is the home of Bruggsmiðjan microbrewery, producing excellent, in-demand Kaldi brews using Czech techniques. The brewery welcomes visitors, but you should call ahead to arrange a tour time. You could also consider joining a food-focused tour with Akureyri-based Saga Travel (p245), which visits this and other local producers.

Sleeping & Eating

★Apartment Hótel Hjalteyri BOUTIQUE HOTEL €€€
(☎462 2770, 897 7070; www.hotelhjalteyri.is; Hjalteyri; d kr39,000, 2-bedroom apt kr49,000, incl breakfast) The wow factor delights at this former school en route to Hjalteyri's harbour. It's renovated to house three double rooms and four apartments of varying sizes (including a delicious penthouse with jacuzzi and terrace), and it's dripping with good taste: big proportions, loads of artworks and books, stylish decor. There's a summer cafe here (open to all, from 2pm to 9pm).

AKUREYRI

POP 18,200

Akureyri (pronounced *ah*-koo-rare-ee) stands strong as Iceland's second city, but a Melbourne, Manchester or Montréal it is not. And how could it be with only 18,000 residents? It's a wonder the city (which would be a 'town' anywhere else) generates this much buzz. Expect cool cafes, quality restaurants, a handful of art galleries and even some late-night bustle – a far cry from other rural Icelandic towns.

Akureyri nestles at the head of Eyjafjörður, Iceland's longest (60km) fjord, at the base of snowcapped peaks. In summer flowering gardens belie the location, just a stone's throw from the Arctic Circle. Lively winter festivals and some of Iceland's best skiing provide plenty of off-peak (and off-piste) appeal. With its relaxed attitude and extensive food and accommodation choices, it's the natural base for exploring Eyjafjörður and around, and it's seeing a growing number of cruise ships calling by (passenger numbers can sometimes overwhelm the town).

Many visitors use Akureyri as a base for visiting Tröllaskagi, Mývatn and Húsavík

Sights

★ Akureyrarkirkja CHURCH

(www.akureyrarkirkja.is; Eyrarlandsvegur; generally 10am-4pm Mon-Fri) Dominating the town from high on a hill, Akureyri's landmark church was designed by Guðjón Samúelsson, the architect responsible for Reykjavík's Hallgrímskirkja. Although the basalt theme connects them, Akureyrarkirkja looks more like a stylised 1920s US skyscraper than its big-city brother.

Built in 1940, the church contains a large 3200-pipe organ and a series of rather untraditional reliefs of the life of Christ. There's also a suspended ship hanging from the ceiling, reflecting an old Nordic tradition of votive offerings for the protection of loved ones at sea. Perhaps the most striking feature is the beautiful central stained-glass window above the altar, which originally graced Coventry Cathedral in England.

The church admits visitors most days; check the board outside for opening times, as they change frequently.

★ Lystigarðurinn GARDENS

(www.lystigardur.akureyri.is; Eyrarlandsholt; 8am-10pm Mon-Fri, 9am-10pm Sat & Sun Jun-Sep) FREE The most northerly botanical garden in the world makes a delightful spot for a fragrant wander on sunny days. The wealth of plant life on display is truly astonishing considering the gardens' proximity to the Arctic Circle. You'll find examples of every species native to Iceland, as well as a host of high-latitude and high-altitude plants from around the world. There's also a beautifully situated cafe.

Akureyri Art Museum MUSEUM

(Listasafnið á Akureyri; www.listak.is; Kaupvangsstræti 12; kr1000; 10am-5pm Jun-Aug, noon-5pm Tue-Sun Sep-May) Stimulate your senses with a browse at the Akureyri Art Museum, which hosts eclectic, innovative exhibitions – from graphic design to portraiture – and is surrounded by a handful of local galleries. It's the heart of a downtown strip the local tourist authorities have optimistically branded the 'Art Alley'.

Akureyri Museum MUSEUM

(Minjasafnið á Akureyri; www.akmus.is; Aðalstræti 58; adult/child kr1200/free; 10am-5pm Jun–mid-Sep, 1-4pm mid-Sep–May) This sweet, well-curated museum houses art and historical items relating to town life, including maps, photos and re-creations of early Icelandic homes. The museum garden became the first place in Iceland to cultivate trees when a nursery was established here in 1899. Next door is a tiny, black-tarred timber church dating from 1846.

Nonnahús MUSEUM

(www.nonni.is; Aðalstræti 54; adult/child kr1200/free; 10am-5pm Jun-Aug) The most interesting of the artists' residences in Akureyri, Nonnahús was the childhood home of renowned children's writer Reverend Jón Sveinsson (1857–1944), known to most as Nonni. His old-fashioned tales of derring-do have a rich local flavour. The house dates from 1850; its cramped rooms and simple furnishings provide a poignant insight into life in 19th-century Iceland.

A combined ticket for Nonnahús and the neighbouring Akureyri Museum is kr2000.

Activities

In winter snowfields draw skiers from all over the country, while independent summertime activities include hiking, golf and hot-pot-hopping. A helpful resource is the collection of Útivist & afþreying hiking maps (there are seven in the series; #1 and #2 focus on the Eyjafjörður area); these are available at Ferðafélag Akureyrar (p245) and the tourist office (p256).

At the time of writing there were no businesses offering bike rental, but it's worth enquiring at the tourist office to see if this has changed.

Akureryi is also the base for a multitude of tours and guided activities all over Iceland's north.

★ Sundlaug Akureyrar SWIMMING

(Þingvallastræti 21; adult/child kr750/200; 6.45am-9pm Mon-Fri, 8am-7.30pm Sat & Sun;) The hub of local life, Akureyri's outdoor swimming pool is one of Iceland's finest. It has three heated pools, hot-pots, water slides, saunas and steam rooms.

Hlíðarfjall Ski Centre SKIING

(462 2280; www.hlidarfjall.is; day pass adult/child kr4900/1400;) Iceland's premier downhill ski slope is 5km west of town. The resort has a vertical drop of 455m; the longest trail is over 2.5km. There are seven lifts and 23 alpine slopes; there are also cross-country ski routes.

The season usually runs between December and late April, with the best

Akureyri

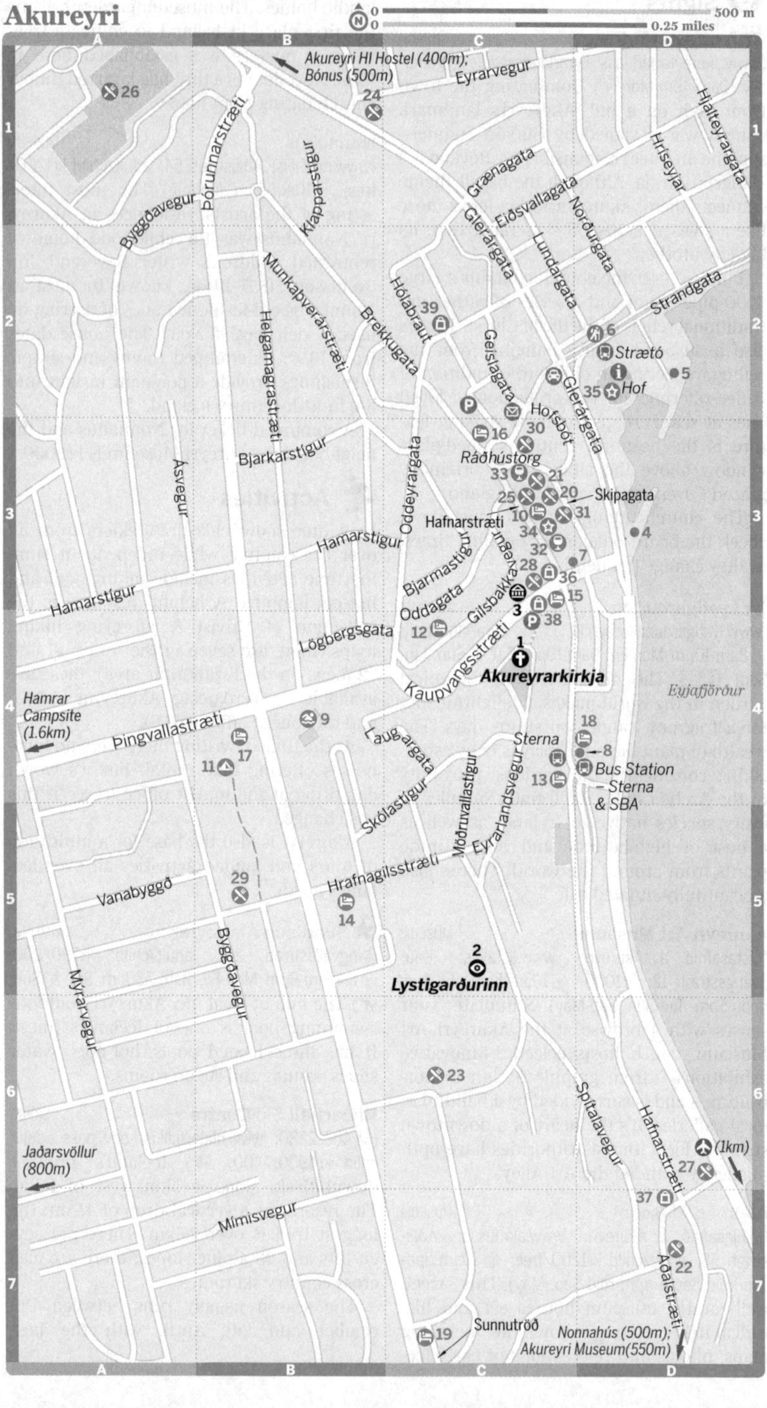
0
500 m
0
0.25 miles
N
A
B
C
D
1
2
3
4
5
6
7
Akureyri HI Hostel (400m);
Bónus (500m)
Eyrarvegur
Hjalteyrargata
Hríseyjar
Grænagata
Eiðsvallagata
Norðurgata
Glerárgata
Lundargata
Strandgata
Þórunnarstræti
Byggðavegur
Klapparstígur
Munkaþverárstræti
Helgamagrastræti
Brekkugata
Hólabraut
Geislagata
Glerárgata
Strætó
Hof
Horfsbót
Ráðhústorg
Skipagata
Hafnarstræti
Bjarkarstígur
Ásvegur
Oddeyrargata
Hamarstígur
Bjarmastígur
Gilsbakkavegur
Hamarstígur
Oddagata
Lögbergsgata
Kaupvangsstræti
Akureyrarkirkja
Eyjafjörður
Hamrar
Campsite
(1.6km)
Þingvallastræti
Laugargata
Sterna
Bus Station
– Sterna
& SBA
Skólastígur
Möðruvallastígur
Eyrarlandsvegur
Hrafnagilsstræti
Vanabyggð
Byggðavegur
Lystigarðurinn
Mýrarvegur
Spítalavegur
Hafnarstræti
(1km)
Jaðarsvöllur
(800m)
Mímisvegur
Aðalstræti
Sunnutröð
Nonnahús (500m);
Akureyri Museum(550m)
1
2
3
4
5
6
7
8
9
10
11
12
13
14
15
16
17
18
19
20
21
22
23
24
25
26
27
28
29
30
31
32
33
34
35
36
37
38
39

Akureyri

Top Sights
1 Akureyrarkirkja C4
2 Lystigarðurinn C5

Sights
3 Akureyri Art Museum C3

Activities, Courses & Tours
4 Ambassador D3
5 Elding D2
6 Ferðafélag Akureyrar D2
7 Saga Travel C3
8 SBA-Norðurleið D4
9 Sundlaug Akureyrar B4

Sleeping
10 Akureyri Backpackers C3
11 City Campsite B4
12 Guesthouse Hvítahúsið C4
13 Hótel Akureyri C4
14 Hótel Edda B5
15 Hótel Kea C3
16 Hrafninn C3
17 Icelandair Hotel Akureyri B4
18 Our Guesthouse D4
19 Sæluhús C7

Eating
20 Akureyri Fish Restaurant C3
21 Berlin C3
Blaá Kannan .... (see 32)
22 Brynja D7
23 Café Laut C6
24 Greifinn B1
Hamborgarafabrikkan .... (see 15)
Icelandair Hotel Akureyri .... (see 17)
25 Indian Curry Hut C3
26 Nettó A1
27 Noa Seafood Restaurant D6
28 Rub23 .... C3
29 Samkaup-Strax B5
30 Serrano C3
31 Strikið C3

Drinking & Nightlife
Akureyri Backpackers .... (see 10)
32 Götubarinn C3
33 R5 .... C3

Entertainment
34 Græni Hatturinn C3
35 Hof D2

Shopping
36 Eymundsson C3
Geysir .... (see 10)
37 Háaloftið D7
38 Sjoppan C3
39 Vínbúðin C2

conditions in February and March (Easter is particularly busy).

In the long hours of winter darkness, all of the main runs are floodlit.

There's ski and snowboard rental, two restaurants and a ski school. In season, buses usually connect the site with Akureyri; check the website for details.

Ferðafélag Akureyrar HIKING
(Touring Club of Akureyri; ☎462 2720; www.ffa.is; Strandgata 23; ⏲3-6pm Mon-Fri May-Aug, 11am-1pm Mon-Fri Sep-Apr) For information on hiking in the area, contact Ferðafélag Akureyrar. Its helpful website details (in English) the huts it operates in northern Iceland and the highlands, plus notes on the Askja Trail, and its program (in Icelandic) of hiking and skiing tours that travellers can join.

Kjarnaskógur OUTDOORS
(♿) About 3km south of town is Iceland's most visited 'forest', the 600-hectare Kjarnaskógur woods. This bushland area has walking and mountain-bike trails, picnic areas and barbecues, and kids' playgrounds. In winter the area is good for cross-country skiing (there's a 7km trail with lighting). The campground (p248) at Hamrar has easy access to the woods.

Jaðarsvöllur GOLF
(☎462 2974; www.golficeland.org; round kr5900-7000; ⏲mid-May–Oct) Up for a game of midnight golf? At only a few degrees south of the Arctic Circle, Akureyri's par-71 Jaðarsvöllur basks in perpetual daylight from June to early August, and you can play golf here around the clock; book ahead for the midnight tee off. Clubs and trolley can be hired.

The course is home to the annual 36-hole **Arctic Open** (www.arcticopen.is; ⏲late Jun), a tournament played under midnight sun over two nights in late June.

Tours

★ **Saga Travel** ADVENTURE TOUR
(☎558 8888; www.sagatravel.is; Kaupvangsstræti 4; ⏲booking office 7.30am-6pm Jun-Aug, reduced hours rest of year) Offers a rich and diverse year-round program of excursions and activities throughout the north – obvious destinations like Mývatn, Húsavík (for whale watching) and Askja in the highlands, but

LONG WEEKEND REMIX: THE DIAMOND CIRCLE

Perfectly positioned between North America and Europe, Iceland has become the *it* destination for a cool weekend getaway. The constant stream of tourists has turned the three-day Reykjavík–Golden Circle–Blue Lagoon trip into a well-worn circuit, so why not blaze a new trail and tackle Iceland's northern triangle of stunning attractions: Mývatn, Húsavík and Akureyri. It's less legwork than you think – when you land at Keflavík International Airport, catch a bus or connecting flight to Akureyri (you will need to travel to the capital's domestic airport).

Day 1: Akureyri

Jump-start your visit to the north with something quintessentially Icelandic: horse riding, preferably with some grand panoramas to enjoy. Then, a half-day is plenty of time to bop around the streets of the city centre. Or for those who can withstand another plane ride, spend the afternoon on Grímsey, Iceland's only slice of the Arctic Circle. For dinner, a good option is **Strikið** (p250) or **Rub23** (p250), followed by a night out on the town.

Day 2: Húsavík & Around

In the morning, head to Húsavík. First, swing by the **Húsavík Whale Museum** (p270) for a bit of background info, then hop aboard a whale-watching tour. Consider heading east for a walk among the canyon walls of Ásbyrgi, check out the roar of thunderous Dettifoss, then recount your whale tales over dinner back at **Naustið** (p274) in Húsavík.

Day 3: Mývatn

For those of you who have been drooling over the photos of Iceland's turquoise-tinted spa springs, fret not. Mývatn has its very own version of the Blue Lagoon: the **Mývatn Nature Baths** (p268). After a leisurely soak, it's time to get the blood flowing again. A three-hour hike around eastern Mývatn takes in a smorgasbord of geological anomalies. A stop at stinky **Hverir** (p269) is a must, and, if time permits, have a wander around the steam vents at Krafla. Then make your way back to Akureyri to catch your flight, but not before visiting one last site: the heavenly waterfall **Goðafoss** (p259).

also innovative tours along themes such as food or art and design. Check out Saga's full program online, or drop by its central booking office.

Quirky 'midnight sun' tours depart at 10pm in June and take you to attractions like Dettifoss and Mývatn in the quiet wee hours. Winter tours are varied (snowmobiling, snowshoeing, Northern Lights viewing – which is, of course, weather dependent, but includes a lesson in photographing them). Private itineraries can be arranged; guides are local and well connected. Tours have a maximum of 16 participants (and usually a minimum of two).

Traveling Viking ADVENTURE TOUR
(☎896 3569; www.ttv.is; 👪) A company doing plenty of local tours, from the expected (Mývatn, Dettifoss, Húsavík) to the more offbeat, including a four-hour family-friendly option focusing on the 'hidden people', or winter ice-fishing. The company gets some buzz for its *Game of Thrones*–themed tour of the Mývatn region; it also offers some cool kayaking options.

Tours generally depart from Hof, or local hotel pick-ups can usually be arranged.

SBA-Norðurleið BUS TOUR
(☎550 0700; www.sba.is; Hafnarstræti 82) This bus company runs a range of sightseeing tours in North Iceland, with popular destinations including Mývatn, Dettifoss, Ásbyrgi and Húsavík.

★ **Skjaldarvík** HORSE RIDING, ADVENTURE TOUR
(☎552 5200; www.skjaldarvik.is; horse ride kr10,900, buggy tour kr19,900) As well as a superb guesthouse (p248) and restaurant, Skjaldarvík offers a couple of top-notch activities from its scenic fjordside locale 6km north of town: horse-riding tours, plus a fun new adrenalin option of buggy rides. These buggies are golf carts on steroids and seat two, and you drive along trails on the surrounding farm (driver's licence required; helmet and overalls supplied).

On the horse-riding front, there are 1½-hour tours along the fjord and into the surrounding hills, departing at 10am, 2pm and 5pm daily in summer.

You can do each activity on its own, or combine them with a package that includes access to Skjaldarvík's outdoor hot-pot and a two-course dinner. See the website for all possibilities (Ride & Bite, Buggy & Bite, Horses & Horsepower). Pick-up in Akureyri can be arranged.

Circle Air FLIGHT TOUR
(☎588 4000; www.circleair.is) Operating out of Akureyri Airport, this company offers sightseeing from the air, or customised photo-flights or hops to Greenland. 'Flightseeing' rates start at kr25,000 for a 40-minute flight over Akureyri and Tröllaskagi; longer flights include the Dettifoss and Mývatn, the central highlands, or a two-hour stop on Grímsey (kr49,000).

Whale-Watching & Boat Tours

Elding WHALE WATCHING
(☎519 5000; www.elding.is; Akureyri harbour; 3hr tour adult/child kr10,900/5450) From a base that's tucked behind the Hof cultural centre, Reykjavík company Elding now operates from Akureyri. There's a regular three-hour whale-watching cruise, with year-round sailings (once daily from October to April), plus the option of an 'express tour' on a RIB (rigid inflatable boat; per person kr19,990, no children under 10) from May to September.

Ambassador WHALE WATCHING, BOAT TOUR
(☎462 6800; www.ambassador.is; Torfunefsbryggja dock; 3hr tour adult/child kr11,490/5745) Ambassador has a growing range of tours on Eyjafjörður, from three-hour whale-watching cruises to fast-paced explorations on RIBs (rigid inflatable boats; two hours, adult/child kr19,990/14,990). A longer offering is the six-hour summertime cruise to Grímsey (adult/child kr29,990/16,990) – enjoy whale watching en route, then a two-hour island stopover. New: winter Northern Lights cruises (adult/child kr11,490/5745), though sightings cannot be guaranteed.

Festivals & Events

The calendar page of the www.visitakureyri.is website lists events big and small. Winter events are growing in stature.

Iceland Winter Games SPORTS
(www.icelandwintergames.com; ⌚Mar) In March snowy activities take centre stage in Iceland's winter-sports capital, including international freeski and snowboard competitions. Tour operators offer ways to get out into gloriously wintry landscapes (like dog sledding, snowmobiling, and super-Jeep or helicopter tours). Rug up!

Summer Arts Festival CULTURAL
(Listasumar; www.listasumar.is; ⌚Jul/Aug) Over six weeks from mid-July into August, Akureyri celebrates the arts with exhibitions, events and concerts.

Akureyri Town Festival CULTURAL
(⌚Aug) Akureyri's biggest summertime fiesta, celebrating the city's birthday on the last weekend of August with various concerts, exhibitions and events.

Sleeping

Akureyri's accommodation scene has undergone a transformation in recent years, with a slew of new, high-quality options. That said, the town still fills up in summer – book ahead.

Akureyri Backpackers HOSTEL €
(☎571 9050; www.akureyribackpackers.com; Hafnarstræti 98; dm kr5800-6300, d without bathroom kr20,300) Supremely placed in the town's heart, this backpackers has a chilled travellers' vibe and includes tour-booking service and popular bar. Rooms are spread over three floors: four- to eight-bed dorms, plus private rooms with made-up beds on the top floor. Minor gripe: all showers are in the basement, as is a free sauna (toilets and sinks on all levels, however).

There's a small kitchen and a laundry. Linen hire (in dorms) costs kr990; breakfast is kr1170.

Akureyri HI Hostel HOSTEL €
(Stórholt; ☎462 3657; www.hostel.is; Stórholt 1; dm kr4550, d with/without bathroom kr18,350/15,350; ⌚Jan–mid-Dec; @) Within the city limits though slightly removed from the action, this friendly, well-run hostel is a 15-minute walk north of the centre. There's a TV lounge and two kitchens in the main house (rooms all have TV), a barbecue deck and two self-contained cottages sleeping up to eight. The owner happily imparts local knowledge. Check-in time (from 3pm) strictly enforced.

HI members get a kr700 discount; linen can be hired.

City Campsite CAMPGROUND €
(Þórunnarstræti; sites per person kr1300, plus lodging tax per site kr100; ⏲ Jun–mid-Sep) This central site is popular for its location, not its charm. It has a washing machine, small dining area and showers (kr300), plus a car-free policy (except for loading and unloading; campervans accepted). Note: no kitchen. Handily, it's close to the swimming pool and a supermarket.

Hamrar Campsite CAMPGROUND €
(☎ 461 2264; www.hamrar.is; sites per person kr1300, plus lodging tax per site kr100; ⏲ mid-May–mid-Oct) This huge site, 1.5km south of town in a leafy setting in Kjarnaskógur woods, has newer facilities than the city campsite, and mountain views. There's a hostel-style building here that has the cheapest beds in town: mattresses on the floor in a sleeping loft for kr2000.

★ **Skjaldarvík** GUESTHOUSE €€
(☎ 552 5200; www.skjaldarvik.is; s/d without bathroom incl breakfast kr18,900/23,900; @) A slice of guesthouse nirvana, Skjaldarvík lies in a bucolic farm setting 6km north of town. It's owned by a young family and features quirky design details (plants sprouting from shoes, vintage typewriters as artwork on the walls). Plus: bumper breakfast buffet, horse-riding and buggy tours, mountain-bike rental, hotpot, and honesty bar in the comfy lounge.

★ **Guesthouse Hvítahúsið** GUESTHOUSE €€
(☎ 869 9890; www.guesthousenorth.is; Gilsbakkavegur 13; d without bathroom kr15,100-16,400) In an elevated, hidden residential pocket behind Kaupvangsstræti, the 'White House' shines with the personal touch of its stylish owner, Guðrún. There are five rooms, plus kitchen with free tea and coffee (note: no breakfast served). Attic rooms are the pick – one has a balcony.

★ **Halllandsnes** APARTMENT €€
(☎ 895 6029; www.halllandsnes.is; Rte 1; apt from kr28,000) There's an unexpected touch of the Mediterranean at this outstanding property 6km east of Akureyri along Rte 1. Its whitewashed buildings and delightful outdoor area enjoy sweeping fjord views, while inside are impeccable, well-furnished apartments with quality appliances, full kitchen including dishwasher, and washer-dryer – you may not want to leave. Each apartment sleeps four or six in comfort.

★ **Sæluhús** APARTMENT €€
(☎ 412 0800; www.saeluhus.is; Sunnutröð; studio/house kr25,700/49,000) This awesome mini-village of modern studios and houses is perfect for a few days' R & R. Each house may be better equipped than your own back home: three bedrooms (sleeping seven), kitchen, washing machine and verandah with hot tub and barbecue. Smaller studios are ideal for couples, with kitchen and access to a laundry (some have hot tub, but these cost extra).

★ **Icelandair Hotel Akureyri** HOTEL €€
(☎ 518 1000; www.icelandairhotels.com; Þingvallastræti 23; d from kr28,100; @) This high-class hotel showcases Icelandic designers and artists among its fresh, white-and-caramel-toned decor; rooms are compact but well-designed. Added extras: outdoor terrace, good on-site restaurant, and lounge (p250) serving high tea of an afternoon and happy-hour cocktails in the early evening.

Hrafninn GUESTHOUSE €€
(☎ 462 2300; www.hrafninn.is; Brekkugata 4; s/d kr23,800/27,300) Branding itself as a 'boutique guesthouse', central Hrafninn (the Raven) feels like an elegant manor house without being pretentious or stuffy. Over three floors, all 12 rooms have bathroom and TV; the common areas feature some cool artworks. There is a small communal kitchenette for guests. Note: no breakfast served.

Hótel Akureyri HOTEL €€
(☎ 462 5600; www.hotelakureyri.is; Hafnarstræti 67; d incl breakfast from kr18,000) Compact, well-equipped rooms are found at this boutique hotel, under friendly, service-minded family ownership and handily placed for the bus station. Front rooms have watery views, back rooms have an outlook on lush greenery (it's worth paying a little extra for fjord views).

Hotel Natur HOTEL €€
(☎ 467 1070; www.hotelnatur.com; Þórisstaðir; s/d incl breakfast kr19,250/27,500) About 15km east of Akureyri along Rte 1, this family-run property offers Nordic simplicity in its minimalist rooms, a huge dining space and breathtaking fjord views. The main accommodation is housed in the farm's old cow barn (but you'd never guess!). Nice attention is given to recreation facilities, including a cool 'sightseeing tower', walking trails, hotpot and billiard table.

Our Guesthouse GUESTHOUSE €€
(☎461 1200; www.ourguesthouse.is; Hafnarstræti 82; dm kr5500, d kr16,600-25,500) Every bus traveller's dream: a decent guesthouse at the bus station. It has a variety of bed options: dorm, rooms with shared bathroom, suite with private bathroom, family- sized apartment. Kitchen access; no breakfast served.

Hótel Edda HOTEL €€
(☎444 4900; www.hoteledda.is; entry on Þórunnarstræti 14; d with/without bathroom kr28,200/17,700; ⊙mid-Jun–late Aug; @) With 200-plus rooms, this vast summer hotel in the local boarding school is not somewhere you'll feel the personal touch. The new wing is modern with bright, well-equipped rooms (bathroom, TV); the cheaper old wing has shared bathrooms and a dated feel. Communal lounge areas are lovely. It's a short walk to the pool and botanical gardens.

Breakfast costs kr2050; there's a well-regarded dinner buffet too (kr6300).

Hótel Kea HOTEL €€€
(☎460 2000; www.keahotels.is; Hafnarstræti 87-89; d incl breakfast kr35,500; @) Akureyri's largest year-round hotel (104 rooms) and popular with groups, super-central Kea has smart business-style rooms with good facilities (including minibar and tea-/coffee-making facilities). There's little local character about it, but some rooms have balconies and fjord views. On site is Múlaberg, a smart restaurant, plus a cosy lounge, but for our money the Icelandair hotel is a fresher (cheaper) option.

TIPS: AKUREYRI ACCOMMODATION

- There are plenty of options outside the town centre – Akureyri is surrounded by excellent rural farmstay properties (you'll need your own car for these). Consult the handy Icelandic Farm Holidays booklet or website (www.farmholidays.is).
- Most accommodation is open year-round (winter weekends are especially busy with skiers).
- The tourist office website (www.visitakureyri.is) lists most options in the area. Knowledgeable staff here may be able to help if you arrive without an accommodation booking (kr500 reservation fee), but only if they have time – which is not common, so don't rely on this service! (We don't recommend arriving in town without a booking.)
- Check accommodation websites for up-to-date rates and low-season discounts.

Eating

There's a surprising array of options, and they get busy – in summer it pays to make dinner reservations. Fast-food-style places cluster around the east side of Ráðhústorg.

★**Berlin** CAFE €
(Skipagata 4; breakfast kr750-1690; ⊙7am-6pm;) Breakfast served all day? Hello Berlin! If you need a fix of bacon and eggs or avocado on toast, this cosy timber-lined cafe is your spot. Good coffee is a bonus, and you can linger over waffles with caramel sauce too. From 11.30am the menu adds lunch-y offerings such as vegetable dhal and chicken wings.

Blaá Kannan CAFE €
(Hafnarstræti 96; lunchtime buffet kr1600; ⊙9am-11.30pm Mon-Fri, from 10am Sat & Sun) Prime people-watching is on offer at this much-loved cafe (the Blue Teapot, in the dark-blue Cafe Paris building) on the main drag. The interior is timber-lined and blinged up with chandeliers; the menu offers panini and bagels, and there's a cabinet full of sweet treats. It's a popular spot for late-night coffee or wine.

Café Laut CAFE €
(Eyrarlandsvegur 30; lunch buffet kr1600; ⊙10am-8pm Jun-Sep) What could be better than a designer cafe in a botanical garden? This cafe has gorgeous picture windows, good coffee, a big sun terrace and a lunchtime soup-and-salad buffet, as well as bagels and panini.

Brynja ICE CREAM €
(Aðalstræti 3; ice cream from kr400; ⊙9am-11pm May, 9am-11.30pm Jun-Aug, 11am-11pm Sep-Apr;) This legendary sweet shop is known across Iceland for the best ice cream in the country (it's made with milk, not cream). It's 500m downhill from the botanical garden.

Serrano FAST FOOD €
(www.serrano.is; Ráðhústorg 7; meals kr1400-1700; ⊙11am-9pm Mon-Sat, from noon Sun) Like your food fast, but fresher than you've been encountering at all those N1 grill-bars? Hit up

Serrano for a bumper burrito, made to order; you can also nosh on tacos and quesadillas, or go green with salads.

★ Strikið INTERNATIONAL €€
(☎462 7100; www.strikid.is; Skipagata 14; lunch kr2400-3200, dinner mains kr3800-6200; ⏲11.30am-10pm Mon-Thu, to 11.30pm Fri & Sat) Huge windows with fjord views lend a magical glitz to this 5th-floor restaurant, and the cool cocktails help things along. The menu showcases prime Icelandic produce (reindeer burger, super-fresh sushi, lamb shoulder, shellfish soup). Passionfruit crème brûlée makes for a sweet end. The three-course signature menu is decent value at kr7600.

Noa Seafood Restaurant SEAFOOD €€
(Örkin hans Nóa; ☎461 2100; www.noa.is; Hafnarstræti 22; mains kr3800-7400; ⏲6-10pm) Part gallery, part furniture store, part restaurant – 'Noah's Ark' is certainly unique, and offers a simple food concept done well. The menu features a selection of fresh fish options, which are pan-fried and served with vegetables, with the pan brought to the table. Classic, effective, tasty. Note that there are quality beef and lamb dishes for non-fish-fans. Bookings recommended.

Icelandair Hotel Akureyri DESSERTS €€
(www.icelandairhotels.com; Þingvallastræti 23; high tea kr2500; ⏲high tea 2-5.30pm) Suffering afternoon sluggishness? Get your sugar rush on courtesy of the great-value high tea served every afternoon in the smart lounge of the Icelandair hotel. You'll be served a three-tiered tray of delight: savoury, sweet and more sweet (coffee/tea included, champagne optional). You're welcome.

If you're after harder stuff, the bar is open from 11.30am to midnight and has happy hour from 4pm to 6pm. The kitchen closes around 9pm.

Greifinn INTERNATIONAL €€
(☎460 1600; www.greifinn.is; Glerárgata 20; mains kr1890-4290; ⏲11.30am-10pm; 👪) Family friendly and *always* full to bursting, Greifinn is one of the most popular spots in town. The menu favours comfort food above all: ribs and wings, juicy burgers, pizzas, pastas, milkshakes and devilish ice-cream desserts. Takeaway available.

Akureyri Fish Restaurant FISH & CHIPS €€
(☎414 6050; ww.reykjavikfish.is; Skipagata 12; mains kr1400-3900; ⏲11am-10pm) The short blackboard at this bustling, casual place highlights piscatorial pleasures: fish and chips is the bestseller, or there's oven-baked salmon, crumbed cod, fish soup, fish burger, mussels and *plokkfiskur* (a tasty, traditional, creamy mashed-fish stew served with rye bread). Fish and chips taste good washed down with local beers.

Hamborgarafabrikkan FAST FOOD €€
(☎575 7575; www.fabrikkan.is; cnr Hafnarstræti & Kaupvangsstræti; burger & fries kr1995-2795; ⏲11.30am-10.30pm Jun-Aug, shorter hours Sep-May; 📶👪) Iceland is one of few countries without McDonald's, but who needs them? Part of a small chain, the Hamburger Factory gives you a choice of 15 square-patty bun-fillings (primarily beef, but also lamb, chicken or portobello mushroom options). Salads, spare ribs and classic desserts (banana split!) round out the menu.

Indian Curry Hut INDIAN €€
(Hafnarstræti 100b; dishes kr1895-2495; ⏲11.30am-1.30pm Tue-Fri, 5.30-9pm Tue-Sun) Add a little heat to a chilly evening with a flavourful curry from this takeaway hut.

Rub23 INTERNATIONAL €€€
(☎462 2223; www.rub23.is; Kaupvangsstræti 6; lunch kr1990-3190, dinner mains kr4290-6690; ⏲11.30am-2pm Mon-Fri, plus 5.30-10pm daily) This sleek, seafood-showcasing restaurant has a decidedly Japanese flavour, but also promotes its use of 'rubs' or marinades (along the lines of sweet mango chilli or citrus rosemary). At dinner, there's a confusing array of menus (including a 'summer menu', sushi menu and tasting menus) – it's a good thing that the food is first-rate. Bookings advised.

Self-Catering

Akureyri has a few supermarkets, but none are very central.

Bónus SUPERMARKET €
(Langholt; ⏲11am-6.30pm Mon-Thu, 10am-7.30pm Fri, 10am-6pm Sat, noon-6pm Sun) Cut-price supermarket.

Samkaup-Strax SUPERMARKET €
(Byggðavegur 98; ⏲9am-11pm Mon-Fri, 10am-11pm Sat & Sun) Near the campsite (p248) west of the centre.

Nettó SUPERMARKET €
(Glerárgata; ⏲10am-7pm) In the Glerártorg shopping mall.

WORTH A TRIP

HRÍSEY

Iceland's second-largest offshore island (after Heimaey) is the peaceful, low-lying Hrísey (population 166), easily reached from the mainland. Thrust out into the middle of Eyjafjörður, the island enjoys spectacular panoramas and is especially noted as a breeding ground and protected area for ptarmigan, as well as being home to an enormous colony of Arctic terns. Tame ptarmigan frequent the village streets. From here, three marked **nature trails** loop around the southeastern part of the island and lead to some good viewpoints.

There's a small **information office** (☎695 0077; ⏱1-5pm Jun-Aug) inside Hús Hákarla-Jörundur, a small museum (admission kr500) on shark-fishing beside the church in the picturesque village where the boat docks. Not to be missed are the tons-of-fun 40-minute **tractor trips** (☎695 0077; adult/child kr1300/free) which plough across the island, passing all the important landmarks. They leave regularly from the boat dock, generally at 10am, noon, 2pm and 4pm daily in summer.

While a leisurely half-day is enough to explore the island, consider staying overnight for a more authentic glimpse of island life. The website www.visithrisey.is outlines a couple of houses for rent on the island. There's a simple **campground** (Austurvegur; sites per person kr1400; ⏱Jun-Aug) with its reception and amenities at the modern swimming-pool complex. Like staying in a comfy share-house, **Wave Guesthouse** (☎695 2277; www.waveguesthouse.is; Austurvegur 9; d without bathroom kr18,500) offers three doubles and one twin room. All share a kitchen, lounge and bathroom.

Verbúðin 66 (☎467 1166; Sjávargata; meals kr1500-2600; ⏱11am-8.30pm Jun-Aug) is asmall, cosy restaurant is close to the boat dock and has a simple lunchtime menu of soup and sandwiches, plus burgers and catch of the day. For self-caterers the village store, **Hríseyjarbúðin** (Norðurvegur; ⏱11am-6pm Mon-Fri, 1-4pm Sat & Sun) sells supplies.

The passenger ferry **Sævar** (☎695 5544; adult/child kr1500/750) runs between Árskógssandur and Hrísey (15 minutes) at least seven times daily year-round; see www.hrisey.is for schedules. Bus 78 from Akureyri doesn't drive into the village at Árskógssandur – it stops about 1km from the ferry harbour.

Drinking & Nightlife

An evening stroll down Hafnarstræti will present you with a few good options, and a chance to see where the crowds are.

Akureyri Backpackers BAR
(www.akureyribackpackers.com; Hafnarstræti 98; ⏱7.30am-11pm Sun-Thu, to 1am Fri & Sat) Always a hub of convivial main-street activity, the fun, timber-clad bar at Akureyri Backpackers is beloved of both travellers and locals for its occasional live music, good-value burgers (and weekend brunches) and wide beer selection – this is a fine spot to sample the local microbrews, Kaldi and Einstök.

Götubarinn BAR
(Hafnarstræti 95; ⏱5pm-1am Thu, to 3am Fri & Sat) The locals' favourite drinking spot, fun, central Götubarinn (the Street Bar) has a surprising amount of cosiness and charm for a place that closes at 3am. There's timber, mirrors, couches and even a downstairs piano for late-night singalongs.

R5 BAR
(www.r5.is; Ráðhústorg 5; ⏱5pm-1am Mon-Thu, to 3am Fri & Sat) An easy-breezy stop for an evening drink, convivial R5 has a mixed bag of decor (tiles, carpeted banquettes, timber tables) and an array of Euro brews, including local drops. Occasional live music, too.

Entertainment

★Græni Hatturinn LIVE MUSIC
(http://graenihatturinn.is; Hafnarstræti 96) Tucked down a lane beside Blaá Kannan, this intimate venue is the best place in town to see live music – and one of the best in the country. If you get the chance, buy a ticket to anything going.

Hof MUSIC, PERFORMING ARTS
(☎450 1000; www.mak.is; Strandgata 12) Modern Hof is a cultural centre for music and other performing arts. Along with conference and exhibition facilities and a good daytime restaurant (1862 Nordic Bistro), it's also home to Akureyri's tourist office; ask here about any scheduled performances.

(Continued on page 256)

1

OZZO PHOTOGRAPHY/500PX ©

1. Ice cave, Vatnajökull **2.** Eyjafjallajökull glacier
3. Farmhouse at foot of Hekla volcano **4.** Magni

3

STOCKWITHME/SHUTTERSTOCK ©

Fire & Ice

'Land of fire and ice' might be an overused marketing slogan, but it's not hyperbole. Serene, majestic scenery belies Iceland's fiery heart – there are some 30 active volcanoes, and many of them lie under thick ice. When their fire-breathing fury is unleashed, the world often has no choice but to take notice (remember Eyjafjallajökull?).

Vatnajökull

The island's ice queen is Europe's largest ice cap and the namesake for its largest national park (p326). Don't miss the chance to explore this endless kingdom of white aboard a snowmobile.

Eyjafjallajökull

We've all heard the name (or at least heard people try to pronounce the name) of the treacherous eruption that spewed impenetrable tufts of ash over Europe in 2010, causing the cancellation of thousands of flights (p142).

Hekla & Katla

Like wicked stepsisters from some Icelandic fairy tale, Hekla (p135) and Katla (p160) are volatile beasts that dominate many of the southern vistas, threatening to belch forth steam, smoke and oozing lava that melts the nearby glaciers and floods the southern plains.

Snæfellsjökull

Jules Verne's famous journey to the centre of the earth starts here – the Snæfellsnes Peninsula's prominent glacial fist (p189) that can be easily glimpsed from Reykjavík on clear days.

Magni & Móði

Iceland's newest mountains (p144) were formed during the eruptions of 2010. Bring a pack of *pýlsur* (hot dogs) with you as you mount Magni – the still-steaming earth will cook them in no time flat.

Icelandic Culture

Weather not conducive for hiking? Never fear – let Iceland's rich culture and creativity take you places. There's a storytelling heritage forged by sagas; music and design that channel nature in inspiring ways; and a celebration of both tradition and experimentation. Above all, it's a willingness to wear your Icelandic identity on your sleeve (or in your knitwear).

BRAGI THOR JOSEFSSON/GETTY IMAGES ©

CHRISTIAN GEHRIG/500PX ©

1. Reykjavík Culture Night
Reykjavikers gather each year in mid-August to celebrate Culture Night (Menningarnótt; p26).

2. Lopapeysur
Locals and visitors alike can be seen wearing these traditional jumpers (p94) made from Icelandic wool.

3. Harpa
Reykjavík's sparkling concert hall (p59) was designed by Henning Larsen Architects, Batteríið Architects and artist Olafur Eliasson.

4. Skyr
This rich and creamy yoghurt-like Icelandic staple (p383) is a must-try.

ROSEMARY CALVERT/GETTY IMAGES ©

 (Continued from page 251)

Shopping

Several shops on Hafnarstræti sell traditional *lopapeysur* Icelandic woollen sweaters, books, knick-knacks and souvenirs. Remember to look for Icelandic-made knitwear (some is now mass-produced in China) and ask about the tax-free scheme.

The Glerártorg shopping mall, on Rte 1 about 1km north of the town centre, is home to a large Nettó supermarket.

★Geysir CLOTHING
(www.geysir.com; Hafnarstræti 98; 9am-10pm) We covet everything in this unique store, from the woollen blankets to the hipster-chic *lopapeysur* and the old Iceland maps. It looks like it dresses all the stylish lumbersexuals in town.

Sjoppan DESIGN
(www.facebook.com/sjoppanvoruhus; Kaupvangs stræti 21) Cute as a button, this tiny store dispenses cool design items and gifts from a hutch out front (you ring the bell for service). It's across from the art museum (p243). Hours vary; check out its Facebook page for these and other details.

Eymundsson BOOKS, SOUVENIRS
(www.eymundsson.is; Hafnarstræti 91-93; 9am-10pm Mon-Fri, 10am-10pm Sat, noon-10pm Sun) First-rate bookshop selling maps, souvenir books and a wide selection of international magazines. There's a tasty cafe on site.

Háaloftið ANTIQUES
(Hafnarstræti 19; 1-5pm Mon-Fri, 11am-3pm Sat) Down near Brynja ice-cream store, 'the Attic', filled with antique and vintage finds, is a rummager's delight. Browse the books, records, porcelain and bric-a-brac for a perfectly unique souvenir. Is there a way to get vintage snowshoes home in your suitcase? Note: cash only.

Christmas Garden GIFTS & SOUVENIRS
(Jólagarðurinn; 10am-9pm Jun-Aug, 2-9pm Sep-Dec, 2-6pm Jan-May) If you can handle the Christmas cheer out of season, this multilevel gingerbread house sells a super-festive selection of locally made decorations and traditional Icelandic Christmas foods. It's 10km south of Akureyri on Rte 821. There's a sweet store next door selling homewares and food products, and out back is possibly Iceland's cutest food hut selling waffles and toffee apples.

Vínbúðin ALCOHOL
(Hólabraut 16; 11am-6pm Mon-Thu & Sat, to 7pm Fri) Government-run alcohol shop.

Information

EMERGENCY

Police (112; nonemergency 464 7700; Þórunnarstræti 138)

MEDICAL SERVICES

Akureyri Hospital (463 0100; www.sak.is; Eyrarlandsvegur) Just south of the botanical gardens.

Apótekarinn (Hafnarstræti 95; 9am-5.30pm Mon-Fri) Central pharmacy.

On-Call Doctor Service (1700; 24hr) Twenty-four-hour number; only for urgent issues.

Primary Health Care Clinic (Heilsugæslustöðin; 460 4600; 3rd fl, Hafnarstræti 99; 8am-4pm Mon-Fri)

MONEY

Banks (open 9am to 4pm) are clustered around Ráðhústorg. All offer foreign exchange and have 24-hour ATMs.

POST

Main post office (Strandgata 3; 9am-6pm Mon-Fri)

TOURIST INFORMATION

Tourist Office (450 1050; www.visitakureyri.is; Hof, Strandgata 12; 8am-6.30pm mid-Jun–mid-Sep, shorter hours rest of year) This friendly, efficient office is inside **Hof** (p251). Staff may also be able to help if you arrive without an accommodation booking (kr500 reservation fee), but only if they have time. (We don't recommend arriving in town without a booking.) There's a complex array of opening hours outside of summer, with the office generally closing at 4pm in winter, 5pm in spring and autumn.

Getting There & Away

AIR

Akureyri Airport (www.akureyriairport.is) is 3km south of the city centre.

Air Iceland (460 7000; www.airiceland.is) runs flights up to eight times daily between Akureyri and Reykjavík (45 minutes), and daily in summer (three times a week in winter) from Akureyri to Grímsey (30 minutes). There's also a weekday link with Vopnafjörður and Þórshöfn in northeast Iceland. All other domestic (and international) flights are routed via Reykjavík.

Icelandair (www.icelandair.com) has one weekly flight from June to September from Keflavík, meaning international travellers arriving into Iceland don't need to travel to Reykjavík's domestic airport to connect to Akureyri. These flights are only bookable as part of an international flight to and from Iceland with Icelandair.

BUS

Bus services are ever-changing in Iceland, so it pays to get up-to-date information on schedules and fares, from the companies themselves (websites are handy) or from tourist information centres.

Akureyri's **bus station** (Hafnarstræti 82) is the hub for bus travel in the north provided by SBA-Norðurleið and Sterna; Strætó operates from a stop in front of **Hof** (p251). (Note: there is talk of building a central bus terminal that will serve all operators, so it pays to double-check departure points.)

If you need to return to Reykjavík, consider taking an all-terrain bus route through the interior highlands, rather than travelling along Rte 1.

SBA-Norðurleið (www.sba.is) services (departing from Hafnarstræti bus terminal):

- Bus 62 to Mývatn (kr4000, two hours, one daily June to mid-September).
- Bus 62 to Egilsstaðir (kr9600, four hours, one daily June to mid-September).
- Bus 62 to Höfn (kr19,000, 9½ hours, one daily June to mid-September).
- Bus 610a to Reykjavík via the Kjölur route (kr17,000, 10½ hours, one daily mid-June to mid-September).
- Bus 641 to Húsavík (kr3800, 1¾ hours, one daily mid-June to August).
- Bus 641 to Ásbyrgi (kr6900, three hours, one daily mid-June to August).
- Bus 641 to Dettifoss (kr9900, 4½ hours, one daily mid-June to August).

Sterna (☎551 1166; www.icelandbybus.is; Hafnarstræti 77) services (beginning at **City Campsite** (p248) before picking up from the Hafnarstræti bus terminal):

- Bus 60a to Reykjavík via Rte 1 (kr8800, 5½ hours, one daily mid-June to early September).

Strætó (☎540 2700; www.straeto.is) services generally run year-round (departing from the **Hof** building):

- Bus 56 to Mývatn (kr2520, 1½ hours, two daily) Drops to four weekly services in winter.
- Bus 56 to Egilsstaðir (kr7560, 3½ hours, one daily) Drops to four weekly services in winter.
- Bus 57 to Reykjavík via Rte 1 (kr9240, 6½ hours, two daily)
- Bus 78 to Siglufjörður (kr2520, 70 minutes, three daily Monday to Friday, one daily Sunday) Runs via Dalvík and Ólafsfjörður.
- Bus 79 to Húsavík (kr2520, 1¼ hours, three daily) Winter services are reduced on weekends (no services Saturday, two on Sunday).
- Bus 79 to Þórshöfn (kr7140, four hours, one daily Sunday to Friday summer, three weekly winter) This service only operates beyond Húsavík to Þórshöfn (via Ásbyrgi, Kópasker and Raufarhöfn) if prebooked. Call Strætó at least four hours before departure.

Airport Express North (www.airportexpress.is) services (from Hof building):

- Direct bus service once a day (June to September) linking Akureyri with Keflavík airport (kr11,000, six hours). The Akureyri–Keflavík service drives through the night. Contact the bus line for less-frequent services in other months.

CAR

After Reykjavík, Akureyri is Iceland's second transport hub. There are several car-hire agencies – all the major firms have representation at the airport. For a fee, most companies will let you pick up a car in Akureyri and drop it off in Reykjavík or vice versa.

Check out www.samferda.is for information about car-pooling, or check hostel noticeboards.

Getting Around

Central Akureyri is quite compact and easy to get around on foot.

BUS

There's a free town bus service on four routes, running regularly from 7am to 7pm weekdays (until 10pm on one route) – look for the yellow buses. Not all routes run on weekends. Unfortunately, no route goes to the airport.

CAR

Akureyri has a unique parking system for Iceland (one that many northern Europeans will be familiar with). When parking in the town centre, you must set a plastic parking clock indicating the time you parked, and display it on the dashboard of your car (so as to be seen through the windshield).

Parking is free, but spaces are signposted with maximum parking times (from 15 minutes to two hours, enforced from 10am to 4pm weekdays). Note: '1 klst' means one hour. You'll be fined if your car overstays the advertised time limit. Pick up a parking clock (free) at the tourist office, banks and gas stations. If this sounds too complicated, there is untimed parking by **Hof** (p251).

TAXI

The **BSO** (☎461 1010; www.bso.is; Strandgata) taxi stand is opposite the **Hof** (p251). Taxis may be booked 24 hours a day.

BSO's website (and a board at the taxi stand) outlines the cost to hire a car and driver to visit nearby sightseeing destinations.

NEW TUNNEL

A new 7.5km-long road tunnel is being built on the eastern side of Eyjafjörður, which will shorten the Rte 1 journey to Húsavík by about 16km. Drivers will be able to avoid the mountain pass Víkurskarð (often blocked by winter snows), and the tunnel will ensure easier winter access to Akureyri's services for residents living east of the town. The tunnel is being built under Vaðlaheiði mountain; it's had a few hiccups since construction began, but is expected to be completed in 2017.

Around Akureyri

If you have time and wheels, it's well worth getting off the Ring Road to explore the region around Akureyri's fjord, Eyjafjörður.

Eyjafjarðarsveit is the valley south of Akureyri, accessed by Rtes 821 and 829. The Eyjafjarðará river runs through fertile farmland with idyllic pastoral views and mountain backdrops.

Eyjafjörður's **eastern shore** is much quieter than its western counterpart, and offers a few good places to pause among the sweeping vistas, including the eclectic **Icelandic Folk & Outsider Art Museum** (Safnasafnið; www.safnasafnid.is; adult/child kr1000/free; ⏲10am-5pm mid-May–Aug), 12km from Akureyri on Rte 1.

Further north, Rte 83 branches off the Ring Road to lead you 20km north to the tiny, tidy fishing village of **Grenivík**, which has a spectacular outlook and good facilities: campground and pool, a small maritime museum, and a small supermarket with attached restaurant. En route (along Rte 83) are the photogenic turf roofs at **Laufás** (www.minjasafnid.is; Rte 83; adult/child kr1200/free; ⏲9am-5pm Jun-Aug) and the acclaimed stables of **Pólar Hestar** (☎463 3179; www.polarhestar.is; Rte 83; 2hr horse ride kr10,000).

Sleeping & Eating

There is a good deal of rural guesthouse accommodation in the Eyjafjarðará river valley. For other options, including camping opportunities, ask at Akureyri's tourist office (p256).

Nollur COTTAGES €€€

(www.nollur.is; 1-bedroom house per week from kr144,000) En route to Grenivík are the architect-designed holiday houses Nollur, rented by the week in high season (minimum two nights from September to May; all bookings done online) and enjoying outstanding views and plenty of creature comforts (including hot-pots). The company also offers high-end properties in Grenivík township.

★**Kaffi Kú** CAFE €

(www.kaffiku.is; Rte 829; dishes kr500-1950; ⏲10am-6pm Apr-Dec, 10am-6pm Sat & Sun Jan-Mar;) Kaffi Kú is a perfect pit stop in pastoral Eyjafjarðarsveit (11km from Akureyri). Dine above a high-tech cowshed (you can watch the cows queue to be milked by a 'robot') on excellent beef goulash or roast-beef bagels, plus waffles that pair perfectly with farm-fresh cream. For a small fee (kr300) you can go inside the cowshed.

Silva VEGETARIAN €€

(☎851 1360; www.silva.is; Rte 829; mains kr1790-3090; ⏲5-9pm Jun-Aug;) About 15km from Akureyri (south on Rte 829), Silva, a small and sweet restaurant with a focus on clean and green homemade dishes (including raw food), is a beacon for vegetarians and vegans. Raw pizzas, veggie burgers, carrot and blueberry cake, smoothies and juices – it all smacks of good health and local produce. Gluten-free options too.

It pays to book. Silva also has lovely self-contained cottages for rent.

Goðafoss

Travellers heading from Akureyri to Mývatn (or Akureyri to Húsavík if you take a small detour) will happen across heavenly waterfall Goðafoss, a magnet that pulls most motorists off the road for a closer look.

Goðafoss access is right on the Ring Road, just east of the Rte 85 turn-off to Húsavík. There are N1 petrol pumps here.

Buses between Akureyri and Mývatn stop here; some buses between Akureyri and Húsavík also stop (others travel Rte 85).

WORTH A TRIP

ALDEYARFOSS

If you're looking for more waterfall wonder after **Goðafoss** and have some time up your sleeve, photogenic **Aldeyarfoss** is worth the journey. It's 41km from the Ring Road on an unsealed road (Rte 842, just west of Goðafoss) and marks the northern entrance/exit of the long, lonely 4WD Sprengisandur route (Rte F26) across the interior highlands.

At the falls, the Skjálfandafljót river churns through a narrow passage and into a deep pool in a canyon lined with intriguing basalt column formations.

Route 842 is generally OK for non-4WDs but it pays to ask locally. Turn left at Mýri farm after about 37km; the last 3.5km to Aldeyarfoss' small parking area are quite rough (take it slowly). This is technically the beginning of the Sprengisandur route – do not venture any further than the falls without a 4WD.

★**Goðafoss** WATERFALL

Goðafoss (Waterfall of the Gods) rips straight through the Bárðardalur lava field along Rte 1. Although smaller and less powerful than some of Iceland's other chutes, it's definitely one of the most beautiful. There are two car parks: one on the Ring Road, the other down the road beside the petrol station. Take the path behind the falls for a less-crowded viewpoint.

Sleeping & Eating

Fosshóll GUESTHOUSE, CAMPGROUND €€

(☎464 3108; www.godafoss.is; sites per person kr1500, d with/without bathroom incl breakfast kr25,935/19,950; ⊗mid-May–mid-Sep) If the sound of pounding water puts you to sleep, a night in the (overpriced) rooms of sunny yellow Fosshóll, next to Goðafoss falls, might be for you. Ask about sleeping-bag rates to save money. There's a camping area, and an evening restaurant here too.

Tourist Complex CAFETERIA €

(Rte 1; ⊗8am-10pm) Right beside Goðafoss is a complex housing info, free wi-fi, a few groceries, a souvenir shop, public toilets and a decent cafeteria. The menu has soups, burgers, pizza etc, and a summer lunch buffet costing kr2990.

Getting There & Away

There are a number of options for reaching Grímsey. Air and boat excursions are normally only an option in summer months.

The Akureyri **tourist office** (p256) can help with information for a visit, or see www.akureyri.is/grimsey.

AIR

From mid-June to mid-August, Norlandair (www.norlandair.is) operates daily flights to/from Akureyri; the rest of the year there are three flights weekly. The bumpy 25-minute journey takes in the full length of Eyjafjörður and is an experience in itself. Ticketing is handled by **Air Iceland** (p256); one-way fares start at around kr12,000.

From mid-June to mid-August, Air Iceland offers half-day excursions from Akureyri (from kr26,000) that include flights and a couple of hours on the island (including a guided walk). You can also do the tour from Reykjavík, taking a short domestic flight first to Akureyri.

A couple of flightseeing operators offer the chance to land for a two-hour stint on the island, including **Mýflug Air** (p262) in Mývatn and **Circle Air** (p247) in Akureyri.

MÝVATN REGION

Undisputed gem of the northeast, Mývatn (pronounced *mee*-vaht) lake and the surrounding area are starkly beautiful, an otherworldly terrain of spluttering mudpots, weird lava formations, steaming fumaroles and volcanic craters, set around a bird-filled lake.

The Mývatn basin sits squarely on the Mid-Atlantic Ridge and the violent geological character of the area has produced an astonishing landscape unlike anywhere else in the country; this is the Iceland you've always imagined.

History & Geology

Ten thousand years ago the Mývatn basin was covered by an ice cap, which was destroyed by volcanic eruptions that also obliterated the lake at its base. The explosions formed the *móberg* peaks (flat-topped mountains formed by subglacial volcanic eruptions) south of today's lake, while volcanic activity to the east formed the Lúdent tephra complex (tephra is solid

GRÍMSEY

Best known as Iceland's only true piece of the **Arctic Circle**, the remote island of Grímsey, 40km from the mainland, is a lonely little place where birds outnumber people by about 10,000 to one. The island is small (5 sq km, with a year-round population of 60) but the welcome is big.

Grímsey's appeal probably lies less in the destination itself, and more in what it represents. Tourists flock here to snap up their 'I visited the Arctic Circle' certificate, pose for a photo with the 'You're standing on the Arctic Circle' monument and appreciate the windswept setting. Scenic coastal cliffs and dramatic basalt formations make a popular home for dozens of species of seabirds, including loads of puffins, plus the kamikaze Arctic tern. We're particularly fond of the anecdote that the airport runway has to be cleared of the terns a few minutes before aircraft are scheduled to arrive. A couple of notes to birders: puffins are not guaranteed beyond about 10 August (they usually arrive in April; viewing is best from May to July). Terns arrive in May and are pretty aggressive in July, when their chicks begin to be active; they commonly leave in early September. And remember to *take care* walking around cliff edges.

Arctic Trip (☎848 1696; www.arctictrip.is) offers some unique island insights, and the chance for a once-in-a-lifetime underwater adventure: Arctic diving in the presence of swimming puffins and guillemots. There are prerequisites, including Open Water scuba dive certification (PADI or the equivalent) and drysuit experience. Tours run from June to early August (two/three days kr230,000/330,000, including food and accommodation).

Snorkelling is also possible (kr49,000), and the company can help with regular island sightseeing too.

Sleeping & Eating

If sleeping inside the Arctic Circle sounds too good to pass up, follow the stairs up through the trapdoor at cosy **Gullsól** (☎467 3190; gullsol@visir.is; r without bathroom per person kr7000) to find teeny-tiny rooms perched above the island's gift shop (which opens in conjunction with ferry arrivals and serves snacks). The full kitchen is handy for self-caterers. Things are slightly more upmarket at **Básar** (☎467 3103; www.gistiheimilidbasar.is; s/d without bathroom incl breakfast kr12,000/17,000) right next to the airport. Sleeping-bag accommodation here is kr6000. There is a guest kitchen and lounge area. Meals can be arranged, as can sailing and sea-angling trips (with notice). There's a small campground (kr500 per person) by the community centre with very basic facilities.

Named after the Arctic tern, (*kría* in Icelandic), the island's only restaurant **Kríán** (☎467 3112; ⊙noon-9pm mid-May–early Sep) is open daily in summer, but has varied winter hours.

matter ejected into the air by an erupting volcano).

Another cycle of violent activity more than 6000 years later created the Ketildyngja volcano, 25km southeast of Mývatn. The lava from that crater flowed northwest along the Laxárdalur valley, and created a lava dam and a new, improved lake. After another millennium or so a volcanic explosion along the same fissure spewed out Hverfell, the classic tephra crater that dominates the modern landscape. Over the next 200 years, activity escalated along the eastern shore and craters were thrown up across a wide region, providing a steady stream of molten material flowing towards Öxarfjörður. The lava dam formed during the end of this cycle created the present Mývatn shoreline.

Between 1724 and 1729 the Mývatnseldar (Mývatn Fires) eruptions began at Leirhnjúkur, close to Krafla, northeast of the lake. This dramatic and sporadically active fissure erupted again in the 1970s (the Kröflueldar or Krafla Fires), with that episode lasting nine years.

In 1974 the area around Mývatn was set aside as the Mývatn-Laxá Nature Conservation Area, and the pseudo-crater field at Skútustaðir, at the southern end of the lake, is preserved as a national natural monument.

Tours

Tourism reigns supreme at Reykjahlíð and for travellers without transport there are numerous sightseeing tours in the area (some originate in Akureyri). Tours fill up fast dur-

It's an agreeable place with an outdoor deck enjoying views over the harbour. Soups and fish dishes are generally available. The Búðin **supermarket** (⊙noon-4pm Mon-Fri, 3-4pm Sat & Sun) is small but well-stocked. If it's closed when you need it, it's usually just a matter of letting a local know and they'll arrange for it to be opened (it's that kind of island).

Getting There & Away

There are a number of options for reaching Grímsey. Air and boat excursions are normally only an option in summer months.

The Akureyri **tourist office** (p256) can help with information for a visit, or see www.akureyri.is/grimsey.

Air From mid-June to mid-August, Norlandair (www.norlandair.is) operates daily flights to/from Akureyri; the rest of the year there are three flights weekly. The bumpy 25-minute journey takes in the full length of Eyjafjörður and is an experience in itself. Ticketing is handled by **Air Iceland** (☎460 7000; www.airiceland.is); one-way fares start at around kr12,000.

Day trips From mid-June to mid-August, Air Iceland offers half-day excursions from Akureyri (from kr26,000) that include flights and a couple of hours on the island (including a guided walk). You can also do the tour from Reykjavík, taking a short domestic flight first to Akureyri. A couple of flightseeing operators offer the chance to land for a two-hour stint on the island, including **Mýflug Air** (p262) in Mývatn and **Circle Air** (p247) in Akureyri.

Boat There is a year-round ferry service between Dalvík and Grímsey. From mid-May to August, the **Sæfari** (☎458 8970; www.saefari.is) ferry departs from Dalvík at 9am Monday, Wednesday and Friday, returning from Grímsey at 4pm (giving you four hours on the island if you're not overnighting). The journey takes three hours and costs kr4830/free per adult/child one way. In winter the ferry departure times remain the same; however, the ship immediately returns to Dalvík once cargo has been discharged and loaded.

If you're coming from Akureyri, the morning bus (Strætó's bus 78) won't get you to Dalvík in good time for the ferry's departure. Without your own wheels you'll need to spend the night before in Dalvík.

From Dalvík, **Arctic Sea Tours** (p240) organises a 10-hour day tour that utilises the Sæfari ferry and gives you four guided hours on Grímsey (kr25,000). **Ambassador** (p247) in Akureyri offers a summer-evening boat excursion with two hours on the island (adult/child kr29,990/16,990). **Gentle Giants** (p272) in Húsavík offers pricey rigid inflatable boat (RIB) day trips to Grímsey (kr72,300).

ing summer, so try to book at least a day before. The visitor centre (p263) can help with bookings.

A number of operators run super-Jeep tours into the highlands, to Askja (p348) and surrounds, from mid-June (when the route opens) until as late into September as the weather permits. From Akureyri it makes for a long day tour (up to 15 hours); 12-hour tours leave from Reykjahlíð. Tour companies pick up and drop off at the car park by the visitor centre.

Geo Travel ADVENTURE

(☎464 4442; www.geotravel.is) A small company owned by two well-connected local guys. They work with the local operators to offer year-round tours, from summer super-Jeep excursions to Askja and Holuhraun ☎(kr38,000), to Northern Lights tours (kr19,500), to winter hikes around Krafla (kr20,000).

Mývatn Activity – Hike&Bike ADVENTURE

(☎899 4845; www.hikeandbike.is; ⊙9am-5pm Jun-Aug) Hike&Bike has a booth by the Gamli Bærinn tavern in Reykjahlíð, offering tour bookings and mountain-bike rental (per day kr4500).

There's a summer program of cycling and hiking tours, including a four-hour walk to Hverfell and Dimmuborgir (p266) (kr12,500); a three-hour pedal through the backcountry (kr12,500); and an evening sightseeing cycle that ends with a soak at

Mývatn & Krafla

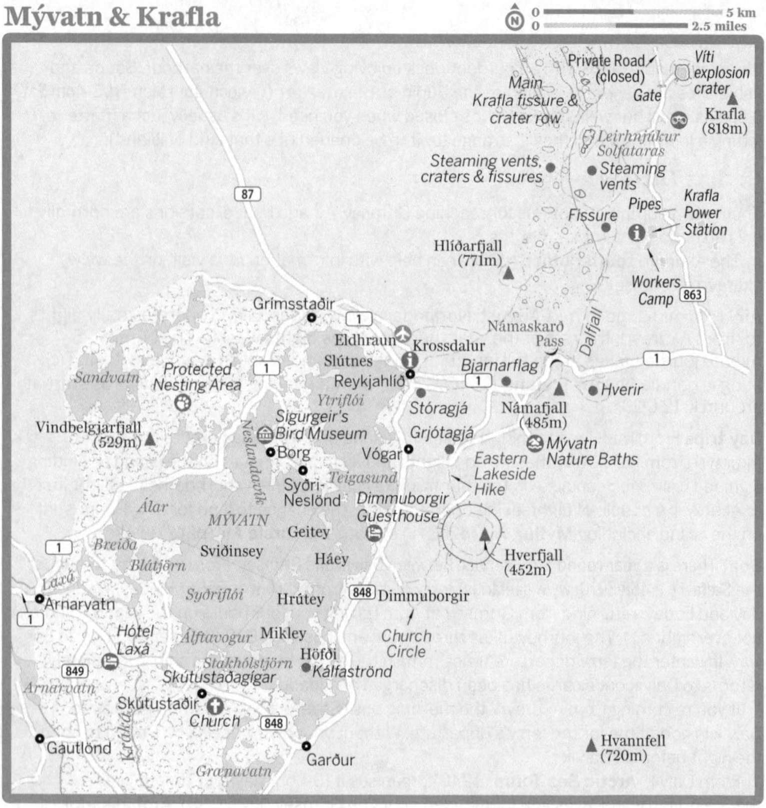

the Nature Baths (p268) (kr12,500, including admission).

Where the company shines is in the local network and knowledge, and the winter pursuits it can arrange (super-Jeep tours, dog sledding, snowshoeing around Dimmuborgir, cross-country skiing and snowmobiling on the frozen lake). It can put together packages that cover accommodation, too.

Saga Travel ADVENTURE
(☎558 8888; www.sagatravel.is) Saga Travel operates an array of fabulous year-round tours in the Mývatn area, including sightseeing, caving, birdwatching and lava walks (see the website for the full selection). Its Northern Lights tours offer photography tips. There is often the option of joining tours from Akureyri or Reykjahlíð.

SBA-Norðurleið BUS TOUR
(☎550 0700; www.sba.is) For an abridged bus tour of Mývatn's top sights, consider linking up with the sightseeing tour operated by SBA-Norðurleið. It starts in Akureyri, but you can hop aboard in Reykjahlíð (from Reykjahlíð at 12.30pm daily June to September: 3½-hour tour, kr8800). There is also a winter version, plus other sightseeing trips in the northeast.

Mýflug Air SCENIC FLIGHT
(☎464 4400; www.myflug.is; Reykjahlíð airport) Mýflug Air operates daily flightseeing excursions (weather permitting). A 20-minute trip over Mývatn and Krafla costs kr15,700; a two-hour 'super tour' (kr51,000) also includes Dettifoss, Ásbyrgi, Kverkfjöll, Herðubreið and Askja. You can also fly north for a one-hour stop in Grímsey (kr43,200).

Snowdogs DOG SLEDDING
(☎847 7199; www.snowdogs.is; tour adult/child kr30,000/15,000; ⊙Nov-Apr/May) On the remote farm Heiði, about 8km off the main road in southern Mývatn (take Rte 849 west

of Skútustaðir), Sæmi and his family run dog-sledding tours across the snow-white wilderness. Tours vary depending on the dogs, people, weather and trail conditions, but guests are generally on the snow for about 45 to 60 minutes, and cover around 8km.

Future plans include the potential for kennel visits; check the website.

Saltvík HORSE RIDING
(☎847 6515; www.saltvik.is; 2hr tour kr9500) Just south of Reykjahlíð, Saltvík operates horseback sightseeing tours around Mývatn (suitable for all skill levels, including beginners). Tours are generally daily at 10am, 2pm and 5pm mid-June to mid-September. Saltvík has a larger operation in Húsavík (p273).

Safarí Hestar HORSE RIDING
(☎464 4203; www.safarihorserental.com; 1/2hr tour kr7000/10,000) Scenic horse tours operate from Álftagerði III farm on the south side of the lake (400m west of Sel-Hótel (p267)) and take in the lakeshore and pseudocraters.

Sleeping & Eating

Mývatn's popularity means that room rates have soared; demand is far greater than supply, so be sure to book ahead. Most prices are very inflated, with €275 being the norm for a run-of-the-mill hotel double in summer's peak. Off-season rates are considerably cheaper. To save money at guesthouses, ask about sleeping-bag options.

Most places to stay and eat are located either in Reykjahlíð or at Vógar, on the lake's eastern shore, with additional options at Dimmuborgir and Skútustaðir. The large hotels all have restaurants.

The local food speciality is a moist, cake-like rye bread known as *hverabrauð* (often translated as 'geysir bread'). It's slow-baked underground using geothermal heat and is served in every restaurant in the area.

Information

Mývatnsstofa Visitor Centre (☎464 4390; www.visitmyvatn.is; Hraunvegur 8, Reykjahlíð; ⊙7.30am-6pm Jun-Aug, shorter hours Sep-May) This well-informed centre in Reykjahlíð (by the supermarket) has good displays on the local geology, and can book accommodation, tours and transport. Pick up a copy of the hugely useful *Mývatn* brochure, which gives a good overview of hiking trails in the area.

Because the Mývatn region is a protected nature reserve, there are rangers here too (from Umhverfisstofnun, the Environment Agency of Iceland), with a staffed desk from 9am to 6pm in summer.

All tours and buses leave from the car park here.

Getting There & Away

All buses pick up/drop off passengers at the **visitor centre** in Reykjahlíð; bus routes 62/62a, 56, 14/14a and 17/17a also stop in Skútustaðir, by the **Sel-Hótel** (p267).

SBA-Norðurleið (www.sba.is) services:

- Bus 62a to Akureyri (kr4000, 1¾ hours, one daily June to mid-September).
- Bus 62 to Egilsstaðir (kr6100, two hours, one daily June to mid-September).
- Bus 62 to Höfn (kr15,500, 7½ hours, one daily June to mid-September).
- Bus 650 to Húsavík (kr3500, 40 minutes, one daily mid-June to August).
- Bus 661 to Krafla (kr1900, 15 minutes, two daily mid-June to early September).
- Bus 661 to Dettifoss (kr4100, one hour, one daily mid-June to early September) From Dettifoss you have the option of linking with bus 641a to Ásbyrgi, Húsavík or on to Akureyri.

Strætó (www.bus.is) services:

- Bus 56 to Akureyri (kr2520, 1½ hours, two daily) Drops to four weekly services in winter.
- Bus 56 to Egilsstaðir (kr5469, two hours, one daily) Drops to four weekly services in winter.

Reykjavík Excursions (www.re.is) services:

- Bus 14a to Landmannalaugar along the highland Sprengisandur route (kr16,500, 10 hours, one daily July to August).
- Bus 17a to Reykjavík along the highland Sprengisandur route (kr20,500, 11½ hours, one daily July to August).

Getting Around

There are wonderful hiking trails around Mývatn, but they're not all connected. Without wheels you may find yourself on long walks along the lakeshore road.

You might consider renting a car in Akureyri. During calmer weather, a good option is to hire a mountain bike from **Hike&Bike** (p261). The 36km ride around the lake can be done in a day.

If you need a taxi (June to August), call ☎893 4389.

Reykjahlíð

POP 150

Reykjahlíð, on the northeastern shore of Mývatn lake, is the main village and Mývatn's

MÝVATN ORIENTATION

Mývatn lake is encircled by a 36km sealed road (Rte 1 on the western and northern shores, and Rte 848 on the southern and eastern shoreline). The main settlement is Reykjahlíð, in the northeast corner – an information centre is here, as are most sleeping and eating options.

Most of the points of interest are linked by the lake's looping road, including the diverse lava formations in eastern Mývatn, the cluster of pseudocraters near southern Mývatn, and the bird-friendly marsh plains around western Mývatn.

In northern Mývatn, the Ring Road (Rte 1) veers east, away from Reykjahlíð, and takes you over the Námaskarð pass to the Hverir geothermal area. Then, a turn-off to the north (Rte 863) leads to Krafla, 14km from Reykjahlíð. Continue along the Ring Road and after another 20km you'll reach the turn-off (sealed Rte 862) to Dettifoss waterfall.

With your own vehicle this whole area can be explored in a day, but if you're using the bus or a bike allow two days. If you want to hike and explore more distant mountains and lava fields, allow at least three.

obvious base. There's little to it beyond a collection of guesthouses and hotels, a supermarket, petrol station and information centre.

Sleeping

Fosshótel plans to open a large new hotel in the northern reaches of Reykjahlíð in summer 2017; see www.fosshotel.is for details.

Bjarg CAMPGROUND €

(☎464 4240; ferdabjarg@simnet.is; site per person kr1600, d without bathroom kr15,900; ⊙mid-May–Sep) This campsite has a gorgeous, peaceful location on the Reykjahlíð lakeshore (almost opposite the supermarket) and features a kitchen tent, laundry service, tour-booking desk, summer rowboat rental and bike hire. Accommodation is also available in a couple of rooms in the main building. Note: no wi-fi.

Hlíð CAMPGROUND, GUESTHOUSE €

(☎464 4103; www.myvatnaccommodation.is; Hraunbrún; sites per person kr1600, dm kr5000, d incl breakfast kr25,000, cottage kr36,500; @) Sprawling, well-run Hlíð is 300m uphill from the church and offers a full spectrum: camping, sleeping-bag dorms and rooms with kitchen access, no-frills huts, self-contained cottages sleeping six, and en-suite guesthouse rooms. There's also a laundry, playground and bike hire.

Helluhraun 13 B&B €€

(☎464 4132; www.helluhraun13.blogspot.com; Helluhraun 13; d without bathroom incl breakfast kr19,000; ⊙Jun-Aug) Ásdis is the sunny host at this small, homely guesthouse with lava-field views. There are just three rooms and one bathroom, but they're bright, spotless and tastefully decorated.

Eldá GUESTHOUSE €€

(☎464 4220; www.elda.is; Helluhraun 9; s/d without bathroom incl breakfast kr17,500/21,500; @) This friendly operation owns three properties along Helluhraun and offers cosy, no-frills accommodation. There are guest kitchens and TV lounges, and buffet breakfast is included. All guests check in at Helluhraun 9.

Vógar GUESTHOUSE, CAMPGROUND €€

(☎464 4399; www.vogahraun.is; Vógar; sites per person/tent kr1500/500, guesthouse d with/without bathroom kr23,600/15,700) There's a range of options here, 2.5km south of Reykjahlíð: camping, hostel-style accommodation in utilitarian prefab huts (double kr11,600), and a newer block of compact guesthouse rooms, with and without bathroom. Sleeping bags reduce the price, as does staying a second night. All rooms have kitchen access; rooms with private bathroom include breakfast.

Vogafjós Guesthouse GUESTHOUSE €€€

(☎464 3800; www.vogafjos.net; Vógar; d incl breakfast from kr29,000) Fresh scents of pine and cedar fill the air in these log-cabin rooms (cosy with underfloor heating), set in a lava field 2.5km south of Reykjahlíð and a few minutes' walk from the Vogafjós restaurant, where breakfast is served. Most rooms sleep two, with family rooms also available.

Hótel Reynihlíð HOTEL €€€

(☎464 4170; www.myvatnhotel.is; s/d incl breakfast from kr28,800/34,400; @) The grand dame of Mývatn hotels is a smartly dressed 41-

room affair. The superior rooms aren't a noticeable upgrade; they only have slightly better views, plus a little more space. Also here is a restaurant, plus lounge-bar and sauna. We like the nine rooms at its cosier annexe, the pretty, lakeside **Hótel Reykjahlíð** (same prices).

Eating

Samkaup-Strax SUPERMARKET €
(9am-10pm mid-Jun–Aug, 10am-6pm Sep–mid-Jun) Busy, well-stocked supermarket (with petrol pumps) next to the visitor centre. Has a burger grill for a cheap feed.

★ **Vogafjós** ICELANDIC €€
(464 3800; www.vogafjos.net; mains kr2500-5400; 10am-11pm Jun-Aug, shorter hours Sep-May;) The 'Cowshed', 2.5km south of Reykjahlíð, is a memorable restaurant where you can enjoy views of the lush surrounds, or of the dairy shed of this working farm (cows are milked at 7.30am and 5.30pm). The menu is an ode to local produce: smoked lamb, house-made mozzarella, dill-cured Arctic char, geysir bread, home-baked cakes, homemade ice cream. It's all delicious.

Gamli Bærinn ICELANDIC €€
(464 4270; www.myvatnhotel.is; snacks & mains kr950-3950; 10am-11pm) The cheerfully busy 'Old Farm' tavern beside Hótel Reynihlíð serves up good-quality pub-style meals all day, ranging from lamb soup to quiche to chicken salad and a pretty great salmon burger with potato salad. In the evening it becomes a local hang-out – the opening hours may be extended during weekend revelry, but the kitchen closes at 10pm.

Daddi's Pizza PIZZERIA €€
(www.vogahraun.is; small pizza kr1720-3115; noon-11pm;) At Vogár campground, this small space cranks out tasty pizzas to eat in or takeaway. Try the house speciality: smoked trout, nuts and cream cheese (tastier than it sounds).

Myllan ICELANDIC €€
(464 4170; www.myvatnhotel.is; mains kr2100-5900; 6.30-9pm) The in-house restaurant at Hótel Reynihlíð is the town's most upmarket and features unsurprising local faves such as smoked lamb, pan-fried Arctic char and T-bone steak with Béarnaise sauce. Locally flavoured desserts appeal (try the *skyr* brûlée). And it wouldn't be a hotel restaurant without club sandwich on the menu!

Information

Post Office (Helluhraun; 9am-4pm Mon-Fri) On the street behind the **supermarket** (p265). Inside is a bank and 24-hour ATM.

Eastern Mývatn

If you're short on time, make this area your first stop in the Mývatn region. The sights along Mývatn's eastern lakeshore can be linked together on an enjoyable half-day hike (p266).

Sights

Grjótagjá CAVE
Game of Thrones fans may recognise this as the place where Jon Snow is, ahem, deflowered by Ygritte. Grjótagjá is a gaping fissure with a 45°C water-filled cave. It's on private property – it's prohibited to bathe here, but the owners allow the public to visit and photograph. This is a beautiful spot, particularly when the sun filters through the cracks in the roof and illuminates the interior. There is easy road access.

★ **Hverfjall** GEOLOGICAL FORMATION
Dominating the lava fields on the eastern edge of Mývatn is the classic tephra ring Hverfjall (also called Hverfell). This near-symmetrical crater appeared 2700 years ago in a cataclysmic eruption. Rising 452m from the ground and stretching 1040m across, it is a massive and awe-inspiring landmark in Mývatn.

The crater is composed of loose gravel, but an easy track leads from the northwestern end to the summit (new toilets here) and offers stunning views of the crater itself and the surrounding landscape. A path runs

INTO THE MADDENING SWARMS

Mývatn's name translates as 'Lake of Midges', and plague-like swarms of these small flies are a lasting memory for many summer visitors. As infuriating as they can be, these midges are a vital food source for wildlife.

If they bother you, consider wearing a head net (which you can buy at the supermarket in Reykjahlíð, and elsewhere) – then splash on the repellent and pray for a good wind to send the little blighters diving.

along the western rim of the crater to a lookout at the southern end before descending steeply towards Dimmuborgir.

Access to the walking track at the ring's northwestern end is via a signed gravel road – it's about 2.5km from the main road to the car park.

★Lofthellir CAVE

The dramatic lava cave at Lofthellir is a stunning destination, with magnificent natural ice sculptures (ice trolls?) dominating the interior.

Although it's one of Mývatn's highlights, the cave is on private property and can only be accessed on a half-day tour run by Saga Travel (p262). The tour involves a 45-minute 4WD journey and a 20-minute walk across a lava field to reach the cave itself, and then special equipment (headlamps, studded boots etc) and some wriggling through tight spaces. Dress warmly.

★Dimmuborgir LAVA FIELD

The giant jagged lava field at Dimmuborgir (literally 'Dark Castles') is one of the most fascinating flows in the country. A series of nontaxing, colour-coded walking trails runs through the easily anthropomorphised landscape. The most popular path is the easy Church Circle (2.3km). Ask at the cafe here about free guided ranger walks in summer.

It's commonly believed that Dimmuborgir's strange pillars and crags were created about 2000 years ago when a lake of lava from the Þrengslaborgir and Lúdentarborgir crater rows formed here, over marshland or a small lake. The water of the marsh started to boil, and steam jets rose through the molten lava and cooled it, creating the pillars. As the lava continued flowing towards lower ground, the hollow pillars of solidified lava remained.

Höfði PARK

One of the area's gentlest landscapes is on the forested lava headland at Höfði. Wildflowers, birch and spruce trees cover the bluffs, while the tiny islands and crystal-clear waters attract migratory birds.

From footpaths along the shore you'll see small caves and stunning *klasar* (lava pillars), the most famous of which rise from the water at **Kálfaströnd** on the southern shore of the Höfði Peninsula.

EASTERN LAKESIDE HIKE

Although easily accessible by car, the sights along Mývatn's eastern lakeshore can also be tackled on a pleasant half-day hike. A well-marked track runs from Reykjahlíð village to **Hverfjall** (p265) (4km), passing **Grjótagjá** (p265) along the way. Then it's on to **Dimmuborgir** (another 3km) with its collection of ruin-like lava. If you start in the late afternoon and time your hike correctly, you'll finish the day with a meal at Dimmuborgir while sunset shadows dance along the alien landscape. As an alternative, the walk from Hverfjall's northwest corner to the **Nature Baths** (p268) is 2.3km – and the sunsets here are pretty special too.

Sleeping & Eating

★Dimmuborgir Guesthouse GUESTHOUSE €€

(☎464 4210; www.dimmuborgir.is; d/cottages incl breakfast from kr22,100/28,500) This lakeside complex close to Dimmuborgir lava field has a block of simple en suite rooms (with shared kitchen-dining area), plus a smattering of timber cottages, which range in size and include modern, well-equipped, family sized options. Breakfast is served in the main house behind big picture windows overlooking the lake.

Kaffi Borgir ICELANDIC €€

(☎4641144; www.kaffiborgir.is; mains kr1950-3950; ⏲10am-9pm Jun-Aug, reduced hours Sep-May, closed mid-Dec–Feb) Kaffi Borgir is a cafe-souvenir shop at the top of the ridge overlooking the Dimmuborgir lava field. Grab a table on the outside terrace, sample the house speciality (grilled trout), and watch the sun dance its shadows across the jagged lava bursts. The lunchtime soup buffet is kr1950; the summertime two-course dinner special (kr3300) is excellent value.

Southern Mývatn

Eastern Mývatn may be the ultimate treasure trove of geological anomalies, but the south side of the lake lures with its epic cache of pseudocraters.

The hamlet of **Skútustaðir** is the only settlement around the lake apart from Reykjahlíð. There's a cluster of tourist activity here, including a couple of hotels, a guesthouse, petrol pump and bus stop.

★ **Skútustaðagígar** GEOLOGICAL FORMATION

The Skútustaðagígar pseudocraters were formed when molten lava flowed into Mývatn lake, triggering a series of gas explosions. These dramatic green dimples then came into being when trapped subsurface water boiled and popped, forming small scoria cones and craters.

The most accessible pseudocrater swarm is located along a short path just across from Skútustaðir, which also takes in the nearby pond, **Stakhólstjörn**, a haven for nesting waterfowl.

Sleeping & Eating

Skútustaðir Farmhouse GUESTHOUSE €€

(☎464 4212; www.skutustadir.is; Skútustaðir; d with/without bathroom incl breakfast kr27,000/21,000; ⊙closed Christmas-New Year) Slightly more accessible prices (in comparison to other options in the area), friendly owners and spotless facilities can be found at this recommended year-round guesthouse. Rooms in the homey farmhouse share bathroom, but there's also an annexe of five en suite rooms, plus a two-bedroom cottage, and a new block of rooms and large guest kitchen.

Hótel Laxá HOTEL €€€

(☎464 1900; www.hotellaxa.is; s/d incl breakfast kr32,800/39,400) Bringing a breath of fresh air to Mývatn is this architecturally arresting, sustainably designed hotel, which opened in mid-2014 about 2km east of Skútustaðir. There are 80 modern, simple rooms – pricey but comfy, with colour schemes complementing the surrounds. The big windows and green sofas of the bar-lounge area invite contemplation; there's also a stylish on-site restaurant.

Dinner mains are priced from kr2550 to kr5750, or you can opt for a buffet (full dinner kr7200, soup and salad buffet kr2900).

This hotel ain't cheap, but note that winter (October to April) rates fall by more than 50%.

Sel-Hótel Mývatn HOTEL €€€

(☎464 4164; www.myvatn.is; Skútustaðir; s/d incl breakfast kr27,000/32,600; @) New rooms and lobby area have reinvigorated the Sel, where there's a mishmash of styles but facilities are good and service friendly. The hotel's best feature is its winter packages, which may incorporate Northern Lights viewing, super-Jeep exploration, snowmobile or go-kart tours on the frozen lake, horse riding etc. Low-season room rates are significantly cheaper.

The hotel's no-frills restaurant offers buffets favoured by tour groups (lunch/dinner buffet kr3500/6900), but there are also evening à la carte options. Check out the brilliant photos in the restaurant of the local area and recent volcanic eruptions.

Hótel Gígur HOTEL €€€

(☎464 4455; www.keahotels.is; Skútustaðir; s/d incl breakfast kr29,800/36,100; @) There's been a makeover at Gígur, with new furniture and a stylish contemporary look, but it doesn't hide the fact that overpriced rooms here are small, even by Icelandic standards. To compensate, there's friendly service, a prime lakeside location in Skútustaðir and ace views. Easily the hotel's best feature is its appealing restaurant, one of the area's best.

Kaffi Sel CAFETERIA €

(Skútustaðir; snacks kr400-1800; ⊙8am-9pm Jun-Aug, 10am-5pm Sep-May) If you're just after a quick bite, grab a hot dog, soup or prepackaged sandwich at this combined souvenir shop-cafeteria next door to the Sel-Hótel.

Western Mývatn

Travellers flock to check out the geological anomalies of Mývatn's eastern shore, but the quieter, less-developed western shore is worth a visit too – especially for its bumper birdwatching.

The Ring Road (Rte 1) actually travels the western shore of the lake, rather than the more-populous eastern shore.

Buses travel the south and east shore, rather than the west.

Sights & Activities

Western Mývatn offers some of the best birdwatching in Iceland, with more than 115 species recorded in the area – including 28 species of ducks. Most species of Icelandic waterfowl are found here in great numbers. Three duck species – the scoter, the gadwall and the Barrow's goldeneye – breed nowhere else in Iceland.

Other species frequenting the area include harlequin and tufted ducks, mallards, scaup, whooper swans, great northern divers, Arctic terns and golden plovers. The area's bogs, marshes, ponds and wet tundra are a high-density waterfowl nesting zone. Off-trail hiking in defined nesting areas is restricted between 15 May and 20 July (when the chicks hatch), but hides near Sigurgeir's Bird Museum allow for birding.

Vindbelgjarfjall HIKING
The steep but relatively easy climb up 529m-high Vindbelgjarfjall (also known as Vindbelgur), on Mývatn lake's western shore, offers one of the best views across the lake and its alien pseudocraters. The trail to the summit starts south of the peak, near the farm Vagnbrekka. Reckon on about a half-hour to reach the mount, and another half-hour to climb to the summit.

★**Sigurgeir's Bird Museum** MUSEUM
(Fuglasafn Sigurgeirs; ☎464 4477; www.fuglasafn.is; adult/child kr1200/600; ⏲9am-6pm Jun-Aug, reduced hours Sep-May) For some birdwatching background, swing by Sigurgeir's Bird Museum, housed in a beautiful lakeside building that fuses modern design with traditional turf house. Inside you'll find an impressive collection of taxidermic avians (more than 180 types from around the world), including every species of bird that calls Iceland home (except one – the grey phalarope). Designer lighting and detailed captions further enhance the experience.

The menagerie of stuffed squawkers started as the private collection of a local named Sigurgeir Stefansson. Tragically, Sigurgeir drowned in the lake at the age of 37 – the museum was erected in his honour. The museum also houses a small cafe and lends out high-tech telescopes to ornithological enthusiasts, plus has hides for rent.

Northern Mývatn

As the lakeshore road circles back around towards Reykjahlíð, the marshes dry up and the terrain returns to its signature stretches of crispy lava.

Eldhraun LAVA FIELD
The lava field along Mývatn's northern lakeshore includes the flow that nearly engulfed the Reykjahlíð Church. It was belched out of Leirhnjúkur (p269) during the Mývatn Fires in 1729, and flowed down the channel Eldá. With some slow scrambling, it can be explored on foot from Reykjahlíð.

Hlíðarfjall HIKING
If you're hiking directly to the Krafla area from Mývatn's northern crest, you'll pass the prominent 771m-high rhyolite mountain Hlíðarfjall just before the halfway mark. Around 5km from Reykjahlíð, the mount can also be enjoyed as a pleasant day hike from the village, affording spectacular views over the lake on one side and the Krafla lava fields on the other.

East of Reykjahlíð

Northern Mývatn's collection of geological gems lie along the Ring Road (Rte 1) as it weaves through the harsh terrain between the north end of the lake and the turn-off to Krafla. There are plenty of paths for exploring the area on foot.

Bjarnarflag GEOTHERMAL AREA
Bjarnarflag, 3km east of Reykjahlíð, is an active geothermal area where the earth hisses and bubbles, and steaming vents line the valley. Historically, the area has been home to a number of economic ventures attempting to harness the earth's powers. (Early on, farmers tried growing potatoes here, but these often emerged from the ground already boiled.)

In the 1960s, 25 test holes were bored at Bjarnarflag to ascertain the feasibility of a proposed geothermal power station. One is 2300m deep and the steam still roars out of the pipe at a whopping 200°C.

Later a diatomite plant was set up, but all that remains of the processing plant is the shimmering turquoise pond that the locals have dubbed the 'Blue Lagoon'. This inviting puddle is actually quite toxic and should not be confused with the Mývatn Nature Baths around the corner (sometimes called the 'Blue Lagoon of the North').

★**Mývatn Nature Baths** SPA
(Jarðböðin; ☎464 4411; www.myvatnnaturebaths.is; adult/child kr4000/free; ⏲9am-midnight Jun-Aug, noon-10pm Sep-May) Northern Iceland's answer to the Blue Lagoon is 3km east of Reykjahlíð. Although it's smaller than its southern counterpart, it's also less hyped (probably a good thing), and it's a gorgeous place to soak in the powder-blue, mineral-rich waters and enjoy the panorama. After a relaxing soak, try one of the two natural steam baths and/or a meal at the on-site cafeteria.

Námafjall MOUNTAIN

Vaporous vents cover the pinky-orange Námafjall ridge, which lies 3km past Bjarnarflag (on the south side of the Ring Road). Produced by a fissure eruption, the ridge sits squarely on the spreading zone of the Mid-Atlantic Ridge. As you travel the Námaskarð pass and tumble down its far side, you enter the alien world of Hverir.

★Hverir GEOTHERMAL AREA

The magical, ochre-toned world of Hverir (also called Hveraröndl) is a lunar-like landscape of mud cauldrons, steaming vents, radiant mineral deposits and piping fumaroles. Belching mudpots and the powerful stench of sulphur may not sound enticing, but Hverir's ethereal allure grips every passer-by.

Safe pathways through the features have been roped off; to avoid risk of serious injury and damage to the natural features, avoid any lighter-coloured soil and respect the ropes.

A walking trail loops from Hverir up Námafjall ridge. This 30-minute climb provides a grand vista over the steamy surroundings.

Krafla

Steaming vents and craters await at Krafla, an active volcanic region 7km north of the Ring Road. Technically, Krafla is just an 818m-high mountain, but the name is now used for the entire area as well as a geothermal power station and the series of eruptions that created Iceland's most awesome lava field. The so-called Mývatn Fires occurred between 1724–29, when many of the fissure vents opened up. The Krafla Fires (1975–84) were very similar in nature: fissure eruptions and magma movements that occurred on and off for nine years.

From Reykjahlíð, a reasonably easy **hike** of around 13km (three to five hours) leads to Hlíðarfjall and Leirhnjúkur along a marked path from near the airstrip. Another walking route (difficult; estimate three to five hours) leads from the Namaskarð pass (opposite Námafjall) along the Dalfjall ridge to Leirhnjúkur.

Krafla Power Station POWER STATION

(⏲visitor centre 10am-5pm Jun-Aug) The idea of constructing a geothermal power station at Krafla was conceived in 1973, and preliminary work commenced with the drilling of holes to determine project feasibility. In 1975, however, after a long rest period, the Krafla fissure burst into activity. The project went ahead regardless and has been expanded since. The power plant's visitor centre explains how it all works.

The viewpoint over the area (continue up Rte 863 to reach it) is impressive.

★Leirhnjúkur LAVA FIELD

Krafla's most impressive, and potentially most dangerous, attraction is the Leirhnjúkur crater and its solfataras, which originally appeared in 1727, starting out as a lava fountain and spouting molten material for two years before subsiding.

In 1975, the Krafla Fires began with a small lava eruption by Leirhnjúkur, and after nine years of on-and-off action Leirhnjúkur became the ominous-looking, sulphur-encrusted mudhole that tourists love today. The earth's crust here is extremely thin and in places the ground is ferociously hot.

A well-defined track leads northwest to Leirhnjúkur from the Krafla parking area; with all the volcanic activity, high temperatures, bubbling mudpots and steaming vents, it's best not to stray from the marked paths.

Víti GEOLOGICAL FORMATION

The dirt-brown crater of Víti reveals a secret when you reach its rim – a green pool of floodwater at its heart. The 300m-wide explosion crater was created in 1724 at the beginning of the destructive Mývatn Fires. There is a circular path around the rim of Víti to the geothermal area to its east.

Note: don't confuse this Víti crater with the Víti crater beside the Askja caldera (you can bathe inside the latter, but not the former). Fun fact: Víti means 'hell' in Icelandic.

ℹ Getting There & Away

Hike here from Reykjahlíð, take the bus (summer only) or drive; it's 15km by road (via the Ring Road and Rte 863).

SBA-Norðurleið (www.sba.is) services:

➡ Bus 661 Reykjahlíð to Krafla (kr1900, 15 minutes, two daily mid-June to early September). Runs at 8am and 11.30am; the latter service continues on to Dettifoss. Return bus from Krafla to Reykjahlíð at 2.15pm.

MÝVATN TO EGILSSTAÐIR (RING ROAD)

Travelling east from Reykjahlíð towards Egilsstaðir, the Ring Road crests Námafjall ridge, passes Hverir (mind the stench!) and offers a turn-off to Krafla. After another 20km you'll encounter the turn-off north to mighty Dettifoss (p280) via Rte 862 (sealed), and then the 4WD-only Rte F88 turn-off south to Askja in the highlands.

Soon you'll cross the bridge over the glacial river Jökulsá á Fjöllum; Rte 864 is signposted north from just east of the bridge; this rough gravel road is generally open June to October, and arrives at Dettifoss (eastern vantage point) after 28km, and Ásbyrgi after 56km.

From the bridge, the Ring Road takes a short cut inland across the stark highlands of the northeast interior. If you won't be travelling into the highlands proper, you'll glimpse them here. The ostensibly barren, grey-toned landscape is dotted with low hills, small lakes caused by melting snowfields, and wandering streams and rivers.

Möðrudalur & Around

This area has always been a difficult place to eke out a living, and farms here are few and far between. Isolated Möðrudalur, a storied oasis in the desert, is the highest farm in Iceland at 469m. Here you'll find a popular mini-village, catering to tourists and bustling in summer. A new information centre is being set up to offer advice to people travelling into the highlands – after visiting Möðrudalur, many folks head into the central highlands via nearby Rte F905 (note you'll need to be well set up for highland exploration, and a 4WD vehicle is essential).

Möðrudalur is 8km south of the Ring Road on Rte 901, with the turn-off about 63km east of Reykjahlíð and 104km west of Egilsstaðir. Petrol is available here (from what may be Iceland's cutest petrol station).

Tours

Volcano Heli SCENIC FLIGHT

(☎647 3300; www.volcanoheli.is) Liechtenstein-born heli-pilot Matthias works from a summer base on Möðrudalur farm, and has epic highland landscapes in his backyard: Askja, Holuhraun, Mývatn and Kverkfjöll are all within a short flying time. The helicopter can carry three passengers, and rates are given for the entire trip (not per person). Prices start at kr106,200 for 30 minutes.

Sleeping & Eating

Fjalladýrð GUESTHOUSE, CAMPGROUND €€

(☎471 1858; www.fjalladyrd.is; Möðrudalur; sites per person kr1350, d with/without bathroom kr35,000/15,900) Fjalladýrð is the name of the tourist service at Möðrudalur farm, and it has a wide array of good accommodation spread over various buildings and budgets: camping, sleeping-bag beds, guesthouse rooms, button-cute turf-roofed cottages, family-sized suites. Outside summer, rates drop by around 30%.

It's worth spending the night if you're interested in tackling some of Iceland's interior – Fjalladýrð runs excellent super-Jeep trips to Askja and Kverkfjöll.

Fjallakaffi ICELANDIC €€

(Möðrudalur; mains kr2290-7490; ⏱7am-10pm May-Sep, 9am-5pm Oct-Apr) Folks simply passing through Möðrudalur should stop for coffee and *kleina* (a traditional twisted doughnut), or try the true farm-to-table dishes at Fjallakaffi, the excellent restaurant here. Dishes range from filet of mountain lamb to goose breast, pan-fried Arctic char and reindeer steak. You can also get a simple soup or toasted sandwich.

HÚSAVÍK

POP 2240

Húsavík, Iceland's whale-watching capital, has become a firm favourite on travellers' itineraries – and with its colourful houses, unique museums and stunning snow-capped peaks across the bay, it's easily the northeast's prettiest fishing town.

Sights & Activities

★ **Húsavík Whale Museum** MUSEUM

(Hvalasafnið; ☎414 2800; www.whalemuseum.is; Hafnarstétt; adult/child kr1800/500; ⏱8.30am-6.30pm May-Sep, 9am-2pm Mon-Fri Oct-Apr) This excellent museum provides all you ever need to know about the impressive creatures that come a-visiting Skjálfandi bay. Housed in an old harbourside slaughterhouse, the museum interprets the ecology and habits of whales, conservation and the history of whaling in Iceland through beautifully curated displays, including several huge skeletons soaring high above (they're real!).

★ Húsavíkurkirkja CHURCH
(Garðarsbraut) Húsavík's beloved church is quite different from anything else seen in Iceland. Constructed in 1907 from Norwegian timber, the delicately proportioned red-and-white church would look more at home in the Alps. Inside, its cruciform shape becomes apparent and is dominated by a depiction of the resurrection of Lazarus (from lava!) on the altarpiece. It's open most days in summer.

★ Skrúðgarður GARDENS
A walk along the duck-filled stream of the endearing town park, which is as scenic as the waterfront area, offers a serene break. Access is via a footbridge on Ásgarðsvegur, or beside Árból guesthouse.

Exploration Museum MUSEUM
(www.explorationmuseum.com; Héðinsbraut 3; adult/child kr1000/500; ⌚2-7pm) Newly opened in 2014, this museum salutes the history of human exploration, covering Viking voyages and polar expeditions (and with a cool 1952 snowcat parked out front). Its most unique exhibition focuses on the Apollo astronauts in Iceland in the 1960s, receiving geology training in the lunar-like landscapes near Askja. There are some great photos from this era.

Culture House MUSEUM
(Safnahúsið; www.husmus.is; Stórigarður 17; adult/child kr1000/free; ⌚10am-6pm Jun–mid-Sep, 10am-4pm Mon-Fri mid-Sep–May) A folk, maritime and natural-history museum rolled into one complex, the Culture House is one of the north's most interesting regional museums. 'Man and Nature' nicely outlines a century of life in the region, from 1850 to 1950 (lots of local flavour), while the stuffed animals include a frightening hooded seal, and a polar bear that was welcomed to Grímsey in 1969 with both barrels of a gun.

Sundlaug Húsavíkur SWIMMING
(Laugarbrekka 2; adult/child kr650/300; ⌚6.45am-9pm Mon-Fri, 10am-6pm Sat & Sun Jun-Aug, shorter hours Sep-May; 👪) The local swimming pool has hot-pots, and water slides for kids.

Tours

Whale Watching

This is why you came to Húsavík. Although there are other Iceland locales where you can do whale-watching tours (Reykjavík and Eyjafjörður, north of Akureyri), this area has become Iceland's premier whale-watching destination, with up to 11 species coming here to feed in summer. The best time to see whales is between June and August when you'll have a near-100% chance of a sighting. This is also, of course, the height of tourist season.

Four whale-watching companies now operate from Húsavík harbour. Don't stress *too* much over picking an operator; prices are similar and services are comparable for the standard three-hour tour (guiding and warm overalls supplied, plus hot drinks and a pastry).

Where the differences are clear, however, is in the excursions that go beyond the standard. When puffins are nesting (from roughly mid-April to mid-August), all companies offer tours that incorporate whale watching with a sail by the puffin-festooned island of Lundey: North Sailing does this on board an atmospheric old schooner over four hours (hoisting sails when conditions are right); Gentle Giants (p272) does it over 2½ hours in a high-speed rigid inflatable boat (RIB).

Trips depart throughout the day (June to August) from around 8am to 8pm, and large signs at the ticket booths advertise the next departure time. Boats also run in April, May, and September to November with less frequency (North Sailing has a daily tour in the last two weeks of March). You can't miss the offices on the waterfront: North Sailing with its yellow flags, Gentle Giants dressed in blue, and smaller Salka (p272) operating from its cafe across the road. A fourth player, Húsavík Adventures (p273), has recently entered the market, offering RIB tours.

When booking a last-minute standard tour, it's worth enquiring about how big the boat is and how many passengers are booked on the tour. Consider taking an early-morning or evening cruise (bus groups visit it in the middle of the day). Note that RIB tours are not suitable for kids under about eight years.

North Sailing WHALE WATCHING
(☎464 7272; www.northsailing.is; Garðarsbraut; 3hr tour adult/child kr10,500/4200) The original whale-watching operator, with a fleet of

Húsavík

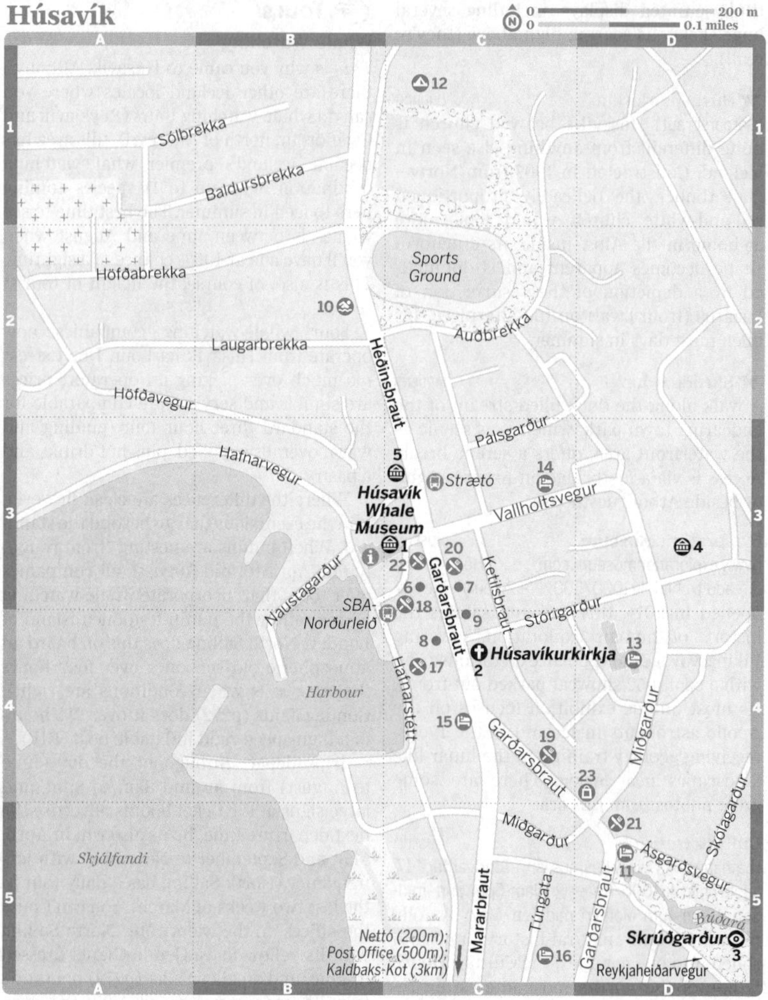

lovingly restored traditional boats. Its four-hour 'Whales, Puffins & Sails' tour (adult/child kr14,000/5600) is on board an old schooner; when conditions are right, sails are hoisted and engines cut. Some tours lasting four hours are on the schedule as a carbon-neutral option (running the ship on renewable energy instead of fossil fuel).

Gentle Giants WHALE WATCHING

(☎464 1500; www.gentlegiants.is; Garðarsbraut; 3hr tour adult/child kr10,300/4200) Gentle Giants has a flotilla of old fishing vessels for its standard three-hour tours, plus a fleet of high-speed rigid inflatable boats (RIBs), offering a way to cover more ground in the bay (RIB tours from kr18,400). It also runs special trips ashore on Flatey (Flat Island) for birdwatching, and fast (and pricey) RIB day trips to Grímsey.

Salka WHALE WATCHING

(☎464 3999; www.salkawhalewatching.is; Garðarsbraut 6; 3hr tour adult/child kr9950/4200; ⏲May-Sep) A relatively new player on the whale-watching scene, taking on the long-established companies with just one 42-passenger oak boat, slightly cheaper

Húsavík

Top Sights
1 Húsavík Whale Museum ... C3
2 Húsavíkurkirkja ... C4
3 Skrúðgarður ... D5

Sights
4 Culture House ... D3
5 Exploration Museum ... C3

Activities, Courses & Tours
6 Gentle Giants ... C3
7 Húsavík Adventures ... C3
8 North Sailing ... C4
9 Salka ... C4
10 Sundlaug Húsavíkur ... B2

Sleeping
11 Árból ... D5
12 Campground ... C1
13 Fosshótel Húsavík ... D4
14 Húsavík Hostel ... C3
15 Port Guesthouse ... C4
16 Sigtún ... C5

Eating
Café Hvalbakur ... (see 18)
17 Fish & Chips ... C4
18 Gamli Baukur ... C3
19 Heimabakarí Konditori ... C4
20 Krambúð ... C3
21 Naustið ... D5
22 Salka Restaurant ... C3

Shopping
23 Vínbúðin ... D4

prices and a tighter menu of offerings. Its base is its light-filled **cafe** (☎464 2551; mains kr1500-4750; ⊙11.30am-10pm) on the main street.

Húsavík Adventures WHALE WATCHING
(☎859 8505; www.husavikadventures.is; Garðarsbraut 5; 2hr RIB tour adult/child kr18,000/12,500) Is there enough room in the bay for a fourth whale-watching operator? Looks like it. This new company offers short, racy two-hour RIB tours three to seven times a day from May to September. From late June to late July, it also has a midnight-sun tour (kr25,000), departing at 10.30pm.

Other Tours

Both major whale-watching operators offer combo tours that involve cruises plus a horse ride at Saltvík. Gentle Giants also offers sea angling expeditions or a two-day hiking trip; North Sailing (p271) offers a unique 'Ski to the Sea' multiday package in April and May, working with ski guides. North Sailing also has week-long sailing trips to Greenland each summer. See websites for full details.

Saltvík Horse Farm HORSE RIDING
(☎847 9515; www.saltvik.is; Rte 85; 2hr tour kr9500) Two-hour coastal rides with glorious views over Skjálfandi bay are available at Saltvík Horse Farm, 5km south of Húsavík. No special riding experience is required. Saltvík also offers week-long rides (around Mývatn, into the more-remote northeast, or along the highland Sprengisandur route), plus farmhouse accommodation.

Húsavík Walking Tours WALKING TOUR
(☎858 5848; francesco@visithusavik.com) Ask at the tourist information centre or Húsavík Hostel if walking tours are happening – at the time of writing they were operating a couple of times a week, with guiding and local insight from Heiðar or Italian-born Francesco. Future plans were still being determined, but a guided walk is a sweet, low-key way to spend some time and learn more about Húsavík.

Fjallasýn ADVENTURE TOUR
(☎464 3941; www.fjallasyn.is) This Húsavík-based company is well established and does a variety of tours in the area – day or multiday, 4WD, hiking, birdwatching etc – both local to Húsavík and further afield to various parts of northeast Iceland and the highlands.

Sleeping

Húsavík Hostel HOSTEL €
(☎858 5848; www.husavikhostel.com; Vallholtsvegur 9; dm/d without bathroom kr6500/15,840) This is the only in-town budget option, and its 21 beds are popular. There are bunk-filled dorm rooms and a couple of private rooms (which include linen), plus kitchen, but no real lounge space. Management is friendly and offers good local information.

Campground CAMPGROUND €
(site per person kr1400; ⊙mid-May–Sep) Next to the sports ground at the north end of town, this well-maintained spot has washing machines and limited cooking facilities, but not nearly enough to cope with summertime

demand. Pay at Sundlaug Húsavíkur swimming pool (p271), or to the warden who visits nightly.

★ **Kaldbaks-Kot** COTTAGES €€
(☎464 1504; www.cottages.is; 2-/4-person cottages excl linen kr18,600/26,300; ⌚May-Sep; @) Located 3km south of Húsavík is this spectacular spread-out settlement of cosy timber cottages that all feel like grandpa's log cabin in the woods (but with considerably more comfort). Choose your level of service: BYO linen or hire it, bring supplies or buy breakfast here (kr1500), served in the magnificent converted cowshed.

Minimum stay is two nights – perfect for enjoying the grounds, the hot-pots, the views, the serenity and the prolific bird life. Options include larger houses sleeping up to 10 people.

★ **Árból** GUESTHOUSE €€
(☎464 2220; www.arbol.is; Ásgarðsvegur 2; s/d without bathroom incl breakfast kr11,100/19,000) This 1903 heritage house has a pretty stream and town park as neighbours. Spacious, spotless rooms are over three levels – those on the ground and top floor are loveliest (the pine-lined attic rooms are particularly sweet). Note: no kitchen.

Port Guesthouse GUESTHOUSE €€
(☎864 0250; http://husavik.timerules.org; Garðarsbraut 14; s/d without bathroom incl breakfast kr10,900/18,900) This guesthouse is located in the converted offices of a fishing company, so don't be put off by the businesslike exterior. It's got winning harbour views, big rooms and good facilities (including kitchen and laundry). There's real effort gone into making Port more inviting than a block of offices, with sweet results.

Sigtún GUESTHOUSE €€
(☎864 0250; www.guesthousesigtun.is; Túngata 13; s/d without bathroom incl breakfast kr10,900/18,900) Free coffee machine, free washing machine and a fancy guest kitchen are draws at this small and cosy, high-quality guesthouse in a quiet residential street. Breakfast is served at the affiliated Port Guesthouse.

Fosshótel Húsavík HOTEL €€
(☎464 1220; www.fosshotel.is; Ketilsbraut 22; d incl breakfast from kr23,600) Fast-growing hotel chain Fosshótel has expanded this hotel (from 67 to 110 rooms) and put its stylish, contemporary stamp on much-needed renovations: charcoal tones, bright colour accents etc. Deluxe rooms are a good step up from standard rooms. The airy lobby creates a great first impression, and the bar and bistro have a subtle whale theme. Still to come: a restaurant.

✕ Eating

Fish & Chips FAST FOOD €
(Hafnarstétt 19; fish & chips kr1700; ⌚11.30am-8pm May-Oct) Doing exactly what it says on the label, this small window-front on the harbour doles out good-value fish (usually cod) and chips, with a few picnic tables out front and a simple seating area upstairs. To find it, walk down the stairs opposite the church, and turn left.

Café Hvalbakur CAFE €
(Garðarsbraut; snacks & meals kr300-1250; ⌚8am-8pm Jun-Aug, 11.30am-8pm Sep-May) With a sun-trap terrace overlooking the waterfront, this friendly cafe – owned by North Sailing (p271) – serves a big cabinet full of baguettes, wraps, muffins and cakes. Good coffee too. It's just down the stairs from the North Sailing ticket office.

Heimabakarí Konditori BAKERY, CAFE €
(Garðarsbraut 15; ⌚7am-6pm Mon-Fri, 8am-4pm Sat & Sun) Sells fresh bread, sandwiches and a cabinet full of sugary cakes and pastries.

★ **Naustið** SEAFOOD €€
(☎464 1520; www.facebook.com/naustid; Ásgarðsvegur 1; mains kr1950-4800; ⌚noon-10pm) In a new location away from the harbour, buttercup-yellow Naustið wins praise for its super-fresh fish and a simple concept well executed: skewers of fish and vegetables, grilled to order. There's also fish soup (natch), fish tacos and langoustine, plus home-baked rhubarb cake for dessert.

Gamli Baukur ICELANDIC €€
(☎464 2442; www.northsailing.is; Hafnarstétt 9; mains kr2220-5940; ⌚11.30am-1am Jun-Aug, shorter hours Sep-May) Among shiny nautical relics, this timber-framed restaurant-bar serves high-quality food (spaghetti with shellfish, wild mushroom barley risotto, organic lamb), plus the pun-tastic dessert *skyramisu*. Occasional live music and a sweeping terrace make it one of the most happening summertime places in northeast Iceland. Kitchen closes at 10pm in summer.

THE WHALES OF HÚSAVÍK

With the help of Edda Elísabet Magnúsdóttir, marine biologist, we investigated the whales of Húsavík and what's gone into making this town the whale-watching capital of Iceland.

Húsavík sits on a super-scenic bay known as Skjálfandi, which is often translated into English as 'Shaky Bay'. The name is apt, since little earthquakes occur very frequently in the bay, usually without being noticed. These tremors occur because the bay sits atop a wrench fault in the earth's crust.

Skjálfandi's bowl-shaped topography and fresh water flowing in from two river estuaries means that there is a great deal of nutrients collecting in the bay. The nutrient deposits accumulate during the winter months, and when early summer arrives – with its long sunlit days – the cool waters of Skjálfandi bay come alive with plankton blooms. These rich deposits act like a beacon, kick-starting each year's feeding season. This is when the whales start appearing in greater numbers.

The first creatures to arrive are the humpback whales *(Megaptera novaeangliae)* and the minke whales *(Balaenoptera acutorostrata)*. The humpback whale is known for its curious nature, equanimity and spectacular surface displays, whereas the minke whale is famous for its elegant features: a streamlined and slender black body and white-striped pectoral fin.

Several minke and humpback whales stay in the bay throughout the year, but most migrate south during the winter. The enormous blue whale *(Balaenoptera musculus)*, undoubtedly the most exciting sight in Skjálfandi, usually starts coming in mid-June and stays until the middle of July.

Other summer sightings in Skjálfandi include the orca, also known as the killer whale (*Orcinus orca;* some come to the bay to feed on fish, others come to hunt mammals), northern bottlenose whales (*Hyperoodon ampullatus;* a mysterious, deep-diving beaked whale), fin whales *(Balaenoptera physalus)*, sei whales *(Balaenoptera borealis)*, pilot whales *(Globicephala melas)* and sperm whales *(Physeter macrocephalus)*.

Self-Catering

Krambúð SUPERMARKET €
(Garðarsbraut 5; 8am-10pm) Centrally located supermarket.

Nettó SUPERMARKET €
(Garðarsbraut 64; 10am-7pm) South of town, by the Olís service station.

Vínbúðin ALCOHOL
(Garðarsbraut 21; 11am-6pm Mon-Thu, to 7pm Fri, to 2pm Sat May-Aug, shorter hours Sep-Apr) Government-run liquor store.

Information

Tourist Information Centre (464 4300; www.visithusavik.is; Hafnarstétt; 8.30am-6.30pm May-Sep, 9am-2pm Mon-Fri Oct-Apr) At the Whale Museum, with plentiful maps and brochures.

Getting There & Away

AIR

Húsavík's airport is 12km south of town. **Eagle Air** (562 4200; www.eagleair.is) flies year-round between Reykjavík and Húsavík.

BUS

SBA-Norðurleið (550 0700; www.sba.is) services (departing from in front of Gamli Baukar restaurant, on the waterfront):

- Bus 641a to Akureyri (kr3700, 1½ hours, one daily mid-June to August).
- Bus 641 to Ásbyrgi (kr2500, 1¼ hours, one daily mid-June to August).
- Bus 641 to Dettifoss (kr6500, 2¾ hours, one daily mid-June to August) From Dettifoss you can connect to bus 661a to Mývatn.
- Bus 650a to Mývatn (kr3500, 55 minutes, one daily mid-June to August).

Strætó (540 2700; www.straeto.is) services (departing from the N1 service station):

- Bus 79 to Akureyri (kr2520, 1¼ hours, three daily).
- Bus 79 to Ásbyrgi (kr2100, one hour, one daily Sunday to Friday summer, three weekly winter) This service only operates from Húsavík to Þórshöfn (via Ásbyrgi, Kópasker and Raufarhöfn) if prebooked. Call Strætó at least four hours before departure.
- Bus 79 to Þórshöfn (kr5040, 2¾ hours, one daily Sunday to Friday summer, three weekly winter) See note above.

CAR

From the Ring Road there are two options to head north to Húsavík: Rte 85 is the shortest route, covering 45km and turning off the Ring Road just west of **Goðafoss** (p259). From northern Mývatn, take Rte 87 55km north. Note that Rte 87 is partially gravel, but fine for small cars.

Húsavík to Ásbyrgi

Heading north from Húsavík along Rte 85 you'll sweep along the coast of the stubby **Tjörnes Peninsula**. The area is known for its fossil-rich coastal cliffs (the oldest layers dating back about two million years). **Mánárbakki Museum** (Rte 85; adult/child kr1000/free; ⏰9am-6pm Jun-Aug), at the tip of the peninsula, is worth checking out.

Giant cracks, fissures and grabens (depressions between geological faults) scar the earth at low-lying **Kelduhverfi**, where the Mid-Atlantic Ridge enters the Arctic Ocean. Like Þingvellir, the area reveals some of the most visible evidence that Iceland is being ripped apart from its core.

There's a great coastal viewpoint about 12km east of Mánárbakki Museum, with information boards giving details of earth movements.

★Tungulending GUESTHOUSE €€
(☎896 6948; www.tungulending.is; off Rte 85; s/d without bathroom incl breakfast kr15,900/22,500; ⏰mid-May–Sep) There's a two-night minimum stay at this unique, well-hidden guesthouse (we applaud policies designed to slow travellers down and help them appreciate the surrounds). The turn-off is about 11km northeast of Húsavík; you then travel 2.5km through farmland (leave gates as you found them) to reach this handcrafted, waterfront, view-enriched outpost. There's no kitchen, but dinner is available. Linger and enjoy.

Hótel Skúlagarður COUNTRY HOTEL €€
(☎465 2280; www.skulagardur.com; s/d incl breakfast kr17,100/23,600) A country hotel behind an unpromising exterior (in a former boarding school), Skúlagarður offers a warm welcome, plus compact, modern, overpriced en suite rooms, and a no-frills restaurant serving good home cooking (oven-baked Arctic char or lamb fillet; mains kr2900 to kr4200). It's 12km west of Ásbyrgi. There's a budget wing here too, the bare-bones **River Guesthouse** (☎463 3390; www.skulagardur.com; Rte 85; s/d without bathroom kr5700/9500).

Keldunes GUESTHOUSE €€
(☎465 2275; www.keldunes.is; s/d without bathroom incl breakfast kr14,500/20,900) Modern guesthouse with good kitchen-dining area, a hot-pot, and large balconies for birdwatching; dinner is available on request. There are decent cottages with bathroom (kr23,900), plus some basic cabins with sleeping-bag beds (per person kr4000). It's 11km west of Ásbyrgi.

JÖKULSÁRGLJÚFUR (VATNAJÖKULL NATIONAL PARK – NORTH)

In 2008 the Vatnajökull National Park – one of Europe's largest protected reserves – was formed when Jökulsárgljúfur National Park merged with Skaftafell National Park to the south. The idea was to protect the Vatnajökull ice cap and all of its glacial run-off under one super-sized preserve.

The Jökulsárgljúfur portion of the park protects a unique subglacial eruptive ridge and a 25km-long canyon carved out by the formidable **Jökulsá á Fjöllum** (Iceland's second-longest river) – the name Jökulsárgljúfur literally means 'Glacier River Canyon'.

Jökulsá á Fjöllum starts in the Vatnajökull ice cap and flows just over 200km to the Arctic Ocean at Öxarfjörður. *Jökulhlaup* (floods from volcanic eruptions beneath the ice cap) formed the canyon and have carved out a chasm that averages 100m deep and 500m wide. The canyon is well known for its waterfalls – Dettifoss is of course the most famous, but there are others.

Sights & Activities

Vatnajökull National Park's northern section can be roughly divided into three parts.

Ásbyrgi The northern entry. A verdant, forested plain enclosed by vertical canyon walls. The visitor centre is here.

Vesturdalur The middle section, with caves and fascinating geological anomalies.

Dettifoss This mighty waterfall anchors the park's southern entrance.

A wonderful two-day hike (p278) weaves along the canyon, taking in all of the major sights en route. If you're not so keen on hiking, the big attractions, such as the waterfalls at the southern end of the park and horseshoe-shaped Ásbyrgi canyon at the northern end, are accessible by good sealed roads. The road between Ásbyrgi and Dettifoss on the western side of the canyon (Rte 862) is being paved in stages over the coming few years.

Note that from mid-June to mid-August, rangers guide free daily interpretive walks that depart from the parking place closest to Ásbyrgi canyon. Check the national-park website, or ask staff.

In the pipeline: rangers are developing a mountain-biking trail through the park (note that this will be for experienced cyclists, not day trippers).

Tours

Summer buses to Ásbyrgi and Dettifoss make it pretty easy to tackle the park on your own. If you're after a tour, several companies can oblige, from Mývatn, Akureyri and Húsavík.

Active North ADVENTURE TOUR
(☎858 7080; www.activenorth.is; 2hr horse ride kr9900) Fancy horse-riding around a canyon said to be formed by a mythical hoof-print? Headquartered opposite the visitor centre, Active North offers easy, scenic two-hour horse-riding trips around the Ásbyrgi canyon, departing at 11am and 2pm. Other trips on horseback, mountain bike or via superJeep are also available, inside the park but also beyond its borders. Mountain bikes can also be hired.

Jeep tours operate year-round (and include a Northern Lights option); horse riding and biking are generally available June to September.

Sleeping & Eating

The store on Rte 85 near the visitor centre at Ásbyrgi has a selection of groceries, plus simple grill-bar options (and a fuel pump). If you're hiking, it's best to purchase supplies in Húsavík; there is also a decent supermarket 35km north in Kópasker.

Ásbyrgi Campsite CAMPGROUND €
(☎470 7100; www.vjp.is; site per adult/teen/child kr1600/750/free; ⏲mid-May–Sep) Camping inside the park boundaries is strictly limited to the official campsites at Ásbyrgi and Vesturdalur (p279), plus Dettifoss for hikers only. The large, easily accessible campsite at Ásbyrgi has a good service building containing showers (kr500) and washing machine (kr500). There are powered sites, but no cooking facilities for campers. No reservations are taken.

Ásbyrgi Store FAST FOOD €€
(Rte 85; mains kr900-2950; ⏲9am-9pm Jun-Aug, 10am-6pm Sep-May) This store on Rte 85, close to the visitor centre, has a selection of groceries, plus simple grill-bar options (soup, lamb, fish, burgers, sandwiches).

Information

Better roads and increased visitor numbers will inevitably result in more facilities and changing transport schedules, so it's worth checking the park website (or with the visitor centre) to see what's new.

Note that there is a ranger station at Vesturdalur.

Gljúfrastofa Visitor Centre (☎470 7100; www.vjp.is; Ásbyrgi; ⏲9am-7pm Jun-Aug, 10am-4pm May & Sep-Oct, 10am-2pm Apr) The super-helpful national-park visitor centre at Ásbyrgi (just off Rte 85) has an information desk with brochures and maps for sale, informative displays on the area, and knowledgeable staff. The office is open until 9pm for about six weeks from late June until early August (ie the Icelandic school-holiday period).

Note: drones are prohibited in the national park, except with permission from park authorities.

MAPS

The park wardens have created several excellent maps of the region. The excellent park map (kr350) is a useful 1:55,000 plan that ranks the local hikes by difficulty.

The Útivist & afþreying maps are also handy; #3 (kr690) zooms in on the Ásbyrgi–Dettifoss route.

Getting There & Away

BUS

Buses stop at the Ásbyrgi store on Rte 85, not far from the **visitor centre**.

SBA-Norðurleið (www.sba.is) services from Ásbyrgi:

- Bus 641a to Húsavík (kr2500, 45 minutes, one daily mid-June to August).
- Bus 641a to Akureyri (kr6900, two hours, one daily mid-June to August).
- Bus 641 to Hljóðaklettar in Vesturdalur (kr2000, 20 minutes, one daily mid-June to August).
- Bus 641 to Dettifoss (kr3600, 1½ hours, one daily mid-June to August) From Dettifoss you can connect to bus 661a to Krafla and Mývatn.

Strætó (www.bus.is) services from Ásbyrgi – note that bus 79 (one daily except Saturday summer, three weekly in winter) only operates between Húsavík and Þórshöfn (via Ásbyrgi, Kópasker and Raufarhöfn) if prebooked. Call Strætó at least four hours before departure:

- Bus 79 to Húsavík (kr2100, one hour).
- Bus 79 to Kópasker (kr1260, 30 minutes).
- Bus 79 to Þórshöfn (kr3360, two hours).

CAR

Rte 85 (sealed) takes you smoothly to the northern section of the park and the **visitor centre** at Ásbyrgi (from Húsavík it's 65km).

There are two north–south roads running parallel on each side of the canyon. Although the national park is open all year, the gravel roads only open from about late May to early October (weather dependent).

- **Rte 862 (west)** From the Ring Road to Dettifoss (24km), the road is sealed. North of Dettifoss, the road is gravel for about 29km past turn-offs to Hólmatungur and Vesturdalur, then sealed for the final 8km to reach Rte 85 and Ásbyrgi. This route is being sealed in stages (a further 8km in 2017); enquire locally about its condition.
- **Rte 864 (east)** This is a gravel road (narrower than Rte 862) for its 60km length; it's passable by 2WD vehicles, but it has a rutted and potholed surface, so take care and drive slowly. There are no plans to improve this road's conditions.

The sealed route from the Ring Road to Dettifoss is open all year, however, Dettifoss access is not guaranteed in winter, when weather conditions may close the road for a few days or more. During this time, you may be able to visit the falls on a super-Jeep tour from Mývatn.

Wherever you are, make sure you stick to roads and marked trails. Off-road driving is hugely destructive to the country's fragile environment, and illegal.

Ásbyrgi

Driving off Rte 85 onto the flat, grassy plain at the northern end of Vatnajökull National Park, there's little to tell you you're standing on the edge of a massive horseshoe-shaped canyon. The lush **Ásbyrgi canyon** extends 3.5km from north to south and averages 1km in width, making it difficult to discern at its widest point.

From the car park near the end of the road, 3.5km south of the visitor centre, several easy short tracks lead through the forest to viewpoints of the canyon. Heading east the track leads to a spring near the canyon wall, while the western track climbs to a good view across the valley floor. The trail leading straight ahead ends at **Botn-**

DETTIFOSS TO ÁSBYRGI HIKE

The most popular hike in Jökulsárgljúfur is the two-day trip (roughly 30km) between Dettifoss and Ásbyrgi, which moves through birch forests, striking rock formations, lush valleys and commanding perpendicular cliffs while taking in all of the region's major sights and offering awesome canyon views.

The hike can be done in both directions; however, the park rangers recommend starting in Dettifoss and heading north.

The suggested itinerary is to drive to Ásbyrgi and park your car. Pick up information and a map from the **visitor centre** (p277), then take the bus to Dettifoss (SBA's current bus service departs from the Ásbyrgi petrol station at 11am in summer, but check the bus timetable at www.sba.is for the latest). The bus stops for half an hour or so at Vesturdalur; consider pitching your tent in this time and leaving your overnight gear at the Vesturdalur campsite, then continuing on the bus to Dettifoss. This way, you can spend the day walking back to Vesturdalur with a lighter load (beneficial if you plan to tackle the difficult Hafragil lowland trail). There's no rush to be back by nightfall – in summer, there's near-endless daylight.

The Dettifoss to Vesturdalur hike takes an estimated six to eight hours. There are two options on this stretch: the considerably more difficult route involves a steep trail and a spectacular walk via the Hafragil lowlands (18km); the easier takes a route north of Hafragil (19.5km). The lowland trail is not suitable for untrained hikers or people afraid of heights.

On the second day of your walk, take some trails around Vesturdalur's highlights, then enjoy a leisurely hike back to Ásbyrgi (12km, three to four hours), opting for either the rim of Ásbyrgi or walking along the Jökulsá river. You'll return to hot showers at the Ásbyrgi **campsite** (p277), and your waiting car.

THE CREATION OF THE CANYON

There are two stories about the creation of Ásbyrgi. The early Norse settlers believed that Óðinn's normally airborne eight-legged horse, Slættur (known in literature as Sleipnir), accidentally touched down on earth and left one hell of a hoof-print to prove it. The other theory, though more scientific, is also incredible. Geologists believe that the canyon was created by an enormous eruption of the Grímsvötn caldera beneath distant Vatnajökull. It released a catastrophic *jökulhlaup* (glacial flood), which ploughed northward down the Jökulsá á Fjöllum and gouged out the canyon in a matter of days. The river then flowed through Ásbyrgi for about 100 years before shifting eastward to its present course.

stjörn, a small duck-filled pond at the head of Ásbyrgi.

Near the centre of the canyon is the prominent outcrop **Eyjan**, and towards the south the sheer, dark walls rise up to 100m. The cliffs protect a birch forest from harsh winds, and the trees here grow up to 8m in height. You can climb to the summit of Eyjan from the campsite (p277) (4.5km return), or take a trail from the visitor centre and ascend the cliffs via one of two ways (it's easiest to go east along the golf course and turn south at the junction).

Vesturdalur

Off the beaten track and home to diverse scenery, Vesturdalur is a favourite destination for hikers. A series of weaving trails leads from the scrub around the campsite to the cave-riddled pinnacles and rock formations of Hljóðaklettar, the Rauðhólar crater row, the ponds of Eyjan (not to be confused with the Eyjan at Ásbyrgi) and the canyon itself.

There is a summer ranger stationed at Vesturdalur.

Vesturdalur Campsite CAMPGROUND €
(☎470 7100; www.vjp.is; site per person kr1600; ⏱early Jun–mid-Sep) Camping inside the park boundaries is strictly limited to the official campsites at Ásbyrgi (p277) and Vesturdalur (plus Dettifoss for hikers only). Vesturdalur's campsite is near the ranger station and has no powered sites, showers or hot water – toilets are the only luxury here.

Vesturdalur is 14km south of Ásbyrgi off Rte 862. At the time of writing, it was 8km from Rte 85 on newly sealed road, a further 4km on gravel to the Vesturdalur turn-off, then 2km to the area.

Hólmatungur is another 16km south; turn off Rte 862 onto Rte 887. Dettifoss is 7km south of Hólmatungur.

Buses run along Rte 862 in summer (p277).

★Hljóðaklettar GEOLOGICAL FORMATION
The bizarre swirls, spirals, rosettes, honeycombs and basalt columns at Hljóðaklettar (Echo Rocks) are a highlight of any hike around Vesturdalur and a puzzling place for amateur geologists. It's difficult to imagine what sort of volcanic activity produced these twisted rock forms. Weird concertina formations and repeat patterns occur throughout, and the normally vertical basalt columns (formed by rapidly cooling lava) show up on the horizontal here.

These strange forms and patterns create an acoustic effect that makes it impossible to determine the direction of the roaring river, a curiosity that gave the area its name.

A circular **walking trail** (3km) from the parking area takes around an hour to explore. The best formations, which are also riddled with lava caves, are found along the river, northeast of the parking area.

Rauðhólar GEOLOGICAL FORMATION
The Rauðhólar (Red Hills) crater row, just north of Hljóðaklettar, displays a vivid array of colours in the cinder-like gravel on the remaining cones. The craters can be explored on foot during a 5km loop walk from the Vesturdalur parking area.

Karl og Kerling GEOLOGICAL FORMATION
Karl og Kerling ('Old Man' and 'Old Woman'), two rock pillars, believed to be petrified trolls, stand on a gravel bank west of the river, a 2km return walk from the Vesturdalur car park. Across the river is **Tröllahellir**, the gorge's largest cave, but it's reached only on a 5km cross-country hike from Rte 864 on the eastern side.

★Hólmatungur OUTDOORS

South of Vesturdalur, lush vegetation, tumbling waterfalls and an air of utter tranquillity make the Hólmatungur area one of the most beautiful in the park. Underground springs bubble up to form a series of short rivers that twist, turn and cascade their way to the canyon.

The most popular walk here is the 4.5km loop from the parking area, which leads north along the Hólmá river to Hólmáfossar, where the harsh lines of the canyon soften and produce several pretty waterfalls.

From here you head south again on the Jökulsá to its confluence with the Melbugsá river, where the river tumbles over a ledge, forming the **Urriðafossar** waterfalls. To see the falls, you need to walk along the (challenging) 2km trail spur to Katlar.

For the best overall view of Hólmatungur, hike to the hill **Ytra-Þórunnarfjall**, just south of the car park.

Hólmatungur is accessed by turning off Rte 862 onto Rte 887. A 4WD is not essential but is advised (you need good ground clearance to travel Rte 887). You can opt to park your vehicle at Vesturdalur and do a long round-trip day hike. Camping is prohibited at Hólmatungur, but it's a great spot for a picnic lunch.

Dettifoss

The power of nature can be seen in all its glory at mighty Dettifoss, one of Iceland's most impressive waterfalls.

Although Dettifoss is only 45m high and 100m wide, a massive 400 cu metres of water thunders over its edge every second in summer, creating a plume of spray that can be seen 1km away. With the greatest volume of any waterfall in Europe, this truly is nature at its most spectacular. On sunny days, brilliant double rainbows form above the churning milky-grey glacial waters, and you'll have to jostle with the other visitors for the best views. Take care on the paths, made wet and slippery from the spray.

The falls can be seen from either side of the canyon, but there is no link (ie no bridge) between the sides at the site itself. Both viewpoints are grand and have pros and cons, and both require a walk from the respective car park of around 15 to 20 minutes to reach the falls. Many photographers rate the east side as their preferred side; road access is easier on the west side (making it busier with tour buses). Consider visiting either side under the summertime midnight sun for smaller crowds.

A sealed road, Rte 862, links the Ring Road with the western bank of Dettifoss, ending in a large car park and toilet facilities. From the car park, a 2.5km loop walk takes in the dramatic, canyon-edge viewpoint of Dettifoss plus views of a smaller cataract, **Selfoss**.

If you visit the eastern side of the falls via unsealed Rte 864, drive a kilometre or two north of the Dettifoss car park and look for the sign to **Hafragilsfoss** – smaller, photogenic falls downriver from Dettifoss with a brilliant viewpoint over the canyon.

NORTHEAST CIRCUIT

Bypassed by the tourist hordes who whiz around the Ring Road, this wild, sparsely populated coastal route around Iceland's re-

VISITING DETTIFOSS

Dettifoss can be reached three ways in summer by car – and only one way in winter (with no guarantee of access).

Rte 862 south from Ásbyrgi (37km) At the time of writing this route was slowly being sealed, in stages (the northern 16km are expected to be sealed by the end of summer 2017). Check locally about its condition. It's open from about June to early October (weather dependent).

Rte 862 north from the Ring Road The turn-off to Dettifoss is 27km east of Reykjahlíð (Mývatn); it's then an easy 24km on sealed road to reach the falls. Note that snowfall may close this road in winter; winter road access is not guaranteed. You may need to join a super-Jeep tour from Mývatn to see the falls when the road is closed.

Rte 864 on the eastern side of the river It's gravel for its 60km length, from the Ring Road to Ásbyrgi. It's not an F road (ie for 4WDs only), but it can be tough going in a 2WD. Route 864 is open from about June to early October (weather dependent).

mote northeast peninsula is an interesting alternative to the direct road from Mývatn to Egilsstaðir. It's an area of desolate moors and beautiful scenery, stretching to within a few kilometres of the Arctic Circle. If you're looking for unspoilt, untouristed, unhyped Iceland – well, you've found it.

Getting There & Around

AIR

Air Iceland (www.airiceland.is) has a weekday air link connecting Akureyri with Þórshöfn and Vopnafjörður.

BUS

Strætó (www.bus.is) services:

- Bus 79 from Akureyri to Húsavík and on to Þórshöfn along Rte 85 (and in reverse; daily except Saturday summer, three weekly winter). Note: this service only operates beyond Húsavík (calling at Ásbyrgi, Kópasker, Raufarhöfn and Þórshöfn) if prebooked. Call Strætó at least four hours before the scheduled departure time from Húsavík.

There's no bus to/from Vopnafjörður.

Kópasker

POP 120

Tiny Kópasker, on the eastern shore of Öxarfjörður 35km north of Ásbyrgi, is the first place you'll pass through before disappearing into the wilds of Iceland's far northeast.

Kópasker HI Hostel HOSTEL €
(☎465 2314; www.hostel.is; Akurgerði 7; dm/d without bathroom kr4700/12,400; ⊙May-Oct) Your best bet for a bed is the homely Kópasker HI Hostel, run by Benni. Rooms are spread across a couple of houses; everything is well maintained, and there's good birdwatching (and sometimes seal-watching) in the neighbourhood. HI members receive a kr700 discount; linen costs kr1500. Note: cash only.

Campsite CAMPGROUND €
(site per person kr1200; ⊙Jun-Aug) Neat little campground at the entrance to town.

Dettifoss Guesthouse GUESTHOUSE €€
(☎869 7672; gisting@kopasker.is; Rte 85; s/d without bathroom kr8475/15,960) Don't be misled by the name: this reasonably priced guesthouse is actually 7km north of Ásbyrgi en route to Kópasker (not south, towards Dettifoss). It's a comfy spot with 12 rooms of varying sizes, guest kitchen and flash shared bathrooms. Breakfast is kr1700. Campers also welcome (kr1200 per person).

Skerjakolla SUPERMARKET, CAFE €
(Bakkagata 10; snacks & pizza kr290-2000; ⊙10am-8pm Mon-Fri, noon-8pm Sat, noon-6pm Sun Jun-Aug, shorter hours Sep-May) Skerjakolla is a sweet surprise: a decent grocery store, with a small and simple cafe inside serving pizza, sandwiches, coffee and cake. There's even a **Vínbúðin** (Bakkagata 10; ⊙4-6pm Mon-Thu, 1-6pm Fri) here too, and a petrol pump out front.

Raufarhöfn

POP 195

Like the setting of a Stephen King novel, distant Raufarhöfn (*roy*-ver-hup), Iceland's northernmost township, is an eerily quiet place with a prominently positioned graveyard. The port has functioned since the Saga Age, but the town's economic peak came early in the 20th century during the herring boom, when it was second to Siglufjörður in volume. Today, Raufarhöfn's rows of dull prefab housing give few clues to its illustrious past. You feel a long way from the gloss and glamour of Iceland's well-oiled tourist machine here.

Arctic Henge MONUMENT
(www.arctichenge.com; ⊙24hr) There are ambitious long-term plans underway to build a massive stone circle on the hill just north of town. When completed, the Arctic Henge will be 50m in diameter with four gates (to represent the seasons) up to 7m in height. The plan is to use the stone henge as a finely tuned sundial to celebrate the solstices, view the midnight sun, and explain the strong local beliefs in the mythology of the Edda poem *Völuspá* (Wise Woman's Prophecy).

Sleeping & Eating

Sólsetur GUESTHOUSE €
(☎849 3536; www.solsetur.com; Víkurbraut 18; d without bathroom incl breakfast kr9900-12,400) A homely guesthouse run by the friendly owner of Kaupfélagið Raufarhöfn, where breakfast is served. There's a full kitchen and living space, and lovely views of the town's bay.

★**Kaupfélagið Raufarhöfn** CAFE €
(Aðalbraut 24; ⊙8-10.30am & 2-9pm) Easily the brightest spark in town, this newly opened cafe and handicrafts gallery has bags of

ROADS IN THE NORTHEAST

A sealed inland Rte 85 has recently been built to link Kópasker with the east, reaching the coast not far from Rauðanes. From the new Rte 85, Rte 874 branches north to Raufarhöfn.

The new road still carries little traffic, but it means that the unsealed but scenic old coastal Rte 85 (now labelled Rte 870) around the bleak and little-visited **Melrakkaslétta** (Arctic Fox Plain) sees little maintenance – 4WDs will face few problems, but it's best to ask locally whether Rte 870 is in a suitable state for 2WDs.

For 55km between Kópasker and Raufarhöfn, Rte 870 passes through the low-lying flatlands, ponds and marshes of this bird-rich area. There are trails and turn-offs to lonely lighthouses on remote headlands. For a long time Hraunhafnartangi was thought to be the northernmost point of the Icelandic mainland, but recent measurements have pinned that prize on its neighbour, Rifstangi, which falls just 2.5km shy of the Arctic Circle.

personality (driftwood, artworks, coffee pots). It's a welcome addition to the town, and opens for a breakfast buffet, afternoon cake and coffee, and simple evening meals.

Rauðanes

There's excellent hiking at **Rauðanes**, where a 7km marked walking trail leads to bizarre rock formations, natural arches, caves and secluded beaches, plus great bird life (including puffins). The turn-off to Rauðanes is about halfway between Raufarhöfn and Þórshöfn (it's a small sign); the road leads 1.5km to an information board (with walking trail details) and small car park. There is a track from here that leads closer to the coastline, but it's only for 4WDs.

Þórshöfn

POP 380

Þórshöfn has served as a busy port since Saga times and saw its heyday when a herring-salting station was established here in the early 20th century. Today it's a very modest place but makes a good base for the remote Langanes peninsula.

For tourist information in town, stop by the swimming-pool/gym complex.

Tours

Þórshöfn Kayak KAYAKING
(☎468 1250; www.baranrestaurant.is; Eyrarvegur 3; ⊙May-Sep) Operating out of Báran restaurant by the harbour, this new outfit offers kayaking tours, from a short and sweet taster (one hour, kr4000), to coastal paddling checking out low cliffs, a lighthouse and lots of seabirds (three hours, kr9700). There's a midnight sun tour, too, in June and July. Prices include drysuits.

Sleeping & Eating

Lyngholt Guesthouse GUESTHOUSE €
(☎897 5064; www.lyngholt.is; Langanesvegur 12; s/d without bathroom kr9500/14,500) This handsome timber guesthouse is situated near the pool. It has good facilities, including kitchen and lounge.

Þórshöfn Campsite CAMPGROUND €
(sites per person kr1200; ⊙Jun-Aug) Neat, grassy campsite close to the heart of town.

Samkaup-Strax SUPERMARKET €
(Langanesvegur 2; ⊙9am-6pm Mon-Fri, 10am-4pm Sat & Sat Jun-Aug, shorter hours Sep-May) For self-catering.

★**Báran** ICELANDIC €€
(http://baranrestaurant.is; Eyrarvegur 3; mains kr1200-3600; ⊙8am-11pm Sun-Thu, to 1am Fri, to 3am Sat May-Sep, shorter hours Oct-Apr) Behind the N1 is a harbourside restaurant that has changed incarnations a few times, but seems to have settled on one – and it's a cool surprise to find a loungey area, wide-ranging menu, high-quality food and some excellent local beer choices. Pizza, pasta and burgers are well-done standards, but there's also good local lamb and fish.

Drop by for a late-night drink with the locals on weekends.

Langanes

Shaped like a goose with a very large head, foggy Langanes is one of the loneliest corners of Iceland. The peninsula's flat terrain, cushioned by mossy meadows and studded with crumbling remains, is an excellent place to break in your hiking shoes and find solitude, should you be seeking it.

Before exploring the region, base yourself at the excellent Ytra Lón Farm Lodge, just off Rte 869 (on a gravel road, but easily done in a small 2WD in summer).

Route 869 ends only 17km along the 50km Langanes peninsula, and although it's possible to continue along the track to the tip at Fontur lighthouse in a 4WD, parts of the road can be difficult to navigate.

If you don't have your own vehicle, you can arrange a transfer to Ytra Lón Farm Lodge from Þórshöfn (for a fee).

★ **Ytra Lón Farm Lodge** APARTMENT €€
(☎846 6448; www.ytralon.is; s/d incl breakfast kr22,300/25,900) For Langanes exploration, base yourself at excellent Ytra Lón, 14km northeast of Þórshöfn and just off Rte 869. It's part of a working sheep farm run by a welcoming Dutch-Icelandic family. Here, colourful studio apartments, each with bathroom and kitchenette, are housed in cargo containers and lined up under a greenhouse-style roof. There's a breakfast buffet of local produce, and a hot-pot.

OFF THE BEATEN TRACK

HIKE OR DRIVE TO THE END OF THE EARTH

Abandoned farms, lonely lighthouses, seal colonies and craggy windswept cliffs home to prolific bird life – there are few places in the world that feel as remote as **Langanes**. The highlight of the area is the new viewing platform over the bird-filled cliffs at **Skoruvíkurbjarg**: it lies above a rock pillar (known as Stóri Karl) that's home to thousands of northern gannets, while nearby are colonies of auks, including guillemots and puffins.

Langanes is perfect for hiking, and to help plot your route it's worth picking up the Útivist & afþreying #7 map, available at Ytra Lón Farm Lodge and local information centres. Another excellent resource is the *Birding Trail* map, which covers birdwatching information in the northeast (from Mývatn to Langanes), with information online at www.birdingtrail.is.

If you're short on time, consider doing a **4WD tour** of Langanes offered by Ytra Lón. A 2½-hour tour to the bird cliffs of Skoruvík costs kr15,900 per person (minimum two people), or you can spend five hours touring, including a visit to the abandoned village of Skálar and the lighthouse at Fontur (kr28,900). Tours run May to September (the best time for birdwatching, though bear in mind that the auks leave the breeding grounds in early August). Prebooking is required.

Vopnafjörður & Around

POP 700

'Weapon Fjord' was once the notorious home of a fearsome dragon that protected northeast Iceland from harm. Today, there are no dragons, and the town is an agreeably sleepy place; it's well known for the superlative salmon rivers in the area (Prince Charles and George Bush Sr have fished here).

Note that Vopnafjörður is considered to be part of East Iceland and online information is found at www.east.is. We have covered it here under North Iceland for the logistics of travelling the Northeast Circuit along Rte 85.

Sights & Activities

Kaupvangur CULTURAL CENTRE
(Hafnarbyggð 4) The town's most significant building is Kaupvangur, a restored customs house. You'll find an excellent cafe and information centre on the ground floor, and a handicrafts store. Upstairs there's a well-curated exhibit about two locals, Iceland's version of the Gershwin brothers. Also on the 2nd floor is a small display about East Iceland émigrés: from 1850 to 1914, a wave of locals purchased boat tickets to North America from this very building.

The **East Iceland Emigration Center** is based here, and can help 'Western Icelanders' (ie North Americans with Icelandic heritage) reconnect with their heritage.

Bustarfell MUSEUM
(adult/child kr900/200; ⏲10am-5pm mid-Jun–mid-Sep) This high-quality folk museum is set in a photogenic 18th-century turf-roofed

WORTH A TRIP

ROUTE 917

East of Vopnafjörður, the truly spectacular 73km mountain drive along mostly unpaved Rte 917 takes you over 655m **Hellisheiði** and down to the east coast. The road may be impassable in bad weather but in summer is generally doable in a small car. It climbs up a series of switchbacks and hairpin bends before dropping down to the striking glacial river deltas on the **Héraðssandur**.

manor house southwest of Vopnafjörður township. The on-site Cafe Croft serves home-baked cake and coffee. It's 8km off Rte 85 about 19km from Vopnafjörður (or reach it on the sealed Rte 920).

Selárdalslaug SWIMMING
(adult/child kr700/350; ⏲noon-10pm May-Aug, shorter hours Sep-Apr) This novel swimming pool lies in the middle of nowhere – it's signed 8km north of Vopnafjörður off Rte 85, just south of the river Selá. Stop for a quick soak in the geothermal waters of the hot-pot (and to admire the candlelit change rooms – there's no electricity out here).

Sleeping & Eating

Under the Mountain/ Refsstaður II GUESTHOUSE €
(☎895 1562; twocats@simnet.is; s/d without bathroom kr6000/9000) Cathy, an American of Icelandic descent, has a special knack for hospitality; her farmhouse feels homey and warm. It's about 9km south of town; first take Rte 917 past the small airstrip, then travel along Rte 919 for 4km. Sleeping-bag beds cost kr4000; there is kitchen access, and discounts for longer stays (call ahead in winter). It's cash only.

Cathy maintains the local emigration exhibit at Kaupvangur (p283) and provides an interesting perspective on life in rural Iceland.

Campsite CAMPGROUND €
(sites per person kr1100; ⏲Jun–mid-Sep) Good campsite with views of the fjord and town below. Follow Miðbraut north and turn left at the school.

★ **Hvammsgerði** GUESTHOUSE €€
(☎588 1298; www.hvammsgerdi.is; s/d without bathroom incl breakfast kr10,900/15,900) Just north of the turn-off to Selárdalslaug, about 9km north of the township, is this welcoming riverside option. It's a cosy, family-friendly guesthouse with agreeable rooms, sweet pets to play with, and farm-fresh eggs at the breakfast table (breakfast kr1500). Sleeping-bag beds are available (kr5500).

★ **Kaupvangskaffi** CAFE €
(www.kaupvangskaffi.com; Hafnarbyggð 4; soup buffet kr1390, pizza kr1360-4620; ⏲10am-10pm) It seems everyone passing through town stops here – and with good reason. Inside Kaupvangur (p283), you'll find sofas to relax on, plus excellent coffee, a big lunchtime soup buffet, pizzas (eat in or take away) and a tempting array of sweet treats.

Kauptún SUPERMARKET €
(Hafnarbyggð; ⏲9.30am-6pm Mon-Fri, noon-4pm Sat) The supermarket shares a car park with Kaupvangur (p283).

Information

Tourist Information Centre (☎473 1331; www.vopnafjordur.com; Hafnarbyggð 4; ⏲11am-5pm Mon-Fri) Good information, inside **Kaupvangur** (p283). Outside of office opening hours you can still get brochures and local info; look for the handy, free guides to local walking routes.

Getting There & Away

There is no bus service to Vopnafjörður.

From Vopnafjörður it's 137km to Reykjahlíð and 136km to Egilsstaðir (via Rte 85 and the Ring Road), so check fuel levels before you leave town.

It's a shorter, more scenic (and more hair-raising) route to Egilsstaðir (95km) via the gravel mountain road Rte 917.

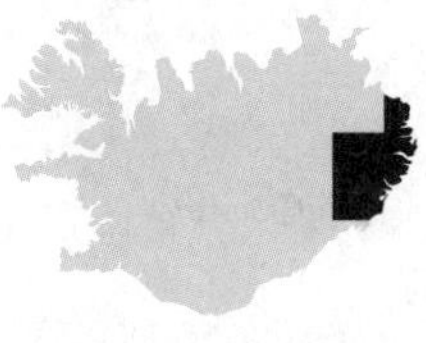

East Iceland

Best Places to Eat

- Randulffs-sjóhús (p304)
- Eldhúsið (p292)
- Klausturkaffi (p294)
- Kaupfélagsbarinn (p306)
- Norð Austur Sushi & Bar (p300)

Best Places to Stay

- Ferðaþjónustan Mjóeyri (p304)
- Hafaldan Old Hospital Hostel (p299)
- Fosshotel Eastfjords (p306)
- Silfurberg (p308)
- Wilderness Center (p293)

Why Go?

As far as you can get (some 650km) from Reykjavík, Iceland's east doesn't announce itself as loudly as other parts of the country, preferring subtle charms over big-ticket attractions. The Eastfjords is the area's most wondrous destination – the scenery is spectacular around the northern fjord villages, backed by sheer-sided mountains etched with waterfalls. If the weather's fine, several days spent hiking here may be some of your most memorable in Iceland.

Away from the convoluted coast, the country's longest lake stretches southwest from Egilsstaðir, its shores lined with perfect diversions. Further inland are the forgotten farms, fells and reindeer-roamed heathlands of the empty east, and Snæfell, one of Iceland's prime peaks.

Don't simply overnight in Egilsstaðir then speed away. The east's spectacular fjords, scenic hiking trails, fascinating geology and friendly villages are some of Iceland's unsung treasures.

Road Distances (km)

	Djúpivogur	Reykjavík	Egilsstaðir	Borgarfjörður Eystri	Seyðisfjörður	Neskaupstaður
Reykjavík	552					
Egilsstaðir	85	698				
Borgarfjörður Eystri	155	702	70			
Seyðisfjörður	111	660	27	92		
Neskaupstaður	164	703	72	140	96	
Breiðdalsvík	64	612	84	153	109	100

East Iceland Highlights

1. **Seyðisfjörður** (p297) Arriving in Iceland in style by sailing up a lovely, long fjord to this bohemian village.
2. **Borgarfjörður Eystri** (p295) Hiking magical trails, chatting with the hidden people and snapping photos of puffin posses in this tiny hamlet.
3. **Lagarfljót** (p292) Touring Lagarfljót's forested lake shores while looking for sea monsters.
4. **Mjóifjörður** (p302) Learning the definition of tranquil isolation in this ruin-strewn fjord.
5. **Stöðvarfjörður** (p306) Marvelling over the magnificent mineral collection in this tiny town.
6. **Wilderness Center** (p293) Exploring highland life and ace walking trails at this remote, unique farm.
7. **Húsey Horse Farm** (p300) Watching birds, seals and spectacular scenery on horseback.
8. **Havarí** (p309) Checking out live music and vegetarian food at this fabulous venue on Berufjörður.

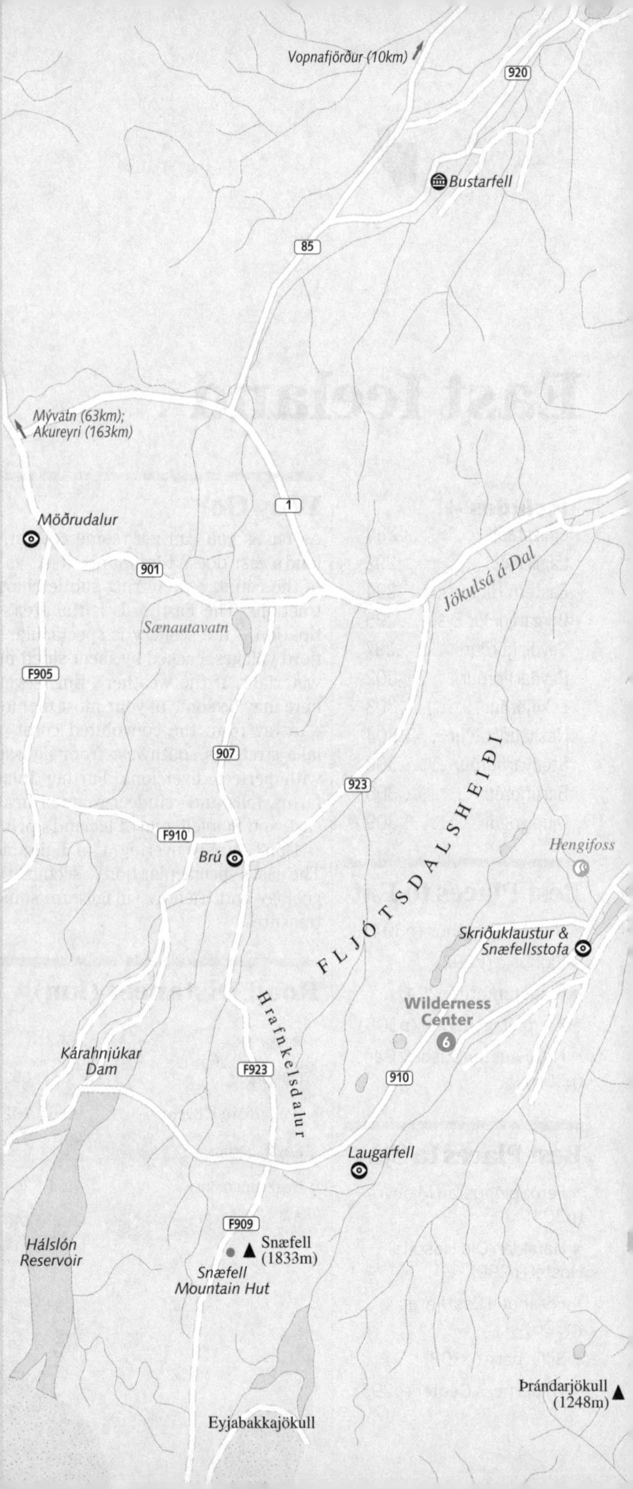

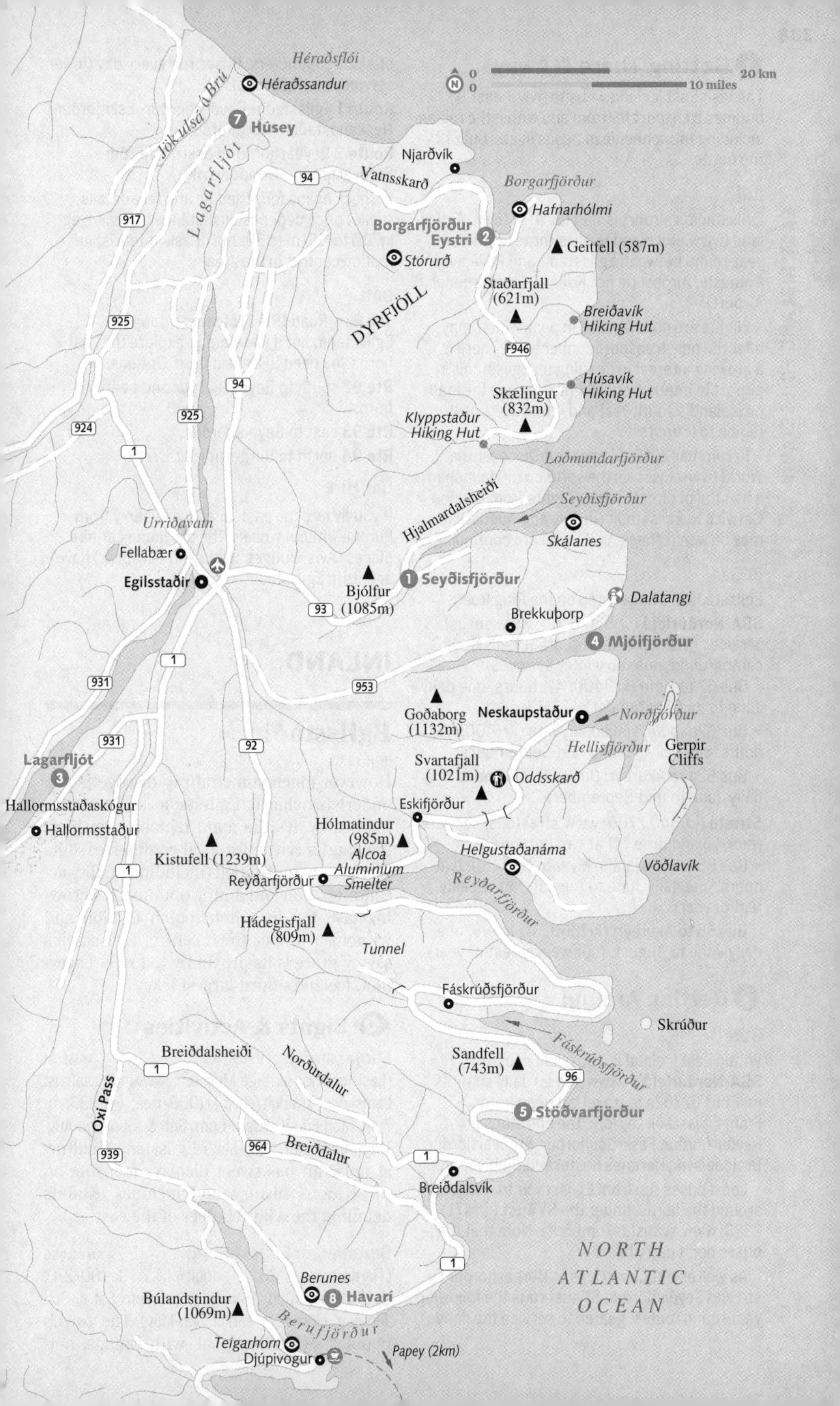

Héraðsflói
Héraðssandur
7 Húsey
Jökulsá á Brú
Lagarfljót
0 20 km
0 10 miles
Njarðvík
94
Vatnsskarð
Borgarfjörður
Hafnarhólmi
917
Borgarfjörður Eystri 2
Geitfell (587m)
Stórurð
Staðarfjall (621m)
DYRFJÖLL
Breiðavík Hiking Hut
925
F946
Húsavík Hiking Hut
94
Skælingur (832m)
925
924
Klyppstaður Hiking Hut
1
Loðmundarfjörður
Seyðisfjörður
Hjalmardalsheiði
Urriðavatn
Skálanes
Fellabær
Egilsstaðir
Bjólfur (1085m)
1 Seyðisfjörður
Dalatangi
93
Brekkuþorp
4 Mjóifjörður
1
931
953
Goðaborg (1132m)
Neskaupstaður
Norðfjörður
931
92
Hellisfjörður
Gerpir Cliffs
Lagarfljót
3
Svartafjall (1021m)
Oddsskarð
Hallormsstaðaskógur
Hallormsstaður
Eskifjörður
Hólmatindur (985m)
Kistufell (1239m)
Alcoa Aluminium Smelter
Helgustaðanáma
1
Reyðarfjörður
Vöðlavík
Reyðarfjörður
Hádegisfjall (809m)
Tunnel
Fáskrúðsfjörður
Skrúður
Breiðdalsheiði
Norðurdalur
Fáskrúðsfjörður
Sandfell (743m)
1
96
Oxi Pass
5 Stöðvarfjörður
964
Breiðdalur
939
1
Breiðdalsvík
NORTH ATLANTIC OCEAN
1
Berunes
8 Havarí
Búlandstindur (1069m)
Berufjörður
Teigarhorn
Djúpivogur
Papey (2km)

Getting There & Away

The Visit East Iceland website (www.east.is) outlines transport to/from and within the region, including the schedule of buses in and out of the fjords.

AIR

Egilsstaðir's airport is 1km north of town. Air Iceland (www.airiceland.is) flies three times daily year-round between Egilsstaðir and Reykjavík Domestic Airport (ie not Keflavík International Airport).

Flights are popular (and in peak winter may offer the only transport connection). There is a growing interest in opening up Egilsstaðir's airport to international flights, to ease the load on Iceland's southwest and introduce a new region to tourists.

In summer 2016 UK operator Discover the World (www.discovertheworld.co.uk) launched a handful of direct charter flights from London Gatwick to Egilsstaðir (in July and August); it may be worth checking if these are continuing.

BUS

Egilsstaðir is a major stop on the Ring Road.

SBA-Norðurleið (☎550 0700; www.sba.is) services (pick-up and drop-off at Egilsstaðir's campground; note no winter services):

- Bus 62 to Höfn (kr9400, 4½ hours, one daily June to mid-September).
- Bus 62a to Reykjahlíð, Mývatn (kr6100, 2½ hours, one daily June to mid-September).
- Bus 62a to Akureyri (kr9600, 4¼ hours, one daily June to mid-September).

Strætó (☎540 2700; www.straeto.is) services (pick-up and drop-off at campground):

- Bus 56 to Reykjahlíð, Mývatn (kr5460, two hours, one daily June to August, four weekly rest of year).
- Bus 56 to Akureyri (kr7560, 3½ hours, one daily June to August, four weekly rest of year).

Getting Around

BUS

Within East Iceland it's possible to use **SBA-Norðurleið's** (www.sba.is) daily summer bus 62/62a to travel between fjords. From Egilsstaðir to Höfn, the bus stops at Reyðarfjörður, Fáskrúðsfjörður, Stöðvarfjörður, Breiðdalsvík, Berunes hostel and Djúpivogur.

Local buses run from Egilsstaðir to villages around the fjords, under the **SVAust** (☎471 2320; www.svaust.is) umbrella. Note that these buses don't carry bikes.

As well as direct services to Borgarfjörður Eystri and Seyðisfjörður, SVAust runs the following year-round routes, geared to service the needs of Alcoa commuters. Buses run every day (fewer services on weekends).

Route 1 Egilsstaðir–Reyðarfjörður–Eskifjörður–Neskaupstaður (Nordfjörður)

Route 2 Reyðarfjörður–Fáskrúðsfjörður–Stöðvarfjörður–Breiðdalsvík

Check online for schedule and fare details (ticket price depends on distance travelled, eg kr700 for 16km to 30km), or ask at tourist information centres in the area.

CAR

The Ring Road (Rte 1) steams through Egilsstaðir, but if you want to explore the Eastfjords you need to leave it here. Options:

Rte 92 south to Reyðarfjörður and nearby fjords.

Rte 93 east to Seyðisfjörður.

Rte 94 north to Borgarfjörður Eystri.

Car Hire

If you fly into the east, or arrive by ferry from Europe without wheels, the big-name car-hire places (Avis, Budget, Hertz and Europcar) have agents in Egilsstaðir.

INLAND

Egilsstaðir

POP 2330

However much you strain to discover some underlying charm, Egilsstaðir isn't a ravishing beauty. It's the main regional transport hub, and a centre for local commerce, so its services are quite good (including quality accommodation and dining options). It's growing fast, but in a hotchpotch fashion and without a proper town centre. Egilsstaðir's saving grace is its proximity to lovely Lagarfljót, Iceland's third-largest lake.

Sights & Activities

Minjasafn Austurlands MUSEUM

(East Iceland Heritage Museum; www.minjasafn.is; Laufskógar 1; adult/child kr1000/free; ⏲11.30am-7pm Mon-Fri, 10:30am-6pm Sat & Sun Jun-Aug, 11am-4pm Tue-Fri Sep-May) Egilsstaðir's cultural museum has sweet displays focusing on the region's history, and includes exhibits detailing the wild reindeer of the east.

Sundlaugin Egilsstöðum SWIMMING

(Tjarnarbraut 26; adult/child kr700/270; ⏲6.30am-9.30pm Mon-Fri, 10am-6pm Sat & Sun Jun-Aug, closes 1hr earlier Sep-May) The town's popular swimming pool, with saunas, hot-

ROUTE OPTIONS

Driving between Egilsstaðir and Djúpivogur, there are three options: two mountain roads and one fjordside route. All three are incredibly panoramic. (Note that routes here are described heading south from Egilsstaðir; for motorists heading north from Djúpivogur, read these directions in reverse.)

➡ **Route 1** From Egilsstaðir, the **Ring Road** heads south, descending steeply from Breiðdalsheiði heath and travelling east through the Breiðdalur valley to Breiðdalsvík, then weaving along the coast to Djúpivogur. This Egilsstaðir–Breiðdalsvík route is 84km (note: not all of this section of the Ring Road is sealed, and in winter, snowfall may close the mountain road at Breiðdalsheiði; any closures are outlined on www.road.is).

➡ **Route 939** A short cut is provided by the rough (gravel) Rte 939 via the **Öxi mountain pass** (this is not a great option in bad weather or fog, and is closed in winter). This pass turns off the Ring Road about 45km south of Egilsstaðir, connecting with the head of Berufjörður after 19km. Note that most GPS units automatically give this route as the shortest option, but do give some consideration as to whether it's the best route for you.

➡ **Routes 92 & 96** A third option is to travel from Egilsstaðir to Breiðdalsvík via Rtes 92 and 96, travelling via the **fjords** Reyðarfjörður, Fáskrúðsfjörður and Stöðvarfjörður. This option is only slightly longer than the Ring Road option (92km), and is sealed the entire length. This is often the only option in winter, when snow closes the Ring Road stretch at Breiðdalsheiði. It has even been mooted that the Ring Road may one day be officially rerouted to take in Rtes 92 and 96.

pots and attached gym, is north of the centre.

Baðhúsið Spa SPA

(☎471 1114; hotel guest/nonguest kr2000/3500; ⏰10am-10pm) Inside Gistihúsið – Lake Hotel Egilsstaðir (p291), this delightfully rustic spa area is a great place to rest weary hiking bones, with hot tub and sauna, plus relaxing lake views. Bookings are required.

Tours

Jeep Tours JEEP TOUR

(☎898 2798; www.jeeptours.is) Knowledgeable Agnar runs excellent 4WD day tours from Egilsstaðir into the highlands: to Askja and Herðubreið (kr44,500), to Snæfell (kr39,500), or on reindeer-spotting safaris. This is also one of few companies visiting Kverkfjöll as a day tour (kr44,500), travelling via (sealed) Rte 910 to Kárahnjúkar dam before tackling remote 4WD tracks. Winter tours are available; check the website.

Wild Boys HIKING TOUR

(☎864 7393, 896 4334; www.wildboys.is) A small operator that arranges guided hikes in the area, including popular day hikes to Snæfell (kr41,000), Dyrfjöll and Stórurð near Borgarfjörður Eystri, or Askja. It also offers multiday hikes in the eastern highland region.

Festivals & Events

Dagar Myrkurs CULTURAL

(⏰early Nov) Over five days in early November, throughout East Iceland, the 'Days of Darkness' celebrates the failing light and the onset of winter with ghost stories, Northern Lights spotting and torch-lit processions.

Sleeping

Rooms and campsites in the area are in hot demand on Wednesday nights in summer, as the ferry to Europe sails from Seyðisfjorður (27km away) on Thursday mornings. If you are taking the ferry, book your accommodation well ahead.

Refer to accommodation websites for up-to-date rates.

Egilsstaðir Camping CAMPGROUND €

(☎470 0750; Kaupvangur 17; sites per person kr1400; @) Camping pitches are in utilitarian rows, but it's central and facilities are reasonable; there's a laundry and on-site cafe, but no camper kitchen. At reception you can rent bikes (kr3900 for 24 hours) and book tours.

Olga Guesthouse GUESTHOUSE €€

(☎860 2999; www.gistihusolgu.com; Tjarnabraut 3; d with/without bathroom incl breakfast kr24,990/20,990) In a good central location, dressed-in-red Olga offers five rooms

Egilsstaðir

Sights

1 Minjasafn Austurlands D3

Activities, Courses & Tours

2 Baðhúsið Spa A4
3 Sundlaugin Egilsstöðum D1

Sleeping

4 Egilsstaðir Camping B5
5 Gistihúsið – Lake Hotel Egilsstaðir A4
6 Hótel Valaskjálf D3
7 Icelandair Hótel Hérað B4
8 Lyngás Guesthouse.............................. C5
9 Olga Guesthouse.................................C4

Eating

10 Bónus B3
11 Café Nielsen......................................C4
Eldhúsið .... (see 5)
12 Nettó B4
13 Salt B4
14 Söluskálinn B4

Shopping

15 Vínbúðin..B4

that share three bathrooms and a small kitchen – all rooms come with tea/coffee-making facilities, TV and fridge. Two doors down is Olga's sister, yellow **Birta Guesthouse**, under the same friendly ownership and with similar high-quality facilities. Both guesthouses have an additional annexe containing en suite rooms.

Lyngás Guesthouse GUESTHOUSE €€
(☎471 1310; www.lyngas.is; Lyngás 5-7; s/d without bathroom kr15,600/19,320) Behind an uninspiring exterior is this fresh, six-room guesthouse, offering fine views, kitchen and a couple of larger, family-friendly rooms. You can save a reasonable amount of krónur using your own sleeping bag (single/double kr12,480/15,456).

Hótel Eyvindará HOTEL, COTTAGES €€
(☎471 1200; www.eyvindara.is; Eyvindará II; s/d incl breakfast kr23,000/28,500; ⏱Apr-Oct) Set 4km out of town (on Rte 94), Eyvindará is a handsome, family-run collection of new hotel rooms, plus good motel-style units and timber cottages. The cottages sit hidden among fir trees, while motel rooms enjoy verandahs and views. There's a decent restaurant too (open mid-May to mid-September), and an inviting lounge area.

Hótel Valaskjálf HOTEL €€
(☎471 1600; www.valaskjalf.is; Skógarlönd 3; s/d incl breakfast kr21,900/28,200) Recipient of an impressive recent makeover, this hotel has petite but well-designed rooms with some colourful retro-style accents. There's a highly rated on-site restaurant, Glóð, and breakfast gets good reports.

Gistihúsið – Lake Hotel Egilsstaðir HOTEL €€€
(☎471 1114; www.lakehotel.is; r incl breakfast kr33,100; @) The town was named after this farm and splendid heritage guesthouse (now big enough to warrant the 'hotel' label) on the banks of Lagarfljót, 300m west of the crossroads. In its old wing, en suite rooms retain a sense of character. In contrast, a new extension houses 30 modern, slightly anonymous hotel rooms. There's a great restaurant (p292) on site, and spa (p289).

Icelandair Hótel Hérað HOTEL €€€
(☎471 1500; www.icelandairhotels.is; Miðvangur 5-7; r from kr33,500; @) This stylish, friendly, business-standard hotel is kitted out with the expected bells and whistles, and appealing splashes of colour. The restaurant (mains kr2200 to kr7600) here is a good place to indulge (house speciality: reindeer). Breakfast buffet kr2600.

LOCAL KNOWLEDGE

MEET THE LOCALS

Tanni Travel (☎476 1399; www.meetthelocals.is) has created some unique experiences in East Iceland. The agency offers a roster of guided village walks (daily from June to mid-September), plus can devise itineraries and put you in touch with activity providers (particularly useful in winter). It also offers visitors the chance to spend an evening dining in the home of locals (per person kr14,500).

Eating

Bókakaffi Hlöðum CAFE €
(www.bokakaffi.is; Helgafelli 2; soup buffet kr1950; ⏱10am-5pm Mon-Fri) In Fellabær, at the western end of the bridge across the river from Egilsstaðir, is this sweet, low-key cafe with quality coffee, retro furniture, vinyl records, secondhand books and baked treats.

Söluskálinn FAST FOOD €
(mains kr900-2100; ⏱8am-11.30pm) Refuel your car and your body at Söluskálinn at the busy N1 service station on the Ring Road.

Café Nielsen INTERNATIONAL €€
(Tjarnarbraut 1; mains kr1800-7400; ⏱11.30am-11.30pm Mon-Fri, 1-11.30pm Sat & Sun mid-May–Sep; 👪) Based in Egilsstaðir's oldest house, cottagey Café Nielsen offers a wide-ranging, crowd-pleasing menu that roams from lobster soup to (pricey) reindeer by way of nachos and barbecue ribs; the kitchen closes at 10pm. In summer there's a leafy terrace and garden. The weekday lunch buffet (soup, salad, pasta) is kr2100.

Salt INTERNATIONAL €€
(www.saltbistro.is; Miðvangur 2; snacks & meals kr900-3900; ⏱10am-10pm Mon-Sat, noon-10pm Sun; 🌿👪) We understand the appeal of this cool cafe-bistro, which offers one of the most diverse menus in regional Iceland. Unfortunately, Salt can struggle with the large crowds it attracts, and service suffers. The food, however, is good: try the gourmet-topped flatbread pizza made with local barley, or opt for a burger, salad or tandoori-baked Indian dish.

★**Eldhúsið** ICELANDIC €€€
(☎471 1114; www.lakehotel.is; lunch kr1390-3990, dinner mains kr3190-6190; ⌚11.30am-10pm) Some of the east's most creative cooking happens at the restaurant inside Gistihúsið – Lake Hotel Egilsstaðir (p291). The menu is an ode to locally sourced produce (lamb, fish, game), and the speciality is the beef, raised right here on the farm. Try a ribeye with Béarnaise foam, or 'surf and turf' tenderloin with tempura langoustine. Desserts are pretty, polished affairs. Bookings advised.

The three-course menu of farm produce costs kr8990 and represents good value for the high standard offered.

Self-Catering

Nettó SUPERMARKET
(⌚9am-8pm Mon-Sat, 10am-7pm Sun) Behind the N1 petrol station.

Bónus SUPERMARKET
(⌚11am-6.30pm Mon-Thu, 10am-7.30pm Fri, 10am-6pm Sat, noon-6pm Sun) On the Ring Road north of the N1.

Vínbúðin ALCOHOL
(Miðvangur 2-4; ⌚11am-6pm Mon-Thu, to 7pm Fri, to 4pm Sat May-Aug, shorter hours Sep-Apr) Government-run liquor store.

ℹ Information

East Iceland Regional Information Centre
(☎471 2320; www.east.is; Miðvangur 1-3; ⌚8.30am-6pm Mon-Fri, 10am-4pm Sat, 1-6pm Sun Jun-Aug, 1-6pm Mon-Fri, 10am-2pm Sat Sep-May) Maps and brochures are plentiful here – you'll find everything you need to explore the entire eastern region. It shares the space with an excellent art and design store.

Egilsstaðastofa Visitor Center (☎470 0750; www.visitegilsstadir.is; Kaupvangur 17; ⌚7am-11pm Jun-Aug, 8.30am-3pm Mon-Fri May & Sep, 8.30am-12.30pm Mon-Fri Oct-Apr) From its info desk at the campground reception, this place focuses on Egilsstaðir and surrounds and can hook you up with bus tickets and various activity tours: hiking, super-Jeep tours, sea-angling etc. Bike hire is available (kr2900 for up to four hours, kr3900 for 24 hours).

ℹ Getting There & Away

Egilsstaðir is the transport hub of East Iceland. There's an airport, and all bus services pass through. The main bus stop is at the campground.

Lagarfljót

The grey-brown waters of the river-lake Lagarfljót are reputed to harbour a fearsome monster, **Lagarfljótsormur**, which has allegedly been spotted since Viking times. The most recent 'sighting' of the serpentine beast (also called the Worm/Wyrm) caused quite a stir – in 2012 a local farmer released footage of a large creature moving in the river. The clip has attracted more than five million hits on YouTube, and garnered international news coverage. Read more at www.lagarfljotsormur.com.

Real or imagined, the poor beast must be pretty chilly – Lagarfljót starts its journey in the Vatnajökull ice cap and its glacial waters flow north to the Arctic Ocean, widening into a 38km-long, 50m-deep lake, often called Lögurinn, south of Egilsstaðir. Whether you see a monster or not, it's a lovely stretch of water to circumnavigate by car.

Rte 931, a mixture of sealed surfaces and gravel (gravel on the less-trafficked western shore), turns off the Ring Road about 10km south of Egilsstaðir and runs around the lake to Fellabær, a circuit of around 70km.

There's useful information about the area at www.hengifoss.is.

Hallormsstaðaskógur

One of Iceland's largest forests, 740-hectare Hallormsstaðaskógur (www.skogur.is) is king of the woods and venerated by the arboreally challenged nation. Although it's small by most countries' standards, it's a leafy reprieve after the stark, bare mountainsides to the north and south of Egilsstaðir. Common species include native dwarf birch and mountain ash, as well as 80 tree species gathered from around the world.

The forest is a popular recreation area, with marked trails and footpaths.

Sleeping & Eating

Bring a picnic to enjoy at one of the many picnic sites in the forest or beside the lake. There's a small store and petrol pump.

Atlavík Campsite CAMPGROUND €
(sites per person kr1400; ⌚mid-May–Sep) In a wooded cove on the lake shore, idyllic Atlavík is a popular campsite, often the scene of summer weekend parties. Pedal boats,

rowing boats and canoes can be hired for watery pursuits.

Höfðavík Campsite CAMPGROUND €
(sites per person kr1400; ⏰mid-May–Sep) A second campsite on the lake shore (the other one is Atlavík Campsite), small and quiet Höfðavík is just north of the petrol station. Powered sites available.

Hótel Hallormsstaður HOTEL €€
(☎471 2400; www.hotel701.is; hotel s/d from kr22,650/28,600, guesthouse s/d without bathroom kr14,050/19,000, all incl breakfast; ⏰mid-May–Sep) A veritable campus of buildings among the trees, this bucolic country retreat offers modern hotel rooms, cottages and the small Grái Hundurinn guesthouse, plus two restaurants (a renowned dinner buffet), spa and an inviting outdoor area.

Activities abound, including horse-riding and quad-bike tours. Bike hire is available.

Hengifoss

★Hengifoss WATERFALL
Crossing the bridge across Lagarfljót on Rte 931, you'll reach the parking area for Hengifoss, Iceland's second-highest waterfall. The falls plummet 118m into a photogenic brown-and-red-striped boulder-strewn gorge.

Getting to Hengifoss requires a return walk of one to two hours (2.5km each way). From the car park, a long staircase leads up the hillside – Hengifoss is soon visible in the distance. It's a steep climb in places but flattens out as you enter the canyon.

Skriðuklaustur

Head south from Hengifoss waterfall for 5km to reach historic Skriðuklaustur, where you can investigate medieval and 20th-century history, plus indulge in excellent local produce. Neighbouring the cultural centre at Skriðuklaustur is the worthwhile visitor centre for the eastern territory of Vatnajökull National Park.

Sights

Skriðuklaustur MUSEUM
(☎471 2990; www.skriduklaustur.is; adult/child kr1000/free; ⏰10am-6pm Jun-Aug, noon-5pm May & Sep) Skriðuklaustur is the site of a late 15th-century monastery and the photogenic home of an Icelandic author feted by the Third Reich. The unusual black-and-white turf-roofed building was built in 1939 by Gunnar Gunnarsson (1889–1975), and now holds a cultural centre dedicated to him. This prolific writer achieved phenomenal popularity in Denmark and Germany – at the height of his fame only Goethe outsold him.

Snæfellsstofa – National Park Visitor Centre VISITOR CENTRE
(☎470 0840; www.vjp.is; ⏰9am-5pm Jun-Aug, 10am-5pm May & Sep) FREE This stylish centre covers the eastern territory of the behemoth that is Vatnajökull National Park. Excellent displays highlight the nature of

WORTH A TRIP

WILDERNESS CENTER

A brilliant new attraction, the **Wilderness Center** (Óbyggðasetur Íslands; ☎440 8822; www.wilderness.is; museum adult/child kr2500/1900) defies easy classification. It's a remote farm that offers museum exhibits, unique accommodation, local food, horse-riding and hiking trails, and the opportunity for tailor-made tours. It's 13km past Skriðuklaustur on Rte 934, at the end of Norðudalur valley, on the edge of the eastern highlands. The historic exhibits here were designed by the farm's owners (a film director and a historian) so are of superb quality – as is the entire farm concept.

Accommodation is offered in simple farmhouse rooms with shared bathroom (double kr16,900) or – more intriguingly – in a dormitory room styled as a *baðstofa*, the traditional living/sleeping room on old Icelandic farms (dorm bed kr6900 to kr7900). Food is available all day (mid-May to September). Guided tours range from three-hour horse rides (kr14,400) to exploration of an abandoned nearby farm (kr8500). Multiday activities are also possible; see the website for information.

If you're staying, give yourself a couple of nights here, and consider walking the **Waterfall Trail**, an easy six-hour riverside hike to Laugarfell (p294) (one-way transfer possible).

OFF THE BEATEN TRACK

HIKING IN DYRFJÖLL

One of Iceland's most dramatic ranges, the Dyrfjöll mountains rise precipitously to an altitude of 1136m between the marshy Héraðssandur plains and Borgarfjörður Eystri. The name Dyrfjöll means Door Mountain and is due to the large and conspicuous notch in the highest peak – an Icelandic counterpart to Sweden's famous Lapporten.

There are walking tracks crossing the range, which allow for plentiful day hikes from Borgarfjörður Eystri. The prime drawcard is Stórurð on the western flank of Dyrfjöll: it's an extraordinary place scattered with huge rocks and small glacial ponds. Along Rte 94, a number of access trails are marked; the best time to hike to Stórurð is from mid-July to mid-September.

There are companies offering guided day hikes of Dyrfjöll mountain and Stórurð from Egilsstaðir, including Wild Boys (p289).

Snæfell mountain and the eastern highlands, and staff sell maps and offer advice to travellers wishing to hike or otherwise experience the park.

Eating

★Klausturkaffi CAFE €€

(www.skriduklaustur.is; lunch buffet adult/child kr2990/1495; ⏲10am-6pm Jun-Aug, noon-5pm May & Sep; 👪) Klausturkaffi, inside Skriðuklaustur (p293), serves an impeccable lunch buffet showcasing local ingredients (seafood soup, reindeer pie, brambleberry *skyr* cake). More tantalising, however, is every sweet-tooth's dream: the brilliant all-you-can-eat cake buffet (adult/child kr1990/995), served from 3pm.

Note that you don't have to pay to enter Skriðuklaustur if you are only visiting the cafe.

Eastern Highlands

The Snæfell peak (at 1833m, Iceland's highest outside the Vatnajökull massif) looms over the southern end of Fljótsdalsheiði, an expanse of wet tundra, boulder fields, perennial snow patches and alpine lakes, stretching westwards from Lagarfljót into the highlands.

Work on the controversial Kárahnjúkar dam and Fljótsdalur hydroelectric power plant brought improved roads around Snæfell, with the paved Rte 910 from Fljótsdalur being the best way up. Along Rte 910, watch for wild reindeer, and bring your swimsuit to stop at the hot springs of Laugarfell. If you want to tour the area with someone else behind the wheel, check offerings from Laugarfell or Egilsstaðir-based Jeep Tours (p289).

The Rte 910 turn-off is just north of Skriðuklaustur (on Rte 934), and the road climbs *fast* but then levels out; it's suitable for 2WDs. No public transport travels here, but a few tours do (largely from Egilsstaðir).

To travel south beyond the Kárahnjúkar-dam viewpoint (to Askja or Kverkfjöll, for example), a large, high-clearance 4WD is required, and a GPS – this area is well off the beaten path.

Kárahnjúkar Dam VIEWPOINT

A scenic 60km drive from the Rte 910 turn-off takes you to the Kárahnjúkar dam and Hálslón reservoir, where information boards and viewing areas allow you to appreciate this vast feat of engineering, as well as observe the incredible **Hafrahvammagljúfur canyon**, below the dam.

Visit between 2pm and 5pm Thursday and Saturday from June to August, when a power-company representative offers free guiding (ie explanations and answering questions) at the dam's car-park area (see www.landsvirkjun.com/company/visitus to confirm times).

★Laugarfell GUESTHOUSE, CAMPGROUND €€

(☎773 3323; www.laugarfell.is; tw/f kr16,000/29,000; ⏲Jun-Sep) Laugarfell is 2km off Rte 910 (OK for 2WD cars) and beckons with hot springs (adult/child kr1000/500) and a cosy guesthouse. Formerly a hostel, the place has moved more upmarket with twin and family rooms (sleeping up to six) and all linen supplied. Note: there's no kitchen, but breakfast (kr1900) and dinner (kr3500) are available, and daytime sandwiches and cakes offered.

Snæfell

No one seems to know whether 1833m-high Snæfell is an extinct volcano, or if it's just having a rest. Iceland's highest peak outside the Vatnajökull massif is relatively accessible, making it popular with hikers and mountaineers.

Although climbing the mountain itself is not difficult for experienced, well-prepared hikers, the weather can be a concern and crampons are advisable. Ascending from the west is most common; it's a hike of six to nine hours, depending on ice conditions. Discuss your route with the hut warden. Consider taking a guided ascent (around kr41,000) with Laugarfell or Wild Boys (p289).

Snæfell Mountain Hut HUT €

(Snæfellsskáli; ☎842 4367; snaefellsstofa@vjp.is; N 64°48.250', W 15°38.600'; sites/dm per person kr1600/6000) The Snæfell mountain hut is run by the national park and can accommodate up to 45 people. It has a kitchen, a camping area and showers. A 4WD is required to reach it. Rangers are based here in summer.

Snæfell is part of the vast Vatnajökull National Park; the park website www.vjp.is has useful information, and the national-park visitor centre, Snæfellsstofa (p293), has info, maps and displays, plus staff ready to answer questions and give guidance.

A 4WD is required to travel Rte F909 (off Rte 910) to reach Snæfell mountain hut at the base of the Snæfell peak. It's 12km from Rte 910 to the hut.

THE EASTFJORDS

Borgarfjörður Eystri

POP 100

This wee hamlet sits in a stunning location, framed by a backdrop of rugged rhyolite peaks on one side and the spectacular Dyrfjöll mountains on the other; the hiking in the area is outstanding. There's very little in the village itself (which is less commonly known as Bakkagerði), although driftwood sculptures, hidden elves and crying seabirds exude a magical charm. As a bonus, this is one of Iceland's most accessible places for up-close viewing of nesting puffins.

For local information, check out www.borgarfjordureystri.is.

Sights

★Hafnarhólmi ISLAND

(www.puffins.is) Five kilometres past the wee church is the photogenic small-boat harbour and islet of Hafnarhólmi, home to a large **puffin colony**. A staircase and viewing platforms allow you to get close to these cute, clumsy creatures (and other seabirds). The puffins arrive by mid-April and are gone by early to mid-August, but other species (including kittiwakes, fulmars and common eiders) may linger longer.

Bakkagerðiskirkja CHURCH

Jóhannes Sveinsson Kjarval (1885–1972), Iceland's best-known artist, was brought up nearby and took much of his inspiration from Borgarfjörður Eystri and surrounds. His unusual altarpiece in this small church depicts the Sermon on the Mount and is directly aimed at this village: Jesus is preaching from Álfaborg, with the mountain Dyrfjöll in the background.

Lindarbakki HOUSE

You can't miss the village's hairiest house: bright-red Lindarbakki (1899) is completely cocooned by whiskery green grass, with only a few windows and a giant pair of antlers sticking out. It's a private home (not open to the public); an information board outside outlines its history.

Álfaborg NATURE RESERVE

Álfaborg (Elf Rock), the small mound and nature reserve near the campsite, is the 'borg' that gave Borgarfjörður Eystri its name. Some locals believe that the queen of Icelandic elves lives here. From the top of the rock there's a fabulous vista of the surrounding fields.

PIT STOP!

Halfway between Egilsstaðir and Borgarfjörður on Rte 94 sits one of East Iceland's quirkier roadside wonders: a pea-green-coloured hut surrounded by miles of nothingness. Built by a local eccentric, the structure is simply a hut to house a solar-powered refrigerated vending machine. If the power is off, flick the 'on' switch (we're not kidding) and wait two minutes (you can sign the guestbook while waiting). Then, voila: a refreshingly cold beverage or snack.

Activities

Musterið Spa SPA

(The Temple; ☎861 1791; www.blabjorg.is; adult/child kr3000/1000; ⊙4-10pm or by appointment) Underneath Blábjörg Guesthouse and enjoying supreme views, this spa features both indoor and outdoor hot tubs and saunas (the brave can take a dip in the sea). It's free for people staying at Blábjörg.

Festivals & Events

Bræðslan MUSIC

(www.braedslan.is; ⊙late Jul) Held in an old herring plant over a weekend in late July, Bræðslan is one of Iceland's best summer concert festivals, earning itself a reputation for great music as well as its intimate atmosphere. Some big local names (and a few international ones) come to play.

Sleeping

Campsite CAMPGROUND €

(sites per person kr1100; ⊙mid-May–Sep) This well-kept site has free kitchen access, plus washing machine and showers.

★ **Blábjörg Guesthouse** GUESTHOUSE €€

(☎861 1792; www.blabjorg.is; s/d without bathroom incl breakfast from kr15,900/18,900) In a cleverly converted fish factory, this well-run, year-round guesthouse houses 11 pristine white rooms (you'll pay a little extra for a sea view), plus guest kitchen and small lounge area. There is also a handful of excellent family sized apartments available (from kr32,900). The standout feature is the downstairs spa, Musterið (free admission for guests).

Álfheimar Country Hotel COUNTRY HOTEL €€

(☎471 2010; www.alfheimar.com; s/d kr20,000/25,200; ⊙May-Sep) Easily the most upmarket option in town (it's the only accommodation with private bathrooms!), Álfheimar has 30 motel-style units in long annexes. The timber-lined rooms have more atmosphere than the newer building, but all are spotless and well equipped. The affable owners are a font of local knowledge; guiding and tours can be arranged.

Borg Guesthouse GUESTHOUSE €€

(☎894 4470, 472 9870; http://gistiheimilidborg.wordpress.com; s/d without bathroom kr10,000/16,000) Borg is a good bet for a bed, since the owner has a few options in the village. Rooms are OK if old-fashioned, with cooking and lounge facilities; breakfast costs kr1700. Cheaper sleeping-bag options are better value (eg a double room excluding linen is kr12,000). Hiking, guiding and 4WD tours can be arranged.

BORGARFJÖRÐUR TO SEYÐISFJÖRÐUR HIKE

Wildly wonderful and unexplored, the rugged country between Borgarfjörður and Seyðisfjörður makes for one of the best multiday hikes in the region. To plan your journey, pick up a copy of the hiking map *Víknaslóðir – Trails of the Deserted Inlets* (kr1000), or contact **Álfheimar** or **Borg** in Borgarfjörður if you're looking for a guide. For hiker huts along this route, see www.ferdaf.is.

Day 1 Start at Kolbeinsfjara, 4km outside the township of Borgarfjörður Eystri, and venture up into the mountains along the Brúnavíkurskarð pass (trail #19 on the map). Turn south (along trail #21) at the emergency hut in Brúnavík, passing beautiful Kerlingarfjall further on. After your five- to six-hour hike (12.5km), settle in for the night at the outfitted farmhouse/campsite in Breiðavík.

Day 2 Next day features another stunning five hours of hiking (13.5km along trail #30). You'll first walk through the grassy leas below Hvítafjall, then link up with the 4WD track heading south to the Húsavík lodge, where you'll spend the second night. The land between Breiðavík and Húsavík is infested with hidden people – the elf sheriff lives at Sólarfjall and the elf bishop lives at Blábjörg further south along the coast.

Day 3 Another 14km of trails are tackled in five hours of hiking (along trail #37) as the path reunites with the sea at silent Loðmundarfjörður. The 4WD track ends at the Klyppstaður lodge on the Norðdalsá river delta at the uppermost point of the fjord.

Day 4 The last day links Loðmundarfjörður to Seyðisfjörður over 12km (trail #41). At the highest point of the mountain pass you'll find a logbook signed by previous hikers. As you venture down into Seyðisfjörður, you'll be treated to a watery fanfare of gushing chutes.

Eating & Drinking

Eyrin Village Store SUPERMARKET €
(11am-6pm Mon-Fri, noon-4pm Sat & Sun Jun-Aug, shorter hours Sep-May) The small supermarket by Fjarðarborg (the community centre) sells groceries.

Já Sæll Fjarðarborg ICELANDIC €€
(472 9920; meals kr1500-3600; 11.30am-midnight Jun-Aug) The menu is simple and the decor uninspiring at this option inside Fjarðarborg (the community centre), but it's worth a visit for its burgers or lamb chops, and a beer among the locals. Ask about the weekly live music held here in summer.

Álfacafé ICELANDIC €€
(472 9900; fish soup kr2200; 10am-10pm Jun-Aug, to 8pm May & Sep) The main venue in town for eating and drinking, with large stone-slab tables and tasty fish soup the headlining act (with decent support from the likes of flatbread with salmon, plus cakes and waffles). Geological stones and souvenirs are also for sale.

Getting There & Away

The village is 70km from Egilsstaðir along Rte 94, about half of which is sealed (accessible by 2WD). It winds steeply up over the Dyrfjöll mountains before dropping down to the coast.

There's a petrol pump close to the entry to the village.

A year-round weekday **bus service** (472 9805, 894 8305; hlid@centrum.is) (kr2000, one hour) operates between the campsite (departs 8am) and Egilsstaðir (departs from the airport and information centre at noon).

Seyðisfjörður

POP 665

If you visit only one town in the Eastfjords, this should be it. Made up of multicoloured wooden houses and surrounded by snow-capped mountains and cascading waterfalls, obscenely picturesque Seyðisfjörður is the most historically and architecturally interesting town in East Iceland. It's also a friendly place with an international community of artists, musicians, craftspeople and students.

If the weather's good, the scenic Rte 93 drive from Egilsstaðir is a delight, climbing to a high pass then descending along the waterfall-filled river Fjarðará.

Summer is the liveliest time to visit, particularly when Smyril Line's ferry sails majestically up the 17km-long fjord to town – a perfect way to arrive in Iceland. Note: you may wish to avoid Seyðisfjörður on Wednesday nights in summer, as the ferry to Europe sails on Thursday mornings and accommodation and meals in town are in hot demand. If you are taking the ferry, book accommodation well ahead.

History

Seyðisfjörður started as a trading centre in 1848, but its later wealth came from the 'silver of the sea' – herring. Its long, sheltering fjord gave it an advantage over other fishing villages, and it grew into the largest and most prosperous town in East Iceland. Most of the unique wooden buildings here were built by Norwegian merchants, attracted by the herring industry.

During WWII Seyðisfjörður was a base for British and American forces. The only attack was on an oil tanker (the *El Grillo*) that was bombed by three German warplanes. The bombs missed their target, but one exploded so near that the ship sank to the bottom of the fjord, where it remains today (a good dive spot).

Seyðisfjörður's steep-sided valley has made it prone to avalanches. In 1885 an avalanche from Bjólfur killed 24 people and pushed several houses straight into the fjord. A more recent avalanche in 1996 flattened a local factory, but no lives were lost.

Sights

Seyðisfjörður is stuffed with 19th-century timber buildings, brought in kit form from Norway; several of these have been transformed into cosy ateliers where local artisans work on various projects. A quick loop around town will reveal half a dozen places to drop some krónur, on art, handicrafts, knitwear and designer homewares.

Bláa Kirkjan CHURCH
(www.blaakirkjan.is; Ránargata) The star of many a tourist photo, the Blue Church has a dramatic mountain backdrop to add to its highly photogenic exterior. It's often locked, but opens for weekly summer concerts (p301).

Avalanche Monument MONUMENT
(Ránargata) The monument near the church dates from the 1996 avalanche, and is made from twisted girders from the factory demolished by the event. The girders were painted white and erected as they were found.

Seyðisfjörður

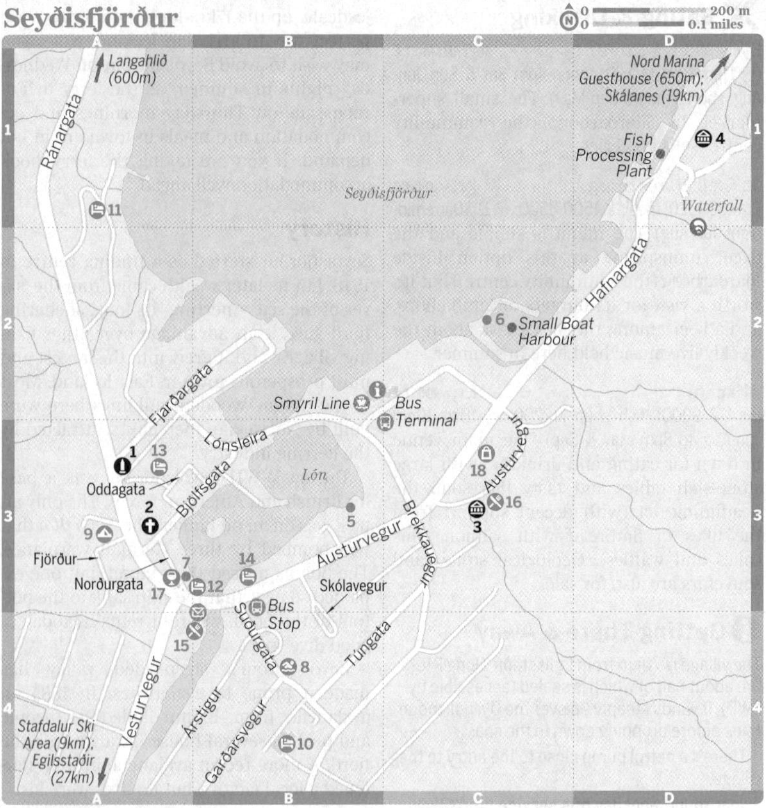

Seyðisfjörður

Sights
1 Avalanche Monument A3
2 Bláa Kirkjan A3
3 Skaftfell – Center for Visual Art C3
4 Tækniminjasafn Austurlands D1

Activities, Courses & Tours
5 Hlynur Oddsson B3
6 Sea Fishing Seyðisfjörður C2
7 Seyðisfjörður Tours A3
8 Sundhöll Seyðisfjarðar B4

Sleeping
9 Campsite A3
10 Hafaldan Old Hospital Hostel B4
11 Halfaldan Harbour Hostel A1
12 Hótel Aldan B3
13 Hótel Aldan (Old Bank) A3
14 Hótel Aldan (Snæfell) B3

Eating
Norð Austur Sushi & Bar (see 12)
Nordic Restaurant (see 12)
15 Samkaup-Strax B4
16 Skaftfell Bistro C3

Drinking & Nightlife
17 Kaffi Lára – El Grillo Bar A3

Entertainment
Blue Church Summer Concerts (see 2)

Shopping
18 Vínbúðin C3

Skaftfell – Center for Visual Art GALLERY
(☎472 1632; www.skaftfell.is; Austurvegur 42; ⊙noon-6pm) It's well worth a look in the gallery space above the Skaftfell Bistro. Skaftfell is a visual art center with a focus on contemporary art, and it stages exhibitions and events, hosts workshops, and facilitates artist residencies. See the website for more.

Tækniminjasafn Austurlands MUSEUM
(www.tekmus.is; Hafnargata 44; adult/child kr1000/free; ⊙11am-5pm Mon-Fri Jun–mid-Sep)

For insight into the town's fishing and telecommunications history, stop by this worthwhile technical museum. It's housed in two buildings on Hafnargata: the impressive 1894 home of Norwegian shipowner Otto Wathne (the old telegraph station), and a mechanical workshop from 1907.

Activities

Short walking trails lead from the museum area uphill to waterfalls, and to the 'sound sculpture' **Tvísöngur** – five interconnected concrete domes. Another short walk leads from the road on the north shore of the fjord (about 6km beyond the Bláa Kirkjan) to the signposted **Dvergasteinn** (Dwarf Rock) – according to folklore, this is a dwarf church that followed the people's church across the fjord.

The hills above Seyðisfjörður are the perfect spot for longer hiking. **Vestdalur** is a grassy valley north of town – just before the Langahlið cottages – renowned for its glorious waterfalls. Following the Vestdalsá river, after two to three scenic hours you'll arrive at a small lake, **Vestdalsvatn**, which remains frozen most of the year (it's generally covered by snow until July).

Trails are marked on the widely available *Víknaslóðir – Trails of the Deserted Inlets* map (kr1000), and the www.visitseydisfjordur.com website outlines some options, including the Seven Peaks Hike (trails climbing seven of the 1000m-plus peaks surrounding the town).

Stafdalur Ski Area SKIING
(www.stafdalur.is; ⏲ 5-7pm Tue-Fri, 11am-4pm Sat & Sun Dec-May) From about December to May there's downhill and cross-country skiing (and gear rental) at Stafdalur, 9km from Seyðisfjörður on the road to Egilsstaðir. Opening hours depend on the day's weather, with weekends being especially popular. Contact the tourist office (p301) for more details.

Sundhöll Seyðisfjarðar SWIMMING
(Suðurgata 5; adult/child kr550/280; ⏲ 6.30-9am & 3-8pm Mon-Fri, 1-4pm Sat) Seyðisfjörður's indoor pool has a sauna and hot-pots.

Tours

Seyðisfjörður Tours TOURS
(☎ 785 4737; www.facebook.com/seydisfjordurtours; Norðurgata 6; ⏲ Jun-Aug, plus Sep by request) From a super-central base next to the reception/restaurant building of Hótel Aldan, this new outfit offers bike rental, guided bike tours around the fjord (two hours kr7000) and walking tours of the town (one hour kr4000). Tailored hiking, boating and fishing tours can be arranged. Confirm tour start times, as these vary.

Hlynur Oddsson KAYAKING TOUR
(☎ 865 3741; hlynur@hotmail.de; Austurvegur 15b; ⏲ Jun-Aug) For a sublime outdoor experience, contact Hlynur, a charming Robert Redford–esque character who spends his summers around town and offers tailor-made tours. Options on the fjord range from one to six hours, visiting a shipwreck or waterfalls (one/three hours kr4000/8000). Experienced kayakers can choose longer trips, including to Skálanes (full day kr25,000, minimum two people).

Sea Fishing Seyðisfjörður BOAT TOUR, FISHING TOUR
(☎ 785 4737; www.facebook.com/seydisfjordurtours; 1hr for 4 people kr25,000-30,000; ⏲ Jun-Aug, plus Sep by request) From the small boat harbour, experienced fisherman Halli can take up to seven people in his boat, for fishing and/or guided sightseeing around the fjord. Great options include a spin out to Skálanes or to neighbouring Loðmundarfjörður. There's a one-hour minimum, but two hours gets you more options and time for fishing. Bookings are handled by Seyðisfjörður Tours.

Sleeping

★ **Hafaldan Old Hospital Hostel** HOSTEL €
(☎ 611 4410; www.hafaldan.is; Suðurgata 8; dm kr5,100, d with/without bathroom kr17,600/13,800; @) Seyðisfjörður's first-class HI budget digs are housed in two locations: the Harbour Hostel is a little out of town and the Old Hospital Hostel is the more-central summertime annexe. The Old Hospital houses the main reception for both buildings from June to August, plus dorms, a handful of en suite rooms and a beautiful kitchen-dining facility.

Halfaldan Harbour Hostel HOSTEL €
(☎ 611 4410; www.hafaldan.is; Ránargata 9; d/quad without bathroom kr12,900/19,800) Cosy, view-enriched dining and lounge areas are the standout feature of Harbour Hostel, found a little out of town past the Blue Church. The thin-walled rooms are unremarkable, and all share bathrooms.

WORTH A TRIP

HÚSEY

Reaching Húsey involves a long but scenic drive, 30km off the Ring Road along the rough, unsealed Rtes 925 and 926 beside the Jökulsá á Brú river (all up, about 60km from Egilsstaðir). The reasons to venture out to this isolated farm are good ones: a simple hostel, horses to ride, birdwatching trails to follow and seals cavorting in the riverine backdrop.

Húsey is has a unique offering: seal-watching tours on horseback. Two-hour rides leave daily at 10am and 5pm; bookings are required (the general public is welcome). Longer horse treks are offered, including two-day treks and weeklong holidays.

It's worth staying a few days to enjoy the natural surrounds and the homey atmosphere of the small, no-frills **Húsey HI Hostel** (☎471 3010; www.husey.de; dm/d without bathroom kr4000/8500; ⊙mid-Jan–mid-Dec). Breakfast is available (kr1800) but you will need to bring other supplies – the closest supermarket is in Egilsstaðir.

With advance notice, pick-up from Egilsstaðir can be arranged through the hostel; the cost is kr19,200 for the car (maximum four passengers).

Campsite CAMPGROUND €
(Ránargata; campsites per person kr1300; ⊙May-Sep) There are two areas for camping – one sheltered, grassy site for tents opposite the Bláa Kirkjan (p297), and another nearby area for vans. The service building houses kitchen, showers and laundry facilities.

★**Hótel Aldan** HOTEL €€
(☎472 1277; www.hotelaldan.com; reception Norðurgata 2; s/d incl breakfast from kr17,900/25,900) This wonderful hotel is shared across three old wooden buildings: reception and a bar-restaurant (where breakfast is served) are at this Norðurgata location (but no guest rooms are here). Ask too about the hotel's central apartments, with full kitchen, lots of space (two and three bedrooms) and some fun retro styling.

➡ **Hótel Aldan (Snæfell)** HOTEL €€
(Austurvegur 3) Snæfell is a creaky, characterful three-storey place with the cheapest rooms, fresh white paintwork and Indian bedspreads. A few new ground-floor family suites have recently been added here.

➡ **Hótel Aldan (Old Bank)** HOTEL €€
(Oddagata 6; s/d incl breakfast kr21,900/29,900) The Old Bank building of Hótel Aldan houses a boutique guesthouse with antique furnishings and a refined air.

Nord Marina Guesthouse GUESTHOUSE €€
(☎787 0701; nordmarina1@gmail.com; Strandarvegur 21; d with/without bathroom kr16,600/13,100; ⊙Apr-Oct) Two kilometres northeast of the supermarket, this unassuming guesthouse enjoys great views from its waterfront position and is home to 13 good-value rooms spread over two buildings; there's kitchen access and a comfy lounge area. It also has two apartments (one sleeps up to seven people for kr36,500).

★**Langahlið** COTTAGES €€€
(☎897 1524; www.langahlid.com; cottages kr35,000-40,000) Book *very* early for these three-bedroom cottages, sleeping up to six in a whole lot of comfort; including a kitchen, lounge, and hot-pot on the deck with astounding views. They're about 2km north of Hótel Aldan, with friendly new Italian owners (who plan to build smaller, one-bedroom cottages on the property, too).

✕ Eating & Drinking

Samkaup-Strax SUPERMARKET €
(Vesturvegur 1; ⊙9am-6pm Mon-Fri, 9am-4pm Sat, 10am-4pm Sun) For self-caterers. Closed Sunday outside summer. ATM out the front.

★**Norð Austur Sushi & Bar** SUSHI €€
(☎787 4000; 2nd fl, Norðurgata 2; mains kr1890-4290; ⊙6-10pm Sun-Thu, to 11pm Fri & Sat mid-May–mid-Sep) Locals rave about this place – and with good reason: the salmon, trout and char served comes straight off the fishers' boats into the hands of accomplished sushi chefs with an international pedigree. Set tasting menus are excellent value (five/seven courses for kr5900/6000); the decor is cool as are the cocktails. Bookings recommended.

★**Skaftfell Bistro** INTERNATIONAL €€
(☎472 1633; http://skaftfell.is/en/bistro; Austurvegur 42; mains kr1300-3500; ⊙8am-10pm; 🔌👪) This fabulous bistro-bar-cultural-centre is perfect for chilling, snacking and/or meeting locals. There's a short menu that changes weekly, plus popular pizza options

(including 'reindeer bliss' and 'langoustine feast'). A new addition is the breakfast menu, with waffles or porridge served until 11am. Be sure to check out the exhibitions in the gallery upstairs. Bookings recommended for larger groups.

Nordic Restaurant ICELANDIC €€
(☎472 1277; www.hotelaldan.is; Norðurgata 2; lunch kr2100-2900, dinner mains kr3650-6250; ⊙11.30am-10pm mid-May–mid-Sep) At the reception building for Hótel Aldan coffee and cakes are served all day in a country-chic setting, and lunches feature the likes of goat's cheese salad or catch of the day. In the evening, flickering candles prettify the tables, and the menu showcases hyperlocal ingredients (lamb, reindeer, fish) with a contemporary touch. Reservations advised.

Kaffi Lára – El Grillo Bar BAR
(Norðurgata 3; ⊙11.30am-1am Sun-Thu, to 3.30am Fri & Sat) When you can't get a table elsewhere in town, there's usually space at this friendly, two-storey cafe-bar offering simple, tasty barbecue dishes and more than 20 different Icelandic beers. The must-try: El Grillo beer, brewed according to a recipe with a great backstory, and named after the bombed British tanker at the bottom of the fjord.

Vínbúðin ALCOHOL
(Hafnargata 4a; ⊙4-6pm Mon-Thu, 1-6pm Fri) Government-run liquor store.

☆ Entertainment

Blue Church Summer Concerts LIVE MUSIC
(www.blaakirkjan.is; Ránargata; adult/child kr3000/free; ⊙8.30pm Wed late Jun–mid-Aug) On Wednesday evenings from late June to mid-August, the Bláa Kirkjan is the setting for a popular series of jazz, classical- and folk-music concerts; see the website for the program. If you're leaving on the Thursday ferry, this is a lovely way to spend your final night in Iceland.

ℹ Information

There's an ATM outside the supermarket.

The website www.visitseydisfjordur.com is invaluable.

Tourist office (☎472 1551; Ferjuleira 1; ⊙8am-6pm Mon-Fri May-Sep) In the ferry terminal building, stocking local brochures, plus info on the entire country. In March, April and October the office is open Tuesdays and Wednesdays during the stops of the Smyril Line ferry. The office is also open during cruise-ship visits.

ℹ Getting There & Away

BOAT

Smyril Line (☎Faroe Islands 298 345900; www.smyrilline.com; Ferjuleira 1) operates a weekly car ferry, the *Norröna*, on a convoluted year-round schedule from Hirsthals (Denmark) through Tórshavn (Faroe Islands) to Seyðisfjörður.

From mid-June to late August, the *Norröna* sails into town at 8.30am on Thursday, departing for Scandinavia two hours later. The rest of the year, the boat pulls in at 9am on Tuesday, leaving Wednesday at 8pm. Winter passage is possible (from October to March, departures are weather-dependent); see the website for more.

BUS

FAS (☎472 1515, 893 2669) runs a bus service between Egilsstaðir and Seyðisfjörður (kr1050, around 45 minutes). Services operate year-round, one to three times daily Monday to Saturday (Sunday services operate from mid-June to August). Services run to coincide with the ferry arrival and departure. An up-to-date schedule can be found on www.visitseydisfjordur.com. The bus stops by the ferry terminal, and also outside the library on Austurvegur).

Around Seyðisfjörður

Skálanes

You might think Seyðisfjörður is the end of the line, but further retreat is possible. The remote farm Skálanes, 19km east of Seyðisfjörður along the fjord edge, is an independent nature reserve and heritage field centre. The owner has restored the once-abandoned farmstead into a veritable Eden for amateur botanists, ecologists, archaeologists (remains from the Settlement Era have been found) and birdwatchers (more than 45 avian species).

Its isolation and experimental nature (it's promoted as a place of learning, not a regular guesthouse) will appeal to naturalists. The goal of Skálanes is sustainability, research and protection of nature. Its facilities are limited, so day visitors are discouraged, and a stay of a few days is recommended.

Sleeping & Eating

★ **Skálanes Mountain Lodge** GUESTHOUSE €€
(☎861 7008, 690 6966; www.skalanes.com; ⊙May-Oct, by arrangement Nov-Apr) A

variety of stay-over packages are available at this remote farm and nature reserve, which usually incorporate guiding and meals; see the website, and contact the lodge for more details. At the time of writing there were upgrades and renovations planned (the addition of private bathrooms to guest rooms, for example). Lodgings are comfortable and homely.

❶ Getting There & Away

Getting to Skálanes is an adventure in itself. You could walk all the way from Seyðisfjörður along a trail (there are footbridges across the three rivers); ride a mountain bike; or paddle a kayak hired in Seyðisfjörður.

In a car, you can drive 13km along the rough unsealed road until you get to the river, then walk about 4km; call to enquire about the state of the road before driving in a small 2WD. In a good-sized 4WD you can drive the whole way to Skálanes (take care fording the rivers), but it's worth considering walking from the first river: the 4km trail is beautiful, and the perfect way to get you in the mood for the eco mindset of the centre.

A final option: overnight guests can be picked up from the river (kr6700 return per vehicle).

Mjóifjörður

The fjord south of Seyðisfjörður is Mjóifjörður (Narrow Fjord), flanked by spectacular cliffs and rows of cascading waterfalls. The gravel road leading into the fjord is slow-going for 2WDs, but once you make it in you'll be surrounded by lush hills peppered with fascinating ruins and schools of farmed fish in the frigid fjord water.

There's some brilliant hiking around Mjóifjörður. For a fee, the folks at Sólbrekka can ferry you across the fjord, from where it's a four-hour hike to Neskaupstaður, or you can climb over northern mountains to reach Seyðisfjörður on a six- to seven-hour trek (it's best to hike in late summer, from mid-July or later, when the high-altitude snow has finally melted).

From the head of Mjóifjörður it's 12km to Brekkuþorp, then the road continues 14km east to the Dalatangi light, Iceland's first lighthouse, from 1895 (next to it is the 'modern' one, dating from 1908 and still in use). Beyond Brekkuþorp a 4WD is advisable, or hire bikes from Sólbrekka.

🛏 Sleeping & Eating

Coffee and light snacks are available at Sólbrekka Cafe (snacks & sandwiches kr350-650; ⊙11am-7pm Jun–mid-Aug), and breakfast and dinner can be arranged for overnight guests. Bring supplies from Egilsstaðir or Reyðarfjörður.

Sólbrekka GUESTHOUSE, COTTAGES €€
(☑476 0007; http://mjoifjordur.weebly.com; cottages excl linen kr18,000; ⊙guesthouse Jun–mid-Aug, cottages Jun-Sep) On the north side of Mjóifjörður, Sólbrekka is the only place to stay. There's a schoolhouse near the sea, offering camping and no-frills rooms with shared bathroom (camping/sleeping-bag accommodation per person kr1200/4500), but the real treat lies up the hill; two self-contained pine cottages sleeping six at a push (one bedroom plus small sleeping loft and a sofa bed).

❶ Getting There & Away

It's 30km from Egilsstaðir to the head of Mjóifjörður (on Rtes 26 and 953), then a further 12km to Brekkuþorp. No transport runs here. The road into and out of Mjóifjörður is impassable from October to sometime in May – during this time, access is by boat twice a week from Neskaupstaður.

Reyðarfjörður

POP 1200

In the Prettiest Fjord pageant, Reyðarfjörður wouldn't be in the running to take home the crown. It's a relatively new settlement with a giant 2km-long aluminium smelter just beyond the town along the fjord.

⊙ Sights

Íslenska Stríðsárasafnið MUSEUM
(http://stridsarasafn.fjardabyggd.is; Spítalakampu; adult/child kr1100/free; ⊙1-5pm Jun-Aug) During WWII around 3000 Allied soldiers (10 times the local population) were based in Reyðarfjörður. At the top end of Heiðarvegur you'll find the excellent Icelandic Wartime Museum, which details these strange few years. The building is surrounded by mines, Jeeps and aeroplane propellers, and holds other war relics. Photographs and tableaux provide a background to Iceland's wartime involvement.

Sleeping

Reyðarfjörður HI Hostel HOSTEL €
(Hjá Marlín; ☎892 0336, 474 1220; www.bakkagerdi.net; Vallargerði 9; dm kr6000, d with/without bathroom kr19,600/14,600, q kr32,000; @) Multilingual Marlín (Belgian, but resident in Iceland for over 20 years) is a warm host at this expanding spot. The primary house has en-suite rooms and a breakfast (kr2000) area; a large second house down the street has simple rooms, a barbecue and a sauna. Nearby on Austurvegur, a newly converted furniture store (!) has 12 four-bed rooms with private bathroom.

Campsite CAMPGROUND €
(sites per person kr1200; ⏲Jun-Aug) At the entrance to town on Rte 92, this neat campground sits beside a duck pond, with decent facilities (including washing machine).

Tærgesen GUESTHOUSE €€
(☎470 5555; www.taergesen.com; Búðargata 4; d with/without bathroom kr24,000/13,000) Timber-lined and dressed with white window shutters, the cosy rooms above Tærgesen (p303) restaurant have loads of cottagey character (and shared bathrooms). They're inside a black corrugated-iron building from 1870. New to the complex: 22 spacious motel-style units with bathroom.

Eating

Sesam Brauðhús BAKERY, CAFE €
(www.sesam.is; Hafnargata 1; ⏲7.30am-5pm Mon-Fri, 9am-4pm Sat) Stop by this first-rate bakery-cafe and choose from a cabinet full of sandwiches, salads and pastries.

Krónan Supermarket SUPERMARKET €
(Hafnargata 2; ⏲11am-6pm Mon-Thu, to 7pm Fri, to 5pm Sat, noon-4pm Sun) Central option for self-caterers.

Tærgesen ICELANDIC €€
(☎470 5555; www.taergesen.com; Búðargata 4; mains kr1350-5250; ⏲10am-10pm) Tærgesen makes much of its connection to the British TV series *Fortitude*. It's known for its pizzas, and for hearty traditional fare that ranges from steak sandwiches to butter-fried trout.

Vínbúðin ALCOHOL
(Hafnargata 2; ⏲11am-6pm Mon-Thu, to 7pm Fri, to 4pm Sat May-Aug, shorter hours Sep-Apr) Government liquor store.

Information

You may see reference on maps and info boards to Fjarðabyggð – this is the municipality that centres on Reyðarfjörður and encompasses fjords from Mjóifjörður south to Stöðvarfjörður. There is excellent info online at www.visitfjardabyggd.is.

Eskifjörður

POP 1060

This friendly, prospering little town is stretched out along a dimple in the main fjord of Reyðarfjörður. Its setting is magnificent: it looks directly onto the mighty mountain Hólmatindur (985m), rising sheer from the shining blue water.

Sights

Helgustaðanáma MINE
The remains of the world's largest spar quarry lie east of Eskifjörður. Iceland spar (*silfurberg* in Icelandic) is a type of calcite crystal that is completely transparent and can split light into two parallel beams. It was a vital component in early microscopes.

To reach the quarry, follow the gravel road past Mjóeyri, driving 6km along the coastline until you reach an information panel; the quarry is then a 500m walk uphill.

Sjóminjasafn Austurlands MUSEUM
(Strandgata 39b; adult/child kr1100/free; ⏲1-5pm Jun-Aug) Inside the 1816 black timber warehouse 'Gamlabuð', the East Iceland Maritime Museum illustrates two centuries of the east coast's historic herring, shark and whaling industry. For more salty-dog stories, be sure to check out Randulffs-sjóhús (p304).

Activities

There are plenty of hiking routes up the nearby mountains. Multiday hikes around the peninsulas east of Eskifjörður abound – particularly popular is the area known as Gerpir. At the time of writing it was tough to obtain a hiking map locally, so ask around for local advice. The owners of Ferðaþjónustan Mjóeyri (p304) are great for hooking you up with guides and activities (and have motorboats for hire if you want to head off to explore).

Gönguvikan (Hiking Week) is a big event on the district's annual calendar, falling the week after the summer solstice.

Oddsskarð
SKIING

Given the right conditions, from December to April skiing is possible on slopes near Oddsskarð, the mountain pass leading to Neskaupstaður. See www.visitfjardabyggd.is for details.

Hólmanes Peninsula
HIKING

The southern shore of the Hólmanes Peninsula, below the peak **Hólmatindur**, is a nature reserve. Hiking in the area offers superb maritime views (look out for pods of dolphins). The Hólmaborgir hike, south of the main road, is a popular loop that takes but an hour or two.

Sundlaug Eskifjarðar
SWIMMING

(Norðfjarðarvegur; adult/child kr700/200; ⊙6am-9pm Mon-Fri, 10am-6pm Sat & Sun) The swimming pool has water slides, hot-pots and a sauna; it's on the main road into town.

🛏 Sleeping

Campsite
CAMPGROUND €

(sites per person kr1200; ⊙Jun–mid-Sep) A simple site in a pretty treed setting not far from the entrance to town.

★Ferðaþjónustan
Mjóeyri
GUESTHOUSE, COTTAGES €€

(☑696 0809, 477 1247; www.mjoeyri.is; Strandgata 120; s/d without bathroom kr14,100/18,800, cottages from kr30,900) On the eastern edge of town, this view-blessed complex juts into the waterway at the tip of a teeny peninsula. There are guesthouse rooms in the main building, but it's the excellent, family sized cottages spread around the property that make Mjóeyri a great choice. There are also camper amenities, and one of the funkiest hot-pots we've seen (in a converted boat).

Hotel Eskifjörður
HOTEL €€

(☑476 0099; www.hoteleskifjordur.is; Strandgata 47; d kr26,000-30,000) In the centre of town, this new hotel has transformed an old bank into a fresh, stylish place to stay, with sweet puffin themes to set the scene. Room prices vary with size and view – the most expensive have a balcony. Breakfast is kr1550.

✗ Eating & Drinking

There are not a lot of places to eat in town, and options shrink outside of summer. In winter you may need to drive to neighbouring towns for a good meal. Quick-eat options include a petrol station with a grill.

Samkaup-Strax
SUPERMARKET €

(Strandgata 50; ⊙9am-6pm Mon-Fri, 10am-2pm Sat) For picnic supplies and self-catering. There's an ATM out front.

★Randulffs-sjóhús
ICELANDIC €€

(☑477 1247; www.mjoeyri.is; Strandgata 96; mains kr3290-4490; ⊙noon-9pm Jun-Aug or by appointment) This extraordinary boathouse dates from 1890, and when new owners entered it in 2008, they found it untouched for 80-odd years. The upstairs sleeping quarters of the fishermen have remained as they were found; downstairs is an atmospheric restaurant among the maritime memorabilia. Unsurprisingly, the tasty, upmarket menu is heavy on fish (including local specialities shark and dried fish).

Kaffihúsið
BAR

(☑476 1150; www.kaffihusid.is; Strandgata 10; ⊙noon-11pm Tue-Thu & Sun, to 3am Fri & Sat) You can't miss the oversized coffee cup announcing this place, primarily a restaurant-bar (kitchen closes at 9.30pm) and hang-out for locals, with pubby happenings like karaoke and a regular quiz night. There's also a cluster of rooms (single/double kr9850/13,500) in the back; they're simple, decent affairs, with shared bathroom.

ℹ Getting There & Away

Eskifjörður is 15km east of Reyðarfjörður on Rte 92, which, at the time of writing, continued up over the Oddsskarð pass (632m) and through a one-lane tunnel to reach Neskaupstaður, 24km northwest. However, the drive from Eskifjörður to Neskaupstaður is set to become a lot less scenic (and hair-raising) when a new 8km tunnel connecting the towns opens in 2017.

The mountain road from Eskifjörður to Oddsskarð will remain open (but not from Oddsskarð to Neskaupstaður); it's worth a drive up to Oddsskarð to enjoy the steep climb and panoramic views.

Neskaupstaður
POP 1500

Although it's one of the largest of the fjord towns, the dramatic end-of-the-line location makes Neskaupstaður (also known as Norðfjörður) feel small and far away from the rest of the world. Attempt to drive further east and you simply run out of road.

As with most towns in the Eastfjords, Neskaupstaður began life as a 19th-century trading centre and prospered during the herring boom in the early 20th century. Its future was assured by the building of the biggest fish-processing and freezing plant in Iceland, Síldarvinnslan (SNV), at the head of the fjord. The east's main regional hospital is located here.

Sights

★Fólkvangur Neskaupstaðar NATURE RESERVE
At the eastern end of town, where the road runs out, is this lovely nature reserve perfect for short strolls. Various paths run over tiny wooden bridges and past boulders, peat pits, cliffs and the sea, with a soundtrack of crying seabirds. You may see whales offshore.

Safnahúsið MUSEUM
(Egilsbraut 2; adult/child kr1100/free; ⏲1-9pm Mon-Sat, 1-5pm Sun Jun-Aug) Three collections are clustered together in one bright-red harbour front warehouse, known as 'Museum House'. **Tryggvasafn** showcases a collection of striking paintings by prominent modern artist Tryggvi Ólafsson, born in Neskaupstaður in 1940. Upstairs, the **Maritime Museum** is one man's collection of artefacts relating to the sea; on the top floor, the **Museum of Natural History** has a big collection of local stones (including spar from the Helgustaðanáma mine), plus an array of stuffed animals, birds, fish and pinned insects.

Tours

★Skorrahestar HORSE RIDING
(☎477 1736; www.skorrahestar.is; Skorrastaður; 2hr hike/ride kr15,500/19,500; ⏲short tours 12.30pm Jun-Sep) Based on a farm west of town, Skorrahestar offers longer treks for experienced riders, including weeklong trips to uninhabited fjords led by Doddi, a storytelling, guitar-playing guide who is a former biologist and teacher (the perfect guide?). A brilliant taster involves two hours of guided riding or hiking in the local landscapes, followed by pancakes and coffee. Good guesthouse accommodation too.

Neskaupstaður Sailing BOATING
(☎477 1950; www.hildibrand.com) Take in the dramatic scenery while hearing about local history and scouting for whales from this old sailing vessel as it tours Neskaupstaður. Tours last 2½ hours (adult/child kr8900/4450) and are scheduled in the afternoon and evening. Sea-angling and customised trips can also be arranged.

Festivals & Events

Eistnaflug MUSIC
(www.eistnaflug.is; ⏲Jul) A beloved metal and punk festival, Eistnaflug ('Flying Testicles') is held every summer in town on the second weekend in July. Sixty bands plus friendly metalheads plus midnight sun.

Sleeping

Campsite CAMPGROUND €
(sites per person kr1200; ⏲Jun–mid-Sep) High above the town, near the avalanche barriers (worth a visit for the great views). It's signposted from the hospital.

Tónspil GUESTHOUSE €
(☎477 1580; www.tonspil.is; Hafnarbraut 22; s/d without bathroom kr7900/13,900) Like an extra in the film *High Fidelity,* you need to ask the dude in the music shop about the rooms above. Which are simple, but there's a handy TV room and kitchen area with a washing machine. Out of season, BYO sleeping bag for reduced prices (kr4900 per person).

★Hildibrand Hotel HOTEL €€
(☎477 1950; www.hildibrand.com; Hafnarbraut 2; d r/apt from kr21,200/29,100) The biggest thing to happen to Neskaupstaður in years, this complex of 15 super-spacious, fully equipped apartments is plumb in the town centre. Each apartment has one to three bedrooms (sleeping up to eight), full kitchen, balcony (those views!) and custom-made furniture – you may be persuaded to move in. In a neighbouring building are standard hotel rooms – small but bright and well-equipped.

Hótel Edda HOTEL €€
(☎444 4860; www.hoteledda.is; Nesgata 40; s/d kr22,200/24,700; ⏲early Jun–mid-Aug; @) On the waterfront at the eastern end of town, this friendly, well-run summer hotel has brilliant views; neat, no-frills rooms (all with bathroom); and a good dinnertime restaurant (mains kr2100 to kr5000). Breakfast is available for kr2050.

Eating

Nesbær Kaffihus CAFE €
(Egilsbraut 5; lunch kr750-2000; ⏲9am-6pm Mon-Wed & Fri, to 10.30pm Thu, 10am-6pm Sat) This cafe-bakery-craft-shop has a quintessential small-town vibe and offers excellent crêpes, cakes, sandwiches, waffles and soup.

Samkaup-Úrval SUPERMARKET €
(Hafnarbraut 13; ⌚10am-7pm Mon-Fri, noon-6pm Sat & Sun) Supermarket in the centre of town, opposite Hildibrand Hotel.

★ **Kaupfélagsbarinn** ICELANDIC €€€
(☎477 1950; www.hildibrand.com; Hafnarbraut 2; lunches kr2000-3200, dinner mains kr3300-7000; ⌚11am-10pm Jun-Aug, noon-9pm Sep-May) Part of the Hildibrand complex, this is easily the most upmarket restaurant in this neck of the woods. In its large, pastel-toned space, say hello to langoustine tails, oven-baked lamb fillet, and *skyr* mousse with citrus infusion and white chocolate. The more casual daytime menu is similarly tempting: try the lamb burger, or fish and chips.

Vínbúðin ALCOHOL
(Hafnarbraut 15; ⌚2-6pm Mon-Fri) Government-run liquor store.

Getting There & Away

A new 8km-long tunnel will open in 2017 to connect the fjord with Eskifjörður, but prior to that the only road access is via the highest highway pass (632m) in Iceland and a nerve-wracking, single-lane, 630m-long tunnel.

There are limited bus services but most travellers rely on their own wheels in this region.

Fáskrúðsfjörður

POP 710

The village of Fáskrúðsfjörður (sometimes known as Búðir) was originally settled by French seamen who came to fish the Icelandic coast between the late 19th century and 1914. In a gesture to the local heritage, street signs are in both Icelandic and French.

Frakkar á Íslandsmiðum MUSEUM
(☎470 4070; Hafnargata 12; adult/child kr1000/free; ⌚10am-6pm May-Sep, other times by appointment) Accessed through the lobby of Fosshotel Eastfjords, this quality museum paints a detailed portrait of the French connection to the fjord. The hotel's reception is in the old doctor's house, and a walkway under Hafnargata links it to the old hospital (now home to hotel rooms). Check out the re-created sailors' quarters in the walkway. Museum entry is free for hotel guests.

Sleeping & Eating

Guesthouse Elín Helga GUESTHOUSE €€
(☎868 2687; elinhelgak99@gmail.com; Stekkholt 20; r without bathroom incl breakfast per person from kr9000) We like this four-room guesthouse, high above town (take Skólavegur then Holtavegur), for its pine-fresh cosiness, sweet host and great views (note: no kitchen, but laundry access is available).

★ **Fosshotel Eastfjords** HOTEL €€€
(☎470 4070; www.fosshotel.is; Hafnargata 11-14; d incl breakfast from kr25,000) This acclaimed new hotel opened in 2014 inside the relocated and restored French hospital. It's all class: 47 high-quality rooms (featuring lovely decor in stylish blues and greys, and a clever mix of old and new), plus a restaurant and lounge-bar with majestic views.

Samkaup-Strax SUPERMARKET €
(Skólavegur 59; ⌚10am-6pm Mon-Fri, to 2pm Sat) For food supplies.

L'Abri ICELANDIC €€
(www.fosshotel.is; Hafnargata 9; mains kr3900-5900; ⌚noon-11pm) As befits its location, L'Abri has a slight French accent, showcasing local produce (seafood soup, beef fillet) plus offering lighter, cheaper bistro dishes (salads and pizzas around kr2500). It's part of the Fosshotel complex, sitting inside the old French hospital and enjoying a splendid fjord view. A good pit stop for coffee and cake.

Café Sumarlína ICELANDIC €€
(www.sumarlina.is; Búðavegur 59; meals kr1050-3570; ⌚11am-10pm) Café Sumarlína, at the entrance to town, is a cosy restaurant-bar in a creaking wooden house, cranking out decent pizzas, burgers and crêpes. Note: the kitchen closes at 8.45pm.

Stöðvarfjörður

POP 200

If you think geology is boring, it's worth challenging that notion in this tiny village. It's small, but it has built a sizeable reputation for both its stone collection and its creativity. Look out for what may be the country's cutest bird hide just west of town, at the head of the fjord.

Sights

★ **Steinasafn Petru** MUSEUM
(www.steinapetra.is; Fjarðarbraut 21; adult/child kr1000/free; ⌚9am-6pm May-Sep, 9am-3pm Oct, Nov & Feb-Apr) The wondrous assemblage at Petra's Stone Collection was a lifelong labour of love for Petra Sveinsdóttir (1922–2012).

Inside her house, stones and minerals are piled from floor to ceiling – 70% of them are from the local area. They include beautiful cubes of jasper, polished agate, purple amethyst, glowing creamy 'ghost stone', glittering quartz crystals...it's like opening a treasure chest.

Creative Centre ARTS CENTRE
(537 0711; www.inhere.is; Bankastræti 1) Going by various names (Fish Factory, Sköpunarmiðstöð, 'In Here'), this once-abandoned fish factory by the harbour is a hive of creativity; it's a collaborative space that's home to artists' studios, a recording studio, workshops and concerts. Keep an eye out for events, or drop by, preferably with advance notice (it's a work space, without fixed opening times, but visitors are generally welcome, and a donation of kr500 is appreciated).

Sleeping & Eating

Campsite CAMPGROUND €
(sites per person kr1200; Jun–mid-Sep) Small, neat, basic campsite just east of the village.

Saxa GUESTHOUSE €€
(511 3055; www.saxa.is; Fjarðarbraut 41; s/d/tr kr9300/16,600/21,000) The town's best option demonstrates that Icelanders have yet to find a building they couldn't convert into a guesthouse! This was a supermarket, and now houses fresh, modern rooms (all with bathroom); note, there's no kitchen. There's a pleasant all-day cafe (snacks and meals kr500 to kr4000) serving homemade fare, including a small but good selection of dishes of an evening.

Brekkan FAST FOOD €
(Fjarðarbraut 44; meals kr500-1500; 9.30am-10pm Mon-Fri, 10am-10pm Sat, 11am-8pm Sun) The low-key local chowhouse, serving up hot dogs, burgers and toasted sandwiches. There's a stack of groceries too.

Shopping

Salthússmarkaður ARTS & CRAFTS
(Fjarðarbraut 43; 11am-5pm Jun-Aug) This market in the community hall sells a variety of charming handmade products (knitwear, carvings, stones etc) and shares a space with a tourist information centre for the Fjarðabyggð municipality.

THE RING ROAD: BREIÐDALSHEIÐI TO DJÚPIVOGUR

This 150km section of the Ring Road covers some very scenic bases: it traverses a mountain pass at the empty moors of Breiðdalsheiði (south of Egilsstaðir), cuts through a broad valley and cruises some great coastline. In summer, there is the option of a shortcut, by taking the 19km Öxi mountain pass (Rte 939) – this cuts about 60km off the journey, but note that Rte 939 is a narrow gravel road and isn't advised in bad weather or fog, or for nervous drivers.

Route 939 is closed in winter, and occasionally Rte 1 (the Ring Road) near Breiðdalsheiði is also closed in bad weather. Never fear – when this happens, you can still travel via the lovely, fully sealed fjord route (Rtes 92 and 96 via Reyðarfjörður, Fáskrúðsfjörður and Stöðvarfjörður), which is only slightly longer than taking Rte 1.

Breiðdalur

As the Ring Road travels from Egilsstaðir to the coast it traverses a mountain pass at Breiðdalsheiði heath before dropping to Breiðdalur ('Wide Valley'). It's a panoramic drive, with the broad valley nestled beneath colourful rhyolite peaks and cut by a popular fishing river, the Breiðdalsá. Take the turn-off to **Flögufoss**, a 60m-high waterfall (19km west of the village of Breiðdalsvík), if you feel like a walk.

Tours

Strengir FISHING TOUR
(660 6890; www.strengir.com) Strengir brings anglers to the region's salmon-rich waters and runs **Eyjar Fishing Lodge**, a high-end, year-round accommodation option open to all. The lodge is located on Rte 964, off Rte 1.

Odin Tours Iceland HORSE RIDING
(475 8088, 849 2009; www.odintoursiceland.com; Höskuldsstaðir) Odin Tours operates year-round horse-riding and hiking tours in Breiðdalur, plus has a cottage for rent. It's about 24km from Breiðdalsvík.

Sleeping & Eating

Hótel Staðarborg HOTEL €€
(475 6760; www.stadarborg.is; r incl breakfast from kr21,850) Once a school, cheerful, plant-filled Hótel Staðarborg has neat, updated

rooms, plus lake-fishing and horse-riding opportunities. Sleeping-bag accommodation is available, and dinner is offered (mains around kr4000). It lies 6km west of Breiðdalsvík.

★**Silfurberg** GUESTHOUSE €€€
(☎475 1515; www.silfurberg.com; Þorgrímsstaðir; d incl breakfast from kr37,500; ⏰Jun–mid-Sep) Silfurberg is a stunning boutique guesthouse on a rural property about 50km south of Egilsstaðir (30km from Breiðdalsvík). Style, humour and craftsmanship have been used to convert a barn into first-class accommodation, containing four rooms, one suite, and delightful, deluxe common areas. The outdoor sauna and dome-enclosed hot-pot are icing on the cake. Meals by arrangement.

Breiðdalsvík

POP 139

Fishing village Breiðdalsvík is beautifully sited at the end of Breiðdalur. It's a quiet place – more a base for walking in the nearby hills and fishing the rivers and lakes than an attraction in itself.

Information is available online at www.breiddalsvik.is.

Travel East ADVENTURE TOUR
(☎471 3060; www.traveleast.is) This agency can arrange any number of local tours and activities, from fishing to cycling to guided hiking. Boat cruises are popular – these leave at 10am and 1.30pm from May to September (kr9700), and puffins and other seabirds are regularly sighted. Jeep tours can also be arranged, including a half-day tour of Breiðdalur highlights (kr22,500).

Sleeping & Eating

Hótel Bláfell HOTEL €€
(☎475 6770; www.hotelblafell.is; Sólvellir 14; s/d incl breakfast kr23,850/27,800) Located in the centre of 'town' (we use that term lightly), Hótel Bláfell has smart monochrome rooms (some timber-lined), a sauna and a superb guest lounge with open fire. Don't be put off by the featureless decor of the restaurant – the evening buffet (kr5900) is justifiably popular, plus there are à la carte options, including pizza (mains kr1500 to kr4100).

The hotel also has excellent two-bedroom apartments in town, plus **Aurora Lodge**, a cosy five-bedroom chalet sleeping 10 (good for groups) on Rte 96 heading towards Stöðvarfjörður.

★**Kaupfjélagið** CAFE €
(Sólvellir 23; light meals kr400-1650; ⏰10am-7pm) Kaupfjélagið stocks groceries and serves up coffee and light meals to passing travellers. Its best feature are the fun displays of vintage general-store items (some for sale) that were discovered in the attic during recent renovations.

Berufjörður

The Ring Road meanders around Berufjörður, a long, steep-sided fjord flanked by rhyolite peaks. There is no village, just a handful of farms strung along the scenic shores. The southwestern shore is dominated by the obtrusive, pyramid-shaped mountain **Búlandstindur**, rising 1069m above the water.

Note that the Ring Road includes an 8km stretch of gravel around Berufjörður.

At the head of the fjord, the Öxi mountain pass (Rte 939) offers a short cut to Egilsstaðir for drivers.

Summer buses between Höfn and Egilsstaðir stop at Berunes HI Hostel.

Teigarhorn NATURE RESERVE
(www.teigarhorn.is; ⏰9am-5pm Jun-Aug) Rockhounds will love the display of zeolites at this farm, now a natural monument and nature reserve 5km northwest of Djúpivogur. It's renowned for its zeolite crystals, and the free museum is open from 1pm to 3pm. The farm has also developed lovely short walking trails around its coast, good for a leg-stretch and birdwatching.

Sleeping & Eating

★**Berunes HI Hostel** HOSTEL €
(☎869 7227, 478 8988; www.berunes.is; dm/d without bathroom kr5300/13,500, cottages from kr22,500; ⏰Apr-Oct; @) Berunes hostel is on a century-old farm run by affable Ólafur and his family. The wonderfully creaky old farmhouse has rooms and alcoves, plus kitchen and lounge; there are also rooms in the newer farmhouse, plus a campsite (kr1500 per person) and en suite cottages. Breakfast includes homemade bread and cakes; there's also a summer restaurant (or BYO food supplies).

HI members receive a discount; linen hire costs kr1500.

The hostel is 22km along the Ring Road south of Breiðdalsvík, and 40km from Djúpivogur. Buses between Egilsstaðir and Höfn stop here. There are excellent hiking trails from the farm.

★Havarí CAFE €
(☎663 5520; www.havari.is; Karlsstaðir; meals kr1200-1800; ⊙11am-9pm;) Continuing the wonderful Icelandic tradition of live music in unlikely places, this warm, creative farm (1km east of Berunes HI Hostel (p308)) is owned by a young family that includes acclaimed musician Prins Póló. A converted barn is now a cafe and music venue; look out for events on Havarí's Facebook page, or stop by to try the tasty farm-made *bulsur* (vegan sausages).

Djúpivogur

POP 460

The neat historic buildings and small harbour are worth a look, but the main reason to visit this friendly fishing village at the mouth of Berufjörður is to catch the boat to Papey (p310).

Djúpivogur (*dyoo*-pi-vor) is actually one of the oldest ports in the country – it's been around since the 16th century, when German merchants brought goods to trade. The last major excitement was in 1627: pirates from North Africa rowed ashore, plundering the village and nearby farms, and carrying away dozens of slaves.

These days the town has embraced the Cittaslow movement ('Slow Cities'; www.cittaslow.org), an offshoot of the Slow Food initiative. Djúpivogur is the only Icelandic member of the Cittaslow network, whose objectives are to promote and spread the culture of good living.

Sights

There's a low-key, creative vibe in the town, and a few quirky artisans work with local stones and driftwood to create jewellery or artful objects.

Eggin í Gleðivík PUBLIC ART
Walk or drive down to the waterfront behind Langabúð and follow the road west to reach this intriguing public artwork: 34 oversized eggs along the jetty, each one representing a local bird. While you're there, check out the old fish factory (Bræðsla) nearby, which hosts contemporary-art exhibitions in summer.

Langabúð Museum MUSEUM
(adult/child kr500/300; ⊙10am-6pm Jun-Aug) Djúpivogur's oldest building is the long, bright-red **Langabúð**, a harbourside log warehouse dating from 1790. It now houses a cafe (p310) and an unusual local museum. Downstairs is a collection of works by sculptor Rikarður Jónsson (1888–1977), ranging from lifelike busts of worthy Icelanders to mermaid-decorated mirrors and reliefs depicting saga characters. Upstairs, in the tar-smelling attic, is a collection of local-history artefacts.

Sleeping

Klif Hostel HOSTEL €
(☎478 2288; www.klifhostel.is; Kambur 1; dm/d without bathroom kr4500/13,200; ⊙May-Oct) Klif is a new-ish addition to town, a small, homey, five-room hostel in the old post office. Dorm beds cost kr4500 per person (BYO sleeping bag or pay extra to hire linen); prices for double rooms include linen.

Campsite CAMPGROUND €
(sites per person kr1550; ⊙Apr-Oct) Behind Við Voginn this campground is run by Hótel Framtíð (pay at the hotel's reception). There are cooking facilities, plus coin showers and a laundry. A new addition: cool new wooden 'barrel' huts, housing three beds and little else (kr15,300, linen not included).

Hótel Framtíð HOTEL €€€
(☎478 8887; www.hotelframtid.com; Vogaland 4; s/d/apt from kr24,200/30,900/37,800) This friendly hotel by the harbour is impressive for a village of this size. It's been around for a while (the original building was brought in pieces from Copenhagen in 1906), and there's an assortment of beds (and budgets) in various buildings. The hotel includes timber-lined hotel rooms, four cute cottages and five apartments (including two sleek, modern options).

There's also a building of rooms with shared bathroom (single/double kr17,900/21,000), and a more budget-friendly hostel (sleeping-bag single/double kr7600/12,100).

Eating & Drinking

Samkaup-Strax SUPERMARKET €
(Búland 2; ⊙9am-6pm Mon-Fri, to 4pm Sat, 10am-4pm Sun) On the main road, with a **Vínbúðin** (⊙4-6pm Mon-Thu, 1-6pm Fri Jun-Aug) attached.

WORTH A TRIP

PAPEY

The name of offshore island Papey (Friars' Island) suggests it was once a hermitage for the Irish monks who may have briefly inhabited Iceland before fleeing upon the arrival of the Norse. This small (2 sq km) and tranquil island was once a farm, but it's now inhabited only by sunbaking seals and nesting seabirds, including a puffin posse. Other highlights include the rock Kastali (the Castle), home to the local 'hidden people'; a lighthouse built in 1922; and Iceland's oldest and smallest wooden church (from 1807).

Papeyjarferðir (862 4399, 478 8119; www.djupivogur.is/papey; adult/child kr10,000/5000) runs four-hour tours to the island, spotting wildlife en route and walking the island trails. Weather permitting, tours depart Djúpivogur harbour at 1pm daily from June to August.

Langabúð Kaffihús CAFE €
(www.langabud.is; lunch kr800-1700; 10am-6pm Sun-Thu, to 1am Fri & Sat May-Sep) The in-demand cafe inside Langabúð Museum has a suitably old-world atmosphere, and serves cakes, soups and sandwiches.

Hótel Framtíð Restaurant ICELANDIC €€€
(478 8887; Vogaland 4; dinner mains kr4650-6160; 10am-9pm) The elegant restaurant at Hótel Framtíð is easily the nicest option in town. Dinner of lobster tails or roast lamb fillet hits the top end of the price scale and palate, but there are all-day pizzas too (from kr1830), and coffee and cake.

Information

Tourist Information Centre (470 8740; Bakki 3; 9am-5pm Mon-Fri, 10am-4pm Sat & Sun mid-May–mid-Sep) Pick up a map of the town – which has decent facilities (bank, post office etc) – from the very helpful tourist office across from Bakkabuð craft store.

Getting There & Away

The summer buses that run between Egilsstaðir and Höfn stop in town (no winter buses).

SBA-Norðurleið (www.sba.is) services:

- Bus 62 to Höfn (kr3800, 1½ hours, one daily June to mid-September)
- Bus 62a to Egilsstaðir (kr5700, 3¼ hours, one daily June to mid-September)

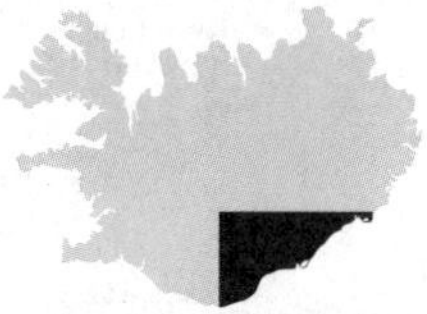

Southeast Iceland

Includes ➡

Best Places to Eat

- Humarhöfnin (p336)
- Pakkhús (p336)
- Jón Ríki (p333)
- Viking Cafe (p337)

Best Places to Stay

- Hrífunes Guesthouse (p316)
- Glacier View Guesthouse (p316)
- Guesthouse Dyngja (p334)
- Árnanes Country Lodge (p333)
- Milk Factory (p334)
- Hólmur (p332)

Why Go?

The 200km stretch of Ring Road from Kirkjubæjarklaustur to Höfn is truly mind-blowing, transporting you across vast deltas of grey glacial sand, past lost-looking farms, around the toes of craggy mountains, and by glacier tongues and ice-filled lagoons. The only thing you won't pass is a town.

The mighty Vatnajökull dominates the region, its huge rivers of frozen ice pouring down steep-sided valleys towards the sea. Jökulsárlón is a photographer's paradise, a glacial lagoon where wind and water sculpt icebergs into fantastical shapes.

The bleak coastal deserts of glacial sand are remnants of calamitous collisions between fire and ice. Further inland is the epicentre of Iceland's worst volcanic event, the Lakagígar fissures. With so much desolation on display, it's not surprising that Skaftafell is so popular. This sheltered enclave between the glaciers and the sands throbs with life and colour, and the footfall of hikers.

Road Distances (km)

	Höfn	Reykjavík	Jökulsárlón	Skaftafell
Reykjavík	459			
Jökulsárlón	79	378		
Skaftafell	135	323	57	
Kirkjubæjarklaustur	200	257	122	69

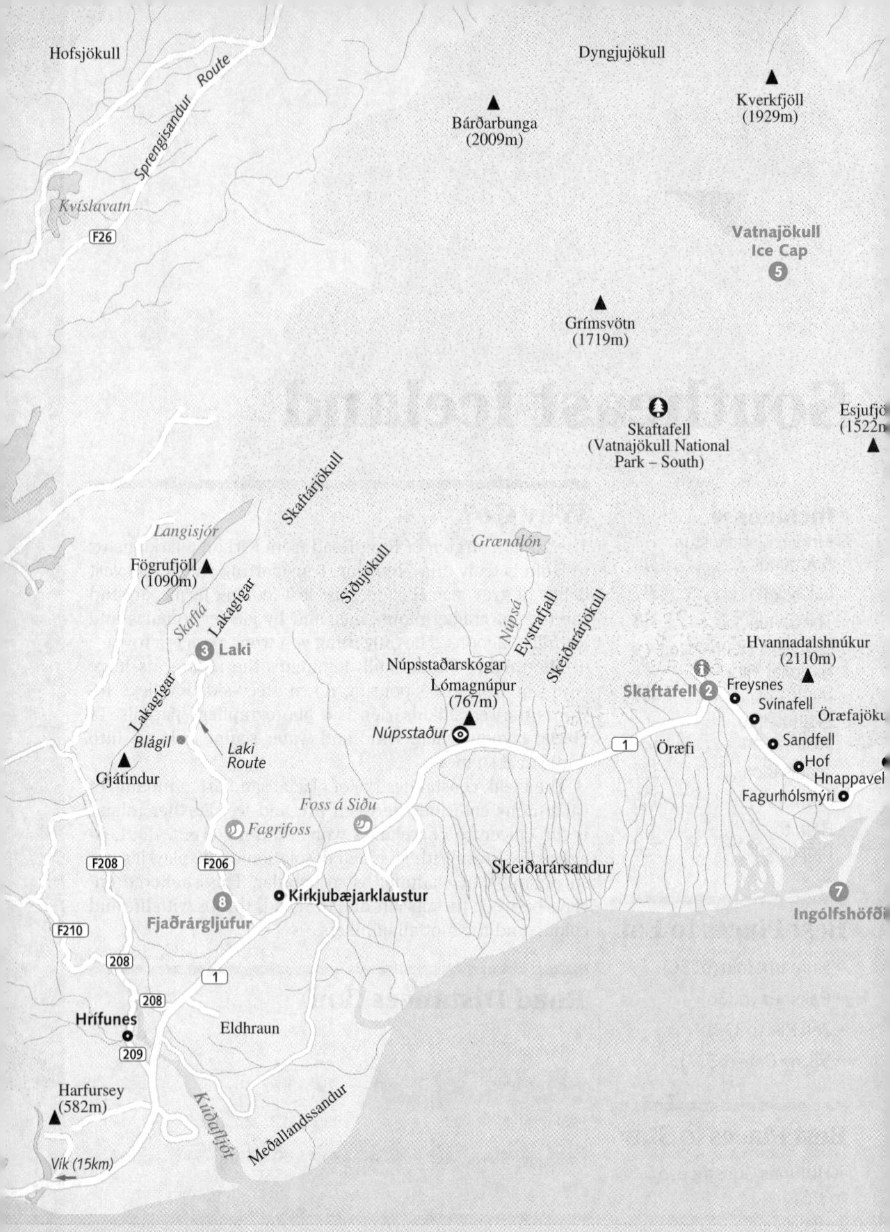

Southeast Iceland Highlights

1 **Jökulsárlón** (p327) Admiring the ever-changing ice sculptures at this bewitching lagoon.

2 **Skaftafell** (p319) Visiting Iceland's favourite national-park pocket, an area of green amid icy masses and vast sand deltas.

3 **Laki** (p317) Striding up Laki for views of three glaciers and an incredible history lesson.

4 **Heinabergslón** (p330) Joining the IceGuide team to paddle around icebergs on this silent glacier lagoon.

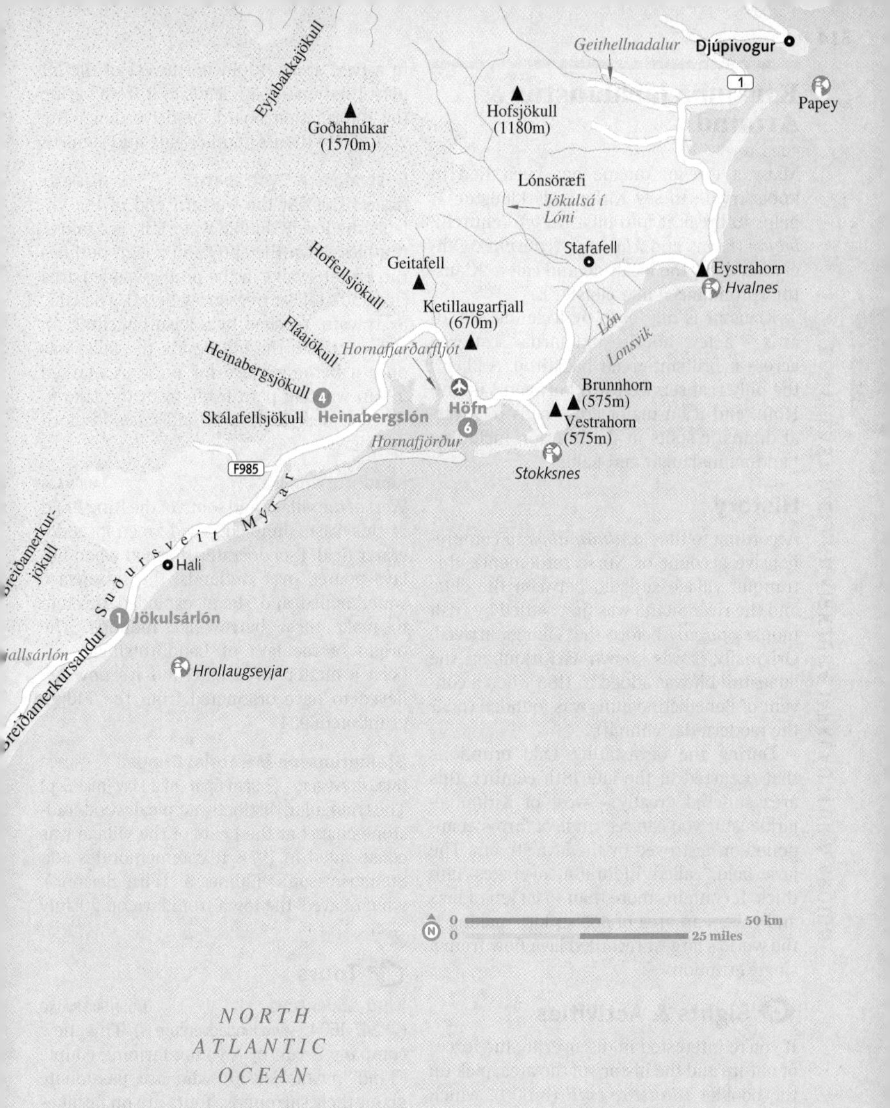

5 Vatnajökull Ice Cap (p329) Trying to wipe the smile off your face as you roar across the ice cap on a snowmobile tour.

6 Höfn (p333) Dining in the town's restaurants to sample delicious seafood treats netted by the local fishing fleet.

7 Ingólfshöfði (p326) Taking a tractor ride and climbing a promontory to check out puffins and dodge dive-bombing skuas.

8 Fjaðrárgljúfur (p325) Peering into the depths from a stunning canyon-edge walking path.

Kirkjubæjarklaustur & Around

POP 120

Many a foreign tongue has been tied in knots trying to say Kirkjubæjarklaustur. It helps to break it into bits: *Kirkju* (church), *bæjar* (farm) and *klaustur* (convent). Otherwise, do as the locals do and call it 'Klaustur' (pronounced like 'cloister').

Klaustur is tiny, even by Icelandic standards – a few houses and farms scattered across a brilliant-green backdrop. Still, it's the only real service town between Vík and Höfn, and it's a major crossroads to several dramatic spots in the interior, including Landmannalaugar and Laki.

History

According to the *Landnámabók* (a comprehensive account of Norse settlement), this tranquil village situated between the cliffs and the river Skaftá was first settled by Irish monks *(papar)* before the Vikings arrived. Originally, it was known as Kirkjubær; the 'klaustur' bit was added in 1186 when a convent of Benedictine nuns was founded (near the modern-day church).

During the devastating Laki eruptions that occurred in the late 18th century, this area suffered greatly – west of Kirkjubæjarklaustur you can see ruins of farms abandoned or destroyed by the lava stream. The lava field, called Eldhraun, averages 12m thick. It contains more than 15 cu km of lava and covers an area of 565 sq km, making it the world's largest recorded lava flow from a single eruption.

Sights & Activities

If you're interested in discovering the forces of nature and the history of the area, pick up the booklet *Klaustur trail* (kr600), which outlines a 20km walking trail that circles the village and takes in many of its natural features. The Katla Geopark also produces a very good map of *Hiking routes in the Skaftárhreppur Region* (kr1890). Maps and info are available from the Skaftárstofa information centre.

Kirkjugólf LANDMARK

The basalt columns of Kirkjugólf (Church Floor), smoothed down and cemented with moss, were once mistaken for an old church floor rather than a work of nature, and it's easy to see why. The honeycombed slab lies in a field about 400m northwest of the N1 petrol station: a path leads to it from beside the information board, or drive down Rte 203, where there's another gate and sign.

Systrafoss & Systravatn WATERFALL

(Sisters' Falls) At the western end of the village, the lovely double waterfall, Systrafoss, tumbles down the cliffs and a sign outlines three short walks in the pretty wooded area (Iceland's tallest trees grow here!). The lake, Systravatn, reached by a leisurely climb up steps cut into the hill beside the falls, was once a bathing place for nuns. A marked 2.5km walking path leads from the lake to descend near Kirkjugólf and takes in glorious views.

Landbrotshólar LANDMARK

West of the village and south of the Ring Road is this vast, dimpled, vivid-green pseudocrater field. Pseudocraters formed when hot lava poured over wetlands; the subsurface water boiled and steam exploded through to make these barrow-like mounds. The origin of the lava of Landbrotshólar has been a matter for debate, but it's now believed to have originated from the Eldgjá eruption of 934.

Steingrímsson Memorial Chapel CHURCH

(Klausturvegur; ⏲9am-6pm mid-May–mid-Sep) The triangular, distinctly atypical wood-and-stone chapel at the heart of the village was consecrated in 1974. It commemorates Jón Steingrímsson's 'Eldmessa' (Fire Sermon), which 'saved' the town from lava on 20 July 1783.

Tours

Kind Adventure MOUNTAIN BIKING

(☎847 1604; www.kindadventure.is) This new company is run by a young farming couple ('kind' means sheep) who are passionate about their surrounds. Tours are on fatbikes (off-road bicycles with oversized tyres) that are perfect for the Icelandic conditions (snow, mud, sand) and enable year-round tours (two to three hours for kr15,500). There's also a two-day adventure to the Laki craters (kr130,000).

Hólasport ADVENTURE TOUR

(☎660 1151; www.holasport.is; ⏲May-Oct) Based at Hótel Laki just south of Klaustur, Hólasport offers super-Jeep tours, including a full-day tour to Laki for kr32,500, or a shorter, river-fording trip into the mountains for kr16,500. There are also fun, frequent quad-bike tours in the pseudo-crater-filled area of Landbrotshólar, or along black-sand beaches (from kr14,500).

Sleeping

Kirkjubær II CAMPGROUND €
(☎894 4495; www.kirkjubaer.com; sites per person kr1300, cottages kr18,000; ⊙camping Jun-Sep, cottages Apr-Oct) Neat green site with sheltering hedges, right in town. Good service buildings include kitchen, showers and laundry. A boon in bad weather: a half-dozen basic huts, each sleeping four in bunk beds (BYO sleeping bag).

Nonna og Brynjuhús HOSTEL €
(www.kiddasiggi.is; Þykkvabæjarklaustur 2; dm kr5300, f kr16,540-17,760) The turn-off to this super-cheerful, family-friendly hostel is 37km west of Klaustur (take Rte 211 south off the Ring Road, signposted 'Álftaver'). It's then another 8km to reach this working dairy and sheep farm. The house here has fun artwork, and 21 sleeping-bag beds (predominantly in bunk rooms), with shared bathroom and kitchen access. Linen can be hired (kr1665).

Kleifar CAMPGROUND €
(www.kleifar.com; sites per person kr750; ⊙Jun-Aug) This very basic campsite (toilets and running water) is scenically situated by a waterfall, 1.5km along Rte 203 (signposted towards Geirland).

Hunkubakkar GUESTHOUSE €€
(☎487 4681; www.hunkubakkar.is; d with/without bathroom incl breakfast kr26,790/22,150; ⊙Feb-Nov) A photogenic option: small, red cottages are spread over a brilliant-green backdrop on this working sheep farm, 7km west of Klaustur (on Rte 206, 2km from Fjaðrárgljúfur canyon). Some rooms have private facilities, others share a bathroom. Breakfast is served in the on-site restaurant (dinner is also available).

Hörgsland CAMPGROUND, COTTAGES €€
(☎487 6655; www.horgsland.is; sites per person kr1250, cottages for 2/6 from kr19,200/35,400, d with/without bathroom incl breakfast kr22,300/18,800) On the Ring Road about 8km northeast of Klaustur is this mini village of 13 spotless, spacious, self-contained cottages that can sleep six (note: on the website, these cottages are called 'guesthouses'). A recent addition is a block of spick-and-span rooms, with and without bathroom. There's also camping, plus outdoor hot-pots, and a simple shop and cafe serving breakfast and dinner.

TIPS FOR THE SOUTHEAST

There are hotels and guesthouses scattered throughout the region, but not nearly enough to satisfy demand. Our advice: book early, and be prepared to pay high rates (some of the country's highest).

The areas around Kirkjubæjarklaustur and Höfn have the most choice; options are very limited around Skaftafell and Jökulsárlón.

Höfn has the best dining selection (with fantastic seafood), and you'll need to stock up on groceries and supplies in Kirkjubæjarklaustur and/or Höfn – there are no supermarkets between these towns, although there are a handful of restaurants and cafes.

Klausturhof GUESTHOUSE €€
(☎567 7600; www.klausturhof.is; Klausturvegur 1-5; d with/without bathroom kr18,200/15,200) With the pretty Systrafoss waterfall as its neighbour, this bright complex offers an assortment of compact rooms at reasonable prices, plus a guest kitchen and an on-site cafe. Winter prices drop considerably, and from October to April you can BYO sleeping bag to save money on private rooms, or book a dorm bed (kr2650). Breakfast is kr1700.

Hótel Laki HOTEL €€€
(Efri-Vík; ☎487 4694; www.hotellaki.is; s/d incl breakfast from kr26,600/30,500) What started as farmhouse accommodation has grown into a sprawling 64-room hotel, on scenic farmland 5km south of Klaustur on Rte 204. As well as comfortable (but overpriced) hotel rooms, there are 15 wee self-contained cottages (cheaper than the rooms), plus a nine-hole golf course, quad-bike and super-Jeep tours, a large restaurant-bar and lake fishing.

Icelandair Hótel Klaustur HOTEL €€€
(☎487 4900; www.icelandairhotels.com; Klausturvegur 6; d from kr28,900) There are few surprises here: the Klaustur has friendly staff and attractive decor in its 57 well-equipped rooms (including a new building of superior rooms), plus a sunny enclosed dining terrace and bar-lounge. The restaurant (dinner mains kr2650 to kr5750) is the town's best and features tantalising local

WORTH A TRIP

HRÍFUNES HOSPITALITY

Hrífunes is a tiny hamlet perfectly placed between Kirkjubæjarklaustur and Vík, in the peaceful and impossibly green surrounds of Skaftártunga. Here, you'll find two warm, hospitable guesthouses that are well worth the detour.

Both guesthouses have memorable dinner options. Note that there are no guest-kitchen facilities.

To reach Hrífunes from Klaustur, travel 24km west along the Ring Road and take Rte 208 then 209. From Vík, travel 39km east along the Ring Road, then take Rte 209 for 6km. With a large 4WD, from Hrífunes you're well placed to tackle some of the stunning southern interior, including Landmannalaugar and the Fjallabak route (Rte F208).

Glacier View Guesthouse (☎770 0123; www.glacierviewguesthouse.is; s/d without bathroom incl breakfast kr15,500/22,000; ⌚May-Oct) Hosts Borgar and Elín are seasoned travel pros – they run a tour company for Icelanders visiting Africa, so they know how to put guests at ease in their cosy home – and yes, in good weather, you can see Vatnajökull *and* Mýrdalsjökull from the lounge. Planned expansion will see the addition of 10 small 'houses' (funky modern cabins) to the scenic property.

Hrífunes Guesthouse (☎863 5540; www.hrifunesguesthouse.is; d with/without bathroom incl breakfast kr36,000/27,000; ⌚Feb-Nov) This old community house has been revived with flair by owners Haukur and Hadda – think stylish country-farmhouse chic, cosy lounge with fire and stunning photos taken by Haukur, who runs photography tours (check out www.phototours.is). Six new en suite rooms are scheduled to be built, to add to the existing six (some with shared bathroom). Two-night minimum in summer.

produce (hot-smoked mackerel, grilled Arctic char, pan-fried lamb fillet, reindeer tartare).

Eating

Most travellers dine at their accommodation, and that's no bad thing – there are not a lot of other options in Klaustur, and in-house restaurants are quite good (most are open to non-guests, too).

Look out for local Arctic char (trout) on menus – it comes from pure water directly under the nearby lava field.

Skaftárskáli FAST FOOD €
(Rte 1; mains kr1350-1950; ⌚9am-10pm Jun-Aug, to 8pm Sep-May) For a quick bite, the usual fast-food suspects at the N1's busy all-day grill-bar may suffice. Kitchen closes at 9.30pm in summer.

Kaffi Munkar CAFE €€
(Klausturvegur 1-5; mains kr1400-3600; ⌚10am-10pm) At the western end of town, Kaffi Munkar serves as the bright cafe-reception of Klausturhof guesthouse. Pop in for soup, spicy chicken, fish stew or 'Arctic char from next door' (according to the cute blackboard menu).

Systrakaffi INTERNATIONAL €€
(☎487 4848; www.systrakaffi.is; Klausturvegur 12; mains kr1100-4600; ⌚noon-10pm Jun-Aug, reduced hours May & Sep) The liveliest place in town is this cafe-bar, which gets slammed in summer. Its wide-ranging menu offers soups, salads, pizzas and burgers – but understandably plays favourites with local char and lamb.

Kjarval SUPERMARKET
(Klausturvegur 13; ⌚9am-9pm) For self-caterers. ATM next door.

Vínbúðin ALCOHOL
(Klausturvegur 15; ⌚4-6pm Mon-Thu, 1-7pm Fri, noon-2pm Sat May-Aug, 4-6pm Mon-Thu, 2-6pm Fri Sep-Apr) Government-run alcohol store.

Information

The helpful tourist office is inside the **Skaftárstofa Visitor Centre** (☎487 4620; www.visitklaustur.is; Klausturvegur 2; ⌚9am-6pm mid-Apr–mid-Oct), with good local info plus coverage and exhibitions on Katla Geopark and Vatnajökull National Park; this is the base for the lesser-visited western pocket of the national park, best accessed from the Fjallabak Route (p139), and only accessible by 4WD or bus. There's also a short film on the Laki eruption.

Getting There & Away

Klaustur is a stop on all Reykjavík–Vík–Höfn bus routes and also serves as a crossroads to Landmannalaugar and Laki. Buses stop at the N1.

Buses travelling east call at Skaftafell and Jökulsárlón.

Sterna (www.sterna.is) services:

- Bus 12 to Höfn (kr4800, five hours, one daily June to mid-September) Stops for an hour at Jökulsárlón for the boat tour.
- Bus 12a to Vík (kr2400, 1¼ hours, one daily June to mid-September).
- Bus 12a to Reykjavík (kr6800, five hours, one daily June to mid-September).

Strætó (www.bus.is) services:

- Bus 51 to Höfn (kr5460, 2¾ hours, two daily).
- Bus 51 to Vík (kr1260, one hour, two daily).
- Bus 51 to Reykjavík (kr7140, 4¼ hours, two daily).

Note that in winter (from mid-September to May), bus 51 drops to one service daily Sunday to Friday.

Reykjavík Excursions (www.re.is) services:

- Bus 10/10a Skaftafell–Klaustur–Eldgjá–Landmannalaugar (one daily mid-June to mid-September) Can be used as a day tour, or as regular transport. Klaustur to Landmannalaugar one way is kr6500.
- Bus 16/16a Skaftafell–Lakagígar via Klaustur (one daily late June to mid-September) Use as a day tour from Skaftafell or Klaustur, with 3½ hours at Laki (from Klaustur kr12,000).
- Bus 20 to Skaftafell (kr3000, one hour, one daily June to mid-September).
- Bus 20a to Vík (kr2500, one hour, one daily June to mid-September).
- Bus 20a to Reykjavík (kr9500, six hours, one daily June to mid-September) Stops for one hour at Vík, 25 minutes at Skógafoss.

Lakagígar

It's almost impossible to comprehend the immensity of the Laki eruptions, one of the most catastrophic volcanic events in human history. Nowadays the lava field belies the apocalypse that spawned it some 230 years ago. Its black, twisted lava formations are overgrown with soft green moss. It's a fascinating place to visit, and one that sees relatively few visitors.

History

In the early summer of 1783, a vast set of fissures opened, forming around 135 craters; the Lakagígar (Laki craters) took it in turns to fountain molten rock up to 1km into the air. These Skaftáreldar (River Skaftá Fires) lasted for eight months, spewing out an estimated volume of volcanic material over 15 cu km, with a resulting lava field (known as Eldhraun) covering an area of 565 sq km. Twenty farms in the area were wiped out by lava; another 30 were so badly damaged they had to be temporarily abandoned.

Far more devastating were the hundreds of millions of tonnes of ash and sulphuric acid that poured from the fissures. The sun was blotted out, the grass died off, and around two-thirds of Iceland's livestock died from starvation and poisoning. Some 9000 people – a fifth of the country's population – were killed and the remainder faced the Móðuharðindin ('Hardship of the Mist'), a famine that followed.

The damage wasn't limited to Iceland, either. Across the northern hemisphere, clouds of ash blocked out the sun. Temperatures dropped and acid rain fell, causing devastating crop failures in Japan, Alaska and Europe (possibly even helping to spark the French Revolution).

Sights & Activities

Laki MOUNTAIN

Although the peak called Laki (818m) did not erupt, it has loaned its name to the 25km-long Lakagígar crater row, which stretches northeastward and southwestward from its base. Laki can be climbed in about 40 minutes from the parking area. From the top there are boundless 360-degree views of the fissure, vast lava fields and glinting glaciers in the distance.

Lakagígar Crater Row LANDMARK

The crater row is fascinating to explore, riddled with black sand dunes and lava tubes, many of which contain tiny stalactites. At the foot of Laki, marked walking paths lead you in and out of the two nearest craters, including an interesting lava tunnel.

Visitor Trail WALKING

An excellent visitor trail has been established over a gentle 500m walk through the crater area; pick up the accompanying brochure (or download it from the national park website) for insight into the fascinating history, geology and ecology of the area. Ensure you stick to the marked paths in this ecologically sensitive region.

Fagrifoss WATERFALL

Fagrifoss (Beautiful Falls) is not a misnomer: this waterfall must be one of Iceland's most bewitching, with rivulets of water pouring over a massive black rock. You'll come to the turn-off on the way to Laki, about 24km along the F206. Tours to Lakagígar invariably stop here.

Sleeping & Eating

Camping is forbidden within the Laki reserve. The nearest campsite, with primitive hut facilities, toilet and fresh water, is at **Blágil**, about 11km from Laki. Beds/campsites are kr4500/1600 per person. These services are operated by the national park and are accessible from the opening of the Laki road (usually mid- to late June) until early September. Contact klaustur@vjp.is for information.

There are no facilities for buying food. You will need to bring your own supplies – all day tours recommend you BYO lunch.

Tours

Visiting the area requires a large, robust jeep and 4WDing experience (as rivers must be forded). If you don't meet these requirements, it's best to join a tour. Departures to the Laki craters are dependent on road and weather conditions.

Reykjavík Excursions BUS TOUR

(☎580 5400; www.re.is) The full-day tour breaks for around 3½ hours of walking in the crater area. It is in brochures as bus route 16 and departs daily from late June to early September, at 8am from Skaftafell (kr17,000) and at 9am from the N1 at Kirkjubæjarklaustur (kr12,000). BYO lunch.

Hólasport JEEP TOUR

(☎660 1151; www.holasport.is) Based at Hótel Laki, just south of Kirkjubæjarklaustur, Hólasport offers eight-hour super-Jeep day tours to Laki (kr32,500) from June to mid-October. BYO lunch.

Kind Adventures MOUNTAIN BIKING

(☎847 1604; www.kindadventure.is) For something more challenging, this new Kirkjubæjarklaustur-based company offers two days of guided mountain biking (on fatbikes) in the Laki craters area (kr130,000, including meals). You reach the area in a jeep, stay overnight in a mountain hut, do a little cave exploration, and ride back (total cycling distance: 64km, mostly downhill). Some mountain-biking experience is required.

Information

The Lakagígar area is contained within the boundaries of Vatnajökull National Park (www.vjp.is). Check the park website for excellent information for travellers. In peak season (mid-July to mid-August), park rangers are available at the Laki car parks from 11am to 3pm.

The **Skaftárstofa Visitor Centre** (p316) in Kirkjubæjarklaustur is a good port of call for advice before visiting.

Getting There & Away

Rte F206 (just west of Kirkjubæjarklaustur) is generally open from mid-June to mid-September (check on www.vegagerdin.is). It's a long and very rugged 50km to the Lakagígar crater row. The road is absolutely unsuitable for 2WD cars as there are several rivers to ford. Even low-clearance 4WD vehicles may not be suitable in the spring thaw or after rain, when the rivers tend to run deep.

The Sandar

The sandar are soul-destroyingly flat and empty regions sprawling along Iceland's southeastern coast. High in the mountains, glaciers scrape up silt, sand and gravel that is then carried by glacial rivers or (more dramatically) by glacial bursts down to the coast and dumped in huge, desert-like plains. The sandar here are so impressively huge and awful that the Icelandic word (singular: *sandur*) is used internationally to describe the topographic phenomenon of a glacial outwash plain.

Skeiðarársandur is the most visible and dramatic, stretching some 40km between ice cap and coast from Núpsstaður to Öræfi. Here you'll encounter a flat expanse of grey-black sands, fierce scouring winds (a cyclist's nightmare) and fast-flowing grey-brown glacial rivers.

Note: *do not* drive off-road in these expanses. It is illegal, and hugely destructive to the fragile environment.

Sights

Lómagnúpur MOUNTAIN

Adding more eye candy to an impressive road trip, a precipitous 767m-tall palisade of cliffs known as Lómagnúpur towers over the landscapes, begging to be photographed. It's full of legends, and looks particularly good as a backdrop to the turf-roofed farm at Núpsstaður.

Núpsstaður FARM

Lómagnúpur towers over the impossibly photogenic old turf-roofed farm at Núpsstaður. The farm buildings date back to the early 19th century, and the idyllic chapel is one of the last turf churches in Iceland. It was once a museum, but at the time of writing the farm was closed to the public.

You can't drive onto the property, but you can park by the road and walk up to the buildings to check them out and take photos.

Skeiðarársandur LANDMARK

Skeiðarársandur, the largest sandur in the world, covers a 1300-sq-km area and was formed by the mighty Skeiðarárjökull. Since the Settlement Era, Skeiðarársandur has swallowed a considerable amount of farmland and it continues to grow. The area was relatively well populated (for Iceland, anyway), but in 1362 the volcano beneath Öræfajökull (then known as Knappafellsjökull) erupted and the subsequent *jökulhlaup* (flooding caused by volcanic eruption beneath ice) laid waste the entire district. After the 1362 eruption the district became known as Öræfi (Wasteland).

Sleeping & Eating

This 70km stretch has very little by way of traveller facilities – only a couple of accommodation options in pretty green oases.

★**Dalshöfði Guesthouse** GUESTHOUSE €€

(☎861 4781; dalshofdi@gmail.com; s/d without bathroom incl breakfast kr13,000/18,300; ⏲Mar-Oct) An appealing option in this area is Dalshöfði Guesthouse, in a remote and scenic farm setting 5km north of the Ring Road. Rooms are bright and spotless, with access to a kitchen and a sunny, plant-filled outdoor deck. There's a two-bedroom apartment here, too (kr33,200), and some lovely hiking trails in the area.

Hvoll Guesthouse GUESTHOUSE €€

(☎487 4785; www.road201.is; d/f without bathroom from kr16,850/27,600) Formerly a HI-affiliated hostel, this well-run guesthouse (also known as Road 201) is on the edge of Skeiðarársandur (3.5km south off the Ring Road via a gravel road) and feels remote despite its large size. There's a busy atmosphere; facilities include several kitchens (bring food – the closest supermarket is 25km away in Klaustur) and a laundry.

HOW TO AVOID BEING SKUA-ED

The great sandar on Iceland's southern coast are the world's largest breeding ground for great skuas (*Stercorarius skua; skúmur* in Icelandic). These large, meaty, dirty-brown birds tend to build their nests among grassy tufts in the ashy sand. You'll often see them harassing gulls into disgorging their dinner, killing and eating puffins and other little birds, or swooping down on *you* if you get too close to their nests.

Thankfully (unlike feather-brained Arctic terns), skuas will stop plaguing you if you run away from the area they're trying to defend. You can also avoid aerial strikes by wearing a hat or carrying a stick above your head.

Fosshótel Núpar HOTEL €€

(☎517 3060; www.fosshotel.is; d incl breakfast from kr28,800) Just west of Hvoll Guesthouse, behind a portacabin-like exterior, this chain hotel offers modern, minimalist rooms, many with good views, and a somewhat soulless restaurant serving buffet dinner.

Skaftafell (Vatnajökull National Park – South)

Skaftafell, the jewel in the crown of Vatnajökull National Park, encompasses a breathtaking collection of peaks and glaciers. It's the country's favourite wilderness: 500,000 visitors per year come to marvel at thundering waterfalls, twisted birch woods, the tangled web of rivers threading across the sandar, and brilliant blue-white Vatnajökull with its lurching tongues of ice, dripping down mountainsides like icing on a cake.

Skaftafell deserves its reputation, and few visitors – even those who usually shun the great outdoors – can resist it. In the height of summer it may feel that every traveller in the country is here. However, if you're prepared to get out on the more remote trails and take advantage of the fabulous hiking on the heath and beyond, you'll leave the crowds behind. Shun the crowds by visiting Svartifoss under the midnight sun.

Skaftafell National Park

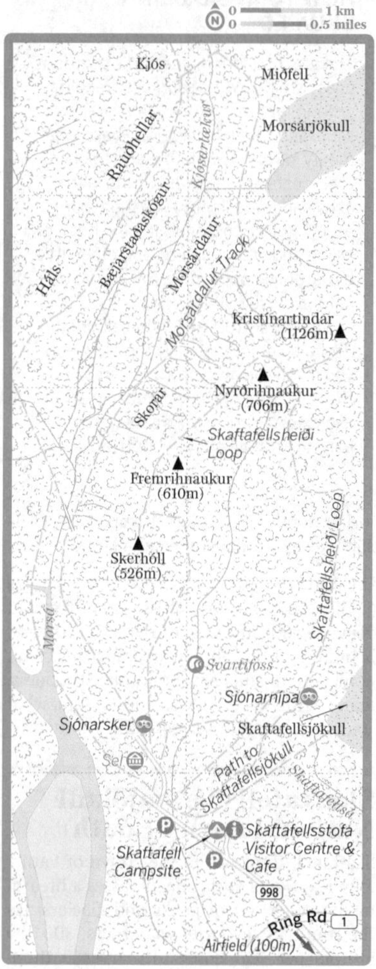

History

The historical Skaftafell was a large farm at the foot of the hills west of the present campsite. Shifting glacial sands slowly buried the fields and forced the farm to be moved to a more suitable site, on the heath 100m above the sandur. The district came to be known as Hérað Milli Sandur (Land Between the Sands), but after all the farms were annihilated by the 1362 eruptions, the district became the 'land under the sands' and was renamed Öræfi (Wasteland). Once the vegetation returned, however, the Skaftafell farm was rebuilt in its former location.

Skaftafell National Park was founded in 1967 by the Icelandic Government and the WWF. In June 2008 it merged with the Jökulsárgljúfur National Park in Iceland's north to form the massive wilderness area of Vatnajökull National Park.

Activities

Skaftafell is ideal for day hikes and also offers longer hikes through its wilderness regions. The park produces good maps outlining shorter hiking trails (kr350), and stocks larger topo maps from various publishers.

Most of Skaftafell's visitors keep to the popular routes on Skaftafellsheiði. Hiking in other accessible areas, such as the upper Morsárdalur and Kjós valleys, requires more time, motivation and planning. Before embarking on more remote routes, speak to the staff at the visitor centre, who are keen to impart knowledge and help you prepare, as well as make you aware of potential risks. You should enquire about river crossings along your intended route; you should also leave a travel plan at www.safetravel.is.

Other possibilities for hikes include the long day trip beyond Bæjarstaðarskógur into the rugged Skaftafellsfjöll. A recommended destination is the 862m-high summit of the **Jökulfell ridge**, which affords a commanding view of the vast expanses of Skeiðarárjökull. Even better is an excursion into the **Kjós** dell.

Note that from mid-June to mid-August, rangers guide free daily interpretive walks that depart from the visitor centre – a great way to learn about the area. Check the website, or ask staff.

Svartifoss

Star of a hundred postcards, Svartifoss (Black Falls) is a stunning, moody-looking waterfall flanked by geometric black basalt columns. It's reached by an easy 1.8km trail leading up from the visitor centre via the campsite.

To take pressure off the busy trail to Svartifoss, park staff recommend you take an alternative path back to the visitor centre. From Svartifoss, continue west up the track to **Sjónarsker**, where there's a view disc that names the surrounding landmarks to help you get your bearings, plus an unforgettable vista across Skeiðarársandur. From here you can visit the traditional turf-roofed farmhouse **Sel**; this 2½-hour, 5.3km return walk is classified as easy.

Alternatively, from Svartifoss head east over the heath to the viewpoint at **Sjónarnípa**, looking across Skaftafellsjökull. This walk is classified as challenging; allow three hours return (7.4km).

Skaftafellsjökull

Another very popular trail is the easy one-hour return walk (3.7km) to Skaftafellsjökull. The marked trail begins at the visitor centre and leads to the glacier face, where you can witness the bumps and groans of the ice (although the glacier is pretty grey and gritty here). The glacier has receded greatly in recent decades, meaning land along this trail has been gradually reappearing. Pick up a brochure that describes the trail's geology. Note: this trail is suitable for those with limited mobility.

Skaftafellsheiði Loop

On a fine day, the five- to six-hour (15.5km) walk around Skaftafellsheiði is a hiker's dream. It begins by climbing from the campsite past Svartifoss and Sjónarsker, continuing across the moor to 610m-high **Fremrihnaukur**. From there it follows the edge of the plateau to the next rise, **Nyrðrihnaukur** (706m), which affords a superb view of Morsárdalur, and Morsárjökull and the iceberg-choked lagoon at its base. At this point the track turns southeast to an outlook point, **Gláma**, on the cliff above Skaftafellsjökull.

For the best view of Skaftafellsjökull, Morsárdalur and the Skeiðarársandur, it's worth scaling the summit of **Kristínartindar** (1126m). The best way follows a well-marked 2km route (classified as difficult) up the prominent valley southeast of the Nyrðrihnaukur lookout, and back down near Gláma.

Tours

Glacier Hikes & Ice Climbing

The highlight of a visit to the southern reaches of Vatnajökull is a glacier hike. It's utterly liberating to strap on crampons and crunch your way around a glacier, and there's much to see on the ice: waterfalls, ice caves, glacial mice (moss balls, not actual mice!) and different-coloured ash from ancient explosions. But – take note: as magnetic as the glaciers are, they are also riven with fissures and are potentially dangerous, so don't be tempted to stride out onto one without the right equipment and guiding.

A number of authorised guides operate year-round in the area (and at lesser-visited glacier tongues further east, toward Höfn). The largest companies, Icelandic Mountain Guides (p323) and Glacier Guides (p323), have info and booking huts in the car park at Skaftafellsstofa Visitor Centre (p324), where you can talk to experts and get kitted out for glacier walks (warm clothes essential, waterproof gear and hiking boots available for hire).

Both companies go further than just easy glacier hikes, offering more challenging options and ice climbs, right up to summiting Iceland's highest peak (Hvannadalshnúkur). Both offer combos, such as a glacier hike plus a lagoon boat trip. See the websites for suggestions and for the most up-to-date rates.

Ice Caves

In hot demand: winter visits to ice caves, glorious dimpled caverns of exquisite blue light, which are accessible (usually at glacier edges) only from around November to March – they can be viewed in cold conditions, and become unstable and unsafe in warmer weather. Temporary ice caves are created anew each season by the forces of nature, and are scouted by local experts. They *must* be visited with guides, who will ensure safety and correct equipment. As with glacier hikes, tours generally involve getting kitted out (crampons, helmets etc), then driving to the glacier edge and taking

FLIGHTSEEING OVER SKAFTAFELL

Atlantsflug (☎854 4105; www.flightseeing.is) offers sightseeing flights offer a brilliant perspective over all this natural splendour, and leave from the tiny airfield on the Ring Road, just by the turn-off to the Skaftafellsstofa Visitor Centre. Choose between six tour options, with views over Landmannalaugar, Lakagígar, Skaftafell peaks, Jökulsárlón and Grímsvötn. Prices start from kr26,100 for 20 minutes on the 'pilot special' surprise route (determined by weather and conditions).

JÖKULHLAUP!

In late 1996 the devastating Grímsvötn eruption – Iceland's fourth largest of the 20th century, after Katla in 1918, Hekla in 1947 and Surtsey in 1963 – shook southeast Iceland and caused an awesome *jökulhlaup* (glacial flood) across Skeiðarársandur. The events leading up to it are a sobering reminder of Iceland's volatile fire-and-ice combination.

On the morning of 29 September 1996, a magnitude 5.0 earthquake shook the Vatnajökull ice cap. Magma from a new volcano, in the Grímsvötn region beneath Vatnajökull, had made its way through the earth's crust and into the ice, causing the eruption of a 4km-long subsurface fissure known as Gjálp. The following day the eruption burst through the surface, ejecting a column of steam that rose 10km into the sky.

Scientists became concerned as the subglacial lake in the Grímsvötn caldera began to fill with water from ice melted by the eruption. Initial predictions on 3 October were that the ice would lift and the lake would spill out across Skeiðarársandur, threatening the Ring Road and its bridges. In the hope of diverting floodwaters away from the bridges, massive dyke-building projects were organised on Skeiðarársandur.

On 5 November, more than a month after the eruption started, the ice *did* lift and the Grímsvötn reservoir drained in a massive *jökulhlaup*, releasing up to 3000 billion litres of water within a few hours. The floodwaters – dragging along icebergs the size of three-storey buildings – destroyed the 375m-long Gígjukvísl Bridge and the 900m-long Skeiðará Bridge, both on the Skeiðarársandur. You can see video footage of the eruption and enormous multi-tonne blocks of ice being hurled across Skeiðarársandur at the **Gamlabúð** (p333) in Höfn.

Some other of Grímsvötn's creations include the Ásbyrgi canyon, gouged out by a cataclysmic flood over just a few days. In 1934 an eruption released a *jökulhlaup* of 40,000 cu metres per second, which swelled the river Skeiðará to 9km in width and laid waste to large areas of farmland.

Grímsvötn erupted again in December 1998, November 2004 and most recently in May 2011, when a huge ash plume was released into the atmosphere, disrupting air traffic (but with nowhere near the disruption caused by 2010's Eyjafjallajökull eruption). There was no *jökulhlaup* on any of these three occasions.

a walk to reach the destination. Reasonable fitness and mobility are required.

With their rapid growth in popularity, the largest and most accessible ice caves can become busy and crowded when tour groups arrive (from as far afield as Reykjavík). It is often the case that guided groups all visit the same cave – some tourists are disappointed to find queues of visitors waiting to enter. Catering to this, a few tour companies offer private tours to more remote caves: these tours are longer, more expensive, and generally require a higher level of fitness to reach.

Local Guide (p322) is the regional expert on ice caves in the south, and can get you to some more remote, private caves if you have more time, stamina and cash. Other good, locally owned companies offering ice-cave exploration include Glacier Adventure (p330), IceGuide (p330) and Glacier Trips (p330).

Tour Companies

Local Guide ADVENTURE TOUR

(☎894 1317; www.localguide.is; Fagurhólsmýri; ⏲9am-5pm) Local Guide's booking agency is at Fagurhólsmýri (there's an N1 fuel pump there), about 26km from Skaftafell. From here, guides run tailored, year-round glacier hikes and ice climbs (the shortest tour offers 1½ hours on the ice for kr11,900). Local Guide is also the long-standing local expert on ice caves, running tours from mid-November to March.

The regular ice-cave tour costs kr18,900, but there are options for longer private tours to more remote caves, or specialised tours for photographers. The website outlines all options and prices.

Many generations of this family have lived at the local farm Hofsnes, so their local knowledge is first-rate (the same family also runs tours to Ingólfshöfði, and ski-mountaineering ascents of Hvannadalshnúkur).

Icelandic Mountain Guides ADVENTURE
(IMG; ☎Reykjavík 587 9999, Skaftafell 894 2959; www.mountainguides.is; ⏰8.30am-6pm May-Sep, reduced hours Oct-Apr) IMG's best-selling walk is the family-friendly 'Blue Ice Experience', with 1½ to two hours spent on the ice at Svínafellsjökull (adult/child kr10,900/5450, minimum age eight years). These tours run from Skaftafell two to six times daily year-round (departures at 10am and 2pm year-round, plus additional tours from June to September).

There are longer three-hour walks up the same glacier (kr15,900), and an option to combine with an introduction to ice climbing (kr18,900).

See the website for IMG's impressive program of multiday mountain-biking, hiking, skiing and super-Jeep tours, including a five-day 'Rivers and Glaciers of Vatnajökull' backpacking trip.

For some trips, IMG can arrange pick-up from Svínafell campsite and Hótel Skaftafell (prebooking required).

Glacier Guides ADVENTURE TOUR
(☎Reykjavík 562 7000, Skaftafell 659 7000; www.glacierguides.is; ⏰8.30am-6pm Apr-Oct, reduced hours Nov-Mar) As well as glacier walks of varying duration and difficulty, Glacier Guides also offers ice climbing, plus wintertime ice-cave visits from Skaftafell. Its beginner-level walk is the family-friendly 'Glacier Wonders', a 3½-hour tour with a one-hour walk on Falljökull (adult/child kr10,990/5495, minimum age 10 years); trips depart from Skaftafell four times daily April to October.

There's also a more demanding 5½-hour tour up the same glacier, with three hours on the ice (kr15,990), and a seven-hour combo trip that includes glacier hiking plus ice climbing (kr24,990).

Sleeping

Inside the park, the only option is to camp. There's very little accommodation close to the park, and hotels in the southeast are in huge demand in summer – you'll need either a tent or a firm hotel booking if you're heading this way.

The nearest hotel is Hótel Skaftafell (p324) at Freysnes, 5km east of the national-park entrance, and there's a handful of options at Hof, a further 15km east.

Skaftafell Campsite CAMPGROUND €
(☎470 8300; www.vjp.is; sites per adult/teen/child kr1600/750/free; ⏰May-Sep) Most visitors bring a tent (or campervan) to this large, gravelly, panoramic campsite (with laundry facilities, and hot showers for kr500). It gets very busy in summer, with a capacity of 400 pitches. Reservations are only required for large groups (40-plus people). No cooking facilities are provided. Wi-fi is available in the visitor centre.

If you're looking for a less-crowded option, consider the campground at Svínafell (p324), 8km east.

Note that winter camping in the car park of the visitor centre is possible, for a fee.

Eating

In summer, there's a cafe inside the park visitor centre, and a food truck nearby, but there are no year-round park options. You can get meals and groceries year-round at Söluskálinn Freysnesi (p325), in Freysnes, 5km east of the national-park entrance.

Bring supplies from the supermarkets at Kirkjubæjarklaustur or Höfn.

Visitor Centre Cafe CAFE €
(light meals kr1190-1990; ⏰10am-8pm May-Sep) There's a busy summertime cafe inside the visitor centre, which sells coffee, soup, grilled panini, cake and waffles. It's closed in winter.

Glacier Goodies FAST FOOD €€
(www.facebook.com/glaciergoodies; mains kr2200-2700; ⏰11.30am-7pm mid-May–Sep) This food truck close to the visitor centre

WINTER IN SKAFTAFELL

There has been a significant growth in winter travel to the region, with the strong draws of Northern Lights and ice caves (caves that form within the ice of a glacier, which become solid and safe for visiting in the coldest months). You can still do glacier walks in winter – and the glaciers look more pristine (taking on that blue hue so beloved of photographers). In the right conditions, Svartifoss freezes in January-February (on the flip side, in winter the falls are not always accessible, due to slippery, unsafe tracks). Between December and March, access to trails is weather dependent, and some may require crampons. There are also restricted daylight hours, so it pays to talk to park staff about your best options.

has a very small menu of well-executed dishes made from local ingredients: lobster soup, fish and chips, baby back ribs and chips.

Information

All flora, fauna and natural features of the park are protected, open fires are prohibited and rubbish must be carried out. It's important to stick to the marked paths to avoiding damaging delicate plant life.

Note that drones are prohibited in the national park without official park permission.

Skaftafellsstofa Visitor Centre (☎470 8300; www.vjp.is; ⏰9am-7pm May-Sep, 10am-5pm Feb-Apr, Oct & Nov, 11am-5pm Dec, 10am-4pm Jan) The helpful year-round visitor centre has an information desk plus maps for sale, informative exhibitions, a summertime cafe and internet access. The staff here know their stuff.

Getting There & Away

Skaftafell is a stop on Reykjavík–Höfn bus routes and also a departure point for wilderness areas such as Landmannalaugar and Lakagígar. There are frequent services to Jökulsárlón.

Buses stop in front of the visitor centre.

Sterna (www.sterna.is) services:

➡ Bus 12 to Höfn (kr2800, 2¾ hours, one daily June to mid-September) Stops for one hour at Jökulsárlón.

➡ Bus 12a to Reykjavík (kr8800, 6¾ hours, one daily June to mid-September).

Strætó (www.bus.is) services:

➡ Bus 51 to Höfn (kr3360, 1¾ hours, two daily June to mid-September, one daily Sunday to Friday mid-September to May) Stops at Freysnes and Jökulsárlón en route.

➡ Bus 51 to Reykjavík (kr9240, 5¼ hours, two daily June to mid-September, one daily Sunday to Friday mid-September to May).

Reykjavík Excursions (www.re.is) services:

➡ Bus 10/10a to Landmannalaugar (kr9000, five hours, one daily mid-June to mid-September) Runs via Eldgjá. Can be used as a day tour, or as regular transport.

➡ Bus 15 to Jökulsárlón (kr2500, 45 minutes, three daily June to mid-September).

➡ Bus 16/16a to Lakagígar (one daily late June to mid-September) Use as a day tour, with 3½ hours at Laki (day tour kr17,000).

➡ Bus 19 to Höfn (kr5500, two hours, one daily June to mid-September).

➡ Bus 20a to Reykjavík (kr11,000, seven hours, one daily June to mid-September) Stops for one hour at Vík.

Skaftafell to Jökulsárlón

Glittering glaciers and brooding mountains line the 60km stretch between Skaftafell and the iceberg-filled lagoon Jökulsárlón, and the unfolding landscape makes it difficult to keep your eyes on the road.

Svínafell & Around

Heading east on the Ring Road from Skaftafell, a sign points the way to the glacier **Svínafellsjökull**. A good dirt road leads 2km to a car park, from where it's a short walk to the northern edge of the glacier. Don't be tempted to stride out onto the glacier unaccompanied – join one of the glacier walks offered by Icelandic Mountain Guides (p323).

The first hamlet you reach east of Skaftafell is **Freysnes**, home to a hotel, and petrol station and store.

The farm Svínafell, 8km southeast of Skaftafell, was the home of Flosi Þórðarson, the character who burned Njál and his family to death in *Njál's Saga*. It was also the site where Flosi and Njál's family were finally reconciled, thus ending one of the bloodiest feuds in Icelandic history. In the 17th century, Svínafellsjökull nearly engulfed the farm, but it has since retreated. There's not much to this tiny settlement now, but there is accommodation.

Tours

Glacier Horses HORSE RIDING

(☎847 7170; www.glacierhorses.is; tours adult/child kr9500/5000; ⏰Jun-Sep) Not far past Svínafell (en route to Hof), this operator offers short (one to 1½-hour) horse rides in view-blessed countryside. Departure times are generally at 10am, 1pm and 4pm (booking essential, by phone or email).

Sleeping & Eating

Ferðaþjónustan Svínafelli CAMPGROUND €

(☎478 1765; www.svinafell.com; sites per person kr1500, cabins & rooms per person kr4300-5000; ⏰campground May-Sep) This well-organised place has a campsite and six basic cabins (sleeping four), and a spotless amenities block with a large dining room. With your own vehicle, it's an alternative to the campsite at Skaftafell. The owner also offers sleeping-bag beds in apartments and rooms scattered about the hamlet (these are available year-round). Check current prices online.

Hótel Skaftafell HOTEL €€€
(☎478 1945; www.hotelskaftafell.is; Freysnes; s/d/tr incl breakfast kr28,500/33,000/39,600) This is the closest hotel to Skaftafell; it's 5km east, at Freysnes, and one of very few hotels in the area, so it's in hot demand – prices reflect this. Its 63 rooms are functional rather than luxurious; staff are helpful. There's a decent restaurant (mains kr3650 to kr5750) plating up local produce such as Arctic char and lamb fillet.

Söluskálinn Freysnesi ICELANDIC €
(mains kr1000-3200; ⏲9am-8pm) The petrol station opposite Hótel Skaftafell has a cafeteria serving a well-priced hot dish of the day alongside burgers, pizzas and a decent selection of groceries.

Hvannadalshnúkur

Iceland's highest mountain, Hvannadalshnúkur (2110m), pokes out from **Öræfajökull**, an offshoot of Vatnajökull. This lofty peak is actually the northwestern edge of an immense 5km-wide crater – the biggest active volcano in Europe after Mt Etna. It erupted in 1362, firing out the largest amount of tephra in Iceland's recorded history. The region was utterly devastated – hence its name, Öræfi (Wasteland).

Tours

The best access for climbing Hvannadalshnúkur is from Sandfellsheiði, about 12km southeast of Skaftafell. Most guided expeditions manage the trip in a very long and taxing day (starting around 5am), and although there are no technical skills required, the trip is both physically and mentally challenging. Total elevation gain is more than 2000m; total distance is around 23km. Independent climbers should carry enough supplies and gear for several days, and must be well versed in glacier travel.

The best time for climbing the mountain is April or May, before the ice bridges melt. Note that each year the ice bridges that make the hike possible are melting earlier and faster, so the climbing season is becoming shorter. Companies may advertise long seasons (April to August, for example), but it is unlikely the conditions will permit ascents beyond June.

DON'T MISS

FJAÐRÁRGLJÚFUR

Carved out by the river Fjaðrá, **Fjaðrárgljúfur** is a darkly picturesque canyon that is a humbling two million years old. A walking track follows its southern edge for a couple of kilometres, with plenty of places to gaze down into its rocky, writhing depths, and to take very Instagram-worthy pics.

The canyon is not far west of Klaustur, 3km north of the Ring Road via Rte 206 – don't turn right at the sign for Laki, but continue for about 1km to reach a car park and toilet facilities.

Icelandic Mountain Guides, Glacier Guides and Local Guide (p322-3; all based in and around Skaftafell) offer guided ascents of Hvannadalshnúkur; briefings are held the night before. Note that prices are always subject to change, as conditions may force companies to hire extra guides per group, raising the costs.

Book in advance, and allow yourself extra days in case the weather causes a cancellation. Check websites for more details.

From Coast to Mountains ADVENTURE TOUR
(Öræfaferðir; ☎894 0894; www.fromcoasttomountains.is; Fagurhólsmýri) Einar, the company owner, holds the world record for ascents of Hvannadalshnúkur (nearly 300!). He offers a ski-mountaineering ascent from late March to mid-May; the price depends on the number of participants (two people costs kr65,000 per person; climbers need their own skis). There is also the possibility of ascent in September/October, under the right conditions.

Icelandic Mountain Guides ADVENTURE TOUR
(☎Reykjavík office 587 9999, Skaftafell 894 2959; www.mountainguides.is) A guided 10- to 15-hour ascent costs kr42,900 per person (minimum two people). Trips run three times a week in the season (conditions permitting). IMG has a second mountain-climbing option in the park: Hrútsfjallstindar Peaks (kr42,900), which reaches 1875m. Based in the car park of Skaftafell National Park.

Glacier Guides ADVENTURE TOUR
(☎Reykjavík 562 7000, Skaftafell 659 7000; www.glacierguides.is) Offers an ascent of Hvannadalshnúkur for kr42,990 per person (minimum two people), daily during the season

(conditions permitting). Based in the car park of Skaftafell National Park.

Hof

At the hamlet of Hof there's a story-book wood-and-peat church, built on the foundations of a previous 14th-century building. It was reconstructed in 1884 and now sits pretty in a thicket of birch and ash with flowers growing on the grassy roof.

Nónhamar COTTAGES €€
(☎616 1247; www.nonhamar.is; cabins kr19,000-22,000; ⊙Mar-Oct) Nónhamar has a trio of super-cosy self-contained cabins sleeping four people in bunks (BYO sleeping bags, or hire linen for kr1800 per person). There's a wee kitchenette and bathroom in each. Note that the property was formerly known as Lækjarhús.

Hof 1 Hotel COUNTRY HOTEL €€€
(☎478 2260; www.hof1.is; d with/without bathroom incl breakfast kr30,600/24,900) Beneath the Öræfajökull glacier, the very civilised Hof 1 harbours an impressive collection of modern Icelandic art, a stylish lounge area, and a sauna and hot-pot area. There's a variety of rooms scattered in various buildings, and a dining area serving dinner (two courses kr3900 to kr4900).

Ingólfshöfði

While everyone's gaze naturally turns inland in this spectacular part of Iceland, there are reasons to look offshore, too – in particular to the 76m-high Ingólfshöfði promontory, rising from the flat lands like a strange dream.

In spring and summer, this beautiful, isolated nature reserve is overrun with nesting puffins, skuas and other seabirds, and you may see whales offshore. It's also of great historical importance – it was here that Ingólfur Arnarson, Iceland's first settler, stayed the winter on his original foray to the country in AD 874.

The signposted departure point for the Ingólfshöfði tours is about 25km east of Skaftafell, close to the Local Guide agency (p322) at Fagurhólsmýri. The departure hut is about 2km off the Ring Road.

VATNAJÖKULL NATIONAL PARK

Vast, varied and spectacular, Vatnajökull National Park was founded in 2008, when authorities created a giant megapark by joining the Vatnajökull ice cap with two previously established national parks: Skaftafell in southeast Iceland and Jökulsárgljúfur in the northeast. With recent additions, the park measures 13,900 sq km – nearly 14% of entire Iceland (it's one of the largest national parks in Europe).

The park boundaries encircle a staggering richness of landscapes and some of Iceland's greatest natural treasures, created by the combined forces of rivers, glacial ice, and volcanic and geothermal activity. The entirety of the Vatnajökull ice cap is protected, including countless glistening outlet glaciers and glacial rivers. There are incredible rock formations around Ásbyrgi canyon, brilliant waterfalls such as Dettifoss and Svartifoss, the storied Lakagígar crater row, Askja and other volcanoes of the highlands, and an unending variety of areas where geology, ecology and history lessons spring to life.

Information

The park's website is www.vjp.is. It's filled with important and useful information; details on trails, campsites, access roads etc, plus it has downloadable maps and brochures.

The park operates five major visitor centres, which all house exhibitions on the park's nature and cultural heritage, and are staffed by rangers who sell maps and provide advice. Not all are open year-round. Visitor centres:

- **Skaftafellsstofa** (p324) At Skaftafell in the southeast.
- **Gamlabúð** (p336) At Höfn in the southeast.
- **Skaftárstofa** (p316) At Kirkjubæjarklaustur in the southeast.
- **Snæfellsstofa** (p293) At Skriðuklaustur (40km southwest of Egilsstaðir, en route to Snæfell mountain) in the east.
- **Gljúfrastofa** (p277) At Ásbyrgi in the north.

From Coast to Mountains ADVENTURE TOUR (Öræfaferðir; ☎894 0894; www.puffintour.is; tours adult/child kr7500/2500; ⏱tours 10.15am & 1.30pm Mon-Sat mid-May–mid-Aug) The Ingólfshöfði reserve is open to visitors. Tours begin with a fun ride across 6km of shallow tidal lagoon (in a tractor-drawn wagon), then a short but steep sandy climb, followed by a 1½-hour guided walk round the headland. The emphasis is on birdwatching, with stunning mountain backdrops to marvel over. Note that puffins usually leave Iceland around mid-August.

Sleeping & Eating

The Local Guide booking agency at Fagurhólsmýri (p322) has a sweet cafe counter, selling coffee, sandwiches and cakes.

Fosshotel Glacier Lagoon HOTEL €€€ (☎514 8300; www.fosshotel.is; Hnappavellir; r incl breakfast from kr33,600) The name is misleading: this large new four-star hotel sits halfway between Skaftafell and Jökulsárlón at Hnappavellir, about 3km east of the departure point for Ingólfshöfði tours. There are *no* lagoon views – Jökulsárlón is a 20-minute drive away. Opened in mid-2016, the newly constructed hotel houses 104 simple but stylish rooms, a good restaurant and an inviting bar area.

Breiðamerkursandur

The easternmost part of the large sandar region, Breiðamerkursandur is one of the main breeding grounds for Iceland's great skuas. Thanks to rising numbers of these ground-nesting birds, there's also a growing population of Arctic foxes. Historically, Breiðamerkursandur also figures in *Njál's Saga,* which ends with Kári Sölmundarson arriving in this idyllic spot to 'live happily ever after' – which has to be some kind of miracle in a saga.

The sandur is backed by a sweeping panorama of glacier-capped mountains, some of which are fronted by deep lagoons. **Kvíárjökull glacier** snakes down to the Kvíá river and is easily accessible from the Ring Roa; look for the sign for Kvíármýrarkambur just west of the bridge over the river. Leave your car in the small car park and follow the path into the scenic valley.

The 742m-high **Breiðamerkurfjall** was once a *nunatak,* a hill enclosed by Breiðamerkurjökull and Fjallsjökull, but the glaciers have since retreated and freed it.

A sign off the Ring Road indicates **Fjallsárlón** – this is an easily accessible glacier lagoon, where icebergs calve from Fjallsjökull. There are some great walking trails around the lagoon, and it's a good alternative to busy Jökulsárlón, 10km further east. If you have the time, we recommend you stop at both lagoons, as they have different qualities: Jökulsárlón is much larger and more dramatic, while from Fjallsárlón's shores you can see the glacier snout. Both lagoons offer boat rides, and Fjallsárlón wins brownie points for building a nice new visitor centre with a cafe.

A walking trail leads 5km east to **Breiðarlón**, another lagoon outlet – this one from Breiðamerkurjökull (also the source of Jökulsárlón).

Fjallsárlón Glacial Lagoon Boat Tours BOAT TOUR (☎666 8006; www.fjallsarlon.is; adult/child kr6200/3500; ⏱tours hourly 10am-5pm May–Sep) It's 600m from the Ring Road to the parking area for Fjallsárlón – and it's here that a new company has set up, offering 45-minute Zodiac boat trips among these lagoon icebergs (as an alternative to the cruises at busy Jökulsárlón, 10km further east and directly on the Ring Road). You can book online.

Fjallsárlón (around 3 sq km) is neither as large nor as dramatic as Jökulsárlón (25 sq km), but it is less crowded, which has its own appeal. The walking trail from the car park to the boat's departure point at the lagoon shore is more intrepid, and there is also an intimacy to a tour on this lagoon – you don't have to travel as far to reach the glacier snout, for example.

Jökulsárlón

A host of spectacular, luminous-blue icebergs drift through Jökulsárlón glacier lagoon, right beside the Ring Road between Höfn and Skaftafell. It's worth spending a couple of hours here, admiring the wondrous ice sculptures (some of them striped with ash layers from volcanic eruptions), scouting for seals or taking a boat trip.

The icebergs calve from Breiðamerkurjökull, an offshoot of Vatnajökull, crashing down into the water and drifting towards the Atlantic Ocean. They can spend up to five years floating in the 25-sq-km-plus, 260m-deep lagoon, melting, refreezing and occasionally toppling over with a mighty splash, startling the birds. They then move on via **Jökulsá**, Iceland's shortest river, out to sea.

Although it looks as though it's been here since the last ice age, the lagoon is only about 80 years old. Until the mid-1930s Breiðamerkurjökull reached the Ring Road; it's now retreating rapidly (up to a staggering 500m per year), and the lagoon is consequently growing.

Activities

The lagoon boat trips are excellent, but you can get almost as close to those cool-blue masterpieces by walking along the shore, and you can taste ancient ice by hauling it out of the water. On the Ring Road west of the car park, there are designated parking areas where you can walk over the mounds to visit the lake at less-touristed stretches of shoreline.

As well as seeing the lagoon, it's highly recommended that you visit the Jökulsá river mouth (there are car parks on the ocean side of the Ring Road), where you'll see ice boulders resting photogenically on the black-sand beach as part of their final journey out to sea.

Tours

Glacier Lagoon Amphibious Boat Tours BOAT TOUR

(☎478 2222; www.icelagoon.is; adult/child kr5000/1500; ⊙9am-7pm Jun-Aug, 10am-5pm Apr, May, Sep & Oct) Take a memorable 40-minute trip in an amphibious boat, which trundles along the shore like a bus before driving into the water. On-board guides regale you with factoids about the lagoon, and you can taste 1000-year-old ice. There is no set schedule; trips run from the eastern car park (by the cafe) regularly – up to 40 a day in summer.

Note that the last boat tour departs about one hour before closing time. Tours may be available from November to March, depending on demand and weather conditions – contact the operators.

The same company also offers a handful of hour-long lagoon tours in Zodiacs (adult/child kr8500/4200; not recommended for kids under 10). These run on a set schedule, and it's worth booking ahead (you can do this online).

Ice Lagoon Zodiac Boat Tours BOAT TOUR

(☎860 9996; www.icelagoon.com; adult/child kr9500/6000; ⊙9am-5.30pm mid-May–mid-Sep) This operator deals exclusively with Zodiac tours of the lagoon. It's a one-hour experience, with a maximum of 20 passengers per boat, and it travels at speed up to the glacier edge (not done by the amphibious boats) before cruising back at a leisurely pace. It pays to book these tours in advance, online; minimum age six years.

The company operates from a huge truck in the western car park – the truck even has toilets for Zodiac customers. It may occasionally be parked in the east car park if conditions require it, but you can't miss it.

Festivals & Events

Fireworks FIREWORKS

(www.visitvatnajokull.is; ⊙mid-Aug) If you're in the area in mid-August, don't miss the annual, one-night fireworks display held at Jökulsárlón as a fund-raiser for the local search-and-rescue team. Entry is usually around kr1000/free for adults/children, and buses run to bring spectators to the event from Höfn, Kirkjubæjarklaustur and Skaftafell.

Sleeping & Eating

The closest accommodation is at the hamlet of Hali, 13km east, and the closest campground is at Hrollaugsstaðir (p331), 10km further east from Hali.

To the west, the closest accommodation is the new Fosshotel (p332) at Hnappavellir, 28km from Jökulsárlón. Camping is 52km away at Svínafell (p324), or 60km at Skaftafell National Park (p323).

Accommodation along this stretch of the Ring Road is in hot demand; book early. (Note that there is no need to book campsites.)

Cafe CAFE €

(snacks kr400-2000; ⊙9am-7pm) The year-round cafe beside the lagoon is a good pit stop for information and a snack, but its small, dated space is totally overwhelmed in summer.

Getting There & Away

Countless tours take in Jökulsárlón. We *don't* recommend trying to do a trip from Reykjavík to the lagoon and back to the capital in one day (it's 375km, or about a 4½-hour drive each way).

DON'T MISS

RIDING ON THE VATNAJÖKULL ICE CAP

Vatnajökull ice cap and its attendant glaciers look spectacular from the Ring Road, and most travellers will be seized by a wild desire to get closer. Guided hikes on icy glacial tongues are a wonderful introduction, but access to the serious bulk of Vatnajökull is only for experienced folks set up for a serious polar-style expedition: the ice cap is riven with deep crevasses, which are made invisible by coverings of fresh snow, and there are often sudden, violent blizzards. But don't be disheartened! You can travel way up into the whiteness on organised snowmobile or super-Jeep tours, now offered by two local companies (including in winter).

Both companies utilise the easiest route up to Vatnajökull: the F985 4WD track (about 35km east of Jökulsárlón, 45km west of Höfn) to the broad glacial spur Skálafellsjökull. At the end of Rte F985, 840m above sea level and with spectacular 360-degree views, most travellers choose to do an awesome **snowmobile ride**. You are kitted out with overalls, helmets, boots and gloves, then play follow-the-leader along a fixed trail. It's great fun, and although it only gives you the briefest introduction to glacier travel, an hour of noisy bouncing about with the stink of petrol in your nostrils is probably enough for most people! If the skidoo isn't your thing, you can also take a **super-Jeep ride** onto the ice, or do a **glacier hike**.

Glacier Jeeps (p330) and a new company, Glacier Journey (p330), both offer snowmobiling and super-Jeep tours; Glacier Jeeps also offers a glacier hike. With the popularity of these tours, it pays to book in advance (online). Children's prices for snowmobile rides are for those aged six to 12 (the rides aren't suitable for younger than six).

Note that winter snowmobile rides are offered only by Glacier Journey, and it bases itself at Jökulsárlón from about mid-December. Check websites for up-to-date rates, schedules and meeting points.

Sterna (www.sterna.is) Bus 12/12a between Reykjavík and Höfn runs once daily from June to mid-September. Travelling in either direction, it stops for one hour at Jökulsárlón (enough time for a boat ride).

Strætó (www.bus.is) Bus 51 between Reykjavík and Höfn runs twice daily from June to mid-September (once daily the rest of the year) and stops here. It simply drops off or picks up passengers, it doesn't linger.

Reykjavík Excursions (www.re.is) has two summer services of note:

- Bus 15 runs a loop between Skaftafellsstofa Visitor Centre and Jökulsárlón (kr2500, 45 minutes, three daily June to mid-September).
- Bus 19 runs from Höfn to Skaftafell and back again each day, stopping for a lengthy spell at the lagoon in either direction (to Höfn kr3500, one hour, one daily mid-June to mid-September).

Jökulsárlón to Höfn

The heavenly 80km stretch of Ring Road between Jökulsárlón and Höfn is lined with around 20 rural properties (many with glaciers in their backyards) offering accommodation, activities and occasionally food.

Gentle, family-friendly lures include a petting zoo (p332), an ice-cream producer (p332), a quality museum, bird-filled wetlands and outdoor hot-pots. Those looking for a little more exertion will find walks to (or on) glacier tongues and visits to wintertime ice caves, plus snowmobile safaris, glacier lagoon kayaking, and horse riding and quad-bike rides taking in spectacular natural splendour.

Sights & Activities

Þórbergssetur MUSEUM

(☎478 1078; www.thorbergur.is; Hali; adult/child kr1000/free; ⌚9am-8pm) This cleverly crafted museum (its inspired exterior looks like a shelf of books) pays tribute to the most famous son of this sparsely populated region – writer Þórbergur Þórðarson (1888–1974). Þórbergur was a real maverick (with interests spanning yoga, Esperanto and astronomy), and his first book *Bréf til Láru* (Letter to Laura) caused huge controversy because of its radical socialist content.

Þórbergssetur also functions as a kind of cultural centre, with changing art exhibitions, and a quality cafe-restaurant (p333). There's a cluster of accommodation surrounding it, including the Hali Country Hotel (p331). Museum entry is free for diners at the restaurant, and for guests at the hotel.

Route F985 SCENIC DRIVE
From the Ring Road, about 35km east of Jökulsárlón and 45km west of Höfn, the F985 4WD track branches off to the broad glacial spur Skálafellsjökull. This 16km-long road is practically vertical in places, with iced-over sections in winter. Glacier Jeeps and Glacier Journey offer a comfortable ride to the top, where you can explore further (on snowmobile or in a super-Jeep).

Please don't even think of attempting to drive Rte F985 in a 2WD car – you'll end up with a huge rescue bill. F roads are *only* for 4WD vehicles. People in small 4WD cars, or inexperienced 4WDers, should likewise not attempt this route.

Tours

★IceGuide ADVENTURE TOUR
(☎661 0900; www.iceguide.is) Óskar and his team operate from Guesthouse Skálafell (p332) in summer (June to September) and have a brilliantly unique offering: kayaking among icebergs on a silent glacier lagoon. The lagoon is the nearby Heinabergslón, at the foot of Heinabergsjökull, and the trip includes a short walk on the glacier itself (adult/child from kr14,900/7900; minimum age 12). Kayaks are 'sit-on-top' style, so experience isn't necessary. Bookings advised.

From November to March, IceGuide leads tours to ice caves from a base at Jökulsárlón (adult/child kr18,900/8900; minimum age eight). These trips involve a 4WD journey to the glacier edge, then a walk on rough terrain to reach the cave. Participants need a reasonable level of fitness and warm clothes; see the website for more information.

Glacier Journey ADVENTURE TOUR
(☎867 0493; www.glacierjourney.is) This new company offers year-round snowmobile and super-Jeep tours (conditions permitting). Glacier Journey works in summer from a base at Guesthouse Skálafell (p332), and accesses its snow course via Rte F985; in winter the base is at Jökulsárlón. Snowmobile tours cost kr23,500/11,750 per adult/child, with two people to a skidoo; solo riders pay an additional kr9000.

If you prefer less exposure to the elements, a super-Jeep tour on the ice is kr23,000/11,500. Summer tours include a midnight-sun offering in June and July. Reservations required.

Glacier Trips ADVENTURE TOUR
(☎779 2919; www.glaciertrips.is) Doing just as its name suggests, this locally owned company leads small-group glacier walks on Fláajökull – a glacier visited by no other operators, so a great chance to get off the beaten track. In summer you can take a late-night walk to experience the midnight sun. The meeting point for glacier walks (from kr15,500) is Hólmur guesthouse.

In winter the focus switches to Northern Lights and visits to ice caves and crevasses, and trips depart from Jökulsárlón (kr19,500).

Glacier Adventure ADVENTURE TOUR
(☎571 4577; www.glacieradventures.is; Hali) The closest guiding company to Jökulsárlón, locally owned Glacier Adventure operates out of the Hali Country Hotel (p331), 13km east of the lagoon. Glacier walks are done on Breiðamerkurjökull, with one to 1½ hours on the ice (adult/child kr15,500/8000). Half-day ice-climbing excursions (kr21,900), and winter ice-cave visits (from kr19,500), including a challenging option to a more remote cave, are also available.

Glacier Jeeps ADVENTURE TOUR
(☎478 1000, 894 3133; www.glacierjeeps.is; ⌚mid-May–mid-Oct) Home base for this long-running snowmobiling company is Vagnsstaðir HI Hostel (p331), which is where its shoulder-season tours meet. From July to October, three-hour tours begin at 9.30am or 2pm from the parking area at the start of Rte F985 (in a small car park by the Ring Road).

Snowmobile tours cost kr23,000 per person, with two people to a skidoo – there's kr8500 extra to pay if you want a skidoo to yourself. Other options include a super-Jeep tour (kr23,000) or glacier walk (kr23,000). All options include transport up and down Rte F985, gear, and about an hour on the ice. Reservations required.

Sleeping

Many of the properties along this stretch have extended their tourist accommodation in the past couple of years – even so, in summer, demand for rooms far exceeds supply (and prices are *high*). Book well ahead, and see websites for up-to-date rates.

We list these options from west to east.

GET YOUR GLACIER ON

Vatnajökull National Park authorities are working with a handful of landowners between Jökulsárlón and Höfn to open up public access to some areas of raw natural beauty (and take pressure off the popular Skaftafell region in the face of rising tourist numbers). These areas are signed off the Ring Road – for now, they are not especially well known, so you stand a good chance of finding yourself a tranquil pocket of glaciated wonder.

Uniquely, three glacier tongues (Skálafellsjökull, Heinabergsjökull and Fláajökull) converge on the Hjallanes and Heinaberg area. A fourth glacier tongue, Hoffellsjökull, lies further east, closer to Höfn. These areas boast some remarkable walking trails and scenery (including glacier lakes and moraines where the glaciers once ended):

Heinabergsjökull is 8km off the Ring Road on a gravel road (signposted not far east of Guesthouse Skálafell). Walking trails from Guesthouse Skálafell (p332) include the 8km Hjallanes loop or a 7.5km hike to Heinabergslón (the icy lagoon at the foot of Heinabergsjökull). From Heinabergslón an 8.3km trail leads to Fláajökull. There are also brilliant kayaking trips that operate on Heinabergslón, operated by IceGuide (p330).

Fláajökull is also 8km off the Ring Road on a gravel road signposted just east of Hólmur guesthouse (p332). A great walking trail (including a new suspension bridge) leads from the small parking area to the glacial tongue. Glacier walks are operated on Fláajökull, led by Glacier Trips (p330).

Hoffellsjökull is accessed from the road to Hoffell guesthouse (p332). A signed, 4km gravel road leads to the glacier, calving into a small lake.

The guesthouses mentioned here act as information points (maps are available), or you can stop by the information centre in Höfn to ask about road conditions, and to find out if any other areas have become newly accessible. Pick up the *Heinaberg, Hjallanes, Hoffell* map produced by the national park at the visitor centres at Höfn or Skaftafellsstofa. Info is also available under 'Destinations' on the national park website, www.vjp.is.

Note that access roads are signed off the Ring Road, and are unsealed and often quite rough (they are not F roads). It pays to ask locally about the condition of roads before setting off in a 2WD (the answer will invariably be, 'it's OK, just go slow', but some roads may be better than others (some have maintenance done on them after the winter).

Hali Country Hotel HOTEL €€€

(☎478 1073; www.hali.is; s/d/apt incl breakfast kr28,500/36,500/55,300) The Þórbergssetur museum acts as reception and restaurant for this smart option, the closest hotel to Jökulsárlón (and one of a cluster of places at Hali settlement). There are high-standard hotel rooms, plus a couple of excellent two-bedroom self-contained apartments.

★ **Skyrhúsid Guesthouse** GUESTHOUSE €€

(☎899 8384; www.facebook.com/skyrhusid; Hali; d/tr without bathroom incl breakfast kr19,000/23,000) This cute, petite guesthouse is in Hali, right by Þórbergssetur. It's a cosy place with just nine fresh rooms (limited kitchen facilities), and a tiny, colourful breakfast area.

Hrollaugsstaðir CAMPGROUND, HOSTEL €

(☎478 1905; sites per person kr1900, s/d without bathroom kr12,500/17,000; ⏲Jun-Aug) There's minimal signage or fanfare for this under-the-radar property, but campers and budget travellers should keep their eyes peeled for the small sign off the Ring Road, about 23km east of Jökulsárlón. It points to a former school that now offers camping and no-frills rooms (including sleeping-bag beds for kr7500), plus kitchen access.

Note that this is a community-owned building and management can change from year to year, so expect changes.

Vagnsstaðir HI Hostel HOSTEL €

(☎478 1048; www.hostel.is; dm/d without bathroom from kr4800/17,400) Snowmobiles litter this Ring Road property, HQ of Glacier Jeeps. It's a small, bunk-heavy hostel with sunny enclosed dining area, plus there are additional six-bed cottages (each with toilet, but no shower) next to the main building. The common complaint is that the limited bathroom facilities and small kitchen are now inadequate for the amount of beds. HI members get a discount of kr700.

DON'T MISS

VATNAJÖKULL BEER

We're a sucker for a good sales pitch, and this beer has it in spades: 'frozen in time' beer brewed from 1000-year-old water (ie Jökulsárlón icebergs), flavoured with locally grown Arctic thyme. It's brewed by Ölvisholt Brugghús near Selfoss, and sold in restaurants around the Southeast. Give it a try for its fruity, malty flavour.

Hótel Smyrlabjörg COUNTRY HOTEL €€€
(☎478 1074; www.smyrlabjorg.is; s/d incl breakfast kr25,000/30,500) A good choice if you're after mod-cons but still want sheep roaming the car park, mountain views, and peace and quiet. This large, welcoming hotel (recently doubled in size) has a restaurant renowned for its good use of local produce (mains kr2550 to kr7500).

★**Guesthouse Skálafell** GUESTHOUSE €€
(☎478 1041; www.skalafell.net; d with/without bathroom incl breakfast kr24,500/20,100) At the foot of Skálafellsjökull, this friendly working farm has a handful of agreeable rooms in the family farmhouse, and also in motel-style units. There are no cooking facilities, but dinner is available. In cooperation with the national park, the knowledgeable owners here offer information and have set up marked walking trails (open to all) in the surrounding glaciated landscapes.

Heinaberg Guesthouse GUESTHOUSE €€
(☎858 2628; heinabergiceland@gmail.com; s/tr/q without bathroom incl breakfast kr11,300/23,400/27,800) Small, chalet-style rooms are offered in a homey lodge on a working dairy farm. It's spick and span, with kitchen access and great views. Room configurations are outside the norm: three very snug singles, a couple of triples, and a family-sized quad. Look for the large, new dairy sheds out front.

★**Hólmur** GUESTHOUSE €
(☎478 2063; www.holmurinn.is; s/d without bathroom from kr10,600/13,800) A perfect pit stop for families, Hólmur offers well-priced farmhouse accommodation (ask about sleeping-bag rates for extra savings) and a sweet, smile-inducing farm zoo (adult/child kr800/600; open 10am to 5pm May to September) with an abundance of feathered and furry friends. Also here is the stand-out restaurant, Jón Ríki (p333).

Lambhús COTTAGE €€
(☎662 1029; www.lambhus.is; cottages excl linen kr18,000-22,000; ⏲Jun-Aug) Ducks and horses, plus 11 cute, compact self-catering cottages (sleeping four to six and ideal for families), are scattered about this vista-blessed property, owned by an affable, multilingual family with years of guiding experience. Linen can be hired (kr2000 per person).

Brunnhóll COUNTRY HOTEL €€
(☎478 1029; www.brunnholl.is; d incl breakfast kr27,750) The hotel at this friendly dairy farm has simple, decent-sized rooms with big views. The good folk at Brunnhóll are also the makers of delicious Jöklaís (this name means 'Glacier Ice cream'), which you can sample at the summertime dinner buffet (full buffet kr6400, soup and salad kr2650), which is open to all. Or stop in any time to buy a scoop/tub.

Hoffell COUNTRY HOTEL, GUESTHOUSE €€€
(Glacier World; ☎478 1514; www.glacierworld.is; d with/without bathroom kr30,500/20,500) The original guesthouse at Hoffell has bright, fresh rooms with shared bathroom and guest kitchen. In mid-2014 a new building opened, housing hotel-style en suite rooms (in a converted cowshed!). Prices include access to the outdoor hot-pots on the property. There's also an on-site restaurant for guests.

As well as friendly owners, the drawcards here are the activities (also accessible to nonguests), including **quad-bike tours** to the glacier (from kr14,000) and a collection of outdoor hot-pots (kr600; open 7am to 10pm).

In cooperation with the national park, Hoffell's owners offer information on their incredible surrounds, including the 4km road to Hoffellsjökull.

Fosshótel Vatnajökull HOTEL €€€
(☎478 2555; www.fosshotel.is; r incl breakfast from kr28,000) This upmarket chain hotel, 14km northwest of Höfn, recently grew from 26 to 66 rooms. The modern timber-and-concrete extension was smartly done, with blue and grey hues that represent the impressive natural surrounds. Older rooms received a welcome makeover too, but the newer deluxe rooms are a nicer pick. There's a restaurant (dinner mains kr2900 to kr5950) on-site.

★**Árnanes Country Lodge** COUNTRY HOTEL €€
(☎478 1550; www.arnanes.is; d with/without bathroom incl breakfast kr29,900/23,700; ⊙Mar-Oct) This polished rural 18-room locale is 6km from Höfn and has motel units and guesthouse rooms. There's an agreeable summertime restaurant (mains kr2600 to kr6900) showcasing produce from neighbouring farms, and horse-riding tours for all skill levels (open to nonguests).

Seljavellir Guesthouse GUESTHOUSE €€
(☎478 1866; www.seljavellir.com; s/d incl breakfast kr26,000/28,500) A newly built complex of 20 smart, minimalist rooms – all with splendid views – and sweet management. Seljavellir is a first-class choice, found opposite Árnanes Country Lodge about 6km from Höfn.

Eating

Many of the places along this stretch have in-house restaurants – open to guests, but often also to nonguests. Self-caterers should stock up on groceries in Kirkjubæjarklaustur or Höfn, as there are no stores.

★**Jón Ríki** ICELANDIC €€
(☎478 2063; www.jonriki.is; mains lunch kr1390-2590, dinner kr2390-6490; ⊙11.30am-2pm Jun-late Aug, 6-9.30pm year-round) This fabulous farmhouse restaurant at Hólmur (p332) is something of a surprise, with funky decor, a small in-house brewery, and beautifully presented, high-quality dishes starring local produce: grilled langoustine, slow-roasted pork belly, white chocolate *skyr* for dessert. Sandwiches and soups feature at lunchtime; pizza is also on the dinner menu. It can get busy, so a dinner reservation is advised.

From September to May, the dinner menu is smaller than in summer, and you're advised to make a booking so the owners know you're coming.

Þórbergssetur Restaurant ICELANDIC €€
(www.hali.is/restaurant; Hali; mains lunch kr1550-3100, dinner kr3200-5500; ⊙11am-9pm) The museum at Hali, Þórbergssetur (p329), is home to a quality cafe-restaurant where the speciality is Arctic char. It's 13km east of Jökulsárlón, and gets very busy.

Höfn

POP 1700

Although it's no bigger than many European villages, the Southeast's main town feels like a sprawling metropolis after driving through the emptiness on either side. Its setting is stunning; on a clear day, wander down to the waterside, find a quiet bench and just gaze at Vatnajökull and its guild of glaciers.

Höfn simply means 'harbour', and is pronounced like an unexpected hiccup (just say 'hup' while inhaling). It's an apt name – this modern town still relies heavily on fishing and fish processing, and is famous for its *humar* (often translated as lobster, but technically it's langoustine).

Bus travellers use Höfn as a transit point, and most travellers stop to use the town's services, so prebook accommodation in summer. On bus timetables and the like, you may see the town referred to as Höfn í Hornafirði (meaning Höfn in Hornafjörður) to differentiate it from all the other *höfn* (harbours) around the country.

Sights & Activities

Activities that explore Vatnajökull's icy vastness – such as glacier walks, super-Jeep tours, lagoon kayaking and snowmobile safaris – are accessed along the Ring Road west of Höfn.

In town, there are a couple of short waterside paths where you can amble and gape at the views; one by Hótel Höfn and another on Ósland.

Gamlabúð NOTABLE BUILDING, MUSEUM
(www.vjp.is; Heppuvegur 1; ⊙8am-8pm Jun-Aug, 9am-5pm May & Sep, to 1pm Oct-Apr) FREE The 1864 warehouse that once served as the regional folk museum has been moved from the outskirts of town to a prime position on the Höfn harbour front. It's been refurbished to serve as the town's visitor centre, with good exhibits explaining the marvels of the region's flagship national park (including flora and fauna), as well as screening documentaries.

Ósland WALKING
This promontory – about 1km beyond the harbour (head for the seamen's monument (Óslandsvegur) on the rise) – boasts a walking path round its marshes and lagoons. The path is great for watching seabirds, though watch out for dive-bombing Arctic terns.

Sundlaug Hafnar SWIMMING
(Víkurbraut 9; adult/child kr800/200; ⊙6.45am-9pm Mon-Fri, 10am-7pm Sat & Sun) The town's

popular outdoor swimming pool has water slides, hot-pots and a steam bath.

Silfurnesvöllur GOLF
(Dalbraut; 9 holes 1/2 people kr3500/5000) There's a nine-hole golf course and small clubhouse at the end of Dalbraut at the northern end of town. How often do you get to play under the midnight sun with a view of glaciers? Club hire is available.

Festivals & Events

Humarhátíð FOOD & DRINK
Every year in late June or early July, Höfn's annual langoustine festival honours this tasty crustacean, hauled to shore in abundance by the local fishing fleet. There's usually a fun fair, dancing, music, lots of alcohol and even a few langoustines.

Sleeping

Along with hotels and guesthouses in Höfn itself, there are numerous good options (most with in-house dining) along the Ring Road west of town. Summer rates in this in-demand region are *high;* check online for up-to-date prices, and for winter discounts.

There are also a number of apartments rented out around town.

Höfn Camping & Cottages CAMPGROUND €
(☎478 1606; www.campsite.is; Hafnarbraut 52; campsites per person kr1500, cottage d/q kr15,000/22,000; ⏲Apr-Oct; @) Lots of travellers stay at the campsite on the main road into town, where helpful owners and plenty of local info are among the draws. There are 11 good-value cottages, sleeping up to six; some have private toilet, but all use the amenities block for showers. There's also a playground and laundry, and some camping gear is sold at the reception.

HI Hostel HOSTEL €
(☎478 1736; www.hostel.is; Hvannabraut 3; dm/d without bathroom kr5500/18,800) Follow the signs from the N1 to find Höfn's sole budget option, hidden away in a residential area. It's a sprawling, dated space (a former aged-care home) that's usually bustling with travellers in summer. It has the requisite facilities (kitchen, laundry) but no lounge areas. There's a kr700 discount for members; linen is kr1850.

★ **Milk Factory** GUESTHOUSE €€
(☎478 8900; www.milkfactory.is; Dalbraut 2; d/q incl breakfast kr24,600/31,750) Full credit to the family – and the designers – behind the masterful restoration of an old dairy factory north of town. Seventeen modern, hotel-standard rooms are here, including two with disabled access. The prize allotments are the six spacious mezzanine suites that sleep four – good for families or friends, although they don't have kitchens. There are also free bikes for guest use.

★ **Guesthouse Dyngja** GUESTHOUSE €€
(☎846 0161; www.dyngja.com; Hafnarbraut 1; d without bathroom incl breakfast kr19,300; @) A lovely young couple own this petite five-room guesthouse in a prime harbour-front locale, and they have filled it with charm and good cheer: rich colours, a record player and vinyl selection, a self-service breakfast, an outdoor deck and good local knowledge. There's also a good new addition: a downstairs suite with private bathroom (kr23,200).

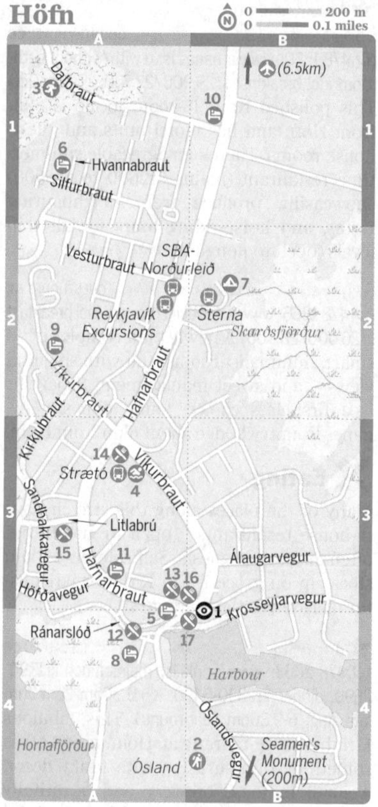

Höfn

Sights

1 Gamlabúð B3

Activities, Courses & Tours

2 Ósland B4
3 Silfurnesvöllur A1
4 Sundlaug Hafnar A3

Sleeping

5 Guesthouse Dyngja A4
6 HI Hostel A1
7 Höfn Camping & Cottages B2
8 Hótel Edda A4
9 Hótel Höfn A2
10 Milk Factory B1
11 Old Airline Guesthouse A3

Eating

12 Hafnarbúðin A4
13 Humarhöfnin A3
14 Kaffi Hornið A3
15 Nettó A3
16 Nýhöfn B3
Ósinn .... (see 9)
17 Pakkhús B4

Shopping

Vínbúðin .... (see 15)

Information

Gamlabúð Visitor Centre .... (see 1)

Old Airline Guesthouse GUESTHOUSE €€
(☎478 1300; www.oldairline.com; Hafnarbraut 24; d without bathroom incl breakfast kr19,200) This new, central guesthouse sparkles under the care of friendly host Sigga. On offer are five fresh rooms with shared bathrooms, plus a large lounge and guest kitchen (with self-service breakfast). Big brownie points to free laundry access. It's attached to a small electronics/IT store.

Dynjandi GUESTHOUSE €€
(☎849 4159; www.dynjandi.com; Rte 1; d/q without bathroom incl breakfast kr17,000/24,000) In a dramatic Ring Road location, at the foot of mountains about 3km east of the Höfn turn-off (a total of 9km from town), Dynjandi is a small and cosy three-room guesthouse on a photogenic horse farm. The friendly Austrian-German hosts are passionate horse breeders and glacier/hiking guides, so they're full of good local info.

Hótel Höfn HOTEL €€
(☎478 1240; www.hotelhofn.is; Víkurbraut; d incl breakfast from kr28,600) Höfn's business-class hotel is often busy with tour groups in summer. Nicely renovated rooms feature safe neutral tones, and views are knockout – you'll want one with a glacier outlook (but bear in mind that so does everyone else!). There's also a fresh-faced on-site restaurant, **Ósinn** (☎478 1240; www.hotelhofn.is; Víkurbraut; mains kr2590-7350; ⏲noon-10pm). Pros: good breakfast. Cons: three storeys, no lift.

Hótel Edda HOTEL €€€
(☎444 4850; www.hoteledda.is; Ránarslóð 3; s/d kr28,700/31,200; ⏲mid-May–Sep; @) With a lovely, view-filled lobby lounge and terrace, the well-located harbour-side Edda makes a decent (albeit overpriced) choice. All neat, no-frills rooms have bathroom, some have great glacier views. Breakfast is kr2050.

Eating & Drinking

Humar (langoustine) is the speciality on Höfn menus – tails or served whole and grilled with garlic butter is the norm, and prices for main dishes range from kr7000 upwards. You'll find cheaper crustacean-centric options too: bisque, sandwiches or langoustine-studded pizza or pasta.

Look out for the **Heimahumar** food truck, parked out front of Nettó in the summer, for the cheapest lobster wraps and panini in town (priced around kr1850).

Hafnarbúðin FAST FOOD €
(Ránarslóð; snacks & meals kr400-2600; ⏲9am-10pm Mon-Fri, 10am-10pm Sat & Sun) A fabulous relic, this tiny old-school diner has a cheap-and-cheerful vibe, a menu of fast-food favourites (hot dogs, burgers, toasted sandwiches) and a fine *humarloka* – langoustine baguette – for kr2000. There's even a drive-up window!

Nýhöfn ICELANDIC €€
(☎478 1818; www.nyhofn.is; Hafnarbraut 2; mains kr3200-5900; ⏲noon-10pm mid-May–mid-Sep) This sweet 'Nordic bistro' is in the home that Höfn's first settler built in 1897, and still retains its refined, old-world atmosphere. The menu spotlights local produce, but is an interesting nod to influences near and far, from langoustine bruschetta to Peruvian ceviche by way of organic vegetarian barley burgers. There's a small bar in the cellar, too.

Kaffi Hornið ICELANDIC €€
(☎478 2600; www.kaffihornid.is; Hafnarbraut 42; lunch buffet kr2350, mains kr2950-6450; ⏲11.30am-10pm) This log-cabin affair is an unpretentious bar and restaurant. Note that although the atmosphere here is less

polished than at fellow Icelandic restaurants Humarhöfnin and Pakkhús, the langoustine dishes are not much cheaper. There's a good lunchtime soup-and-salad buffet, and a menu stretching from steak sandwiches to grilled salmon, plus an excellent craft-beer selection.

★ Pakkhús ICELANDIC €€€

(☎478 2280; www.pakkhus.is; Krosseyjarvegur 3; mains kr3100-6790; ⏲noon-10pm mid-May–mid-Sep, 5-9pm mid-Sep–mid-May) Hats off to a menu that tells you the name of the boat that delivers its star produce. In a stylish harbour-side warehouse, Pakkhús offers a level of kitchen creativity you don't often find in rural Iceland. First-class local langoustine, lamb and duck tempt taste buds, while clever desserts end the meal in style; who can resist a dish called '*skyr* volcano'?

No reservations taken – you may have to wait for a table, but there is a bar area downstairs.

★ Humarhöfnin ICELANDIC €€€

(☎478 1200; www.humarhofnin.is; Hafnarbraut 4; mains kr2900-8400; ⏲noon-10pm Mar-Sep, to 9pm Oct-Nov) Humarhöfnin offers 'Gastronomy Langoustine' in a cute, cheerfully Frenchified space with superb attention to detail: herb pots on the windowsills, roses on every table. Mains centred on pincer-waving critters cost upwards of kr7000, but there are also more budget-friendly dishes including a fine langoustine baguette (kr4300) or pizza (kr2900).

Nettó SUPERMARKET

(Miðbær; ⏲9am-8pm Mon-Sat, 10am-7pm Sun) Supermarket (with bakery) in the central Miðbær shopping centre. Stock up – in either direction, it's miles to the next grocery selection. The bakery sells ready-made meals such as sandwiches, salads and sushi. There's an ATM out the front of the shopping centre.

Vínbúðin ALCOHOL

(Miðbær; ⏲11am-6pm Mon-Thu, to 7pm Fri, to 4pm Sat May-Aug, reduced hours Sep-Apr) Government-run liquor store.

ℹ Information

Gamlabúð Visitor Centre (☎470 8330; www.visitvatnajokull.is; Heppuvegur 1; ⏲8am-8pm Jun-Aug, 9am-5pm May & Sep, 9am-1pm Oct-Apr) Harbour-front Gamlabúð houses a national-park visitor centre with excellent exhibits, plus local tourist information and maps for sale. Ask about activities and hiking trails in the area.

ℹ Getting There & Away

AIR

Höfn's airport is 6.5km northwest of town. Eagle Air (www.eagleair.is) flies year-round between Reykjavík and Höfn (one way from kr18,600).

BUS

Bus companies travelling through Höfn have different stops, so make sure you know what operator you're travelling with and confirm where they pick up from.

Buses heading from Höfn to Reykjavík stop at all major towns and landmarks, including Jökulsárlón, Skaftafell, Kirkjubæjarklaustur, Vík, Skógar, Hvolsvöllur, Hella and Selfoss. See websites for up-to-date rates and schedules.

Note that there is no winter bus connection between Egilsstaðir and Höfn (ie bus 62a doesn't run).

SBA-Norðurleið (☎550 0720; www.sba.is) services (stop at N1 petrol station):

- Bus 62a to Egilsstaðir (kr9400, five hours, one daily June to mid-September; stops at Djúpivogur, Breiðdalsvík and fjords along Rtes 92 and 96).
- Bus 62a to Mývatn (kr15,500, 7½ hours, one daily June to mid-September).
- Bus 62a to Akureryi (kr19,000, 9¼ hours, one daily June to mid-September).

Sterna (☎551 1166; www.icelandbybus.is) services (pick-up/drop-off at campground):

- Bus 12a to Reykjavík (kr11,600, 10¼ hours, one daily June to mid-September).

Strætó (☎540 2700; www.straeto.is) services (pick-up/drop-off out front of the swimming pool):

- Bus 51 to Reykjavík (kr12,180, 7¼ hours, two daily June to mid-September, one daily Sunday to Friday the rest of the year).

Reykjavík Excursions (☎580 5400; www.re.is) services (stop at N1 petrol station):

- Bus 19 to Skaftafell (kr5500, 4¼ hours, one daily June to mid-September). Stops at Jökulsárlón for 2½ hours. Can be used as a day tour returning to Höfn (with 5¼ hours at Skaftafell).

Höfn to Djúpivogur

The 105km stretch around Iceland's southeast corner, between Höfn and Djúpivogur, is another impossibly scenic stretch, the road curving past only a handful of farms backed by precipitous peaks.

DON'T MISS

STOKKSNES

About 7km east of the turn-off to Höfn, just before the Ring Road enters a tunnel through the Almannaskarð pass, a signposted road heads south to Stokksnes. After 4.5km, in a wild setting under moodily Gothic Vestrahorn mountain, you'll find a cool little outpost: the **Viking Cafe** (www.vikingcafe.is; waffles & cake kr900; ⌚9am-7pm May-Oct), where coffee, waffles and cake are served.

The farm-owner runs the cafe, and he charges visitors kr800 to explore his incredible property, including a photogenic Viking village **film set** and miles of **black-sand beaches**, where seals laze and the backdrop of Vestrahorn creates superb photos.

Note that the film set (built in 2009 by Icelandic film director Baltasar Kormakúr) may finally see action soon, when Baltasar directs *Vikings*, a long-gestating film project he started writing more than a decade ago. The set will hopefully remain in place after its film duties are done.

You can camp in the area (with permission from the farm-owner; per person kr1500, including farm entry).

Stafafell

In the middle of nowhere, Stafafell is a lonely farm, lost under the mountains. It's a good hiking base for exploring Lónsöræfi.

There are a number of day hikes in the hills and valleys north of Stafafell. Perhaps the best day hike is a well-marked, 14.3km, four- to five-hour return walk from Stafafell to **Hvannagil**, a colourful rhyolite canyon on the eastern bank of the river Jökulsá í Lóni; pick up a route description from the farmhouse.

A trio of brothers own the farm; one operates a guesthouse (☎478 1717; www.stafafell.is; r without bathroom per person kr4000, cottages incl linen kr18,000-22,000) and has a couple of simple cottages for rent, while another runs a basic campsite (sites per person kr1500) in summer.

The website www.stafafell.is is rich in local information.

Lónsöræfi

If you're in Iceland to get in touch with your inner hermit, the remote, rugged nature reserve Lónsöræfi could be on your hitlist. This protected wilderness, inland from Stafafell, contains some colourful rhyolite mountains, and at 320 sq km is one of Iceland's largest conservation areas.

Hiking in this region is challenging and only for experienced hikers (some trails require substantial river crossings). Longer treks range towards the eastern part of Vatnajökull, and northwest to Snæfell. Although Lónsöræfi isn't part of Vatnajökull National Park, the park's website (www.vjp.is) has details of hiking trails, and the visitor centres at Skaftafell, Höfn and Skríðuklaustur (in the east, covering the Snæfell region of the national park) can advise on options and sell topo maps, which you will certainly require. There is good info (especially on access to the area) at www.stafafell.is, though it is not always up to date.

The only road into the reserve is the F980, a rough track off the Ring Road that ends after 25km at Illikambur. It's only suitable for super-Jeeps and experienced drivers – there is a deep, fast-flowing river to cross (small 4WDs will simply not cut it here). Contact **Glacier Journey** (☎478 1517; www.glacierjourney.is; ⌚mid-Jun–mid-Oct) if you want hiker transport to/from Lónsöræfi (kr11,900 one way, minimum two people).

Tours

South East ehf JEEP TOURS

(☎846 6313; www.southeasticeland.is) Siggi offers well-reviewed customised super-Jeep tours in the southeast, including a five-hour tour from Höfn into the Lónsöræfi area (kr25,000 per person). Prebooking is required.

Icelandic Mountain Guides HIKING

(IMG; ☎587 9999; www.mountainguides.is) IMG offers a five-day, 50km backpacking tour through Lónsöræfi (from kr152,000), staying in mountain huts (travelling north to south). It's in its program under the name 'In the Shadow of Vatnajökull'.

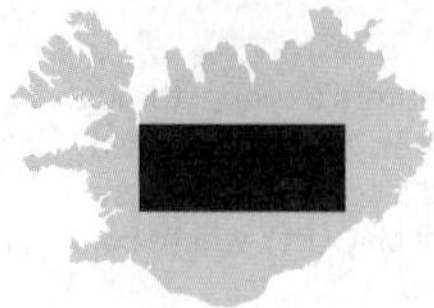

The Highlands

Includes ➡

Best Natural Wonders

- Askja (p348)
- Herðubreið (p348)
- Hveravellir (p342)
- Kverkfjöll (p349)
- Drekagil (p348)
- Kerlingarfjöll (p343)
- Holuhraun (p348)

Best Places to Take a Dip

- Víti (p348)
- Hveravellir (p342)
- Laugafell (p344)
- Kerlingarfjöll (p343)

Why Go?

You may have travelled the Ring Road thinking that Iceland is light on towns; that sheep seem to outnumber people; that you haven't encountered an N1 service station for many a mile. Well, you ain't seen nothing yet. In the interior highlands, there are practically no services, accommodation, bridges over rivers – or guarantees if something goes wrong.

Gazing across the desolate expanses, you could imagine yourself in the Australian outback or, as many have noted, on the moon. Those aren't overactive imaginations at work – *Apollo* astronauts trained here before their lunar landing.

The isolation, in essence, is the reason that people visit (plus the opportunity to bring geology lessons to life). Although some travellers are disappointed by the interior's ultra-bleakness, others are humbled by the sight of nature in its rawest form. The solitude is exhilarating, the views are vast – and the access is limited, so prepare well.

Good to Know

- **Kjölur route** (Rte 35) North–south route across the country. Served by summer buses. All rivers bridged.
- **Sprengisandur route** (Rte F26) North–south route across the country. Served by summer buses.
- **Askja route** (Öskjuleið; Rte F88 or F905/910) Access from Iceland's north to Askja caldera, Herðubreið mountain and the new Holuhraun lava field. Served by numerous tour operators, primarily from Mývatn.
- **Kverkfjöll route** (Rte F905, F910, then F902) Access from Iceland's north (or east, via Rte 910) to Kverkfjöll ice caves. Served by a few tour operators.

Kjölur Route

If you want to sample Iceland's central deserts but don't like the idea of ford crossings, the 200km Kjölur route has had all of its rivers bridged. In summer there are even scheduled daily buses that use it as a 'short cut' between Reykjavík and Akureyri.

From the south, Rte 35 starts just past Gullfoss, passing between two large glaciers before emerging near Blönduós on the northwest coast. It reaches its highest point (around 700m) between the Langjökull and Hofsjökull ice caps, near the mountain Kjalfell (1000m). Its northern section cruises scenically past Blöndulón, a large reservoir used by the Blanda hydroelectric power station. Road conditions in the north are better than those in the south.

The Kjölur route usually opens in mid-June, and closes sometime in September, depending on weather conditions.

Tours

A bit of online digging will reveal hiking and horse-riding tours along the Kjölur route (also search 'Kjalvegur'), plus a few jeep tours.

You can use the scheduled summertime buses as a day tour, or as a regular bus service.

Saga Travel JEEP TOUR
(☎558 888; www.sagatravel.is) From July to October (weather permitting), Saga Travel does a one-day cross-country guided tour from Reykjavík to Akureyri (kr59,990), visiting the Golden Circle highlights before taking the Kjölur route north and stopping at Hveravellir en route (with time for bathing). You can opt to stay in Akureyri, or fly back to Reykjavík (not included in the price).

Sleeping & Eating

As well as the popular options at Kerlingarfjöll and Hveravellir, two organisations operate huts along the route (BYO sleeping bag); campers can also pitch by the huts. It's necessary to prebook hut beds.

Kerlingarfjöll and Hveravellir offer food, but you need to bring self-catering supplies for all other overnighting options. Huts generally have kitchen access, but utensils are not guaranteed.

Gljásteinn HUTS €
(☎486 8757; www.gljasteinn.is; sites per person kr1200, dm kr6000; ⊙mid-Jun–Aug) Has three well-appointed huts on or just off the route, suitable for drivers, hikers and horse riders. Huts are listed from south to north.

➡ **Fremstaver**
(N 64°45.207', W 19°93.699') Cosy hut that sleeps 25, has cooking facilities. Located on the south slopes of the mountain Bláfell.

➡ **Árbúðir**
(N 64°609.036', W 19°702.947') This good hut sleeps 30, has cooking facilities and hot showers. Located on the banks of the Svartá river, right on Rte 35 about 42km north of Gullfoss. There's a small cafe here, where you can buy food and handicrafts.

➡ **Gíslaskáli**
(N 64°744.187', W 19°432.508') Excellent hut operated by Gljásteinn; sleeps up to 50, has cooking facilities, dining and sitting rooms, hot showers. Located 4km north of the turn-off to Kerlingarfjöll, and 1km off Rte 35.

Ferðafélag Íslands HUTS €
(☎568 2533; www.fi.is; sites per person kr1800, dm kr5000-5500) Runs the following huts, which have toilets and a kitchen (no utensils though). Huts are listed from south to north: beds must be reserved.

TOURS TO THE HIGHLANDS

Aside from the day tours to Askja and Kverkfjöll, and the summertime buses servicing the Kjölur and Spengisandur routes, there are multiday tours that explore the central highlands area.

Icelandic Mountain Guides (www.mountains.is) has an eight-day tour travelling throughout the region, plus visiting Mývatn and Landmannalaugar (from kr315,000).

Eldhestar (www.eldhestar.is) offers eight-day wilderness horse-riding treks along the Kjölur and Spengisandur routes, for very experienced riders.

With limited time, you can get a wonderful overview of the landscapes courtesy of sightseeing flights; check out the small-plane options from Akureyri and Mývatn, and the helicopter flights from Möðrudalur.

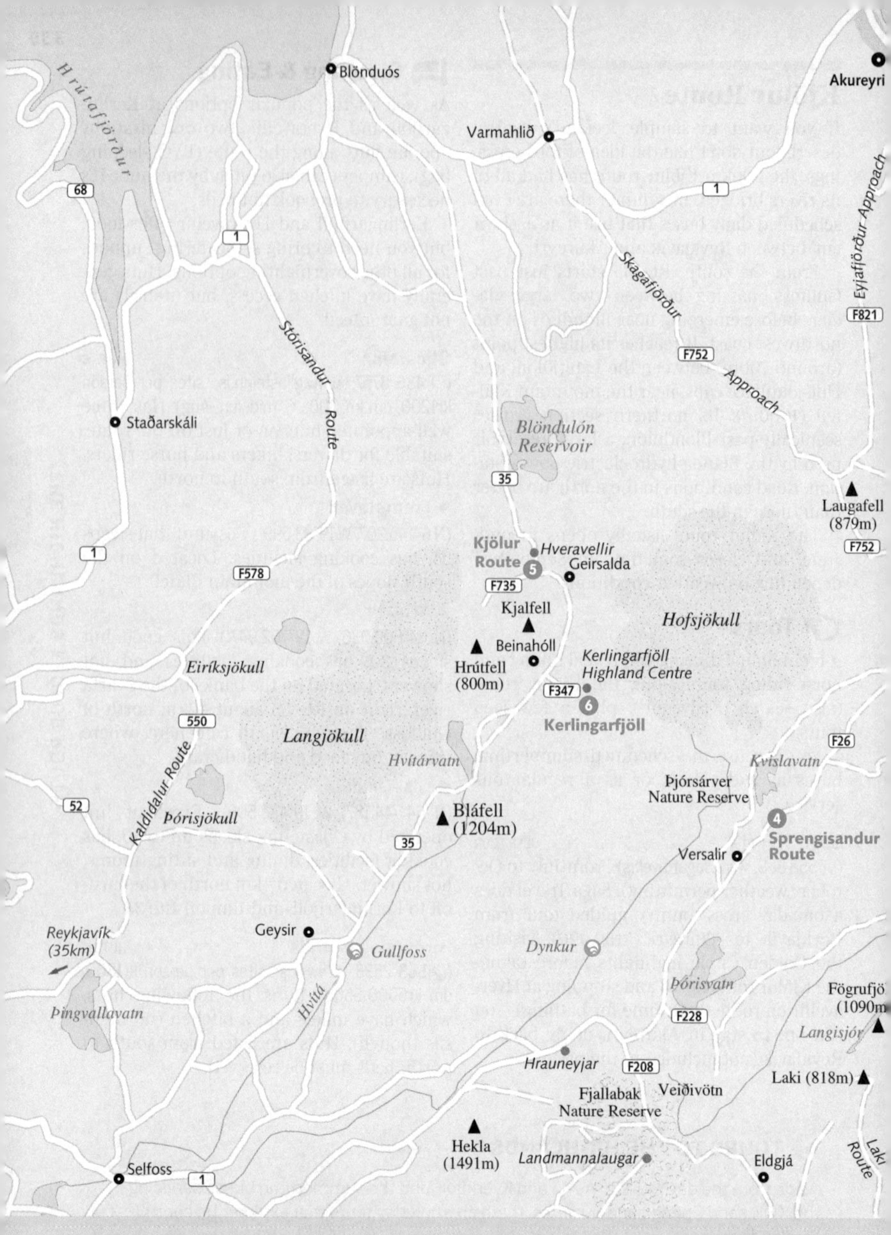

The Highlands Highlights

1 **Askja** (p348) Hiking across the lava field, drinking in the caldera views, then soaking in the waters of Víti crater.

2 **Kverkfjöll** (p349) Marvelling at icy sculptures hidden in the geothermal caves.

3 **Herðubreið** (p348) Paying homage to the Queen of the Mountains.

4 **Sprengisandur route** (p344) Pitying the melancholy ghosts and

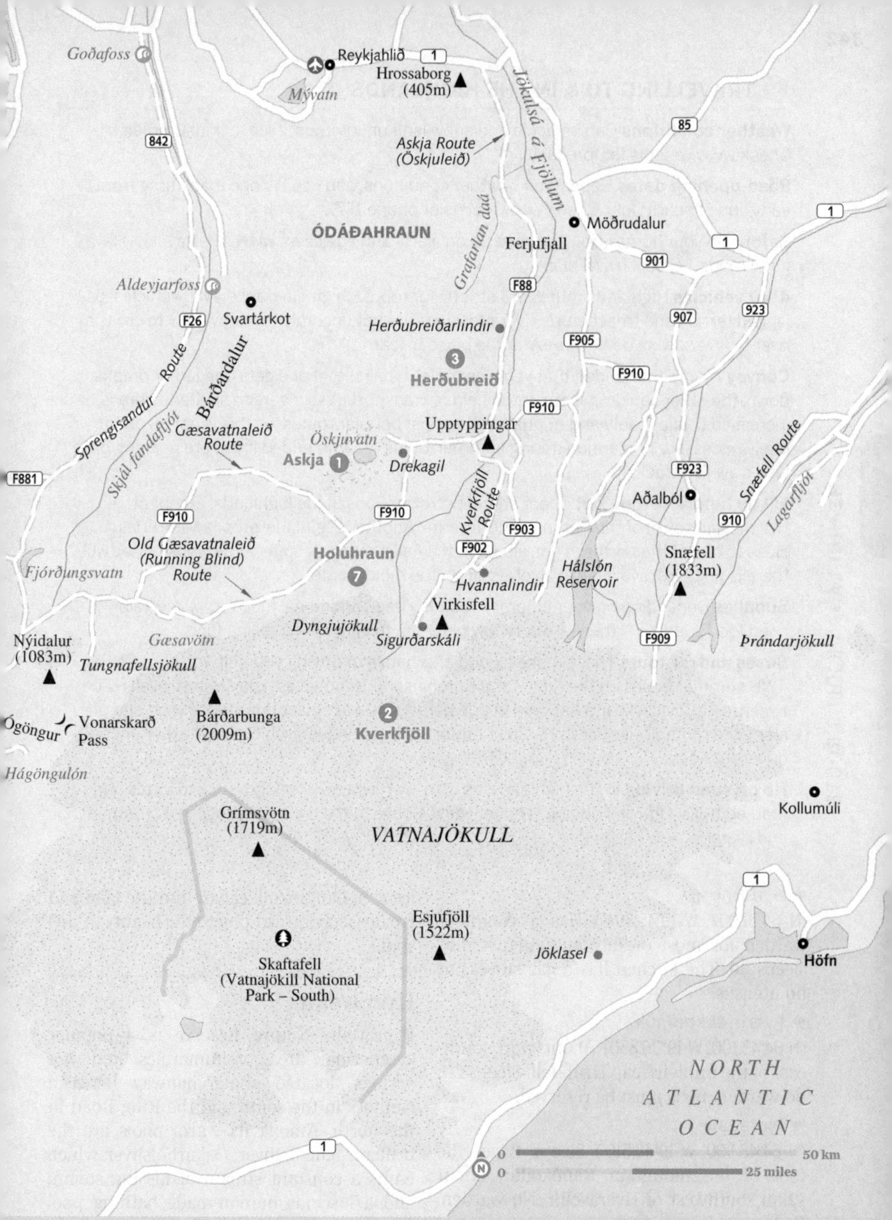

outlaws on Iceland's longest, loneliest north–south track.

5 Kjölur route (p339)
Spicing up the endless vistas of desolation with stops at hot springs and climbable crags.

6 Kerlingarfjöll (p343)
Investigating the new, improved hiking trails around the majestic massif.

7 Holuhraun (p348)
Getting an impressive geology lesson and treading gingerly on Iceland's newest lava field.

TRAVELLING TO & IN THE HIGHLANDS

Weather conditions Can be fickle and snow isn't uncommon, even in midsummer. Check www.vedur.is for forecasts.

Road-opening dates Depend on weather conditions, and usually occur any time from early June to early July. Check www.road.is or phone 1777.

Safety Do your homework, and read up on alerts and advice on www.safetravel.is. Have good maps. Leave a travel plan.

4WD vehicles Highlands routes are strictly for robust, high-clearance 4WD vehicles, as jagged terrain and treacherous river crossings are not uncommon. Know how to cross a river before setting out – this is not the place to learn.

Convoy It's recommended that vehicles travel in pairs, so if one gets bogged or breaks down, the other can drag it out, fetch help or transport passengers to shelter. There is increased traffic in July and August on the most popular routes, so this is not an absolutely necessary precaution during summer, but is recommended if you are heading onto less-travelled tracks.

Fill up before setting out There are no petrol stations in the highlands, except at Hrauneyjar, south of the Sprengisandur route. Another useful fuel stop is Möðrudalur, close to one of the northern entrances to the Askja route. Despite some websites' advice, there is no petrol available at Hveravellir on the Kjölur route.

Supplies Depending on your itinerary you may need additional fuel. You will certainly need food supplies – there are very few places in the highlands selling food.

Buses and/or tours These make a good alternative to driving yourself. You can use the 4WD summer buses on the Kjölur and Sprengisandur routes as a day tour (travelling between, say, Reykjavík and Akureyri in one burst), or as a regular bus, hopping on and off along the route. Tour operators offer comfortable super-Jeep vehicles and experienced drivers/guides.

No off-road driving In the highlands, as with everywhere in Iceland, stick to roads and marked trails. Off-road driving is hugely destructive to the country's fragile environment, and illegal.

➡ **Hvítárnes**

(N 64°37.007', W 19°45.394') Has a volunteer warden for most of July and August; hut sleeps 30. The kitchen has a gas stove, but no utensils.

➡ **Þverbrekknamúli**

(N 64°43.100', W 19°36.860) About 4km southeast of the mini-ice cap Hrútafell. Sleeps 20; no warden. Beds must be reserved.

➡ **Þjófadalir**

(N 64°48.900', W 19°42.510') Sleeps 12, at the foot of the mountain Rauðkollur, about 12km southwest of Hveravellir. No warden. Beds must be reserved.

Hvítárvatn

The pale-blue lake Hvítárvatn, 35km northeast of Gullfoss, is the source of the glacial river Hvítá – a popular destination for Reykjavík-based white-water rafting operators. A glacier tongue of Iceland's second-largest ice cap, Langjökull, calves into the lake and creates icebergs, adding to the beauty of this spot.

Hveravellir

Hveravellir Nature Reserve is a popular geothermal area of fumaroles and hot springs, located about halfway between Gullfoss in the south and the Ring Road in the north. Among its warm pools are the brilliant-blue Bláhver; Öskurhólshver, which emits a constant stream of hissing steam; and a luscious human-made bathing pool (kr500 for day guests; included in the rates for overnight guests). Another hot spring, Eyvindurhver, is named after the outlaw Fjalla-Eyvindur. Hveravellir is reputedly one of the many highland hideouts of this renegade.

Hveravellir is signposted 30km north of the Kerlingarfjöll turn-off (approximately

90km north of Gullfoss, and 90km south of the Ring Road in the north). Buses stop here, usually for an hour.

Petrol is no longer available at Hveravellir.

Sleeping & Eating

Self-cater (there are limited cooking facilities at Hveravellir – enquire about access when you book your hut bed), or visit the small all-day cafe here. Breakfast is kr1800, and during the day you can purchase soups, sandwiches, cakes, and hot dishes like hamburgers, fish stew, or chicken and potatoes (mains kr1800 to kr2500).

Hveravellir HUT €
(☎ summer 452 4200, year-round 894 1293; www.hveravellir.is; sites per person kr1800, dm kr7500-9300; ⏲ Jun-Sep/Oct) There are two hikers' huts with about 50 beds (linen available for kr2000; private rooms possible). There's also a campsite, limited cooking facilities (only available for guests staying in the Old Hut, not campers), and a simple cafe and store. Helpful staff can assist with information on local hiking trails.

Kerlingarfjöll

Until the 1850s Icelanders believed that this mountain range (10km off Rte 35 on Rte F347) harboured the worst outlaws. It was thought they lived deep in the heart of the 150-sq-km range in an isolated Shangri-la-type valley. So strong was this belief that it was only in the mid-19th century that anyone ventured into Kerlingarfjöll, and it was only in 1941 that the range was properly explored by Ferðafélag Íslands (Iceland Touring Association).

It's certainly dramatic. The colourful landscape is broken up into jagged peaks and ridges, the highest of which is Snækollur (1477m), and it's scattered with hot springs. A stunningly colourful 5km (90-minute) walk leads from the Kerlingarfjöll Highland Centre to the geothermal area of **Hveradalir**, a highlight of any visit. Alternatively, you can drive 15 minutes to a parking area at Mt Keis, from where Hveradalir is a short walk.

Access to Kerlingarfjöll is 10km off Rte 35 on Rte F347. The bus stops here.

Sleeping & Eating

Self-cater (there are cooking facilities at Kerlingarfjöll Highland Centre), or visit the small restaurant here. The breakfast buffet is kr1750; sandwiches and soups are served during the day; and there are simple, tasty evening options (fish stew, baked salmon, lamb soup).

Kerlingarfjöll Highland Centre GUESTHOUSE €€
(☎ summer 664 7878, year-round 664 7000; www.kerlingarfjoll.is; sites per person kr1850, d with bathroom incl breakfast kr27,850; ⏲ mid-Jun–mid-Sep) There is a handful of huts and houses at this great, remote centre, with various bathroom configurations and linen options (sleeping-bag accommodation kr4650 to kr6100). There's also a campsite, guest kitchen, simple restaurant (dinner mains kr3100 to kr3500) and natural hot-pots. Check the website for up-to-date rates, and details of local trails.

Getting There & Away

BUS

In summer scheduled buses travel along the Kjölur route between Reykjavík and Akureyri (in both directions). You can use it as a day tour, or as a regular bus service. These services are included in a number of bus passports.

SBA-Norðurleið (www.sba.is) services:

➡ Bus 610 Reykjavík–Akureyri, 610a Akureyri–Reykjavík (once daily mid-June to mid-September) SBA's service takes 10½ hours for the complete journey, with half-hour stops at Geysir and Gullfoss. There's a 15-minute stop at Kerlingarfjöll, and an hour at Hveravellir (time for a dip). The entire journey costs kr17,000 one way.

Note that the bus may be an appealing option at first; however, we've received comments from readers that while the first hour of outback desolation is riveting, the other nine hours can be snooze-inducing if you aren't planning to disembark anywhere along the way.

CAR

Note that the Kjölur route is labelled Rte 35 (not F35), but it is still a mountain road, and while it is technically possible to drive a 2WD along the route, it is absolutely not recommended (there are potholes/puddles that could near-swallow a small car, you'll do damage to the car's underside, and your journey will be slow and very bumpy). Car-hire companies expressly forbid the use of 2WD rentals on the route.

Drivers with 4WD vehicles will have no problems on the Kjölur route. Note that if you're in a 2WD and curious for a taste of the highlands, the first 14km of the route (north of Gullfoss) are sealed.

Sprengisandur Route

To Icelanders, the name Sprengisandur conjures up images of outlaws, ghosts and long sheep drives across the barren wastes. The Sprengisandur route (F26) is the longest north–south trail, and crosses bleak desert moors that can induce a shudder even today in a 4WD.

Sprengisandur offers some wonderful views of Vatnajökull, Tungnafellsjökull and Hofsjökull, as well as Askja and Herðubreið from the western perspective. An older route, now abandoned, lies a few kilometres west of the current one.

The Sprengisandur route proper begins at Rte 842 near Goðafoss in northwest Iceland. Some 41km later, you'll pass through a red metal gate as the road turns into F26. After 2.5km there's a poster explaining the sights and finer points of the route, and 1km later you'll happen upon one of Iceland's most photogenic waterfalls, **Aldeyjarfoss**. Churning water bursts over the cliff's edge as it splashes through a narrow canyon lined with the signature honeycomb columns of basalt.

After the falls, the Sprengisandur route continues southwest through 240km of inhospitable territory all the way to Þjórsárdalur. There are two other ways to approach Sprengisandur, both of which link up to the main road about halfway through.

The route generally opens around the start of July.

Laugafell

The main site of interest on the Skagafjörður approach is Laugafell, an 879m-high mountain with some hot springs bubbling on its northwestern slopes. You can stay at the **Ferðafélag Akureyrar** (Jul-Aug 822 5192; www.ffa.is; N 65°01.630', W 18°19.950'; sites per person kr1800, dm kr6500) hut complex, with 35 beds, a kitchen and a magnificent, geothermally heated, natural swimming pool. There's a warden on-site in July and August. Outside of July and August, contact FFA via its website.

Laugafell is on the Eyjafjörður approach to the Sprengisandur route. It's 87km south of Akureyri via Rte 821 and F821. There is no bus service.

You will also reach Laugafell if you take the Skagafjörður approach. It's 93km via Rte 752 and F752.

A few tour companies out of Akureryi offer 4WD day tours to this area, including the Traveling Viking (p246).

Nýidalur

Nýidalur (also known as Jökuldalur), the range just south of the Tungnafellsjökull ice cap, was discovered by a lost traveller in 1845. With facilities including a **campsite and huts** (Jul-Aug 860 3334; www.fi.is; N 64°44.130', W 18°04.350'; sites per person kr1800, dm kr7500), plus appealing hiking trails, it's the most popular rest spot for travellers along the Sprengisandur route. The huts have kitchen facilities (no utensils), showers (kr500) and a summer warden (July and August). Book your bed in advance. It's about 100km from Hrauneyjar.

There are two rivers – the one 500m from the hut may be difficult to cross (even for a 4WD). Ask the warden for advice on conditions.

The Sprengisandur buses stop here.

Hrauneyjar

Somewhat unexpectedly, in the bleakest position imaginable (west of Þórisvatn in the Hrauneyjar region), you'll find a year-round guesthouse and hotel. They lie at the crossroads of the Sprengisandur route (F26) and the F208 to Landmannalaugar, so are handy

KJÖLUR HIKING

Looking for an independent multi-day hike in the area?

Old Kjalvegur route (www.fi.is) An easy and scenic three-day hike (39km) from Hvítárvatn to Hveravellir (or vice versa). The trail follows the original horseback Kjölur route (west of the present road), via the Hvítárnes, Þverbrekknamúli and Þjófadalir mountain huts (p342).

Hringbraulin (www.kerlingarfjoll.is/routes) A challenging three-day circuit (47km) around Kerlingarfjöll, starting and ending at Kerlingarfjöll Highland Centre (p343), with huts at Klakkur and Kisubotnar.

THE BADLANDS

Historically in Iceland, once a person had been convicted of outlawry they were beyond society's protection and aggrieved enemies could kill them at will. Many outlaws *(útilegumenn)*, such as the renowned Eiríkur Rauðe (Erik the Red), voluntarily took exile abroad. Others escaped revenge-killing by fleeing into the mountains, valleys and broad expanses of the harsh Icelandic interior, where few dared pursue them.

Undoubtedly, anyone who could live year-round in these bitter, barren deserts must have been extraordinary. Icelandic outlaws were naturally credited with all sorts of fearsome feats, and the general populace came to fear the vast badlands, which they considered to be the haunt of superhuman evil. The *útilegumenn* thereby joined the ranks of giants and trolls, and provided the themes for popular tales such as the fantastic *Grettir's Saga*.

One particular outlaw has become the subject of countless Icelandic folk tales. Fjalla-Eyvindur ('Eyvindur of the Mountains'), a charming but incurable 18th-century kleptomaniac, fled into the highlands with his wife, and continued to make enemies by rustling sheep to stay alive. Throughout the highlands you'll see shelters and hideouts attributed to him and hear tales of his ability to survive in impossible conditions while always staying one jump ahead of his pursuers.

for highland attractions and have marked walking trails in the area.

Petrol and diesel are available at the Hrauneyjar complex. There is sealed road to Hrauneyjar from the west on Rte 32 (it branches off Rte 30 between Selfoss and Flúðir), or you can access it from Rte 26 (off the Ring Road near Hella).

The guesthouse also cleverly offers 4WDs for rent (a pricey kr36,500 for 12 hours), so you can consider some highland exploring from here even if you're touring in a 2WD; or if you come by bus.

Buses travelling the Sprengisandur route call at Hrauneyjar.

Sleeping & Eating

The Hrauneyjar accommodation options have high rates, but are in great demand due to their proximity to Landmannalaugar.

Hrauneyjar Guesthouse GUESTHOUSE €€
(☎487 7782; www.hrauneyjar.is; s/d incl breakfast from kr19,800/22,500; @) Offers small, no-frills guesthouse rooms of varying standards, and a pricey sleeping-bag option (single/double, not including breakfast, for kr9600/11,800). There's also a decent restaurant serving lunch and dinner (mains kr1500 to kr4900).

Hotel Highland HOTEL €€€
(☎487 7782; www.hotelhighland.is; s/d incl breakfast kr32,050/36,250; ⌚Jun-Sep; @) If you want luxuries – comfier rooms, bar and smart gourmet restaurant, hot-pot and sauna – head for Hotel Highland, under the same owners and 1.4km from Hrauneyjar Guesthouse. These extra comforts come at a premium; the restaurant gets a big rap.

Veiðivötn

This beautiful area just northeast of Landmannalaugar is an entanglement of small desert lakes in a volcanic basin, a continuation of the same fissure that produced Laugahraun in the Fjallabak Nature Reserve. This is a wonderful place for wandering, following 4WD tracks that wind across the tephra sands between the numerous lakes (very popular for trout fishing).

Access to this area is via Rte F228, east of Hrauneyjar.

Getting There & Away

BUS

In July and August, Reykjavík Excursions (www.re.is/iceland-on-your-own/) operates two scheduled services along the Sprengisandur route (start dates are determined by road-opening dates). These services are included in a number of bus passports.

Reykjavík Excursions services:

➡ **Bus 14 Landmannalaugar–Mývatn, 14a Mývatn–Landmannalaugar** (daily late June to early September) Total journey 10 hours. Although it's a scheduled bus, it's used as a tour of sorts, with extended pauses at Nýidalur, Aldeyjarfoss and Goðafoss. Fare for the entire route is kr16,500.

➡ **Bus 17 Reykjavík–Mývatn, 17a Mývatn–Reykjavík** (daily late June to early September) Total journey 12 hours. Although it's a scheduled bus, it's also used as a tour, with breaks at Nýidalur, Aldeyjarfoss and Goðafoss. Fare for the entire route is kr20,500.

Note that the summertime scheduled buses along the Sprengisandur carry bikes (kr3500).

CAR

There's no fuel along the route. Goðafoss to Hrauneyjar is 240km, so plan accordingly.

The nearest petrol stations are at Akureyri (from the Eyjafjörður approach); Varmahlíð (from the Skagafjörður approach) or Fosshóll, near Goðafoss (if you're coming from the north along the main route through Bárðardalur). There is petrol at Hrauneyjar if you're driving from the south.

Eyjafjörður Approach From the north, the F821 from southern Eyjafjörður (south of Akureyri) connects to the Skagafjörður approach at Laugafell.

Skagafjörður Approach From the northwest the 81km-long F752 connects southern Skagafjörður (the nearest town is Varmahlíð on the Ring Road) to the Sprengisandur route. The roads join near the lake Fjórðungsvatn, 20km east of Hofsjökull.

Askja Route

The Askja route (Öskjuleið) runs across the highlands to Herðubreið (1682m), the Icelanders' beloved 'Queen of the Mountains', and to the desert's most popular marvel, the immense Askja caldera.

The usual access road is Rte F88, which leaves the Ring Road 32km east of Mývatn. Askja is also accessible further east via Rtes F905 and F910 (close to Möðrudalur).

Rte F88 leaves the Ring Road at **Hrossaborg**, a 10,000-year-old crater shaped like an amphitheatre, used as a film set for the Tom Cruise sci-fi film *Oblivion* (2013). For much of the way the F88 is a flat journey, following the western bank of the Jökulsá á Fjöllum glacier river, meandering across tephra wasteland and winding through rough, tyre-abusing sections of the 4400-sq-km **Ódáðahraun** (Evil Deeds Lava Field).

After a long journey through the lava- and flood-battered plains, things perk up at the lovely oasis of **Herðubreiðarlindir**, at the foot of **Herðubreið**. The route then wanders westwards through dunes and lava flows past the **Dreki** huts and up the hill towards Askja, where you leave your car to walk the remaining 2.5km to the caldera.

Activities

For independent hikers, the website of Ferðafélag Akureyrar, the Touring Club of Akureyri (www.ffa.is), outlines details of the **Askja Trail**, known in Icelandic as Öskjuvegurinn. This is the organisation's walking trail with huts across the Ódáðahraun, starting from Herðubreiðarlindir and ending at Svartárkot farm in upper Bárðardalur valley (Rte 843). Hut beds must be booked well in advance with FFA; see the website.

Also see the national-park website (www.vjp.is) for hiking information.

Independent long-distance hikers should inform a park ranger of their plans; and leave a travel plan at safetravel.is.

For hiker transport in the area, your best best is Mývatn Tours (p347). It can drop you at a hut and arrange to pick you up a few days later.

Tours

Hiking Tours

Ferðafélag Akureyrar HIKING TOUR
(Touring Club of Akureyri; FFA; ☎462 2720; www.ffa.is; Strandgata 23, Akureyri) A couple of times a year (in summer), Ferðafélag Akureyrar organises five-day hut-to-hut hiking tours (kr68,000 per person) along the Askja Trail. See 'Touring Program' on its website for details; the program is in Icelandic, so look for 'Öskjuvegur' in July and August to see specific dates.

Icelandic Mountain Guides HIKING TOUR
(IMG; ☎587 9999; www.mountainguides.is) IMG runs guided multi-day backpacking hikes in the area, including a five-day, 95km traverse from Mývatn to Askja (from kr205,000), or a seven-day, 95km trek from Askja to Nýidalur (from kr239,000).

Super-Jeep Tours

A number of operators run super-Jeep tours to Askja, from mid-June (when the route opens) until as late into September/October as weather permits.

From Akureyri it makes for a long day (up to 15 hours); a better base is Reykjahlíð at Mývatn (even then, tour time is around 11 to 12 hours). If you want a more relaxed pace (and a chance to experience highland evening stillness), consider a two day-tour.

For all tours, you are expected to bring/order a packed lunch; some operators stop for a late-afternoon coffee at Möðrudalur en route home; others head further south to the new lava field at Holuhraun. Don't forget your swimsuit and towel, too, should you fancy a dip in Víti crater at Askja.

It's worth noting that with the growth of tourism, many of these companies are offering more highland exploration, including customised multi-day tours, guided hikes, and 4WD treks to lesser-known natural features. There is also a notable growth in winter tours (in huge, weather-defying super-Jeep vehicles).

See websites for latest prices and offerings, and for advice on what to bring.

Fjalladýrð JEEP TOUR
(☎471 1858; www.fjalladyrd.is) Based at Möðrudalur farm on Rte 901 – perfectly placed for Askja access via F905 and F910. Day tours to Askja cost kr36,000. It can also arrange visits to Kverkfjöll (over one or two days; prices depend on numbers). Has excellent accommodation and eating options right at its departure point.

Geo Travel JEEP TOUR
(☎864 7080; www.geotravel.is) A great small company owned by two local guys. Small-group day tours run from Reykjahlíð and visit Askja and Holuhraun (kr37,000). Also has a two-day tour to Holuhraun, Askja and Kverkfjöll (kr95,000).

Saga Travel JEEP TOUR
(☎558 8888; www.sagatravel.is) Very reliable small-group option, departing daily from both Akureyri and Mývatn (from Akureyri/Mývatn kr49,500/41,900 – note that the trip from Akureyri heads off at 6.30am and may be up to 16 hours). Saga also offers a slower-paced two-day trip, overnighting in either a mountain hut or campsite (from Akureyri/Mývatn kr139,000/133,000).

Jeep Tours JEEP TOUR
(☎898 2798; www.jeeptours.is) Jeep Tours runs unique tours out of Egilsstaðir in east Iceland, contrary to the other companies that approach Askja from the north. Visit Askja (kr44,500) or Kverkfjöll as a day tour (kr44,500). Tours travel via the (sealed) Rte 910 to Kárahnjúkar dam before tackling lesser-known 4WD tracks.

Mývatn Tours BUS
(☎464 1920; www.askjatours.is) Tours in a large 4WD bus daily from late June to early September (kr20,000), from Reykjahlíð. This is the best option if you want hikers' transport to the area, and to be picked up another day; sample one-way fare from Reykjahlíð to Dreki is kr12,000.

North Travel BUS
(☎898 4499; ww.northtravel.is) Works with bus company SBA-Norðurleið to run a popular three-day Askja–Kverkfjöll–Vatnajökull tour (including Holuhraun), operating from late June to late August. It departs weekly (Monday) from Akureyri and picks up in Mývatn. Cost is kr55,000, which includes transport and guide (but not food or accommodation; hut reservations arranged).

Herðubreiðarlindir

The oasis Herðubreiðarlindir, a nature reserve thick with green moss, angelica and the pinky-purple flower of the Arctic river beauty Epilobium latifolium, was created by springs flowing from beneath the Ódáðahraun lava. You get a superb close-up view of Herðubreið from here (unless, of course, you're greeted by dense fog and/or a wall of blowing sand).

PROPOSED HIGHLANDS NATIONAL PARK

A broad coalition of Icelandic organisations and associations (diverse interest groups including recreational associations, nature conservationists, government agencies and the travel industry) have banded together in the hopes of establishing a national park in the central highlands of Iceland. The goal is to protect the vast wilderness and its unique unspoilt landscapes, plus ensure responsible future management. The area proposed for protection is some 40,000 sq km (including all of the existing Vatnajökull National Park).

The vision of a highlands national park is partially a measure against Iceland's expanding energy industry. By protecting the area, the coalition hopes to ensure only limited development and construction within the area, and to prevent rivers and geothermal areas from future energy harnessing (which could involve the construction of dams, hydroelectric power stations and high-voltage pylons).

Polls indicate popular support among Icelanders for the creation of such a national park (61% in favour). International backing is also important; and there is a petition seeking support. Read more about the proposal at www.halendid.is.

The mini tourist complex at Herðubreiðarlindir has an information office staffed by summer wardens, a campsite and the 30-bed **Þorsteinsskáli hut** (☎822 5191; www.ffa.is; N 65°11.544', W 16°13.360'; site/dm per person kr1800/6500), a cosy lodge with showers (kr500) and kitchen. Book your hut beds in advance.

Behind the hut is a Fjalla-Eyvindur 'convict hole': outlaw Eyvindur is believed to have occupied it during the winter of 1774–75, when he subsisted on angelica root and raw horsemeat stored on top of the hideout to retain heat inside.

Herðubreiðarlindir is about 60km from Hrossaborg, at the northern point of Rte F88, and another 35km on to Drekagil.

Herðubreið

Iceland's most distinctive mountain (1682m) has been described as a birthday cake and a lampshade, but Icelanders call it (more respectfully) the 'Queen of the Mountains'. It crops up time and again in the work of local poets and painters, entranced by its beauty.

If Herðubreið (meaning 'Broad Shoulders') appears to have been made in a jelly mould, that's not far off base. It's a *móberg* mountain, formed by subglacial volcanic eruptions. In fact, if Vatnajökull was to suddenly be stripped of ice, Grímsvötn and Kverkfjöll would probably emerge looking more or less like Herðubreið.

Drekagil

The name of the gorge Drekagil, 35km southwest of Herðubreið, means 'Dragon Canyon', after the shape of a dragon in the craggy rock formations that tower over it. The canyon (behind the Dreki huts) resembles something out of Arizona or the Sinai; bitter winds and freezing temperatures just don't suit this desert landscape!

The **Dreki huts** (Askja Camp; ☎822 5190; www.ffa.is; N 65°02.503', W 16°35.690'; site/dm per person kr1800/7500; ⏲mid-/late Jun–early Sep) are an ideal base for exploring the area. The huts, operated by Ferðafélag Akureyrar, sleep a total of 60, and there are showers, a kitchen, an information centre and a warden here. Day use of the facilities at Dreki (bathroom etc) costs kr500 per person. Camping is also permitted, but the wind and cold may become oppressive for tent campers (who may want to consider the lusher site at Herðubreiðarlindir, 35km away).

Not only does the dramatic Drekagil ravine offer an easy stroll up to an impressive waterfall, but you can also walk 8km up the marked trail to Askja. There is also a marked 20km trail to the Bræðrafell hut.

There is a ranger station (☎842 4357) at Drekagil in the summer. From Drekagil, it's 8km by road to reach the Askja car park.

At Drekagil the Gæsavatnaleið route (F910) turns off the Askja route to cross some intimidating expanses and connect with the Sprengisandur route at Nýidalur, some 125km away. This involves a number of river crossings and is only for large vehicles.

Askja

The utterly desolate Askja caldera is the main destination for all tours in this part of the highlands. This immense 50-sq-km caldera shouldn't be missed – it's a 2.5km walk from the car-park area, and as you approach the site you'll find it difficult to imagine the sorts of forces that created it.

Your first sighting of the sapphire-blue lake **Öskjuvatn**, at the heart of the crater, is guaranteed to be memorable. The lake stands in contrast to the milky waters inside the small crater known as **Víti**, adjacent to the caldera.

Although a bit on the chilly side (temperatures range between 22°C and 30°C), a dip in Víti's milky blue pool is one of the highlights of an Askja adventure (and is sometimes done sans swimsuit). The route down is slippery but not as steep as it looks; it may be closed for safety reasons by park officials.

From Drekagil there's an 8km road to reach the Askja car park, and it's then a scenic 2.5km walk (easy to moderate, depending on snow melt and weather conditions) across lava fields to reach the caldera.

Free, ranger-led, one-hour hikes leave from the Askja car park at 1pm daily mid-July to mid-August.

Holuhraun

Iceland's huge new lava field dates from 2014–15 and still smoulders in some areas (sightseeing flights grant you a sense of its vastness). By road, Holuhraun is accessible from Drekagil; follow the signs to a marked trail that's been set up, enabling you to walk on a small section of the lava (it's fragile, and sharp and jagged, so take care). At this access point you can clearly see the difference

ASKJA HISTORY

The cataclysm that formed the lake in the Askja caldera (and the Víti crater) happened relatively recently (in 1875) when 2 cu km of tephra was ejected from the Askja volcano. The force was so strong that bits of debris actually landed in Continental Europe. Ash from the eruption poisoned large numbers of cattle in northern Iceland, sparking a wave of emigration to America. It's quite daunting to realise that such cataclysmic events could be replayed at any time.

After the initial eruption, a magma chamber collapsed and created a craterous 11-sq-km hole, 300m below the rim of the original explosion crater. This new depression subsequently filled with water and became the lake Öskjuvatn, the second-deepest in Iceland at 220m.

In 1907 German researchers Max Rudloff and Walther von Knebel were rowing on the lake when they completely vanished; their bodies were never found. It was suggested that the lake may have hazardous quirks, possibly odd currents or whirlpools; but a rickety canvas boat and icy water could easily explain their deaths. There's a stone cairn and memorial to the men on the rim of the caldera.

In the 1875 eruption a vent near the northeastern corner of the lake exploded and formed the tephra crater Víti, which contains geothermal water. This is one of two well-known craters called Víti, the other being at Krafla near Mývatn. (FYI: Víti means 'hell' in Icelandic.)

between the old lava field and the new, and note the interplay of the lava and river.

Park rangers at Drekagil can provide information about Holuhraun, and about safety precautions to take if you are visiting – this is a volcanically active area. Stay on the tracks and signed trails at all times.

Signs point the way to Holuhraun from Drekagil; head south on the F910 and follow these signs (it's a distance of around 24km).

Getting There & Away

There's no public transport along the Askja route, but there are plentiful tours. Alternatively, hire a large 4WD and prepare for a rocky ride (seek advice on fording rivers). The route usually opens in mid- to late June.

If you take F88 into Askja, it's a good idea to leave along F910 so you don't have to retrace all of your steps. Other options from Askja include heading east towards Egilsstaðir, or west on the Gæsavatnaleið route (F910) to Sprengisandur (ask locally for advice on conditions). To reach Kverkfjöll ice caves, head east on F910, then south on F902.

There are no fuel stops anywhere on the route. The nearest ones are at Möðrudalur (90km from Askja) and Mývatn (120km from Askja). Plan accordingly.

Kverkfjöll Route

The Kverkfjöll route creeps across the highlands to the Kverkfjöll area at the northern margins of the Vatnajökull ice cap.

Kverkfjöll is actually a cluster of peaks formed by a large central volcano. It is partially capped by the ice of Kverkjökull (a northern tongue of Vatnajökull). Over time, the name Kverkfjöll has also come to refer to the hot-spring-filled ice caves that often form beneath the eastern margin of the Dyngjujökull ice due to the heavy geothermal activity in this area.

Along the access road F902 (off Rte F10) are several sites of interest, including the twin pyramid-shaped **Upptyppingar hills** near the Jökulsá á Fjöllum bridge, and the **Hvannalindir** oasis, about 20km north of Sigurðarskáli hut (Kverkfjöll's accommodation and information base).

A 2km-return marked hike from behind the hut takes you up **Virkisfell** (1108m) for a spectacular view over Kverkfjöll and the headwaters of the Jökulsá á Fjöllum.

Kverkfjöll

Besides being the source of the roiling Jökulsá á Fjöllum, central Iceland's greatest river, Kverkfjöll is also one of Iceland's largest geothermal areas.

The lower **Kverkfjöll ice caves** lie 3km from the Sigurðarskáli hut; they're about a 15-minute walk from the 4WD track's end. Here the hot river flows beneath the cold glacier ice, clouds of steam swirl over the river and melt shimmering patterns on the ice walls, and there you have it – a spectacular tourist attraction. Perhaps this was the source of the overworked fire-and-ice cliché

ICELAND'S NEWEST LAVA FIELD – FOR NOW

On 16 August 2014, sensors began picking up increased seismic activity in and around Bárðarbunga, one of many volcanoes that lie underneath Vatnajökull ice cap. (This immense volcano system is under the ice cap's northwest area.)

The magma in the Bárðarbunga caldera formed an 'intrusive dike' (tunnel of magma) through the ground under an outlet glacier named Dyngjujökull. On 29 August, the magma surfaced – a fissure eruption, complete with spectacular lava fountains, began in Holuhraun, a 200-year-old lava field about 5km away from the Dyngjujökull glacial edge.

The eruption continued for almost six months and came to be Iceland's largest lava eruption for 230 years. Its stats are impressive: the new basaltic lava field is about 85 sq km in area (considerably larger than the island of Manhattan), is an average of 10m to 14m thick, and weighs about the same as a herd of 600 million elephants. The lava was around 1180°C when it reached the surface. The river system and land around the lava are still undergoing change.

that pervades almost everything ever written about Iceland.

Large blocks of ice frequently crash down from the roof – don't enter the ice caves or you risk being crushed. Also, the giant blocks of ice can alter the entrance to the cave – it's best to ask where the safest access point is currently located (there's only one point of entry, and it's not an issue if you are on a tour). There can be a danger of sulphur inhalation further inside the cave.

From the lower ice caves, ranger-led tours continue up onto the glacier itself. Longer guided tours head over the glacier to the remarkable Hveradalur geothermal area.

Tours

Without a robust 4WD vehicle, the only way to visit Kverkfjöll is on a tour. If you do have your own vehicle, you can park and walk up to the ice caves – anywhere further is strictly ill-advised without a guide.

As well as short walks in the area, the park rangers stationed at Sigurðarskáli hut offer guided hikes in good weather: three hours onto the **Kverkjökull outlet glacier** (kr10,500), or eight to 10 hours to the geothermal area at 1700m, known as **Hveradalur** (kr17,000); prices include equipment. Call 863 9236 (in summer) for tour details, or email ferdafelag@egilsstadir.is.

Besides the ranger-led tours, there are tour packages involving transport and guiding. From the east, Wild Boys (864 7393, 896 4334; www.wildboys.is) has hiking tours in the area, and Jeep Tours (p347) offers a day trip here in a super-Jeep from Egilsstaðir. Fjalladyrð (p347) has a two-day tour from Möðrudalur. From Mývatn, Geo Travel (p347) has a two-day Askja–Kverkfjöll tour, and there's the popular three-day Askja–Kverkfjöll–Vatnajökull tour run by North Travel (p347), which picks up in Akureyri and Mývatn.

Sleeping

Sigurðarskáli Hut HUT €
(summer 863 9236, year-round 863 5813; www.ferdaf.is; N 64°44.850', W 16°37.890'; sites per person kr1800, dm kr7500; mid-Jun–early Sep) The large Sigurðarskáli hut has comfortable sleeping accommodation (sleeps 75) in a new hut, plus a well-maintained campsite. There are cooking facilities, toilets and showers. Campers pay an additional kr800 for access to cabin facilities like the kitchen.

Information

Kverkfjöll is part of the vast Vatnajökull National Park; check the park website (www.vjp.is) for information.

The road to Kverkfjöll usually opens mid- to late June. It's good to get to Kverkfjöll early in the season because there's a higher chance of accessing the caves (warmer weather = tumbling ice blocks and bouts of glacial melting). Ask the ranger first about cave conditions and for recommendations for a successful exploration of the area; we strongly advise joining a tour to take advantage of ranger expertise.

Getting There & Away

The road to Kverkfjöll (F902; in Icelandic known as Kverkfjalaleið) usually opens mid- to late June.

The Kverkfjöll route connects Möðrudalur (70km east of Mývatn, off the Ring Road) with the Sigurðarskáli hut, 3km from the lower caves, via the F905, F910 and F902. After visiting Askja, you can follow up with a 70km trip to Kverkfjöll by driving south along the F902.

Drivers note: the petrol station at Möðrudalur is the last place to fill up.

Understand Iceland

Iceland Today

Iceland's tourism has boomed in recent years. Thirty per cent growth each year since 2010 has helped the country stabilise its economy following the 2008 banking crash. Tourism has also brought a host of changes, and infrastructure and logistical planning are rushing to keep up. Meanwhile, the country is easing the capital controls put in place during the crash, and the populace is pressuring the government to respond to high-profile scandals.

Best on Film

Heima (2007) Follow band Sigur Rós as they perform throughout Iceland.

Rams (*Hrútar*; 2015) Engrossing tale of two brothers and their sheep.

The Homecoming (*Blóðberg*; 2015) Sly modern comedy-drama where a 'perfect' family's life goes topsy-turvy.

Of Horses and Men (2013) A surreal portrait of the intertwining lives of men and horses.

101 Reykjavík (2000) Dark comedy exploring sex, drugs and the life of a loafer in downtown Reykjavík.

Jar City (2006) Carefully crafted detective thriller based on the novel by Arnaldur Indriðason.

Best in Print

The Draining Lake (Arnaldur Indriðason; 2004) One of many engrossing tales from a master of Nordic Noir.

Independent People (Halldór Laxness; 1934–35) Bleak tragi-comedy from the Nobel Laureate.

The Sagas of Icelanders (Jane Smiley et al; 2001) Excellent, readable translations of Iceland's epic, often brutal, tales.

Devil's Island (Einar Kárason; 1983) American culture clashes with rural tradition in postwar Reykjavík.

The Blue Fox (Sjón; 2003) Poetic 19th-century fantasy-adventure tale.

Tourism Boom

Curious travellers started to arrive following the 2010 Eyjafjallajökull eruption and a smart publicity campaign led by the Iceland tourism board, which helped spread word of Iceland's charms. The tourism boom saw a 264% increase from 2010 to 2015, with about 1.3 million visitors arriving in 2015. Businesses catering to tourists also boomed, and tourism now accounts for 31% of Iceland's export of goods and services (up from 18.8% in 2010) and 4.6% of the GDP, and employs 14.1% of the country's workforce. There are no signs of a slowdown. The country continues to provide spectacles that capture attention: from rumbling volcanoes like Katla to the victories of Iceland's football (soccer) team in the 2016 European League championship, and as a top filming destination for the likes of *Game of Thrones* and sci-fi blockbusters.

Tourism Repercussions

The strengthening of the economy as a result of tourism income is indisputable, and many locals appreciate the new activities and services, and the increase in international profile that the industry brings. When polled, 56% of Icelanders acknowledge the job opportunities created by tourism, and 62% say that it has increased their interest in Iceland's natural landscapes.

But there's a flipside. Short-term apartment rentals such as Airbnb in the centre of Reykjavík are pushing locals out of the rental market. News reports consistently feature the destruction of the environment, or rescues of stranded tourists from glaciers, mountainsides and wave-swept beaches by Iceland's search and rescue team, a volunteer- and donation-based operation. In 2016 more than 75% of Icelanders considered the pressure from tourism on the environment to be too high.

Responses include limits on Airbnb-type rentals, additional cautionary signs and barriers at some sights, restrictions on free camping in campervans, an educational campaign (http://inspired.visiticeland.com/academy), and improved methods for learning about safety and logging hikes (www.safetravel.is).

Protecting Iceland

Important debate is taking place about how Iceland's fragile environment can withstand the pressure it's under. The country's unspoilt natural landscape is a major tourist draw, and if current growth continues, Iceland could host close to 3 million visitors in 2020. How much tourism can Iceland's waterfalls, trails and lava fields sustain, and how can they be adequately protected, for both locals and visitors to enjoy?

Tourism authorities are currently placing huge emphasis on promoting responsible travel and preparing visitors for how to experience and protect the unusual environment. About 53% of Icelanders polled in 2016 say that better infrastructure and organisation is where national efforts should be placed, and 34% say improved transport and roads.

Iceland also benefits from its copious sources of renewable energy (primarily geothermal and hydro power). This helps fuel life on the island and also attracts large energy users – (controversial) aluminium smelters here for cheap power, and lower impact computing 'server farms' are on the rise.

Political Hi-jinks

One of the world's few nations to prosecute the bankers held responsible for the financial collapse in 2008, Icelanders maintain a sharp watch on their leaders. In April 2016 when the Panama Papers document leak from law firm Mossack Fonseca revealed financial improprieties by Prime Minister Sigmundur Davíð Gunnlaugsson and his wife, huge protest ensued. As a result, Gunnlaugsson appeared to resign as prime minister, then quickly, and controversially, pivoted to indicate he would take a leave of absence only and not relinquish his seat in government nor his leadership role in the Progressive Party. Sigurður Ingi Jóhannsson (also of the Progressive Party) became acting prime minister.

On a wave of ensuing anti-establishment sentiment, in June 2016 Iceland elected its first new president in 20 years: historian and author Guðni Thorlacius Jóhannesson, a political outsider. In the same year, capital controls put in place during the economic meltdown began to be eased (made possible partially by the tourism boom).

Early parliamentary elections were held in October 2016, with the centre-right Independence Party (which shared power with the Progressive Party in the outgoing government) winning 29% of the vote, the Left-Green Movement 15.9% and the Pirate Party 14.5%. The Progressive Party fell to only 11.5%. At the time of research, talks were still underway to see if a coalition government could be formed.

POPULATION: **330,000**

AREA: **103,000 SQ KM**

TOURISTS: **1.3 MILLION (2015)**

SHEEP: **481,000**

ELECTRICITY PRODUCTION FROM RENEWABLES: **100%**

if Iceland were 100 people

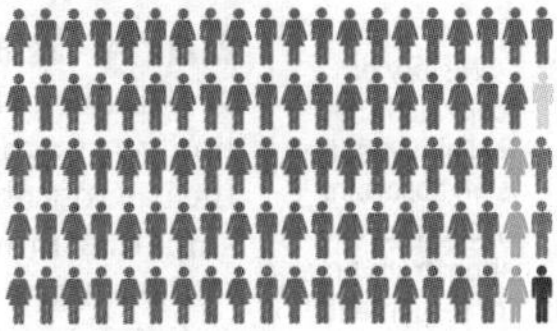

93 would be Icelandic
3 would be Polish
1 would be Nordic
2 would be other
1 would be Asian

belief systems

(% of population)

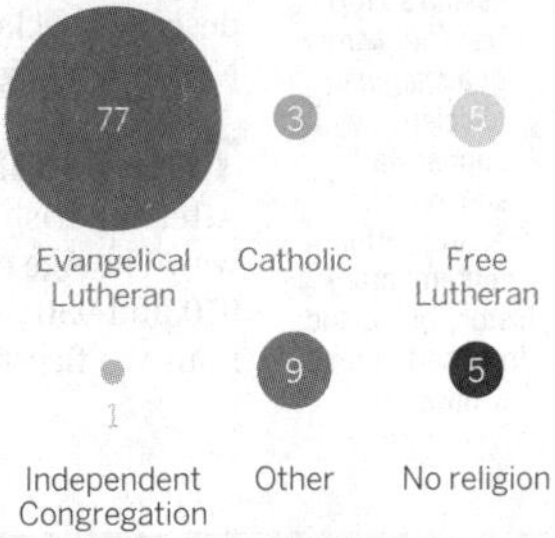

population per sq km

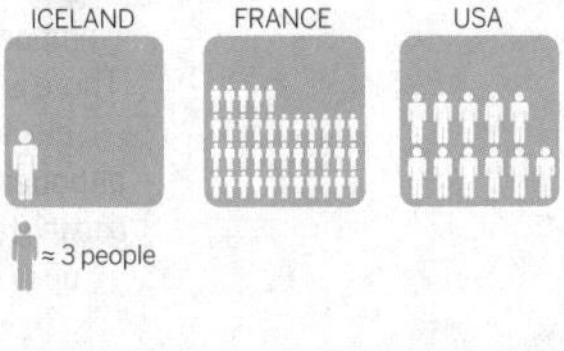

History

Geologically young, staunchly independent and frequently rocked by natural (and more recently financial) disaster, Iceland has a turbulent and absorbing history of Norse settlement, literary genius, bitter feuding and foreign oppression. Life in this harsh and unforgiving landscape was never going to be easy, but the everyday challenges and hardships have cultivated a modern Icelandic spirit that's highly aware of its stormy past, yet remarkably resilient, fiercely individualistic, quietly innovative and justifiably proud.

History of Iceland, by Jon R Hjalmarsson, is an absorbing account of the nation, from time of settlement to the book's publication in the 1990s.

Early Travellers & Irish Monks

A veritable baby in geological terms, Iceland was created around 20 million years ago. It was only around 330 BC, when the Greek explorer Pytheas wrote about the island of Ultima Thule, six days north of Britain by ship, that Europeans became aware of a landmass beyond the confines of their maps, lurking in a 'congealed sea'.

For many years rumour, myth and fantastic tales of fierce storms, howling winds and barbaric dog-headed people kept explorers away from the great northern ocean, *oceanus innavigabilis*. Irish monks were the next to stumble upon Iceland: they regularly sailed to the Faroes looking for solitude and seclusion. It's thought that Irish *papar* (fathers) settled in Iceland around the year 700. The Irish monk Dicuil wrote in AD 825 of a land where there was no daylight in winter, but on summer nights 'whatever task a man wishes to perform, even picking lice from his shirt, he can manage as well as in clear daylight'. This almost certainly describes Iceland and its long summer nights. The *papar* fled when the Norsemen began to arrive in the early 9th century.

Iceland's 1100 Years: The History of a Marginal Society, by Gunnar Karlsson, provides an insightful, contemporary history of Iceland from settlement onwards.

The Vikings are Coming!

After the Irish monks, Iceland's first permanent settlers came from Norway. The Age of Settlement is traditionally defined as the period between 870 and 930, when political strife on the Scandinavian mainland caused many to flee. Most North Atlantic Norse settlers were ordinary Scandi-

TIMELINE

AD 600–700

Irish monks voyage to uninhabited Iceland, becoming the first (temporary) settlers. There is little archaeological evidence, although the element *'papar'* (fathers) crops up in certain place names.

850–930

Norse settlers from Norway and Sweden arrive, call the island Snæland (Snow Land), then Garðarshólmi (Garðar's Island), and finally Ísland (Iceland). Scattered farmsteads rapidly cover the country.

871

Norwegian Viking Ingólfur Arnarson, credited as the country's first permanent inhabitant, sails to the southwest coast; in time he makes his home in a bay that he names Reykjavík.

navian citizens: farmers, herders and merchants who settled right across Western Europe, marrying Britons, Westmen (Irish) and Scots.

It's likely that the Norse accidentally discovered Iceland after being blown off course en route to the Faroes. The first arrival, Naddoddr, sailed from Norway and landed on the east coast around 850. He named the place Snæland (Snow Land) before backtracking to his original destination.

Iceland's second visitor, Garðar Svavarsson, circumnavigated the island and then settled in for the winter at Húsavík on the north coast. When he left in the spring some of his crew remained, or were left behind, thereby becoming the island's first residents.

Around 860 the Norwegian Flóki Vilgerðarson uprooted his farm and family and headed for Snæland. He navigated with ravens, which, after some trial and error, led him to his destination and provided his nickname, Hrafna-Flóki (Raven-Flóki). Hrafna-Flóki sailed to Vatnsfjörður on the west coast but became disenchanted after seeing icebergs floating in the fjord. He renamed the country Ísland (Iceland), and returned to Norway; although he did eventually come back to Iceland, settling in the Skagafjörður district on the north coast.

Credit for the first intentional settlement, according to the 12th-century *Íslendingabók,* goes to Ingólfur Arnarson, who fled Norway with his blood brother Hjörleifur. He landed at Ingólfshöfði (Southeast Iceland) in 871, then continued around the coast and set up house in 874 at a place he called Reykjavík (Smoky Bay), named after the steam from thermal springs there. Hjörleifur settled near the present town of Vík, but was murdered by his slaves shortly after.

As for Ingólfur, he was led to Reykjavík by a fascinating pagan ritual. It was traditional for Viking settlers to toss their high-seat pillars (a symbol of authority and part of a chieftain's paraphernalia) into the sea as they approached land. The settler's new home was established wherever the gods brought the pillars ashore – a practice imitated by waves of settlers who followed from the Norwegian mainland.

Where to Find Viking Vibes

- *National Museum (Reykjavík)*
- *Settlement Exhibition (Reykjavík)*
- *Þingvellir National Park (near Selfoss)*
- *Víkingaheimar (Njarðvík)*
- *Eiríksstaðir (reconstruction; Dalir)*
- *Stöng farmstead (Þjórsárdalur)*
- *Settlement Center (Borgarnes)*
- *Njál's Saga sites (Hvolsvöllur)*

Assembling the Alþingi

By the time Ingólfur's son Þorsteinn reached adulthood, the whole island was scattered with farms, and people began to feel the need for some sort of government. Iceland's landowners gathered first at regional assemblies to trade and settle disputes, but it became apparent that a national assembly was needed. This was a completely novel idea at the time, but Icelanders reasoned that it must be an improvement on the oppressive system they had experienced under the Nordic monarchy.

In the early 10th century Þorsteinn Ingólfsson held Iceland's first large-scale district assembly near Reykjavík, and in the 920s the

The word Viking is derived from *vík,* which means bay or cove in Old Norse and probably referred to Viking anchorages during raids.

930

The world's oldest existing parliament, the Alþingi, is founded at Þingvellir. The Icelanders' law code is memorised by an elected law speaker, who helps to settle legal matters at annual parliamentary gatherings.

986

Erik the Red founds the first permanent European colony in Greenland, building the settlements of Eystribyggð and Vestribyggð in the southwest of the country.

1000

Iceland officially converts to Christianity under pressure from the Norwegian king, though pagan beliefs and rituals remain. Leif the Lucky lands in Newfoundland, becoming the first European to reach America.

1100–1230

Iceland's literary Golden Age, during which the Old Norse sagas are written. Several are attributed to Snorri Sturluson – historian, poet and the sharpest political operator of the era.

self-styled lawyer Úlfljótur was sent to study Norway's law codes and prepare something similar that would be suitable for Iceland.

At the same time Grímur Geitskör was commissioned to find a location for the Alþingi (National Assembly). Bláskógar, near the eastern boundary of Ingólfur's estate, with its beautiful lake and wooded plain, seemed ideal. Along one side of the plain was a long cliff with an elevated base (the Mid-Atlantic Ridge), from where speakers and representatives could preside over people gathered below.

THE VIKINGS

Scandinavia's greatest impact on world history probably occurred during the Viking Age. In the 8th century, an increase in the numbers of restless, landless young men in western Norway coincided with advances in technology, as Nordic shipbuilders developed fast, manoeuvrable boats sturdy enough for ocean crossings.

Norwegian farmers had settled peacefully in Orkney and the Shetlands as early as the 780s, but the Viking Age officially began in bloodshed in 793, when Norsemen plundered St Cuthbert's monastery on Lindisfarne, an island off Britain's Northumberland coast.

The Vikings took to monasteries with delight, realising that speedy raids could bring handsome rewards. They destroyed Christian communities and slaughtered the monks of Britain and Ireland, who could only wonder what sin they had committed to invite the heathen hordes. However, the Vikings' barbarism was probably no greater than the standard of the day – it was the suddenness and extent of the raids that led to their fearsome reputation.

In the following years Viking raiders returned with great fleets, terrorising, murdering, enslaving and displacing local populations, and capturing whole regions across Britain, Ireland, France and Russia. They travelled to Moorish Spain and the Middle East, attacking Constantinople six times, and even served as mercenaries for the Holy Roman Empire.

Icelandic tradition credits the Norse settlement of Iceland to tyrannical Harald Hårfagre (Harald Fairhair), king of Vestfold in southeastern Norway. Filled with expansionist aspirations, Harald won a significant naval victory at Hafrsfjord (Stavanger) in 890. The deposed chieftains chose to flee rather than surrender, and many wound up in Iceland.

While Viking raids continued in Europe, Eiríkur Rauðe (Erik the Red) headed west with around 500 others to found the first permanent European colony in Greenland in 986. Eiríkur's son, Leif the Lucky, went on to explore the coastline of northeast America in the year 1000, naming the new country Vínland (Wineland). Permanent settlement was thwarted by the *skrælings* (Native Americans), who were anything but welcoming.

Viking raids gradually petered out, and the Viking Age ended with the death of King Harald Harðráði, last of the great Viking kings, who died in battle at Stamford Bridge, England, in 1066.

1104

Hekla's first eruption in human-historical times. The volcano covers Þjórsárdalur valley and its prosperous medieval farms with a thick layer of ash, rock and cinders.

1200

Iceland descends into anarchy during the Sturlung Age. The government dissolves and, in 1281, Iceland is absorbed by Norway.

1241

Seventy armed men arrive at Snorri Sturluson's home in Reykholt, ordered to bring him to Norway to face treason charges. Snorri never leaves – he is stabbed to death in his cellar.

1397

On 17 June the Kalmar Union is signed in Sweden, uniting the countries of Norway, Sweden and Denmark under one king. As part of this treaty, Iceland comes under Danish control.

In 930 Bláskógar was renamed Þingvellir (Assembly Plains). Þorsteinn Ingólfsson was given the honorary title *allsherjargoði* (supreme chieftain) and Úlfljótur was designated the first *lögsögumaður* (law speaker), who was required to memorise and annually recite the entire law of the land. It was he, along with the 48 *goðar* (chieftains), who held the actual legislative power.

Although squabbles arose over the choice of leaders, and allegiances were continually questioned, the new parliamentary system was a success. At the annual convention of the year 1000, the assembled crowd was bitterly divided between pagans and Christians, and civil war looked likely. Luckily, Þorgeir, the incumbent law speaker, was a master of tact. The *Íslendingabók* relates that he retired to his booth, refusing to speak to anyone for a day and a night while he pondered the matter. When he emerged, he decreed that Iceland should accept the new religion and convert to Christianity, although pagans (such as himself) were to be allowed to practise their religion in private. This decision gave the formerly divided groups a semblance of national unity, and soon the first bishoprics were set up at Skálholt in the southwest and Hólar in the north.

Over the following years, the two-week national assembly at Þingvellir became the social event of the year. All free men could attend. Single people came looking for partners, marriages were contracted and solemnised, business deals were finalised, duels and executions were held, and the Appeals Court handed down judgements on matters that couldn't be resolved in lower courts.

The Althing at Thingvellir, by Helmut Lugmayr, explains the role and history of the oldest parliament in the world and includes a section on Þingvellir's unique geology.

Anarchy & the Sturlung Age

The late 12th century kicked off the Saga Age, when epic tales of early settlement, family struggles, romance and tragic characters were recorded by historians and writers. Much of our knowledge of this time comes from two weighty tomes, the *Íslendingabók*, a historical narrative from the Settlement Era written by 12th-century scholar Ari Þorgilsson (Ari the Learned), and the detailed *Landnámabók*, a comprehensive account of the settlement.

Despite the advances in such cultural pursuits, Icelandic society was beginning to deteriorate. By the early 13th century the enlightened period of peace that had lasted 200 years was waning. Constant power struggles between rival chieftains led to violent feuds and a flourishing of Viking-like private armies, which raided farms across the country. This dark hour in Iceland's history was known as the Sturlung Age, named for the Sturlungs, the most powerful family clan in Iceland at the time. The tragic events and brutal history of this 40-year era is graphically recounted in the three-volume *Sturlunga Saga*.

Iceland Saga, by Magnús Magnússon, offers an entertaining introduction to Icelandic history and literature, and explains numerous saga events and settings. *The Sagas of Icelanders* (Jane Smiley et al; 2001) provides excellent saga translations.

1402–04

The Black Death sweeps across Iceland, 50 years after its devastating journey across mainland Europe, and kills around half of the population.

1550

King Christian III's attempts to impose Lutheranism finally succeed after the Catholic bishop Jón Arason is captured in battle and beheaded at Skálholt, along with two of his sons.

1590

Bishop Guðbrandur Þorláksson's lovely – and quite accurate – map of Iceland is published. The sea is sprinkled with whale-like monsters, and it notes that Hekla 'vomits stones with a terrible noise'.

1602

Denmark imposes a trade monopoly, giving Danish and Swedish firms exclusive trading rights in Iceland. This leads to unrestrained profiteering by Danish merchants and Iceland's slow impoverishment.

As Iceland descended into chaos, the Norwegian king Hákon Hákonarson pressured chieftains, priests and the new breed of wealthy aristocrats to accept his authority. The Icelanders, who saw no alternative, dissolved all but a superficial shell of their government and swore their allegiance to the king. An agreement of confederacy was made in 1262. In 1281 a new code of law, the *Jónsbók,* was introduced by the king, and Iceland was absorbed into Norwegian rule.

Norway immediately set about appointing Norwegian bishops to Hólar and Skálholt and imposed excessive taxes. Contention flared as former chieftains quibbled over high offices, particularly that of *járl* (earl), an honour that fell to the ruthless Gissur Þorvaldsson, who in 1241 murdered Snorri Sturluson, Iceland's best-known historian and writer.

Meanwhile, the volcano Hekla erupted three times, covering a third of the country in ash; a mini–ice age followed, and severe winters wiped out livestock and crops. The Black Death arrived, killing half the population, and the once indomitable spirit of the people seemed broken.

The Complete Sagas of Icelanders, edited by Viðar Hreinsson, is a must for saga fiends. It's a summary translation of saga tales, featuring all the main yarns, along with a few shorter fantasy tales.

Enter the Danes

Iceland's fate was now in the hands of the highest Norwegian bidder, who could lease the governorship of the country on a three-year basis. In 1397 the Kalmar Union of Norway, Sweden and Denmark brought Iceland under Danish rule. After disputes between Church and state, the Danish government seized Church property and imposed Lutheranism in the Reformation of 1550. When the stubborn Catholic bishop of Hólar, Jón Arason, resisted and gained a following, he and his two sons were taken to Skálholt and beheaded.

In 1602 the Danish king imposed a crippling trade monopoly whereby Swedish and Danish firms were given exclusive trading rights in Iceland for 12-year periods. This resulted in large-scale extortion, importation of spoilt or inferior goods, and yet more suffering that would last another 250 years. However, one positive eventually emerged from the monopoly. In an attempt to bypass the embargo and boost local industry, powerful town magistrate Skúli Magnússon built weaving, tanning and wool-dyeing factories, which would beome the foundations of the modern city of Reykjavík.

Even More Misery

If impoverishment at the hands of Danish overlords was not enough, Barbary pirates got in on the action, raiding the Eastfjords and the Reykjanes Peninsula before descending on Vestmannaeyjar in 1627. The defenceless population attempted to hide in Heimaey's cliffs and caves, but the pirates ransacked the island, killing indiscriminately and loading 242 people onto their ships. The unfortunate Icelanders were taken

1625–85

Period of the notorious Westfjords witch-hunts: 21 Icelanders are executed, beginning with Jón Rögnvaldsson, burned at the stake for 'raising a ghost' and possessing sinister-looking runic writing.

1627

The 'Turkish Abductions' take place: Barbary pirates raid the east of Iceland and the Vestmannaeyjar, taking hundreds of people prisoner and killing anyone who resists them.

1703

Iceland's first census reveals that the country's population is a tiny 50,358; 55% are female. Men – physical labourers – are more affected by malnutrition and famine.

1783–84

The Laki crater row erupts, pouring out poisonous gas clouds that kill 25% of the population and more than 50% of livestock. The haze covers Europe, causing freak weather conditions, flooding and famine.

to Algiers, where most were sold into slavery. Back home, money was scrimped and saved as ransom, and eventually 13 of the captives were freed. The most famous was Guðríður Símonardóttir, who returned to Iceland and married Hallgrímur Pétursson, one of Iceland's most famous poets – the three bells in Hallgrímskirkja are named after the couple and their daughter.

During the same period, Europe's witch-hunting craze reached Icelandic shores. Icelandic witches turned out mostly to be men – of the 130 cases that appear in the court annals, only 10% involve women. The luckiest defendants were brutally flogged; 21 of the unluckiest were burned at the stake, mostly for supposedly making their neighbours sick or for possessing magical writing or suspicious-looking amulets.

It may have been the Age of Enlightenment in Europe, but it's a wonder any Icelanders survived the 18th century. In this remote outpost in the North Atlantic, the population of 50,000 was holding on for dear life, in the face of a powerful smallpox epidemic, which arrived in 1707 and killed an estimated 18,000 people, and a series of volcanic eruptions: Katla in 1660, 1721 and again in 1755; Hekla in 1693 and 1766; and Öræfajökull in 1727.

Things got worse. In 1783 the Laki crater row erupted, spewing out billions of tonnes of lava and poisonous gas clouds for a full eight months. Fifty farms in the immediate area were wiped out, and the noxious dust and vapours and consequent Haze Famine went on to kill around 9000 Icelanders; first plants died, then livestock, then people. Ash clouds from the eruption affected the whole of Europe, causing freak weather conditions, including acid rain and floods. Authorities in Denmark contemplated relocating the remaining Icelandic population, which by 1801 numbered just 47,000, to Denmark.

Island on Fire, by Alexandra Witze and Jeff Kanipe, examines the Laki eruptions – the cataclysmic event by which Icelanders measure all other volcanic eruptions.

Return to Independence

After five centuries of oppressive foreign rule, Icelandic nationalism flourished in the 19th century, conscious of a growing sense of liberalisation across Europe. By 1855 Jón Sigurðsson, an Icelandic scholar, had successfully lobbied for restoration of free trade, and by 1874 Iceland had drafted a constitution and regained control of its domestic affairs.

Iceland's first political parties were formed during this period, and urban development began in this most rural of countries. Still, it wasn't enough to stave off the wave of emigration that had started: between 1870 and 1914, some 16,000 Icelanders left to seek a better life in North America. Reasons for emigrating included lack of opportunity – the growing fishing industry could not employ all the workers who wished to escape the hard labour of rural life and move to the new urban centres – and

Burial Rites, by Hannah Kent, is a novel based on the true story of the last public execution in Iceland. It's set in 1829 and is meticulously researched, evoking the hardships of rural Icelandic life.

1786

The official founding of Reykjavík (currently inhabited by fewer than 200 souls). The settlement is granted a trade charter, and merchants are enticed to settle here with tax breaks.

1855–90

Iceland moves towards independence, with the restoration of free trade and a draft constitution. Not everyone sticks around to see it: many Icelanders emigrate to start life afresh in North America.

1917–18

Iceland is struck by the 'Winter of the Great Frosts'. Temperatures plummet to a record low of −38°C (−36.4°F), and icebergs block all ports.

1918

Denmark's grip on Iceland gradually loosens. Following Home Rule in 1904, the Act of Union is signed on 1 December 1918, making Iceland an independent state within the Kingdom of Denmark.

yet another volcanic eruption, Askja, in 1875, which spewed livestock-poisoning ash.

By 1918 Iceland had signed the Act of Union, which effectively released the country from Danish rule, making it an independent state within the Kingdom of Denmark.

Iceland prospered during WWI as wool, meat and fish exports gained high prices. When WWII loomed, however, Iceland declared neutrality in the hope of maintaining its important trade links with both Britain and Germany.

On 9 April 1940 Denmark was occupied by Germany, prompting the Alþingi to take control of Iceland's foreign affairs once more. A year later, on 17 May 1941, Icelanders requested complete independence. The formal establishment of the Republic of Iceland finally took place at Þingvellir on 17 June 1944 – now celebrated as Independence Day.

Wasteland with Words: A Social History of Iceland, by Sigurður Gylfi Magnússon, draws on the detailed diaries and letters of Icelanders in past centuries, with a particular focus on the years from 1850 to 1940.

WWII & the USA Moves In

As a result of Germany's occupation of Denmark in 1940, Iceland was in charge of its own wartime foreign affairs (and on the path to full independence, to be established before the war's end). Wartime Iceland's complete lack of military force worried the Allied powers and so in May 1940 Britain, most vulnerable to a German-controlled Iceland, sent in forces to occupy the island. Iceland had little choice but to accept the situation, but ultimately the country's economy profited from British construction projects and spending.

When the British troops withdrew in 1941 the government allowed US troops to move in, on the understanding they would move out at the end of the war. Although the US military left in 1946, it retained the right to re-establish a base at Keflavík should war threaten again. Back under their own control, Icelanders were reluctant to submit to any foreign power. When the government was pressured into becoming a founding member of NATO in 1949, riots broke out in Reykjavík. The government agreed to the proposition on the conditions that Iceland would never take part in offensive action and that no foreign military troops would be based in the country during peacetime.

These conditions were soon broken. War with Korea erupted in 1950, and in 1951 at NATO's request the US, jumpy about the Soviet threat, once again took responsibility for the island's defence. US military personnel and technology at the Keflavík base continued to increase over the next four decades, as Iceland served as an important Cold War monitoring station. The controversial US military presence in Iceland only ended in September 2006, when the base at Keflavík finally closed.

1940–41

After the Nazis occupy Denmark, the UK sends British troops to invade and occupy neutral Iceland, concerned Germany might acquire a military presence there. A US base is later established at Keflavík.

1944

A majority of Icelanders vote for independence from Denmark, and the Republic of Iceland is formally established on 17 June. King Christian X telegrams his congratulations.

1966

Icelandic State Television begins its first broadcasts in September.

1974

The Ring Road around the island is completed when the Skeiðarárbrú bridge opens on 14 July. Until now, Höfn has been one of the most isolated towns in Iceland.

Modern Iceland

In the 20th century Iceland transformed itself from one of the poorest countries in Europe to one of the most developed.

Following the Cold War, Iceland went through a period of growth, rebuilding and modernisation. The Ring Road was completed in 1974 – opening up transport links to the remote southeast – and projects such as the Krafla power station in the northeast and the Svartsengi power plant near Reykjavík were developed. A boom in the fishing industry saw Iceland extend its fishing limit in the 1970s to 200 miles (322km). This, however, precipitated the worst of the 'cod wars', as the UK refused to recognise the new zone. During the seven-month conflict, Icelandic ships cut the nets of British trawlers, shots were fired, and ships on both sides were rammed.

The fishing industry has always been vital to Iceland, although it's had its ups and downs – quotas were reduced in the 1990s so stocks could regenerate after overfishing. The industry went into recession, leading to an unemployment rate of 3% and a sharp drop in the króna. The country slowly began a period of economic regeneration as the fishing industry stabilised. Today the industry still provides 22% of export goods and services earnings, 12% of GDP, and employs 4.2% of the workforce. It remains sensitive to declining fish stocks.

In 2003 Iceland resumed whaling as part of a scientific research program, despite a global moratorium on hunts. In 2006 Iceland resumed commercial whaling, in spite of condemnation from around the world. Hunting of minke whales continues, drawing further international rebukes; hunting of endangered fin whales was suspended in 2016.

One of the most famous essays on Iceland's financial crash of 2008 is Michael Lewis' 'Wall Street on the Tundra', written for *Vanity Fair* in 2009. Search for it online – it's a cracking read. Follow it with 'Lost', from *The New Yorker* (March 2009).

Financial Crisis & Beyond

Iceland's huge dependence on its fishing industry and on imported goods means that the country has always had relatively high prices and a currency prone to fluctuation. Its exact vulnerability was brought into focus in September 2008, when the global economic crisis hit the country with a sledgehammer blow. Reykjavík was rocked by months of fierce protest, as the then-government's popularity evaporated along with the country's wealth.

Prime Minister Geir Haarde resigned in January 2009. His replacement, Jóhanna Sigurðardóttir, hit international headlines as the world's first openly gay prime minister. Her first major act was to apply for EU membership, with the eventual aim of adopting the euro as the country's new currency, in an effort to stabilise the economy. EU membership was then and continues to be a contentious issue.

1975

The third in a series of 'cod wars' takes place between Iceland and the UK. These disputes over fishing rights in the North Atlantic flare up in the 1950s and 1970s, as Iceland expands its territorial waters.

1980

Vigdís Finnbogadóttir becomes president of Iceland, the first woman in the world to become elected head of state.

1986

The beginning of the end of the Cold War? General Secretary Mikhail Gorbachev and President Ronald Reagan agree to meet at a summit in Höfði House, Reykjavík.

2006

The controversial US military base at Keflavík closes down after 45 years in service; the government also approves the resumption of commercial whaling.

ICELAND'S ECONOMIC MELTDOWN

Between 2003 and early 2008, Iceland was full of confidence and riding high. But much of the country's wealth was built over a black hole of debt – its banks' liabilities were more than 10 times the country's annual GDP. The ripples of the worldwide financial crisis became a tidal wave by the time they reached Icelandic shores, washing away the country's entire economy.

By October 2008 the Icelandic stock market had crashed; the króna plummeted, losing almost half its value overnight; all three national banks went into receivership; and the country teetered on the brink of bankruptcy.

Help came for Iceland in November 2008 with a US$2.1 billion International Monetary Fund (IMF) loan and a US$3 billion bailout from Scandinavian neighbours. Nevertheless, spiralling inflation, wage cuts and redundancies meant that Icelanders' incomes fell by a quarter in real terms. Protestors rioted in Reykjavík, furious with a government they felt had betrayed them by not downsizing the bloated banking system.

The crash was a terrible blow to Icelanders – its legacy included high household debt, high inflation, record unemployment (peaking at 9.4% in early 2009) and the need to emigrate for work – some 5000 Icelanders moved to Norway in the four years following the crash.

Incredibly, however, the economic situation has begun to right itself. Where other countries in financial straits chose to bail out their financial institutions, the Icelandic government refused to use taxpayers' money to prop up the failing banks. Instead, it made the Icelandic social welfare system its priority, choosing to help those citizens who were worst affected by the crash and let the private banks' creditors take the hit. Though bank creditors (many of them hedge funds) are still trying to recoup their money, Iceland's approach won praise from the IMF and from numerous economists.

This unique decision appears to be paying off. While other nations are floundering in the financial mire and dealing with record unemployment rates, Iceland is on the rise again. As of 2016, unemployment is back down to around 2.9% and capital controls put in place during the recovery are beginning to be eased.

Iceland again hit global headlines in April 2010, when ash cloud from the eruption under Eyjafjallajökull ice cap shut down European air traffic for six days, causing travel chaos across much of the continent. In comparison, the Grímsvötn volcano, which erupted the following year, was a mere trifle – its ash cloud caused just three days of air-traffic disruption. In 2014, Bárðarbunga's rumblings shone a spotlight onto Iceland's volatility once again, as have Katla's jolts in 2016.

But events in Iceland have proven there's no such thing as bad publicity: triggered by the 2010 eruption and the free press it generated for Iceland, plus a concerted Icelandic effort to build airline routes and expo-

2008
The worldwide financial downturn hits Iceland particularly hard, precipitating the worst national banking crisis ever when all three of the country's major banks collapse.

2009
Iceland formally applies for EU membership – a contentious issue among the population. Formal accession talks begin in 2010, are suspended in 2013, and the application withdrawn by a new government in 2014.

2009
Jóhanna Sigurðardóttir becomes the first female Prime Minister of Iceland and the world's first openly gay head of government of the modern era.

2010
The volcano under Eyjafjallajökull glacier begins erupting in March. In April its 9km-high ash plume brings European flights to a standstill for six days. The eruption is declared over in October.

sure, tourism has boomed, increasing 264% from 2010 to 2015. The country has become the fastest-growing travel destination in Europe, with all the benefits (economic growth and employment) and headaches (infrastructure issues and environmental impact) that such status entails.

Icelanders went to the polls in April 2013 with the national economy on the path to recovery, but with the population smarting from the government's tough austerity measures (higher taxes, spending cuts). The results showed a backlash against the ruling Social Democrats; the centre-right camp (comprising the Progressive Party and the Independence Party) successfully campaigned on promises of debt relief and a cut in taxes, as well as opposition to Iceland's application to join the EU.

The two parties formed a coalition government. In early 2014 the government halted all negotiations with the EU – despite promising a referendum on whether or not to proceed with membership negotiations. Although polls show a majority of Icelanders still oppose joining the EU, making such a move without the promised referendum was deeply unpopular.

In April 2016 the Panama Papers document leak from the law firm Mossack Fonseca revealed financial improprieties implicating three Icelandic ministers, including Prime Minister Sigmundur Davíð Gunnlaugsson. As a result of massive protests, Gunnlaugsson stepped aside as prime minister. Sigurður Ingi Jóhannsson became the acting prime minister, and early elections were scheduled for October 2016, with polls indicating a close contest between the Independence Party and the direct-democracy-based Pirate Party.

In June 2016, on a wave of anti-establishment sentiment, Iceland elected its first new president in 20 years: historian and author Guðni Thorlacius Jóhannesson.

2013

In parliamentary elections, voters deliver a backlash against the Social Democrats' austerity measures in the wake of the financial crisis. A new coalition of centre-right parties forms government.

2013

The number of international visitors to Iceland numbers 807,000 (up from 320,000 in 2003). A year later, that number hovers around 1 million, and in 2015 it's 1.3 million.

2014–16

From August 2014 through mid-2015, volcanic eruptions occur at Bárðarbunga, a large volcano system under the Vatnajökull ice cap. In mid-2016 increased seismic activity is detected at Katla .

2016

As a result of financial improprieties revealed by the Panama Papers document leak from the law firm Mossack Fonseca and the protests that follow, Prime Minister Sigmundur Davíð Gunnlaugsson steps aside.

Natural Wonders

It's difficult to remain unmoved by the amazing diversity of the Icelandic landscape. Prepare to explore everything from lunar-like landscapes of ornate lava flows and towering volcanoes with misty ice caps to steep-sided glistening fjords, lush emerald-green hills, glacier-carved valleys, bubbling mudpots and vast, desert-like expanses. It is this rich mix of extraordinary scenery and the possibility of experiencing such extremes, so close together, that attracts and then dazzles visitors.

Volatile Iceland

Situated on the Mid-Atlantic Ridge, a massive 18,000km-long rift between two of the earth's major tectonic plates, Iceland is a shifting, steaming lesson in schoolroom geology. Suddenly you'll be racking your brains to remember long-forgotten homework on how volcanoes work, what a solfatara is (spoiler: it's a volcanic vent emitting hot gases), and why lava and magma aren't quite the same thing.

Iceland is one of the youngest landmasses on the planet, formed by underwater volcanic eruptions along the joint of the North American and Eurasian plates around 20 million years ago. The earth's crust in Iceland is only a third of its normal thickness, and magma (molten rock) continues to rise from deep within, forcing the two plates apart. The result is clearly visible at Þingvellir, where the great rift Almannagjá broadens by between 1mm and 18mm per year, and at Námafjall (near Mývatn), where a series of steaming vents mark the ridge.

Volcanoes

At 103,000 sq km, Iceland is roughly the size of Portugal, or the US state of Kentucky. Within its borders are some 30 active volcanoes. Its landscape is comprised of 3% lakes, 11% ice caps and glaciers, 23% vegetation, and 63% lava and other raw terrain.

Thin crust and grating plates are responsible for a host of exciting volcanic situations in Iceland. The country's volcanoes are many and varied – some are active, some extinct, and some are dormant and dreaming, no doubt, of future destruction. Fissure eruptions and their associated craters are probably the most common type of eruption in Iceland. The still-volatile Lakagígar crater row around Mt Laki mountain is the country's most extreme example. It produced the largest lava flow in human history in the 18th century, covering an area of 565 sq km to a depth of 12m.

Several of Iceland's liveliest volcanoes are found beneath glaciers, which makes for dramatic eruptions as molten lava and ice interact. The main 2010 Eyjafjallajökull eruption was of this type: it caused a *jökulhlaup* (flooding caused by volcanic eruption beneath an ice cap) that damaged part of the Ring Road, before throwing up the famous ash plume that grounded Europe's aeroplanes. Iceland's most active volcano, Grímsvötn, which lies beneath the Vatnajökull ice cap, behaved in a similar fashion in 2011.

Iceland not only has subglacial eruptions, but also submarine ones. In 1963 the island of Surtsey exploded from the sea, giving scientists the opportunity to study how smouldering chunks of newly created land are colonised by plants and animals. Surtsey is off-limits to visitors, but you can climb many classical-looking cones such as Hekla, once thought to be the gateway to Hell; Eldfell, which did its best to bury the town of Heimaey in 1974; and Snæfellsjökull on the Snæfellsnes Peninsula.

Recent eruptions in Iceland have tended to be fairly harmless – they're often called 'tourist eruptions' because their fountains of magma, electric storms and dramatic ash clouds make perfect photos but cause relatively little damage. This is partly due to the sparsely populated land, and partly because devastating features such as fast-flowing lava, lahars (mudslides) and pyroclastic surges (like the ones that obliterated Pompeii and Herculaneum) are usually absent in this part of the world.

The main danger lies in the gases that are released: suffocating carbon dioxide, highly acidic sulphur-based gases, and the deadly fluorine that poisoned people and livestock during the Laki eruptions of 1783. The Icelandic Met Office (Veðurstofa Íslands; www.vedur.is) keeps track of eruptions and the earthquakes that tend to proceed them, plus the emissions that follow. Its work during 2014–15 Bárðarbunga seismic events and volcanic activity included daily factsheets. As of 2016, the volcanoes to watch are Katla and Hekla, both well overdue for eruption.

For background information about the country's diverse geology, check out the revised 2nd-edition 2014 publication of *Iceland – Classic Geology in Europe*, by Þór Þórdarson and Armann Hoskuldsson.

Geysers, Springs & Fumaroles

Iceland's Great Geysir gave its name to the world's spouting hot springs (it comes from the Icelandic for 'to gush'). It was once very active, frequently blowing water to a height of 80m, but earthquakes have altered the pressures inside its plumbing system and today it is far quieter. Its neighbour, Strokkur, now demonstrates the effect admirably, blasting a steaming column into the air every five to 10 minutes.

Geysers are reasonably rare phenomena, with around a thousand existing on earth. However, in Iceland, water that has percolated down through the rock and been superheated by magma can emerge on the surface in various other exciting ways. Some of it boils into hot springs, pools and rivers – you'll find naturally hot water sources all around Iceland, including the springs at Landmannalaugar, the river at Hveragerði and the warm blue-white pool in the bottom of Víti crater at Askja. Icelanders have long harnessed these soothing gifts of nature, turning them into geothermal swimming pools and spas. The country's smartest spas are Mývatn Nature Baths and the Blue Lagoon, but note that they are not natural hot springs – they are human-made lagoons fed by the water output of the nearby geothermal power plants.

Fumaroles are places where superheated water reaches the surface as steam – the weirdest Icelandic examples are at Hverir, where gases

GEOLOGICALLY SPEAKING

Everywhere you go in Iceland you'll be bombarded with geological jargon to describe the landscape. These terms will let you one-up geological neophytes.

Basalt The most common type of solidified lava. This hard, dark, dense volcanic rock often solidifies into hexagonal columns.

Igneous A rock formed by solidifying magma or lava.

Moraine A ridge of boulders, clay and sand carried and deposited by a glacier.

Obsidian Black, glassy rock formed by the rapid solidification of lava without crystallisation.

Rhyolite Light-coloured, fine-grained volcanic rock similar to granite in composition.

Scoria Porous volcanic gravel that has cooled rapidly while moving, creating a glassy surface with iron-rich crystals that give it a glittery appearance.

Tephra Solid matter ejected into the air by an erupting volcano.

literally scream their way from sulphurous vents in the earth. Lazier, messier bloops and bubblings take place at mudpots, for example at Seltún (Krýsuvík) on the Reykjanes Peninsula, where heated water mixes with mud and clay. The colourful splatterings around some of the mudpots are caused by various minerals (sulphurous yellow, iron-red), and also by the extremophile bacteria and algae that somehow thrive in this boiling-acid environment.

Ice & Snow

Glaciers and ice caps cover around 11% of Iceland; many are remnants of a cool period that began 2500 years ago. Ice caps are formed as snow piles over millennia in an area where it's never warm enough to melt. The weight of the snow causes it to slowly compress into ice, eventually crushing the land beneath the ice cap.

Iceland isn't truly an Arctic country – the mainland falls short of the Arctic Circle by a few kilometres. To cross that imaginary boundary, you'll need to travel to the island of Grímsey, Iceland's only real piece of Arctic territory.

Iceland's largest ice cap, Vatnajökull in the southeast, covers about 8% of the country and is the largest in the world outside the poles. This immense glittering weight of ice may seem immovable, but around its edges, slow-moving rivers of ice – glaciers – flow imperceptibly down the mountainsides. Like rivers, glaciers carry pieces of stony sediment, which they dump in cindery-looking moraines at the foot of the mountain, or on vast gravelly outwash plains such as the Skeiðarársandur in Southeast Iceland. This can occur very quickly, if volcanoes under the ice erupt and cause a *jökulhlaup:* the *jökulhlaup* from the 1996 Grímsvötn eruption destroyed Iceland's longest bridge and swept jeep-sized boulders down onto the plain.

Several of Iceland's glaciers have lakes at their tips. Jökulsárlón is a stunning place to admire icebergs that have calved from Breiðamerkurjökull. Luminous-blue pieces tend to indicate a greater age of ice, as centuries of compression squeeze out the air bubbles that give ice its usual silvery-white appearance. Icebergs may also appear blue due to light refraction.

Glaciers have carved out much of the Icelandic landscape since its creation, forming the glacial valleys and fjords that make those picture-postcard photos of today. The ice advances and retreats with the millennia, and also with the seasons, but there are worrying signs that Iceland's major ice caps – Vatnajökull, Mýrdalsjökull in the southwest, and Langjökull and Hofsjökull in the highlands – have been melting at an unprecedented rate since 2000. Glaciologists believe the ice cap Snæfellsjökull in the west (with an average ice thickness of only 30m), as well as some of the outlet glaciers of the larger ice caps, could disappear completely within a few decades. Others have lost their glacier status due to melting, such as West Iceland's Ok (formerly Okjökull) in 2014.

Wildlife

Mammals & Marine Life

In 2002 scientists discovered the world's second-smallest creature, *Nanoarchaeum equitans,* living in near-boiling water in a hydrothermal vent off the north coast of Iceland. The name means 'riding the fire sphere'.

Apart from birds, sheep and horses, you'll be lucky to have any casual sightings of animals in Iceland. The only indigenous land mammal is the elusive Arctic fox, best spotted in remote Hornstrandir in the Westfjords. In East Iceland, herds of reindeer can sometimes be spotted from the road. Reindeer were introduced from Norway in the 18th century and now roam the mountains in the east. Polar bears very occasionally drift across from Greenland on ice floes, but armed farmers make sure they don't last long.

In contrast, Iceland has a rich marine life, particularly whales. On whale-watching tours from Húsavík in northern Iceland, you'll have an excellent chance of seeing cetaceans, particularly dolphins, porpoises, minke whales and humpback whales. Sperm, fin, sei, pilot, orca and blue whales also swim in Icelandic waters and have been seen by visitors.

LITTLE NORTHERN BROTHERS

Cute, clumsy and endearingly comic, the puffin (*Fratercula arctica*, or *lundi* as they're called in Icelandic) is one of Iceland's best-loved birds. Although known for its frantic fluttering and crash landings, the bird is surprisingly graceful underwater and was once thought to be a bird-fish hybrid.

The puffin is a member of the auk family and spends most of its year at sea. For four or five months it comes to land to breed, generally keeping the same mate and burrow (a multiroom apartment!) from year to year.

Until very recently, 60% of the world's puffins bred in Iceland, and you could see them in huge numbers around the island from late May to August. However, over the last decade, the puffin stock has gone into a sudden, sharp decline in the south of Iceland. They still visit the south – Vestmannaeyjar Islands' puffins are the largest puffin colony in the world – but in smaller numbers and with considerably less breeding success. The reason is uncertain, but it's thought that warming ocean temperatures have caused their main food source – sand eels – to decline. It's also possible that hunting and egg collection have had an effect.

The good news for twitchers is that puffins in the north and west seem less affected (for now). The photogenic birds continue to flitter around the cliffs of Grímsey and Drangey, as well as in Borgarfjörður Eystri, the Westfjords and Snæfellsnes.

Seals can be seen in the Eastfjords, on the Vatnsnes Peninsula in Northwest Iceland, in the Mýrar region on the southeast coast (including at Jökulsárlón), in Breiðafjörður in the west, and in the Westfjords.

Birds

Bird life is prolific, at least from May to August. On coastal cliffs and islands around the country you can see a mind-boggling array of seabirds, often in massive colonies. Most impressive for their sheer numbers are gannets, guillemots, gulls, razorbills, kittiwakes, fulmars and puffins. Less numerous birds include wood sandpipers, Arctic terns, skuas, Manx shearwaters, golden plovers, storm petrels and Leach's petrels. In the southern Westfjords you can occasionally spot endangered white-tailed eagles. In addition, there are many species of ducks, ptarmigans, whooping swans, redwings, divers and gyrfalcons, and two species of owls.

Flowers & Fungi

Although Iceland was largely deforested long ago, its vegetation is surprisingly varied – you just need to get close to see it. Most vegetation is low-growing, spreading as much as possible to get a better grip on the easily eroded soil. Wind erosion and damage from off-road drivers are big conservation issues. Even the trees, where there are any, are stunted. As the old joke goes, if you're lost in an Icelandic forest, just stand up.

If you're visiting in summer, you'll be treated to incredible displays of wildflowers blooming right across the country. Most of Iceland's 450 flowering plants are introduced species – especially the ubiquitous purple lupin, once an environmental help, now a hindrance. A nationwide poll held in 2004 voted for the mountain avens *(Dryas octopetala)*, known as *holtasóley* (heath buttercup) in Icelandic, as the national flower. Look out for it on gravel stretches and rocky outcrops – its flowers are about 3cm in diameter, each with eight delicate white petals and an exploding yellow-sun centre.

Coastal areas are generally characterised by low grasses, bogs and marshlands, while at higher elevations hard or soft tundra covers the ground.

Another common sight when walking almost anywhere in Iceland is fungi. There are about 2000 types growing here, and you'll see everything

Imported by the Vikings, the purebred Icelandic horse *(Equus scandinavicus)* is a small, tough breed perfectly suited to the country's rough conditions. Icelandic horses have five gaits, including the unusual *tölt* – a running walk so smooth that riders can drink a glass of beer without spilling a drop.

from pale white mushrooms to bright orange flat caps as you walk along trails, by roadsides or through fields.

In southern and eastern Iceland new lava flows are first colonised by mosses, which create a velvety green cloak across the rough rocks. Older lava flows in the east and those at higher elevations are generally first colonised by lichens. Confusingly, Icelandic moss *(Cetraria islandica)*, the grey-green or pale brown frilly growth that you'll see absolutely everywhere, is actually lichen.

A Guide to the Flowering Plants and Ferns of Iceland, by Hörður Kristinsson, is the best all-round field guide to Icelandic flowers.

National Parks & Reserves

Iceland has three national parks and more than 100 nature reserves, natural monuments and country parks, with a protected area of 18,806 sq km (about 18% of the entire country). A proposed Highland National Park (www.halendid.is) would protect a vast section of Iceland's interior (40,000 sq km), comprising a full 40% of the country.

Umhverfisstofnun (Environment Agency of Iceland; www.ust.is) is responsible for protecting many of these sites. Its website contains information on its work to promote the protection as well as sustainable use of Iceland's natural resources, including on how travellers can tread lightly. The agency also recruits summer volunteers each year, to work in conservation projects within the parks.

Þingvellir National Park (p111), Iceland's oldest national park, protects a scenic 84-sq-km lake, the geologically significant Almannagjá rift, and is the site of the original Alþingi (National Assembly). The park is a Unesco World Heritage Site. Snæfellsjökull National Park (p189) in West Iceland was established in June 2001. The park protects the Snæfellsjökull glacier (made famous by author Jules Verne), the surrounding lava fields and coast. Vatnajökull National Park (p326) is the largest national park in Europe and covers roughly 13% of Iceland. It was founded in 2008 by uniting two previously established national parks: Skaftafell in Southeast Iceland, and Jökulsárgljúfur further north. The park protects the entirety of the Vatnajökull ice cap, the mighty Dettifoss waterfall and a great variety of geological anomalies.

Garden angelica *(Angelica archangelica)* grows wild in many parts of Iceland. It's been valued as a medicinal herb since Viking times, and these days is appearing in more and more recipes. Kaldi beer even has a brew (known as Stinnings Kaldi) with angelica as an ingredient.

Energy Agendas

Iceland's small population, pristine wilderness, lack of heavy industry and high use of geothermal and hydroelectric power (66% and 20% of primary energy use, respectively, in 2014) give it an enviable environmental reputation. Its use of geothermal power is one of the most creative in the world, and the country's energy experts are now advising Asian and African industries on possible ways to harness geothermal sources.

However, power supplies provided free by bountiful nature are not just of interest to Icelanders. Foreign industrialists in search of cheap energy also have their eye on the country's glacial rivers and geothermal hot spots. Alcoa, an American aluminium-smelting company, was responsible for one of Iceland's most controversial schemes: the Kárahnjúkar hydroelectric station (p369) in East Iceland, completed in 2009, was the biggest construction project in Iceland's history. It created a network of dams and tunnels, a vast reservoir, a power station and miles of power lines to supply electricity to a fjordside smelter 80km away in Reyðarfjörður.

Alcoa makes much of its efforts to reduce its carbon footprint – and it's true that the aluminium it manufactures in Iceland uses cheap, green energy from renewable sources (this was the whole point of closing two US smelters and setting up here). What can't be denied, however, is that the mega-dam built specifically to power the Alcoa plant has devastated the landscape. Environmentalists raised serious objections to the project, on a number of grounds, but locals were less vocal with objections – many were grateful for work opportunities coming to the area. Bear in mind that East Iceland has a population of only 12,500; imagine how hard it might be to fight government decisions and multinational corporations.

The Power of Power

The Kárahnjúkar dam and aluminium smelter are a dramatic illustration of the dilemma Iceland faces. To ensure economic prosperity, Iceland is seeking to shore up its position as a green-energy superpower. Thanks to its rich geothermal and hydroelectric energy sources, and new wind turbines (read more at www.nea.is), Iceland generates more electricity per capita than any other country in the world – and double as much as second-placed Norway. Interestingly, Iceland also uses more energy per capita than any other nation. Eighty per cent of Iceland's electricity is sold to a handful of international companies based in Iceland, such as aluminium smelters, but exporting electricity would bring in new revenue.

Iceland and the UK are moving through the initial feasibility studies of exporting clean hydroelectric energy via a 1000km subsea power cable running from Iceland to the UK (known as IceLink in the UK; read more at www.atlanticsuperconnection.com). Iceland is also continuing

WHALING IN ICELAND

In the late 19th century, whale hunting became a lucrative commercial prospect with the arrival of steam-powered ships and explosive harpoons. Norwegian hunters built 13 large-scale whaling stations in Iceland, and hunted until stocks practically disappeared in 1913. Icelanders established their own whaling industry in 1935, until whale numbers again became dangerously low and commercial hunting was banned by the International Whaling Commission (IWC) in 1986. Iceland resumed commercial whaling in 2006, to the consternation of environmentalists worldwide. The question of why Iceland is whaling today is not a simple one to answer.

Iceland's authorities stress that the country's position has always been that whale stocks should be utilised in a sustainable manner like any other living marine resource. Its catch limits for common minke whales and fin whales follow the advice given by the Marine Research Institute of Iceland regarding sustainability – the advice for the 2014 and 2015 seasons was for an annual maximum catch of 229 minke whales and 154 fin whales, respectively.

Those numbers stir passions, especially given that fin whales are classified as endangered globally on the International Union for Conservation of Nature (IUCN) Red List. In 2016 fin whaling was halted due to trade difficulties with Japan, though it is unclear what the future will bring.

Members of Iceland's tourism board are strong objectors to whaling, stating that Iceland's whaling industry will have a detrimental effect on whale watching (although this is disputed by the Ministry of Industries and Innovation). With the boom in tourist numbers, the idea is that a whale is worth more alive (for watching) than dead (for eating). Ironically, estimates are that from 40% to 60% of Icelandic whale meat consumption is by curious tourists, with only 3% of Icelanders eating whale meat regularly; much is exported to Japan, though demand has declined there, too. In 2012 the International Fund for Animal Welfare (IFAW) and IceWhale (Icelandic Whale Watching Association) launched a high-profile 'Meet Us Don't Eat Us' campaign to encourage visitors to go whale watching rather than whale tasting, and their 2016 petition garnered more than 100,000 signatures. Their website and *Whappy* app list whale-friendly restaurants in Iceland.

Icelandic whaling has attracted other international condemnation – in 2014, a formal diplomatic protest (known as a démarche) against whaling was delivered to the Icelandic government from 35 nations, including the US, Australia and members of the EU. A US-based campaign, 'Don't Buy From Icelandic Whalers' (www.dontbuyfromicelandicwhalers.com), encourages the public not to buy fish from suppliers and retailers who source from Icelandic companies linked to whaling. But, for the moment, whaling continues.

to expand its power-intensive industries, including becoming a global data-centre hub, home to the servers housing all our digitised information.

But if such initiatives go ahead, the power must still be harnessed, and power plants and power lines must be built for such a purpose. Where will these be located? What other tracts of Iceland's highland wilderness may be threatened by industrial megaprojects? NGO organisation Landvernd (www.landvernd.is), the Icelandic Environment Association, has proposed that the central highlands be protected with the establishment of a national park. Economic profit versus the preservation of nature – it's an age-old battle. Watch this space.

The Forlagið (Mál og Menning) series of maps now includes some fun themed ones: *Fuglakort* (Birdwatcher's Map), *Höggunarkort* (Tectonic Map), *Jarðfræðikort* (Geological Map) and *Plöntukortið* (Botanical Map). The text is in Icelandic, English and German.

The Impact of Tourism on Nature

Well over 1.5 million visitors per year head to Iceland for their dream holiday in a vast natural playground. And guess what? This boom in numbers is threatening the very thing everyone is travelling to see: Iceland's unspoilt nature.

Icelanders are voicing a valid concern that the population of 330,000 and its existing infrastructure is ill-equipped to handle the demands and behaviour of visitors. Media consistently reports instances of tourists disrespecting nature or taking dangerous risks: hiking in poor weather without proper equipment, getting vehicles stuck in rivers, driving cars onto glaciers, falling off cliffs or being swept off beaches. In February 2016, for example, tourists hopped across icebergs in Jökulsárlón. Footage and social media showing cavalier, risky behaviour like this (see also Justin Bieber rolling in fragile moss in his 2015 'I'll Show You' video) further encourages a disregard for rules, signs and common sense.

The people on the hook for rescues are the extraordinarily competent and well-respected Icelandic Association for Search and Rescue (ICE-SAR; www.icesar.com). It is an all-volunteer operation paid for by donation. A good article on the organisation, 'Life Is Rescues', appeared in *The New Yorker* in November 2015. ICE-SAR puts a huge emphasis on accident prevention and education with its informative website (www.safetravel.is) and '112 Iceland' app that allows travellers to register hikes and trips.

Icelanders have responded by erecting more signs – despite the fact locals tend to abhor them (they mar the landscape); ropes along some walkways – which some visitors continue to flout; and an educational campaign (http://inspired.visiticeland.com/academy). The government has also instituted camping rules requiring campervans to spend the night in organised campgrounds rather than on roadsides or in car parks, to address the problem of people using the roadside as their bathroom.

Ultimately the protection of Iceland's environment will be a joint project between Icelanders – by building out their infrastructure and rules, and fostering an attitude of environmental protection – and visitors – who can heed local advice and respect the country they are visiting.

Dreamland: A Self-Help Manual for a Frightened Nation by Andri Snær Magnason critically examines the government's decisions over Kárahnjúkar dam. The powerful documentary based on the book, *Dreamland* (2009), won critical acclaim.

Proposed Visitor Fees & Caps

A continuously debated proposal involves the introduction of a one-off fee, ensuring travellers contribute to the protection and maintenance of natural sites – perhaps an arrival tax payable at the airport, or a nature pass purchased according to the length of your stay. It doesn't seem like an unreasonable request – especially when one looks at it in the context of Iceland's tiny population, now hosting hordes of trekkers and buses full of holidaymakers all requiring car parks, toilet blocks, picnic tables, rubbish bins, improved signage, not to mention rangers providing information and safety advice.

There's occasional talk of lotteries or limits on visitor numbers in certain regions or on certain trails (such as the Laugavegurinn hike), but so far no new policies or legislation have been set down. Stay tuned.

Icelandic Culture

Iceland blows away concerns such as isolation, never-ending winter nights and its small population with a glowing passion for all things cultural. The country's unique literary heritage begins with high-action medieval sagas and stretches to today's Nordic Noir bestsellers. Every Icelander seems to play in a band, and the country produces a disproportionate number of world-class musicians. The way of life and grand landscapes inspire visual artists who use film, art and design to capture their unique Icelandic perspectives.

Literature

Bloody, mystical and nuanced, the late 12th- and 13th-century sagas are some of Iceland's greatest cultural achievements. Reverend Hallgrímur Pétursson's 1659 *Passíusálmar* (Passion Hymns) were an Icelandic staple, sung or read at Lent. Nobel Prize–winning author Halldór Laxness put Iceland on the 20th-century literary map. But Icelanders aren't resting on their laurels: today the country produces the most writers and literary translations per capita of any country in the world.

The Sagas

Iceland's medieval prose sagas are some of the most imaginative and enduring works of early literature – epic, brutal tales that flower repeatedly with wisdom, magic, elegiac poetry and love.

Written down during the 12th to early 14th centuries, these sagas look back on the disputes, families, doomed romances and larger-than-life characters (from warrior and poet to outlaw) who lived during the Settlement Era. Most were written anonymously, though *Egil's Saga* has been attributed to Snorri Sturluson. Some are sources for historical understanding, such as *The Saga of the Greenlanders* and *Saga of Erik the Red,* which describe the travels of Erik and his family, including his son Leif (a settler in North America).

The sagas, written over the long, desperate centuries of Norwegian and Danish subjugation, provided a strong sense of cultural heritage at a time when Icelanders had little else. On winter nights, people would gather for the *kvöldvaka* (evening vigil). While the men twisted horsehair ropes and women spun wool or knitted, a family member would read the sagas and recite *rímur* (verse reworkings of the sagas).

The sagas are very much alive today. Icelanders of all ages can (and do) read them in Old Norse, the language in which they were written 800 years ago. Most people can quote chunks from them, know the farms where the characters lived and died, and flock to cinemas to see the latest film versions of these eternal tales. Check out the Icelandic Saga Database (www.sagadb.org) for more.

An old Icelandic saying is *Betra er berfættum en bókarlausum að vera* ('It's better to be barefoot than bookless'). Icelanders remain passionate about the written word, so it's fitting that Reykjavík is a Unesco City of Literature, with tours and programs to match.

Eddic & Skaldic Poetry

The first settlers brought their oral poetic tradition with them from other parts of Scandinavia, and the poems were committed to parchment in the 12th century.

TOP ICELANDIC SAGAS

Egil's Saga Revolves around the complex, devious but sensitive Egill Skallagrímsson, and much of it is set near modern-day Borgarnes. A renowned poet or *skald*, triumphant warrior and skilled negotiator, Egill is also the grandson of a werewolf/shapeshifter, and unlike most Saga protagonists, lived to a ripe old age.

Laxdæla Saga A tragic saga set in Northwest Iceland around Breiðafjörður and the Dalir: bitter marriages, thwarted love and murder abound.

Njál's Saga Two of Iceland's greatest heroes, Njál and Gunnar, are drawn into a fatal, 50-year family feud.

Gisli Sursson's Saga The quintessential outlaw story, Gisli's tale involves revenge, fratricide and banishment.

Völsungasaga (Saga of the Völsungs) Parts of this saga may seem familiar – Richard Wagner *(Der Ring des Nibelungen)* and JRR Tolkien *(Lord of the Rings)* both swiped episodes.

Eyrbyggja Saga A minor saga set around the Snæfellsnes Peninsula, worth reading for its offbeat, supernatural tone; definitely the only medieval Icelandic work where ghosts are taken to court over their hauntings.

Eddic poems were composed in free, variable meters with a structure very similar to that of early Germanic poetry. Probably the most well known is the gnomic *Hávamál,* which extols the virtues of the common life – its wise proverbs on how to be a good guest are still quoted today.

Skaldic poems were composed by *skalds* (Norwegian court poets) and are mainly praise-poems of Scandinavian kings, with lots of description packed into tightly structured lines. As well as having fiercely rigid alliteration, syllable counts and stresses, Skaldic poetry is made more complex by *kennings,* a kind of compact word-riddle. Blood, for instance, is 'wound dew', while an arm might be described as a 'hawk's perch'.

The most renowned *skald* was saga anti-hero Egill Skallagrímsson. In 948, after being captured and sentenced to death, Egill composed the ode *Höfuðlausn* (Head Ransom) for his captor Eirík Blood-Axe. Flattered, the monarch released Egill unharmed.

Iceland publishes the greatest number of books per capita in the world, and the literacy rate is a perfect 100%.

Modern Literature

Nobel Prize–winner Halldór Laxness is Iceland's modern literary genius. Also well known is the early-20th-century children's writer Reverend Jón Sveinsson (nicknamed Nonni), whose old-fashioned tales of derring-do have a rich Icelandic flavour and were once translated into 40 languages; *At Skipalón* is the only one readily available in English. Sveinsson's house in Akureyri is now an interesting museum. Two other masters of Icelandic literature are Gunnar Gunnarsson (1889–1975; look for *The Sworn Brothers, a Tale of the Early Days of Iceland,* 2012) and Þórbergur Þórðarson (1888–1974; look for *The Stones Speak,* 2012).

For more contemporary fare, try Einar Kárason's outstanding *Devil's Island,* the first of a trilogy about Reykjavík life in the 1950s; unfortunately, the other two parts haven't yet been translated into English. Hallgrímur Helgason's *101 Reykjavík* is the book on which the cult film was based. It's a dark comedy following the torpid life and fertile imagination of out-of-work Hlynur, who lives in downtown Reykjavík with his mother. Even blacker is *Angels of the Universe,* by Einar Már Gudmundsson, which is about a schizophrenic man's spells in a psychiatric hospital. Svava Jakobsdóttir's *Gunnlöth's Tale* blends contemporary life with Nordic mythology.

Currently surfing the Nordic Noir tidal wave is Arnaldur Indriðason, whose Reykjavík-based crime fiction permanently tops the bestseller lists. Many of his novels are available in English, including *Voices,* the award-winning *Silence of the Grave, The Draining Lake* and, our favourite, *Tainted Blood* (also published as *Jar City,* and the inspiration for a film of the same name). Yrsa Sigurðardóttir's thrillers have also been widely translated – her latest are *Someone to Watch Over Me* and *The Undesired.* Dip into Ragnar Jónasson's Dark Iceland series with *Snowblind,* set in remote Siglufjörður.

Also look for Guðrún Eva Mínervudóttir's *The Creator,* a dark psychological novel. Former Sugarcube collaborator Sjón's *The Blue Fox* is a fantasy-adventure tale set in the 19th century; or try his most recent: *Moonstone – The Boy Who Never Was.*

Music

Pop, Rock & Electronica

Iceland punches above its weight in the pop- and rock-music worlds. Internationally famous Icelandic musicians include (of course) Björk and her former band, The Sugarcubes. From her platinum album *Debut* (1993) to her most recent, *Vulnicura* (2015), Björk continues to be a force.

Sigur Rós followed Björk to stardom. Try their albums *Ágætis Byrjun* (1999) or *Takk* (2005), which garnered rave reviews around the world, or their most recent, *Kveikur* (2013). The band's concert movie *Heima* (2007) is a must-see. Lead singer Jónsi had success with his joyful solo album *Go* (2010).

Indie-folk Of Monsters and Men stormed the US charts in 2011 with their debut album, *My Head is an Animal.* The track 'Little Talks' from that album reached number one on the Billboard US Alternative Songs chart in 2012. Their latest album, *Beneath the Skin* (2015), debuted at number three on the US Billboard 200.

HALLDÓR LAXNESS

Over his long lifetime, Nobel Prize–winner Halldór Laxness (1902–98) succeeded in reshaping the world of Icelandic literature, and reviving the saga-scale story. Today he is Iceland's most celebrated 20th-century author.

Laxness was born as Halldór Guðjónsson, but he took the name of his family's farm Laxnes (with an extra 's') as his nom de plume. Ambitious and inquisitive, Laxness had his first work published at the age of 14, and began his restless wanderings at 17. He wrote his first novel, *Undir Helgahnúk* (Under the Holy Mountain), from a monastery during a period of fervent Catholicism. Laxness then left for Italy, where his disaffection with the Church and increasingly leftist leanings led to the writing of *Vefarinn Mikli frá Kasmír* (The Great Weaver from Kashmir). In the 1930s he moved to America to try his luck in the fledgling Hollywood film industry, before becoming enthralled with communism and travelling widely in the Soviet Bloc. In 1962 the author settled at Laxnes, near Þingvellir, for good; his home is now a museum. It was here that he wrote *Skáldatími* (Poets' Time), a poignant recantation of everything he'd ever written in praise of the Communist Party.

In 1955 Laxness won the Nobel Prize for Literature and became, in true Icelandic style, a hero of the people. His works are masterpieces of irony, and his characters, however misguided, are drawn with sympathy. Unfortunately, only a portion of his 51 novels and countless short stories, articles, plays and poems are currently available in translation, the most famous of which is *Independent People* (1934–35). This bleak tragi-comedy is told in lush, evocative language and deals with the harsh conditions of early-20th-century Icelandic life. It focuses on the bloody-minded farmer Bjartur of Summerhouses and his toiling family, and creates a detailed depiction of traditional farmstead life. Also fascinating is *Iceland's Bell,* a saga-like portrait of extreme poverty and skewed justice, set in an Iceland subjugated by Danish rule. Other translated works are *World Light, The Fish Can Sing, Paradise Reclaimed, The Atom Station* and *Under the Glacier*.

Ásgeir Trausti, who records simply as Ásgeir, had a breakout hit with *In the Silence* (2014), an English-language album, and sells out concerts internationally.

Reykjavík has a flourishing music scene with a constantly changing line-up of new bands and sounds – see www.icelandmusic.is for an idea of the variety.

Seabear, an indie-folk band, have spawned several top music-makers such as Sin Fang (try *Flowers* from 2013) and Sóley (*We Sink* from 2012, *Ask the Deep* from 2015). Árstíðir record minimalist indie-folk, and had a 2013 YouTube hit when they sang a 13th-century Icelandic hymn a cappella in a train station in Germany. They released *Verloren Verleden* with Anneke van Giersbergen in 2016. Kiasmos is a duo mixing moody, minimalist electronica; check out their album also called *Kiasmos* (2014).

Reykjavík's cutting-edge Harpa concert hall, with its facade of glimmering hexagons, has four state-of-the art stages and amazing acoustics. It's a great place to catch a show.

GusGus, a local pop-electronica act, have nine studio albums to their credit and opened for Justin Timberlake at his sold-out 2014 concert in Reykjavík. In September 2016, Sturla Atlas, the Icelandic hip hop/R&B phenom opened for the other Justin (Bieber); Bieber's video *I'll Show You* was shot in Iceland. Another well-known Icelandic rapper is Gisli Pálmi.

FM Belfast, an electronica band, set up their own recording label to release their first album, *How to Make Friends* (2008); their latest is *Brighter Days* (2014).

Múm makes experimental electronica mixed with traditional instruments (their latest is *Smilewound*; 2013). Their member Sigurlaug Gísladóttir released *Mr. Silla* in 2015. Prins Póló, named after a candy bar, records lyric-heavy dance-pop. Also check out Hafdís Huld, whose latest pop album is called *Home*, and ebullient garage-rockers Benny Crespo's Gang. Just Another Snake Cult heads towards the psychedelic with *Cupid Makes a Fool of Me* (2013). Or check out Singapore Sling for straight-up rock and roll. The list goes on. And on.

Tips on Finding Music

Similarly, Reykjavík's live-music venues are ever-changing – the best thing to do is to check the free publication *Reykjavík Grapevine* (www.grapevine.is) or its app (called Appening) for current news and listings. Increasingly, live local music can be found all over Iceland. If your trip coincides with one of the country's many music festivals, go! The fabulous Iceland Airwaves (p27) festival (held in Reykjavík in November) showcases Iceland's talent along with international acts, as does Secret Solstice (June).

Traditional Music

Until rock and roll arrived in the 20th century, Iceland was a land practically devoid of musical instruments. The Vikings brought the *fiðla* and the *langspil* with them from Scandinavia – both a kind of two-stringed box rested on the player's knee and played with a bow. They were never solo instruments but merely served to accompany singers.

Reykjavík Arts Festival (late May to early June) is a great chance to see the intersection of Icelandic visual, literary, musical and performing arts.

Instruments were generally an unheard-of luxury and singing was the sole form of music. The most famous song styles are *rímur* (poetry or stories from the sagas performed in a low, eerie chant; Sigur Rós have dabbled with the form), and *fimmundasöngur* (sung by two people in harmony). Cut off from other influences, the Icelandic singing style barely changed from the 14th century to the 20th century; it also managed to retain harmonies that were banned by the church across the rest of Europe on the basis of being the work of the devil.

You'll find choirs around Iceland performing traditional music, and various compilation albums, such as *Inspired by Harpa – The Traditional Songs of Iceland* (2013), give a sampling of Icelandic folk songs or *rímur*.

Cinema & Television

Iceland's film industry is young – regular production started around the early 1980s – but it has created some distinctive work to date. Both short-form and feature-length Icelandic films have received all kinds of international awards and prestige, and they often contain thought-provoking subject matter and superb cinematography, using Iceland's powerful landscape as a backdrop.

For the latest on Icelandic feature films, documentaries and animation, visit the website www.icelandicfilmcenter.is.

In 1992 the film world first took notice of Iceland when *Children of Nature* was nominated for an Academy Award for Best Foreign Film. In it, an elderly couple forced into a retirement home in Reykjavík make a break for the countryside. The director, Friðrik Þór Friðriksson, is something of a legend in Icelandic cinema circles. *Cold Fever* (1994), *Angels of the Universe* (2000) and *The Sunshine Boy* (2009) are well worth watching, and he also produces many films.

Another film to put Reykjavík on the cinematic map was *101 Reykjavík* (2000), directed by Baltasar Kormákur and based on the novel by Hallgrímur Helgason. This dark comedy explores sex, drugs and the life of a loafer in downtown Reykjavík. Kormákur's *Jar City* (2006) stars the ever-watchable Ingvar E Sigurðsson as Iceland's favourite detective, Inspector Erlendur, from the novels by Arnaldur Indriðason. Kormákur's 2012 film, *The Deep,* based on a true story of a man who saved himself from a shipwreck in the Vestmannaeyjar Islands, was a hit, and in 2013 he launched into Hollywood with *2 Guns,* starring Denzel Washington and Mark Wahlberg. *Everest* (2015) starred Keira Knightley, Robin Wright and Jake Gyllenhaal. Kormákur has established RVK Studios, which also produced the hit TV series *Ófærð* (Trapped; 2015), an excellent, moody crime drama set in Seyðisfjörður in East Iceland (though filmed in Siglufjörður in the north). His thriller *The Oath* (*Eiðurinn*) was released in 2016.

Benedikt Erlingsson's 2013 *Of Horses and Men* was an indie sensation for its surreal portrait of the lives of men and horses, from the horses' perspective. It was nominated as Iceland's entry to the Academy Awards. Erlingsson is also an actor, and had a role in Rúnar Rúnarsson's 2011 *Volcano* (Eldfjall), about an aging couple who evacuated the Vestmannaeyjar

READY FOR ITS CLOSE-UP

Iceland has become a Hollywood darling for location shooting. Its immense, alien beauty and the government's 20% production rebate for film-makers have encouraged Hollywood directors to make movies here. Try to spot the Icelandic scenery in blockbusters such as *Tomb Raider* (2001), *Die Another Day* (2002), *Batman Begins* (2005), *Flags of Our Fathers* (2006), *Stardust* (2007), *Journey to the Centre of the Earth* (2008), *Prometheus* (2012), *Oblivion* (2013), *Star Trek: Into Darkness* (2013), *The Secret Life of Walter Mitty* (2013), *Noah* (2014) and the HBO series *Game of Thrones* (locations from Mývatn to Gjáin). Christopher Nolan–hit *Interstellar* (2014) and recent Star Wars installment *The Force Awakens* (2015) were shot here too. The TV series *Fortitude* is an English production filmed in Reyðarfjörður in East Iceland (though set in Norway). And then there are films such as *Land Ho!* (2014), both set and shot in Iceland.

Film and TV directors aren't the only ones who ditch the CGI and get the real thing in Iceland. Musicians shoot videos here, too, including Icelandic talents Björk, Of Monsters and Men and Sigur Rós. Don't miss Sigur Rós' inspiring concert film *Heima* (2007), starring the Icelandic people and their roaring falls and towering mountains. Bon Iver's 2011 video 'Holocene' is six minutes that the Icelandic Tourist Board should co-opt for its ad campaigns. And Justin Bieber's 2015 'I'll Show' You is an advertisement in what not to do (moss destruction and glacial lagoon bathing).

Some tour companies offer tours tailored to film locations; also check out the app *Iceland Film Locations* (www.filmlocations.is).

islands during the eruption of Eldfjall, and how they reconcile illness with family. *Sparrows* (Þrestir), Rúnarsson's disturbing portrait of the growing pains of a young man moved from Reykjavík to a remote town in the Westfjords (much was filmed in Flatey), saw success in 2015.

Hrútar (Rams; 2015), directed by Grímur Hákonarson, is an engrossing comedy-drama about two estranged brothers and their sheep. It was a break-out hit internationally, winning the prize Un Certain Regard at Cannes and becoming the Icelandic entry at the 2016 Academy Awards.

For lighter fare, watch *The Homecoming* (Blóðberg; 2015), a sly modern comedy-drama where a 'perfect' family's life goes topsy-turvy. Or find 2015's *Albatross,* where city boy Tommi shores up for the summer at the Bolungarvík golf club with a nutty cast of characters.

Other titles can be found at www.icelandiccinema.com.

Many Icelandic painters and musicians are serious creative artists in multiple disciplines. Some are making a splash overseas, such as Ragnar Kjartansson, who represents a new breed of Icelandic artist: part painter, part actor, director and musician. Reykjavík Art Museum's Hafnarhús and Reykjavík galleries do a great job showcasing such artists.

Painting & Sculpture

Many of Iceland's most successful artists have studied abroad before returning home to wrestle with Iceland's enigmatic soul. The result is a European-influenced style, but with Icelandic landscapes and saga-related scenes as key subjects. Refreshingly, you'll find museums stocked with wonderful works by men and women alike.

The first great Icelandic landscape painter was the prolific Ásgrímur Jónsson (1876–1958), who produced a startling number of Impressionistic oils and watercolours depicting Icelandic landscapes and folk tales. You can see his work at the National Gallery in Reykjavík.

One of Ásgrímur's students was Johannes Kjarval (1885–1972), Iceland's most enduringly popular artist, who grew up in the remote East Iceland village of Borgarfjörður Eystri. His first commissioned works were, rather poignantly, drawings of farms for people who were emigrating, but he's most famous for his early charcoal sketches of people from the village and for his surreal landscapes. A whole beautiful building of the Reykjavík Museum of Art (Kjarvalsstaðir) is named for him.

Iceland's most famous contemporary painter is probably pop-art icon Erró (Guðmundur Guðmundsson, 1932–), who has donated his entire collection to Reykjavík Art Museum's Hafnarhús. Danish-Icelandic artist Olafur Eliasson (1967–) creates powerful installations and also designed the facade of Reykjavík's dazzling concert hall, Harpa. Páll Guðmundsson (1959–) is a working artist in Húsafell who makes evocative sculptures and paintings, and unusual stone and rhubarb *steinharpa* (similar to a xylophone), which he has played with the band Sigur Rós.

The tiny Museum of Design and Applied Art (www.honnunarsafn.is) in Garðabær, just south of Reykjavík, showcases the local design scene from the early 20th century to today and has a small Kraum design outlet.

Architecture & Design

Iceland's Viking longhouses have succumbed to the ravages of time, but traditional turf-and-wood techniques were used right up until the 19th century. There is a good example at Glaumbær (North Iceland).

Guðjón Samúelsson (1887–1950), perhaps one of Iceland's most famous 20th-century architects, worked to create a distinctive Icelandic style, and you will find his minimalist buildings all over the country, from Hallgrímskirkja and the nearby swimming pool, Sundhöllin, in Reykjavík, to Þingvallabær (farmhouse at Þingvellir) and Héraðsskólinn, formerly a school in Laugarvatn. *A Guide to Icelandic Architecture* (Association of Icelandic Architects) looks at 250 Icelandic buildings and designs.

Iceland's coterie of unique designers, artists and architects tend to be Reykjavík based, though that trend is changing with the tourism boom. Many practitioners form collectives and open shops and galleries, which are full of handmade, beautiful works: everything from striking bowls made out of radishes to cool couture. Reykjavík's Iceland Design Centre (p59) has loads more information, and its DesignMarch (p24) annual event opens hundreds of exhibitions and workshops to the public.

Icelandic Attitudes

Centuries of isolation and hardship have instilled particular character traits in the small, homogenous Icelandic population. Their connection to their homeland, history and countrypeople is deeply felt, even if the land reciprocates that love with some sharp edges. The nation's 330,000 souls tend to respond to life's challenges with a compelling mix of courage, candour and creativity, edged with a dark, dry humour.

'Þetta reddast' & the National Psyche

Icelanders have a reputation as tough, hardy, elemental types, and rural communities are still deeply involved in the fishing and/or farming industries. Geographically speaking, 'rural' could be said to define most of the country outside the capital region, which is home to only 36% of Iceland's total population.

Naturally enough for people living on a remote island in a harsh environment, Icelanders are self-reliant individualists who don't like being told what to do. But these steadfast exteriors often hide a more dreamy interior world. Iceland has always had a rich cultural heritage and an incredibly high literacy rate, and its people have a passion for all things artistic. This enthusiasm is true of the whole country, but it's particularly noticeable in downtown Reykjavík, where seemingly everyone plays in a band, dabbles in art or design, makes films or writes poetry or prose – they're positively bursting with creative impulses.

This buoyant, have-a-go attitude was hit hard during the 2008 financial meltdown. Soup kitchens sprang up in the city and thousands of younger people left Iceland to try their luck in Norway. But Icelanders are resilient – within just a few years, emigration rates fell, and confidence started springing up around the country, mushrooming along with new businesses catering to the tourist boom. The country maintains its belief in the old saying *'Þetta reddast'* (roughly translated, 'It will all work out okay'). The phrase is so frequently used it has been described as the country's motto.

Icelanders are happily patriotic. Witness their Euro 2016 football (soccer) victories, with their Viking thunderclap, and the fact that approximately 10% of the country went to France for the tournament. Icelandair wishes a heartfelt 'Welcome home!' to its Icelandic passengers when the plane touches down at Keflavík. Citizens who achieve international success are quietly feted: celebrities such as musicians Björk and Sigur Rós reflect prestige onto their entire homeland.

Town layouts, the former US military base, and the prevalence of hot dogs and Coca-Cola point to a heavy US influence, but Icelanders consider their relationship with the rest of Scandinavia to be more important. Although they may seem to conform to the cool-and-quiet Nordic stereotype, Icelanders are curious about visitors and eager to know what outsiders think: 'How do you like Iceland?' is invariably an early question. And an incredible transformation takes place on Friday and Saturday nights, when inhibitions fall away and conversations flow as fast as the alcohol.

Iceland is the world's most peaceful country according to the Global Peace Index, which has ranked the country top of the pops every year since 2008. The GPI bases its findings on factors such as levels of violent crime, political instability and the percentage of a country's population in prison.

The Little Book of the Icelanders, by Alda Sigmundsdóttir, is a wonderful collection of 50 miniature essays on the 'quirks and foibles' of the Icelandic people, written by an insightful Icelander who returned to live in the country after 22 years abroad.

Work Hard, Play Hard

In the last century the Icelandic lifestyle has shifted from isolated family communities living on scattered farms and in coastal villages to a more urban-based society, with the majority of people living in the southwestern corner around Reykjavík. Despite this change, family connections are still very strong. Though young people growing up in rural Iceland are likely to move to Reykjavík to study and work, localised tourism is bringing entrepreneurial and job options to the hinterlands once again.

Iceland has one of the world's highest life expectancies – 81.8 years for men and 84.5 years for women.

Icelanders work hard (and long – the retirement age is 70), often at a number of jobs, especially in summer's peak when there is money to be made feeding, accommodating, driving and guiding thousands of tourists. The locals have enjoyed a very high standard of living in the late 20th and early 21st centuries – but keeping up with the Jónssons and Jónsdóttirs came at a price. For decades, Icelanders straight out of university borrowed money to buy houses or 4WDs and spent the rest of their days living on credit and paying off loans. Then, in 2008, the crash occurred, and huge amounts of debt suddenly had to be paid back. People wondered how Iceland would ever work itself out of its economic black hole. And yet, with characteristic grit, resilience, adaptability and imagination, Icelanders have hauled their country back from economic disaster.

The Icelandic commitment to hard work is counterbalanced by deep relaxation. The bingeing in Reykjavík on Friday and Saturday nights is an example of R&R gone wild. But, also keep your eye out for the hundreds of summer houses you'll see when you're driving in the country, and the exceptional number of swimming pools, which form the social hub of Icelandic life.

Women in Iceland

In 2015 Iceland held the top spot (for the seventh consecutive year) in the World Economic Forum's Global Gender Gap Index. The index ranked 136 countries on gender equality by measuring the relative gap between women and men across four key areas: health, education, economics and politics. Iceland continues to be the country with the narrowest gender gap in the world – this means Icelandic women have greater access to health and education, and are more politically and economically empowered than women in other countries.

The Viking settlement of Iceland clearly demanded toughness of character, and the sagas are full of feisty women (for example, Hallgerður Höskuldsdóttir, who declines to save her husband's life due to a slap that he gave her years earlier). For centuries Icelandic women had to take care of farms and families while their male partners headed off to sea.

Even though Icelanders speak the nearest thing to Viking in existence, Iceland is the least purely Scandinavian of all the Nordic countries. DNA studies have shown that much of Icelanders' genetic make-up is Celtic, suggesting that many Viking settlers had children by their British and Irish slaves.

Though women and men struggled equally through Iceland's long, dark history, modern concepts of gender equality are a pretty recent phenomenon. Women gained full voting rights in 1920, but it wasn't until the 1970s protest movements reached Iceland that attitudes really began to change. Particularly powerful was the 'women's day off' on 24 October 1975: the country ceased to function when 90% of Icelandic women stayed away from work and stay-at-home mums left children with their menfolk for the day.

In 1980 Iceland became the first democracy to elect a female president, the much-loved Vigdís Finnbogadóttir. In 2009 the world's first openly gay prime minister, Jóhanna Sigurðardóttir, came into power. Iceland has among the highest rate of women's participation in the labour market among OECD countries, at 78.5%.

The social care system is so good that women have few worries about the financial implications of raising a child alone: maternity-leave provisions are excellent; childcare is affordable; there is no sense that motherhood precludes work or study; and there's no stigma attached to unmarried mothers. The country isn't perfect – sexual violence and unequal pay are still issues – but Icelandic women are well educated and independent, with the same opportunities as Icelandic men.

Iceland had just one TV channel until 1988 – and even that went off air on Thursdays so that citizens could do something more productive instead. It's said that most children born before 1988 were conceived on a Thursday...

Religious Beliefs

Norse

At the time of the Settlement Era, Iceland's religion was Ásatrú, which means 'faith in the Aesir' (the old Norse gods). Óðinn, Þór (Thor) and Freyr were the major trinity worshipped across Scandinavia. Óðinn, their chief, is the god of war and poetry, a brooding and intimidating presence. In Iceland most people were devoted to Þór (Icelandic names such as Þórir, Þórdís and Þóra are still very popular). This burly, red-haired god of the common people controlled thunder, wind, storm and natural disaster, and was a vital deity for farmers and fishers to have on their side. Freyr and his twin sister Freyja represent fertility and sexuality. Freyr brought springtime, with its romantic implications, to both the human and the animal world, and was in charge of the perpetuation of all species.

Icelanders peacefully converted to Christianity more than a thousand years ago, but the old gods linger on. The Ásatrú religion evolved in the 1970s, almost simultaneously in Iceland, the US and the UK. Whereas membership of other religions in Iceland has remained fairly constant, Ásatrúarfélagið (Ásatrú Association) is growing. It is now Iceland's largest non-Christian religious organisation, with approximately 3187 members in 2016 (an increase of 19% from 2015).

Christianity

Traditionally, the date of the decree that officially converted Iceland to Christianity is given as 1000, but research has determined that it probably occurred in 999. What is known is that the changeover of religions was a political decision. In the Icelandic Alþingi (National Assembly), Christians and pagans had been polarising into two radically opposite

WHAT'S IN A NAME

Icelanders' names are constructed from a combination of their first name and their father's (or, more rarely, mother's) first name. Girls add the suffix *dóttir* (daughter) to the patronymic and boys add *son*. Therefore, Jón, the son of Einar, would be Jón Einarsson. Guðrun, the daughter of Einar, would be Guðrun Einarsdóttir.

Because Icelandic surnames only usually tell people what a person's father is called, Icelanders don't bother with 'Mr Einarsson' or 'Mrs Einarsdóttir'. Instead they use first names, even when addressing strangers. It makes for a wonderfully democratic society when you're expected to address your president or top police commissioner by their first name. And yes, trivia buffs, the telephone directory is alphabetised by first name.

About 10% of Icelanders have family names (most dating back to early Settlement times), but they're rarely used. In an attempt to homogenise the system, government legislation forbids anyone to take on a new family name or adopt the family name of their spouse.

There's also an official list of names that Icelanders are permitted to call their children, and any additions to this list have to be approved by the Icelandic Naming Committee. For the 5000 or so children born in Iceland each year, the committee reportedly receives about 100 applications and rejects about half. Among its requirements are that given names must be 'capable of having Icelandic grammatical endings', and shall not 'conflict with the linguistic structure of Iceland'.

factions, threatening to divide the country. Þorgeir, the *lögsögumaður* (law speaker), appealed for moderation on both sides, and eventually it was agreed that Christianity would officially become the new religion, although pagans were still allowed to practise in private.

Today, as in mainland Scandinavia, most Icelanders (around 80%) belong to the Protestant Lutheran Church – but many are nonpractising. Church attendance is very low.

Those interested in exploring their Icelandic heritage should consult the East Iceland Emigration Center (www.hofsos.is), at Hofsós, and the Snorri Program (www.snorri.is).

Icelandic Ancestry & Genetic Research

Biotech research is big in Iceland – thanks, in part, to the 12th-century historian Ari the Learned. Ari's *Landnámabók* and *Íslendingabók* mean that Icelanders can trace their family trees right back to the 9th century.

In 1996, neuroscience expert Dr Kári Stefánsson recognised that this genealogical material could be combined with Iceland's unusually homogenous population to produce something unique – a country-sized genetic laboratory. In 1998 the Icelandic government controversially voted to allow the creation of a single database, by presumed consent, containing all Icelanders' genealogical, genetic and medical records. Even more controversially, the government allowed Kári's biotech startup company Decode Genetics to create this database, and access it for its biomedical research, using the database to trace inheritable diseases and pinpoint the genes that cause them.

The decision sparked public outrage in Iceland and arguments across the globe about its implications for human rights and medical ethics.

SUPERNATURAL ICELAND: THE HIDDEN PEOPLE

Once you've seen some of the lava fields, eerie natural formations and isolated farms that characterise much of the Icelandic landscape, it will come as no surprise that many Icelanders believe their country is populated by *huldufólk* (hidden people) and ghosts.

In the lava live *jarðvergar* (gnomes), *álfar* (elves), *ljósálfar* (fairies), *dvergar* (dwarves), *ljúflingar* (lovelings), *tívar* (mountain spirits) and *englar* (angels). Stories about them have been handed down through generations, and many modern Icelanders claim to have seen them...or at least to know someone who has.

There are stories about projects going wrong when workers try to build roads through *huldufólk* homes: the weather turns bad; machinery breaks down; labourers fall ill. In mid-2014 Iceland's 'whimsy factor' made international news when a road project to link the Álftanes peninsula to the Reykjavík suburb of Garðabær was halted after campaigners warned it would disturb elf habitat.

As for Icelandic ghosts, they're substantial beings – not the wafting shadows found elsewhere in Europe. Írafell-Móri (*móri* and *skotta* are used for male and female ghosts, respectively) is said to need to eat supper every night, and one of the country's most famous spooks, Sel-Móri, gets seasick when stowing away in a boat. Stranger still, two ghosts haunting the same area often join forces to double their trouble.

Rock stacks and weird lava formations around the country are often said to be trolls, caught out at sunrise and turned to stone. But living trolls are seldom seen today – they're more the stuff of children's stories.

Surveys suggest that more than half of Icelanders believe in, or at least entertain the possibility of, the existence of *huldufólk*. But a word of warning: many Icelanders tire of visitors asking them whether they believe in supernatural beings. Their pride bristles at the 'Those cute Icelanders! They all believe in pixies!' attitude...and even if they don't entirely disbelieve, they're unlikely to admit it to a stranger.

If you want to know more, and ask all the questions you can, join a tour in Hafnarfjörður, 10km south of Reykjavík, or sign up for a course at the Icelandic Elf School (Álfaskólinn; www.elfmuseum.com) in Reykjavík. Yes, there really is such a place, and it runs four-hour introductory classes most Fridays.

Should a government be able to sell off its citizens' medical records? And is it acceptable for a private corporation to use such records for profit?

While the arguments raged (and investors flocked), the company set to work. The database was declared unconstitutional in 2003, Decode was declared bankrupt in 2010, and sold to US biotech giant Amgen in 2012. By that time, Decode had built a research database using DNA and clinical data from more than 100,000 volunteers (one third of the population), and had done work in isolating gene mutations linked to heart attacks, strokes and Alzheimer's disease.

Decode continues to unravel the mysteries of the human genome, and in 2014 began a controversial drive to encourage more Icelanders to voluntarily donate their genetic material to its database. With its completed research, it has also been able to 'impute' the genetic make-up of Icelanders who have not participated at all – leading to ethical questions: should they inform carriers of dangerous gene mutations even if those people have not agreed to participate? So far, the answer has been that it remains illegal to do so.

In his book *The Almost Nearly Perfect People,* author Michael Booth seeks to explore 'the truth about the Nordic miracle'. He presents some great stats and entertaining insights on Icelanders, from financial-crash culprits to *huldufólk* (hidden folk) superstitions.

Icelandic Cuisine

If people know anything about Icelandic food, it's usually to do with a plucky population tucking into boundary-pushing dishes such as fermented shark or sheep's head. It's a pity the spotlight doesn't shine as brightly on Iceland's delicious, fresh-from-the-farm ingredients, the seafood bounty hauled from the surrounding icy waters, the innovative dairy products (hello, *skyr!*) or the clever, historic food-preserving techniques that are finding new favour with today's much-feted New Nordic chefs.

North: The New Nordic Cuisine of Iceland, by chefs Gunnar Karl Gíslason and Jody Eddy, is a beautiful book that profiles traditional Icelandic food producers, many of them suppliers to Gunnar's first-class Dill restaurant.

Food Heritage

For much of its history, Iceland was a poverty-stricken hinterland. Sparse soil and cursed weather produced limited crops, and Icelandic farmer-fishers relied heavily on sheep, fish and seabirds to keep them from starving. Every part of every creature was eaten – fresh or dried, salted, smoked, pickled in whey or even buried underground (in the case of shark meat), with preserving techniques honed to ensure food lasted through lean times.

Local food producers and chefs today are rediscovering old recipes and techniques with a renewed sense of pride in the country's culinary heritage, and the results can be quite special. The strong Slow Food Movement prioritises locally grown food over imports, with restaurants proudly flagging up regional treats.

Staples & Specialities

Fish & Seafood

'Half of our country is the sea', runs an old Icelandic saying. Fish is still the mainstay of the Icelandic diet: you'll find it fresh at market stalls and in restaurant kitchens, from where it emerges boiled, pan-fried, baked or grilled.

In the past, Icelanders merely kept the cheeks and tongues of *þorskur* (cod) – something of a delicacy – and exported the rest; but today you'll commonly find cod fillets on the menu, along with *ýsa* (haddock), *bleikja* (Arctic char) and meaty-textured *skötuselur* (monkfish). Other fish include *lúða* (halibut), *steinbítur* (catfish), *sandhverfa* (turbot; nonindigenous), *síld* (herring), *skarkoli* (plaice) and *skata* (skate). During summer you can try *silungur* (freshwater trout) and *villtur lax* (wild salmon). *Eldislax* is farmed salmon; it's available year-round and appears on countless menus in smoked form.

Harðfiskur, a popular snack eaten with butter, is found in supermarkets and at market stalls. To make it, haddock is cleaned and dried in the open air until it has become dehydrated and brittle, then it's torn into strips.

Rækja (shrimp), *hörpudiskur* (scallops) and *kræklingur* (blue mussels) are harvested in Icelandic waters; mussels are at their prime during the very beginning and the end of summer. *Humar* (or *leturhumar*) are a real treat: these are what Icelanders call 'lobster'; the rest of us may know them as langoustine. Höfn, in Southeast Iceland, is particularly well known for *humar* and even has an annual lobster festival.

Where to Find Fresh...

Langoustines: Höfn

Tomatoes: Flúðir

Reindeer: Egilsstaðir and East Iceland

Hverabrauð ('hot springs bread'): Mývatn

Mussels: Stykkishólmur

Foal: Skagafjörður

Meat

Icelandic lamb is hard to beat. During summer, sheep roam free to munch on chemical-free grasses and herbs in the highlands and valleys, before the September *réttir* (sheep roundup), after which they are corralled for the winter. The result of this life of relative luxury is very tender lamb with a slightly gamey flavour. You'll find lamb fillets, pan-fried lamb or smoked lamb on most restaurant menus.

Beef steaks are also excellent but not as widely available, and are consequently more expensive. Horse is still eaten in Iceland, although it's regarded as something of a delicacy; if you see 'foal fillets' on the menu, you're not imagining things.

In eastern Iceland wild reindeer roam the highlands, and reindeer steaks are a feature of local menus. Hunting is highly regulated; reindeer season starts in late July and runs well into September.

Birds have always been part of the Icelandic diet. *Lundi* (puffin) used to appear smoked or broiled in liver-like lumps on dinner plates, although it's a rarer sight these days following a worrying crash in puffin numbers. Another seabird is *svartfugl;* it's commonly translated as 'blackbird' on English-language menus, but what you'll actually get is guillemot. High-class restaurants favouring seasonal ingredients may have roasted *heiðagæs* (pink-footed goose) in autumn.

Food lovers may be tempted by food-focused tours such as 'Culinary Coastline' out of Akureyri, run by Saga Travel (www.sagatravel.is), or tours around West Iceland, operated by Crisscross (www.crisscross.is).

Sweets & Desserts

Don't miss *skyr,* a delicious yoghurt-like concoction made from pasteurised skimmed milk. Despite its rich flavour, it's actually low in fat and is often mixed with sugar, fruit flavours (such as blueberry) and cream to give it an extra-special taste and texture. *Skyr* can be found in any supermarket and as a dessert in restaurants.

Icelandic *pönnukökur* (pancakes) are thin, sweet and cinnamon flavoured. Icelandic *kleinur* (twisted doughnuts) are a chewy treat, along with their offspring *ástarpungar* (love balls), deep-fried, spiced balls of dough. You'll find these desserts in bakeries, along with an amazing array of fantastic pastries and cakes – one of the few sweet legacies of the Danish occupation.

TASTEBUD TOURING

We think that the incredible local fish and lamb should be high on your hit-list in Iceland. You may be considering the 'novelty value' of sampling the likes of whale, puffin and even *hákarl* (fermented Greenland shark), but please do consider your actions. Try these delicious blasts of local flavour instead.

Skyr Rich and creamy yoghurt-like staple, sometimes sweetened with sugar and berries. You can consume it in yoghurt-style drinks or local desserts, playing a starring role in cheesecake and crème brûlée (or even 'skyramisu') concoctions.

Hangikjöt Literally 'hung meat', usually smoked lamb, served in thin slices (it's traditionally a Christmas dish).

Harðfiskur Brittle pieces of wind-dried haddock ('fish jerky'?), usually eaten with butter.

Pýlsur Icelandic hot dogs, made with a combination of lamb, beef and pork, and topped with raw and deep-fried onion, ketchup, mustard and tangy remoulade (ask for *'eina með öllu'* – one with everything).

Liquorice Salt liquorice and chocolate-covered varieties fill the supermarket sweets aisles.

Rúgbrauð Dark, dense rye bread. Look for *hverabrauð* in Mývatn – it's baked underground using geothermal heat.

A BANQUET OF BODY PARTS

Eyeball a plate of old-fashioned Icelandic food, and chances are it will eyeball you back. In the past nothing was wasted, and some traditional specialities look more like horror-film props than food. You won't be faced with these dishes on many menus, though – they're generally only eaten at *þorramatur* (literally, 'food of Þorri') buffets during the Þorrablót midwinter feast (named for the month of Þorri in the Old Norse calendar, and corresponding to mid-January to mid-February). Plentiful *brennivín* (caraway-flavoured schnapps) is the expected accompaniment.

Svið Singed sheep's head sawn in two, boiled and eaten fresh or pickled.

Sviðasulta (head cheese) Made from bits of *svið* pressed into gelatinous loaves and pickled in whey.

Slátur (the word means 'slaughter') Comes in two forms: *lifrarpylsa* is liver sausage, made from a mishmash of sheep intestines, liver and lard tied up in a sheep's stomach and cooked (kind of like Scottish haggis). *Blóðmör* has added sheep's blood (and equates to blood pudding).

Súrsaðir hrútspungar Rams' testicles pickled in whey and pressed into a cake.

Hákarl Iceland's most famous stomach churner, *hákarl* is Greenland shark, an animal so inedible it has to rot away underground for six months before humans can even digest it. Most foreigners find the stench (a cross between ammonia and week-old roadkill) too much to bear, but it tastes better than it smells… It's the aftertaste that really hurts. A shot of *brennivín* is traditionally administered as an antidote.

Local dairy farms churn out scrumptious scoops of homemade ice cream, often featured on menus of nearby restaurants.

Drinks

Nonalcoholic

Life without *kaffi* (coffee) is unthinkable. Cafes and petrol stations will usually have an urn of filter coffee by the counter, and some shops offer complimentary cups of it to customers. Snug European-style cafes selling espresso, latte, cappuccino and mocha are ever-more popular, popping up even in the most isolated one-horse hamlets (the coffee isn't always good, though). Tea is available, but ranks a very poor second choice – the brand sitting on most supermarket shelves makes a feeble brew.

Check out *50 Crazy Things to Taste in Iceland*, by Snæfríður Ingadóttir (including great photos by Þorvaldur Örn Kristmundsson), for a few fun pictorials of Iceland's traditional eats.

Besides all that coffee, Icelanders drink more Coca-Cola per capita than most other countries. Another very popular soft drink is Egils Appelsín (orange soda) and the home-grown Egils Malt Extrakt, which tastes like sugar-saturated beer.

It isn't a crime to buy bottled water in Iceland, but it should be. Icelandic tap water generally comes from the nearest glacier, and is some of the purest you'll ever drink.

Alcoholic

For some Icelanders, drinking alcohol is not about the taste – getting trollied is the aim of the game. Particularly in Reykjavík, it's the done thing to go out at the weekend and drink till you drop.

You must be at least 20 years old to buy beer, wine or spirits, and alcohol is only available from licensed bars, restaurants and the government-run Vínbúðin liquor stores (www.vinbudin.is). There are roughly 50 shops around the country; most towns have one, and the greater Reykjavík area has about a dozen. In larger places they usually open from 11am to 6pm Monday to Thursday and on Saturdays, and from 11am to 7pm on Fridays (closed Sundays). In small communities, the Vínbúðin store may only open for an hour or two in the late afternoon or evening. Expect queues around 5pm on a Friday. The cheapest bottles of imported wine cost from kr1200. Beer costs about a third of what you'll pay in a bar.

Petrol stations and supermarkets sell the weak and watery 2.2% brew known as pilsner, but most Icelanders would sooner not drink it at all. The main brands of Icelandic beer – Egils, Gull, Thule and Viking – are all fairly standard lager or pils brews; you can also get imported beers. In recent years a slew of good local distilleries and breweries has sprung up all over Iceland, concocting whisky, vodka and dozens of high-calibre craft beers – check our cheat sheet (p88) for your next bar-room order. Look out, too, for seasonal beers – the ones brewed for the Christmas period are especially popular.

Chef Anthony Bourdain described *hákarl* (fermented Greenland shark) as 'probably the single worst thing I have ever put in my mouth'.

Reports of astronomical prices for boozing in Iceland are not altogether true – a pint of beer in a bar costs around kr1000 to kr1600. In Reykjavík, many venues have early-evening happy hours that cut costs to between kr500 and kr700 per beer. Download the smartphone Reykjavík Appy Hour app to gladden your drinking budget.

The traditional Icelandic alcoholic brew is *brennivín* (literally 'burnt wine'), a potent schnapps made from fermented potatoes and flavoured with caraway seeds. It has the foreboding nickname *svarti dauði* (black death) and it's essential drinking if you're trying any tasty traditional titbits (p384).

Where to Eat & Drink

Restaurants

Iceland's best restaurants are in Reykjavík, but some magnificent finds are mushrooming up beyond the capital, catering to travellers looking for authentic local flavours. These restaurants are tapping into the network of unsung local producers: barley farmers, mussel harvesters, veggie growers, sheep farmers and fishers. At many places, your meal's food miles will be very low.

Beer Day (1 March) dates back to the glorious day in 1989 when beer was legalised in Iceland (it was illegal for most of the 20th century). As you'd expect, Reykjavík's clubs and bars get particularly wild.

Bear in mind that the price difference between an exceptional restaurant and an average one is often small, so it can be well worth going upmarket. Often, though, in rural Iceland you may not have a huge choice – the town's only eating place may be the restaurant in the local hotel, supplemented by the grill bar in the petrol station. And in peak summer, you may struggle to get a table without a reservation, and/or face long waits.

À la carte menus usually offer at least one fish dish, one veggie choice (invariably pasta) and a handful of meat mains (lamb is the star). Many restaurants also have a menu of cheaper meals such as hamburgers and pizzas. Soup will invariably appear – either as a lunchtime option (perhaps in the form of a soup-and-salad buffet) or as a dinnertime starter. *Fiskisúpa* (fish soup) comes courtesy of various family recipes, while *kjötsúpa* (meat soup) will usually feature veggies and small chunks of lamb.

In Reykjavík, and to a lesser extent Akureyri, there are some ethnic restaurants, including Thai, Japanese, Italian, Mexican, Indian and Chinese.

PRICE RANGES

Eating reviews are divided into the following price categories based on the cost of an average main course:

€ Less than kr2000 (€15)

€€ kr2000–5000 (€15–39)

€€€ More than kr5000 (€39)

You can also stumble across some welcome surprises – Ethiopian in Flúðir and Moroccan in Siglufjörður.

Opening hours for restaurants are usually 11.30am to 2.30pm and 6pm to 10pm daily. Note that even in summer, restaurants may stop serving meals around 9pm.

Cafes & Pubs

Sweet, peppery caraway is used to flavour Icelandic cheese, coffee, bread and *brennivín* (schnapps). In late August, after the plant has flowered, some Reykjavikers head to Viðey island to gather caraway seeds.

Downtown Reykjavík has a great range of bohemian cafe-bars where you can happily while away the hours sipping coffee, people-watching, scribbling postcards or tinkering on your laptop. Menus range from simple soups and sandwiches to fish dishes and designer burgers. Recent years have seen cafe menus morph into more restaurant-like versions (with an attendant hike in prices). The cafe scene is spreading, too, with some cool new spots scattered around the country.

Many of Reykjavík's cafes morph into wild drinking dens in the evenings (mostly on Fridays and Saturdays). DJs suddenly appear, coffee orders turn to beer, and people get progressively louder and less inhibited as the evening goes on, which is usually until sometime between 4am and 5am. Outside the capital, things are considerably more subdued, although Friday and Saturday nights do see action in Akureyri.

Hot Dog Stands & Petrol Stations

Icelanders do enjoy fast food. If you see a queue in Reykjavík, it probably ends at a *pýlsur* (hot dog) stand. Large petrol stations often have good, cheap, well-patronised grills and cafeterias attached. They generally serve sandwiches and fast food from around 11am to 9pm or 10pm. Some also offer hearty set meals at lunchtime, such as meat soup, fish of the day or plates of lamb. Cafeterias at N1 service stations anywhere along the Ring Road are invariably busy.

Supermarkets & Bakeries

Salt Eldhús (www.salteldhus.is) is a small cooking school in Reykjavík that offers hands-on, gourmet cooking classes using local ingredients.

Every town and village has at least one small supermarket. The most expensive is 10-11, but it's generally open late hours. Bónus (easily recognised by its yellow-and-pink piggy sign) is the country's budget supermarket chain. Others include Hagkaup, Kjarval, Krónan, Nettó, Nóatún, Samkaup-Strax and Samkaup-Úrval. Opening times vary greatly; in Reykjavík most are open from 9am to 11pm daily, but outside the capital hours are almost always shorter. Sunday hours may be limited or nonexistent.

We can't praise the old-school Icelandic *bakarí* (bakeries) enough. Most towns have one (it may be part of a supermarket), which is generally open from 7am or 8am until 4pm on weekdays (sometimes also Saturdays). These sell all sorts of inexpensive fresh bread, buns, cakes, sandwiches and coffee, and usually provide chairs and tables to eat at.

Iceland has to import most of its groceries, so prices are steep – roughly two or three times what you'd pay in North America or Europe. Fish (tinned or smoked) and dairy products represent the best value and are surprisingly cheap. Some fruit and vegetables are grown locally, and these tend to be fresh and tasty, but imported vegetables sometimes look pretty sad by the time they hit supermarket shelves.

Vegetarians & Vegans

Vegetarians and vegans will have no problem in Reykjavík – there are some excellent meat-free cafe-restaurants in the city, and many more eateries offer vegetarian choices (you'll probably want to eat every meal at Gló). Outside the capital most restaurants have at least one veggie item on the menu – this is routinely cheese-and-tomato pasta or pizza, though, so you could get very bored. Vegans usually have to self-cater.

Survival Guide

Directory A–Z

Accommodation

Iceland's accommodation ranges from basic hikers' huts to business-standard hotels, hostels, working farms, guesthouses, apartments, cottages and school-based summer rooms. Luxury and boutique hotels are predominantly found in Reykjavík and tourism hot spots in the southwest, with a select few in regional pockets.

There's been a boom of new hotels and guesthouses, and many existing options have expanded and upgraded to cater to the rapid increase in visitor numbers. Even still, demand often outstrips supply in popular tourist centres (eg Reykjavík, the south and Mývatn). Summer prices are *high,* and getting higher with increasing demand.

For the cost, accommodation is often of a lower standard than you might expect from a developed European destination. Although rooms are generally spotless, they are usually small, with thin walls and limited facilities.

Please note the following:

- We recommend that between June and August travellers book *all* accommodation in advance (note there is no need to prebook campsites). May and September are following this trend. Reykjavík is busy year-round.
- Tourist information centres will generally have details of all the accommodation in their town/region. Larger centres might have a booking service, where they will book accommodation for a small fee (usually around kr500). Note, this service is for walk-in visitors, not for prebooking via email. And don't rely on it – areas can and do book out quickly, or you may find the nearest available room is miles from your intended stop.
- The best rate can often be found by contacting the property directly. A number of properties don't have their own websites, however, preferring all bookings via third-party websites – Booking.com is widely used across Iceland and is useful for checking all available accommodation in a town/region on a specified date. These properties may also have a Facebook page – it's worth checking.
- Prices for summer 2016 are generally listed in our reviews (or for summer 2017, when these were readily available). Travellers must expect that prices will rise from year to year. Websites will invariably list up-to-date prices.
- From September to May, most guesthouses and hotels offer discounts of 10% to 50% on their summer prices. Check websites for up-to-date prices.
- Some hotels and guesthouses close during winter; where this is the case, opening times are given in our reviews. Many hotels and guesthouses close over the Christmas–New Year period. If no opening times are given, accommodation is open year-round.
- Some accommodations list prices in euro, to ward against currency fluctuations, but payment is made in Icelandic krónur (kr).
- Guesthouses and farmstays can offer numerous options, eg camping; rooms with/without bathrooms, with made-up beds or sleeping bags; cottages with/without kitchen and/or bathroom. Check websites for full coverage.

BOOK YOUR STAY ONLINE

For more accommodation reviews by Lonely Planet authors, check out http://lonelyplanet.com/hotels/. You'll find independent reviews, as well as recommendations on the best places to stay. Best of all, you can book online.

➡ Our reviews indicate whether a private bathroom is offered; whether linen is included or if there is a sleeping-bag option; and if breakfast is included in the price.

Camping

Tjaldsvæði (organised campsites) are found in almost every town, at some rural farmhouses and along major hiking trails. The best sites have washing machines, cooking facilities and hot showers, but others just have a cold-water tap and a toilet block. Some are attached to the local *sundlaug* (swimming pool), with shower facilities provided by the pool for a small fee.

Icelandic weather is notoriously fickle, and if you intend to camp it's wise to invest in a good-quality tent. There are a few outfits in Reykjavík that offer rental of camping equipment, and some car-hire companies can also supply you with gear such as tents, sleeping mats and cooking equipment.

With the increase in visitors to Iceland, campgrounds are getting busier, and service blocks typically housing two toilets and one shower are totally insufficient for coping with the demand of dozens of campers. If the wait is long, consider heading to the local swimming pool and pay to use the amenities there.

It is rarely necessary (or possible) to book a camping spot in advance. Many small-town campsites are unstaffed – look for a contact number for the caretaker posted on the service block, or an instruction to head to the tourist information centre or swimming pool to pay; alternatively, a caretaker may visit the campsite in the evening to collect fees.

A few things to keep in mind:

➡ When camping in parks and reserves the usual rules apply: leave sites as you find them; use biodegradable soaps; and carry out your rubbish.

➡ Campfires are not allowed, so bring a stove. Butane cartridges and petroleum fuels are available in petrol stations. Blue Campingaz cartridges are not always readily available; the grey Coleman cartridges are more common.

➡ Camping with a tent or campervan/caravan usually costs kr1200 to kr1800 per person. Electricity is often an additional kr800. Many campsites charge for showers.

➡ A 'lodging tax' of kr111 per site exists; some places absorb this cost in the per-person rate, others make you pay it in addition to the per-person rate.

➡ Consider purchasing the good-value Camping Card (www.campingcard.is), which costs €110 and covers 28 nights of camping at 41 campsites throughout the country for two adults and up to four children. Note that the card doesn't include the lodging tax, or any charges for electricity or showers. Full details online.

➡ Most campsites open mid-May to mid-September. Large campsites that also offer huts or cottages may be open year-round. This is a fluid situation, as an increasing number of visitors are hiring campervans in the cooler months and looking to camp with facilities – ask at local tourist offices for info and advice.

➡ If camping in summer, be aware that if the weather turns bad and you'd like to sleep with a roof over your head, you'll be extremely lucky to find last-minute availability in guesthouses or hostels.

➡ Free accommodation directory *Áning* (available from tourist information centres) lists many of Iceland's campsites, but is not exhaustive.

SLEEPING PRICE RANGES

The following price categories are based on the high-season price for a double room:

€ less than kr15,000 (€110)

€€ kr15,000–30,000 (€110–225)

€€€ more than kr30,000 (€225)

Emergency Huts

Bright-orange survival huts are situated on high mountain passes and along remote coastlines (and are usually marked on maps of the country). Huts are stocked with emergency rations, fuel and blankets (and a radio to contact help). Note that it is illegal to use the huts in nonemergency situations.

Farmhouse Accommodation

Many rural farmhouses offer campsites, sleeping-bag spaces, made-up guestrooms, and cabins and cottages. Over time, some 'farmhouses' have evolved into large country hotels.

Facilities vary: some farms provide meals or have a guest kitchen, some have outdoor hot-pots (hot tubs), and many provide horse riding or can organise activities such as fishing. Roadside signs signal which farmhouses provide accommodation and what facilities they offer.

Rates are similar to guesthouses in towns, with sleeping-bag accommodation around kr6500 and made-up beds from kr10,000 to kr15,000 per person. Breakfast is usually included in the made-up room price, while an evening meal (generally served at a set time) costs around kr7000.

Some 170 farm properties are members of **Icelandic Farm Holidays** (www.farmholidays.is), which publishes an annual map called *Discover Iceland,* available free from most tourist information centres. Its website allows you to helpfully search by area, type (hotel, B&B, self-catering, hostel etc) and to further narrow down the search with categories such as farmstay, or local food on-site. The company can arrange package self-drive holidays.

Guesthouses

The Icelandic term *gistiheimilið* (guesthouse) covers a broad range of properties, from family homes renting out a few rooms, to a cluster of self-contained cottages, to custom-built blocks of guestrooms.

Guesthouses vary enormously in character, from stylish, contemporary options to those with plain, chintzy or dated decor. A surprisingly high number offer rooms only with shared bathroom.

Most are comfortable and cosy, with guest kitchens, TV lounges and buffet-style breakfasts (either included in the price or for around kr2000 extra). If access to a self-catering kitchen is important to you, it pays to ask beforehand to ensure availability.

Some guesthouses offer sleeping-bag accommodation at a price significantly reduced from that of a made-up bed. Some places don't advertise a sleeping-bag option, so it pays to ask.

As a general guide, sleeping-bag accommodation costs kr7000 per night, double rooms in summer kr18,000 to kr24,000, and self-contained units excluding linen from kr17,000. Guesthouse rooms with own bathroom are often similarly priced to hotel rooms.

Hostels

There are 35 well-maintained hostels administered by **Hostelling International Iceland** (www.hostel.is). In Reykjavík, Akureyri and a handful of other places, there are also independent backpacker hostels. Bookings are recommended at all of them, especially from June to August.

About half the HI hostels open year-round. Check online for opening-date info.

All hostels offer hot showers, cooking facilities and sleeping-bag accommodation, and most offer private rooms (some with private bathroom). If you don't have a sleeping bag, you can hire linen (prices vary, but reckon on around kr2000 per person per stay).

Breakfast (where available) costs kr1750 to kr2000.

Join **Hostelling International** (www.hihostels.com) in your home country to benefit from HI member discounts of kr700 per person. Nonmembers pay around kr5000 for a dorm bed; single/double rooms cost kr7500/12,000 (more for private bathrooms). Children aged five to 12 get a discount of kr1500.

SLEEPING-BAG ACCOMMODATION

Iceland's best-kept secret is the sleeping-bag option offered by hostels, numerous guesthouses and some hotels. For a fraction of the normal cost, you'll get a bed without a duvet; you supply your own sleeping bag.

Taking the sleeping-bag option doesn't mean sleeping in a dorm – generally you book the same private room, just minus the linen. The sleeping-bag option usually means BYO towel, too, and it's also worth packing a pillowcase.

Sleeping-bag prices never include breakfast, but you'll often have the option to purchase it.

Note that the option to use your own sleeping bag is more prevalent outside the peak summer period.

Hotels

Every major town has at least one business-style hotel, usually featuring comfortable but innocuous rooms with private bathroom, phone, TV and sometimes minibar. Invariably hotels also have decent restaurants.

Summer prices for singles/doubles start at around kr20,000/28,000 and usually include a buffet breakfast. Rates for a double room at a nice but nonluxurious hotel in a popular tourist area in peak summer can easily top kr34,000.

Prices drop substantially outside high season (June to August), and cheaper rates may be found online.

The largest local chains are **Icelandair Hotels** (www.icelandairhotels.is), **Fosshótel** (www.fosshotel.is), **Keahotels** (www.keahotels.is) and **CenterHotels** (www.centerhotels.is). New chain **Stracta Hótels** (www.stractahotels.is) has plans to expand beyond its first base in Hella.

Many international hotel chains are eyeing the growing Reykjavík market – Hilton has recently added to its portfolio in the capital, and a new five-star Marriott Edition is set to open in 2018.

SUMMER HOTELS

Once the summer school holidays begin, many boarding schools, colleges and conference centres become summer hotels offering simple accommodation. Most open from early June to late August (some are open longer), and 11 of them are part of a chain called **Hótel Edda** (www.hoteledda.is), overseen by the Icelandair Hotels chain.

NEW CAMPING LAWS

New laws regarding camping were introduced in late 2015, primarily to curtail the boom in campervans and caravans pulling over on roadsides or in car parks for the night instead of at organised campgrounds. This habit is offensive to locals, and has resulted in a big increase in people using nature as their bathroom – not cool.

The new laws are wordy, and outlined under the heading 'Where can I camp in Iceland?' on the website of Umhverfisstofnun, the Environment Agency of Iceland (www.ust.is). The bottom line – if you have a camping vehicle of any type (campervan, caravan, tent trailer etc), you must camp in proper, marked campgrounds.

Laws are slightly more relaxed for hikers and cyclists, but there are still rules to follow regarding obtaining landowner permission, being an acceptable distance from official campgrounds, the number of tents allowed to be set up, and not camping on cultivated land.

Accommodation tends to be simple: rooms are plain but functional, usually with twin beds, a washbasin and shared bathrooms, although a number of summer hotels have rooms with private bathroom, and a handful offer 'Edda Plus' rooms of a higher standard, with private bathroom, TV and phone.

A couple of Edda hotels have dormitory sleeping-bag spaces; most Edda hotels have a restaurant.

Expect to pay around kr3000 for sleeping-bag accommodation in a dorm (where available); kr28,000/18,000 for a double room with/without private bathroom; and around kr2000 for breakfast.

Mountain Huts

Private walking clubs and touring organisations maintain *skálar* (mountain huts; singular *skáli*) on many of the popular hiking tracks. The huts are open to anyone and offer sleeping-bag space in basic dormitories. Some huts also offer cooking facilities, campsites and have a summertime warden.

The huts at Landmannalaugar, Þórsmörk and around Askja are accessible by 4WD; huts in Hornstrandir are accessed by boat; many other mountain huts are on hiking trails and accessible only by foot.

GPS coordinates for huts are included in our reviews.

The main organisation providing mountain huts is **Ferðafélag Íslands** (Iceland Touring Association; Map p56; ☎568 2533; www.fi.is; Mörkin 6), which maintains 15 huts around Iceland (some in conjunction with local walking clubs). The best huts have showers (for an additional fee, around kr500), kitchens, wardens and potable water; simpler huts usually just have bed space, toilet and a basic cooking area. Beds cost kr5000 to kr7500 for nonmembers. Camping is available at some huts for kr1800 per person.

Other organisations include **Ferðafélag Akureyrar** (Touring Club of Akureyri; Map p244; ☎462 2720; www.ffa.is; Strandgata 23; ⊙3-6pm Mon-Fri May-Aug, 11am-1pm Mon-Fri Sep-Apr), which operates huts in the northeast (including along the Askja Trail), and **Útivist** (Map p56; ☎562 1000; www.utivist.is; Laugavegur 178; ⊙noon-5pm Mon-Fri), which has huts at Básar and Fimmvörðuháls Pass in Þórsmörk.

It's essential to book with the relevant organisation, as places fill up quickly.

Children

Iceland may not be equipped with adventure parks or high-profile attractions for children, but the whole country is an adventure with its wide-open spaces, wildlife and science projects brought to life. It's a fairly easy place to travel with kids, and parents will find it free of most urban dangers, but do keep toddlers away from those cliffs and unfenced waterfalls!

Dramatic scenery, an abundance of swimming pools and the friendliness of the locals help to keep kids happy, and they will probably love the bird colonies, waterfalls, volcanic areas and glaciers. A number of activities can keep them busy, such as short hikes, super-Jeep tours, horse riding, whale watching, boat rides and easy glacier walks (for the latter, the minimum age is around eight to 10 years).

Reykjavík is the most child-friendly place simply because it has the greatest variety of attractions and facilities. Distances can be long in the rest of the country, so you may want to limit yourselves to one or two regions.

Families might like to check out the *Íslandskort barnanna* (Children's Map of Iceland), aimed at young kids and published by Forlagið (Mál og Menning) with text in Icelandic and English.

Practicalities

- Admission for kids to museums and swimming pools varies from half-price to free. The age at which children must pay adult fees varies (anywhere from 12 to 18 years).
- On internal flights and tours with Air Iceland (www.

Climate

Akureyri

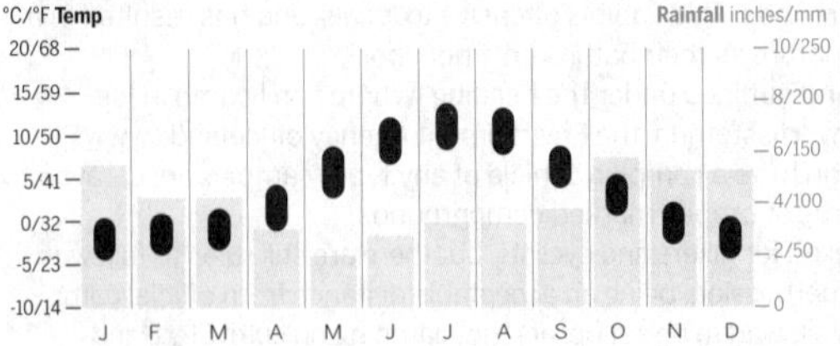

Reykjavík

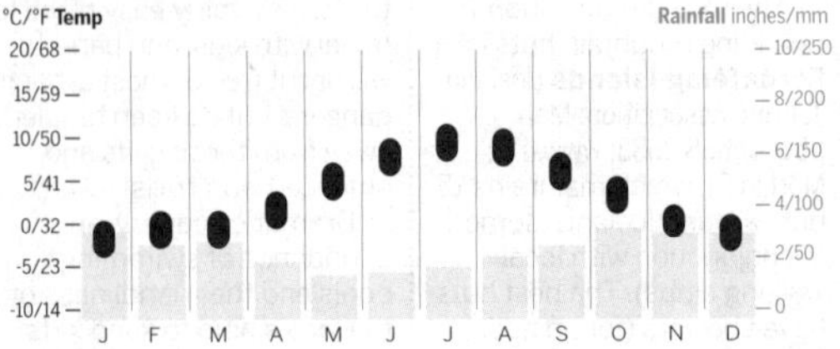

Vík

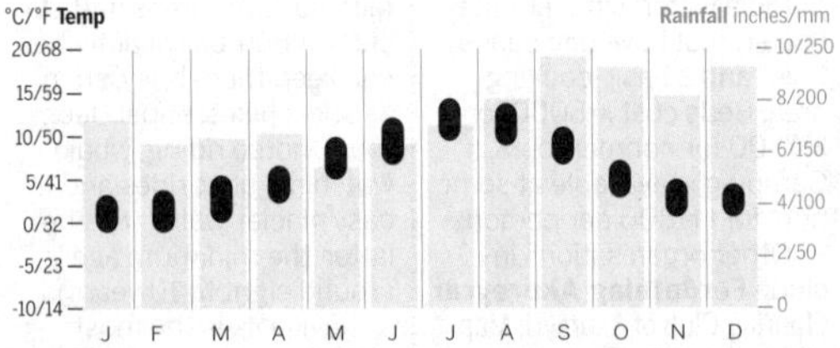

airiceland.is), children aged two to 11 years pay half-fare and infants under two fly free.

➡ Most bus and tour companies offer a 50% reduction for children aged four to 11 years; Reykjavík Excursions (www.re.is) tours are free for under 11s, and half-price for those aged 12 to 15.

➡ International car-hire companies offer child seats for an extra cost (book in advance).

➡ Changeable weather and frequent cold and rain may put you off camping with kids, but children aged two to 12 are usually charged half-price for camping, hostel, farmhouse and other accommodation. Under-twos usually stay for free.

➡ Many places offer rooms accommodating families, including hostels, guesthouses and farmstays. Larger hotels often have cots (cribs), but you may not find these elsewhere.

➡ Many restaurants in Reykjavík and larger towns offer discounted children's meals, and most have high chairs.

➡ Toilets at museums and other public institutions may have dedicated baby-changing facilities; elsewhere, you'll have to improvise.

➡ Attitudes to breastfeeding in public are generally relaxed.

➡ Formula, nappies (diapers) and other essentials are available everywhere.

Customs Regulations

Iceland has quite strict import restrictions. For a full list of regulations, see www.customs.is.

Alcohol duty-free allowances for travellers over 20 years of age:

➡ 1L spirits and 750mL wine and 3L beer, or

➡ 3L wine and 6L beer, or

➡ 1L spirits and 6L beer, or

➡ 1.5L wine and 12L beer, or

➡ 18L beer

Additionally:

➡ Visitors over 18 years can bring in 200 cigarettes or 250g of other tobacco products.

➡ You can import up to 3kg of food (except raw eggs, some meat and dairy products), provided it's not worth more than kr25,000. This may help self-caterers to reduce costs.

➡ To prevent contamination, recreational fishing and horse-riding clothes require a veterinarian's certificate stating that they have been disinfected. Otherwise officials will charge you for disinfecting clothing when you arrive. It is prohibited to bring used horse-riding equipment (saddles, bridles etc). See www.mast.is.

➡ Many people bring their cars on the ferry from Europe. Special duty-waiver conditions apply for stays of up to one year.

Embassies & Consulates

A handful of countries have formal embassies in Reykjavík. Up-to-date details of embassies and consulates within Iceland can be found on the Icelandic Ministry of Foreign Affairs website (www.mfa.is; click on Diplomatic Missions, then Foreign Missions).

Electricity

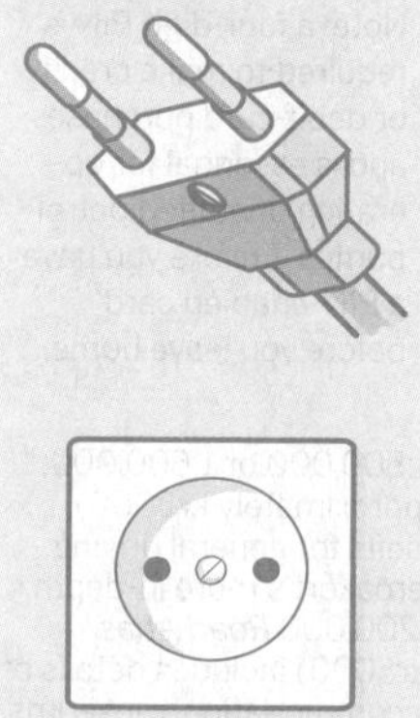

230V/50Hz

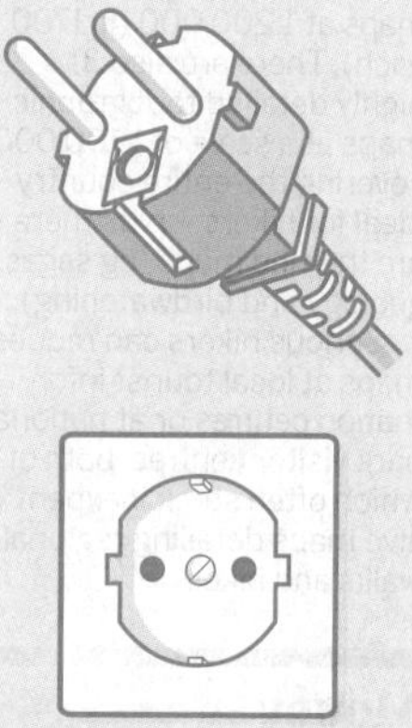

230V/50Hz

Health

Travel in Iceland presents very few health problems. Tap water is safe to drink; the level of hygiene is high, and there are no endemic nasties.

Health Insurance

A travel insurance policy that covers medical mishaps is strongly recommended. Always check the policy's small print to see if it covers any potentially dangerous sporting activities you might be considering, such as hiking, diving, horse riding, skiing or snowmobiling.

Vaccinations

There are no required or recommended vaccinations.

Availability & Cost of Health Care

The standard of healthcare is extremely high, and English is widely spoken by doctors and medical-clinic staff. Note, however, that there are limited services outside larger urban areas.

For minor ailments, pharmacists can dispense valuable advice and over-the-counter medication; pharmacies can be identified by the sign *apótek*. Pharmacists can also advise as to when more specialised help is required.

Medical care can be obtained by visiting a healthcare centre, called *heilsugæslustöð*. Find details of centres in greater Reykjavík at www.heilsugaeslan.is; in regional areas, ask at a tourist office or your accommodation for advice on the closest healthcare centre.

Citizens of Nordic countries need only present their passport to access healthcare. Citizens of the European Economic Area (EEA) are covered for emergency medical treatment on presentation of a European Health Insurance Card (EHIC). Apply online for a card via your government health department's website.

Citizens from other countries can obtain medical assistance but must pay in full (and later be reimbursed by their insurance provider, if they have one). Travel insurance is advised. For more information on healthcare for visitors, see www.sjukra.is/english/tourists.

Hypothermia & Frostbite

The main health risks are caused by exposure to extreme climates; proper preparation will reduce the risks. Even on a warm day in the mountains, the weather can change rapidly – carry waterproof outer gear and warm layers, and inform others of your route.

Acute hypothermia follows a sudden drop of temperature over a short time. Chronic hypothermia is caused by a gradual loss of temperature over hours. Hypothermia starts with shivering, loss of judgement and clumsiness. Unless rewarming occurs, the sufferer deteriorates into apathy, confusion and coma. Prevent further heat loss by seeking shelter, wearing warm, dry clothing, drinking hot, sweet drinks and sharing body warmth.

Frostbite is caused by freezing and the subsequent damage to bodily extremities. It is dependent on wind chill, temperature and the length of exposure. Frostbite starts as frostnip (white, numb areas of skin), from which complete recovery is expected with rewarming. As frostbite develops, however, the skin blisters and becomes black. Loss of damaged tissue eventually occurs. Your should wear adequate clothing, stay dry, keep well hydrated and ensure you have adequate kilojoule intake to prevent frostbite. Treatment involves rapid rewarming.

Tap Water

Iceland has some of the cleanest water in the world: tap water is completely safe to drink. Locals find it amusing to see travellers buying bottled water when quality water is available from the tap.

Geothermal hot water smells of sulphur, but cold water doesn't smell.

Insurance

Although Iceland is a very safe place to travel, theft does occasionally happen, and illness and accidents are always a possibility. A travel insurance policy to cover theft, loss and medical problems is strongly recommended.

Always check the policy's small print to see if it covers any potentially dangerous sporting activities you might be considering, such as hiking, diving, horse riding, skiing or snowmobiling.

Internet Access

Wi-fi is common in Iceland.

➡ Most accommodation and eating venues across the country offer online access, and often buses do, too. Access is usually free for guests/customers, but there may be a small charge. You may need to ask staff for an access code.

➡ Most of the N1 service stations have free wi-fi.

➡ To travel with your own wi-fi hot spot, check out Trawire (http://iceland.trawire.com) for portable 4G modem rental with unlimited usage from US$10/day (up to 10 laptops or mobile devices can be connected).

➡ Some campervan-hire companies offer portable modem devices as an optional extra.

➡ Most Icelandic libraries have computer terminals for public internet access, even in small towns; there's often a small fee.

➡ Tourist information centres often have public internet terminals, often free for brief usage.

Legal Matters

Icelandic police are generally low-key and there's very little reason for you to end up in their hands. Worth knowing:

➡ Drink-driving laws are strict. Even two drinks can put you over the legal limit of 0.05% blood-alcohol content; the penalty is loss of your driving licence plus a large fine.

➡ If you are involved in a traffic offence – speeding, driving without due care and attention etc – you may be asked to go to the station to pay the fine immediately.

➡ Drunk and disorderly behaviour may land you in a police cell for a night; you will usually be released the following morning.

➡ Penalties for possession, use or trafficking of illegal drugs are strict (long prison sentences and heavy fines).

LGBTI Travellers

Icelanders have a very open, accepting attitude towards homosexuality, though the gay scene is quite low-key, even in Reykjavík (p90).

Maps

In recent years Iceland has been busy building new roads and tunnels, and sealing gravel stretches. We recommend you purchase a recently updated country map.

Tourist information centres have useful free maps of their town and region. They also stock the free tourist booklet *Around Iceland*, which has information and town plans.

Tourist info centres, petrol stations and bookshops all sell road atlases and maps.

Map publisher Ferðakort (www.ferdakort.is) sells online and has a dedicated map department at **Iðnú bookshop** (Map p56; ☎517 7200; www.ferdakort.is; Brautarholt 8; ⏰10am-5pm Mon-Thu, to 4pm Fri) in Reykjavík. Forlagið (Mál og Menning) is another reputable map publisher with a wide range; browse at its **store** (Map p60; ☎580 5000; www.bmm.is; Laugavegur 18; ⏰9am-10pm Mon-Fri, 10am-10pm Sat; 📶) in the capital or online (www.forlagid.is – click on 'landakort').

Both companies have good touring maps of Iceland (1:500,000 or 1:600,000; approximately kr2000), useful for general driving. Ferðakort's more in-depth 1:200,000 *Road Atlas* (kr5000) includes details of accommodation, museums and swimming pools. Both companies also produce plenty of regional maps – Forlagið (Mál og Menning) has a series of eight regional maps at 1:200,000 (kr1700 each). There are also 31 highly detailed topographic maps at a scale of 1:100,000, covering the entire country – ideal for hikers – plus there are themed maps (eg sagas, geology and birdwatching).

Serious hikers can request maps at local tourist information centres or at national park visitor centres, both of which often stock inexpensive maps detailing regional walks and hikes.

ESSENTIAL: CREDIT CARD PIN

Note: a four-digit PIN is required to make credit- or debit-card purchases, and is essential for operating unstaffed petrol pumps. Ensure you have a PIN-enabled card before you leave home.

Money

ATMs

➡ As long as you're carrying a valid card, you'll need to withdraw only a limited amount of cash from ATMs.

➡ Almost every town in Iceland has a bank with an ATM *(hraðbanki)*, where you can withdraw cash using MasterCard, Visa, Maestro or Cirrus cards.

➡ Diners Club and JCB cards connected to the Cirrus network have access to all ATMs.

➡ You'll also find ATMs at larger petrol stations and in shopping centres.

Credit & Debit Cards

- Locals use plastic for even small purchases.
- Contact your financial institution to make sure that your card is approved for overseas use – you will need a PIN for purchases.
- Visa and MasterCard (and to a lesser extent Amex, Diners Club and JCB) are accepted in most shops, restaurants and hotels.
- You can pay for the Flybus from Keflavík International Airport to Reykjavík using plastic – handy if you've just arrived in the country.
- If you intend to stay in rural farmhouse accommodation or visit isolated villages, it's a good idea to carry enough cash to tide you over.

Currency

The Icelandic unit of currency is the króna (plural krónur), written as kr or ISK.

- Coins come in denominations of kr1, kr5, kr10, kr50 and kr100.
- Notes come in denominations of kr500, kr1000, kr2000, kr5000 and kr10,000.
- Some accommodation providers and tour operators quote their prices in euro to ward against currency fluctuations, but these must be paid in Icelandic currency.

Taxes & Refunds

The standard rate of value-added tax (VAT) in Iceland is 24%. A reduced rate of 11% applies to certain products and services, including food and accommodation. VAT is included in quoted prices.

Tipping

As service and VAT taxes are always included in prices, tipping isn't required in Iceland. Rounding up the bill at restaurants or leaving a small tip for good service is appreciated.

Travellers Cheques

Travellers cheques and banknotes can be exchanged for Icelandic currency at all major banks, but be aware that bank branches are only found in towns of a reasonable size.

Opening Hours

Opening hours vary throughout the year (some places are closed outside the high season). In general hours tend to be longer from June to August, and shorter from September to May. Standard opening hours:

Banks 9am–4pm Monday to Friday

Cafe-bars 10am–1am Sunday to Thursday, 10am to between 3am and 6am Friday and Saturday

Cafes 10am–6pm

Offices 9am–5pm Monday to Friday

Petrol stations 8am–10pm or 11pm

Post offices 9am–4pm or 4.30pm Monday to Friday (to 6pm in larger towns)

Restaurants 11.30am–2.30pm and 6pm–9pm or 10pm

Shops 10am–6pm Monday to Friday, 10am–4pm Saturday; some Sunday opening in Reykjavík malls and major shopping strips.

Supermarkets 9am–8pm (11pm in Reykjavík)

Vínbúðin (government-run alcohol stores) Variable; many outside Reykjavík only open for a couple of hours per day.

Post

The Icelandic postal service (www.postur.is) is reliable and efficient, and rates are comparable to those in other Western European countries.

A postcard/letter to Europe costs kr180/310; to places outside Europe it costs kr240/490. Full list of rates, branches and opening hours online.

Public Holidays

Icelandic public holidays are usually an excuse for a family gathering or, when they occur on weekends, a reason to rush to the countryside and go camping. If you're planning to travel during holiday periods, particularly the Commerce Day long weekend, you should book mountain huts and transport well in advance.

National public holidays in Iceland:

New Year's Day 1 January

Easter March or April. Maundy Thursday and Good Friday to Easter Monday (changes annually)

First Day of Summer First Thursday after 18 April

Labour Day 1 May

TAX-FREE SHOPPING

Anyone who has a permanent address outside Iceland can claim a tax refund on purchases when they spend more than kr6000 at a single point of sale. Look for stores with a 'tax-free shopping' sign in the window, and ask for a form at the register.

Before you check in for your departing flight at Keflavík, go to the refund office at Arion Banki and present your completed tax-free form, passport, receipts/invoices and purchases. Make sure the goods are unused. Opening hours of the office match flight schedules.

If you're departing Iceland from Reykjavík airport or a harbour, go to the customs office before check-in.

Full details outlined at www.globalblue.com.

TIPS ON SEASONAL OPENINGS

Some regional attractions and tourist-oriented businesses in Iceland are only open for a short summer season, typically from June to August. Reykjavík attractions and businesses generally run year-round.

As tourism is growing at a rapid pace, some regional businesses are vague about opening and closing dates; increasingly, seasonal restaurants or guesthouses may open some time in May, or even April, and stay open until the end of September or into October if demand warrants it.

With the growth of winter tourism, an increasing number of businesses (especially on the Ring Road) are feeling their way towards year-round trading. Note that many Icelandic hotels and guesthouses close from Christmas Eve to New Year's Day.

Check websites and/or Facebook pages of businesses, and ask around for advice.

Note that most museums (especially outside the capital) only have regular, listed opening hours during summer (June to August). From September to May they may advertise restricted opening hours (eg a couple of hours once a week), but many places are happy to open for individuals on request, with a little forewarning – make contact via museum websites or local tourist offices.

Ascension Day May or June (changes annually)

Whit Sunday and Whit Monday May or June (changes annually)

National Day 17 June

Commerce Day First Monday in August

Christmas 24 to 26 December

New Year's Eve 31 December

School Holidays

The main school holiday runs from the first week of June to the third week of August; this is when most of the Edda and summer hotels open.

The winter school holiday is a two-week break over the Christmas period (around 20 December to 6 January). There is also a spring break of about a week, over the Easter period.

Safe Travel

Iceland has a very low crime rate and in general any risks you'll face while travelling here are related to road safety, the unpredictable weather and the unique geological conditions.

A good place to learn about minimising your risks is **Safetravel** (www.safetravel.is). The website is an initiative of the Icelandic Association for Search and Rescue (ICE-SAR); it also provides information on ICE-SAR's **112 Iceland app** for smartphones (useful in emergencies), and explains procedures for leaving a travel plan with ICE-SAR or a friend/contact.

Road Safety

- Unique hazards (p406) exist for drivers, such as livestock on the roads, single-lane bridges, blind rises and rough gravel roads.
- The numerous F roads (p406) are suitable only for 4WDs, often involve fording rivers, and are often only open for a few months each year, in summer.
- For road conditions, see www.road.is or call ☎1777.

Weather Conditions

- Never underestimate the weather. Proper clothing and equipment is essential.
- Visitors need to be prepared for inclement conditions year-round. The weather can change without warning.
- Hikers must obtain a reliable forecast before setting off – call ☎902 0600 (press 1 after the introduction) or visit www.vedur.is/english for a forecast in English. Alternatively, download the **weather app** of the Icelandic Meteorological Office (IMO), called Veður.
- Emergency huts are provided in places where travellers run the risk of getting caught in severe weather.
- If you're driving in winter, carry food, water and blankets in your car.
- In winter, hire cars are generally fitted with snow tyres.

Geological Risks

- When hiking, river crossings can be dangerous, with glacial run-off transforming trickling streams into raging torrents on warm summer days.
- High winds can create vicious sandstorms in areas where there is loose volcanic sand.
- Hiking paths in coastal areas may only be accessible at low tide; seek local advice and obtain the relevant tide tables.
- In geothermal areas, stick to boardwalks or obviously solid ground. Avoid thin crusts of lighter-coloured soil around steaming fissures and mudpots.
- Be careful of the water in hot springs and mudpots – it often emerges from the ground at 100°C.

➡ In glacial areas beware of dangerous quicksand at the ends of glaciers, and never venture out onto the ice without crampons and ice axes (even then, watch out for crevasses).

➡ Snowfields may overlie fissures, sharp lava chunks or slippery slopes of scoria (volcanic slag).

➡ Always get local advice before hiking around live volcanoes.

➡ Only attempt isolated hiking and glacier ascents if you know what you're doing. Talk to locals and/or employ a guide.

➡ It's rare to find warning signs or fences in areas where accidents can occur, such as large waterfalls, glacier fronts and cliff edges. Use common sense, and supervise children well.

Telephone

➡ Public payphones are elusive in Iceland. You may find them outside post offices, bus stations and petrol stations. Many accept credit cards as well as coins. Local calls are charged at around kr20 per minute.

➡ To make international calls from Iceland, first dial the international access code ☎00, then the country code, the area or city code, and the telephone number.

➡ To phone Iceland from abroad, dial your country's international access code, Iceland's country code (☎354) and then the seven-digit phone number.

➡ Iceland has no area codes.

➡ Toll-free numbers begin with ☎800; mobile (cell) numbers start with 6, 7 or 8.

➡ Online version of the phone book with good maps at http://en.ja.is.

➡ Useful numbers: directory enquiries ☎118 (local), ☎1811 (international).

Mobile Phones

➡ The cheapest and most practical way to make calls at local rates is to purchase an Icelandic SIM card and pop it into your own mobile phone (tip: bring an old phone from home for that purpose).

➡ Before leaving home, make sure that your phone isn't locked to your home network.

➡ Check your phone will work on Europe's GSM 900/1800 network (US phones work on a different frequency).

➡ Buy prepaid SIM cards at bookstores, grocery stores and petrol stations throughout the country, and also on Icelandair flights. Top-up credit is available from the same outlets.

➡ Iceland telecom Síminn (www.siminn.is/prepaid) provides the greatest network coverage; Vodafone (http://vodafone.is/english/prepaid) isn't far behind. Both have voice-and-data starter packs including local SIM cards; Síminn's costs kr2000 (including kr2000 voice and data credit).

Phonecards

The smallest denomination phonecard (for use in public telephones – which are very rare) costs kr500, and can be bought from grocery stores and petrol stations. Low-cost international phonecards are also available in many shops and kiosks.

Time

➡ Iceland's time zone is the same as GMT/UTC (London).

➡ There is no daylight saving time.

PRACTICALITIES

Discount Cards Students and seniors qualify for discounts on internal flights, some ferry and bus fares, tours and museum entry fees. You'll need to show proof of student status or age.

Laundry Public facilities are tough to find. Campgrounds, hostels and guesthouses may have a washing machine for guest use (for a fee). Business hotels may offer a pricey service. Some apartments include a washing machine.

Newspapers & Magazines *Morgunblaðið*(www.mbl.is) is a daily paper in Icelandic; its website has local news in English.*Iceland Review* (www.icelandreview.com) has news and current affairs, including tourist-related news.*Reykjavík Grapevine* (www.grapevine.is) has excellent tourist-oriented and daily-life articles about Iceland, plus listings of what's on. A paper copy of the *Grapevine* is widely available and free.

Radio RÚV (Icelandic National Broadcasting Service; www.ruv.is) has three radio stations: Rás 1 (news, weather, cultural programs), Rás 2 (pop music, current affairs) and Rondó (classical music).

Smoking Illegal in enclosed public spaces, including in cafes, bars, clubs, restaurants and on public transport. Most accommodation is nonsmoking.

Weights & Measures The metric system is used.

EMERGENCY NUMBERS

For police, ambulance and fire services in Iceland, dial ☎112.

- From late October to late March Iceland is on the same time as London, five hours ahead of New York and 11 hours behind Sydney.
- In the northern hemisphere summer, Iceland is one hour behind London, four hours ahead of New York and 10 hours behind Sydney.
- Iceland uses the 24-hour clock system, and all transport timetables and business hours are posted accordingly.

Toilets

It may surprise you to learn that public toilets are newsworthy in Iceland – the shortage of them hits the headlines every so often, and stories of tourists doing their business in public, in inappropriate places (eg car parks and cemeteries), are guaranteed to madden the locals. Many Icelanders view the increase in human waste being found in nature as being directly linked to campers and campervan travellers who shun campgrounds, and this has led to new laws prohibiting such camping.

Reykjavík and larger towns have public restrooms, but natural sights (including major Ring Road sights such as Jökulsárlón and Seljalandsfoss) often have too few facilities for the increasing number of visitors. Long queues can form at the small number of toilets available, especially when buses pull in. There are also long stretches of road without any facilities at all (eg the 100km stretch of Ring Road between Höfn and Djúpivogur).

Our advice: plan your trip well; stop at facilities wherever you see them (eg N1 gas stations); and be prepared to fork out a small fee (eg kr200) for the use of some facilities. Do not do your business in public because you'd rather not pay. If there's an emergency, find an appropriate place (do not dig up fragile land) and do not leave your toilet paper behind.

And keep your fingers (and legs) crossed that Icelandic authorities tackle this issue soon!

Tourist Information

Websites

Official tourism sites for the country:

Visit Iceland (www.visiticeland.com)

Inspired by Iceland (www.inspiredbyiceland.com)

Each region also has its own useful site/s:

Reykjavík (www.visitreykjavik.is)

Southwest Iceland (www.visitreykjanes.is; www.south.is)

West Iceland (www.west.is)

The Westfjords (www.westfjords.is)

North Iceland (www.northiceland.is; www.visitakureyri.is)

East Iceland (www.east.is)

Southeast Iceland (www.south.is; www.visitvatnajokull.is)

Smartphone Apps

Useful and practical smartphone apps include the vital 112 Iceland app for safe travel, Veður (weather), and apps for bus companies such as **Strætó** (☎540 2700; www.bus.is) and **Reykjavík Excursions** (☎580 5400; www.re.is). Offline maps come in handy.

There are plenty more apps that cover all sorts of interests, from history and language to aurora-spotting, or walking tours of the capital. Reykjavík Grapevine's apps (Appy Hour, Craving and Appening) deserve special mention for getting you to the good stuff in the capital.

Travellers with Disabilities

Iceland can be trickier than many places in northern Europe when it comes to access for travellers with disabilities.

For details on accessible facilities, contact the information centre for people with disabilities, **Þekkingarmiðstöð Sjálfsbjargar** (National Association of People with Disabilities; ☎550 0118; www.thekkingarmidstod.is).

A good resource is the website God Adgang (www.godadgang.dk), a Danish initiative adopted in Iceland. Follow the instructions to find Icelandic service providers that have been assessed for the accessibility label.

Particularly good for tailor-made accessible trips around the country are **All Iceland Tours** (www.alliceland tours.is) and **Iceland Unlimited** (www.iceland unlimited.is). **Gray Line Iceland** (www.grayline.is) runs sightseeing and day tours from Reykjavík and will assist travellers with special needs.

Reykjavík's city buses have a 'kneeling' function so that wheelchairs can be lifted onto the bus; elsewhere, however, public buses don't have ramps or lifts.

Download Lonely Planet's free *Accessible Travel* guide from http://lptravel.to/AccessibleTravel.

Visas

Iceland is one of 26 member countries of the Schengen Convention, under which the EU countries (all but Bulgaria, Croatia, Romania, Cyprus, Ireland and the UK) plus Iceland, Norway, Liechtenstein and Switzerland have abolished checks at common borders.

The visa situation for Iceland is as follows.

- Citizens of EU and Schengen countries – no visa required for stays of up to three months.
- Citizens or residents of Australia, Canada, Japan, New Zealand and the USA – no visa required for tourist visits of up to three months. Note that the total stay within the Schengen area must not exceed three months in any six-month period.
- Other countries – check online at www.utl.is.

To work or study in Iceland a permit is usually required – check with an Icelandic embassy or consulate in person or online.

For questions on visa extensions or visas and permits in general, contact the Icelandic Directorate of Immigration, Útlendingastofnun (www.utl.is).

Volunteering

A volunteering holiday is a worthwhile (and relatively inexpensive) way to get intimately involved with Iceland's people and landscapes. As well as the below options, a stint at the **Arctic Fox Center** (Melrakkasetur; ☎456 4922; www.arcticfoxcenter.com; adult/child kr1200/free; ⏰9am-6pm Jun-Aug, 10am-4pm Sep-May; 📶) in the wilds of the Westfjords is also possible.

Iceland Conservation Volunteers (www.ust.is/the-environment-agency-of-iceland/volunteers) Iceland's Environment Agency, known as Umhverfisstofnun (UST), recruits around 200 volunteers each summer for work on practical conservation projects around the country, which mainly create or maintain trails in Vatnajökull National Park. Places on its short-term programs (under four weeks) are usually arranged through its partner volunteer organisations, such as Working Abroad (www.workingabroad.com) or Iceland-based SEEDS. Longer-term placements are also possible on Trail Teams that work together for 11 weeks over summer; see the UST website for details.

SEEDS (www.seeds.is) Iceland-based SEEDS organises work camps and volunteering holidays (generally two to three weeks in length), primarily focusing on nature and the environment (building trails, ecological research), but also construction or renovation of community buildings, or assistance at festivals and events.

Volunteer Abroad (www.volunteerabroad.com) Offers an overview of possible projects in Iceland. Note that many of the projects listed are under the remit of Umhverfisstofnun, but arranged through various international volunteering organisations.

Workaway (www.workaway.info) This site is set up to promote exchange between travellers/volunteers and families or organisations looking for help with a range of activities (from au pair work to farm assistance). It has dozens of Icelandic hosts looking for unpaid help in return for accommodation.

Worldwide Friends (www.wf.is) Iceland-based Worldwide Friends runs short-term work camps that largely support nature and the environment. There are also options for involvement in community projects, and art and cultural events.

WWOOF (www.wwoofindependents.org) World Wide Opportunities On Organic Farms (also known as Willing Workers On Organic Farms) has a handful of farm properties in Iceland that accept wwoofers, although there is no national WWOOF organisation. In return for volunteer help, WWOOF hosts offer food, accommodation and opportunities to learn about organic lifestyles.

DIRECTORY LISTINGS

Due to the unique way in which surnames are formed in Iceland (girls add the suffix *-dóttir*, daughter, to their father's first name; boys add the suffix *-son*), telephone directories are alphabetised by first name.

Work

The increasing flow of tourists to Iceland requires more workers. To be hired for in-demand summer seasonal work (eg housekeeping and hospitality in hotels, guesthouses and restaurants) you must be from the EU/EEA. If you're after a professional job, Icelandic language skills may be a prerequisite (exceptions exist in the growing computer programming and gaming industries, and in tourism).

For non-EU/EEA nationals, things aren't so easy – you must have a work permit, which most commonly requires sponsorship from a local company. Full details are outlined on the Directorate of Immigration's site: www.utl.is.

One of the best places to start gathering information and contacts is the website of Vinnumálastofnun, the Icelandic Directorate of Labour (www.vinnumalastofnun.is). It provides information on work in Iceland, plus links to agencies that may be able to help.

Transport

GETTING THERE & AWAY

Iceland has become far more accessible in recent years, with more flights arriving from more destinations. Ferry transport (from northern Denmark) makes a good alternative for Europeans wishing to take their own car.

Flights, cars and tours can be booked online at lonelyplanet.com/bookings.

Entering the Country

Iceland is part of the Schengen Agreement, which eliminates border passport control between Schengen countries in Europe.

There is passport control when entering Iceland from a country outside the Schengen area. Some nationalities need a visa to enter Iceland.

For entry into the Schengen area, you must have a passport valid for three months beyond your proposed departure date.

As long as you are in possession of the right documentation, immigration control should be a quick formality.

Air

Airports & Airlines

Keflavík International Airport (KEF; ☎525 6000; www.kefairport.is) Iceland's main international airport is 48km southwest of Reykjavík.

Reykjavík Domestic Airport (Reykjavíkurflugvöllur; Map p56; www.reykjavikairport.is; Innanlandsflug) Internal flights and those to Greenland and the Faroes use this small airport in central Reykjavík.

A growing number of airlines fly to Iceland (including budget carriers) from destinations in Europe and North America. Some airlines have services only from June to August. Find a list of airlines serving the country at www.visiticeland.com (under Plan/Travel to Iceland).

Icelandair (www.icelandair.com) The national carrier has an excellent safety record.

Air Iceland (www.airiceland.is) The main domestic airline (not to be confused with Icelandair). Also flies to destinations in Greenland and the Faroe Islands.

WOW Air (www.wowair.com) Icelandic low-cost carrier, serving a growing number of European and North American destinations.

Sea

Smyril Line (www.smyrilline.com) operates a pricey but well-patronised weekly car ferry, the *Norröna*, from Hirtshals (Denmark) through Tórshavn (Faroe Islands) to Seyðisfjörður in East Iceland. It operates year-round, although winter passage is weather-dependent – see website for more.

Fares vary greatly, depending on dates of travel, what sort of vehicle (if any) you are travelling with, and

CLIMATE CHANGE & TRAVEL

Every form of transport that relies on carbon-based fuel generates CO_2, the main cause of human-induced climate change. Modern travel is dependent on aeroplanes, which might use less fuel per kilometre per person than most cars but travel much greater distances. The altitude at which aircraft emit gases (including CO_2) and particles also contributes to their climate change impact. Many websites offer 'carbon calculators' that allow people to estimate the carbon emissions generated by their journey and, for those who wish to do so, to offset the impact of the greenhouse gases emitted with contributions to portfolios of climate-friendly initiatives throughout the world. Lonely Planet offsets the carbon footprint of all staff and author travel.

ESSENTIAL WEB RESOURCES

Four websites every traveller should know about:

Safetravel (www.safetravel.is) Learn about minimising risks while travelling in Iceland.

Icelandic Met Office (www.vedur.is) Never underestimate the weather in Iceland, or its impact on your travels. Get a reliable forecast from this site (or call ☎902 0600, and press 1 after the introduction). Download its app, too (called Veður).

Vegagerðin (www.road.is) Iceland's road administration site details road openings and closings around the country. Vital if you plan to explore Iceland's little-visited corners and remote interior, and for information about winter road access.

Carpooling in Iceland (www.samferda.is) Handy site that helps drivers and passengers link up. Passengers often foot some of the petrol bill. It's a savvy alternative to hitching (for passengers), and a way to help pay for car rental and fuel (for drivers).

cabin selection. The journey time from Hirtshals to Seyðisfjörður is 47 hours.

It's possible to make a stopover in the Faroes. Contact Smyril Line or see the website for trip packages.

GETTING AROUND

There is no train network in Iceland. The most common way for visitors to get around the country is to drive a rental car.

There's a decent bus network operating from around June to mid-September between major destinations; bus services are more limited outside of summer. Don't overlook internal flights to help you maximise your time.

Air

Iceland has an extensive network of domestic flights, which locals use almost like buses. In winter a flight can be the only way to get between destinations, but weather at this time of year can play havoc with schedules.

Domestic flights depart from the small **Reykjavík Domestic Airport** (Reykjavíkurflugvöllur; Map p56; www.reykjavikairport.is; Innanlandsflug), not from the major international airport at Keflavík.

A handful of airstrips offer regular sightseeing flights – eg Mývatn, Skaftafell, and Reykjavík and Akureyri domestic airports – and helicopter sightseeing is increasingly popular.

Airlines in Iceland

Air Iceland (Flugfélag Íslands; ☎570 3030; www.airiceland.is) Not to be confused with international airline Icelandair. Destinations covered: Reykjavík, Akureyri, Grimsey, Ísafjörður, Vopnafjörður, Egilsstaðir and Þórshöfn. Offers some fly-in day tours.

Eagle Air (☎Reykjavík 562 4200; www.eagleair.is) Operates scheduled flights to five small airstrips from Reykjavík: Vestmannaeyjar, Húsavík, Höfn, Bíldudalur and Gjögur. Also runs a number of day tours.

Bicycle

Cycling is an increasingly popular way to see the country's landscapes, but be prepared for harsh conditions.

Gale-force winds, driving rain, sandstorms, sleet and sudden flurries of snow are possible year-round. We recommend keeping your plans relatively flexible so you can wait out bad weather if the need arises.

You'll be forced to ride closely alongside traffic on the Ring Road (there are no hard shoulders to the roads).

The large bus companies carry bikes, so if the weather turns bad or that highlands bike trip isn't working out as planned, consider the bus. Note that space can't be reserved. It's free to take a bike on **Strætó** (☎540 2700; www.bus.is) services; other companies, such as **Sterna** (☎551 1166; www.icelandbybus.is), **SBA-Norðurleið** (☎550 0700; www.sba.is) and **Reykjavík Excursions** (☎580 5400; www.re.is), charge around kr3500.

Puncture-repair kits and spares are hard to come by outside Reykjavík; bring your own or stock up in the capital. On the road, it's essential to know how to do your own basic repairs.

If you want to tackle the interior, the Kjölur route has bridges over all major rivers, making it fairly accessible to cyclists. A less-challenging route is the F249 to Þórsmörk. The Westfjords also offers some wonderful, challenging cycling terrain.

Transporting Bicycles to Iceland

Most airlines will carry your bike in the hold if you pack it correctly in a bike box.

At Keflavík International Airport, a new facility (a container 100m east of the Arrivals exit) is available to assemble or disassemble bikes. **Reykjavík City Hostel** (Map p56; ☎553 8110; www.hostel.is; Sundlaugavegur 34; dm from kr4750, d with/without bathroom kr17,900/12,900; P@🛜) 🍃 also offers such facilities and will store bike boxes. At Keflavík airport, **Bílahótel** (www.bilahotel.is) is a garage (in the same building as Geysir Car Rental) that offers luggage storage, including bike boxes.

The **Smyril Line ferry** (www.smyrilline.com) from Denmark transports bikes for €15 each way.

Hire

Various places rent out mountain bikes, but in general these are intended for local use only, and often aren't up to long-haul travel.

If you intend to go touring, it's wise to bring your bike from home or purchase one when you arrive; alternatively, **Reykjavík Bike Tours** (www.icelandbike.com) has touring bikes for rent.

Resources

Cycling Iceland (www.cyclingiceland.is) Online version of the brilliantly detailed *Cycling Iceland* map, published annually.

Icelandic Mountain Bike Club (http://fjallahjolaklubburinn.is) The English-language pages of this website are a goldmine of information.

The Biking Book of Iceland Keep an eye out for a new series of cycling books by Ómar Smári Kristinsson, covering trails in the Westfjords, West, Southwest and South Iceland. Not all are available in English.

Boat

Several year-round ferries operate in Iceland. Major routes all carry vehicles, but it's worthwhile booking ahead for car passage.

➡ **Herjólfur** (www.herjolfur.is) Connecting Landeyjahöfn in South Iceland to Vestmannaeyjar islands.

➡ **Sævar** (www.hrisey.net) Frequent and easy connections from Árskógssandur in North Iceland, north of Akureyri, to the island of Hrísey.

➡ **Baldur** (www.seatours.is) Connecting Stykkishólmur in West Iceland to Brjánslækur in the Westfjords.

➡ **Sæfari** (www.saefari.is) Connecting Dalvík in North Iceland to Grímsey island on the Arctic Circle.

From June to August, regular boat services run from Bolungarvík and Ísafjörður to points in Hornstrandir (Westfjords).

Bus

Iceland has an extensive network of long-distance bus routes, with services provided by a handful of main companies. The free *Public Transport in Iceland* map has an overview of routes; pick it up at tourist offices or view it online at www.publictransport.is.

From roughly June to mid-September regular scheduled buses run to most places on the Ring Road, into the popular hiking areas of the southwest, and to larger towns in the Westfjords and Eastfjords, and on the Reykjanes and Snæfellsnes Peninsulas. The rest of the year, services range from daily, to a few weekly, to nonexistent.

In summer, 4WD buses run along some F roads (mountain roads), including the highland Kjölur, Sprengisandur and Askja routes (inaccessible to 2WD cars).

Many bus services can be used as day tours: buses spend a few hours at the final destination before returning to the departure point, and may stop for a half-hour at various tourist destinations en route.

Bus companies may operate from different terminals or pick-up points. Reykjavík has several bus terminals; in small towns, buses usually stop at the main petrol station, but it pays to double-check.

Many buses are equipped with free wi-fi.

Many buses have GPS tracking, so you can see when your bus is approaching your stop.

Companies

Main bus companies:

Reykjavík Excursions (☎580 5400; www.re.is)

SBA-Norðurleið (☎550 0700; www.sba.is)

Sterna (☎551 1166; www.icelandbybus.is)

Strætó (☎540 2700; www.bus.is)

Bus Passports

Bus operators offer 'bus passports' every summer (valid from early or mid-June to the first week of September), with the aim of making public transport around the island as easy as possible. At the time of research, none of the passports cover the Westfjords, but services along the highland Sprengisandur and Kjölur routes can be included.

If you're considering touring Iceland by bus, do your homework before buying a bus passport. They're not cheap, and it's significantly more convenient (and maybe be cheaper, if you are two or more) to hire your own vehicle.

Some passports lock you into a time restriction, others (eg circular routes) allow you to travel at leisure, provided you travel in one direction.

Passports lock you into using the services of one company, and no Icelandic bus company offers the perfect network – each has significant geographic gaps in service, and most routes only run once per day. Strætó has the biggest network and most frequent services but is not a part of any passports. You may be better off buying separate tickets for each leg of your journey, using the bus service that offers you the best route at the time. Find up-to-date rates on websites.

ICELAND ON YOUR OWN PASSPORTS

Reykjavík Excursions and SBA-Norðurleið work together to offer Iceland On Your

Own passports; full details at www.ioyo.is.

Pros:

➡ Services along both the highland Kjölur and the Sprengisandur routes.

➡ Good services in the south (using the strong Reykjavík Excursions network).

➡ Coverage in the north that includes Akureyri to Húsavík, Ásbyrgi and Dettifoss (using SBA-Norðurleið's network).

Cons:

➡ A gap in Ring Road coverage in West Iceland, with circular passes heading north via the highland Kjölur route, then taking the Ring Road.

The passports:

Circle Passport Reykjavík to Varmahlíð via the Kjölur route, then follows the Ring Road around the country (kr42,000).

Beautiful South Passport Travel along the full south coast (Reykjavík to Höfn); includes routes to Gullfoss, Þórsmörk, Landmannalaugar and Lakagígar (3/5/9/11 days kr24,500/36,000/ 53,000/60,500).

Beautiful South Circle Passport South coast (Reykjavík to Skaftafell), plus Landmannalaugar (kr22,000).

Highlights Passport Kjölur and the Sprengisandur routes, plus south coast and northern area around Akureyri and Húsavík; no coverage in the east, from Mývatn to Höfn (7/11/15 days kr46,500/66,000/80,000).

Highland Circle Passport Valid for one circular route taking in the Sprengisandur and Kjölur routes; also covers Reykjavík to Skaftafell (kr44,000).

Combo Passport Combines the Ring Road (except for the western part) and the two highland routes, plus a few additional routes in the north and south (7/11/15 days kr58,000/77,000/91,500).

Hiking Passport This is the best-seller, and with good reason. If you're hiking Laugarvegur, you can be dropped off at Landmannalaugar and picked up at the route's end in Þórsmörk (or vice versa). If you're hiking Fimmvörðuháls, you can transfer between Skógar and Þórsmörk (kr12,500).

ICELAND BY BUS PASSPORTS

Sterna has four passports utilising its network. Details are at www.icelandbybus.is.

Pros:

➡ Services the entire Ring Road (including the west), and has a highland route – Kjölur.

➡ Passports don't specify a time limit.

Cons:

➡ Limited routes off the Ring Road.

East Circle Passport Reykjavík to Varmahlíð via the Kjölur route, then follows the Ring Road around the country (kr42,900).

Full Circle Passport Travels the Ring Road, pure and simple (kr36,900).

Ultimate Passport Travels the Ring Road, plus Landmannalaugar and Þórsmörk, and includes two day trips from Reykjavík, covering the Golden Circle and Reykjanes Peninsula (kr69,900).

Highland Hikers Passport Covering Landmannalaugar, Þórsmörk and Skógar; valid for bus transfer to the start of your hike, and from the end point (kr12,500).

Car & Motorcycle

Driving in Iceland gives you unparalleled freedom to discover the country and, thanks to (relatively) good roads and (relatively) light traffic, it's all fairly straightforward.

➡ The Ring Road (Rte 1) circles the country and, except for a couple of small stretches in East Iceland, is paved.

➡ Beyond the Ring Road, fingers of sealed road or gravel stretch out to most communities.

➡ Driving coastal areas can be spectacularly scenic, and incredibly slow as you weave up and down over mountain passes and in and out of long fjords.

➡ A 2WD vehicle will get you almost everywhere in summer (note: *not* into the highlands, or on F roads).

➡ In winter heavy snow can cause many roads to close; mountain roads generally only open in June and may start closing as early as September. For up-to-date information on road conditions, visit www.road.is.

➡ Don't be pressured into renting a GPS unit – if you purchase a good, up-to-date touring map, and can read it, you should be fine without GPS. If you are planning to take remote trails, it will be worthwhile.

Bring Your Own Vehicle

Car hire in Iceland is expensive, so bringing your own vehicle may not be as crazy as it sounds. The Smyril Line ferry from Denmark is busy in summer bringing vehicles to Iceland from all over Europe (book well ahead).

For temporary duty-free importation, drivers must carry the vehicle's registration documents, proof of valid insurance (a 'green card' if your car isn't registered in a Nordic or EU-member country) and a driving licence.

Permission for temporary duty-free importation of a vehicle is granted at the point of arrival for up to 12 months, and is contingent upon agreeing to not lend or sell your vehicle. For more information, contact the Directorate of Customs (www.customs.is).

If you're staying for a long period, you might consider shipping your own vehicle via **Eimskip** (www.eimskip.is) shipping services. Be aware that this is far from cheap, and involves heavy paperwork, but it may be useful for long-stayers who have lots of gear or a well set-up camper/4WD. Eimskip has five shipping lines in the North Atlantic.

Driving Licences

You can drive in Iceland with a driving licence from the US, Canada, Australia, New Zealand and most European countries. If your licence is not in Roman script, you need an International Driving Permit (normally issued by your home country's automobile association).

Fuel & Spare Parts

➡ Petrol stations are regularly spaced around the country, but in the highlands you should check fuel levels and the distance to the next station before setting off.

➡ At the time of research, unleaded petrol and diesel cost about kr205 (€1.60) per litre.

➡ Some Icelandic roads can be pretty lonely, so carry a jack, a spare tyre and jump leads just in case (check your spare when you pick up your rental car).

➡ In the event of a breakdown or accident, your first port of call should be your car-hire agency.

➡ Although the Icelandic motoring association **Félag Íslenskra Bifreiðaeigenda** (FÍB; www.fib.is) is only open to locals, if you have

CROSSING RIVERS

While trekking or driving in Iceland's highlands you're likely to face unbridged rivers that must be crossed. There are a few rules to follow.

➡ Melting snow causes water levels to rise, so the best time to cross is early in the morning before the day warms up, and preferably no sooner than 24 hours after a rainstorm.

➡ Avoid narrow stretches, which are likely to be deep – the widest ford is likely to be shallowest.

➡ The swiftest, strongest current is found near the centre of straight stretches and at the outside of bends. Choose a spot with as much slack water as possible.

➡ Never try to cross just above a waterfall and avoid crossing streams in flood (identifiable by dirty, smooth-running water carrying lots of debris and vegetation).

For Hikers

➡ A smooth surface suggests that the river is too deep to be crossed on foot. Anything more than thigh-deep isn't crossable without being experienced and having extra equipment.

➡ Before attempting to cross deep or swift-running streams, be sure that you can jettison your pack midstream if necessary.

➡ Lone hikers should use a hiking staff to probe the river bottom for the best route and to steady themselves in the current.

➡ Never try to cross a stream barefoot. Bring wetsuit boots or sandals if you want to keep your hiking boots dry.

➡ While crossing, face upstream and avoid looking down or you risk getting dizzy and losing balance. Two hikers can steady each other by resting their arms on each other's shoulders.

➡ If you fall while crossing, don't try to stand up. Remove your pack (but don't let go of it), roll onto your back and point your feet downstream, then try to work your way to a shallow eddy or to the shore.

For Drivers

➡ If you're not travelling in convoy, consider waiting for other traffic.

➡ Watch where and how experienced drivers cross.

➡ You may need to check the depth and speed of the river by wading into it (using techniques described for hikers, including a hiking staff). A good rule of thumb: if you would not want to wade through a river you should not drive through it.

➡ Work with the water – drive diagonally across in the direction of the current, making sure you're in a low gear. Drive steadily, without stopping or changing gear, just slightly faster than the water is flowing (too slow and you risk getting stuck, or letting water up the exhaust).

breakdown cover with an automobile association affiliated with ARC Europe you may be covered by the FÍB – check with your home association.

➡ FÍB's 24-hour breakdown number is ☎511 2112. Even if you're not a member, it can provide information and phone numbers for towing and breakdown services.

Car Hire

Travelling by car is the only way to get to some parts of Iceland. Although car-hire rates are expensive by international standards (actually the most expensive in Europe, according to one recent study), they compare favourably to bus or internal air travel, especially if there are a few of you to split the costs. Shop around and book online for the best deals.

To rent a car you must be 20 years old (23 to 25 years for a 4WD) and hold a valid licence.

The cheapest cars, usually a small hatchback or similar, cost from around kr10,000 to kr12,000 per day in high season (June to August). Figure on paying from around kr15,000 for the smallest 4WD that offers higher clearance than a regular car but isn't advised for large river crossings, and from kr20,000 for a larger 4WD model.

Rates include unlimited mileage and VAT (a hefty 24%), and usually collision damage waiver (CDW).

Weekly rates offer some discount. From September to May you should be able to find considerably better daily rates and deals.

Check the small print, as additional costs such as extra insurance, airport pick-up charges and one-way rental fees can add up.

In winter you should opt for a larger, sturdier car for safety reasons, preferably with 4WD (ie absolutely not a compact 2WD).

In the height of summer many companies run out of rentals. Book ahead.

Many travel organisations (eg Hostelling International Iceland, Icelandic Farm Holidays) offer package deals that include car hire.

Most companies are based in the Reykjavík and Keflavík areas, with city and airport offices. Larger companies have extra locations around the country (usually in Akureyri and Egilsstaðir). Ferry passengers arriving via Seyðisfjörður should contact car-hire agencies in nearby Egilsstaðir.

Car-hire companies:

Átak (www.atak.is)

Avis (www.avis.is)

Budget (www.budget.is)

Cars Iceland (www.carsiceland.com)

Cheap Jeep (www.cheapjeep.is)

Europcar (www.europcar.is) The biggest hire company in Iceland.

Geysir (www.geysir.is)

Go Iceland (www.goiceland.com)

Hertz (www.hertz.is)

SADcars (www.sadcars.com) Older fleet, therefore (theoretically) cheaper prices.

Saga (www.sagacarrental.is)

CAR SHARING

A peer-to-peer car-sharing platform called **Cario** (www.cario.com) offers people the chance to hire privately owned cars from locals. If you take up this option, do your homework and assess the costs and the small print – from our research, some prices were not much different than those of car-rental companies; cars were much older; and you don't have the reassurance of a company behind you to help if things go wrong.

CAMPERVAN HIRE

Combining accommodation and transport costs into campervan rental is a booming option – and has extra appeal in summer, as it allows for some spontaneity (unlike every other form of accommodation, campsites don't need to be prebooked). Campervanning in winter is possible, but we don't particularly recommend it – there are few facilities open for campers at this time, and weather conditions may make it unsafe.

Large car-hire companies usually have campervans for rent, but there are also more offbeat choices, offering from backpacker-centric to family-sized, or real 4WD set-ups. Some companies offer gear rental to help your trip go smoothly (GPS, cooking gear and stove, barbecue, sleeping bags, camping chairs, fishing equipment, portable wi-fi hot spots etc).

Camper Iceland (www.campericeland.is)

Go Campers (www.gocampers.is)

Happy Campers (www.happycampers.is)

JS Camper Rental (www.js.is) Truck campers on 4WD pick-ups.

Rent Nordic (www.rent.is)

MOTORCYCLE HIRE

Biking Viking (www.rmc.is/en/biking-viking) offers motorcycle rental, tours and service.

Insurance

A vehicle registered in Nordic or EU-member countries is considered to have valid automobile insurance in Iceland. If your vehicle is registered in a non-Nordic or non-EU country, you'll need a 'green card', which proves that you are insured to drive while in Iceland. Green cards are issued by insurance companies in your home country; contact your existing insurer.

When hiring a car, check the small print; most vehicles come with third-party insurance and CDW to cover you for damage to the car. Also check the excess (the initial amount you will be liable to pay in the event of an accident) as this can be surprisingly high.

Hire vehicles are not covered for damage to tyres, headlights and windscreens, or damage caused to the car's underside by driving on dirt roads, through water or in ash- or sandstorms. Many companies will try to sell you additional insurance to cover these possibilities. You need to consider whether this is appropriate for you and your plans, and how prepared you are to cough up in the event of such occurrences (and the cost of the insurance versus factors such as the length of your rental and what regions you plan to visit). There is no way of predicting what climatic conditions you might meet on your trip.

Road Conditions & Hazards

Good main-road surfaces and light traffic (especially outside the capital and southwest region) make driving in Iceland relatively easy, but there are some specific hazards. Watch the 'Drive Safely on Icelandic Roads' video on www.drive.is for more.

Livestock Sheep graze in the countryside over the summer, and often wander onto roads. Slow down when you see livestock on or near roadsides.

Unsurfaced roads The transition from sealed to gravel roads is marked with the warning sign 'Malbik Endar' – slow right down to avoid skidding when you hit the gravel. Most accidents involving foreign drivers in Iceland are caused by the use of excessive speed on unsurfaced roads. If your car does begin to skid, take your foot off the accelerator and gently turn the car in the direction you want the front wheels to go. Do not brake.

Blind rises In most cases roads have two lanes with steeply cambered sides and no hard shoulder; be prepared for oncoming traffic in the centre of the road, and slow down and stay to the right when approaching a blind rise, marked as 'Blindhæð' on road signs.

Single-lane bridges Slow down and be prepared to give way when approaching single-lane bridges (marked as 'Einbreið Brú'). Right of way is with the car closest to the bridge.

Sun glare With the sun often sitting low to the horizon, sunglasses are recommended.

Winter conditions In winter make sure your car is fitted with snow tyres or chains; and carry a shovel, blankets, food and water.

Ash and sandstorms Volcanic ash and severe sandstorms can strip paint off cars; strong winds can even topple your vehicle. At-risk areas are marked with orange warning signs.

F roads Roads suitable for 4WD vehicles only are F-numbered.

River crossings Few interior roads have bridges over rivers. Fords are marked on maps with a 'V'.

Tunnels There are a number of tunnels in Iceland – a couple are single lane, and a little anxiety-inducing! Before you enter such tunnels, a sign will indicate which direction has right of way. There will be a couple of pull-over bays inside the tunnel (signed 'M'). If the passing bay is on your side in the tunnel, you are obligated to pull in and let oncoming traffic pass you.

Road Rules

- Drive on the right.
- Front and rear seatbelts are compulsory.
- Dipped headlights must be on at all times.
- Blood alcohol limit is 0.05%.
- Mobile phone use is prohibited when driving except with a hands-free kit.
- Children under six years must use a car seat.
- Do not drive off-road (ie off marked roads and 4WD trails).

F ROADS

We can think of a few choice F words for these bumpy, at times almost-nonexistent tracts of land, but in reality the 'F' stands for *fjall* (mountain). Do not confuse F roads with gravel stretches of road (regular gravel roads are normally fine for 2WDs, although some of them are bumpy rides for small, low-clearance cars).

- F roads are indicated on maps and road signs with an 'F' preceding the road number (F26, F88 etc).
- Opening dates vary with weather conditions, but are generally around mid- to late June.
- F roads only support 4WDs. If you travel on F roads in a hired 2WD you'll invalidate your insurance. F roads are unsafe for small cars: do yourself a favour and steer clear, or hire a 4WD (or take a bus or super-Jeep tour).
- Before tackling any F road, educate yourself about what lies ahead (eg river crossings) and whether or not the entire route is open. See www.road.is for mountain-road opening details.
- While some F roads may almost blend into the surrounding nature, driving off marked tracks is strictly prohibited everywhere in Iceland, as it damages fragile ecosystems.

BUYING FUEL

Most smaller petrol stations are unstaffed, and all pumps are automated. There is the (time-consuming) option of going inside a staffed service station to ask staff to switch the pump to manual, enabling you to fill up and pay for your fuel afterwards. To fill up using the automated service:

- Put your credit card into the machine's slot (you'll need a card with a four-digit PIN) and follow the instructions.
- The next step is determined by the type of payment machine. On newer touchscreens you can press 'Full Tank', or you input the maximum amount you wish to spend, then wait while the pump authorises your purchase. Entering a maximum amount pre-approves your card for that capped amount, but you are only charged for the cost of the fuel put into your vehicle (this can be any amount you wish, up to the pre-approved capped amount).
- Select the pump number you are using.
- Fill tank.
- If you require a receipt, re-enter your card into the slot.

The first time you fill up, visit a staffed station while it's open, in case you have any problems. Note that you need a PIN for your card to use the automated pumps. If you don't have a PIN, buy prepaid cards from an N1 station that you can then use at the automated pumps.

Speed Limits

- Built-up areas: 50km/h.
- Unsealed roads: 80km/h.
- Sealed roads: 90km/h.

Hitching & Ride-Sharing

Hitching is never entirely safe, and we don't recommend it. Travellers who hitch should understand that they are taking a small but potentially serious risk. Nevertheless, we met scores of tourists who were hitching their way around Iceland and most had positive reports. Single female travellers and couples tend to get a lift the quickest.

Patience is a prerequisite of hitching, and logic is important, too – be savvy about where you position yourself. Try standing at junctions, near petrol stations or even by Bónus supermarkets.

When you arrive at your accommodation it can't hurt to let people know where you're aiming for the next day. There may be another traveller going that way who can give you a ride. Check out **Carpooling in Iceland** (www.samferda.is) for rides – note there is an expectation that passengers will contribute to fuel costs.

Local Transport

Bus

Reykjavík has an extensive network of local buses connecting all the suburbs, and running to Akranes, Borgarnes, Hveragerði, Selfoss and Hvalfjarðarsveit. See www.straeto.is for information on routes, fares and timetables.

Local bus networks operate in Akureyri, Ísafjörður, and the Reykjanesbær and Eastfjords areas.

Taxi

Most taxis in Iceland operate in the Reykjavík area, but many of the larger towns also offer services. Outside of Reykjavík, it's usually wise to prebook.

Taxis are metered and can be pricey. Tipping is not expected.

At the time of research, there were no Uber and Lyft services in Iceland (yet).

Language

Icelandic belongs to the Germanic language family, which includes German, English, Dutch and all the Scandinavian languages except Finnish. It's related to Old Norse, and retains the letters 'eth' (*ð*) and 'thorn' (*þ*), which also existed in Old English. Be aware, especially when you're trying to read bus timetables or road signs, that place names can be spelled in several different ways due to Icelandic grammar rules.

Most Icelanders speak English, so you'll have no problems if you don't know any Icelandic. However, any attempts to speak the local language will be much appreciated.

If you read our coloured pronunciation guides as if they were English, you'll be understood. Keep in mind that double consonants are given a long pronunciation. Note also that öy in our pronunciation guides is like the '-er y-' in 'her year' (without the 'r') and that kh is like the 'ch' in the Scottish *loch*. Stress generally falls on the first syllable in a word.

BASICS

Hello.	*Halló.*	*ha*·loh
Good morning.	*Góðan daginn.*	*gohth*-ahn *dai*-in
Goodbye.	*Bless.*	bles
Good evening.	*Gott kvöld.*	khot kverld
Good night.	*Goða nótt.*	*khoh*-th-ah noht
Thank you	*Takk./Takk fyrir.*	tak/tak *fi*·rir
Excuse me.	*Afsakið.*	*af*·sa·kidh
Sorry.	*Fyrirgefðu.*	*fi*·rir·gev·dhu

WANT MORE?

For in-depth language information and handy phrases, check out Lonely Planet's phrasebooks range. You'll find them at **shop.lonelyplanet.com**.

READING ICELANDIC

Letter	Pronunciation
Á á	ow (as in 'how')
Ð ð	dh (as the 'th' in 'that')
É é	ye (as in 'yet')
Í í	ee (as in 'see')
Ó ó	oh (as the 'o' in 'note')
Ú ú	oo (as in 'too')
Ý ý	ee (as in 'see')
Þ þ	th (as in 'think')
Æ æ	ai (as in 'aisle')
Ö ö	eu (as the 'u' in 'nurse')

Yes.	*Já.*	yow
No.	*Nei.*	nay

How are you?
Hvað segir þú gott? — kvadh *se*·yir thoo got

Fine. And you?
Allt fínt. En þú? — alt feent en thoo

What's your name?
Hvað heitir þú? — kvadh *hay*·tir thoo

My name is ...
Ég heiti ... — yekh *hay*·ti ...

Do you speak English?
Talar þú ensku? — *ta*·lar thoo *ens*·ku

I don't understand.
Ég skil ekki. — yekh skil *e*·ki

It will be OK.
Þetta reddast. — *thah*-tah *rah*-dohst

DIRECTIONS

Where's the (hotel)?
Hvar er (hótelið)? — kvar er (*hoh*·te·lidh)

Can you show me (on the map)?
Geturðu sýnt mér (á kortinu)? — *ge*·tur·dhu seent myer (ow *kor*·ti·nu)

What's your address?
Hvert er heimilisfangið þitt? — kvert er *hay*·mi·lis·fan·gidh thit

EATING & DRINKING

What would you recommend?
Hverju mælir þú með? — *kver*·yu *mai*·lir thoo medh

Do you have vegetarian food?
Hafið þið grænmetisrétti? — *ha*·vidh thidh *grain*·me·tis·rye·ti

I'll have a ...
Ég ætla að fá ... — yekh *ait*·la adh fow ...

Cheers!
Skál! — skowl

I'd like a/the ..., please.	*Get ég fengið ..., takk.*	get yekh *fen*·gidh ... tak
table for (four)	*borð fyrir (fjóra)*	bordh *fi*·rir (*fyoh*·ra)
bill	*reikninginn*	*rayk*·nin·gin
drink list	*vínseðillinn*	*veen*·se·dhit·lin
menu	*matseðillinn*	*mat*·se·dhit·lin
that dish	*þennan rétt*	*the*·nan ryet
bottle of (beer)	*(bjór)flösku*	(*byohr*)·*fleus*·ku
(cup of) coffee/tea	*kaffi/te (bolla)*	*ka*·fi/te (*bot*·la)
glass of (wine)	*(vín)glas*	(*veen*)·glas
water	*vatn*	vat
breakfast	*morgunmat*	*mor*·gun·mat
lunch	*hádegismat*	*how*·de·yis·mat
dinner	*kvöldmat*	*kveuld*·mat

EMERGENCIES

Help!	*Hjálp!*	hyowlp
Go away!	*Farðu!*	*far*·dhu
Call ...!	*Hringdu á ...!*	*hring*·du ow ...
a doctor	*lækni*	*laik*·ni
the police	*lögregluna*	*leu*·rekh·lu·na

I'm lost.
Ég er villtur/villt. (m/f) — yekh er *vil*·tur/vilt

Where are the toilets?
Hvar er snyrtingin? — kvar er *snir*·tin·gin

SHOPPING & SERVICES

I'm looking for ...
Ég leita að ... — yekh *lay*·ta adh ...

How much is it?
Hvað kostar þetta? — kvadh *kos*·tar *the*·ta

SIGNS

Inngangur	Entrance
Útgangur	Exit
Opið	Open
Lokað	Closed
Bannað	Prohibited
Snyrting	Toilets

NUMBERS

1	*einn*	aydn
2	*tveir*	tvayr
3	*þrír*	threer
4	*fjórir*	*fyoh*·rir
5	*fimm*	fim
6	*sex*	seks
7	*sjö*	syeu
8	*átta*	*ow*·ta
9	*níu*	*nee*·u
10	*tíu*	*tee*·u
20	*tuttugu*	*tu*·tu·gu
30	*þrjátíu*	*throw*·tee·u
40	*fjörutíu*	*fyeur*·tee·u
50	*fimmtíu*	*fim*·tee·u
60	*sextíu*	*seks*·tee·u
70	*sjötíu*	*syeu*·tee·u
80	*áttatíu*	*ow*·ta·tee·u
90	*níutíu*	*nee*·tee·u
100	*hundrað*	*hun*·dradh

That's too expensive.
Þetta er of dýrt. — *the*·ta er of deert

It's faulty.
Það er gallað. — thadh er *gat*·ladh

Where's the ...?	*Hvar er ...?*	kvar er ...
bank	*bankinn*	*bown*·kin
market	*markaðurinn*	*mar*·ka·dhu·rin
post office	*pósthúsið*	*pohst*·hoo·sidh

TRANSPORT

Can we get there by public transport?
Er hægt að taka rútu þangað? — er haikht adh *ta*·ka *roo*·tu *thown*·gadh

Where can I buy a ticket?
Hvar kaupi ég miða? — kvar *köy*·pi yekh *mi*·dha

Is this the ... to (Akureyri)?	*Er þetta ... til (Akureyrar)?*	er *the*·ta ... til (*a*·ku·ray·rar)
boat	*ferjan*	*fer*·yan
bus	*rútan*	*roo*·tan
plane	*flugvélin*	*flukh*·vye·lin

What time's the ... bus?	*Hvenær fer ... strætisvagninn?*	*kve*·nair fer ... *strai*·tis·vag·nin
first	*fyrsti*	*firs*·ti
last	*síðasti*	see·dhas·ti
One ... ticket (to Reykjavík), please.	*Einn miða ... (til Reykjavíkur), takk.*	aitn *mi*·dha ... (til *rayk*·ya·vee·kur) tak
one-way	*aðra leiðina*	*adh*·ra *lay*·dhi·na
return	*fram og til baka*	fram okh til *ba*·ka
I'd like a taxi ...	*Get ég fengið leigubíl ...*	get yekh *fen*·gidh *lay*·gu·beel ...
at (9am)	*klukkan (níu fyrir hádegi)*	*klu*·kan (*nee*·u *fi*·rir *how*·de·yi)
tomorrow	*á morgun*	ow *mor*·gun

How much is it to ...?
Hvað kostar til ... ? kvadh *kos*·tar til ...

Please stop here.
Stoppaðu hér, takk. *sto*·pa·dhu hyer tak

Please take me to (this address).
Viltu aka mér til (þessa staðar)? *vil*·tu *a*·ka myer til (*the*·sa *sta*·dhar)

GLOSSARY

See the Icelandic Cuisine chapter (p382) for useful words and phrases dealing with food and dining.

á – river (as in Laxá, or Salmon River)
álfar – elves
austur – east

basalt – hard volcanic rock that often solidifies into hexagonal columns
bíó – cinema
brennivín – local schnapps
bær – farm

caldera – crater created by the collapse of a volcanic cone

dalur – valley

eddas – ancient Norse books
ey – island

fell – see *fjall*
fjall – mountain
fjörður – fjord
foss – waterfall
fumarole – vents in the earth releasing volcanic gas

gata – street
geyser – spouting hot spring
gistiheimilið – guesthouse
gjá – fissure, rift
goðar – political and religious leaders of certain districts in the times before Christianity (singular *goði*)

hákarl – putrid shark meat
hestur – horse
höfn – harbour
hot-pot – outdoor hot tub or spa pool, found at swimming baths and some accommodation; in Icelandic, hot-pot is *heitur pottur*
hraun – lava field
huldufólk – hidden people
hver – hot spring

ice cap – permanently frozen glacier or mountain top
Íslands – Iceland

jökull – glacier, ice cap

kirkja – church
kort – map

Landnámabók – comprehensive historical text recording the Norse settlement of Iceland
laug – pool; one that is suitable for swimming
lava tube – underground tunnel created by liquid lava flowing under a solid crust
lón – lagoon
lopapeysa/lopapeysur (sg/pl) – Icelandic woollen sweater
lundi – puffin

mörk – woods or forest; colloquially *mörk* also refers to the goals in football, and the earmarks of sheep
mudpot – bubbling pool of superheated mud

nes – headland
norður – north

puffling – baby puffin

reykur – smoke, as in Reykjavík (literally 'Smoky Bay')

safn – museum
sagas – Icelandic legends
sandur – sand; can also refer to a glacial sand plain
scoria – glassy volcanic lava
shield volcano – gently sloped volcano built up by fluid lava flows
sími – telephone
skáli – hut, snack bar
stræti – street
suður – south
sumar – summer
sundlaug – heated swimming pool

tephra – rock/material blasted out from a volcano
tjörn – pond, lake
torg – town square

vatn – lake, water
vegur – road
vestur – west
vetur – winter
vík – bay
vogur – cove, bay

Behind the Scenes

SEND US YOUR FEEDBACK

We love to hear from travellers – your comments keep us on our toes and help make our books better. Our well-travelled team reads every word on what you loved or loathed about this book. Although we cannot reply individually to your submissions, we always guarantee that your feedback goes straight to the appropriate authors, in time for the next edition. Each person who sends us information is thanked in the next edition – the most useful submissions are rewarded with a selection of digital PDF chapters.

Visit **lonelyplanet.com/contact** to submit your updates and suggestions or to ask for help. Our award-winning website also features inspirational travel stories, news and discussions.

Note: We may edit, reproduce and incorporate your comments in Lonely Planet products such as guidebooks, websites and digital products, so let us know if you don't want your comments reproduced or your name acknowledged. For a copy of our privacy policy visit lonelyplanet.com/privacy.

OUR READERS

Many thanks to the travellers who used the last edition and wrote to us with helpful hints, useful advice and interesting anecdotes: Anna Brunner & Jessica Brooke, Bart Streefkerk, Cliff & Helen Elsey, Daniel Crouch, Elena Kagi, Eyþór Jóvinsson, Fiorella Taddeo, Gudrun Stefansdottir, Helen Simpson, Ildiko Lorik, Janire Echevarri, John Gerrard, John Malone, Joshua Wood, Keela Shackell-Smith, Klavs Hendil, Linda Moore, Ling-Shao Chang, Lisa Romano, Lori Zoras, Marco Conti, Marianne Backman, Marlies Van Hoef, Martin Fettke, Matt Kurz, Melanie Zahnd, Peter Gordon, Peter Madsen, Peter Stern, Richard Owen, Ryan Nix, Sarah Britton, Sebastian Steel, Semir Jahic, Sonia Martinez, Steve Eldridge, Sylvia Perez, Terry Bedard, Victoria Courtney, Vidal de Freitas Mansano

WRITER THANKS

Carolyn Bain

I wish I had the space to thank every Icelander (and expat and fellow traveller) who, over the course of my visits, has helped me see more, understand more and enjoy more – from guesthouse owners and national park rangers to highland tour drivers. A heartfelt *takk fyrir* to so many people for great conversations, invaluable information and so many acts of kindness. Cheers to James Smart for my favourite gig, and bouquets to my superb project collaborator, Alexis Averbuck.

Alexis Averbuck

My work on Iceland was a labour of love supported by many. Big thanks to Heimir Hansson (Westfjords), Jón Björnsson (Hornstrandir), Dagný Jóhannsdóttir (Southwest), Kristján Guðmundsson (West), Ragnheiður Sylvía Kjartansdóttir (Reykjavík and everywhere!), Einar Sæmundsen (Þingvellir) and Helga Garðarsdóttir (Laugavegurinn). Svava Guðjónsdóttir kept my statistics accurate. Edda and Páll made Húsafell so, so special! Carolyn was once again a brilliant, generous, astute collaborator. Respect to James for his great care. Rachel, Jenny, Oren and Timothy were amazing BOB-sters, making Icelandic escapades a family adventure. Ryan = peachy.

ACKNOWLEDGEMENTS

Climate map data adapted from Peel MC, Finlayson BL & McMahon TA (2007) 'Updated World Map of the Köppen-Geiger Climate Classification', *Hydrology and Earth System Sciences*, 11, 163344.

Cover photograph: Geothermal field, Kerlingarfjöll, Martin M303/Shutterstock ©

THIS BOOK

This 10th edition of Lonely Planet's *Iceland* guidebook was researched and written by Carolyn Bain and Alexis Averbuck. The previous edition was also written by Carolyn and Alexis. The 8th edition was written by Brandon Presser, Carolyn Bain and Fran Parnell.

This guidebook was produced by the following:

Destination Editor James Smart

Product Editor Tracy Whitmey

Senior Cartographer David Kemp

Book Designers Cam Ashley, Gwen Cotter

Assisting Editors Michelle Bennett, Bella Li, Anne Mulvaney, Kristin Odijk, Charlotte Orr, Susan Paterson, Saralinda Turner

Cartographer James Leversha

Cover Researcher Naomi Parker

Thanks to Imogen Bannister, Dan Corbett, Gemma Graham, Jane Grisman, Paul Harding, Victoria Harrison, Andi Jones, Elizabeth Jones, Claire Naylor, Karyn Noble and Victoria Smith, Tony Wheeler

Index

ALPHABETICAL ORDER

The Icelandic letters Þ and Ö appear at the end of the alphabet after the letter Z.

Map Pages **000**
Photo Pages **000**

Map Pages **000**
Photo Pages **000**

N

O

P

INDEX M-P

Map Pages **000**
Photo Pages **000**

Ö

CLAARTJE SCHOUTEN

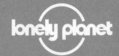

Map Legend

Sights
- Beach
- Bird Sanctuary
- Buddhist
- Castle/Palace
- Christian
- Confucian
- Hindu
- Islamic
- Jain
- Jewish
- Monument
- Museum/Gallery/Historic Building
- Ruin
- Shinto
- Sikh
- Taoist
- Winery/Vineyard
- Zoo/Wildlife Sanctuary
- Other Sight

Activities, Courses & Tours
- Bodysurfing
- Diving
- Canoeing/Kayaking
- Course/Tour
- Sento Hot Baths/Onsen
- Skiing
- Snorkelling
- Surfing
- Swimming/Pool
- Walking
- Windsurfing
- Other Activity

Sleeping
- Sleeping
- Camping

Eating
- Eating

Drinking & Nightlife
- Drinking & Nightlife
- Cafe

Entertainment
- Entertainment

Shopping
- Shopping

Information
- Bank
- Embassy/Consulate
- Hospital/Medical
- Internet
- Police
- Post Office
- Telephone
- Toilet
- Tourist Information
- Other Information

Geographic
- Beach
- Hut/Shelter
- Lighthouse
- Lookout
- Mountain/Volcano
- Oasis
- Park
- Pass
- Picnic Area
- Waterfall

Population
- Capital (National)
- Capital (State/Province)
- City/Large Town
- Town/Village

Transport
- Airport
- Border crossing
- Bus
- Cable car/Funicular
- Cycling
- Ferry
- Metro station
- Monorail
- Parking
- Petrol station
- S-Bahn/S-train/Subway station
- Taxi
- T-bane/Tunnelbana station
- Train station/Railway
- Tram
- Tube station
- U-Bahn/Underground station
- Other Transport

Note: Not all symbols displayed above appear on the maps in this book

Routes
- Tollway
- Freeway
- Primary
- Secondary
- Tertiary
- Lane
- Unsealed road
- Road under construction
- Plaza/Mall
- Steps
- Tunnel
- Pedestrian overpass
- Walking Tour
- Walking Tour detour
- Path/Walking Trail

Boundaries
- International
- State/Province
- Disputed
- Regional/Suburb
- Marine Park
- Cliff
- Wall

Hydrography
- River, Creek
- Intermittent River
- Canal
- Water
- Dry/Salt/Intermittent Lake
- Reef

Areas
- Airport/Runway
- Beach/Desert
- Cemetery (Christian)
- Cemetery (Other)
- Glacier
- Mudflat
- Park/Forest
- Sight (Building)
- Sportsground
- Swamp/Mangrove

OUR STORY

A beat-up old car, a few dollars in the pocket and a sense of adventure. In 1972 that's all Tony and Maureen Wheeler needed for the trip of a lifetime – across Europe and Asia overland to Australia. It took several months, and at the end – broke but inspired – they sat at their kitchen table writing and stapling together their first travel guide, *Across Asia on the Cheap*. Within a week they'd sold 1500 copies. Lonely Planet was born.

Today, Lonely Planet has offices in Franklin, London, Melbourne, Oakland, Dublin, Beijing and Delhi, with more than 600 staff and writers. We share Tony's belief that 'a great guidebook should do three things: inform, educate and amuse'.

OUR WRITERS

Carolyn Bain

A travel writer and editor for 16 years, Carolyn has lived, worked and studied in various corners of the globe, including London, Denmark, St Petersburg and Nantucket. She is regularly drawn north from her base in Melbourne, Australia, to cover diverse destinations for Lonely Planet, from dusty outback Australia to the luminous Greek islands, by way of Maine's lobster shacks and Slovenia's alpine lakes. The Nordic region stakes a large claim to her heart, with repeated visits to Iceland and Denmark for work and pleasure. Carolyn writes about travel and food for a range of publishers; see carolynbain.com.au for more.

Alexis Averbuck

Alexis Averbuck was born in Oakland, CA, and earned a degree at Harvard University. She has travelled and lived all over the world, from Sri Lanka and India to Mexico, Europe and Antarctica. In more recent years she's been living in Hydra, Greece, and exploring her adopted homeland; travelling to France to sample oysters in Brittany and careen through hill-top villages in Provence; and adventuring along Iceland's surreal lava fields, sparkling fjords and glacier tongues. A travel writer for over two decades, Alexis has lived in Antarctica for a year, crossed the Pacific by sailboat and written books on her journeys through Asia, Europe and the Americas. She also appears in videos and on television promoting travel and adventure, and is a painter – visit www.alexisaverbuck.com.

Published by Lonely Planet Global Limited
CRN 554153
10th edition – May 2017
ISBN 978 1 78657 471 8

10 9 8 7 6 5 4 3 2 1
Printed in China